ISBN 0-9746749-0-7

Printed in the United States of America by The Cricket Press,
Summer Street, Manchester-by-the-Sea, MA 01944

Published by Manchester Historical Society, 10 Union Street,
Manchester-by-the-Sea, MA 01944

JEFFREY'S CREEK

A Story of People, Places and Events in the Town That Came to Be Known as

MANCHESTER-BY-THE-SEA

by Gordon Abbott, Jr.

Published by Manchester Historical Society
Manchester-by-the-Sea, Massachusetts 01944
2003

COVER PHOTO

This photograph taken from Spy Rock Hill around 1887, shows Jeffrey's Creek (foreground) and Manchester harbor at low tide prior to its first dredging in 1896. It is clearly all mud flats except for a trickle of water making its way seaward. Misery Island is visible in the far distance as is the Tower House at Norton's Point and the house at Read's Island. The present stone causeway at Beach Street, which you can see in the middle of the photo, had yet to be constructed. It was built in 1888. Note the small boats grounded out just beyond the open culvert as well as the schooner in the outer harbor. The house to the right of the bridge was constructed on pilings. It was later destroyed in a storm. Although there is a railroad siding, at the time a single track proceeded to Gloucester.

In the foreground is Jeffrey's Creek for which the settlement was originally named. As late as 1887, it was still a tidal waterway and a part of the harbor where fishermen moored their dories. Once surrounded by salt marsh, it no longer exists. Filled with earth and surfaced primarily with asphalt, it is now the site of Harbor Point and the shopping center with Allen's Drug Store. Beach Street was first built in 1873. Prior to that, Smith Point residents approached the town via Masconomo Street, Sea Street and Summer Street. If you look closely at Beach Street from the Town Pier today, you can see the arch of the stone culvert, now sealed with granite blocks, through which the waters of the creek ran as the tide rose and fell.

More than a century and a half ago, before its shore line was developed and the railroad causeway installed in 1847, Manchester harbor, like many along the coast, was ringed with hundreds of acres of salt marsh. Masconomo Park was once marshland as were the shores of the inner harbor from the marina to where the Legion and town's sewer treatment plant are located. Indeed, that marshland behind Town Hall was filled and the granite seawall built just after World War II. Sections of salt marsh may still be seen at Tuck's Point in Whittier Cove and at Day's Creek. State environmental laws today protect salt marsh which, with its creeks and estuaries, provides a fertile breeding ground for fin and shell fish. The photo is believed to have been taken by John Rufus Cheever. It is provided through the courtesy of his great-grandson, Doug Heath.

This photograph, which appears throughout the book as the masthead for chapter headings, is a view of the Town of Manchester from Powder House Hill sometime in the 1880's. In the foreground is the "Channel," originally acquired for fire fighting purposes and much enjoyed during winters in the old days for ice skating. The back of the Baptist Church is recognizable as is the Old School House, the fourth structure to the right of the church. Built in 1818, it was later moved to Elm Street to make way for a new fire house constructed on its approximate location in 1891. The present fire house occupies the same site. Visible on the skyline, center, is the roof of the Masconomo House.

PREFACE

The Manchester Historical Society is proud to sponsor the publication of this exciting new illustrated history of the small coastal village first known as Jeffrey's Creek. The town's transformation from a simple seafaring economy to the affluent commuter/retirement community we know today as Manchester-by-the-Sea is a fascinating story as readers are about to discover.

Many things make Manchester-by-the-Sea unique, not the least of which is its spectacular natural beauty. But what I think makes our community truly special are the people who live and work here—people who care deeply about the rich heritage we all share. Some trace their local roots back many generations, others are fairly new residents, attracted to Cape Ann by its superb location and the quality of life we are privileged to enjoy.

None have done more to preserve the character of Manchester than the men and women who have served the Manchester Historical Society since its founding in 1886. These dedicated individuals have been the stewards of town history, the caretakers of the artifacts, documents and collections that so dramatically trace the many chapters in our 358-year existence.

No one better exemplifies the spirit of this stewardship than the author of this book, Gordon Abbott, Jr. A third generation resident, Gordon has been a member of the Historical Society's Board for more than a decade (serving earlier as a Vice President in the 1960's). He is best known as the author and editor of REFLECTIONS, a series of well-researched and entertaining papers on various aspects of town history. A selection of these is included in this current publication.

In 1995, Gordon volunteered to write a brief history of the town for its 350th Anniversary celebration. With this material as a resource, he then embarked on a more ambitious project—writing and editing this more comprehensive story of the town. It includes much new material, fascinating in itself, but what is especially notable is the abundance of photographs and illustrations, many of which appear in print for the first time.

A former journalist and newspaper editor, Gordon's passion for history and love of Manchester comes alive on every page. Thank you, Gordon, for your years of research, your literary skills, and your commitment to keeping Manchester's history alive for generations to come. The Historical Society is honored and delighted to be the publisher of JEFFREY'S CREEK, <u>A Story of People, Places and Events in the Town That Came to Be Known as MANCHESTER-BY-THE-SEA</u>.

John Jay Huss
President
Manchester Historical Society
September, 2003

FOREWORD

The production of this history of Manchester-by-the-Sea evolved first, from the pleasure that I had writing a shorter summary for the celebratory volume published in 1995 on the occasion the town's 350th anniversary, and second, from the series of papers, entitled REFLECTIONS, that I have produced over the past decade for the Manchester Historical Society.

In each case, what I found most fascinating are the people, both living and dead, who have made the town what it is today. They are truly extraordinary, and it is their lives and their accomplishments that this book is primarily designed to celebrate and to reflect.

We are enormously fortunate to be a part of a wonderfully livable community. It is a hope as well that a knowledge, understanding and appreciation of the past will help us chart a better course for the future.

The text of the book is divided into several sections, each of which may be read, and hopefully, enjoyed independently. First, is a chronology of the town from the time of its earliest settlement to the present day, really a much extended version of the brief history which I wrote for the 350th anniversary book. Next comes a series of early photographs, some of which have not been shown before, many of which were discovered and acquired for the Manchester Historical Society by Reginald Foster, III, its past President, who did so much to help with the collection of all the photos for this book.

Third is a section entitled A Closer Look which describes and discusses in greater detail people, places and events connected with our wonderfully varied and interesting past. Following that is another collection of historic photographs. And finally, because of their content, I have chosen to reproduce six selected issues of REFLECTIONS. These are mailed only to members of the Manchester Historical Society and thus may not have been seen by most of the community.

They cover such topics as Masconomo and his Indians; fires and firefighters; the Dana family, our first summer residents; the Booths and other celebrities; the history of the Manchester Police Department; a profile of publisher and summer resident James T. Fields and stories of local shipwrecks; the Manchester Electric Company; life at Manchester's Grand Summer Hotel; the Masconomo House; the great Sea Serpent and the Manchester Yacht Club.

Once again, I owe thanks to three major authors who preceded me: Reverend Darius F. Lamson, whose History of the Town of Manchester 1645-1895 was published by the town in honor of its 250th anniversary; Frank L. Floyd, former Town Clerk, State Representative and owner of Floyd's News Store, whose Manchester-by-the-Sea was published in 1945; and Benjamin B. Merrill, Jr., long-time feature writer and reporter for The Manchester Cricket and author of A History of Twentieth Century Manchester published in 1990.

The single, most useful source of information throughout has been The Manchester Cricket. I am enormously grateful to Editor Dan Slade, to his brother, David, Vice President of The Cricket Press, to Harry Slade, President, and to every member of their staff for their hospitality and generosity which permitted me access to original bound volumes of the paper as well as to the publication which preceded it, the Beetle & Wedge. Other publications used for reference purposes are named in the Bibliography. Photo credits appear in the captions. The transition from manuscript to type could not have been accomplished without the interest, experience and abilities of Linda Bossio, with whom it has been a delight to work. The book is better because of her meticulous attention to both the quality of the print and of the graphics.

I am also grateful to a number of individuals who have been invaluable as sources of information, inspiration and support. They include especially Slim Proctor, Librarian at the Manchester Historical Society; John Huss, President of the Society; the late Frances L. Burnett, whose knowledge of town history was unrivaled; and Lottie Calnek, MHS board member and former Curator. Mary Crane Kirby and Jerry Noonan both read, corrected and suggested additions to the original manuscript, a priceless contribution. The Honorable Ellen Flatley, Justice of Gloucester's District Court, and a third generation resident of Manchester, also very kindly read a final version of the book itself.

The following reviewed specific chapters and added immeasurably to their accuracy, content and interest: Tim Averill, Mary Baker, Helen Bethell, Don Belin, Connie Brown, Ted Brown, Mary Bundy, Finney Burke (who also made possible the acquisition of photos of Stuffy McInnis courtesy of <u>The Boston Globe</u>), John Cabot, Hon. William Fitzgerald, Charles Filias, Hon. Ellen Flatley, Reg Foster, Kathy Greenslet, Miles and Lee Herter, John Herrick, Kitty Coolidge Lastavika, MD and William J. Otto, MD, Joe Hyland and Hardy Nalley, Dorothy Jodice, Town Engineer Bob Moroney, Susan Kenny Carroll, Craig Lentz, Sally Means Loring, Chris Nahatis, Pat Noonan, Charles Shurcliff, Dan Slade, Peter Spang, Gardner Read, Priscilla Triebs, Vin Terrill and Ann Wigglesworth. Special thanks as well to Carl Triebs, whose extensive research and writing has enabled him to know more about Manchester's role in the Civil War than any living resident.

I have also from time to time used material from chapters of that impressive publication which commemorates our 350th anniversary. Information and direct quotes are attributed to the author or authors involved.

Finally, I am most grateful to my dear wife Katharine, a writer herself (her own book, <u>Nantucket Summers</u>, was published in 1996) who has provided continuing advice and encouragement, is always there to answer any question I may have, and who has lived with this project patiently and with good humor for more than a year. I appreciate, too, more than I can say, the interest and enthusiasm of my four children and the excellent suggestions they have offered along the way.

Any errors or omissions can be blamed only upon the author. As in every work of this sort there are sure to be some, and for these I apologize in advance.

G.A. Jr.
Manchester-by-the-Sea
Massachusetts
September, 2003

A CHRONOLOGICAL HISTORY

The story of the town from the first English settlement at Cape Ann in 1623; the incorporation of Manchester in 1645; the early years, the American Revolution and the War of 1812; the prosperous era of furniture manufacturing and the Civil War; the growth of Manchester as a seasonal residential community; the heroes and heroines of World War I and World War II; to, finally, its emergence as modern-day Manchester-by-the-Sea.

1630: ARBELLA ARRIVES OFF SALEM

A hazy sun illuminates ARBELLA in mid-ocean in this drawing from the Bradlee Collection at the Peabody-Essex Museum, Salem. With Governor of the Bay Colony John Winthrop and his followers aboard, the 350-ton "stout, well-found" vessel was manned by a crew of 52 seamen and armed with 28 guns. ARBELLA left England on April 7, 1630 and on June 12 dropped anchor in Salem Bay, a voyage of two months.

FIRST SETTLEMENT

In 1623, Dorchester Company Chooses Cape Ann as Site for Fishing Village

The first organized English settlement on the north shore of Massachusetts Bay was established at Cape Ann in 1623 by the Dorchester Company of Adventurers.

The brainchild of Master (the term reverend had not yet come into use) John White, rector of the 13th century parish church at Stanton St. John, just east of Oxford, England, it was to be a business venture for its 120 shareholders who also agreed with the good pastor that it could provide steady employment for West Country fishermen and, if a clergyman could be enlisted, used to teach Christianity to the Indians.

Both fisher folk and planters sailed from Weymouth aboard the FELLOWSHIP landing at Cape Ann in the fall of 1623. There they set up stages or flakes to dry cod, haddock and other species, and built a house for shelter at what is now Stage Fort Park. About 14 men spent the winter, but nothing seemed to go right. The rocky soil, too poor to farm, failed to generate produce necessary to sustain the settlement. Because of bad management and worse timing, the company's ships were unable to find a decent market for what fish had been caught. And a clergyman arrived too late to be of benefit to anyone. The result was that by 1626, the Dorchester Company, had run out of money. Not a success either socially, spiritually or financially, it was soon dissolved and most of its disgruntled and discontented people returned to England.

Some of the settlers, however, chose to remain. Led by a young man named Roger Conant, and armed with a promise, again from the ever-optimistic Master John White, of a new grant of land, they decided to leave Cape Ann. In the fall of 1626, carrying their belongings, some 30 of them followed an Indian trail west along the shore past Jeffrey's Creek, some day to become the Town of Manchester, until they arrived at a place that the Indians called Naumkeag. There they built a few thatched-roofed cottages on the peninsula between the North River and the Danvers River which is now a part of the City of Salem.

By 1627, John White, who was never to see America himself, had convinced other investors to back a second venture. It was known as The New England Company for Massachusetts Bay and with a patent, it laid claim to all lands from three miles north of the Merrimack River to three miles south of the Charles River, a sizable piece of real estate. Its goals, somewhat simpler than those of the Dorchester Company, were to colonize the area and to convert the Indians to Christianity.

But what it needed more than anything to protect its prodigious claim to new lands was a royal charter. This time its backers included an influential group of London merchants. Among them was Sir Richard Saltonstall, nephew and heir to the Lord Mayor of London, and an ancestor of Manchester's longtime resident and former State Senator William L. Saltonstall of Summer Street. Men of influence and wealth, they were able in March, 1629, to acquire the necessary patent authority from the King.

With the charter now came a new name for the enterprise: the Governor and Company of the Massachusetts Bay in New England. Remarkably, for more than 50 years, its concepts and principles served as the foundation for life in the Colony of Massachusetts Bay. Leader of the settlement this time was to be a soldier, Captain John Endecott, a man known and widely respected for his discipline, courage and attention to duty.

In the summer of 1628, 50 men, women and children, including Endecott, were aboard the ABIGAIL when she arrived at Naumkeag. The Governor had received orders to accord the Old Planters, still led by Roger Conant, equal rights with the new. But from the beginning this was not to be. Endecott himself appropriated the framing of the house that had been built in Gloucester by the Dorchester Company to make a dwelling of his own. Newcomers were unfairly allowed to take over the gardens, lots and even houses of the old. Finally, Conant negotiated an agreement whereby lands were set aside along the Bass River. There the Old Planters established a village which "in their lifetime," writes historian Samuel Eliot Morison in his Builders of the Bay Colony, "grew into the township of Beverly." Much to Conant's chagrin, however, it was known derisively by those who remained in Salem as "Beggarly." But over time, the community belied its nickname, producing such eminent Massachusetts families as the Conants, the Balches, the Palfreys and the Woodburys.

In 1629, some 300 additional settlers stepped ashore from the TALBOT, the LION'S WHELP, and the GEORGE BONAVENTURE. With this group were two clergymen, there to organize the first church at Naumkeag which in that same year was christened Salem, the Hebrew name for "peace." One, Francis Higginson, was obviously pleased with what he saw around him which must have included at least a portion of the shoreline of Manchester. A "fyne and sweet harbor [most likely Salem Bay]," he writes in his journal, "where 20 ships might easily ride therein…" Four men were soon put ashore and returned "with ripe strawberries, gooseberries and sweet, single roses…" Again, Higginson delightedly described the landscape we know and love today: "It was wonderful to behold so many islands," he said, "replenished with thicke wood and high trees, and many fayere green pastures…"

It was in 1630, however, with the arrival of John Winthrop aboard ARBELLA that began what historians call the Great Migration. During the next 13 years, it would add 20,000 persons to the population of New England. A year earlier, conditions worsened for those whose Puritan beliefs separated them from the Church of England. Unlike the Pilgrims, whose mission, it is said, was "glorified by faith, hope and charity, but necessarily and always limited by the slender resources of the poor and humble men who originated it," those who came to Salem in 1630 were family men, accompanied by their wives and children and comparatively well-to-do. Guided by a Higher Power, they sought a place to practice their religion in their own way and to establish what was to become the first "commonwealth" in the New World.

Leaders of the group met in Cambridge, perhaps at Emmanuel College, and agreed that the best way to accomplish their objectives was to transfer the charter and government of the new Massachusetts Bay Colony from old England to the new. Those going would themselves provide the necessary financing so that there should be no obligations to any merchant or banker in England.

Winthrop, a well-educated patrician, and squire in his own town of Groton, was elected Governor of the colony and in March, 1630, less than a year after the agreement, he was ready to depart. It was an extraordinary organizational achievement. ARBELLA, with Peter Milbourne as Master, was an able vessel of 350 tons, fast and seaworthy. Manned by 52 seamen, she carried 28 "pieces of ordinance." She served as flagship of the expedition. Accompanying her were the TALBOT which had made the crossing before, the AMBROSE and the JEWEL. A fleet of four ships. Seven others were to follow. Aboard ARBELLA besides John Winthrop, with their families, were Sir Richard Saltonstall, Simon Bradstreet and Thomas Dudley. Master John White, who must have been pleased with their success so far, joined them if only to say farewell.

The crossing itself was uneventful, although with England still at war with France, decks were cleared for action when eight sail, which later proved to be friendly, were sighted off Dunkirk. Finally, on Tuesday, June 10, 1630, according to John Winthrop's celebrated Journal, gale winds from the south bore ARBELLA towards Cape Ann. One afternoon she sighted English fishermen at the Isles of Shoals, their ship at anchor and five or six shallops (open pulling boats) under sail.

PAST LITTLE MISERY
John Winthrop Anchors Off Plum Cove; Masconomo Is Welcomed Aboard

"We took many mackerel," Winthrop writes, "and met another shallop which stood [out from] Cape Anne." (Named for Queen Anne, Cape Ann was originally spelled with an "e.") On Saturday, June 12, "about four in the morning," he continued, "we were near our port. We shot two pieces of ordinance to meet Mr. Pierce [William Pierce, Master of the LYON]." His ship, which lay in the harbor, had arrived some days before. An hour earlier, ARBELLA had also welcomed aboard Isaac Allerton of Plymouth Colony, a fur trader, who in his shallop was bound for Pemaquid, Maine. There was obviously no shortage of local knowledge available as the ship neared her destination.

"As we stood towardes the harbor," the Journal states, "we sawe another shallop comeing to us, so we stood in to meet her & passed throughe the narrow streight between Baker's Ile & Kettle Ile & came to an Anchor a litle within the Illandes." What a handsome sight ARBELLA must have been, her sails filled with a light easterly breeze and all colors flying.

A note in the latest reprint of The Journal of John Winthrop, 1630-1649, edited by Richard S. Dunn, James Savage and Laetitia Yeandle, and published by The Belknap Press of Harvard University Press, corrects Winthrop's reference to

"Kettle Ile." It reads: "JW [John Winthrop] seems to have mixed up the names of two islands. He had passed Kettle Island while rounding Cape Ann, but was now passing between Little Misery Island and Bakers Island to enter Salem Harbor..."

It is generally agreed that ARBELLA came to anchor off the Beverly shore, perhaps at Plum Cove, and not, despite tales told for years, in Manchester's outer harbor. Maritime historian Samuel Eliot Morison makes the case by tracing ARBELLA's log of her voyage from England to America which appears in Winthrop's Journal and explains his reasoning in an article he wrote in 1930 for the Publications of the Colonial Society of Massachusetts. A portion of the article is reprinted elsewhere in this history.

Winthrop's sketch of the Massachusetts coast from Gloucester to Salem which accompanies his Journal is remarkably accurate and shows what looks like House Island, Ram Islands, Bakers Island, Misery, Little Misery, and, off the Salem shore, Little Haste, Great Haste and Coney Island. Gloucester, Beverly and Salem harbors appear in some detail. Manchester may be seen behind House and Ram Islands as a small dent in the coastline.

With many at sea and on the land taking note of her arrival, the welcome for ARBELLA was a merry one. As Governor Winthrop writes (always with old English spelling; I have taken the liberty of modernizing it): "After Mr. Pierce came aboard and returned to fetch Mr. Endecott [Winthrop replaced him as Governor]...with him, Mr. Skelton [Rev. Samuel Skelton who came to Salem with Rev. Francis Higginson], and Captain Levett [Christopher Levett of Casco, Maine], we...and some other gentlemen and some of the women and our Captain returned with them to Naumkeag [they must have rowed there in a skiff] where we supped with good venison pastry and good beer and at night returned to our ship. Some of the women stayed behind. In the meantime, most of our people went ashore upon the land of Cape Anne which lay very near us and gathered a store of strawberries..."

Affairs in Salem, however, were not as happy as they may have immediately appeared. Winthrop was told that nearly 80 of the 300 colonists who had arrived from 1628 to 1629 had died. Others were ill and nearly out of food. Little provision had been made for the hundreds of other settlers yet to come that year. The growing season was well advanced and with insufficient room at Salem, leaders of the colony had to decide quickly where else to settle and provide housing before winter was upon them.

Sunday, the day after ARBELLA's arrival, Winthrop reports that Masconomo, Sagamore of Agawam (soon to be called Ipswich), and one of his men, came aboard and spent the day. Then on Monday, the ship weighed anchor and with a head wind most likely from the southwest, was forced to kedge her way to the inner harbor which Morison again believes was the mouth of the North River in Beverly.

A likeness of ARBELLA appears on Manchester's Town Seal. In the foreground is a shallop or a canoe making for the ship perhaps carrying Masconomo. Other ships in Winthrop's fleet struggled in later, the poor TALBOT taking three months for the crossing during which she lost 14 passengers to illness and disease. By fall, nearly 1,000 people and 200 cattle had been landed at Salem.

BOSTON BECKONS
Settlement Is Moved: New World Embraces Mass Bay Charter

Winthrop and the others soon became convinced that Boston Bay should be the site of the new settlement, not Salem. And on August 23, 1630, leaders of the colony met at Charlestown for their first political assembly, officially marking the transfer of the charter from the old world to the new. Soon the Bay Colony which now embraced the shores of Boston Harbor as well as Salem would include three times as many people as New Plymouth founded by the Pilgrims a decade earlier.

For the colonists, the North Shore must have seemed an inviting place. Wood was plentiful for housing, for fuel and for building skiffs, shallops and larger vessels as well. Unlike the rocks and ledges of outer Cape Ann, soils could be found that were adequate for planting. Game of every sort was abundant. Salt marsh and swamp provided open land for grazing. And bays and rivers, full of fish, offered sheltered anchorages for ships of every size.

In those early times, what we know today as Manchester was a part of Salem. Most settlers in the area were "freemen," or members of the church, and thus permitted rights in common lands. In Manchester, some 400 acres, including what is now the center of town, had been designated "common land" and was ruled by a number

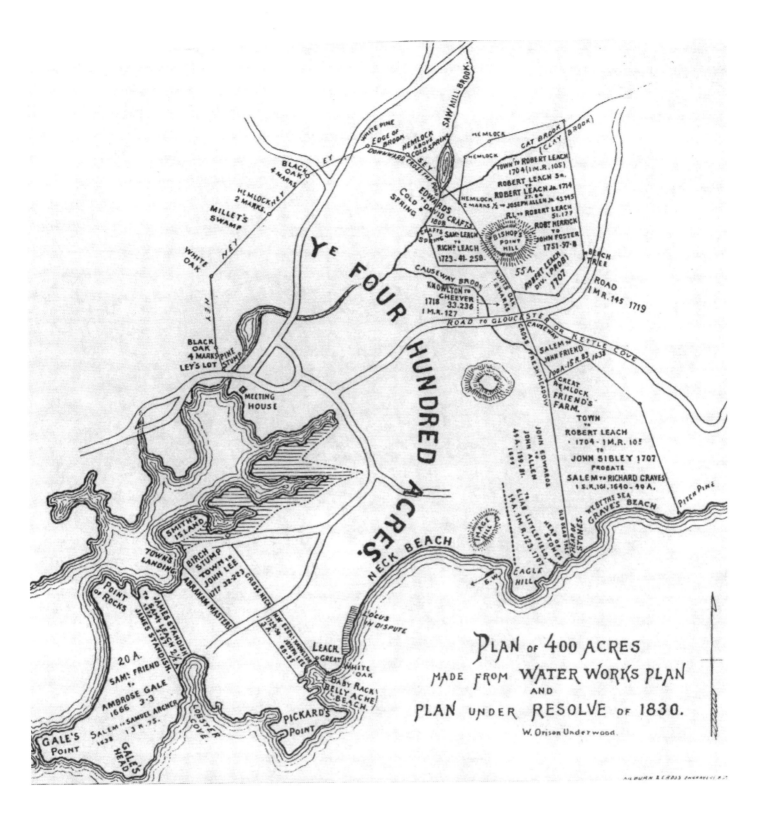

This map of the original 400 acres at Jeffrey's Creek appears in the Reverend Darius Lamson's <u>History of the Town of Manchester, 1645-1895</u>. Originally a part of Salem, records show that in February, 1636, the land was ordered to be subdivided into from 40 to 60-acre parcels to be owned by nine persons or "freemen," each required to be a member of the church. Later, land owners were known as Proprietors. In 1634, the General Court of Massachusetts Bay Colony appointed a Commission to determine town boundaries. Two years later, legislators adopted a landmark Act which gave cities and towns the power to establish their own independent governments, grant ownership of lots, maintain law and order, and elect or appoint their own officials. Note the names of early settlers as well as place names, many of which are the same today. In 1645, in response to a petition from 17 landowners to the General Court "for power to erect a village," the name Jeffrey's Creek was changed to Manchester. John Winthrop and Simon Bradstreet were charged with the responsibility of determining its boundaries. How the name Manchester was chosen is a mystery. Was it because of associations with Manchester, England or the Duke of Manchester, a "warm friend of the American colonies?" What is known is that there is a town or city called Manchester in every New England state except Rhode Island.

of "Proprietors." Areas such as these were used by the residents of the community for grazing animals, to provide firewood and for cultivation. The waters nearby, both fresh and salt, were filled with an abundance of finfish and shell fish. And although there is no accurate record of what life here was like, we can presume from what transpired later, that a settlement developed at the head of the harbor and that there were families here, primarily English men, women and children, who were going about the business of surviving in a new and very different environment. What held them together was not only their dependence upon each other, but as Puritans, a deep and abiding belief in their religion, a faith which called for a decentralized church, which placed a heavy emphasis on the Bible as the word of God, and which dealt with each individual's struggle for contact with the Almighty.

THE ORIGINAL 400 ACRES
Jeffrey's Creek Residents Petition for the Right to Hold Property in 1636

In 1635, recognizing that residents of these Puritan communities that had been established along the North Shore and elsewhere, wanted and indeed, needed, to control their own destinies, the General Court approved an Act which would enable them to dispose of their lands and woods… to grant lots…to pass laws, to levy fines and to "choose their own particular officers."

Salem records show that settlers at Jeffrey's Creek—for that is how Manchester was first known—petitioned for the right to hold property, and in February, 1636, the original 400 acres of common land was ordered to be divided. It included not only the center of town but a portion of Smith's Point, Singing Beach and Eagle Head, part of the land now owned by the Essex County Club, Millet's Swamp and Central Pond. How the settlement acquired the name of Jeffrey's Creek is not known for certain. It is said to be named for William Jeffrey or Jefferys, a property agent and early resident of Weymouth who was not even one of Manchester's original nine landowners, but is heard of later in Ipswich where today there is a Jeffery's Neck. As many fishermen and sailors know, there is also a Jeffery's Ledge offshore. Some say William Jeffrey built a cabin where Day's Creek enters the harbor at Masconomo Park giving

his name to what was then a tidal inlet. What is known is that Jeffrey was an educated man. Born in Sussexshire, England, he graduated from Cambridge University in 1606 and received a master's degree in 1610. He later served as Governor of Rhode Island and died in Newport in 1675. His grave may be seen there today.

The list of those first landowners or Proprietors in Manchester includes family names which still exist: William Allen, Samuel Archer, John Sibley, George Williams, John Moore, John Black, Sergeant Dixy, Sergeant Wolfe and the widow of Thomas More. The lots they acquired varied between 30 and 60 acres. Some grantees built houses on a portion of their lands. Others chose not to settle here at all. Grants were also made to Norman and William Bennett, Robert Allyn, James Standish, John Pickworth and Richard Gardner. The handsome house at 13 Washington Street, owned for many years by attorney Betram Allen, is located on land which was a part of the original Allen grant.

By 1640, there were 63 people living at Jeffrey's Creek, and that year 17 of them sought the right from the General Court "to erect a village." On June 18, 1645, the name of Jeffrey's Creek was changed to Manchester. Origin of the name may be geographic—Manchester, England—or personal—the Duke of Manchester. No one can be certain. The community's first Town Meeting (for which records do exist) took place on February 25, 1657. Thus was established a democratic form of government which is still prevalent throughout New England.

Although travel in those days was primarily by boat or on Indian trails along the shore and inland, in 1646 settlers recognized the need for a "way between the ferry in Salem and the head of Jeffery's Creek" as well as the need of "a footebridge at Mackrell Cove." Efforts to create the infrastructure of a town had begun.

Life was not easy in the new world. There were wild animals, even wolves in Manchester, Beverly and Wenham which preyed upon sheep and cattle and at times were a menace to human beings. Rattlesnakes made working in the woods hazardous. Winters were long and cold. Primitive heating facilities did little to increase personal comfort. "Extraordinary Cold Storm of Wind and Snow," reports Judge Samuel Sewall of Salem in 1717. (Sewall was the only one of three presiding judges at the Witch Trials in 1692 to admit later that he had been in error.) "At six o'clock my ink freezes so that I can hardly write by a good fire in my [wife's] chamber." Unlike the Judge, many early settlers were illiterate.

But wood was plentiful as was game. A musket was always kept handy and wild turkeys taken in the forest often weighed as much as 40 pounds. The Judge mentions in his diary such delicacies as boiled pork, bacon and venison as well as roast beef, roast fowl, pork and beans, and even mince pie and "chockolette." But the average family was lucky if it could salt down a hog or quarter of beef in the autumn. There was porridge and rye bread, and to drink—milk, cider and on rare occasions, tea.

Work for both men and women was hard and lasted from sun-up to long after sundown. It included clearing forests, tilling gardens, caring for domestic animals, hunting game, fishing, erecting houses, building ships and caring for families which often numbered as many as 12 to 15 persons all living under one roof in houses that, in general, were tiny by today's standards. Despite the hardships of life, however, these farmers and artisans believed that theirs was a freer and better world than the one they had left behind, a world which recognized the dignity of the individual, and which offered opportunities for riches, if risks could be overcome, which far exceeded anything they had ever known.

INDIAN PROBLEMS

Manchester Is Generally Spared, but Our Militiamen Are Slain in Deadly Ambush

By 1637, the Indians, watching the incursion of English settlers upon their lands, began to grow more hostile. Because of its location on the ocean shore, Manchester escaped the Indian attacks which devastated such inland towns as Lancaster and Deerfield. But Manchester men serving in the military were less fortunate and many were slain, particularly in the ambush at Bloody Brook, South Deerfield in 1675. At one point, 70 men from Manchester were drafted and served with the Essex County Regiment which fought both the Indians and the French.

During the last decades of the seventeenth century, news of Indian uprisings, raids and massacres cast a long shadow of fear and apprehension across communities throughout the Common-

wealth. No house was without its muskets and many women as well as men learned how to use them effectively to protect their families. Butchery and brutality were common on both sides. Animosities and hatred were fueled by battles between the British and the French, each side recruiting its own Indian allies. Finally, with the fall of King Philip and the capture of his wife and son who were sold into slavery in the West Indies, the conflict subsided.

The costs were enormous. In Massachusetts, 16 towns were destroyed or abandoned. Expenses rose dramatically as, of course, did taxes. Manchester was no exception. But the fact that colonists had won possession of their lands and property by their own hands, with the expenditure of their own coin and their own blood, without aid of any kind from England, was to have dramatic consequences in shaping the national character in the years to come.

As the colonies grew more confident in themselves and more independent of the Mother Country, signs of unrest began to appear. New England, now populated almost entirely by a second generation of settlers born in the New World, was especially independent. Well educated, comparatively prosperous, the heirs to early Puritanism were themselves philosophically exploring the questions of liberty and sovereignty and who should direct their lives. All this was particularly galling to the Crown. As one Frenchman wrote: "the English who dwell near Boston will not worry about the prohibitions which the King of England may issue because they hardly recognize his authority." Trade with the West Indies and Europe was booming and British merchants were complaining that they were being undersold and that Massachusetts especially was ignoring the Navigation Acts.

By 1684, the Crown, angry with the errant colonists, had revoked the Charter of the Massachusetts Bay Colony and installed former Governor of New York Edmund Andros with a Royal Council to rule the Dominion. The Governor's policies affecting land ownership and taxes, designed to destroy local autonomy, met with bitter opposition and in Ipswich, with open resistance. Manchester was equally indignant and on May 17, 1689, the town petitioned elected officials in Boston to restore the Commonwealth's Charter. The high-handed Andros, however, lasted only a few months before he was overthrown and imprisoned. The seeds of rebellion had been planted. Loyalty to legitimate royal power, however, continued and ties to England remained strong.

With the Indian menace ended and with relations with the Crown improved, Manchester shared the benefits of a new era of prosperity and growth for the colony of Massachusetts. A road was constructed to Gloucester and the first store opened on Sea Street run by that redoubtable entrepreneur, Sally Samples. The town's first tavern appeared on North Street and was quickly followed by the establishment of two others, for in those early days the tavern was the center of town activity.

In 1691, Manchester residents—there were then 350 of them—voted to construct a new and larger Meeting House to replace the old which first appeared in 1672. Its specifications called for a structure measuring 30 by 25 feet with a belfry "suitable for a good bell of 100 weight." By 1700, a sizable number of buildings including another schoolhouse, a tide mill, a saw mill and a blacksmith's shop—the latter owned by Joseph Knight—had made the Cove "quite the largest precinct in town." A number of vessels also had been built by Asa Kitfield who was engaged in fishing and in trading lumber. The town, like others, lived quietly attending to its own interests.

Then, in 1745, men from Manchester joined a combined British and American force which traveled by sea and, in a daring amphibious maneuver, captured the French fort at Louisburg, Nova Scotia, giving England title to the entire coast of North America. Manchester resident Benjamin Craft, who with Stephen Low, William Allen and Joseph Emerton, was a member of the Louisburg expedition, ran the commissary for his regiment.

Although the long war between Britain and France had a minimal effect upon life in the Colonies (there was fear of a French fleet attacking Manchester and Cape Ann in 1746), the peace that followed brought additional prosperity until about 1760. That year, public records provide a glimpse of how successful some settlers had become. For example, John Herrick: his annual worth—28 Pounds (a goodly sum in those days); one dwelling and money at interest, 20 Pounds. He also had "two horses, six oxen, six cows, five sheep, two hogs; 100 acres of pasture, 10 acres of tillage; 150 bushels of grain and 10 barrels of cider." Life had been good to Herrick but he had achieved his success by the strength of his back and by the sweat of his brow.

TENSIONS WITH BRITAIN
Feelings For and Against the King Run High; Residents Fund 'Minutemen'

From 1700 to 1775, the country's population increased dramatically from some 250,000 to more than 2.5 million. In large part this was due to natural growth—births over deaths—but immigration from Ireland and from Germany also played an important role. One fifth of the population of America was black, almost all of them slaves. The church, too, had undergone massive changes which led to a loss of power by religious leaders in their communities and a new growth of denominationalism. And there were dramatic if underlying differences between the political philosophies of England proper and those of her citizens who lived in the American Colonies.

Gradually, tensions between the two mounted and the story is as old as history: the arrogant and despotic policies of George III and his Prime Minister, Lord North. The clumsy, irritating and insensitive search for revenue from the Colonies. The Sugar Act. The Stamp Act. The indignant outrage of the Americans. The emergence of the Sons of Liberty. The rise of Samuel Adams and popular politics. The Tea Act and the Boston Tea Party. The argument: taxation without representation. And, finally, the end of respect for British authority and the rise of revolutionary fervor. The reaction in England: anger and impatience. The dispatch of a British warship. The Boston Massacre—five civilian deaths. The arrival of additional troops with General Gage, now Governor of the Colony of Massachusetts. The Coercive Acts of 1774. Military rule and a crackdown on the Colonists. And finally, open rebellion. The battles of Lexington and Concord and Bunker Hill. The Continental Congress and in 1775, the Declaration of Independence.

Meanwhile, in Manchester, less than 30 miles from Boston, now hot-bed of the Revolution, feelings were running high both for and against the King. According to the History of Manchester, 1645–1895, by D.F. Lamson, Captain Thomas Leach told the story of how his grandfather, Ezekiel Leach, had warned "his children one day when they were going to school, that if the teacher

8

asked them to spell 'English' not to do it." There were Tory families who left for New Brunswick and Nova Scotia. There were others who chose to stay but painted their chimneys white to show their loyalty to the Crown. Residents at Town Meeting in 1775 voted to raise funds to support the "Minutemen," while others agreed to keep watches from Chubbs Creek to Kettle Cove for a British landing.

Although Salem and Marblehead were well defended, less could be said of the area between Beverly and Cape Ann except for the placement of a small battery at Glass Head in Manchester. Finally, a Committee of Correspondence was formed in town to deal with the military business of the war. Its members were John Edwards, Eleazer Crafts, Samuel Forster, Jonathan Herrick, Jacob Hooper, Aaron Lee, Isaac Lee, John Lee and Isaac Proctor.

Watches now were kept around the clock. Entrenchments were dug. And Dr. John Whipple, Manchester's first physician, was appointed Captain of the "Coast Guards" with orders that he and his soldiers should carry their "arms to meeting every meeting day." The Town provided a bonus of 14 pounds for each man who enlisted in the Continental Army. And taxes were levied to pay for the war. On that celebrated April 19, 1775, Manchester men also set out for Concord to help defend military supplies stored there. At Medford, however, they learned of the battle at the North Bridge and of the British retreat and they returned home. Twenty-one citizens of the town joined the Continental Army. Others manned earthworks and served aboard privateers authorized to plunder enemy vessels. With men away and trade and fishing at a standstill, the war for Manchester meant hard times financially, but its citizens gave all the funds they could raise to support the Revolution, even those monies which had been specifically dedicated for the ministry.

In 1777, Eleazar Crafts, was a Major in Manchester's Militia unit. Ten years earlier, at the age of 22, he had married 33-year-old Sally Allen Samples, a young widow with children who was famous as the town's first storekeeper. But with the war increasing in intensity and the British on their way to recapture the Fort at Ticonderoga, Crafts was ordered to join American troops at Saratoga, New York.

Men traveled on foot in those days under the most difficult conditions using woodland trails for there were few roads. But they were young, hardy and committed to defend the cause of free-dom. Craft's diary, from the Historical Collection, Volume VI, at the Peabody-Essex Museum, tells of the march north in his own words. The simplicity of his remarks enhances the extraordinary drama of his experiences,

"September 9, 1777. Left home, bound to join the Northern Army. Reached Cambridge. September 10. Rainy morning. Marched to Sudberry [Sudbury]. Dined at Tilton's. Afternoon reached Shrewsbury. September 11. Marched on. Reached Ware. Rain. Put up. September 12. This day reached Northampton. Put up at Toppan's. September 13. Head out for Bennington. Reached Worthington. September 14. Sabbath Day. Marched on. Reached New Providence. Put up. Lodged on the floor for the first time. September 15. This day reached Bennington [Vermont]. About 8 o'clock." Twenty-four hours later, he was bivouacked with other American troops on the outskirts of Saratoga.

British General John Burgoyne with an army of 8,000 men, approached Ticonderoga from Canada by way of Lake Champlain. His goal, and that of other English forces, was to isolate New England and thus end the rebellion. But the Americans had other ideas. With his supply lines increasingly stretched, Burgoyne's ponderous force was attacked continually on its flanks by New England militia units such as the one led by Eleazar Crafts. When 900 British regulars tried to seize supplies from an American arsenal in Bennington, they were all but destroyed by a force of 2,000 New England patriots commanded by General John Stark.

The delaying action allowed American forces in the Hudson River valley to organize and by the time Burgoyne reached Saratoga he faced American General Horatio Gates and an army of 10,000 men. Hopelessly outnumbered and out-fought in two bloody battles, Burgoyne surrendered his entire force.

'A SHOWER OF GRAPE'

Turning Point: Burgoyne Is Defeated by the Americans at Saratoga

Major Crafts describes his own role and reactions to the battle. "October 7. This day pleasant...the enemy were out of their lines. We were now all well, alert and gay, but...we were soon met by a shower of grape shot and small arm balls. Capt. Flint fell close by me the first minute we got up. The engagement lasted two hours. We, through God's goodness, drove them into their lines and got possession of some of their works. October 9. Rainy day. The enemy fled today. All is quiet until October 14. This day a flag of truce was sent out from Mr. Burgoyne which caused a cessation of arms...I was ordered on picket guard with 160 men and within 40 rods of the [enemy's] lines. October 17. A pleasant day and glorious for Americans. The great General Burgoyne marched out and laid down his arms to who he often called the rebel army. November 30. Sabbath day. This morning the brigade discharged at 9 o'clock. Began our march for home. God grant us a safe journey."

The victory at Saratoga was a turning point in the Revolutionary War. It convinced the British that they might not be able to defeat the rebels as easily as they thought. And it gave confidence to France which soon entered the war on the side of the Americans.

Eleazar Crafts did reach Manchester safely and when peace came he and his wife Sally turned their house into Craft's Tavern. It was located on the Town Common near where the Library is today. Major Crafts died at 50 years of age of consumption (now known as tuberculosis) probably contracted during the war. The couple's granddaughter was Abigail Hooper who married Captain Richard Trask. The Trask house, built in 1823, is preserved today on Union Street as headquarters of the Manchester Historical Society.

With Massachusetts Bay blockaded by British ships, General Washington was desperately short of gun powder and ammunition. The enemy, on the other hand, unable to obtain supplies locally, hauled its war material in vessels which proceeded in a steady stream to Boston from Nova Scotia, the West Indies and from England. What was needed was an American navy to intercept these ships and to capture their cargoes for the Continental Army. To undertake such a task, Washington turned to a feisty Marbleheader, Colonel John Glover, who leased his schooner HANNAH for the purpose. The HANNAH was followed by scores of other vessels including the LEE which, under command of Captain John Manley of Marblehead, captured the 250-ton British transport NANCY on her way to Boston.

Aboard was the answer to Washington's dream: some 2,000 muskets and bayonets, 100,000 flints, 8,400 fuses, 31 tons of musket shot and an immense brass mortar. It was a treasured cargo and Manches-

ter militia men were among those who stood guard as it was off-loaded at Freshwater and Kettle Coves.

BOLD, BRAVE & BRASSY
Privateers Play a Major Role; Manchester Sailors Foil Attempt to Take Their Ship

But while Washington's navy was successful in providing material for the Continental Army at the expense of John Bull, privateering also played a critical role during the war, harassing enemy ships and seizing supplies. More than 600 Letters of Marque were issued to privately-owned Massachusetts vessels by the Continental Congress and some 1,000 more by the Commonwealth's General Court. The documents authorized ship owners, as private citizens, to capture vessels and to appropriate goods of an enemy nation.

Of little use in battle, privateers were lightly armed and manned by fishermen and other sailors who came from coastal towns such as Manchester. They were small, fast, close-winded vessels which engaged in daring feats of seamanship while attacking British supply lines as far away as the English Channel. Swooping down on slower British merchantmen, they seized stores, munitions and clothing, putting a skeleton crew aboard to sail the ships into protected American harbors. Early on, following a review by an admiralty court, it was agreed that officers and crews would be awarded prizes totaling one-third the value of captured, non-military cargo. Needless to say, this added significantly to the incentive to succeed, and in the early years of the war sizable profits were made by everyone connected with privateering.

But this kind of "legalized piracy" although glamorous in its execution had its hazards. Among the most serious disasters suffered by Manchester during the war was the loss of the privateer GLOUCESTER. After capturing two prizes, she disappeared without a trace in July, 1776, with a crew of 130 men. Eighteen men aboard the brig were from Manchester including her surgeon, the town's beloved Dr. Joseph Whipple, who left a widow and seven children. Ten other residents of the town were also lost aboard the privateer BARRINGTON, which sailed out of Newburyport. In 1778, Captain Jeremia Hibbert of Manchester drowned in a storm off Portland, Maine, with the sinking of the brig CIVIL USAGE. His brother Joseph, also master of a privateer, died in the naval battle at Penobscot. All four Hilton brothers were lost at sea in the same year.

But Yankee audacity as well as heroism enabled other Manchester seamen not only to survive but to triumph. Take the story of two Manchester men, Captain William Tuck (for whom Tuck's Point is named) and his mate, Daniel Leach. Their ship had been captured by the British, and Tuck, famous for his "gift of the gab," had managed to ingratiate himself with British officers aboard and was taken ashore to dinner in Nova Scotia. Leach, in the meantime, while the English prize crew was in the rigging tricing up, smashed open the arms chest, and retook the ship. When the officers returned, Leach announced that they were his prisoners and with Captain Tuck in command again, the ship promptly got underway for Boston.

Then there was the tale of 21-year-old William Kitfield of Manchester who with two other young men his age was captured aboard an American craft and imprisoned in Britain. The three managed to escape and, pretending to be English, shipped aboard a vessel bound for Jamaica and Halifax. Each purchased a sword before they sailed and planned to seize the ship while underway. As an account in the Salem Register explains: "About midnight, when all three were in the same watch, [one] was placed at the cabin door while Kitfield went to the second mate, who was at the helm, and told him the anchor was off the bow. Thus they got charge of the deck and the officers were [kept] prisoner below. The crew, being promised a share of the prize, readily joined [the Americans]. The next day they ran alongside an American privateer and were taken to Salem where the vessel was given up to the three daring youngsters. According to the Register, "The [British] Captain cried bitterly and said he would not care so much about it if it were not the first time he had been [in command]!"

HIGH SPIRITS

Captured Captain Sails His Ship Back to Boston; Surprised British Surrender

William Pert, another Manchester skipper, was carrying a cargo of provisions and fine liquor when his ship, too, was taken by the English off Boston and a prize crew put aboard to sail her to Halifax. The officers, however, soon discovered the spirits and were enjoying them hugely when night fell.

Being in strange waters, they asked Captain Pert to work the vessel. He readily agreed, leaving the helm to go below on occasion to urge his captors to sample other varieties of wine and brandy. Throughout the night, while enemy officers entertained themselves, Captain Pert quietly tacked the ship and sailed her back to Boston. When morning came, the bewildered British, suffering mightily from their indulgences of the night before, found themselves under the guns of the fort at Boston Harbor where they were taken prisoner.

Americans patrolling the shore west of Manchester's Tuck's Point as members of Colonel Glover's regiment, captured one of two British coasters which sought shelter from the weather in the cove at Great Misery Island. Aboard, the patriots were delighted to find provisions for the English army at Annapolis, Nova Scotia, which they turned over to General Washington's headquarters at Cambridge.

By 1787, the War of Independence had ended successfully. The Articles of Confederation had been adopted, and the Peace of Paris had been signed by Britain. Men from Manchester had served their new country well. Nearly a seventh of the town's male population, 137 men, had been members of the Continental Army. Eighty women were widows, and in 1778 when the General Court ordered the town to send five men to be conscripted, only three could be found. The result was a fine of 200 pounds. It was quickly appealed, however, and the community exonerated. Manchester, it was agreed, had done more than her share. But the war had taken its toll and people were in desperate economic circumstances. Fishing was at a standstill and trade all but non-existent. Slowly, however, as men did return home, conditions improved. Then in 1794, another calamity struck as some 70 residents died of what was probably an epidemic of typhoid fever.

Daily life continued to be difficult. Science had not yet discovered the answers we have today and superstition was rife. Fear and suffering were a part of everyone's existence. Manchester even had its own "witch," a poor, harmless woman named Molly Sennitt who lived on North Street.

The sea, however, still proved to be Manchester's greatest asset. Fishermen and merchant sailors made the name of the town known throughout the world. At one time it was said that Manchester had more captains in the merchant service than any other community in Essex County. In 1810 alone,

A schooner-rigged Chebacco boat ghosts along in a light breeze. Named for the Parish of Chebacco which was once a part of Ipswich, the vessels, which preceded the graceful Gloucester schooners like the one at left background, were smaller with a sharp or "pinky" stern and were designed to fish along the shores of Cape Ann. Many Chebacco boats were moored in Manchester during the early years of the 19th century. Photo courtesy of Cape Ann Historical Association.

Fisherman Edward Woodbury Heath with his "wheelbarrow boat" at the Cove. Born on January 3, 1855, Edward Heath was the son of John Gardner and Nancy (Nichols) Heath. He began fishing at age 14 and continued in the industry for 54 years of his life. He died December 15, 1921 leaving a daughter, Mrs. Gladys Karlen. Photo from the collection of Nathaniel C. Andrews.

there were 50 men, each of whom served as master of a ship at sea. Two vessels bore the name of the town. The schooner MANCHESTER, built in 1784 for coastal trading, was afloat in Gloucester in 1878. Another schooner named MANCHESTER was built for fishing in 1845 in Essex.

THE 'SACRED COD'

After the Revolution, Fishing Becomes a Major Industry for Manchester

Throughout the history of Massachusetts and, indeed, New England, fishing has been a mainstay of the region's economy (at least until the 1960's when overfishing all but destroyed traditional species). In his "A Description of New England," a report of his voyages here as early as 1616, Captain John Smith not only names the area for posterity, but extols its fisheries as one of its outstanding assets. John Winthrop, too, exclaims that "among the grounds [for] settling a plantation in New England" is its "infinite variety & store of fishes."

On Beacon Hill, in the chambers of the House of Representatives today, in a place of honor above the Speaker's platform, hangs an historic carved replica of the "sacred cod" acquired in 1784. John Adams himself is said to have declared: "[the fisheries] were to us what wool was to England and tobacco was to Virginia, the great staple which became the basis of power and wealth." One of the major features, too, of the Peace of Paris which the new United States of America signed with England in 1783, included a definition of its rights to the fisheries of Newfoundland. And on the North Shore, the purpose of the first English settlement at Cape Ann, as explained to King James, was "to worship God and catch fish."

Before fleets of graceful schooners made their way east off shore to the Grand Banks, there were coastal fishermen here who ventured as far as the Bay of Fundy in shallops, open boats with sails and oars. In the early days with smaller populations, there was little need to voyage far for fish so plentiful were they in waters nearby. But after the Revolution, ambitions and markets grew, and at Manchester, Essex and Gloucester, shipwrights produced larger craft. One, the "Chebacco boat," named for the Parish of Chebacco, which was then a part of Ipswich, had a sharp or pinky stern. Another with a flat stern was called by the unlikely name of "Dogbody." Both were rigged as "cat-schooners" without a bowsprit or a jib. These craft, and there were scores of them in harbors around Cape Ann, rarely exceeded 40 feet in length and "usually had two or more [open] cockpits in which the crew stood when fishing," according to Howard I. Chapell's History of American Sailing Ships.

These two types remained in favor until about 1820, when, Chapell explains, the Chebacco boat developed into the "Jigger" and then into the "Pinky," a small schooner with a square stern. More attention was now being paid to fishing off shore and the size of vessels increased to some 65 feet overall. Primarily schooner rigged, these boats were shaped like a barrel with short, high quarterdecks and full bows. Known locally as 'Heeltappers," they were again rigged fore and aft as schooners "with an occasional main topmast staysail."

Finally, in Essex in 1846, Andrew Story, Chapell writes, "designed and built a schooner on speculation which was the expression of his own ideas of what a fisherman should be." Using the lines of a "Baltimore Clipper" as inspiration, the vessel had "more deadrise and shaper ends than had yet been seen in the fishing fleet." Christened ROMP, she was very different from her predecessors and was greeted with some skepticism by the always conservative fishing community. Her speed and sea-keeping qualities, however, soon won enthusiastic approval and she is considered to have led to a complete change in the character and design of New England fishing vessels, one which lasted throughout the great age of sail.

Meanwhile, first in shallops, then in Chebacco boats, jiggers and pinkies and small schooners, Manchester men put to sea. With a Bible in one hand, and after 1800, a copy of Nathaniel Bowditch's Practical Navigator in the other, they ranged far and wide from Newfoundland to Bermuda and the Caribbean. Fish were plentiful—cod, haddock and halibut, pollack, herring and mackerel. But whether carrying cargo or fish, following the sea was a dangerous occupation. As poet Oliver Wendell Holmes wrote:

"Ah, many a lonely home is found
Along the Essex shore,
They cheered the goodman outward bound,
And see his face no more."

A RUGGED LIFE

'Wooden Ships and Iron Men:' Trademark of the New England Fishing Industry

It was also a life of few comforts. In 1895, Reverend Lamson quotes a survivor of the time when fishing was the business of the town. His name was Deacon A.E. Low and he reports on what it was like during the early 19th century, fishing off Labrador aboard the schooner RICHMOND, Abram Stone, Master. "When I was 13 years of age," the Deacon says, "I was put into the business. We fished for several weeks and then on September 15, we sailed for home, encountering a line gale off Cape Breton. The strong current rushing from the gulf [of St. Lawrence] raised a sharp and dangerous sea. At the height of the gale, the wind would lull suddenly, the vessel falling into the trough of the sea, the waves breaking 20 feet above the deck. When the [storm] subsided, one boat with davits had gone from the stern and three boats stowed on deck were stove.

"Cape Ray was sighted and...the night being cloudy and dark, a timber ship crashed upon us, striking abaft the main chains, down [came] the mainsail...knocking the captain overboard, who was saved by the sail hanging from the side...The next day we were in tow for Miramichi. The schooner cast off outside the bar. We landed at a small village with a tavern and...needed repairs being made, we were off again on our passage. Beating around the eastern point of Prince Edward Island, the vessel struck on a reef...as the tide went down, the decks went up which looked much like the end of the voyage; but when the tide turned the wind changed with a strong breeze off the shore. Again afloat, we passed through the Straights of Canso with a fine leading breeze, under the foretopsail. Clearing the Straights we made sail and were six days to Cape Ann." At the time, it was all in a day's work.

The loss of two vessels, the BLOOMING YOUTH and the SENATOR on the sands of Sable Island in May, 1840, was still "being talked about" as Reverend Lamson was writing his history of the town in 1895. Crew of the BLOOMING YOUTH managed to get ashore safely but the ship herself was a total loss. Built in Essex, she was about 70 tons. The men, who included at least two (one a boy) from Manchester, remained with an island resident for 24 days before they were able to get to Halifax and then to Boston. The crew of SENATOR was rescued by fishermen from Cape Cod who bought the vessel for a few dollars, kept her afloat and towed her home where she was fitted out again for fishing.

In the 29 years between 1745 and 1774, 90 Manchester men perished at sea. Other terrors for seaman included slaughter by Indians ashore and boarding by pirates on the open ocean.

By the early 1800's, the fisheries in Manchester had reached a zenith. Assessors' lists show vessels ranging from 54 tons to 130 tons. The latter, the brig ALONZO, Captain Abiel Burgess, was the largest and first square-rigged ship to visit Manchester's Town Landing. Her arrival, obviously at high water, drew an excited crowd of all ages. By 1835, however, fishing and coastal vessels in Manchester totaled less than 1,200 tons. The use of coastal weirs and traps used particularly for catching mackerel and herring, reduced the fleet to 13 craft with landings in 1845 totaling $21,435. Cabinet making soon began to take over where fishing left off.

As Lamson states, "The inhabitants of Manchester...have owed much of their pluck, their persistence, their success in life, to the ocean with whose waves they sported from childhood, and which presented at their very doors a field for their skill and an area for their prowess." It all came to an end, however, with the War of 1812.

With American seamen being seized or impressed at sea and made to work as crew on British warships, and American merchant vessels being boarded and harassed, the United States declared war upon Great Britain in 1812. As a part of the nation's policy to pressure Britain to change its ways, President Jefferson had earlier (1807) declared an embargo which closed American ports and prohibited foreign commerce. The results were significantly more disastrous for our own citizens than they were for the English.

Manchester sought relief from the Great and General Court. A petition was drafted and sent to Beacon Hill. However, an article in July, 1812 which appeared in The Messenger, a Boston newspaper, stated that the protest was "so literate and so comparatively reserved that it apparently went unheard in Washington, perhaps overshadowed by [another from] Gloucester which addressed the President himself."

"Our home is on the ocean," petitioners in Manchester wrote, "our wealth we draw from the deep, and by dangers and suffering...we support ourselves. While our fish are perishing in our stores, our vessels rotting at the wharves, we look with sorrow and dismay upon the poverty which must be our lot unless government in its wisdom should speedily provide relief..." None came, however, and exports, the heart and soul of coastal economies, dropped dramatically in value. The result was that in New England support of Federalism grew in popularity and Federalists in Congress bitterly opposed war with England.

WAR OF 1812
Local Skippers Run the British Blockade; Our Powder House Is Built on the Hill

With its inevitable arrival, watches for the enemy were once again set along the coast as English men-of-war, still part of the mightiest Navy in the world, sailed just off shore ready to raid towns and villages. Norton's Point became the site of a new breastwork. And to store ammunition, a Powder House, which still stands today, was built of brick on a hill behind the town.

There was a resurgence also in privateering. Especially built in shipyards in Salem, Newburyport and along the New England coast, "the privateers of 1812," writes Alan Villiers in Men, Ships and the Sea, "were swift brigs and schooners... their sleek hulls were bare of ornament; they carried high raking masts and stout rigging to support a cloud of canvas. The British admired them, and used those they captured" to further their own cause.

The London Statesman, too, was flattering in its appraisal. "These sea-going Americans," it declared, "will be found a different sort of enemy than the French. They possess a nautical knowledge with equal enterprise to ourselves. They will...attempt deeds which a Frenchman would never think of..." The records clearly show they did.

The account that follows, taken from Lamson's history of the town, quotes a story, told, apparently from memory, by "two old inhabitants of Salem and Beverly" which appeared in The Beverly Times prior to 1895.

"...Ebenezer Tappan, who kept a store on Central Street [in Manchester] believed it possible to evade the enemy's ships and get some supplies from Boston. His topsail schooner NANCY was noted for her sailing qualities, and Captain Jerry Danforth, Nathan Carter, and his son, Benjamin Tappan, were placed in charge. They kept along the shore, entered Boston Harbor by Shirley Gut at night; [then] having secured their cargo, which consisted of flour, sugar, molasses, rum and lumber, they started homeward. All went well until they had passed Baker's Island and they were congratulating themselves upon the success of their trip for they were almost home.

"Suddenly, the fog lifting, disclosed the much dreaded cruiser quite near. A shot from her was a hint to stop, but, as there was a breeze, they kept on their course for Manchester. They could see two barges being made ready for a chase. When they reflected on the damage they might inflict on the unprotected village, they resolved to run inside [west of] Misery Island and [to] endeavor to reach the protection of the fort below Salem. But the wind became lighter and the barges were gaining so fast it was decided to run her on shore which they did at Mingo Beach in Beverly.

"The men landed under cover of the vessel but as they reached the high land near the road they were fired upon by their pursuers. The English used every effort to get their prize afloat, but, failing that, they took some of the goods, stripped the sails and set her on fire. The militia from Beverly and Manchester soon arrived, extinguished the blaze and hastened the departure of the barges by some musket shots. The vessel was afterwards taken to Manchester and repaired."

According to Lamson, "the late Captain Leach witnessed the affair with his father and grandfather, with whom he rode to the scene in a 'square-topped chaise.'" Lamson also reports that a piece of shot from a swivel (a small canon that turns on a pivot), a ball about two inches in diameter, picked up just after it was fired by one of the barges, was, in 1895, possessed by Manchester resident Oliver T. Roberts.

Manchester also petitioned the General Court for two six-pound cannon. Captain Hooper's Company of Foot, some 80 men with Sergeants Ebenezer Tappan Jr. and Amos Knight, drilled on the Common, much as their fathers had before them during the Revolution. Afterwards, they retired to the Tavern for a welcome cider or flip (like egg nog)—citizen soldiers who throughout the nation's history have rallied to protect their ideals, their homes and their country in times of need.

But although British ships landed, burned villages and seized livestock and other foodstuffs elsewhere in New England, Manchester escaped damage from the enemy. One incident, however, a near confrontation, is famous in the annals of the town.

CALLING THEIR BLUFF
Manchester Militiamen Turn Back the Dreaded Enemy at Crow Island

Early in the war, an English ship, preparing to launch her boats, was sighted off Kettle Cove and the alarm was sounded. Militiamen quickly mustered in front of the Congregational Church. The cannon was loaded with powder and a single ball and, towing the gun, the column set out for Crow Island. Once there, men and boys, gripping their muskets, crouched behind rocks and bushes while the cannon was pointed out to sea as the enemy approached.

Hearing the sounds of fife and drum and seeing heads and the cannon on shore, the English, assuming they would be facing a larger force than actually existed, turned about and rowed back to their ship. As soon as the pulling boats were far enough off shore, the brave defenders stood up and, gleefully proclaiming their success at vanquishing the enemy, set out for town again tugging the old cannon and followed by a crowd of "noisy-boys."

When they reached the bottom of "the great hill" on Summer Street, however, to their amazement and chagrin, they discovered by the side of the road the cannon ball which they had loaded so carefully earlier. There it sat, having fallen from the gun as it was being pulled up the hill on its way to confront the enemy. But loaded or not, the cannon had accomplished its objectives and nothing could dampen the enthusiasm of the militia. It marched proudly home to be greeted by welcoming townsfolk who heartily cheered the heroes who had saved them from invasion.

As many of the men were away fighting, when the alarm sounded that an enemy ship was offshore, the women of the town would head for the woods taking with them whatever valuables they could carry. One story has it that someone's good wife reached the woods with the silver intact, but in her haste she discovered she had forgotten the baby!

A Manchester resident was aboard the U.S. frigate CHESAPEAKE, 38 guns, when she fought His Britannic Majesty's ship SHANNON, also 38 guns, off Boston in June, 1813. His name was Lambert Flowers. CHESAPEAKE suffered 146 casualties in the battle, SHANNON, 83. Flowers was among the American wounded. With an inexperienced and poorly disciplined crew, CHESAPEAKE was forced to strike her colors . Her captain, James Lawrence, was killed during the action. It is said his last words were, "Don't give up the ship!" which became a rallying cry for the U.S. Navy. A prize crew of 50 sailed CHESAPEAKE to Halifax, Nova Scotia. Flowers recovered and served as a boatswain in the Navy for many years.

Hundreds of people watched the battle which, unfortunately, was over too quickly. Most were on shore, but Stephen Danforth of Manchester was an eyewitness on the water. According to The Cricket which interviewed him as an older man years later in December, 1888, "he was fishing with his father near Middle Bank...and during the first of the engagement, several shots passed over their boat. The frigates afterwards changed positions and the shot went south...He did not see much of the frigates during the battle [because] of the smoke.

"At another time during the War of 1812, [Danforth] said [that] two barges from a British frigate captured his father while [he was] fishing in the Bay. They pulled for Kettle Cove [in] Manchester, intending to make him pilot them into the harbor. When near shore [the British] asked, 'how many militia men [are] in town?' He replied, 'two hundred.'

The answer frightened them," The Cricket continued, "and they carried him back to his boat, contenting themselves by stealing all his fresh fish and [his] mainsail..."

Other men from Manchester served in the Navy as well, some at sea and some on Lake Erie with Master Commander Oliver Hazard Perry, whose exploits in battle have made him an American hero. Ephraim Clements, John Babcock, Joseph Camp and his brother William were with Lieutenant Thomas Macdonough during his great victory as leader of the U.S. squadron on Lake Champlain. Some were captured and others killed (the Camp brothers never returned and were presumed lost), but all fought for their country with bravery and distinction.

The War of 1812 established the freedom of the new nation forever and won it international recognition as a naval power. Manchester's reputation

This house at 22 Sea Street was first owned by Sally Allen who married sailor and Scotsman Samuel Samples. Legend has it that after her marriage, Sally helped to build the house herself carrying bricks and walking to Salem to buy nails and glass for its window panes. After a decade, Samuel was lost at sea, and Sally, then a widow with four children, resourcefully opened a store in the parlor, walking to Boston during the Revolution and crossing British lines to acquire pins and needles for her customers. (She later wed Major Eleazar Crafts.) In 1864, the property was purchased by Shakespearean actor Joseph Proctor, a venerated figure in Manchester's community of artists. This photo shows Proctor standing tall in the center with his daughter Anna at his right and his wife Elizabeth at his left. Photo courtesy of Ogden White.

Baker Homestead at 187 School Street in 1884. Located at the junction of School Street and Route 128, the house bought by Robert Baker in 1818 still stands today. Baker Farm was a popular local source of milk, strawberries and Christmas trees. From left are Lorenzo Baker driving the wagon with Dolly the black mare; John Baker, Jr. holding Dolly's bridle; the dog Fannie; standing, Hattie Barnes, Mrs. Rollins' sister; Mrs. Rollins; seated, Nancy A. Baker (1835- 1918), wife of John Baker, Sr.; standing, Nancy Burnham; seated, Mary Dade Baker (1860-1893, Hattie's mother); standing, Lucy Baker (1860-1930). Photo courtesy of Bernice Baker Lipsett.

17

as a maritime community grew as its vessels not only engaged in coastal trade but visited ports in Europe, Spain and the Mediterranean, as well as in the West Indies.

By 1815, peace had been agreed upon and a treaty signed with the British at Ghent in Belgium. Two wars in 40 years had exhausted the country, but its victories had established the United States as a member of the world community. In Manchester, the war's end was celebrated with a "great dinner at the tavern where the emotions of the people found vent in speeches, patriotic songs and shouts of merriment until the wee hours of the morning."

CABINET-MAKING ERA

Fishing Declines but Furniture Factories Spring Up; Offer New Employment

The town had a reason to hail its growth and increasing prosperity. In 1816, it was home to three grist mills, three lumber mills, one mahogany veneering mill, one bakery, 12 carpenters, one cooper's (or barrel) shop, one wheelright, three painters, one tailor, one brickyard, six shoemakers' shops, two blacksmiths, one manufacturer of ships' steering wheels and one tannery as well as a number of livestock and produce farms. No longer were fishing and farming the only activities. Women, too, were beginning to play a role in industry, particularly in milling, both wool and cotton, and in the making of clothes. Despite its size and the reverses of its early years, Manchester was coming of age.

By 1845 there were as few as 18 boats engaged in mackerel fishing. But another industry was in its ascendancy—furniture manufacturing—which was to make the town famous throughout the country. As early as 1837, there were 12 so-called "cabinet shops" in Manchester employing 120 of a population of 1,600 inhabitants.

Mills were among the first buildings constructed by early settlers. There were saw mills to produce lumber for housing and for ships, and grist mills to produce flour for bread. Colonists brought some of their household furnishings from England such as favorite chests of drawers, desks and tables, but room was scarce on the tiny ships of the day and much of the settlers' furniture was made after they arrived. Initially, it was crude, just enough to serve the purpose. But as time passed, skilled craftsmen turned out pieces which were as handsome as those made in the finest European shops by Chippendale or Hepplewhite.

Many of these craftsmen were right here in Manchester. Moses Dodge began work in 1775 launching a dynasty of Dodge furniture makers which lasted until the late 1950's when the Dodge Mill was closed. Other names involved in the cabinet business since its early days were Ebenezer Tappan, Caleb Knowlton, John P. Allen and Larkin Woodberry. Shops were filled with the sweet smells of pine, birch, cherry and such exotic woods as mahogany and walnut. The furniture produced was shipped by water and often sold at auction. Some auctions resulted in so many orders that it was difficult to find men skilled enough to respond to them. Once a craft industry, cabinet-making quickly came to depend upon woodworking tools that grew more sophisticated each year. One shop in Manchester, owned by John Perry Allen, skilled at sawing, produced wood veneers for furniture makers throughout the country. Unfortunately, Allen's shop, located on Saw Mill Brook where it enters the inner harbor, was destroyed by fire in 1836. Damage was estimated at $30,000, a sizable sum in those days. But the mill was soon rebuilt.

Besides cabinets, dressers, chairs, beds and tables, it is not well known that Manchester also manufactured musical instruments. Upright piano cases were produced in the late nineteenth century by Rust & Marshall whose shop was located on Elm Street. Later, when the firm purchased Rockport's Manning Organ Company, it also made pipe organs. Unfortunately, according to a paper read to members of the Historical Society by I.M. Marshall, founder and editor of The Manchester Cricket, upright pianos had yet to become popular and thus cases were not easy to sell. However, a few pianos, Marshall wrote, were completed in their entirety "by a German named Hazelhurst who lived on Beach Street...a remarkably skillful mechanic, [he was] capable of doing every part of the work including tuning..." When it came to organs, Rust & Marshall apparently met with greater success "turning out a goodly number of these instruments which were considered equal to the Esty and [those of] other first class [manufacturers]." One, built in Manchester, is today preserved in the Hattie Lee Harris Living Room at the Historical Society.

Much of the less expensive furniture manufactured here found its way to New Orleans and there was shipped up the Mississippi River to the burgeoning mid-west. To protect their delicate finishes before they were boxed, chairs, tables and dressers were often wrapped in copies of the LIBERATOR, a radical, anti-slavery publication beloved by many liberal New Englanders. When the cases were opened on a windy day in the slave-owning states and the newspaper packing was blown far and wide, it must have outraged Southern planters to read the moral utterances of the North's most outspoken abolitionists right in their own back yards. Word was soon sent back to use some other packing material!

The mass market for furniture shifted to the west after 1835 where lumber and labor were cheap. But Manchester's skilled artisans continued to meet the demand for carefully crafted pieces which were considered among those who knew "as fine as any turned out in the United States." The work day was long. As many as 14 hours were spent at the bench or the lathe.

JOBS AND MONEY
Regular Hours and a Paycheck Lead to More Time for Leisure and Learning

But with new money provided by the success of Manchester's now major industry, workers and their families began to enjoy life as they never had before. Many of the mills employed 50 or more people, one as many as 100. Unlike fishing or farming, working hours in industry were defined and thus there was more time not only for leisure but for learning. And this was relished as a family with young and old taking part. As Manchester and the rest of America experienced a new prosperity, circumstances were providing the beginnings of the emergence of a middle class.

Although religion and the Puritan ethic still tended to exert their influences, there was a greater emphasis on pleasure as described to Reverend Lamson by Deacon Low who recalled the celebration of Independence Day in 1826. First, residents "were awakened by the joyful ringing of bells and booming of cannon, announcing the dawn of the nation's birthday." This was followed by a parade led by Captain Benjamin Knowlton's company of militia in handsome uniforms with blue coats and white trousers; then exercises at the church; a reading of the Declaration of Independence; an oration by Deacon D.L. Bingham; and,

finally, dinner for all at Town Hall. Other celebratory occasions included feasting, speeches, toasts and games, at other locations around town including "Poplar Field and Lobster Cove." There were fireworks, more speeches, band music and always rum which was dispensed freely and exuberantly from wood casks.

On quieter days, sea captains and merchants from Salem and Boston might also visit Manchester in their sporty square-topped chaises (a light carriage with two or four wheels and a folding top drawn by one horse) and curricles (a two-wheeled carriage drawn by two horses abreast). Here they met at the beech grove with others of their kind (remember, Manchester had more than her share of ship's Masters) "eating cold fowl and chowder, discussing Federalist politics, and exchanging ponderous jokes" until late afternoon when it was time to head for home.

From those days in the mid-1700's when each student was taxed five pence per week for the support of the teacher, the town's school system had matured significantly. In the early days, a series of independent regional schools located in the Cove, at the Row, at the Plain, at the Center and in Newport or West Manchester, had taught the basics using "the horn book" and the psalter for reading, and the goose quill pen for writing. Teachers, wielding birch twigs, kept disciplinary problems to a minimum. Finally, in 1848, a high school was established "for the benefit of the whole town." It was housed in a portion of Town Hall and had no building of its own until the mid-1850s when the first Story High was built on Cheever's Hill.

A BEAUTIFUL BUILDING
Congregational Church Is Constructed in 1809; Religion Plays a Major Role

By 1804, Manchester also had its own "social library." And in 1809, the Proprietors received permission to "erect a meeting house" and construction of the Congregational Church, as we know it today, began. Workers received one dollar a day and the results of their labors have given us the most beautiful building in town. Its first bell came from the old Meeting House.

The church, of course, in those days played a major role in people's lives. William H. Tappan's history of Manchester (1888) says that townspeople first met to worship beneath the branches of a tree at "Gale's Point." John Winthrop's <u>Journal</u> also mentions that in 1645, "the village at Jefferyes Creeke was named Manchester & the people there (not being yet in Churche state) had procured mr Smithe (sometymes Pastor of the Church of Plymouthe) to preach to them…"

By 1650, minister Nathaniel Marston "was granted free seed for his cattle and timber to build him a house." Other ministers followed, some popular, some less so. One was even asked to "provide for himself and his family some other place," but differences were ironed out and he remained.

Until 1821, the church building was unheated. During the winter, parishioners, men, women and children, would sit, as Tappan writes "on hard, board seats, where the temperature [within] was the same as that which raged and howled over the snow and ice without, and listen to the long services of the period…their forebearance, he adds, "can only be explained by a much greater degree of zeal and endurance than is possessed by their descendants."

There were even those members who voted against the purchase of a church stove, questioning its effect "on the health of the congregation and [fearing] that [it] would make the young puny and effeminate." The original cast-iron heater, ridiculously small, "stood in front of the pulpit and was connected to the chimney at the opposite end of the church by a long pipe which ran the length of the central aisle." During its first day in use, two young women fainted, reportedly overcome by the "baked air." Later, some ladies brought a foot stove filled with hot coals to the service, but long before it was over it was usually stone cold.

Throughout history, ministers everywhere have varied in popularity, but one of those in Manchester held in highest esteem by his congregation and the town as a whole was Reverend Ariel Parish who joined the church in 1791. A graduate of Dartmouth College, he died at the early age of 30 ministering to his beloved parishioners and other townspeople during an "epidemic of fever" which swept the community in 1794.

His obituary is heartfelt in its praise for what seems to have been a cleric whose attributes were ideal. "While he was one of the strictest of the Calvinistic school," it read, "no man ever manifested a more candid or placid temper toward those who had adopted a different creed. The uniform decision with which he embraced his own opinions, led him decidedly to yield the same privilege to others. His sermons were uniformly plain and practical, without harshness or controversy or the show of ornament. His elocution in the pulpit was manly, distinct and pathetic [able to arouse pity], and doubtless had his days been prolonged, he would have risen to eminence. While he lived he was distinguished for his easy and social suavity of manners by which he won the affections and reigned in the hearts of his people; for he shared their joys and sympathized in their sorrows. A letter from a member of his church thus closes: 'he was cut off in the morning of life and the tears of many watered his grave. Even children followed with endearing wile, and plucked his gown to share the good man's smile.' "

By 1810, another minister had taken over, parishioners were worshipping in the new church building and 110 additional souls had joined the congregation.

THE IRON HORSE
Railroad Arrives in Manchester in 1847; Single Track, 65 Cents to Boston

The network of roads and streets, too, had multiplied and there were major ways to Gloucester, to Beverly and Salem, and to Wenham. By the early 1800's, a stage coach ran from Gloucester to Salem three times each week, and teams were often changed in Manchester on the way. To make it easier for horses, the steep hill at Bennett Street, once the only access to town, was bypassed in 1827 by extending Bridge Street from Bennett to Pine. At Salem, passengers would transfer to the coaches of the Salem to Boston Stage Company which charged a fare of one dollar each way. But in 1847, tracks were laid to Manchester and an exciting new service began on the right-of-way acquired by the Eastern Railroad Company.

Initially, there were two passenger trains and one freight each day on the single track to Boston (a second track was laid in 1893). The fare was 65 cents, actually, five cents less than it was in 1945 when the cost of a ticket included a tax of nine cents. The depot and freight siding in Manchester, first located on the north side of the tracks, was constructed with considerable effort. Salt marsh and lowland near Jeffrey's Creek were filled by Irish laborers, many of whom, according to Frank L. Floyd's history of the town, <u>Manchester-by-the-Sea</u> were

Steam engine sits at the railroad depot at Manchester in the early 1900's. Although there is a motor truck at far right, horses and carriages wait for their passengers, and ladies on the platform wear dresses down to their ankles. Steam engines like this were used by the Boston & Maine Railroad through the 1940's. After World War II, diesel engines became increasingly popular. Note that without as many trucks on the road then, there is a baggage car behind the engine for freight and, as trains were the major method of transportation, a sizable number of cars for passengers. Prior to World War I, the railroad offered deluxe service with parlor cars aboard "The Flying Fisherman" which ran from Boston to Gloucester. Photo courtesy of SPNEA.

Bridge tender poses by his heated shelter in this photo in 1894 of the railroad draw bridge leading to the inner harbor. View is towards town showing the Dow Block (1894) at left. The new railway station, which was built in 1895, had yet to be constructed. Double tracks had just been installed to Ashland Avenue. A single set of rails proceeds across the bridge and continued then all the way to Rockport. In 1896, double tracks were laid to Magnolia (making a new draw bridge necessary at Manchester), and by 1908 they had finally reached the City of Gloucester. The siding in the foreground could have been used by passing trains or by Fenton's Boat Yard which shipped yachts by rail on flat cars.

quartered "in the old mill which was remodeled into a tenement house in that vicinity where Lincoln Street crosses Saw Mill Brook." Laying tracks on the right of way and the building of the bridge and causeway across the inner harbor required drilling and blasting, horses and wagons and scores of men wielding picks and shovels, activities which entertained "sidewalk superintendents" of all ages. After the railroad was completed, many of the Irish families stayed and became much respected citizens of the community. The Eastern Railroad was leased and later, in 1890, purchased by the Boston & Maine. A passenger station in West Manchester was erected in 1895, and a new depot downtown in 1896. A station was also built at the end of Kettle Cove Avenue primarily to provide service for Magnolia and its great summer hotel, the Oceanside. By 1945, 32 trains stopped at Manchester each day. Today, a much reduced schedule competes for commuters with the automobile.

By 1803, Manchester also had acquired its first Post Office. Later the four-horse coaches which linked Salem and Gloucester brought mail to town twice a day. In the early days, the Post Office moved frequently, usually to the residence of whoever served as Postmaster. In 1885, however, with the appointment of Julius F. Rabardy, it came to rest in the Rabardy Block. A native of France and a Union veteran who lost a leg in the Civil War, Rabardy also established what is now Floyd's News Store. Operated for many years by his great-granddaughter Alice Rice, Floyd's sadly closed its doors in 2002.

In 1903, the Post Office moved to the Pulsifer Block at the corner of Union and Beach Streets where it resided until the present brick structure was built during the Roosevelt Administration in 1939. Mail was delivered by hand twice each day. Letter carriers, equipped with their familiar leather bags, walked their routes every season no matter what the weather. Mail was heaviest in the afternoon and especially during the summer months when copies of the magazine North Shore Breeze added to their burden. Trucks owned by the Postal Service—and Manchester had one before World War II, a Model A Ford—were painted olive drab.

In recent years, the following have served Manchester as Postmasters: John Gavin, 1936-1941; Harry Swett, 1941-1948; Jake Greenberg, 1948-1968 (Greenberg, appointed by Harry S Truman,

was the last to be named to the post by a President of the U.S.); Jeremiah J. Noonan, Jr., 1968-1981; Patrick J. Ring, 1982-1986; Peter C. Milner, 1987-1995; Michael Donlon, 1995-1998; and Jon M. Erna, 1998 to the present day. Postal employee Benjamin Stasiak holds the record as the longest-serving member of the Board of Selectmen in the history of the town, 14 years from 1960 until 1974. Jerry Noonan was also a member and chairman of the Board of Assessors for many years.

FIRE!
Wood buildings, Candlelight and Open Hearths Keep the TORRENT Busy

With wood houses lit by candle and heated either by fire places or wood-burning stoves, fire in the 19th century was a major concern. To deal with its hazards, Manchester purchased its first pump fire engine, the "Eagle," in 1828 for $600. By 1832, it had acquired the "Torrent" built by local resident Colonel Eben Tappan. The "Torrent," which retired from active service in 1885, is still in existence today. It has been restored, is owned by the Manchester Historical Society and is on display at SEASIDE NO. 1.

Fires took their toll regularly. In 1836, flames destroyed John P. Allen's sawing and veneering mill, as well his dwelling house and outbuildings. Other cabinet shops and houses also burned. Throughout the next two decades, the "Torrent" and her accompanying bucket brigades were kept busy fighting flames which razed mills, furniture shops, dwelling houses, warehouses and stables. Thankfully, however, there were no major conflagrations such as those which inflicted such devastation to Boston (1872) and to Salem (1914).

There was time now, too, for entertainment and even adult education. In 1830, Manchester formed its own Lyceum as a "Society for Mutual Improvement." Anyone could join for 50 cents and listen to lectures—some given by local folk—as well as take part in discussions about the issues of the day. Topics were serious. They varied from the way county roads were repaired to whether property ownership should be required to permit a resident to vote. Enthusiasm for the Lyceum led to the establishment of a town library of nearly 1,000 volumes. But with the average wage still at $1.25 per day (board was $2.25 a week), minds were on the practicalities of living and it would be some years yet before the aesthetic qualities of the community were addressed. An exception to this was the planting of a series of American elms whose grandeur for more than a century shaded the town's streets. Future generations, alas, because of Dutch elm disease, will never know what it was like to walk the streets of small towns throughout New England, to hear the rustle of leaves overhead, and to admire the beauty and majesty of these great trees.

With a wealthier and more diverse society which now had time for leisure and conversation, an interest in learning from books and lectures, and a mobility made possible by improved roadways and later by the arrival of the railroad, new ideas began to find their way to Manchester.

One of these was Second Adventism promoted in town, according to Reverend Lamson, by the powerful preaching of Elam Burnham of Essex. During the winter of 1842-1843, it made many converts. Manchester resident John Lee writes in his diary: "There is a very great Reformation in this town. The work shops and grocery stores are shut up...business is suspended, and all sorts of people attend meetings [at which] men, women and children speak and pray..."

Local ministers had little to say in favor of the movement, but Lamson, a clergyman himself, admitted that not all was bad. "With a good deal of fanaticism and extravagance," he writes, "there was much sincerity and pious feeling [and] many [were] moved by deep religious convictions and led into serious and devout living." One of the results of the devotion to Second Adventism, he reports, was the establishment in 1884 of the Baptist church on School Street, although the ideology itself failed to survive "in any organic form."

A second enthusiasm involved temperance, and in 1829 a Temperance Society was formed to support "the principle of total abstinence from ardent spirits..." Seven years later, with Larkin Woodberry as President, the Society could list some 400 members.

'HORRORS OF SLAVERY'
Manchester Ends It by 1775; the Missouri Compromise Makes It a National Issue

But of all the movements which swept the country as the nineteenth century progressed, none could rival efforts in the North to abolish slavery. It is difficult today to understand the emotions that then surrounded the issue. In Manchester, "ser-vants for life" were noted in the Assessors' books in 1760. Earlier in 1696, William Tappan's history of the town notes that "Samuel Leach and John Lee were owners of slaves." Early abolitionists, especially in Boston, which carried on a lively trade with the South, were often considered rabble-rousers and dangerous to the peace and tranquillity of the community.

Manchester declared itself for freedom as early as 1775. That year, a lecturer, name unknown today, regaled residents about "The Beauties of Civil Liberty and the Horrors of Slavery." He seems to have made an impression for from that year on no mention of indentured servants can be found in town records.

In 1853, voters at Town Meeting, swept with fervor, approved a formal, four paragraph Resolution, opposing repeal of the Missouri Compromise which prohibited slavery from existing in territories acquired from France with the Louisiana Purchase. "We view with alarm and indignation," residents declared, "this attempt...to enlarge the area of slavery by a violation of contracts and trampling on the rights of man..." The Town Clerk was instructed to forward a copy of the resolves to local Congressman Charles W. Upham in Washington.

That same year, Manchester residents elected their fellow townsman, attorney Richard Henry Dana, Jr. to represent them as delegate to the Massachusetts Constitutional Convention. An ardent Free Soiler, Dana, son of the town's first summer resident and celebrated author of Two Years Before the Mast, a story of his voyage around Cape Horn to California aboard the brig PILGRIM, was delighted. "I had the compliment of being elected from Manchester by a clear majority over all others on the first ballot," he wrote in his diary. An ardent abolitionist, Dana served as defense counsel, albeit unsuccessfully, for two escaped slaves, who were captured in Boston under the provisions of the Fugitive Slave Act. A compromise among parties in Congress, it confirmed that slaves were legal property of their owners and thus should be returned.

The Free Soil Party, moderate in its demands compared to others, was immensely popular in New England. It called for removal of all Federal sanctions for slavery by ending it in the District of Columbia; by banning it in the territories; and by using every constitutional means to deprive it of national support. By 1856, Free Soilers had merged with anti-slavery Democrats and powerful Whigs to create the new Republican Party. Its candidate for the Presidency was Colonel John C. Fremont whose activities in the west helped the nation secure California as a free state.

Hugely popular in the northeast, Fremont campaigned in Manchester. A rally at Gale's Point drew more than 8,000 people, many times the population of the town. Large delegations attended from every community in Essex County. Wagons and horses were parked everywhere. Massive tents were erected to shelter speakers and the crowd. Bands played and banners rippled in the wind. The town itself was decorated with red, white and blue. Arches were built and covered with garlands of flowers. Slogans urged allegiance to the candidates and to the party. Manchester's Henry Kitfield was chairman of the Committee on Arrangements. And one of the featured and much-acclaimed speakers was our own Richard Henry Dana, Jr. Fremont collected a surprising popular vote and remarkably would have been elected President, defeating Democrat James Buchanan, if he had carried Illinois and Pennsylvania.

UNDERGROUND RAILWAY

Salem the Main Line, But a Desperate Man Here Is Helped to Canada

Meanwhile, abolitionists in town, according to Lamson, met frequently and kept informed by reading anti-slavery publications like the Liberator and the National Era. Many conservative and wealthy Whigs, still sympathetic with Southern gentry, were critical of the abolitionist movement. But the voices of freedom here were not to be stilled. Outrage was expressed with the Fugitive Slave Act. There were resolutions and prayer meetings, readings and discussions all related to emancipation.

A few courageous souls in town belonged to a secret organization which had pledged its efforts to shield and defend slaves who were seeking a way north to freedom. The abilities of the group were tested, Lamson relates, "sometime in the fifties." On a cold and rainy spring evening, a fugitive appeared in Manchester having "missed the main track of the Underground Railroad at Salem." He was warmed, fed, clothed and sent on his way by three sympathetic residents who also provided him with money. Next heard from, he was safe and sound in Canada. This was a time, as one municipal leader declared, which "lifted the moral sense of the community to a higher plane...and purified and energized the public conscience" for the great struggle yet to come.

In 1860, Abraham Lincoln, candidate of the Republican Party, was elected President of the United States. John Brown's righteous uprising at Potawatomie Creek had taken place a year earlier and the nation's drift towards civil war accelerated. South Carolina, had already seceded and by 1861, Mississippi, Florida, Alabama, Georgia, Louisiana and Texas had followed. The struggle was not only about slavery. It involved more complicated questions of states' rights, the role of the federal government and the age-old conflict between majority rule and minority rights. Feelings ran high on both sides and there were many here and abroad who wondered if the Republic would survive.

At 4:30 a.m. on April 12, 1861, the war between North and South began in earnest as General Beauregard's artillery at Charleston, South Carolina launched a bombardment of Fort Sumter. Thirty-four hours later, his ammunition gone, Major Robert Anderson and his garrison of some 70 Union soldiers surrendered.

THE SOUTH REBELS

Manchester Men Respond to a Call to the Colors; Nation Is Plunged into Civil War

In Manchester, as in thousands of other northern cities and towns, the news of the firing on Fort Sumter united people of every political party behind the defense of the Union. As the call went out for men to join the Colors, the town responded gallantly. But an accurate count of the number of local men who served with Union forces is difficult to come by.

No one in recent years has better researched Manchester's relationship to the Civil War than has Carl R. Triebs, a longtime resident and a former Treasurer of the Manchester Historical Society. As Triebs writes in a paper presented to Historical Society members in 2001, the answer resides "in a large number of disjointed and sketchy records."

A report issued by the Board of Selectmen in March, 1866, lists 159 men. The names memorialized on the bronze tablet which is affixed to the large boulder on the Town Common number 184. Triebs believes the total is closer to 194. His information comes from records of the Town Clerk, Census Reports, newspapers in Gloucester and Salem, military records collected by the State Adjutant General, service records and Federal pension records at the National Archives in Washington, DC, and, finally, from a comprehensive nine volume work published by the Commonwealth in 1931 entitled <u>Massachusetts Soldiers, Sailors and Marines In the Civil War</u>.

Unlike World Wars I and II, no universal draft existed during the War of the Rebellion until 1863. The Federal government simply announced its need for a certain number of volunteers. States were provided with quotas and each city and town was asked for a specific number of men. For example, when Fort Sumter fell to Southern troops on that April day in 1861, President Lincoln called for 75,000 men to serve for 90 days. The quota for Massachusetts was 1,560 which it immediately exceeded by activating its already organized militias. Eight men from Manchester, most probably members of a militia company in Beverly or Gloucester, responded. Until 1850, Triebs reports, Manchester had its own unit of citizen soldiers known as the Manchester Mechanic Light Infantry.

Less than a month after its first call, the White House asked for additional volunteers, some 42,000 men, to form 40 new Union regiments. Volunteers were asked to serve for nine months, one year or two years. Seventy-seven Manchester men enlisted and were posted primarily for three years. Seven also signed up for the Navy. But there were discrepancies. Triebs cites Union soldier Edmund Morgan who died in a Confederate prison. His name appears on a memorial plaque at the Library but it is not included in the Selectmen's report in 1866. Jefford Decker, too, who married Harriet Lee of Manchester, lived here at least from 1841 to 1849. The couple had five children. Decker served as commander of Manchester's military unit and was Postmaster here from 1845 to 1849. But in 1861, he was a resident of Lawrence and thus was left off the list.

As the war increased in its intensity, the Administration made further requests: in 1862, 300,000 men for three years; and later that same year 300,000 more for nine months. Time in service varied significantly. Men also reenlisted and those who came up with the numbers at the end of the war may not have had access to the latest data. Triebs is continuing his efforts to clarify the total number and to learn more about those here who served the Union cause.

Bounties attracted men to enlist, especially the unemployed. With markets in the South no longer within reach and with growing competition from furniture now mass-produced elsewhere, the number and size of cabinet shops in Manchester was shrinking. To men without a job, even a modest Federal bonus and a bounty from the Town of $125 was attractive.

UNCLE SAM WANTS YOU
Bonus Program Spurs Enlistments; a Few from Manchester Pay for a Substitute

But volunteer enlistments failed to meet the manpower needs of the Federal government and in March, 1863, Congress passed the Enrollment Act which meant that every able-bodied male citizen and immigrant between ages 17 and 50 was eligible for military service. Quotas were assigned to each Congressional district. If the number of volunteers fell short, a lottery system was used to fill it. The first year of the draft, according to Triebs, Manchester's quota was 14 men. Three enlisted and 11 were drawn by lottery. One man provided (probably hired) a substitute; three paid to purchase outright exemption from the draft, all of which was perfectly legal. More than $1,000 was often paid to some luckless youth by a man who could afford to buy his way out of army service. It was this unfair feature of the Act, which caused extraordinary hostility towards conscription throughout major cities in the North including Boston. In New York, Union troops were finally called out to suppress a riot which lasted for three days and caused much destruction of property.

In 1864, Manchester was again asked for 14 men. This time, thanks to enlistments and reenlistments, plus other credits, the town was able to satisfy its quota. By 1865 when the war ended, out of a total of 183 men sought, Triebs' research shows that Manchester had provided 191 for military service.

During the war, Massachusetts raised a total of 68 infantry units. With those from other northern states, these formed the heart of the Union Army. According to Triebs, men from Manchester were members of 38 different units; 35 men participated in some form of combat; 20 men saw service with

In the blue uniform of the Union Army, George Washington Tucker of 13 School Street, Manchester, poses for this formal tintype photograph. Tucker who was born in 1824 and lived for 70 years until 1894, was a musician. He first enlisted for 90 days with 8th Massachusetts Volunteer Militia which was assigned to guard railway facilities in Washington and Baltimore. He then re-enlisted and served with the Massachusetts Volunteer Heavy Artillery.

Civil War soldier Enoch Crombie posed for this photo on October 5, 1919 with his wife Sarah Lee Crombie. His uniform was one worn by veterans who had served with the Grand Army of the Republic (G.A.R). Crombie was a member of Allen Post, Number 67, G.A.R. Its headquarters were located in The Memorial Library and Grand Army Hall given to the town in 1887 by Thomas Jefferson Coolidge whose brother Sidney, a battalion commander, was killed at the Battle of Chickamauga in 1863.

Stone cabinet mill which once stood at the end of Elm Street just below Powder House Hill. In Manchester, the heyday of furniture making was from the early 1800's to about 1850. The total of some 43 shops in town offered employment to hundreds of people. The financial impact on the community was significant. It created new wealth and with regular hours, the industry offered adults time for leisure and learning which few had during the more demanding and dangerous days of commercial fishing.

the artillery; six joined the cavalry; and 12 enlisted in the Navy. Most of these were aboard ships enforcing the blockade of southern ports. Navy recruits, all volunteers, received no bonus which may explain in part why a coastal town had so few serving at sea.

Men who joined the Union Army were not always combat infantrymen. Sergeant Frederick W. Smith, 23rd Massachusetts Volunteer Infantry, was posted to Long Island in Boston Harbor where for four months he supervised and helped to train draftees. Gilman Andrews was named a Brigade Postmaster, and Andrew Jewett became a regimental clerk.

"Of the Army units in which Manchester men served and saw combat," Triebs writes, "24 operated in the eastern theater—in the army of the Potomac, Army of Virginia, Army of the James [River], or other eastern commands. Seven were assigned to Louisiana and the lower Mississippi, four [to] Tennessee." Charles Juhnke and Thomas Welch, Manchester men who enlisted in 1861, fought with the 2nd Massachusetts Volunteer Infantry in 1862 in the (Shenandoah) Valley Campaign, at Cedar Mountain and at Antietam. In 1863, they were at Chancellorsville and at Gettysburg. They also accompanied the regimental contingent that was sent to New York to subdue the Draft Riots.

In 1864, still with the 2nd Massachusetts, they were sent west to join General William Tecumseh Sherman in his celebrated "March to the Sea" from Tennessee to Atlanta, and from the coast of Georgia, north to the Carolinas. Juhnke and Welch were with the regiment when Confederate General Joseph E. Johnson surrendered to Sherman in April, 1865. Remarkably, both survived four years of bloody combat, were discharged, and presumably returned to Manchester when the regiment was disbanded at the war's end.

12TH MASSACHUSETTS
Infantry Regiment in the Thick of the Action; Antietam Takes Its Toll

Twelve men from Manchester, according to Triebs, were members of the 12th Massachusetts Volunteer Infantry, a regiment raised by Colonel Fletcher Webster, son of the great statesman. Their average age was 24; four were married with children and seven of the 12 had worked as cabinet-makers. Unfortunately, Triebs reports, all but one were killed in action (as was Colonel Webster),

wounded, died in prison camps or received a discharge for service disabilities. They included Daniel S. Pert, Laban Cushing, Josiah Ober and George Glenn.

Each was a member of Company K which suffered heavy casualties during the battle at Antietam in September, 1862. Isaac Allen was killed. Edward F. Allen and William H. Allen were wounded as was Julius Rabardy, who lost a leg. (His dramatic account of the action appears later in this book.)

In December, 1862, at Fredericksburg, a battle described by Triebs as "a blood bath for Union forces," Edward Allen and William Allen were wounded once again as was Samuel Knowlton and William Hooper. Knowlton's wounds were severe enough to merit transfer in 1864 to the Veterans Reserve Corps. Samuel N. Lendall of Manchester joined the 12th Massachusetts Volunteer Infantry in 1863. He lost an arm in the battle at Spotsylvania Courthouse in mid-1864 and was discharged later that year.

Summer resident Russell Sturgis, Jr., Captain of Company A, 45th Massachusetts Volunteer Militia, looking for enlistees in September, 1862, set up a recruiting booth at the old fire house on School Street. Twenty-two Manchester men signed up for a term of nine months. Fifteen of these, Triebs reports, had worked in the then declining furniture industry. Indeed, William H. Wheaton, who owned a small cabinet-making shop in town, closed its doors and enlisted with all of his employees. He was named Sergeant.

Francis B. Pert and William J. Pert were wounded at the battle of Kinston; Luther V. Allen was also wounded later in a battle at Whitehall, both in North Carolina. When the regiment was disbanded in July, 1863, Stephen A. Ferguson and Joseph A. Morgan returned to Manchester but died later most probably of typhoid fever contracted while on duty in North Carolina.

In December, 1864, 18 men, most just 18 years of age, significantly younger than earlier volunteers, enlisted for one year with the 25th Unattached Militia Company. The infantry unit, a part of the home guard, was stationed at Fort Miller, Marblehead. All were discharged in June, 1865 at the war's end. The fort, located at Naugus Head, overlooking Winter Island at the entrance to Salem Harbor, had served as a military post both in the Revolution and in the War of 1812.

CASUALTIES MOUNT
194 Manchester Men Wear Union Blue; 25 Die in War; 35 Are Wounded

The carnage of the war was well known and Manchester was no exception. Of its 194 men who served with Union forces, seven were killed in action or died of wounds; six died in Confederate prisons; 11 died of disease; and one died in an accident, a total of 25. Thirty-five were wounded and recovered. There were 60 casualties in all, or 31 percent of those who served. Twenty-one men were discharged for disabilities. "Thus of the 194 [total]," Triebs concludes, "almost half could be considered victims of the conflict."

The war dragged on for four years. Unlike those in earlier days, Manchester's sons who were fighting for the Union were far away. News of their activities came only from letters and from personal accounts when they were able to return home. Otherwise, names like Bull Run, Shiloh, Vicksburg, Cold Harbor and the Wilderness could have been on the other side of the world.

Finally, on April 9, 1865, in the Court House of the small Virginia town of Appomattox, General Robert E. Lee surrendered his Confederate forces to General Ulysses S. Grant, Commander-in-Chief of Union armies.

According to a special summary report on the war presented in 1866 by the Board of Selectmen, the town handed out $7,885 in bonuses to meet its enlistment quotas. Later, to families of soldiers who needed financial assistance, it paid $17,498 which was reimbursed by the Commonwealth. The war caused an estimated increase in town debt of $10,000.

Manchester could review its contribution to the victory with pride and satisfaction. "Few towns of a like population can show a better record as regards the number of her own citizens sent into the conflict," Selectmen wrote. "The town may well congratulate herself on the record she has made in the great work of preserving the unity, integrity and freedom of the nation, in-as-much as so many of her own sons went forth to do and to die for the common weal." The best memorial to their deeds of heroism is preserved in the records of Allen Post 67, Grand Army of the Republic, which are today accessible at the Manchester Public Library.

The end of the war was celebrated in town with "triumphant shouts of joy, excited congratulations and the ringing of bells...Flags were unfolded and flung out to the breeze, drums and fifes were brought out, processions formed and marched to the depot...several speeches were made and loud and repeated cheers were given for the speakers, for President Lincoln, his generals and the heroic soldiers of the Army. 'America,' 'Rally Round the Flag Boys,' and 'John Brown' were sung with thrilling effect...in the afternoon the Fire Department turned out and, with citizens, escorted four wounded soldiers..." Prayers were said and hymns were sung. "Tears were in many eyes...[and] altogether it was a day of Jubilee..."

Six days later, however, the mood changed to one of sadness and grief as the news of Lincoln's assassination was received. "Funeral services for the President were held at the Congregational Church by the Reverend F.V. Tenney and, chastened and subdued by the solemn lesson of the hour, the people slowly dispersed to their homes." Today, more than a century after the Civil War ended, the monument on the Town Green recognizes the sacrifices made by Manchester men in their heroic efforts to preserve the Union.

During the late 1860's, West Manchester, earlier known as Newport, was the center of a small but flourishing shoemaking industry. Located in private houses along Bridge Street between Harbor Street and Jersey Lane, these were small shops with two to four men and women. One was owned by Joseph Morse whose daughter, Mary Butler Morse, was said to be as good with "waxed ends" as anyone in the shoemaking trade.

Others, according to a paper presented in 1939 to the Manchester Historical Society by Isaac Marshall, veteran Editor of The Manchester Cricket, were owned by Daron W. Morse and Andrew Roberts. "Mary Ann Roberts, a portly woman, broad of beam...rugged in build with a kindly soul," writes Marshall, worked with her brother Andrew at a regular shoemaker's bench.

In winter, fishermen, farmers and merchant seamen often took up shoemaking to add to their seasonal incomes. One of these was West Manchester resident Captain Israel Goodrich who, in command of the schooner LILY RICH, sailed between Perth Amboy, New Jersey and Manchester delivering coal. Further west on Bridge Street, Captain David Goodrich and his son Charles also made shoes during the off season but later migrated to the Willamette Valley in Oregon where they owned a small farm.

Elegant architecture of the Forster-Leach house is evident even beneath the bunting in this photo probably taken before the Water Celebration parade in 1892. Built in 1804 by Israel Forster for his bride Hannah Lee, the house, which still stands today at the corner of Bridge and Pine Streets, includes a hand-carved stairway, a McIntyre fireplace and wall-paper imported from England. Sadly, the first Hannah died at age 24 leaving a baby daughter, but another Hannah took her place and lived here for many years raising three children of her own. Israel Forster owned the mill at Bennett's Brook, as well as the schooner HANNAH, a waterfront warehouse and wharf.

A small boy, who could be a Dana, poses with his dog in front of the Richard Henry Dana house overlooking Dana's Beach and Grave's Island. In 1845, Richard Henry Dana, Sr., who acquired the land and built the structure, became Manchester's first summer resident. A poet of some note and a founder of the famed literary magazine, The North American Review, Dana was father of Richard Henry Dana, Jr., a Harvard graduate, an attorney, an early and ardent abolitionist and, perhaps most important, author of Two Years Before the Mast, a story of his odyssey aboard the brig PILGRIM which sailed from Boston around Cape Horn to Monterey, California. Dana, a common seaman, was aboard to improve his health. The book, a huge success, set new standards for writing about the sea.

North Street was also the site of a shop operated by Thomas Morse. Others were on Bennett Street. One, "in the lee of the high school yard," was owned by Solomon Allen. It was not only a shoe-making shop, Marshall recalled, but a gathering place for "the men of leisure" in town who exchanged gossip there and discussed the issues of the day. Indeed, the place was so popular that it became known as "Solomon's Temple." A man of many talents, Allen made ladies' shoes to order and was also a barber.

SUMMER RESIDENTS
In 1845, Richard Henry Dana, Sr. Becomes Our First Seasonal Cottage Owner

In 1845, 15 years before the War Between the States began, Manchester entered a new era in its history by taking its first step towards becoming a "summer resort." On April 9 of that year, attorney Richard Henry Dana, Jr., purchased for his father some 30 acres off Summer Street overlooking what became known as Dana's Beach. There, Richard Henry Dana, Sr., who had come to Manchester by way of Rockport where he had summered since 1840, built a modest cottage on the hillside with a magnificent view of the water.

A poet and journalist, Dana was a founder of The North American Review which became one of America's best-known literary magazines. He was also the forerunner of a host of distinguished summer residents who were soon to follow. They included Charles Frederic Adams who purchased Crow Island in 1848; Captain Robert Bennet Forbes, who in 1857 retired from the China Trade and built his cottage in West Manchester (he later moved to Milton); and Chicago native John Crown-inshield Dodge, Dr. Jedidiah Cobb and Russell Sturgis, a Major in the Union Army who had recruited and led a company of Manchester men during the War Between the States. Each of these three bought land at Singing Beach. The rush to enjoy the sylvan charms of Manchester had begun.

A Story of People, Places and Events in the Town That Came to Be Known as Manchester-by-the-Sea

THE GRANDEUR OF THE GILDED AGE

Owners of Highwood, the largest property in town, Mr. and Mrs. William B. Walker of Chicago and Manchester epitomized the luxurious lifestyle of the Gilded Age in America, 1880-1914. Here they are, at left, welcoming guests on a summer day around 1900. Much of the landscape at Highwood was designed by architect and planner Frederick Law Olmsted, famous for Boston's Emerald Necklace as well as for New York's Central Park. Visitors could stroll the grounds on its many paths or admire distant views of the ocean and Massachusetts Bay over the tops of the trees. Horse and carriage rides through the woods were also popular and on hot afternoons iced tea was served on shaded terraces.

WATERING SPOT

Railroad Makes Manchester Accessible as a Summer Resort Community

In the 1830's, Nahant was the first "watering spot" on the North Shore for Boston families now wealthy enough to be able to afford to escape the diseases and discomforts of the city during the summer months. But the railroad, roadways of increasing quality, and steamship service, opened the door to other towns to the East—Swampscott, Marblehead and Beverly—including Prides Crossing and Beverly Farms—Manchester, Magnolia, Gloucester—especially Eastern Point—and, finally, Rockport on the tip of Cape Ann.

There were beaches, fewer to be sure than on Cape Cod, but spectacular just the same; the rocky coast whose beauty became the subject for scores of celebrated painters from Fitz Hugh Lane to Winslow Homer; and thousands of acres of woodland with a magnificent mix of ponds, hills and granite ledges, most of it wild but some open to carriages, riders on horseback and those who preferred to walk. And then there was the sea itself, a view of eternity, with islands near the shore, its waters in constant motion with the tides and wind. It could be enjoyed by those who looked upon it in wonder; by others who ventured closer in boats which varied from simple skiffs to hundreds of feet of steam or sailing yacht; and, of course, by those hardy souls who enjoyed a refreshing dip in its usually chilly waters. It was this magnificent landscape that attracted seasonal residents and visitors alike to Manchester.

The mid-to-late nineteenth century was the heyday also of the Grand Summer Hotel and Manchester had one of its own—the Masconomo House. It was located on 12 acres at the corner of Beach and Masconomo Streets overlooking Singing Beach, one of the town's natural treasures. It was huge—three stores high—and, with its 106 rooms and a dining room that seated some 300 guests, it was a symbol of the elegance and refinement of the Gilded Age.

Built in 1878 by actor Junius Brutus Booth, older brother of John Wilkes Booth, the assassin who shot and killed President Abraham Lincoln, the hotel was attached to a private residence that Booth and his actress wife Agnes had constructed in 1869. Both were popular members of Manchester's then small circle of artistic and literary people which included the Booths, comic actor John Gibbs Gilbert and Boston publisher James T. Fields.

A fabled rendezvous for the rich and famous, the Masconomo House, enlarged in 1887, boasted a gigantic octagonal hall with four massive fireplaces, bowling alleys and a billiard room. Bath houses beckoned braver guests to Singing Beach a short distance away. And there were theatrical presentations to entertain not only those who were staying at the hotel but many who came from as far away as Boston aboard special trains to see actors work their wonders on the stage. It was said that the opulence of the Masconomo House rivaled "the best hotels in Europe." And somehow, throughout its life, its popularity seemed in no way to be diminished by its owner's relationship to the assassin of a beloved national leader. The Masconomo House was torn down in 1920, marking an end to an era. A portion of the Booth cottage and a bit of the hotel still stand today.

Fields, one-time editor of the Atlantic Monthly as well as a partner of the publishing house Ticknor & Fields which owned the Old Corner Book Store, built his summer house atop Thunderbolt Hill. But he and his wife Annie were perhaps best known locally for re-christening the town "Manchester-by-the-Sea" which they proudly had printed on their letter paper. It was immediately popular with many residents, but to others, such as the celebrated jurist Oliver Wendell Holmes, Jr., who for some years had rented a summer cottage near the railroad station in Beverly Farms, it was an affectation too tempting to ignore. Holmes teased his friend by referring to his own community as "Beverly-by-the-Depot." Not to be outdone, some wag also coined "Gloucester-by-the-Smell" as a nick-name for Cape Ann's historic fishing port.

Although it was used informally for nearly a century, the town legally became Manchester-by-the-Sea in 1990. In a move led by former Selectman Ed Corley who said it would recognize the community's unique character, the proposal won Town Meeting approval by just two votes. It was then sent to the state legislature where a 33 vote margin made it official. Objections to the change in name were not of a substantive nature. They dealt primarily with the time it took to write "Manchester-by-the-Sea" on legal documents and other papers and how much it would cost to change the lettering on signs and municipal vehicles.

Of all of those interested in the development of Manchester as a summer resort, no one was more

Verandah at the three-and-one-half story Masconomo House hotel at Beach and Masconomo Streets stretches across the front of the 230-foot building. Woman in white dress and apron was most probably a member of the hotel staff. Men in the background may have been as well. On the lawn is a wagon which most likely belonged to the small boy in the photo. Note the chairs which could be used by the establishments' up to 300 guests. This photo is one half of a stereoscope photograph which provided a three dimensional view. They were very popular at the time.

South side of the Masconomo House hotel looks out over the pasture to Singing Beach and the ocean beyond. At right is Booth Cottage built in 1869 by Agnes and Junius Brutus Booth, Jr. and still located at the corner of Masconomo and Beach Streets. The Masconomo House was constructed in 1877. For more than 30 years it flourished as a great summer hotel welcoming the rich and famous from all over the world including U.S. President Grover Cleveland and actress Lillian Russell. It was finally torn down in 1920. **Courtesy of Essex Institute, Salem.**

perceptive than the Reverend Cyrus Augustus Bartol. Pastor of the West Church on Cambridge Street in Boston, Reverend Bartol, perhaps looking towards his retirement, focused a practical eye on the value of Manchester real estate and in 1870 purchased a sizable portion of shorefront known as Glass Head Pasture west of what is now the Manchester Yacht Club. There he built for himself a three-story Victorian, shingle-style house, complete with a separate studio for his artist daughter and an observation tower from which he could see most of the town as well as his new acquisition, 75 acres of land at Smith's Point which he sold to newcomers interested in joining the growing summer colony. Soon, he purchased Norton's Point as well, mindful of the fact, as he is reported to have said, that the Lord created only so much shorefront property.

CHANGING SKYLINE

Manchester's Roberts & Hoare Lead the Way as Builders of Summer Homes

Although a number of builders changed the skyline of Manchester with the construction of new summer homes, none can compare either in quality or in quantity with Roberts & Hoare. Oliver T. Roberts, son of one of the town's many distinguished sea captains, was born in West Manchester in 1850. He began his working life as a 13-year-old cabin boy aboard a clipper, one of the magnificent sailing ships of the era. But unlike his father, the sea was not in his blood. Back on shore in 1882, he formed a partnership with William Hoare, a cabinetmaker who as a youngster had come to the United States from England. Each was in his early thirties. Roberts & Hoare soon became one of the most respected and successful building contractors in the country.

By 1895, the partners had built 32 houses and 21 barns or stables for summer residents of the North Shore including some notable structures in Manchester such as the River House at Norton's Point and "Kragsyde" which overlooked Lobster Cove from Smith's Point. In their heyday, Roberts & Hoare provided employment for as many as 200 men in all of the building trades. At the turn of the century, eight or ten projects—located from Tuck's Point to Norton's Point and from Smith's Point to Magnolia—were often underway at once.

Oliver Robert's own house, still standing at 18 Bridge Street, according to architect Stephen Roberts Holt of Manchester, his great grandson, "overlooked a huge staging area [which stretched] from Knight's Wharf to Sinnicks' barn just off Ashland Avenue." There lumber, delivered by barge, was piled high as was stone for foundations and bricks for fireplaces and chimneys. Sinnicks, mason for Roberts & Hoare, was "in those days before poured concrete, the most important subcontractor in town."

Shop space was located in a former thread mill on Elm Street. There, Holt writes in the town's 350th anniversary yearbook, "steam-driven machinery milled out the sash, doors and finished trimwork for all the large homes under construction. At the job site, however... finish work was accomplished with basic hand tools—hammers, chisels and saws." Both men died in the same year, 1922. But by then the great building boom had ended.

In his chapter entitled Cottages Great and Small, which appears in the town's commemorative 350th anniversary book, Holt explains that architectural styles in Manchester run the gamut from Colonial to Modern with Georgian, Federal, Greek Revival, Gothic Revival, Stick Style, Shingle Style and Colonial Revival in between. Architects whose drawings and designs created the character, dimensions and details of houses we admire today include Peabody & Stearns, Arthur Little, William R. Emerson, Everett & Mead, Hollis Larcom Roberts, C.H. Blackall, Bigelow & Wadsworth, Andrews, Jacques & Rantoul and Parker and Thomas & Rice, firms that designed the first and present Essex County Club buildings.

Many of the great "cottages" are gone or were remodeled as life changed through the years, but the vestiges of some still remain. Two have been lovingly restored to their former glory. One is at 65 Harbor Street, West Manchester, a tudor-style dwelling built in 1906 for Eben D. Jordan, Jr. The other is at Norton's Point. Known originally as the "Barn House," it was built in 1885 for William A. Tucker and includes a boat house facing Whittier's Creek. Architect for the restoration was Stephen Roberts Holt.

Other historic structures that have recently been restored include the more than 100-year old Chowder House at Tuck's Point where two years ago a new building was also added to house the area's restrooms. It was designed by architect John Olson of Olson, Lewis & Dioloi, Elm Street, Manchester, to harmonize with the park's late nineteenth century landscape.

One of the most magnificent and inspiring examples of architecture style is Manchester's First Congregational Church built in 1809. A special regional committee of the clergy originally proposed it be located on North Hill, but it was constructed by "carpenters, cabinetmakers and shipbuilders" for $8,500 just where it stands today on the Town Common. The design of the steeple is attributed to Colonel Jacob Smith, but the structure itself follows concepts outlined in Asher Benjamin's book The American Builder's Companion published in 1809. Benjamin's drawings and ideas, Stephen Holt points out, were "inspired by [those of] Sir Christopher Wren in the late 17th century."

SPANISH-AMERICAN WAR
Letters in THE CRICKET: Shells, Bullets and the Capture of San Juan Hill

On February 15, 1898, a fatal explosion aboard the battleship USS MAINE in Havana harbor changed the course of U.S. foreign policy forever. The country's cries for revenge led finally to a war with Spain and ultimately to the acquisition of an American Empire.

In the Philippines, Commodore George Dewey's Squadron made short work of the Spanish fleet at Manila Bay. On the other side of the world, at Santiago, Cuba, Admiral Cevera's ships suffered the same fate at the hands of the Navy's Atlantic Squadron.

The land war which featured President-to-be Theodore Roosevelt's heroic charge up San Juan Hill, was short and sweet as well with more casualties recorded from disease than from combat. But as glamorous as the war seemed in the press, as always, to those who fought ashore in Cuba, it was a different story.

In October, 1898, Daniel Sheehan of Manchester received a letter from his nephew, D.J. O'Mahoney, who was with Company I of the 9th Massachusetts, U.S. Volunteers. Dated August 11, it was written in Cuba somewhere "Outside Santiago" and later published in The Cricket.

O'Mahoney had landed with his regiment at Siboney on July 1, 1898 and had marched all night to reach the front. "Mud up to our waists in some parts," he wrote, "mud that glued itself to our shoes and the rest of our clothing...shortly the sound of firing reached us and at the top of the hill we waited for orders. Over our heads we heard the continual ping! ping! of Spanish bullets and the shrieks of their shells which every now and then landed with effect. We were held in reserve with the 2nd Regulars up front.

"At about [10 a.m.] the Spanish resolved on an assault to retake the hill. Soon we were lying on the ground, our guns loaded, waiting for what might come our way...It is a most peculiar sensation when for the first time, you hear bullets clipping the grass by your side, and [are] not allowed to fire...we held out for about three-quarters of an hour when the enemy finally withdrew with heavy losses...It's a wonder that not more than two were wounded...Company I escaped untouched..." Within a few days, the City of Santiago surrendered and a truce was declared.

"Now that the fighting is finished," O'Mahoney continued, "both the 2nd and the 9th are anxious to move. Men of [each] regiment have suffered from malaria, but up to the present I am in the best of health. Dannie Sheehan is the same stout lad as ever, and sends his best wishes to all. We would both enjoy a trip to Manchester-by-the-Sea and here's hoping that affairs will soon turn in such a manner as to make it possible. [Signed] Your nephew, D.J. O'Mahoney."

By October, The Cricket reported that O'Mahoney was not "in the best of health" but was confined to Boston City Hospital where he was "seriously ill," most likely a victim of malaria.

As its reputation as a summer colony grew, Manchester's quiet charm attracted men of significant ability and substance. Among them were financier Thomas Jefferson Coolidge whose generosity provided the town with its elegant cut stone library designed by architect Charles Follen McKim, and Augustus Hemenway, who built his house on Pickworth Point overlooking Ballyrack (known as Belly-ache) Cove. By the 1890's, the improvement of the railroad, the coming of the automobile, and new wealth and new leisure, had increased Manchester's summer population dramatically.

To answer the demands of these new residents for leisure activities, the Essex County Club with its golf course and tennis courts was founded in 1893. The Manchester Yacht Club was established a year earlier. By 1904, the club listed 81 yachts owned by its members. Ten had an overall length of 100 feet or more. One, ISIS, measured more than 200 feet overall. The Essex County Club which, before mechanized lawn mowers were invented, used flocks of sheep to keep the grass trimmed on its fairways, soon developed a reputation which attracted the Massachusetts Amateur Golf Championship won by club member Andrew Carnegie II in 1904, and the Ladies Invitational Tennis Tourney, an annual event until 1969, which over the years welcomed tennis greats from Alice Marble to Billie Jean King.

The Curtis sisters, Harriet and Margaret, Manchester summer residents all their lives (their forebear was General Greely Curtis who purchased waterfront land off Summer Street at the end of the Civil War), began playing golf at the Essex County Club as children. Remarkable athletes, each later won the Women's National Golf Championship, one in 1906, the other in 1907. The next year, Margaret, skilled at tennis as well, was a member of the team that won the Women's National Doubles Championship.

During these extraordinary years, signs of wealth were everywhere and in some circles Manchester was referred to as "a playground for millionaires." Chauffeur driven Cadillacs, Packards and LaSalles moved swiftly about the streets and were cared for by skilled mechanics at Standley's Garage, then occupying the entire corner of Beach and Summer Streets where Richdale is now. The markets—Hooper's (founded in 1868), Sheldon's and Bullock's—offered home delivery of fresh vegetables, meats and other delicacies. Scores of summer houses boasted spectacular gardens which produced not only great pleasure and satisfaction for their owners, but bouquets of fresh flowers daily which decorated elegant rooms and hallways. Many of them, pictured in garden books of the time, went on to win awards from horticultural societies around the nation.

CELEBRITIES ARRIVE

Embassies Move to Manchester; 2 U.S. Presidents Enjoy Our Hospitalities

Manchester, too, was always a favorite of the diplomatic community. In 1904 alone, 11 ambassadors, each with a sizable retinue, summered in town. They were here (long before air conditioning) to escape the heat and humidity of the nation's capitol, and swimming at Singing Beach was one of their most enjoyable pleasures. Starting in 1899 with the Minister from Spain, Duke D'Arcos and his wife the Duchess, plenipotentiaries from France, Italy, Germany, Austria-Hungary, England, Russia, Brazil, Turkey and other countries, set forth on an annual pilgrimage to Manchester which continued until 1914, the start of the Great War.

One of the drawing cards also was the social season at the Masconomo House which in 1905 was even considered as a location for the Peace Conference hosted by President Theodore Roosevelt, which brought an end to the Russo-Japanese War. Despite its size, however, it proved to be too small for the number of international delegates attending and the conference was moved to the Wentworth Hotel at Newcastle, New Hampshire.

During the first decade of the twentieth century, the more than 100 rooms of the Masconomo House were rarely vacant. Miss Charlotte Brown's Brownland Cottages on Old Neck Road, which accommodated some 70 persons, were booked as well. Among Miss Brown's most distinguished guests for at least one summer was inventor Alexander Graham Bell. The Brownland Cottages held out until 1940 when they, too, were razed, victims of a changing social scene.

Other celebrities who spent their summers in Manchester or visited the town included Charles W. Fairbanks, Vice President of the United States from 1905 to 1909 (T.R. was President), who rented here for two years. While vacationing in Beverly, President William Howard Taft played golf regularly at the Essex County Club and once attended the Sunday morning service at the Congregational Church. In 1918, thanks to the generosity of Thomas Jefferson Coolidge, Jr., President and Mrs. Woodrow Wilson occupied the "Marble Palace" at Coolidge Point for a week. Colonel Edward M. House, the President's aide and confidant, regularly vacationed nearby in Magnolia. The Crown Prince and Princess of Sweden visited Coolidge's son, T.J. C. III, who was appointed Undersecretary of the Treasury by President Franklin D. Roosevelt during his first term. President Theodore Roosevelt's children were frequent visitors to Manchester. One child was married here. And until the beginning of World War I when he returned to Germany, Baron Frans Von Papen summered here as well. During World War II, Von Papen served as the German Ambassador to Turkey. J.P. Morgan, Jr., was also

Highwood, one of the largest of Manchester's summer estates, was owned by Mr. and Mrs. William B. Walker of Chicago. Reached from Pine Street or Jersey Lane, portions of the landscape were designed by Francis Law Olmsted, Jr., whose father was most famous for plans which led to the creation of New York's Central Park. The "Mansion," as it was called, is much like many which decorate the English countryside. With magnificent views over the treetops to the ocean beyond, it was torn down after World War II. Like Woodholm, much of the property was then developed, but vestiges of the original remain.

Greenhouses and the elegantly designed "crystal palace" were features at Woodholm, property of Mr. and Mrs. William B. Walker's son, Charles Cobb Walker whose property adjoined Highwood owned by his father and mother. A graduate of Harvard College, Class of 1892 and Harvard Law School, he was for many years a practicing attorney in Boston. He died in 1950. Like Highwood, much of Woodholm has been subdivided for single residence dwellings. During the Great Depression, even the Walker family cut back on expenses, halting greenhouse construction at least temporarily.

a regular summer visitor aboard his steam yacht CORSAIR whose sleek black hull lay in the outer harbor while Mrs. Morgan visited her sister, Mrs. Rita Crosby. Mrs. Morgan and Mrs. Crosby also had roots in Manchester as daughters of long-time summer resident Henry Grew. Joseph Clark Grew, U.S. Ambassador to Japan at the time of the attack on Pearl Harbor, had a house for many years in West Manchester.

In land area alone, the two largest of Manchester's grand estates were owned by Philip Dexter of Boston and by William B. Walker of Chicago. On his 260 acres, Dexter employed some 150 men in 1910 to build a summer house complete with tennis courts and a pond which today in winter is used by the town for ice skating.

OLMSTED LANDSCAPE

An English Country House, 3 Stories Tall & Paneled Everywhere with Dark Oak

Portions of the landscape at Highwood, the Walker estate, were designed by Olmsted Brothers of Brookline, a firm established by Frederick Law Olmsted, legendary planner for Boston's Emerald Necklace and New York's Central Park. (After his death, the office was continued by his son, F.L. Olmsted, Jr. who added other partners including, at one time, landscape architect Charles Eliot, founder of The Trustees of Reservations.)

The house itself, a half-timbered, Tudor style mansion some 160 feet long and three stories tall, was built in 1896 and 1897 for Mr. and Mrs. Walker by Roberts & Hoare as were the stable, outbuildings and greenhouse. Sited on top of one of Manchester's highest hills (the area included First Hill and Fowler's Hill), it had its own water tower as pressure from the municipal system proved insufficient.

The interior of the structure matched the character and look of an English country house: a massive front hall; quartered oak floors; huge open fireplaces in all but one room; dark oak paneling everywhere; a living room which measured 26 by 36 feet with fluted oak columns; intricate carvings and a 14-foot high ceiling, itself paneled with oak and recessed plaster; and a 12-sided dining room with a series of windows on its south side which provided a magnificent view of the water from Magnolia to Salem Bay.

Downstairs also was a den whose walls were lined with books; a sizable smoking room and the service area which included a china closet, pantry, kitchen and a cold room for the ice chest which was filled regularly with natural ice cut during the winter at local ponds. (After the turn of the century, this was replaced by an electric Frigidaire.) A grand staircase led to the floors above. On the second were eight bedrooms and three baths. And on the third, five bedrooms and two baths.

Some distance away was the barn which housed a small herd of Jersey cows, stables for horses, room for carriages, wagons and harnesses, and living quarters for a coachman. Livestock also included pigeons, poultry and turkeys, all white according to orders given by Mrs. Walker. Even the family's English bull terrier, Rollo, matched the required color.

Remarkably, by April, 1897, less than a year after the building contract had been signed, part of the house was ready for occupancy by the family. They moved in for the summer while work continued elsewhere.

The grounds, primarily forested, were traversed by some seven miles of roadways. The house itself was surrounded by lawn and there were walking paths everywhere. Granite steps reached down from the house to woodlands below which, in spring, were alive with wildflowers.

Tulips, lilies of the valley, violets and banks of yellow and purple pansies brightened areas around the house. Patches of forget-me-nots grew among the boulders and, as one visitor wrote, "masses of Scilla Siberica seemed to reflect the blue of the sky." Roadways were lined with hedges of rhododendrons which added gloriously to the colors of spring.

The rose garden was enclosed with a high stone wall covered with ivy and "scarlet ramblers." Wildflowers inhabited the ledges. Nearby was a goldfish pond framed with dwarf evergreens. During the winter, spruce, pine and hemlock provided a charming contrast of color to the white snow. An impounded pond (now on Forster Road) which attracted a variety of wildlife through the seasons, was christened "Lake Louise" after its owner. And during the warm summer months, outside the living room, the terrace, guarded by two life-sized stone statues of seated lions brought from Venice, was the site of many delightful gatherings for cocktails and after-dinner coffee. Tea was also served there regularly in the afternoon, weather permitting, of course.

Highwood was paid for and presented to Louise Cobb Walker, by her father, a wealthy Chicago businessman who, in failing health, lived there with his daughter and her husband for five years. When the old man grew too infirm to manage the property himself, he persuaded his son-in-law to leave his own business in the mid-West and to take his place. Until the arrival of the Great Depression and another generation, there were apparently funds enough to accomplish whatever the family wished.

With their son's decision to settle in the East after his graduation from Harvard (Class of 1892) and Harvard Law School, and the death of Mrs. Walker's mother, the couple decided to move to Manchester year round. What the luxuries of life were like in one of the great houses that were built here in that era of opulence is charmingly told in an illustrated "Appreciation" written in 1928 by Belle S.B. Harvey, a devoted friend of Mrs. Walker's and one who was often her guest.

HOUSEHOLD STAFF
Servants Play a Vital Role in Running & Maintaining Great Country Houses

First, there is no doubt that little would have been possible in that era without a sizable household staff to manage activities both inside and out. The cook, senior in rank, was English, according to Mrs. Harvey, and had been with the household for many years. Much beloved, in retirement she was generously given a house of her own in town. Even in her senior years, she continued to provide the Mansion, as it was called, with wild berry preserves from her personal kitchen.

The head chauffeur, Mrs. Harvey continues, also played a major role at Highwood delivering the mails, running family errands, meeting trains during the day and taking Mrs. Walker on drives to explore the surrounding countryside. There was a houseman, too, whose duty it was to lay wood for the fires and to oversee the operation of plumbing, electrical and other systems necessary to daily life.

The laundress, too, writes Mrs. Harvey, "is of long residence. She presides [over her domain] with absolute authority, arranging the time allowed to each employee for her work, and she takes a keen delight in her task of renovation and the accuracy of her reckoning of household linen supplies."

Fresh cut flowers, of course, were delivered daily from the greenhouses and there were vases in every room. "One of the maids," adds Mrs. Harvey, "is most tasteful in their arrangement." Finally, besides helpers on the household staff, maids upstairs and downstairs, gardeners and grooms, there was the English butler and his wife who joined the Walkers once again after brief employment elsewhere because of health.

Each year there was a party for the staff with musical entertainment and gifts for everyone and for their children. "It is an extraordinary household," Mrs. Harvey concludes. "I wish I could name all whose services render life here so delightful. [Every] position is capably filled and each takes pride in his or her special occupation." Those were different times. Ones which we shall not see again.

In 1917, when the United States entered World War I, Highwood devoted itself to aid the Allies. Led by Mrs. Walker's patriotism and commitment, friends and staff rallied to the cause. "We are all soldiers now," she exclaimed, "and we are not satisfied unless we are doing our utmost!" Despite the exigencies of war, arrangements were made to ship, particularly wool clothing, directly by Cunard Line abroad. "I am sending a token of sympathy from Manchester, Massachusetts to Manchester, England," Mrs. Walker declared in an enclosed message. "It is a personal contribution and I beg of you to distribute it as you think best. The garments are plain and simple, warm and all new."

"Five hundred and fifty-five articles were sent to the Belgians," Belle Harvey reports, "including blankets, all kinds of woolen underwear, costumes and wraps [and] Christmas toys for children. In other shipments, 277 articles were sent to Lady William Osler at Oxford, England; 407 garments were given to the Red Cross for distribution in France; and 37 articles went to the Army and Navy YMCA for wounded soldiers." Fifty soldiers' kits, which included personal items such as soap, toothpaste, a pipe, harmonica, candy, pencils and writing paper, were delivered abroad to "Doughboys" in time for Christmas, 1917.

And "Mrs. Walker did all the shopping herself, buying materials by the bolt." In one case, "a whole counter of shoes of different sizes" was shipped overseas. The kitchen at Highwood produced canned vegetables and jellies for Army camps around the United States. Finally, at the end of hostilities, to express her own gratitude and to salute their service to the nation, Mrs. Walker presented a special medal to each of her volunteers. With its own colorful ribbon, it was inscribed "Highwood War Relief."

Throughout the war, Mrs. Walker also found time to compile a scrapbook history of events both here and overseas—a collection of newspaper clippings, journal articles, letters and photographs all related to the momentous happenings in the world. The 30 large volumes, bound in red vellum, were presented to the University of Chicago.

For many decades, son Charles Cobb Walker, an attorney in Boston, lived next door with his family at Woodholm. His death in 1950 signaled the end of an extraordinary era. Much of the Walker's land today has been subdivided for single residence use. The big houses are gone, but the names of the original properties were retained by developers.

In West Manchester, Eben D. Jordan, Jr., patron of the arts, father of the Boston Opera House and son of the founder of Jordan Marsh, built himself a tudor-style summer house in 1906 with a waterfront view of the outer harbor. Overlooking Long Beach, self-made millionaire George Robert White, replaced his simple summer cottage with a shingle-style mansion which in 1912, he enclosed completely with brick and stone. White, a bachelor, and the originator of Cuticura Soap, as well as President of Potter Drug and Chemical Corporation, lived at "Lilliothea" for the remaining summers of his life. When he died in 1922, he had established the George R. White Fund to benefit the people of Boston. "But," as veteran Town Clerk and news store owner Frank N. Floyd wrote in his history of the town published in 1945, "he gave no recognition to Manchester in his will." It may have been because when White offered to build a new high school bearing his name, the town turned him down. The money instead was used to construct the White Building at Massachusetts General Hospital.

Another titan, Albert C. Burrage, inhabited West Manchester where his estate, "Seahome," reached by what is known today as Boardman Avenue, was made possible with the money he had made investing in Chilean copper. Burrage, an attorney, was celebrated for his collection of orchids which grew in greenhouses in both Manchester and in Beverly Farms.

He was also owner for nearly 40 years of the handsome steam yacht AZTEC designed by William Gardner and built by Lewis Nixon in 1902. A veteran of service in both World Wars (first with the U.S. and then with Canada), AZTEC measured 260 feet overall and was one of the ten largest yachts in the country. She often lay anchor in Manchester's outer harbor.

One of the great luxuries, too, in an earlier era for some was commuting to Boston by boat. Before the Second World War, attorney and long-time Manchester summer resident Edward Taft used to do this regularly aboard his 65-foot GITANA with a crew of three, a captain, engineer and steward. Usually he would meet the yacht at the Manchester Yacht Club where he was taken by his chauffeur.

"I'd have my pajamas on under my overcoat," he recalled some years ago. "We'd get underway and I'd go below to shave. When we were off the easterly end of Misery [Island], we'd heave to and I'd go for a swim. Then into a bathrobe and breakfast with the morning paper. When we reached Boston Light, it was time to get dressed. I landed at the Northern Avenue bridge, and had a seven-minute walk to the office. I got up at the same time as if I'd taken the train. I told the captain that no matter what time we started, we shouldn't get to Boston before 9:15. That was when the train arrived. And it was an easier walk from Northern Avenue than from the North Station." GITANA, handsome at her mooring in Proctor's Cove with her white hull and bright Lawley tender on a boat boom, was powered with two 250 horsepower gasoline engines.

THE JOY OF FLOWERS
Many of the North Shore's Most Exquisite Gardens Are Located in Manchester

Besides the great houses, many with dramatic views of the harbor or the blue waters of Massachusetts Bay, there were once again the gardens, magnificent in their design and inspiring in their colorful displays of floriculture. Louise Sheldon's book, Beautiful Gardens in America, published by Charles Scribner of New York in 1924, includes in its contents a series of photographs of the elegant gardens of the North Shore. Its cover features the dramatic white marble statue of the goddess Diana which appeared in the gardens of Mrs. Gordon Abbott, Sr. at Glass Head. (In a later generation, this property won the silver medal of the Massachusetts Horticultural Society.) Also pictured are gardens at Grafton Wood owned by Dr. and Mrs. J. Henry Lancashire; those at Crowhurst owned by

Postcard view shows Italian gardens at the Randolph Tucker's at Norton's Point overlooking Whittier's Creek and Tuck's Point. A showplace of the North Shore, the gardens were visited in 1917 by President and Mrs. Woodrow Wilson who lunched with the Tuckers following a game of golf at Essex County Club. The Wilsons had arrived in Gloucester earlier aboard the Presidential yacht MAYFLOWER.

Lily pads decorate the garden pool at Graftonwood, home of Dr. and Mrs. J. Henry Lancashire overlooking Graves Island. The gardens, which recently celebrated their 100th anniversary, were designed by landscape architect Martha Brookes Hutcheson and are still a showcase of the North Shore. Architect Herbert D. Hale drew the plans for the original house shown above which was built in 1902 for Boston businessman Charles Head. Known as Undercliff, it was purchased by the Lancashires about 1913 and rechristened. Like many other summer dwellings, it was modified significantly in 1940. At that time, too, the landscape was extended by architect Umberto Inocenti. Photo courtesy of SPNEA.

Mr. and Mrs. Francis W. Whitehouse; and those at The Chimneys owned by Mrs. Gardiner M. Lane. The present owners of the Lancashire's property, now called simply Grafton, recently celebrated the 100th anniversary of the garden which looks as magnificent today as it did a century ago.

Others which should be mentioned as well are gardens owned by William A. Tucker at The Moorings, Norton Point; Mr. and Mrs. Stephen Van Rensselaer Crosby's gardens at Appletrees on Bridge Street (Mrs. Crosby was the second president of the heralded Garden Club of America); gardens at Coolidge Point owned by Mr. and Mrs. Thomas Jefferson Coolidge, Jr.; and the landscaping by Fletcher Steele at Uplands at the top of Highland Avenue and later rock gardens there by owner Rear Admiral and Mrs. Harry Hull. Included, of course, at most of these properties besides the gardens themselves were greenhouses tended with care by scores of dedicated and knowledgeable professionals.

As Louise Sheldon writes in 1924, "probably no other section of the Union contains as many gardens, old and new, as does [Massachusetts]...the luxuriance of bloom is most noticeable on the coast where all plants, especially certain less long-lived annuals such as Poppies, Salpiglossis and Mallows reach their limit of perfection and continue their best for an unusual period." Other plants and shrubs she mentions appearing in gardens of the era throughout the season were German iris, Sweet William, delphinium, hollyhocks, wild flowers, cherry and pear trees, box, lemon lilies, peonies, flag and, of course, roses.

Each year after 1917 when it was completed, Manchester's Horticultural Hall on Summer Street hosted flower and vegetable shows with blue, white and red ribbons awarded to the winners. (Almost every large property raised its own fruit, especially strawberries, and vegetables—beans, tomatoes, lettuce, cauliflower, squash and corn—which were delivered with fresh flowers daily to the great houses in season.) Especially proud of their contributions were the chief gardeners at each estate who competed for honors. Sponsored by the North Shore Horticultural Society which was founded in 1899, these summertime shows were hugely popular events drawing entries from properties throughout the region from Swampscott to Gloucester.

The activities of the high and mighty were chronicled in The North Shore Blue Book and Social Register and the regularly published North Shore Breeze, which not only carried text describing social doings, but black and white photos of such events as the St. John's Church Fair in Beverly Farms (the nearest year-round Episcopal parish; Emmanuel Church was built in 1882 for summer services only), tennis and golf tournaments at Essex, as the County Club was known, and the annual Water Sports at the Manchester Yacht Club.

News of the town appeared in the Beetle & Wedge, a monthly newspaper founded in 1875 by storekeeper, Postmaster and telegraph operator Julius F. Rabardy. After three years, however, the paper ceased to exist and it wasn't until 1888 that The Manchester Cricket was born. First published by The Beverly Times, it was acquired in 1889 by its long-time editor I.M. Marshall. In 1922, Marshall joined with Harry E. Slade and his newly-established Cricket Press. Thankfully, the Cricket has been with us weekly ever since.

SELF-MADE MAN
Isaac Marshall, Redoubtable Editor and Founder of The Manchester Cricket

Born in Manchester in 1865, Isaac M. Marshall was a remarkable man. A graduate of Story High School in the days before a college degree was a requirement for success and self-made men were often the rule rather than the exception, he held various jobs until 1888 when he established The Manchester Cricket and became its first Editor. At his desk daily for some 60 years, he was a determined reporter and an excellent writer honored by The Boston Globe as its local correspondent for 54 years.

A great traveler, he tells about an epic trip that he took with Mrs. Marshall in 1929 in his book Around the World in 136 Days. His obituary in The Cricket includes a collection of photographs taken of the couple from the pyramids of Egypt to the temples of China and in many of the most remote corners of the earth. In the fashion of the time, they show the pair posing in local costumes in front of well-known landmarks.

A member of the National Editorial Association, in 19 years he never missed its annual meetings around the country enabling him to visit each of the then 48 states, the Provinces of Canada as well as Alaska and Mexico. In all, he toured Europe on three occasions, saw the British Isles and cruised to the North Cape. He wrote two books about his voyages as well as a series of recollections of what life was like in Manchester from 1895 to 1945 some of which he presented at meetings of the Manchester Historical Society.

Although he chose not to seek elective office, he served his town as a member of the Finance Committee from 1930 until 1936 and as President of the Historical Society. A charter member of the Manchester Club, he was known for his ability to tell a story, his sense of humor and his broad perspective on life.

Today, The Manchester Cricket is published by The Cricket Press. Its Editor is Daniel B. Slade who continues a family tradition of 80 years. Dan was preceded by his father, Daniel F. Slade, and by his grandfather, Harry E. Slade who, with his Speed Graphic news camera, was a familiar and welcome presence at events in Manchester throughout the years.

Another publication much enjoyed by residents of Manchester particularly in the 1930's and 1940's was the magazine North Shore Breeze, as its masthead proclaimed: A Weekly Journal Devoted to the Best Interests of the North Shore. Its news articles and photographs dealt primarily with the social activities of summer residents but also featured the natural attractions of the region as well as cultural and other events which took place during the "season" from Gloucester to Salem. Founded in 1905, its publisher and editor was J. Alex Lodge.

TRANSFORMATION
Wealthy Summer Residents Change the Character of a Tiny, Close-Knit Town

Manchester had changed significantly since the days before the great Civil War. The boom in building summer houses had brought new business to local carpentry firms and employment had been provided for hundreds of heads of local families as plumbers and electricians and year-round household caretakers. There were new retail stores serving the increasing population and with all this came a new prosperity for the town as a whole. The growth in property values meant new tax receipts to care for old infrastructure and to build new as needed. When a particularly worthy public project presented itself, a remarkable number of generous summer residents responded with contributions of cash or of land which might be needed for a building site.

As the Reverend Darius F. Lamson states in his landmark history of Manchester prepared for the town's 250th anniversary, "Acres once covered with tangled growth of wildwood, and considered too valueless for taxation, have been threaded by romantic avenues, and beautified by lawns and gardens." But Lamson, writing at the end of the nineteenth century, also pondered the effects of the town's inevitable transformation from a small, closely-knit community to an international seaside resort. "Year by year," he writes, "the transformation has been going on until it is doubtful if the fathers, were they to revisit this earthly scene, would know the ancient town...The magnates of the wealthy and society and letters who have built and domiciled among us, and made the old roads of Cape Ann alive with their varied and brilliant equipages, have introduced changes 'surpassing fable, and yet true,' creating," as Dr. Lamson declares thoughtfully, "a new social problem...." Whether the period will be considered as a time of " prosperity and glory" or "of decline and decay" he left to future historians. The invasion of Manchester by wealth and what was then considered "society" dramatically changed relationships within the community. There was summer and there was winter, each with a population of a very different character. Also, there was "Town" and there was "Gown" where no such distinction had existed before.

Major Russell Sturgis, too, one of 14 speakers at the dedication of the Memorial Library and Grand Army Hall in 1887, recognized the changing social fabric of the town. Expressing special sympathy to those whose land had been purchased by summer residents or who, because of the development of seasonal housing had lost access to precious places of their youth as, indeed, he had himself, he said, "if this be my feeling after less than 30 years [of residency], is it a wonder that those whose ancestors have occupied these shores for a century or more should chafe under its transfer to strangers?

"Still," he countered cheerfully, there are "many advantages...employment for men and women, enlargement of stores, lighting and watering of our streets, funds to be able to make further improvements of buildings, and today the one we now occupy...[the] judicious gift of an adopted citizen [Thomas Jefferson Coolidge]...So let us acknowledge," he added, "our mutual dependence [upon each other and] continue [to] respect and appreciate [our] happy union..."

In his own history, written in 1945 just after World War II, Frank Floyd observed that the "wealthy are getting poorer and the homes are getting smaller…Perhaps someday soon," he said wistfully, "we will pass into a town enlarged and enriched by many smaller permanent homes…and become a community made up of nice year-round dwellings inhabited by commuters." He was to get his wish.

By 1914, Manchester's population had grown to some 2,900 people. Besides the Congregational Church, for those of Roman Catholic faith there was Sacred Heart, a magnificent stone structure built of granite in 1907 by local contractors Roberts & Hoare and Morley & Flatley. It replaced a wooden building now a private dwelling located on Friend Street and Sumac Lane. Father William F. Powers, a priest much beloved by the community as a whole, is reported to have said that "it was the best Catholic Church built with Protestant money that he ever saw," for there were people of every faith and many wealthy summer residents who made its construction possible.

According to The Manchester Cricket in 1905, "An unnamed Protestant donated the land" upon which the church was built. As the number of seasonal houses grew in town during the early years of the nineteenth century, Sacred Heart Church saw the total of its parishioners increase accordingly, due in no small measure to the number of Irish Catholic serving as domestic help. As early as 1843, Baptists had "organized themselves into a Christian Church" and built a handsome house of worship on School Street. Episcopalians, too, benefitted from the generosity of Civil War Major Russell Sturgis, Jr., a summer resident of Smith's Point who, in 1882, provided funds for the construction of Emmanuel Church on Masconomo Street.

According to the Reverend John G. Hughes, III, pastor of Manchester's First Congregational Church and author of Ecumenical History, a chapter which appeared in the town's 350th anniversary yearbook, Sturgis was "influenced in his early life by [American evangelist and missionary] Dwight L. Moody [1837-1899]." During the Civil War, Hughes writes, Sturgis offered "spiritual consolation and guidance to the wounded and dying." During these ministrations, he met his second wife, Margaret McCullock of Baltimore. The two were married in 1866. In a diary, written in 1894 for his children, Major Sturgis declares: "in the spring of 1892, your Mother said to me, 'you have often said you wish to make me an Easter present. Now I have a wish. I want a church!'"

Emmanuel was built in three months and held its first service in July, 1882. Hubbard Sturgis, according to Hughes, Russell's brother, was the architect (Sturgis and Bingham of Boston). "The other summer church," Hughes continues, "was the First Unitarian Church [also on Masconomo Street] built in 1895." Today, deconsecrated, its steeple and its three Tiffany stained-glass windows gone, it is a distinctive private dwelling.

By the eve of World War I, Story High School had been named for Dr. Asa Story, one of the town's most beloved physicians, born in Essex in 1796, and the George A. Priest School (Dr. Priest was a School Board member for two decades) had been erected at the corner of North Street and Norwood Avenue. Manchester was equipped with a three-door, three-story engine house located on School Street, site of the present fire station. Wells had been established especially for fire fighting and, in 1873, the channel behind the fire house had been purchased as an additional water supply. Fire equipment in 1910 included the latest Knox combination chemical and hose wagon.

There was also a police station on the west side of the Town Common overlooking the inner harbor which had an office for the Chief and a series of cells for those who broke the law. (Its building had once housed Seaside I, a steam fire engine purchased by the town in 1885.) A new Town Hall, which occupied the site of the present building, had been built in 1868 and enlarged in 1893. The Elder Brethren, an organization of men over 50 years of age who gather annually for chowder at Tuck's Point, had been established and was thriving. Tuck's Point itself had been purchased from Dr. Bartol for $5,000 and the town had acquired the Tappan salt marsh and tidal flats for $19,000. Both sites were to become popular public parks, the latter to be named Masconomo. The community had its own bank as well—the Manchester Trust Company—founded in 1911.

UTILITIES INSTALLED
By 1890, We Can Take Pride in a New Water System, Electric Power & the Telephone

By the 1890's, the telephone had replaced the telegraph. Miss Annabel Haraden was the town's first telephone operator and many still living recall the personal services provided telephone subscribers by these gallant ladies. In emergencies, they could be lifesavers. There was always a pleasant voice at the other end of the line when you raised the receiver. And until the dial arrived after World War II, phone numbers were no more than three digits. By 1912, there were 283 telephone lines, most of them underground, and 470 stations which averaged 3,000 calls each day.

Until the turn of the century, the town was lit with gas lamps and kerosene was used to fuel lights at home. All this changed, however, in 1903 with the founding of the Manchester Electric Company. The installation of wires started shortly thereafter. Most, like the telephone, went underground. Despite the added cost, the town wished to avoid the unsightliness of poles and overhead cables. By 1915, most of the town's streets were illuminated with electricity.

In the 1890's, too, it was agreed that because of Manchester's size and impending growth it needed a public water supply as well as a sewage system downtown. Following exhaustive research and the passage of the necessary legislative act, test wells were drilled and on the thirtieth try, one yielding "a remarkable flow" of fresh water was found "near the junction of Eastern and Northern Valleys." A pump house was constructed off Lincoln Street. A storage tank was erected on Powder House Hill. Manufactured of riveted iron plates, it was filled for the first time in February, 1892, and reported to be "practically watertight."

By 1894, Manchester's water system included 14.4 miles of piping, 120 hydrants and 381 service pipe lines. To commemorate the accomplishment, residents earlier had staged a "Water Celebration" which included a parade, speeches, prayers of thanks, an illuminated fountain near Town Hall, a procession of boats up and down the harbor, and in the evening, a band concert. To meet future needs, far-sighted town officials soon proposed that a new standpipe be erected on Moses Hill and that legislation be sought to give Manchester the right to pump water from Gravelly Pond in Hamilton. Today, Manchester's water supply is the envy of many towns twice its size throughout the Commonwealth.

As the town's population increased, so did the need for a modern system of sewage disposal. By the turn of the century, the contamination of brooks, streams and harbor became a problem which threatened public health. An engineering report in 1911 called for immediate action and Town Meeting voters responded, 112 to 76. Pipes were laid and a pumping station constructed in 1914. It was originally proposed that the pumping station be located at House Island, but wiser heads decided that the outfall should discharge directly into the sea. The following year, the system was in operation. While outlying houses still employed cesspools and septic tanks (many of which continue to operate successfully today), the more settled sections of town had their wastes removed by a new municipal sewer.

WOMEN'S SUFFRAGE
The Ladies Battle for Political Equality; 1919: National Amendment Passes

Meanwhile, in June of 1914, the heir of the Austro-Hungarian Empire was assassinated by Serbian nationalists in Sarajevo, igniting the fires of World War I. Although Europe seemed far away to most Americans, the Allies and the cause they fought for were to grow in importance in the months ahead.

That year a battle was raging across the United States which involved women's right to vote. In August, 1914, an audience of more than 500 people gathered at the Town Common to hear Miss Louise Stanwood, chief of Manchester's Suffrage League, introduce spokeswoman Miss Margaret Foley, who pleaded for the passage of suffrage legislation.

"We women want to vote," declared Miss Foley, according to The Manchester Cricket, "not because we want to be like men, but because we are women. Men vote in the spirit in which they think, women want to vote in the spirit in which they think. We do not claim to be superior to men [or] able to run politics better...we women might make as bad a mess of it as you men have..." Laughter rippled through the audience.

"You say a woman's place is in the home," she continued. "One hundred years ago that was true...[but] in the great struggle to free the slaves women fought alongside you and now we are fighting for our freedom and when you vote for suffrage, you do no more than 10 other states have already done. This is not a sex war. I suppose men are doing the best they can, but they cannot see things from a woman's point of view."

Eight years later, in 1922, Mrs. George Silva rose at Town Meeting to express support for a

Sheep were used to "mow" the grass on fairways at Essex County Club in 1898. In the background is the original club house. Designed by Boston architects Andrews, Jacques & Rantoul, it was built in 1893 by Roberts & Hoare of Manchester. Construction took four months and cost $15,381. The shingle-style structure was destroyed by fire in 1913 and replaced by the present brick building. Tennis courts are at right.

The Marble Palace, designed by celebrated architects McKim, Mead & White in 1902, was built of brick and white marble for Thomas Jefferson Coolidge, Jr. whose father was the benefactor of Manchester's Memorial Library. President Woodrow Wilson vacationed at the house for two weeks during World War I. The structure was torn down in 1958. Its Italian gardens were famous throughout the region.

46

proposal to construct a new sewer to service a section of town which included Forest Street where she lived. Women had won the right to vote and Mrs. Silva was the first woman in Manchester to be able to speak her mind at Town Meeting

WORLD WAR I

Manchester's Youth Are Called to Serve on the Far Off Battlefields of France

In 1915, a German submarine sank the Cunard liner LUSITANIA with the loss of 128 American lives. Although the ship was carrying munitions, the incident provoked a storm of protest and emotion. Feelings against the Germans ran high. Finally, in April, 1917, German U-boats torpedoed four unarmed American merchantmen. The U.S. could stand by no longer and President Wilson asked for a declaration of war.

In Manchester, The Cricket, according to Ben Merrill's History of Manchester, 1900–1990, printed the names of some 35 young men who were likely to be drafted. They included Gordon Cool, Thomas L. O'Donnell, Frank Floyd and Michael Anning. Some were conscripted and some enlisted. Immigrant workers from France and Italy left to join their own colors, depleting the supply of labor for summer estates which finally did open on schedule. But instead of garden parties, their activities included rolling bandages, making surgical dressings, knitting woolen socks and scarves and hosting programs and parties to benefit Belgian Relief. Manchester's Miss Charlotte Read joined a unit of lady ambulance drivers in France and won the Croix de Guerre for bravery.

Mothers, wives, sons and daughters in town learned about their loved ones overseas from letters. "I am living with another fellow in a dugout for two," wrote Sergeant Harry D. Baker to his mother... "I'm glad I carry my slicker with me. It comes in handy these nights...ran across Walter Smith and we had quite a chat...am still fine and must close this in order to have it censored..."

Gordon Cool also wrote: "Dear Mother...Keep a stiff upper lip and be cheerful because we'll all be home again soon and believe me we will be the happiest boys in the world...[As] I was walking around camp...met Irving Baker, Joe Chadwick, Frank Amaral and Walter Smith, so you see I am not lonesome...tell father I'm a regular old sailor and also a soldier now...your loving son, Gordon."

There were other letters, too. One datelined "American Expeditionary Force, France" read "Dear Sir: It is with the deepest regret that I must inform you of the death of Pvt. Michael J. Coughlin on April 28, 1918...Pvt. Coughlin was an excellent soldier and well liked by all who knew him... He gave his life for the greatest cause for which men die, and while we extend to you the sincerest sympathy of his officers and comrades, we cannot help but admire the manly manner of his passing and assure you that it shall not be in vain..." It was signed "Officers and Men of Co. 'A,' 1st U.S. Engineers, W.S. Corkran, Captain Engrs. U.S.A." The letter was addressed to Michael Coughlin's father, James Coughlin, of Norwood Avenue, Manchester.

By the end of the summer of 1918, thanks in large measure to fresh American troops which bolstered the weary Allies, the Germans were on the run. In July of that year, President and Mrs. Wilson were in Manchester at the "Marble Palace" on Coolidge Point. Mrs. Coolidge had turned the property over to the Wilsons and their entourage for a week. The President, protected by U.S. Marines camped about the grounds, met with his advisor Colonel House and talked about a unifying institution which he hoped would be established after the war ended. It was to be called the League of Nations.

By November, 1918, the war was over and an armistice had been signed. In all, scores of young men from Manchester had answered the call to the colors. Five had failed to return. Post 113 of the American Legion is named for one of them, Frank Amaral, the town's first battle casualty of the Great War. Today the Legion is known as the Amaral-Bailey Post. Richard Bailey was the Town's first casualty in World War II. Other casualties of World War I included Joseph McNeary, Michael Coughlin, Edward Goldthwaite and Ammi Lancashire.

LOCAL HERO

Corporal Frank Amaral Is Manchester's First Casualty; Decorated for Bravery

Amaral, a Corporal with Company H of the 104th Regiment of the American Expeditionary Force, died of wounds received in action in April, 1918. According to The Manchester Cricket, Amaral first enlisted in Salem with Company H of the First Massachusetts Infantry which saw service during the Mexican Border war. Initially, he was turned down because of problems with his teeth, but he persisted and "after many visits to the dentist" he was finally accepted by the Army. With General John J. Pershing's Punitive Expedition, he fought against bandit leader Pancho Villa in Mexico in 1916. He enlisted again in 1917 and was assigned to the 104th Regiment.

After training in the U.S., Amaral's was among the first units to be sent to France. "The last [that was] heard from him," The Cricket reported, "was [some three weeks before he died] when he wrote telling of his experiences in the trenches and saying he would never forget his first night in No Man's Land. His letter, however, was full of hope and comfort" for those at home.

Born in Gloucester and orphaned in his teens, Frank Amaral was brought up and cared for by Mrs. Virginia Perry of Manchester. For six years prior to his Army service, he had worked on the William Hooper estate in West Manchester. Just before his departure for the front, The Cricket concludes, he had become engaged to Ethel Andrews, daughter of Mr. and Mrs. Everett Andrews of Manchester.

Corporal Amaral was later awarded the Croix de Guerre by the government of France. The citation reads: "for conspicuous coolness and courage in the direction of his squad under heavy fire. He inspired his men until he was killed in action on April 13, 1918." He was 23 years old.

Amaral, however, who died in an engagement with the enemy, was not the first casualty of the war to come from Manchester. That sad distinction belonged to Jeremiah Joseph McNeary, a resident of Summer Street, whose skull was fractured in an accident in France when he was kicked in the head by an Army mule in December, 1917. Born in October, 1890, McNeary had worked as a blacksmith for Horace Standley. He was assigned to the artillery section of the 101st Corps of Engineers.

An epidemic of influenza which caused thousands of deaths in this country and abroad also visited Manchester in 1918. Horticultural Hall, built only the year before, was converted into a dispensary. Children were among the first victims. Schools and churches were closed to discourage transmission of the disease. Nurses visited ill families throughout the town. Some 300 sandwiches were made daily for those unable to shop for themselves. Among those afflicted, according to The Cricket, were the Patrick Mulvey family and their six children. More than 400 cases of influenza and

at least one death were reported. It was a fearful and sobering time for Manchester residents prior to the discovery of antibiotics.

Throughout its lifetime, Horticultural Hall, headquarters of the North Shore Horticultural Society, served the community in many ways: as the site of a much appreciated annual flower show; as a movie theater; for wedding receptions; for Story High School graduation ceremonies; for the Junior Prom and the Senior Reception; and as a basketball court for Story High and for students at the Price School. The building, which was located on Summer Street diagonally opposite the depot, was torn down in 1963. It is the site today of Harbor Hill apartments, soon to become part of a building project offering units of affordable housing.

PROHIBITION
Rum-runners Operate Off Our Coast; the Great Depression Arrives

The Roaring Twenties were famed for their prosperity and self-indulgence as well as for their intolerance, isolationism and machine-driven politics. But one of the activities of the decade most felt by individual Americans was the prohibition of alcoholic beverages. There were "drys" and there were "wets" and what went into supplying the latter with illegal spirits gave rise to stories of outrageous adventure and intrigue.

In coastal regions, the choice of transportation for bootleggers was often the "rum-runner," a sleek, speedy power boat that could outrun Coast Guard patrol craft while dropping off cases of contraband liquor at pre-arranged destinations along the shore, usually at night. One rum-runner grounded on Half Tide Ledge in Manchester's outer harbor. Her consignment, destined originally for a reportedly "prominent Beverly Farms resident," was seized by authorities. As in most cases, however, what eventually became of it was difficult to determine. Another rum-runner, recalled Pine Street resident Henry Hall, then Club Captain at the Manchester Yacht Club, ended up in the harbor itself. "I went down to the Club one Sunday morning," Henry explained, "and there was a boat in Tuck's Point Cove. She was loaded with liquor. I called the Police Chief and we towed her up the harbor. The Coast Guard came over from Gloucester for the boat. l never did find out what happened to that liquor," he added with a smile.

This historic postcard photo of Masconomo Park shows its landscape at the time from Beach Street. Across the harbor, red buildings of Walter B. Calderwood's Yacht Yard are visible. Land for the park, a great deal of it salt marsh, was purchased for $19,300. In 1910, Olmsted Brothers of Brookline, the celebrated firm of landscape architects, was engaged to draw up plans which included winding gravel paths for pedestrians and horse-drawn carriages and a sizable amount of fill. The plans were only partially followed. A bandstand was built in 1923. In 1977, the area was redesigned to meet modern-day needs. The impressive bronze statue of a Manchester "Doughboy" from World War I carrying the country's colors rendered by sculptor Philip Sears, was erected in 1931. It lists and commemorates the dead, honors those who served in the Great War and celebrates America's and the Allies' victory over tyranny.

"Smithies" at Horace Standley's blacksmith shop at the corner of Beach and Summer Streets in 1910. Horses and carriages were then the primary mode of transportation. By 1915, with the automobile becoming increasing popular, Wes Standley, one of Horace's sons, established Standley's Garage at the same location. David Hersey, great-grandson of Horace Standley, is owner and operator of the business today.

During the summer of 1924, however, things got more serious. Just after midnight, acting on a tip that bootleggers were in the area, Police Chief George Dean and his men, tried to flag down two speeding Packard cars seen earlier on Ocean Street near White Beach. Both, however, broke free of a roadblock set up by Manchester Police, and the chase began with officers—one of them perched on the running board of the Dodge cruiser as it sped through town—firing their pistols at the fleeing vehicles. At West Manchester, opposite Harbor Street, police caught the first Packard, forced it over and arrested two men. The other vehicle was located not far away. Its driver was persuaded to surrender after trying to escape across Winthrop Field. According to The Cricket, "about 60 cases of whiskey, gin and champagne" were seized with the two cars. At Dana's Beach, the officers found another 60 cases including 10 gallons of pure alcohol. Prohibition ended in 1933 with the repeal of the 18th Amendment.

The buoyant hopes of the 1920's, however, disappeared overnight in the stock market crash of 1929. That fall, one year-round West Manchester resident reported that he could hear the sound of music and laughing voices as a wealthy financier who lived nearby held a party nearly every night. "When the crash came," he said, "there was nothing but silence and darkness at the house. The man's fortune had been completely wiped out."

During the Great Depression, Manchester was no exception to the nation's problems of unemployment. As The Cricket reported in 1934, Emergency Relief Administrator Chester L. Standley, who had served as Chairman of the Board of Selectmen from 1923 to 1929 (and was Norm Hersey's uncle and the brother of Wes Stanley, Norman's grandfather, who founded Standley's Garage), announced that he was able to keep a crew of 14 men at work spreading gravel on town roads. Standley also successfully sought grants from the state to provide another 16 to 18 jobs improving Central Pond and building a new dam. Following a meeting of store owners and merchants, a businessman's association was established at the suggestion of Peter Brown, owner of Manchester Fruit Store, to encourage residents and others to "shop in Manchester." Its officers were Thomas Lee, Henry Tappan, attorney Edward Morley and bank president Harrison Cann. Also in attendance was State Representative

Frank Floyd, proprietor of Floyd's News Store, who said that a businessmen's association "could accomplish a great deal for the community."

But news from the depression years was not all bleak. On August 4, 1930, Manchester helped to commemorate the Tercentenary of the Massachusetts Bay Colony with a gala, day-long celebration. The schedule shows there was a children's field day at the town playground, a "Shore Dinner" (luncheon) at Tuck's Point, a parade, and a band concert and fireworks at Masconomo Park. A film, "Three Centuries of Massachusetts," was shown to students at Story High and the George A. Priest School at Horticultural Hall. As part of the program on Sunday, August 3, two church services were held at the Congregational Church to which every resident was invited. Drummers in colonial costume marched through the town to summon people to morning and afternoon events.

WEATHERING IT
Summer Residents Help Provide Jobs, Income During the Lean Years

By 1929, Manchester's Boy Scouts had their own headquarters on School Street, thanks to the generosity of summer residents Francis M. Whitehouse and Mr. and Mrs. Russell Codman. Rosedale Cemetery had expanded into the former Goldsmith Gravel Pit, land owned by the town. A franchise to provide natural gas for Manchester's stoves and furnaces had been awarded to the North Shore Gas Company of Ipswich. As proponent Alex Sjorlund, one of the most quotable attendees at Town Meetings, declared: "...no one has found out yet how to broil a steak (with) electricity..."

For the most part, Manchester managed to keep its head above water during the depression. There was work for painters, plumbers, carpenters and cleaning people putting summer houses to bed in the fall and opening them up in the spring. Moving vans carted trunks and other equipment back and forth to Boston. As the owner of one of the town's leading businesses declared, "people had to eat," and so the markets survived as well. There was a mini-boom in swimming pool construction as wealthy summer residents sought to escape the increasingly crowded sands of Singing Beach. In the 1930's, a row of bathhouses, each painted a shade of green, topped the bluff in back of the beach. Many were quite elaborate with porches and seats. In front of the bathhouses was a board-walk and even a few sand dunes. But a winter storm in January, 1933, was too much for the frail structures. Many were washed out to sea. Others, upended by the surf, were salvaged by their owners and turned into backyard tool sheds. Some of these still exist today. One was carted off to New Hampshire where for years it served as an outhouse.

The 1920's had given the country a host of new inventions—the radio, motion pictures, electric-powered washing machines and kitchen gadgets such as mixers and coffee makers—all of which radically changed peoples lives. By the fall of 1931, more than one-third of the nation listened to "Amos 'n' Andy," the most popular comedy show on radio. And people everywhere were humming and whistling jingles celebrating the wonders of Campbell's soup and Rinso soap. But of all of the inventions that came to America in the 20th century, none affected its life as much as the automobile.

In Manchester, auto traffic was increasing annually and with Route 127 the only road to Gloucester, running through the middle of town, discussions began about the need to widen Central Street opposite Town Hall. For two years, 1939 and 1940, the debate continued at Town Meetings. At issue primarily was the future of the magnificent American elm trees which in those days lined the curb from Bridge Street to Summer Street. There were arguments pro and con. Police Chief George Dean was concerned about public safety: "I have watched this situation for 15 years [with its] ever increasing traffic problems," he said. "The time to do it is this fall when the traffic is light and the men need the work."

Alfred Needham thought otherwise. "We have become slaves of the demi-god gasoline engine," he declared. "Because of the automobile must we destroy the beauty and quaintness of Manchester? Cutting down the elm trees will ruin the Common." An alternative plan called for the construction of a road to bypass the business district, running behind Town Hall and joining Beach Street at the railroad tracks. But despite the fervor and the feelings, Central Street was never widened as dramatically as proposed. Perhaps a part of the reason was that plans had already been drawn for Route 128 (indeed, a section of the road in Danvers was built prior to World War II) which would avoid the town altogether on its way to Cape Ann.

With the election of Franklin Roosevelt as President in 1933, the country slowly began to fight its way out of the depression. But while America focused on its own problems scarcely 20 years after the end of World War I, war was brewing again in Europe. In 1938, Adolf Hitler, now head of a newly militarized Nazi Germany, marched into Austria. That same year in Asia, Japan, also on the march, had occupied most of the important cities of China. By the end of 1939, Hitler had seized Poland, and Britain and France joined to declare war on Germany.

'WINDS OF WAR'
Japanese Planes Attack Pearl Harbor; Scores Sign Up for Armed Services

Americans dearly wanted to stay out of what was to become World War II, but few alive that day will forget where they were on Sunday, December 7, 1941, when the first news came from Hawaii that the Japanese had attacked and bombed the U.S. Naval Base at Pearl Harbor. From that moment on, there was no turning back.

For the 47 members of the Class of 1941 at Story High School, life changed dramatically as it did for millions of other Americans. According to Ben Burgess, three members of his class lost their lives in combat: Richard Bailey, Otis Standley and Anthony Santamaria. Bailey, for whom the Amaral-Bailey American Legion Post is named, was lost with his ship, the cruiser USS QUINCY, which was sunk in August, 1942, during the battle of Savo Island. About half the Class of 1941 saw service in the Army, Navy or Marines. At least one joined the Waves. Burgess himself, with the 91st Armored Cavalry Reconnaissance Squadron, fought his way from Casablanca in North Africa to Sicily, Naples, Rome and Monte Casino. And while Corporal Burgess was on the peninsula of Italy, his classmate, Quartermaster 2nd Class Jerry Noonan, was aboard the Sims class destroyer USS ROE (DD-418), first on convoy duty in the Atlantic and later in the Pacific providing shore bombardment prior to the invasions of Guam, Saipan, Tinian and Iwo. His brother, Pat, an Electrician's Mate 2nd Class, served at a top secret Navy base in Greenland which intercepted wireless messages from German submarines and warned convoys of their presence. It was also part of a LORAN chain, a hush-hush electronic invention which enabled ships and planes to navigate more accurately.

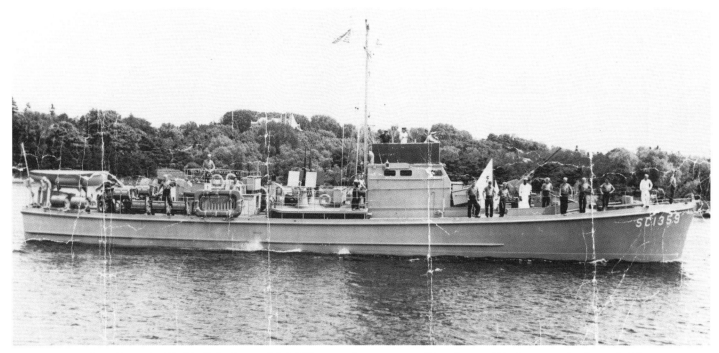

Commissioned on June 3, 1943, Subchaser SC 1359, seen here exiting Manchester Harbor, was built at Calderwood Yacht Yard where Manchester Marine is today. Her keel was laid on November 3, 1942. Measuring 110 feet, 10 inches overall with a 17 foot beam and a draft of six feet, six inches, these ships were armed with one three inch 50 caliber deck gun, two 50 caliber machine guns and racks for 14, 300 pound depth charges. Despite their small size, SC's crossed both oceans and operated in European and Asian theaters of war. Shortly after her commissioning, with a green crew aboard, SC 1359 ran aground on Hardy's Ledge in Salem Bay. She was towed off and taken to Gloucester where she was repaired. Altogether, eight SC's were built in Manchester. Photo courtesy of J. Borden Foster and Daniel A. Curran.

Sergeant and Squad Leader Larry Kirby, Jr., of Manchester and the Army's 101st Airborne Division, uses a field telephone to call for helicopter support during the battle for Lamar Plain, Vietnam. Wounded at Tam Key, Sergeant Kirby served in combat for 13 months. He was awarded the Bronze Star with V for Valor, the Purple Heart and the Air Medal for his participation in 24 helicopter assaults. Thousands of young men lost their lives fighting for their country in this bitter jungle war on the Vietnam peninsula. Their bravery and commitment, too often overlooked in what was an era of enormous controversy and social upheaval, deserves the nation's everlasting recognition and gratitude. Photo courtesy of Mr. & Mrs. Larry Kirby, Sr.

Lieutenant Bob Hooper, Story High Class of 1942, who had left Dartmouth College at the end of his freshman year to join the Army Air Corps, became navigator and bombardier of a B-26 engaged in tactical bombing missions over France and Germany. Hooper's classmate, Lieutenant Tom Hurley, was leading an infantry platoon across Europe with the Third Army commanded by another North Shore resident, General George S. Patton of Hamilton. While on the other side of the world, Marine Lieutenant Dan Slade waded ashore at Iwo Jima to help capture a vital stepping stone on the way to Tokyo, and Guy Bailey, an ordnance man with a squadron of B-29's on Tinian, saw the heavily-guarded shed where the first A-bomb was kept before it was dropped on Hiroshima.

A priceless scrapbook of news clippings and photographs from The Manchester Cricket and The Beverly Times, kept faithfully during World War II by Mrs. Harold Day, shows that Manchester's Leonard Andrews served as a technician in the Army. (His brother Nat was also an Army veteran.) Felix "Pop" Radack became a Naval Air Cadet. Both men were later to become Chiefs of the town's Police Department. Brothers and sisters enlisted in the service. Clippings show they included the four Scullys—Francis, James, William and Edward; the Corleys—Joseph, Edward, George and Richard; the Filiases—Bill and Alex; the Wogans—Philip and Richard; the Ferraras—James and Richard; the Cranes—Vincent, Wallace, Melvin and Claud; Robert Crane, a cousin was listed as missing in action in the South Pacific; the Baileys—Robert, Guy and Richard (see above); the Morrisons—John and Norman; the Conlons—Dennis, Francis, John, James and Thomas; the Doanes—Clifford, Alfred, Raymond and Donald; the Magnusons—Herman, Paul and Philip; the Hurleys—Patricia, Thomas and William; the Marshalls—John and Robert; the Hoopers—Stanwood and Bob; the Slades—Dan and Harry; the Noonans—Jerry and Pat; the O'Mearas—Harry and Nancy and the Kraczynskis—Steven and Joe.

Other brothers and sisters listed as in the Armed Services included, in the U.S.Navy, John F. Marshall, Electricians Mate 1st Class and Robert L. Marshall, Fireman 1st Class, sons of Mr. and Mrs. John S. Marshall; and in the Army, Private First Class Gordon C. Burnham, Marietta Burnham Steade, Women's Army Corps, and Irene Burn-

ham, Army Nurse Corps, son and daughters of Mr. and Mrs. Ralph Burnham.

Manchester women volunteered. June Ericson, Marjorie Cragg, Patricia Hurley, Eunice Fleetwood Therrien, Anna Crocker, Marjorie Jones, Marjorie Marshall, Dorothy Sjorlund, Doris Cressy and Lucille Plasman were among those who joined the WAVES. Katherine Flatley and Bessie Kassanos served in the U.S. Coast Guard. Mary Radack, Mary Ellen Cool, Virginia Diggdon and Marjorie Kelleher were members of the Army Nurse Corps. Mabel Mantjouranis and Sarah Rudden joined the Women's Army Corps or WACS. Mabel, then a T/4, was married to T/5 Clayton L. Sweatland, Jr. of California when the two were stationed in far away Dutch New Guinea.

By April, 1944, more than 300 men and women from Manchester were in uniform with the Navy, the Army, the Marines, the Army Air Corps and the Coast Guard. They included Navy Captain Berisford Waller, skipper of the cruiser TUSCALOOSA, whose family summered at Smith's Point for many years, and Colonel Gil Irvin, one of the first summer residents to live in Manchester year-round, who was with Headquarters of the 8th Air Force in Europe.

THE HOME FRONT
Gas and Food Rationing; Blackouts at Night; at the Yard, Sub-Chasers Are Being Built

On the home front, life during the war years was different as well. Gold-framed flags with blue stars, signifying that a family member was in the service, were proudly displayed in windows throughout the town. The young and the too old to serve joined ration boards, civil defense units, fire and police auxiliaries, the Red Cross and the United Service Organization, or USO, which entertained service men and women on leave or liberty. Students worked parttime in stores and at garages while their parents took jobs in defense plants producing materials for war. Many of these operated 24 hours a day. Veterans of World War I served in the State Guard, usually without pay. At Story High, youngsters studied airplane silhouettes and were trained as observation tower "spotters." To this day, one life-long Manchester resident, now in her 70's, can recognize a P-38 Lightning or a P-40 fighter.

People planted Victory gardens, held drives for household fat used in making munitions, scrap metal, paper and other products that could help the war effort. All bought Victory Bonds. Heading the Hit Parade on radio were songs like I'll Be Seeing You, The White Cliffs of Dover, and even the poignant Lilly Marlene, beloved by both German and Allied soldiers alike. Food items were rationed as was gasoline. The amount of fuel each vehicle could receive was determined by ration cards marked A, B and C. With rubber in short supply, cars were limited to five tires each. And, as silk and nylon went into parachutes, stockings for the ladies soon were scarce luxuries.

As night came, houses everywhere in Manchester drew blackout curtains to eliminate skyglow and make it difficult for enemy submarines to find a ship silhouetted against the shore. Auto headlights were half blacked out as well. The aircraft spotting tower on Town Hill behind the Manchester Historical Society was manned by resident volunteers 24 hours a day. And armed U.S. Coast Guard personnel, on the lookout for saboteurs, patrolled the shorefront from Beverly to the Gloucester line around the clock. Anyone who ventured upon the water for commercial fishing or for pleasure needed a Coast Guard identification card.

On August 10, 1944, veterans from the Spanish-American War in 1898, members of the 8th Regiment, Massachusetts Volunteers, both officers and enlisted men, were still spry enough to celebrate a reunion at Tuck's Point. In late September, a seasonal hurricane swept up the coast downing tree limbs which fell on a house owned by Charles Dodge and damaged John L. Silva's taxi. The Right Reverend Monsignor George F. Leahy of Sacred Heart Church also celebrated his 50th anniversary as a priest.

At Walter B. Calderwood's Boat Yard at the end of Ashland Avenue behind a chain link security fence, more than 125 men were at work building wooden, 110-foot submarine chasers for the Navy. From 1942 to 1944, eight ships were launched and joined the fleet. Some were involved in coastal patrol. One vessel took part in the Normandy invasion. Another operated in the Mediterranean.

Although mail from home meant everything to servicemen and women, it was the arrival of The Cricket that was looked forward to with equal anticipation. Letters of thanks addressed to Harry Slade, Sr., then Editor and Publisher, from Donald Bentley, Francis Coughlin, Eddie Scully, Russell Fears, Brud Fritz, John Gillis, Sergeant Ben Stasiak (later to become a long-time selectman) and scores of others show how much news of Manchester meant to her sons and daughters far away.

In May of 1945, Germany surrendered. Three months later the free world celebrated V-J Day. Two atomic bombs dropped on Hiroshima and Nagasaki by order of President Harry S. Truman ended the war in the Pacific and saved the millions of lives that would have been lost on both sides, had the planned invasion of Japan's home islands taken place.

The heroes came home, millions of them, through receiving stations from California to New York where they acquired not only final physicals, mustering-out pay and bonuses provided each GI by a grateful Congress, but, most important, that "ruptured duck," a patch bearing a gold eagle surrounded by a circle, which was sewn above the left breast pocket of every uniform, proudly proclaiming that the wearer was honorably discharged and once again a civilian.

By the end of 1945, three of the community's senior officers, who had grown close to each other in the service, were back at work. Dr. Charles Herrick, Commander, U.S. Naval Reserve, had re-opened his office at 21 Union Street. Navy Commander Whit Kimball, former Principal of Story High School, returned to school administration and teaching. And Commander Gordon Abbott had purchased Calderwood's Yacht Yard and re-christened it Manchester Marine Construction Company.

NAVY CROSS

Heroism and Skill Are Recognized as Local Residents Receive Medals

Abbott had been awarded the Navy Cross, the nation's second highest decoration for valor, for "extraordinary heroism" as commanding officer of the fleet minesweeper USS DEFENSE while on the "picket line" north of Okinawa. There were other medal winners in town as well. Mrs. Harold Day's scrapbook shows that Bronze Stars were presented to Army Lieutenants Russell M. Dennis and William J. Dean, Jr., and to Lieutenant Charles Burnett, USNR; Distinguished Flying Crosses went to Lieutenants Bob Hooper and Ralph H. Lane, Jr.; Captain Vincent M. Crane was awarded the Silver Star, Distinguished Flying Cross and Air Medal; and Carpenters Mate 1st Class Gerard

Halloran was among those honored with the Presidential Unit Citation. A number of Manchester's young men were wounded in action and received the Purple Heart. Thirteen from Manchester gave their lives for the cause of freedom. They were Richard E. Bailey, Robert S. Crane, John Gavin, Jr., John D. Kelleher, Harry Mercer, James A. Murray, Russell S. Noyes, Charles E. Saco, Anthony Santamaria, Jarvis H. Saulnier, Compton Sargent, Charles R.L. Sturgis and Otis H. Stanley.

As the war neared its end, others from Manchester also entered the service. Although technically veterans of World War II, these youngsters primarily served with naval, land and air forces occupying the defeated nations of Germany and Japan. Their names appear on the town's Honor Roll. It should be noted as well that many distinguished combat veterans settled in Manchester after the war. They included Marines Larry Kirby and Val Hollingsworth, the latter losing a leg at Iwo, as well as Naval Academy graduate Rear Admiral Harry Hull, a submarine skipper during the war, who later flew his flag aboard the cruiser USS BOSTON as Commanding Officer, Cruiser-Destroyer Flotilla 10.

On the home front, one of the most remarkable characteristics of World War II was the united spirit of the country and its wholehearted commitment to the support of its armed services and to ultimate victory. People faced hardships and deprivation with humor and understanding, worked long and odd hours in war factories, and volunteered for countless tasks without pay and without complaint, knowing that on battlefields far away there were young men and women who were prepared to make the ultimate sacrifice to keep the world free.

A NEW LIFE

G.I. Loans Spur Sales of New Homes; Veterans Marry and Settle Down

As millions of veterans headed home, long-postponed desires were waiting to be fulfilled. At the top of the list was marriage and settling down to raise a family. New family units needed shelter and the first step of their lives together was to purchase a house. In most cases, this was made easy with a new national policy which perpetuated the American dream of home ownership—the Gl Mortgage Loan. The housing boom that followed World War II also initiated a revolution in living. A symbol of what America had fought for was the single family dwelling—for each man and woman, their own castle—with its picture window (a term developed at the time) and a yard large enough to support a lawn and perhaps a small garden.

Many of these young marrieds were the sons and daughters of first or perhaps second generation immigrants who had fought for the right to improve their own lot and to provide their children with the benefits of a new society which they themselves would help to build. It was called 'suburbia" and it later created a new urban infrastructure which soon established a culture of its own. Within the next decade, Manchester was to become part of this revolution and, as a suburban town, to change forever. New wealth and new education, thanks to the Gl Bill, seemed to make every dream a possibility.

"Society," as the town once knew it before the war, had all but disappeared. Domestic servants—household maids, chauffeurs and gardeners—became occupations of the past as Manchester turned into a year-round community. Many of the largest estates such as Eagle Head and the Walker property were subdivided into smaller house lots. Other great houses of an earlier era still in family hands were reduced in size to meet the needs of a new and simpler life. To make way for the changes it knew were sure to come and to preserve its rural character, the town wisely adopted zoning as early as 1944, restricting the shoreline to single residences only and designating areas for business, light industry (north of Route 128) and residential. Slowly, vacant lots throughout the town itself began to disappear as new housing took their place.

Early subdivisions included Highwood, a part of the Walker property. There were others at Old Essex Road, University Lane, at Hickory Hill, off Forest Street, on Harold Street and at Spy Rock Hill. Houses were constructed off Pine and Pleasant Streets, on Crooked Lane and at Moses Hill. But Manchester, unlike many towns in the Commonwealth, grew slowly. In 1945, its population was 2,539. By 1976, 31 years later, it had doubled to 5,100 persons. In the last nearly 20 years, it has increased to some 5,600. In eastern Massachusetts, the greatest growth took place primarily in towns south and west of Boston. Manchester's granite ledges, its unforgiving soils and its size—just seven and one-half square miles—discouraged major developments which could have had a dramatic impact upon life in what has always been a small town.

Despite the lure of other states and regions which they may have seen in the service, an impressive number of young people returned after the war to the town where they grew up. Stanwood and Bob Hooper became the third generation to operate Hooper's Market. Dan and Harry Slade soon took over The Cricket Press although Harry, Senior, still remained active. The Brown family banded together and established Manchester's first supermarket, a local landmark. Herman and Phil Magnuson assumed responsibility for the family's florist business. Ben Stasiak became an employee of the Postal Service and served on the Board of Selectmen for a record 14 years. (Runner up was Louis Barrier who was a member of the board for 12 years.) Jake Greenberg was appointed Postmaster, followed by Jerry Noonan who also served for decades on the Board of Assessors. Ed French returned to Manchester Marine as chief painter. George Burchstead joined the Manchester Electric Company and eventually was named its General Manager. Karl Amalia started his own business as a landscape contractor and tree surgeon. The Demarkis family's Seaside Cafe became the Harborside Restaurant with John Demarkis as its genial host. Bill and Nick Filias established the Manchester Food Mart on Brook Street. Ed Corley worked at The Cricket Press, became a life guard at Singing Beach and later a Selectman and holder of other municipal positions. Kenny Bohaker was part of the team at Hooper's Market. Perry Allen returned to Allen's Drug Store. Nat Andrews became a successful plumbing contractor. His brother Alan took over once again as Chief of Police.

New residents who came to town purchased real estate in the late 1940's at prices that would make the average citizen wish now that he'd bought some of it himself as an investment. Shorefront properties that were later to sell for many millions of dollars, went for $50,000 to $75,000. Older buildings such as the Priest School and even the railroad depot that had served their usefulness in another era were razed to make way for progress. One, the Manchester House, the town's only hotel on Central Street opposite Town Hall, was destroyed by fire in 1952. And if it hadn't been for the skill and persistence of Manchester's firemen, much more of the community than the Manchester House might have been lost in the blaze.

THE RED MENACE
Communist North Korea Invades South; U.S. Troops, Manchesterites, Respond

While America was recovering from the effects of World War II, the trumpets of war sounded again, this time in far-off Korea. In June 1950, Communist North Korean Forces had invaded the South, and President Truman, with the support of the United Nations, decided to fight aggression which he believed might lead to World War III. Again, Manchester's young men and women answered the call to arms.

By September, 1950, it had already been announced by the Department of Defense that Lieutenant L. W. T. Waller, U.S. Marine Corps, had been wounded. Waller, son of retired Navy Rear Admiral and Mrs. Beresford W. Waller, who with their children had spent many summers here at a family house off Proctor Street, landed at Inchon, fought his way north, and then with the entry into the war of Red China, turned around with the Marines and through bitter winter weather, battled his way back to safety from the Chosin Reservoir where he was wounded once again.

Also wounded in combat on the Korean peninsula was Corporal Rene Imbeault of School Street who wrote home from a hospital at Osaka, Japan that he had been hit in the shoulder while on patrol "about 15 miles north of Taegu in the mountains and had to walk three miles to an aid station [all the] while losing...blood." There he was given plasma but was on the move again as North Korean mortars opened up on the position. "We struck out cross country," he said, "until we reached a rear Aid Station. From there we went by truck and then by train to [the port city of] Pusan. All the while all I had over my wound was a rag bandage and my bloody clothes. I also had a good dose of morphine in me that really helped..." From the hospital at Osaka, Corporal Imbeault was soon on his way to the United States.

Other Manchester residents in the reserves were called back to active duty to serve in the Army, in the Navy, in the Air Force and in the Marines. Many of them were veterans of World War II. Few seemed to question the wisdom of President Truman's decision to intervene militarily, although many were critical of General MacArthur's leadership which they believed led to the involvement of Red China.

By 1953, an armistice had been signed and a wary peace restored at the 38th Parallel. Today, 40 resident veterans of the Korean War are members of the Amaral-Bailey Post of the American Legion.

FOREST FIRE, 1957
Massive Blaze Menaces Entire Town; Firemen, Volunteers Are Heroic

In May, 1957, Fire Chief Richard A. Hammond and his men were heroes once again as a forest fire burned more than 1,000 acres of tinder-dry woodland in Manchester and threatened the very existence of the town itself. For three days the blaze raged in the wooded area from Pine and Bridge Streets to Route 128 and Beverly Farms. Members of the Massachusetts National Guard and employees of the State Department of Public Works as well as firemen from as many as 40 communities as far away as Wilmington, Malden and Lawrence, joined members of the local fire and police forces, highway department and other residents to help battle the blaze. Businessmen who regularly commuted to Boston stayed home from work to wield brooms and shovels. Story High was closed as students pitched in to help. Houses on Highland Avenue, Jersey Lane and Forster Road were particularly threatened, but quick action at the last minute managed to save them. During the conflagration, scores of volunteers working with the Red Cross served firefighters as many as 1,000 meals three times a day. Finally, the blaze was under control. Said Chief Hammond, praising the work of everyone involved, "By the Grace of God there wasn't a life lost or a building damaged to any degree..."

With a growing number of young families in town, Manchester soon turned to the need for new schools. In 1952, elementary grades were moved into the newly-constructed Memorial School building off Lincoln Street. That same year, Story High School, having outgrown its hilltop quarters on Bennett Street, moved to the John Price School building at the corner of Brook Street and Norwood Avenue. A decade later, this building, too, became obsolete and the present Junior-Senior High School structure was built. It was originally proposed to site the high school where the Eagle Head Playground or Sweeney Park (named in honor of former Superintendent of Streets P. Edward Sweeney) is located on Summer Street, but the characteristics of the subsoil there made this an impossibility. The land, however, was eminently suited for recreation and conservation and soon became another of the community's attractive public parks.

A rising population and an increase in the complexities of government forced the town to examine the need for a new Town Hall. Debate about a new building had been heard off and on since the 1920's. It seemed as though an endless number of Building Committees had been appointed and had presented their reports, all to no avail. As resident Frank Kirby wrote The Cricket at one point in the 1960's: "As night follows day, Town Meeting is coming, and with [it] the question of new Town Hall..." Finally, in 1969, voters agreed to fund the construction of the present structure. Now it, too, is considered by some as too small to meet the needs of the community.

With the Police Department in new quarters at Town Hall, discussions began about a new building for the fire department. Again, a number of study committees examined a series of sites in town, but in 1974 it was recommended that a new building be constructed on the site of the old. The proposal won Town Meeting approval by just three votes.

By now, Manchester had become to a great extent what Frank Floyd had hoped. Thanks to rail and Route 128 it was, as he suggested, "45 minutes from State Street," and, indeed, "a community made up of nice year-round dwellings, inhabited by commuters." To be sure, there were many who still made their living in town, but a significant number of residents, old and new, commuted out of town to work. Where in earlier days they might have gone primarily to Boston, in the new era of mobility with better roads, they could work anywhere in the region within what they considered a reasonable commuting distance.

In recent years, Manchester has done its best to retain its character as primarily a residential community. In the late 1950's, with a utopian eye on the possibility of increasing tax receipts and providing additional job opportunities for local residents, the town zoned the area north of Route 128 as "Limited Commercial." What many envisioned was an attractively landscaped industrial park which could become host to a small number of firms housed in low-rise buildings and manufacturing sophisticated, high-value products such as those used in the electronics industry. Utopia, however, failed to materialize. Instead, over time, the primary impact on the area was made by a gravel and stone-crushing operation. The Manchester Athletic Club, which has proved popular, exists nearby as do several smaller businesses. Agassiz Rock Reservation, public open space owned by The Trustees of Reservations, borders the area to the north and includes Beaverdam Hill and a portion of the wetlands of Saw Mill Brook.

CATHEDRAL PINES

Property Is Preserved for Public Enjoyment North of Route 128 as Early as 1879

Before the turn of the century, upper School Street and Southern Avenue in Manchester and Essex were immensely popular as a place to drive carriages. In 1879 a number of citizens were concerned that logging practices would destroy the beauty of the area. They banded together to form the Woodland Park Trust to purchase property on either side of the roadway to preserve it as forest land. Included in the Trust's acquisitions was Cathedral Pines in Manchester. In recent years, thanks to the efforts of the Manchester Conservation Trust (now Manchester-Essex Conservation Trust) and action at Town Meeting which designated tax title land as open space, major portions of the surrounding woodlands have been protected for conservation purposes. Although there are still some inholdings of private property, the land looks much the same as it must have to carriage riders in the 1890's.

One of the leaders of efforts to protect the carriage drive in Manchester and Essex at the end of the nineteenth century was summer resident Alice Towne Lincoln, 24-year-old daughter of John Henry Towne, a wealthy Philadelphia industrialist who in 1875 bequeathed his 85 acres near the Magnolia line to the University of Pennsylvania. The land was sold and later developed with access provided by University Lane. Lincoln Street was named for Alice Lincoln's husband, Roland C. Lincoln. The Lanesville marble drinking fountain at the Town Common was given by Mrs. Lincoln in memory of her parents in 1895 at the time of Manchester's 250th Anniversary celebration.

Open spaces and public parks continue to make Manchester a desirable place to live. Singing Beach, perhaps the town's best known attraction, was acquired under the authority of the Common-

wealth's Park Act in 1892. After two celebrated court cases which dealt with damages, the property cost the town a bargain $110,000. Other parks and open spaces include Tuck's Point, acquired in 1895; Masconomo Park, acquired in 1903; Powder House Hill protected in 1940; White and Black Beaches acquired in 1921; the Brick Pond Area on Summer and Forest Street given to the town in 1943; Cheever Commons and Millstone Hill Conservation Areas north of Route 128 acquired by the town in 1963; Wyman Hill Conservation Area given in 1965; Sweeney Park, part of land originally purchased by the town for school building purposes; and Winthrop Field bequeathed to the town by Miss Clara Winthrop in 1970. Agassiz Rock Reservation off School Street, the Coolidge Reservation at Coolidge Point and a number of conservation restrictions all given to The Trustees of Reservations are also a part of the town's collection of appealing open spaces.

In 2001, a new open space project was proposed on Raymond Street at the Manchester-Magnolia town line. The parcel of land had once been the site of the Surf Restaurant. Today, thanks to contributions from local residents, an expenditure approved at Town Meeting, and a grant from the Commonwealth, the property has been purchased, structures have been removed and the area has been attractively landscaped and is now a small neighborhood park.

Manchester's burial grounds add beauty and historic interest to the community as well. According to early accounts, the dead were most likely first laid to rest northeast of the Congregational Church for, in Colonial times, church yards, in the English tradition' were used as cemeteries.

Frank Floyd, in his history of the town, Manchester-by-the-Sea recalls records in 1873 which authorize Selectmen to sell a lot of land at the Cove known as "Old Burying Ground Pasture" thus apparently indicating that some of the early inhabitants were interred in that area as well. And, as Reverend Lamson states, there were those in his era (1895) who remember at least one white marble headstone in the Cove bearing the name "Abigail Gilbert."

But the first real evidence of land being set aside for cemetery purposes appears in 1661. It resulted in the establishment of the old burying ground at the corner of Summer and Washington Streets. As the road to Gloucester in those days followed Sea Street to Eagle Head and crossed land later owned by the Dana family, the cemetery appears to have included a portion of what is now Summer Street.

REST IN PEACE
Manchester Cemeteries Tell the Story of the Town Through the Years

In the 1700's, the property was fenced and then protected by a stone wall and gate, none of which were able to deal with the primary problems of the time which involved the growth of briers. Indeed, the warrant for the Town Meeting in 1772 addressed the issue directly seeking a plan to assist "those who are Called to follow their Deceased Friends to the Grave [hoping that they] may be delivered from those Briers..." The solution was to allow Jacob Tewxbury "use and Improvement of the Burying Ground free and Clear of Rent until he shall accomplish destruction of the Briers..."

Hearing nothing more, we must assume that Jacob was able to complete the task. Subsequent town meetings gave others the right to graze sheep on the property to continue to keep briers under control. Headstones here bear dates from the early 18th century.

On the east side of School Street is Union Cemetery, resting place for many sea captains and cabinet makers, established as a private association in 1845. Its proprietors agreed to turn it over to the town in 1888. The original cost of the land with improvements was recorded at $765.21.

Foreseeing Manchester's growth in population, another private corporation in 1857 founded Rosedale Cemetery which borders School Street, opposite Pleasant Street. It, too, was transferred to the town in 1888 with the neighboring Knight cemetery plot which the family had owned since 1875. With these new acquisitions, Manchester also appointed a Cemetery Commission to manage all of its burying grounds. In 1890, as the Reverend Lamson reports, a lot was set aside by the town and dedicated to Manchester's Post 67, Grand Army of the Republic, for the use of veterans of the Civil War. Then in 1902, the town authorized the expenditure of $8,800 to acquire additional land to be added to the original cemetery parcel.

That same year, Susan E. Crowell gave to the town, in memory of her brother, what is now B.F. Crowell Memorial Chapel. The handsome granite structure, completed in 1904, is available without cost "to all people and creeds for mortuary services." In recent years, weddings and concerts have taken place there as well.

In the late 1940's, land north of Pleasant Street was acquired to again expand Rosedale Cemetery. And finally, in 1952, the need for further burial spaces led to the acquisition of Pleasant Grove Cemetery off Pine Street.

PRECIOUS ASSET
Manchester's Harbor Offers a Livelihood for Fishermen; Boating Businesses

But perhaps Manchester's most valuable public open space is its harbor which gave the town its original name—Jeffrey's Creek. Through the years, its waters and its shoreline have supported shell and fin fisheries for native Americans and for early settlers. They continue to enable a significant lobster fishery to exist today. They have also provided pleasure and refuge for countless residents and visitors who have chosen boating as a pastime. The harbor and its tributaries have supported tidal grist and timber mills. They have been filled to permit the construction of Beach Street and the railroad. And starting in 1894, they were dredged to permit navigation at any tide to town landings both behind Town Hall and at Masconomo Park. This led to the establishment of two building and repair yards for yachts which today are Crocker's Boat Yard and Manchester Marine Corporation.

In recent years, the number of moorings has grown significantly. Because of this, many yachts find themselves assigned to Area 7, the outer harbor. Area 7 has been used as an anchorage and mooring area for yachts, both large and small, for more than a century. Many residents still recall the 1930's when the outer harbor was host to the steam yacht AVALON, chartered by Miss Eleanora Sears, a ten-meter boat and an eight-meter boat, a number of smaller cruising yachts and down the way, off West Beach, WINSOME, a magnificent yawl of some 70 feet in length owned by Neil Rantoul, a resident of Beverly Farms. Not long ago, WHEN AND IF, a handsome schooner, once the property of General George S. Patton, called Manchester her home port and also moored in the outer harbor.

VIETNAM

Difficult, Controversial War Sends Many Young Americans in Harm's Way

When President John F. Kennedy was elected in 1961, problems involving Vietnam were already of significant concern. Kennedy was convinced that the struggle in Southeast Asia was primarily a battle to halt the spread of communism throughout that part of the world and by November, 1963, there were 16,000 American military advisors in the country. Continuing the administration's policies, President Johnson pledged to the nation that he was "not going to lose South Vietnam" and the war escalated. Few issues have so split the country politically. Yet like any war, young men and women were called to serve the colors, right or wrong, and too many paid the supreme sacrifice.

One of these was Navy Airman William K. Hinkley, Jr. of 50 Pleasant Street, 21 years old, who, while serving aboard the aircraft carrier USS FORRESTAL was killed in a tragic accident on July 29, 1967. A 1963 graduate of Manchester High School, Hinkley is buried at Pleasant Grove Cemetery.

Three other Manchester servicemen were wounded in Vietnam. Joe Lazisky, U.S. Army, was hit by enemy fire while his unit was engaged in combat in the Delta region. With shrapnel in his thigh, he was taken by helicopter to the 24th Evacuation Hospital. He expected to return to his Brigade shortly. Bruce Gilson was injured in January, 1967, when the truck he was driving ran over a land mine and was demolished. He suffered shrapnel wounds in his leg, arm and hip but returned to action within a week. He had served in combat for nearly a year. And Larry Kirby, Jr., Specialist 4, a member of the U.S. Army's famed 101st Airborne Division received his Purple Heart as a land mine exploded when he was on patrol as a squad leader near the DMZ. He was evacuated to Japan and thence to the United States. Kirby, a veteran of 13 months of combat, was also awarded the Bronze Star for Valor.

An ugly war, Vietnam became America's longest running conflict, lasting until January, 1973 when the Nixon Administration finally extricated the United States from Southeast Asia. Some 57,000 Americans had been killed; 300,000 had been wounded. More than a million Vietnamese had lost their lives. This country had learned a bitter lesson.

The turbulent sixties brought all sorts of new problems to society. Some of them are explained in the issue of REFLECTIONS appearing later in this book which tells the story of the Manchester Police Department.

In 1962, problems with summer traffic again plagued the town. Reacting to continuing complaints, both the Board of Selectmen and the Planning Board revived an idea that had been originally suggested in 1938. It called for the construction of a by-pass roadway which would run behind Town Hall and join Route 127 again at the railroad station. The plan included one-way traffic and even a stop light. Voters wisely defeated the proposal, which would have chopped up the heart of the community. In the decade that followed, the town first rejected and then in 1982, agreed to the fluoridation of its water supply. It also said a sad goodbye to the last of its great elm trees, victims of Dutch elm disease, and made way for changes downtown which included Peele House Square and such additional subdivisions as Greenbriar, Sea Rock Estates, Woodholm II, Deer Hill and Rockwood Heights.

'AFFORDABLE HOUSING'

Rising Real Estate Prices Make It Tough in Town for Both Young and Old

The price of real estate everywhere rose dramatically and Manchester was no exception. Indeed, by the early 1980's, some houses acquired in the 1950's were worth 10 times what they were purchased for. The down side of this was a major concern that youngsters who grew up in town could not afford to stay here when they needed housing of their own. Another worry was that new municipal employees would be forced to live out of town because local housing was too expensive. Finally, elderly residents who hoped to stay where they were, found their real estate taxes rising proportionately. The answer had to be some sort of "affordable housing," and, working with the appropriate state agencies, officials began to press for it.

In the 1970's, a new tide gate and concrete retaining wall were constructed for Central Pond behind the Fire Station. Police patrolmen enrolled at the State's police academy brought a new level of professionalism to the department. The Harbor Committee initiated a numbering system for moorings to control and monitor an increasing demand. The Highway Department built a new parking lot at Eaglehead Playground. New street lights were installed downtown. The residents of Walker Road continued to deal with problems of flooding. And residents of the community on both sides of the issue squared off with each other about whether a halfway house for teenage boys should be established on Lincoln Street.

In February, 1978, a major northeast storm buried Manchester in more than three feet of snow. High tides and winds up to 80 knots produced surf which destroyed the sea wall at Singing Beach and damaged scores of other waterfront structures. Trains and auto traffic came to a standstill as communities along the shore dug themselves out. Those who were fortunate to escape damage really rather enjoyed the storm which for nearly a week saw residents getting around town on foot and on cross-country skis.

By the late 1980's, Manchester, like many towns throughout the region, was suffering from the effects of drought. In 1988, a paucity of rain had left Gravelly Pond reservoir 53 inches below normal and a cycle of water bans began. Water Commissioners reported that the level of the pond was so low that "whirlpools could be seen forming over the intake pipes." Over time, however, the rains did come replenishing both Round Pond and Gravelly Pond. Meanwhile, the town began to plan for the establishment of a water filtration facility mandated by state regulations.

Throughout history, Manchester women have played a major role in their town's achievements, but it took until 1985 for voters to elect a woman—Sue Noble—to represent them on the Board of Selectmen. Polly Townsend, Mary Hardwick, Dawn Grohs and Sue Thorne continue the tradition. Another distinguished Manchester woman, former Town Counsel Ellen Flatley, has been Justice of the District Court in Gloucester since 1988. Helen Bethell, Joan Brown, Frances Burnett, Candy Bergquist, Ann Brewer, Adele Ervin, Joanne Graves, Sue Hall, Ann Harrison, Virginia Hughes, Dr. Katherine Lastivica, Helen Mitchell, Gail Ramos, Charlotte Wilson, Carroll Cabot and others have served the community as members of its School Committee, Planning Board, Board of Appeals, Board of Health, Conservation Commission and Finance Committee. Business women, too, from store owners Sally Samples and Abigail Trask in the town's early days, to Grace Hall, Alice Rice, Connie Brown, Andrea Ramos, Bernice Thompson, Regina Villa, Elaine Perkins, Mary Ellen Otto, Sally Huss, Kip Abbott and Patty Cardinale-Cohen today, contribute immensely to causes which foster the community's success and well-being.

FINALLY, REGIONALIZATION
After Many Attempts, Town Meeting Voters Approve Link with Essex

As the 1980's progressed it became harder and harder for the municipality to meet budget goals. Squeezed by Proposition 2 1/2, the Finance Committee did its best to keep up with demands. With the assistance and guidance of professional planner Jon Witten, the Planning Board was able to modernize the Zoning By-law and complete a Master Plan for the community's future. And with school choice approved by the State Legislature, the town received a welcome injection of cash as students from Gloucester and Essex took advantage of the opportunity to attend Manchester schools. By 2001 town meeting voters authorized the start of planning which would end with new facilities for what is now Manchester-Essex Regional High School.

In the early 1990's, the quest for "affordable housing" continued and treatment plants for both water and sewer were overdue. By 1999, a handsome new medical building had been erected off School Street at the junction of Route 128, enabling a group of physicians to offer a series of medical services under one roof.

At the heart of every decision in government, however, was the issue of cost—whether what was proposed was needed and how much the town was willing to pay for it. In this regard, Manchester was much the same as any other city or town in the Commonwealth, and little different in this present decade than it has been throughout its history. There did seem to be a few years, however, in the late 1990's, thanks to the nation's booming economy, a stock market with the Dow Jones average reaching new highs, and a general air of consumer confidence, when no one at Town Meeting quibbled with funding requests. But this may have been a rare moment in time.

In an earlier era, a distinguished summer resident of Manchester played a leading role in the establishment of a new concept of investing in the market which was to affect wealth in America for years to come. It was the invention of the mutual fund. One of the founding fathers of the new industry was Merrill Griswold, a summer resident of Manchester for many years who, with his family, lived at Arbor Vitae, a property on Masconomo Street. From 1932 to 1953, Griswold served as Chairman of Massachusetts Investors Trust, the first mutual fund company in America. It was his genius in acquiring the necessary Federal legislation in the 1930's and in providing and implementing ideas about his new and attractive investment opportunity which made possible today's multi-billion dollar mutual fund business. Another pioneer was Henry T. Vance, also a resident of Manchester at Eagle Head. Vance and his corporation, Vance, Saunders & Company, were allied with Massachusetts Investors Trust and responsible for providing its underwriting and marketing services. Griswold and the country's mutual fund industry, as one investment professional declared, "brought Wall Street to Main Street."

STATISTICAL PROFILE

State Survey & Census Figures Tell the Story; They Show Our Population Is Shrinking

A summary profile of the town and where it stands statistically is provided every five years by the Commonwealth's Executive Office of Communities and Development. The latest report available, dated 1995, which also uses data from the 1990 Census, shows that the population of the Town of Manchester that year was 5,286 persons, 2,515 of them male, 2,771 female. This is 138 persons less than in 1980. And estimates say population here will shrink further to 5,231 persons by the year 2010.

According to census findings, 15 percent of the population was 65 years of age or older; 24.7 percent, ages 45 to 64; 42 percent, ages 15 to 44, 11 percent, ages 5 to 14 and 6.3 percent, under five years old. Of these, 99.1 percent were white, 0.4 percent were Asian or Pacific Islander, 0.4 percent were of Hispanic origin, and 0.1 percent were American Indian, Eskimo or Aleut. Two persons were African-Americans. Department of Public Health figures for 1995 show that there were 69 resident births that year and 37 resident deaths.

The 1990 Census reports that the average household in Manchester included 2.48 persons; 58.4 percent of these were married couples, 2.0 were male, 7.8 percent were female and 31.8 percent were listed as "non-family households."

Most households, or 1,618, received their incomes from wages and salaries. The average was $63,141. There were 524 self-employed persons with an average annual income of $35,647. Sixty households were listed as receiving public assistance. And 1,391 received income from interest which averaged $17,915 per household annually. Just less than four percent of the town's population, or 205 persons, were listed as being below the poverty level.

Household income was distributed as follows: $25,000-$34,999, 10.9 percent of the population; $35,000-$49,999, 14.5 percent; $50,000-$74,999, 21.9 percent; $75,000-$99,999, 13 percent and $100,000 or more, 18.8 percent. The median income for households was $52,806, 42.9 percent higher than the state average.

In 1990 (U.S. Census), Manchester had a total of 2,315 housing units. If occupied by their owners, their median value was $306,800. Just over 69 percent of the structures were single units; 20.4 percent had two to four units; and 8.6 percent included five or more units. There were 84 conventional state-assisted units of public housing.

Forty-six percent of the town's dwellings were built in 1939 or earlier and 41.3 percent were built between 1950 and 1970. In recent years, home construction has slowed: 5.1 percent of the existing stock was built from 1980 to 1988. The median sales price according to Banker & Tradesman, increased 12.1 percent from $235,000 to $263,000 between 1990 and 1991; decreased 20.3 percent to $210,000 in 1992; increased again 14.3 percent from $210,000 to $240,000 between 1992 and 1993. And in 1994, slipped to $229,500 per dwelling unit. Eight building permits for new home construction were issued in 1994; 10 were issued in 1992.

Of a student population of 760 reported by the Department of Education in 1991–1992, 77.6 percent attended public schools; 22.4 percent attended independent schools. The Town of Manchester spent $6,930 per pupil compared to a state average of $5,034. More than 94 percent of students here received a high school diploma; 47.1 percent continued their studies in college and received a Bachelor's degree or higher. The dropout rate was 0.4 percent in 1993–1994. Statewide it was 3.7. Again in 1993–1994, teachers here received an average salary of $45,801, while the average across the state was $39,023.

Of the 2,793 persons in Manchester listed as employed by the 1990 Census, most, or 1,112, worked in the service sector of the economy; 539 worked in wholesale and retail trade; 336 were in manufacturing; and 307 in finance, insurance and real estate. In 1993, the largest employer was the town itself with 166 persons on its payroll. Next came the Manchester Athletic Club with 85; Oakwood Nursing Home with 50; The Cricket Press with 25 and Brown's Market with 20 employees. (Brown's was sold in 1996.)

To reach work, the 1990 U.S. Census reports that 72 percent of Manchester's residents drove their cars alone; 10.4 percent walked or worked at home; 9.4 percent used carpools; and 6.3 percent depended upon public transportation.

According to the State's Office of Environmental Affairs in 1985, 27.2 percent of the land in Manchester, or 1,356 acres, was devoted to residential use. Some 16 acres were used for commercial purposes; 130 acres for transportation (roads, rail); 145 acres for recreation; and three acres for industry.

5,286 RESIDENTS

Our Land Area Totals 7.84 Square Miles; We Are a 'Bookish' Community

The land area of the town totals 7.84 square miles. With a population of 5,286, it accommodates 674 persons per square mile. Those include, according to the Secretary of State in 1994, 900 Republicans, 548 Democrats and 2,087 unenrolled Voters.

The state Board of Library Commissioners reports that in 1993–1994, books circulated by Manchester's Memorial Library totaled 51,045. This is a per capita average per year of 9.24 books compared to a statewide average of 4.91 books.

By far the largest of the town's recreation facilities is its Wilderness Conservation Area which totals some 216 acres of public land preserved for environmental education, hiking, ski touring, nature walks and picnicking. Other areas include parks, playgrounds, the Essex County Club (169 acres), and open spaces such as Agassiz Rock Reservation, Coolidge Point Reservation, Wyman Hill Conservation Area, Eaglehead Wildlife Study Area and Owl's Nest Nature Preserve.

In 1993, the Office of Public Safety reported 86 crimes in Manchester, an average rate of 16.27 crimes per 1,000 people. This compared to a statewide rate of 47.95 crimes per 1,000 people.

According to the Department of Public Welfare, in 1994 three people received Emergency Aid; 16 persons received Supplemental Security Income—Aged; 16 received Supplemental Security—Disabled; and there were seven cases of Aid to Families with Dependent Children. A total of 76 received Food Stamps only.

As might be expected, in Fiscal Year 1994, with a total assessed value of $702,424,000, by far the largest percentage of the town's total revenue, or $7,361,000, came from residential real estate taxes. With income from commercial, industrial and personal property taxes, levies totaled $8,020,000. Including state aid, local receipts and other income, revenues for FY1994 came to $10,497,000.

Operating expenditures, again for FY1994, totaled $9,037,000. The largest amount, $3,995,000, was spent on education. The next largest expenditure was for the town's fixed costs, $1,387,000. That year we spent $1,027,000 for Public Works including highways; $734,000 for Police and $438,000 for Fire. General government cost $528,000; Culture and Recreation, $222,000 and Debt Service $331,000. From Moody's, Manchester received a bond rating of A.

Thanks to its traditionally conservative voting record, the efforts of its Finance Committee and Boards of Selectmen through the years, of its other elected officials and appointed committee members, and of those able and dedicated public officials at Town Hall, Manchester appears to be in excellent financial health.

Any town anywhere would be proud of the professional abilities of our department heads: Rosemary Cashman, Town Administrator; Charlie Lane, Town Accountant; Gretchen Wood, Town Clerk; Bob Moroney, Director of Public Works and Town Engineer; Ron Ramos, Chief of Police; Andrew Paskalis, Fire Chief; Caroline Johnson, Treasurer; Virginia Noyes, Principal Assessor.

Also, Robert Shaps, Superintendent of Schools; Jolene Larson, Librarian; Nancy Hammond, Council on Aging; Paul O'Brien, Veterans' Agent, and Betsy Rickards, Conservation Administrator.

Most important, the community itself continues to be held in rare affection by all who live or have lived within its boundaries. Although it has changed from a small town to a suburb, it still retains many small town characteristics. The human scale of its buildings and roadways provide it with an appealing warmth and charm. Its people generally know each other and wave and talk when they pass or meet on streets and sidewalks. Shopping is a personal pastime with clerks and store owners who are friends and associates. Municipal employees are often neighbors or acquaintances as well.

Despite healthy disagreements about political issues, most residents respect each others' opinion and individuality, share a common devotion to the welfare of the community, are proud of the town's rich heritage and genuinely enjoy associating with their fellow human beings. Thankfully, courtesy, honesty and goodwill are still the traits which govern our lives together. And when the chips are down, Manchester has shown throughout her lifetime that her people can pull together, amicably and enthusiastically, to solve the problems of the moment.

As the town now celebrates 358 years since its incorporation in 1645, the wise words of Henry C. Leach, Chairman of the town's 250th Anniversary Celebration, a gala event in 1895, are worth recalling. What he said then in the somewhat flowery prose of the era, is equally appropriate today.

"We recognize the changes that have come over the town," he declared in his closing remarks at a special commemorative ceremony in July, more than 100 years ago. "The little village by the sea with its homogeneous population, has become metropolitan in its habits and cosmopolitan as to population. The primitive has given place to the modern. The 'good old times' are only a tradition...

"Unchanged and unchangeable," he continued, "is our love for the old town and the old associations. Unchanged also is 'the ocean's wild and solitary waste...' And so long as the waves of ocean shall 'dash themselves to idle foam' upon [our] rock-bound shore, the sons and daughters of Manchester, at home and abroad, will be true to all that makes for the peace, prosperity and happiness of this embryo city by the sea." Amen.

Late autumn view of Central Square in the late 19th century, shows the Manchester House, far left, a popular boarding hostelry with dining room and bar which was extensively damaged by fire in 1952. Police officers Alex Backry and Fred Lear led guests to safety through smoke and flame. Two Manchester firemen, Wilbur Stanley and Richard Wogan, were injured fighting the blaze. Located just west of the Rabardy Block with Beaton's Hardware store out of the photo to the left, the structure was originally constructed in 1712. A third floor was added in 1900 after an earlier fire. The building was never rebuilt. The only sign of life in town is the horse and wagon at center. The drinking fountain is covered for winter. Gas lamps have yet to be replaced with electricity. Photo courtesy Manchester Historical Society, Elliott Crocker collection.

Looking down School Street from Central Square in the early 1900's. Notice the mix of autos and the two horses and wagons. The handsome vehicle coming down School Street appears to be driven by a uniformed chauffeur. An elegant lady in white is seated in back. Signs advertise Whalen Drugs, Hair Dressing, and Confectionaries. Two young boys frolic on the corner. Again, many of the buildings visible are still there today. Photo courtesy of SPNEA.

View from the gardens of the Henry L. Higginson estate at Sunset Hill around 1900. Black Beach is in the foreground. The present sea wall along the roadway had yet to be built. The Old Fort House on the point was originally a barn later converted to a summer dwelling by Benjamin G. Boardman. In 1872 it was assessed for $3,500. Outer Ram Island and House Island are visible in the distance. Photo Peabody-Essex Museum.

View looking west from the Congregational Church steeple in the late 1800's. In the foreground is Knight's lumber yard which borders the inner harbor. The building just beyond Knight's is Jewett's Mill. At lower right, facing Central Street, is the Police Station, a converted fire house with the hose tower still in existence. Bridge Street is visible at upper left. Few houses had been built along the waterfront. Note also the homogeneity of the architecture. The vernacular style called for white clapboard, a practical and attractive pitch on the roof, simple brick chimneys and rectangular windows, a combination pleasing to the eye that became popular in New England.

Intersection of Bridge Street, Pine Street and Bennett Street prior to 1900. All roadways were unpaved. On the side of the harness maker's shop at the corner of Bennett and Bridge Streets is a billboard which reads "Visite Dry Goods and Carpeting Salem." Again, American elms are a striking characteristic of the streetscape.

Central Square, Manchester, on a busy day in the mid-1890's. Horses and carriages come and go. Two children, one with a bicycle, wait to cross School Street. Many of the buildings visible are still standing. The building at left was, in 1792, the home of Dulcena Lathrop Bingham, who in 1803 was appointed Manchester's first postmaster. Building at right was the site for many years of Allen's Drug Store which used to have a soda fountain with white marble counters. Elegant carriage with the top-hatted coachman is owned by J.O. Weatherbee. The photograph was a gift of Mrs. Theodore L. Badger of Chestnut Hill, granddaughter of the Weatherbees.

Summer Street and Manchester's railroad depot around 1915. Beach Street is visible in mid-photo with the harbor beyond looking out to Misery Islands in the distance. Note that Horticultural Hall had yet to be constructed. It was built in 1917. Buildings at right include Horace Standley's blacksmith shop, now Standley's Garage. This photo appeared on the cover of the <u>North Shore Breeze</u>, a weekly magazine published regionally prior to World War II, on November 5, 1915. The orchard today, of course, is the site of proposed affordable housing.

With double tracks extended to Magnolia in 1896 and then in 1908 to Gloucester, Magnolia became a busy railroad stop on the Boston & Maine Railroad's Gloucester Branch especially during the summer months when visitors flocked to the Oceanside Hotel. Coolidge Point residents also used the station which was razed in 1942. It was located in Manchester at the end of Magnolia Avenue.

Winter scene at the junction of Union and Beach Streets around 1885 after a snow fall. Sidewalks have been shoveled and the two horses may be making their way to work on the streets which were often rolled to accommodate sleighs. There were many sizable residential buildings downtown in those days. The photo appears to have been taken from the house at the east corner of Beach and Union which was built by cabinetmaker John C. Long in 1833 and today is the site of Zak's Handcrafts & Gifts.

Four-story ice house at Ayers' Pond off Loading Place Road about 1900. Ice was also harvested at Lake Louise or Bennett's Pond and at Gravelly Pond. Most was sold locally. Winter temperatures in those days often reached below zero and cutting began in late January when ice was from 10 to 12 inches thick. Some 30 men were employed in Manchester during the heyday of the industry. Blocks sawed by hand were hauled up the slipway to the ice house on a continuous belt operated by a donkey engine and, insulated with saw dust and hay, most of them lasted through the hot summer months into late fall. They were distributed by "ice men" wearing rubber cloaks to protect their clothing as they carried ice on their backs to "ice boxes" throughout town. Motor trucks soon replaced wagons as delivery vehicles. Raymond Crocker was cutting ice at Gravelly Pond as late as 1943. His house at 52 Bridge Street was equipped with an ice house for storage and was much admired for the luxuriant quality of its front lawn.
Photo from the Manchester Historical Society gift of Elliott Crocker.

Horticultural Hall on Summer Street was for many years one of the town's most elegant structures. Built in 1917 by general contractors Roberts & Hoare, its foundation was completed by Austin Morley, its masonry by George Sinnicks; its heating by Robert Robertson; its lighting by Gustav A. Knoerr; and its painting by Edward A. Lane, all of Manchester. Headquarters of the North Shore Horticultural Society, the Hall served the town in many ways: as the site of annual flower shows; as a movie theater (evening features cost 28 cents); for wedding receptions; for Story High School graduation ceremonies; for the Junior Prom and Senior Receptions; as a gym and basketball court for Story High and students at the Price School; and as a home for the American Legion and the Masons. During the great flu pandemic in 1918, the building was used as an infirmary to isolate patients who had the highly infectious disease. Despite an offer which could have purchased and preserved the property, Horticultural Hall was torn down in 1963. Today it is the site of Harbor Hill apartments now being renovated for affordable housing.

For more than 100 years, municipal offices in Manchester were located in the Town Hall pictured above. The Odd Fellows Lodge was also quartered on the third floor. Town Meetings were regularly held in the auditorium on the second floor as were social events such as Saturday night dances. This view in a photo probably taken in the 1880's from the marsh at Cheever's Point off Ashland Avenue, shows Town Hall with two public outdoor toilets perched on the stone seawall with an appropriate portion hanging over the inner harbor; the Franklin Building next to the Congregational Church; the Police Station with its tower (now Seaside No. 1); and Knight's Wharf and lumber yard. Town Hall was built in 1868 and razed in 1969 to make way for the present brick structure.

A CLOSER LOOK

Selected subjects in detail. This section includes chapters describing <u>ARBELLA and her route to the New World</u>; the early days of <u>Manchester harbor</u>, how it was turned from mud flats to a deep water anchorage and about its fishermen and yachtsmen; how our privateers helped win both the <u>American Revolution and the War of 1812</u>; two of Manchester's celebrated <u>merchant captains</u>; <u>the industrious era of furniture-making</u>; Manchester's role in <u>the Civil War</u> and some personal experiences of courage on the field of battle; <u>the life and times of Thomas Jefferson Coolidge</u> whose generosity made possible The Memorial Library and Grand Army Hall; a profile of <u>the Reverend Cyrus A. Bartol</u> who became one of Manchester's most successful real estate investors; <u>the story of Manchester's schools and our prize-winning debate team</u>; the <u>embassy era</u> when scores of foreign diplomats fled the heat of Washington each year to enjoy Manchester's cooler climes; <u>the arrival of new families from lands far away</u> in the 19th and early 20th centuries who settled here to find happiness and success; how Manchester men and women helped win victory in <u>two World Wars</u> and what life was like on the home front; how two Manchester sisters began golf and tennis at an early age and went on to become national champions; <u>how high school students from this small town managed through the decades to compile so many championships in athletics</u>; what residents did for transportation before the automobile when <u>horses, carriages and wagons</u> traversed dirt roadways; Manchester's beloved <u>physicians</u>; celebrations and <u>parades</u>; our <u>artists, writers and musicians</u>; parks and <u>open spaces</u>; the <u>islands</u> around us; our own <u>major league ball player</u>; and distinguished residents who served both their state and nation as <u>elected representatives and diplomats</u>.

'BETWEEN BAKERS ILE & LITTLE ILE'

John Winthrop (1588-1640) led the way to the New World aboard ARBELLA landing in Salem in 1630. Well-educated, strong-minded, deeply devout, self-confident and a born leader, Winthrop has been called "the Puritan Squire." Pioneer of the Great Migration, which brought more than 1,000 settlers to Massachusetts in 1630 alone, he carried the charter of the Massachusetts Bay Colony to Boston and later became its Governor. Photo, courtesy of the Peabody-Essex Museum, is of a portrait of Winthrop which is hung at the State House.

THE ADMIRAL'S VIEW

Naval Historian Samuel Eliot Morison Uses Winthrop's Log to Trace Course

For more than 100 years, residents here have been told that John Winthrop's ARBELLA, bound for Salem from England in 1630, came to anchor at the end of her voyage in the waters of Manchester's outer harbor. Indeed, her replica adorns the Town Seal. Another version, however, indicates that ARBELLA may have bypassed Manchester altogether and anchored west of Misery Islands in Plum Bay off the Beverly shore.

The original version of the story that ARBELLA visited Manchester first was presented by the Reverend Darius F. Lamson in his History of the Town of Manchester, 1645–1895 which was published by the town and written for its 250th Anniversary. Lamson's conclusion has been accepted by two centennial celebrations, in 1895 and in 1995, and the reenactment of this portion of the town's history has been a popular highlight of each occasion.

To make his point, Reverend Lamson presents what he calls an "extract" from Winthrop's JOURNAL. The language, however, has been modernized. ARBELLA, it states, "...passed through the narrow straight between Baker's Island and another little island and came to anchor within the harbor..." Note 1, page 18, below the quote in Lamson's 425-page book, states that the "little island" was House Island which, indeed, would have put ARBELLA within Manchester's outer harbor. But even Lamson seemed in doubt for following Note 1 and the words "House Island," is a question mark like this: (?).

The other version is held by the late Harvard historian and author of the official history of the U.S. Navy in World War II, Rear Admiral Samuel Eliot Morison. It also appears in The Journal of John Winthrop, 1630-1649, published by The Belknap Press of Harvard University Press in 1996. In this latest presentation of the famous JOURNAL, Winthrop writes with his original spelling: "...as we stood towards the harbour, we saw another shallop coming to us, so we stood in to meet her, and passed throughe the narrowe streight betweene Bakers Ile & Kettle Ile, & came to an Anchor a little within the Islandes..." Unlike Lamson's history, the JOURNAL's Note 21, on page 34, is explicit: "...JW," it states, "seems to have mixed up the names of two islands. He had passed Kettle Island while rounding Cape Ann... but was now passing between Little Misery and Baker's Island to enter Salem harbor. Morison [Samuel Eliot]," it adds, "postulates that the ARBELLA anchored off Plum Cove on the Beverly shore."

Admiral Morison addressed the issue himself in an article which appeared in the Publications of The Colonial Society of Massachusetts, Volume 21, Transactions 1927-1930, pages 285 to 306. Entitled The Course of the ARBELLA from Cape Sable to Salem, it describes how the vessel encountered, as Winthrop's JOURNAL states, a shallop—an open boat fitted with oars and sail—sailing to Pemaquid. Aboard, explains Morison, was "Isaac Allerton [again substantiated by the JOURNAL], a Pilgrim Father, more renowned for sharp trading than for piety, [who] was thoroughly acquainted with these waters and doubtless gave Captain Milborne [of ARBELLA] the proper directions for the ship channel and the anchorage beyond."

Morison's exact words are crucial for they best explain his reasoning, thus the quote continues. "If the ARBELLA 'stood in' to meet the second shallop," he explains, "she had probably been sailing further off shore than the straight course demanded. She then took the narrow straight 'between Bakers Ile & Little Ile,' which still is the main ship channel to Salem Harbor. Little Island has been called Little Misery for the last two hundred and fifty years...Winthrop's chart [a hand-drawn sketch] shows Bakers and the Little Island in their correct relative position, together with Great Misery Island and two others which I take to be House Island and Saul's Rock.

"...I believe, for the following reasons," Morison declares, "that she anchored at about 10 a.m., June 12, [1630] from a quarter to a half mile off Plum Cove. 1) Winthrop says she anchored a little within the islands, hence she must have been nearer to the islands than the harbor. 2) High water came that morning at a little after nine, so that by the time ARBELLA reached Plum Cove sailing 2 to 2 1/2 knots with a light wind (if my calculations are correct), the ebb tide would have been setting against her, and further progress would have been difficult until the wind freshened or the tide changed. 3) This spot off Plum Cove is one of two places in Salem Bay where Bowditch [Nathaniel, the great navigator] places the symbol for a good anchorage on his chart of 1806. It is a favorite anchorage today for deep water vessels such as oil tankers."

Never one to mince words where maritime history is concerned, Morison gives short shrift to the theory that ARBELLA visited Manchester at all. "There are several reasons, each conclusive," he writes, "why the Arbella could not have anchored in Manchester Harbor. 1) Winthrop distinctly states that he passed through the straight between Baker's Island and Little Island, which there is no doubt means Little Misery. The Manchester people assert that the Little Island means House Island; but there is no straight between Baker's Island and House Island. They lie a mile apart with a ledge [Whaleback] between. 2) The ARBELLA's destination was Salem, and there is no reason why she should have gone out of her way to enter a bad harbor with a dangerous entrance when the day was yet young and wind and tide favoring. 3) It would have been a five mile row from Manchester Harbor to the settlement at Salem. 4) Winthrop's own chart shows a very slight indentation of the coast line at a point corresponding to Manchester Harbor."

So there you have it. I am certainly not one to quibble with Professor Morison except with his criticisms of Manchester Harbor which today rivals few on the east coast for its protection and charm at least for small boats. Remember, even Lamson raised a question about the identity of "Little Ile." But with the evidence presented, readers must make up their own minds about where ARBELLA anchored that first day in the New World. Especially if they plan to continue the tradition, as we did in 1895 and 1995, of using a replica of the ship and a costumed crew as a highlight of the next centennial in 2095.

As ARBELLA appears on the Town Seal with an Indian canoe approaching her, we can take heart that Winthrop's JOURNAL does record that "In the morning the Sagamore of Agawame, & one of his men came aboard our shippe & stayed with vs all daye." And he notes as well that on the first day "most of our people went on shore vpon the lande of Cape Anne which laye verye neere vs, & gathered store of strawber[rie]s."

Again, Notes in the Harvard reprint of the JOURNAL explain that our own Masconomo "was the Sachem of the Pawtucket Indians who lived N of Salem. His base at 'Agawam' [which means fish curing place] was soon renamed Ipswich by the colonists." We do know that Indians roamed all over the area, including what is now Manchester, seeking game, fish and shellfish. And we could suppose that those who went ashore "on Cape Anne" might have visited at least a portion of West Manchester. But all evidence points to the fact that Salem was Winthrop's objective and lands to the east where Manchester is located were of little interest except to those who would eventually settle there.

'A WELL-FOUND SHIP'

A Former Privateer, ARBELLA Displaced 350 Tons; Was Manned by 52 Seamen

In 1629, when John Winthrop was chosen to lead the "Great Migration" to establish the Massachusetts Bay Colony at Salem, his first need was for ships to transport what ultimately turned out to be more than 1,000 settlers to the New World.

Two aspects of the proposed expedition were unusual. First, its numbers. No earlier voyages came anywhere near equaling its size. For example, just 101 persons were aboard the MAYFLOWER when she landed at Plymouth in 1620. Second, the trip was primarily financed by the colonists themselves, middle-class yeomen of moderate means—merchants, farmers and their families—who sought opportunities not only for spiritual freedom as did the Pilgrims, but for "the right to profit by the toil of their own hands."

Ships of the early 17th century were not designed to carry passengers. Until Winthrop's adventure, there was little demand. England's sizable merchant marine was devoted to transporting cargo and the few travelers who existed adapted to what sparse accommodations were available aboard.

Although vessels of every size and quality of construction were available, there was a special class of merchantmen used to carry wine from ports in the Mediterranean which were known admiringly as "sweet ships." Because of their precious contents, they were unusually well built and leaked little, if any, unlike the average transport. The MAYFLOWER was one of these and it is probable that Winthrop and other leaders of his expedition did their best to select from this category.

ARBELLA, at 350 tons, was the largest of what became, according to maritime historian Samuel Eliot Morison, a fleet of 14 vessels (others say the total was 11). "She was a stout, well-found ship," writes Morison in Builders of the Bay Colony,

Costumed Puritans, playing the part of Governor Winthrop, here portrayed by Richard Henry Dana, III, and his party, pose at the Manchester Yacht Club in 1895, to commemorate the 250th Anniversary of the Town of Manchester, much as they did in 1995, 100 years later. They then boarded a replica of ARBELLA designed and built for the occasion in Salem using the hull of an old sloop, and were towed up the harbor. There they were met by the Great Sachem Masconomo in the person of Police Sergeant Leonard Andrews, grandfather of our own Sergeant Neil Andrews who portrayed Chief Masconomo in 1995. A one-day affair, the 250th Anniversary celebration included an impressive and lengthy parade. The event is told about in detail in the chapter entitled "Celebrations."

"larger than the average emigrant vessel." As the EAGLE, ARBELLA had seen service as a privateer owned by Sir Kenelm Digby. She was renamed for Lady Arbella Johnson, daughter of the Earl of Lincoln, whose husband, Isaac, was an organizer of the expedition. Her Master was Peter Milbourne. She was manned by 52 seamen and was equipped with 28 pieces of ordnance. In contrast, MAYFLOWER was described as "180 tons" and was armed with 10 to 12 guns. (Tonnage is measured in various and confusing ways, but in those days it was related to the carrying capacity of a vessel's hold which determined the tax her owner paid.)

ARBELLA, reportedly nine years old at the time, was purchased by a number of underwriters of the expedition and chartered for the occasion. Like many 17th century ships, according to Charles Edward Banks, author of The Winthrop Fleet of 1630, her "bow with [its] high forecastle deck was occupied by…seaman…the still higher poop deck on the stern…sheltered the quarters of the officers. The space between these two towering structures," Banks adds, "…was used for the cargo, the ordnance and the stowing of the long boats."

In the central portion of the ship as well, "some cabins" had been constructed. These were probably "rough compartments of boards for women and children, while hammocks for the men were swung from every available point of vantage." Governor Winthrop, Lady Arbella Johnson and others of their station, had quarters that were somewhat better than those afforded the rank and file. Indeed, of the voyage Governor Winthrop wrote to his wife in England: "Our boys are well and cheerful, have no mind of home. They lie both with me, sleep as soundly in a rug (for we use no sheets here)…and so do I myself."

Proper food was not easy to come by and scurvy was common in voyages which lasted as long as six to 12 weeks. The antidotes, of course, were fresh vegetables and citrus fruits such as limes or lemons, impossible to keep aboard for more than a few days without refrigeration. And so the colonists relied upon beer which was known at least as a mild preventative of scurvy. It also kept better than water. ARBELLA carried about 10,000 gallons of beer in wood casks, and 3,500 gallons of drinking water. For solid food there was beef and pork, preserved according to the "art or mystery" of the day, salt cod, biscuits, butter and flour used to make bread. Dried peas, some 40 bushels of

them, were the only vegetable aboard. When possible, as it was when ARBELLA arrived off the Grand Banks south of Newfoundland, passengers were able to supplement their diets with fresh cod and haddock. Many, of course, brought special treats from home which they may have shared with fellow passengers. These tidbits included wine and other spirits.

A large tripod kettle which swung over a "hearth box" in the forecastle was used for cooking. Fires were lit with charcoal to reduce the discomfort and hazards of smoke. There were few lights aboard— some "lanthornes" and a few dozen candles—and when darkness came it was time for bed. The only heat was from the fire in the galley. Cows and bullocks were carried in a pen at the aft end of the gun deck. But as these were for the beginnings of a herd of precious draft and dairy animals which would become a vital part of the new community, they were not consumed as food. All in all, ocean voyaging in the 17th century offered few comforts. For solace, passengers relied upon the powers of religion as well as on the knowledge that the voyage would ultimately end.

LITTLE ROOM FOR LUGGAGE
Passage to the New World Could Cost a Family of Eight as Much as $1,000

For the passage, people could take little from their homes in England; some clothes, perhaps, and a few pieces of furniture, but room for more was at a premium. There was cost to consider as well. A family of eight, which may have included children as well as a servant or two, would pay as much as $1,000 for their passage, estimates author Charles Banks in The Winthrop Fleet. There were additional charges for animals and baggage. It cost, for example, some 10 Pounds to ship a horse across the Atlantic to New England.

ARBELLA like other vessels of her era, was rigged as a three-masted "ship." Her bowsprit, gammoned (fastened with lashing) to the stem, had considerable upward rake. On its underside was a yard on which was set a "spritsail" which helped to keep the ship on course as her bulbous bow pulled her to windward as it plowed through the water. Bobstays did not exist, appearing first after 1670. The foremast was stepped well forward in the forecastle. The topmast, according to Professor F. Alexander Magoun of MIT's Department of Naval

Architecture and author of The Frigate Constitution and other Historic Ships published in 1928, would have been a separate spar which could be lowered to the deck. The mainmast was similar to the foremast, while the mizzen "was still probably a pole mast."

There were yards on the fore and mainmast carrying "square" sails (actually shaped; more like a trapezoid, wider at the heads than along the foot) which could be raised and lowered with ties. The topsail yards were short. The mizzen was rigged with a lateen, a relic of early Mediterranean vessels which remained in use for many years. The standing rigging was secured with dead-eyes. Running rigging was belayed to cleats at the foot of her masts. Her sails were of cotton canvas and her lines, including her anchor rode, were of hemp. ARBELLA, like other vessels of her time, was steered with a whip-staff with which, in light air, a single seaman could move the tiller and rudder. When it was rough, however, blocks and tackles were employed to steer the ship. Her guns, if they resembled the MAYFLOWER's, as many did at the time, were of brass. A "saker" fired a three pound ball: a "minion," a four pounder. She also would have carried a number of small pulling boats perhaps nested on deck.

Her hull was of wood, of course, held together with thousands of treenail or "trunnel" fastenings, wood pegs driven into the hull by mallet. Oak was used in her construction, as was elm. The MAYFLOWER, again according to Professor Magoun, was planked with Spanish chestnut. There are no records to show how the ARBELLA was constructed.

Except for the scare she had off Portland Bill when she cleared her decks and prepared for action with a small fleet of what she thought were "Dunkirkers" (they turned out to be friendly sail), the voyage of the ARBELLA to the New World was uneventful. Accompanied by the AMBROSE, TALBOT and the JEWELL, she found her way across the Atlantic using dead reckoning and a cross-staff to ascertain her latitude. Captain Milbourne chose a latitude line of 43 degrees, 15 minutes North, as his course to the westward which brought him south of Cape Sable, Nova Scotia. From there he sailed across the Bay of Fundy to raise Mount Desert Island, weathered Boon Island and arrived at Cape Ann. His landing in Salem Bay off Manchester took place on Saturday, June 12, 1630.

History tells us little about ARBELLA after she arrived in Salem, but her voyage with Governor Winthrop and her role as flagship of England's Great Migration to the New World and the settlement at Salem, has been celebrated ever since.

It was a primary feature of Manchester's 250th Anniversary event in July, 1895. As an article in HARPER'S WEEKLY at the time declared, "the maritime character of the town suggested...a reproduction of governor Winthrop's good ship ARBELLA." Months were consumed in preparation. A naval architect, David M. Little of Salem, agreed to take on the project, as HARPER'S put it "con amore." Little discovered an old fishing sloop, the HARD CHANCE, which was rebuilt for the occasion. Another key figure in the effort was Boston landscape painter and decorative artist Ross Turner whose talents helped to brighten the little vessel in the manner of her day. "As she glided into the beautiful little harbor," HARPER'S reported, "she was seen to be possessed by all the characteristics pictured in the old books—the high poop, the queer masts and spars [and] the rich and elaborate ornamentation about the stern..." She was, of course, towed by a "modern" steam launch, but this seems to have detracted little from her appeal. Her crew was dressed in historic costumes and, appropriately, her commanding officer was architect David Little who played the part of Peter Milbourne.

Another replica of ARBELLA was produced for the Tercentenary of the Massachusetts Bay Colony which was celebrated with great fanfare statewide in 1930. Then officials, perhaps taking a leaf out of Manchester's book, found the coastal schooner LAVOLTA and, with Captain Osgood A. Gilbert of New Bedford in charge of the project, rebuilt her as a reproduction. She was said to have been within six inches of the length of the original ARBELLA.

The replica played a major role at a special celebration in Salem on June 12, 1930 reportedly watched by more than 50,000 people. She was then towed to Boston where she was put on display dockside in the Charles River Basin and opened for public visitation. Her cabins were filled with furnishings of the era obtained from an antique dealer in Ipswich.

In the fall of 1995, a new "ARBELLA" entered Manchester harbor to help celebrate the 350th anniversary of the town's founding. Actually, she was a chartered replica of Henry Hudson's ship HALF MOON. Hudson, an English navigator and explorer from 1607 to 1610, became famous when he discovered the river and the bay that bear his name on the way to seeking a northwest passage to China on behalf of the Dutch East India Company.

The new HALF MOON, spotted by supporters of the town's anniversary in the fall of 1994 as she lay alongside a dock in Gloucester where she had come for repairs, is much like ARBELLA must have been at least in the character of her rig and in the lines of her hull. At 95 feet overall, she is somewhat smaller but she performed her task most satisfactorily. And with her 250 horsepower diesel, she had no need of a steam launch to tow her up harbor, although with her 10 foot draft she carefully chose to appear on the scene at the time of high water.

A Story of People, Places and Events in the Town That Came to Be Known as Manchester-by-the-Sea

BY THE SEA...BY THE BEAUTIFUL SEA

Singing Beach looking east at Eagle Head, Grave's Island and Coolidge Point about 1900. Although the ladies are out with their umbrellas and parasols, no one is bathing so it was probably not a hot summer day. Only the child at right appears to have the courage to go wading. Privately owned until 1892, Singing Beach was appropriated by the town as a public park using authority granted by the Park Act, a Massachusetts General Law. A court settlement awarded the owners $110,000, which today seems a bargain for the beach's just more than 12 acres.

A TIDAL CREEK
Until It Was Dredged in 1896, Manchester Harbor Was Navigable Only at High Tide

Some 12,000 years ago when the great glacier retreated from the North American continent, it presented Manchester-by-the-Sea with what today is one of the finest harbors on the New England coast.

Its entrance and outer anchorage are protected from prevailing southwesterly winds by Great and Little Misery Islands; from northerlies by Glass Head and the shore to Chubb Point; and from winds from the south and southeast by House and Ram Islands and Gale's Point. Once inside the narrow entrance to the harbor between Tuck's Point and Proctor's Point, coves open up on either hand to provide small, shallow-draft vessels with an ideal refuge from fall northeasters and even from blows of hurricane force. With a mud bottom, the holding ground for moorings or for anchors is excellent as well.

In Colonial times, however, Manchester harbor—or Jeffrey's Creek as it was then called—had a very different look. Until the initial dredging project was completed in 1896, navigation to the head of the harbor was possible only at high water. When the tide fell, mud flats, traversed by a narrow stream, stretched from the municipal float behind Town Hall where Saw Mill Brook enters the harbor to where the outer pair of channel buoys are located today. Sizable vessels did make their ways to docks and wharves near the town itself (the 130-ton brig ALONZO, owned by Captain Abiel Burgess, once visited the Town Landing), but as water levels dropped with the tide, they either left to anchor in the outer harbor or grounded out in the soft mud.

But if the rise and fall of the tide was a hazard for mariners in Manchester's early days, it was a convenient source of power for grist and saw mills. In 1638, William Bennett built a tidal grist mill where Bennett's Brook runs into the harbor between Norton's Point and Crocker's Boat Yard. It was replaced by another built by Israel Forster which stood for more than a century and is pictured in early photos and post cards. Another mill was constructed in 1845 by furniture-maker Cyrus Dodge at the end of the stone dam which extends north from Marsh Island opposite Masconomo Park. The mill, later purchased by John Perry

Allen to saw veneers, burned in 1851. Piles which supported the structure may still be seen at low water at the end of the dam at Day's Creek. Other mills which made use of the tide's ebb and flow were located at Chubb Creek where the railroad trestle is today (Easkot's Mill) and as early as 1644 where Causeway Brook enters the harbor at SEASIDE NO. 1.

In its early days, the harbor included a significant amount of salt marsh. Abounding with bird life, it was (as it is today) a nursery for many important species of fish. Its salt hay, too, was harvested as fodder and bedding for horses. The area between Summer and Tappan Streets was all marshland traversed by a tidal stream. When Beach Street was built in 1873, a causeway with a wood bridge (replaced in 1888 by the present stone structure) limited access to the marsh to small boats only. The site was finally filled in the late 1800's to accommodate the construction of a railway passenger station and freight depot.

Early charts show that Masconomo Park, acquired by the town in 1903, also included salt marsh. There are still small parcels of marsh in the inner harbor which was created in 1847 by the railroad embankment. The drawbridge was added later. The area where American Legion Hall is located was salt marsh until the 1950's when it was filled with dredge spoil. The largest area of marsh still in existence includes Marsh Island and is located on the east side of the harbor at Day's Creek. At Kettle or Manchester Cove on the Magnolia side of town, Ocean Street looks out on a sizable stretch of salt marsh. Marsh also lines the shore of Whittier's Cove in West Manchester and both sides of Bennett's Brook from Bennett Street to the harbor. There is still a tiny patch of marsh at Black Beach in West Manchester and the town shares a huge area of salt marsh at Chubb Creek with the City of Beverly.

Fishing was among the most important activities engaged in by the town's first settlers. Timber was readily available for building boats of every size and skiffs and larger vessels were soon constructed to harvest the quantity of marine life which flourished along the shore and in Massachusetts Bay. The sound of adzes shaping frames and spars, and the ring of caulking mallets were heard on the waterfront as double-ended "pinkies," shallops, small ketches, and "Chebacco boats" were planked, rigged and launched. Public landings,

View of the beach at Tuck's Point about 1890 from the grassy pier where the yacht club was constructed in 1895. The Chowder House was then sited on the shoreline. It was moved inland to its present location about 1896. That year also, to provide townspeople with a view of their harbor, the Rotunda, or Pavilion, was built by contractors Roberts & Hoare. Now one of Manchester's most distinctive landmarks, it was designed by architect E.A.P. Luscomb of Boston and cost $1,820. In the background is Norton's Point and, from left, above the Chowder House roof, the Barn House, First House and the River House, all originally built to provide rental income for the Reverend Cyrus A. Bartol.

Old tide mill at the mouth of Bennett's Brook. Photo taken between 1888 and 1898. the building was razed in 1903. Man in the foreground at left with a top hat is said to be Charles Lee who, with Dr. Blaisdell, founded the first pharmacy in Manchester. A mill was first built at this site in 1638 by William Bennett. This mill was probably built by Israel Foster. Captain Augustus W. Smith farmhouse on Proctor Street may be seen across the harbor. Note Friendship sloop rigged but without sail.

essential to provide access to inshore waters for local fishermen, were established at Tuck's Point, in the inner harbor behind Town Hall, at Proctor's Cove, at Lobster Cove, at Kettle Cove, at Magnolia Beach and at Black Cove in West Manchester.

Cod, hake and pollock were salted and dried on flakes and stages at the outer ends of the harbor, both at Gale's Point and at Glass Head. Weirs were erected in the coves and, unlike today, few fishermen were disappointed with their catch. As Governor John Winthrop wrote in his Journal in 1639, "one boat with three men would take in a week ten hundreds [of exceedingly large and fat mackerel] which was sold in Connecticut for 3.12 Pounds the hundred…"

The Reverend Francis Higginson of Salem speaks of lobsters weighing 25 pounds and exclaims that "the abundance of other fish was beyond believing." But it was the cod that symbolized the region's success. Indeed, the Peace of Paris in 1883 which brought an end to the American Revolution, not only set the boundaries of the new United States but was explicit about our rights to the fisheries of the Grand Banks south of Newfoundland.

Coastal trade expanded, too, and by 1700, Manchester resident Asa Kitfield is reported to have built "a large number of vessels" engaged in fishing and carrying lumber. Schooners (the rig appeared about 1820) ventured as far away as George's and even to Canadian waters to harvest cod. South to the West Indies and to Europe went vessels which carried cargoes of salt fish, barreled beef and pork, wood bowls, buckets, brooms and ox-bows and later finished furniture to be traded for sugar, rum, salt, wines and bolts of wool and cotton. By 1810, there were 50 Masters of merchant ships who were residents of Manchester. One of the most famous vessels of the day was the schooner MANCHESTER. Another MANCHESTER, some 64 tons, was built in Essex in 1845. In his History of Manchester, 1645–1895, written for the town's 250th anniversary, Reverend Darius Lamson was able to interview Manchester men who had been born in the early 1800's and had been to sea all their lives. The tales they told of pirates, of foreign ports, of storms and shipwrecks, are filled with daring adventure.

During the Revolution and the War of 1812, Manchester seamen served aboard the many privateers which sank and captured British merchantmen and harassed the Royal Navy. But although swashbuckling tales of bravery were commonplace and the achievements of Manchester's captains, mates and sailors were legendary, life at sea was never easy and there were many widows and fatherless children at home to prove it. After the hated Embargo which all but banned the movement of American vessels, and the War of 1812, Manchester's fishing industry declined dramatically. To be sure, there were still boats which fished along the coast, but the heyday of the fisheries here was over. Merchant vessels were larger, too, and although Manchester could still be proud of the number of ship's Masters who lived here, they sailed from other ports which offered larger and deeper harbors.

But a renaissance was in sight. It came in the form of a growing number of summer residents who enthusiastically sought out the harbor as a site for recreation—rowing, sailing, power boating and swimming—and as a much desired visual attraction for those whose mansions were beginning to line its shores.

To meet this new demand for water-related pleasures, the Manchester Yacht Club was established in 1892. Its club house, still a prominent part of the waterfront, was designed by architect Ernest M.A. Machado of Salem. On land purchased from the Reverend Cyrus A. Bartol, the cornerstone was laid in mid-June, 1895. The structure was dedicated some five weeks later and its look has changed little in its century of existence. The location of the new club house, however, was of some concern to the town which earlier had constructed a picnic house just back of the beach at Tuck's Point (also on land bought from the Reverend Bartol). The view out the harbor from this building was now blocked by the yacht club and it was with some indignation that the town moved its structure from the shore to its present site.

It was perhaps with an eye to recapturing its view at Tuck's Point that the town commissioned architect E.A.P. Luscomb of Boston to design the Rotunda, still the harbor's most distinctive manmade landmark. Built by Robert & Hoare in 1896, it cost $1,820 and did, indeed, extend far enough to the south to provide an excellent view of the channel and Misery Islands.

The beach at Tuck's Point was originally rocky, but starting in the 1930's sand was brought annually from Singing Beach to give it a more comfortable surface for bathers. A concrete block bath house was built just before World War II.

The yacht yard at Cheever's Point (where Manchester Marine is now located) was owned by Fenton & White and later by David Fenton alone as Timothy White opened a yard next door (now Crocker's Boat Yard). Both yards built a remarkable number of successful racing boats including a few of what were then called "scows," flat-bottomed, 40 to 50 feet overall, without ballast except for two, 135-pound bronze or steel bilge boards. This photo taken in 1910 shows a scow built by Fenton & White which may be the <u>MASSACHUSETTS</u>. (Timothy White, center, is wearing the vest and holding a child.) Owned by a Manchester Yacht Club syndicate, that same year she successfully defended her title winning the Sewanaka International Challenge Cup defeating in Manchester waters the <u>ST. LAWRENCE</u> representing the Royal St. Lawrence Yacht Club of Canada. Photo courtesy of Mrs. John L. Allen.

In recent years, the building housing the Manchester Yacht Club has been removed and replaced with a new structure which, although somewhat larger, perfectly captures the architectural character of the old. At Tuck's Point, too, an attractive new building has taken the place of the concrete block bath house; the Chowder House has been repaired and restored and new flowers, shrubs and trees added to improve the scenic beauty of the landscape.

Although North Shore waters, because of their temperatures, were never as inviting as those south of Cape Cod, Manchester's beaches and the ocean nearby provided welcome relief during the hot summer days of July and August. Bathers dotted the sands of Black Beach, White Beach, Grave's Beach, Long Beach, and Gray Beach, but it was musical sounds of Singing Beach which won it early and lasting recognition throughout the region. Sand which produces a distinct, audible sound when scuffed appears at a number of localities around the world, according to a research paper by Joel W. Block which appeared some years ago in The Manchester Cricket. It has been found on the island of Eigg off the west coast of Scotland, at Kauai in the Hawaiian Islands and at a few beaches in England. But while other sands may produce a "ring, a roar, or a hum," Singing Beach, writes Joel Block, "produces a sound similar to a sneaker squeaking on a gymnasium floor." It gives the beach a characteristic all its own. And it is due, explains Block, to the qualities of the sand itself: a very narrow grain size distribution; angular and spherically shaped grains; and a lack of impurities. Over the years, Singing Beach has appeared in scores of paintings and photographs and has provided pleasure for many millions of people who have lived in town or who have made the trek by rail and by foot to the end of Beach Street where the musical sands meet the sea.

'MUSICAL SAND'

Henry Thoreau Visits Singing Beach in 1858; Town Acquires It in 1899

One of these in earlier times was no less than naturalist, writer, and philosopher Henry David Thoreau. In 1939, author Bertha Stevens selected and arranged a series of his writings in a book entitled Thoreau, Reporter of the Universe. Among them was this description of Singing Beach which Thoreau visited on September 22, 1858. "A clear day...Leave Salem for Cape Ann on foot...One mile southeast of the village of Manchester struck the beach of 'musical sand,' just this side of a large, high, rocky point called Eagle Head! This is a curving beach; maybe one-third of a mile long and some twelve rods wide. We found the same kind of sand on a similar but shorter beach on the east side of Eagle Head [Dana's Beach]. We perceived the sound when we scratched with an umbrella or the finger swiftly...through the sand; also still louder when we struck [the beach] forcibly with our heels, 'scuffing' along. The wet or damp sand yielded no particular sound, nor did that which lay loose and deep next [to] the bank, but only the more compact and dry." Seemingly unimpressed, Thoreau added, "The sound was not at all musical nor was it loud." Four years later in Concord, he was to die of tuberculosis.

Long used and enjoyed by residents, Singing Beach, once private property, was finally acquired by the town using authority granted it by the so-called Park Act, General Laws, Chapter 154, Acts of 1892. A court settlement in 1899 established the cost: $111,434.02.

With the growth of boating, new demands were made for dredging and enlarging Manchester harbor. In August, 1876, the town's monthly newspaper, the Beetle & Wedge, reported with some irritation that the "schooner LILLA RICH had arrived on Monday last and remains fast in the mud." Little more than a decade later, the Federal government had begun to make Manchester a deep water port. By 1896, dredging had provided a channel 60 feet wide and four feet deep at low water which ran from Proctor's Point to the coal dock at Knight's wharf where Peele House Square is located today. Coal was regularly delivered by barge to this wharf until the end of World War II.

A major impediment to navigation was removed in 1888. With an appropriation of only $2,500, dynamite was used to break up a large portion of Bow Bell Ledge opposite what is now the Rotunda. This allowed the channel to be widened to 60 feet with four feet of water at mean low tide.

The dredged entrance channel first followed the bed of the creek. It began about halfway between Glass Head and Gale's Point, curving past Long Beach to join the main channel opposite the yacht club. The present straight-line entrance channel was dredged in 1911. In 1907, according to an article written by Julie Harrison in 1979, "Manchester entered into a long-lasting partnership with the state" which provided funds annually on a matching basis for dredging purposes. Additional dredging took place in 1935 creating mooring basins throughout the harbor and deepening the channel to eight feet at low water. Two years later a dredging project enlarged the inner harbor and provided fill for the area where Legion Hall is located. Since then, Whittier's Cove, Crocker's Cove and Proctor's Cove have been dredged regularly to provide room for moorings. One proposal to expand the harbor, however, was defeated because of its cost. It called for the dredging of the flats inside Ram Islands and the construction of a breakwater to protect what could have been another sizable mooring area.

During the nineteenth century, navigation was also restricted by ice during the winter months. Many still alive today recall skating on the inner harbor which, if it had been calm, could be frozen in a smooth sheet as thick as 13 inches. But that was child's play compared to the old days. In February, 1899, The Manchester Cricket reported "a solid sheet of ice from Town Wharf to House Island, and from there the ice field extends in an irregular line to Misery [Islands]." Before World War II, the harbor was regularly covered with slush ice as far out as Ram Islands.

Although scores of vessels were built on the shoreline of Manchester harbor in the early days, it was the growing interest in yachting that in 1892 encouraged E.P. Crooker to apply for a license to construct a marine railway on land at Cheever's Point leased from Daniel Leach. According to a talk given by Thomas P. Sturtevant who purchased the yard in 1969, it took the Commissioners of the Board of Harbors and Lands one year to grant his request. By 1895, David Fenton and Timothy White had formed a partnership to establish the town's first boat yard where Manchester Marine is now located. Four years later, White started his own yard next door which after World War II became Crocker's Boat Yard.

'BUILDERS OF YACHTS'
Manchester's Ship and Yacht Yards Are a Part of the Fabric of the Waterfront

Meanwhile, Walter B. Calderwood, a native of Rockport, Maine, joined Fenton and for a nearly a decade the two operated the yard at the foot of Ash-

land Avenue. Finally, Calderwood bought out Fenton who moved his building operations to a boat shed at the head of the inner harbor which today is a private residence. Calderwood, a quiet man of immense physical strength, served the town as a selectman from 1923 to 1925. In the 1930's, he advertised his yard as "Builders of Yachts, Launches and Tenders" and offered to store "Boats for the Winter at Owner's Risk in Case of Fire."

Yachts serviced locally in those days varied from dinghies to classes of Manchester 15-footers, 17-footers and 18-footers, small cruising boats— yawls, ketches, cutters and sloops—to the larger yachts, both sail and power, which were characteristic of the times. As early as 1904, for example, 81 yachts were listed as owned by members of the Manchester Yacht Club. Ten of these had an overall length of 100 feet or more. One, ISIS, measured more than 200 feet. Each of these vessels could cruise anywhere in the world but required a sizable professional crew and, of course, a budget to match. Because of the size of their railways, it is unlikely that any yard in Manchester prior to World War II could accommodate a vessel much larger than 70 or 80 feet.

Professional sailing masters, so-called "yacht captains" (although traditionally the owner can only be called "Captain") were a vital part of waterfront activities before and after World War II. Not only were these men able to "hand, reef and steer" with the best, they could splice wire and rope, repair engines and with paint and varnish, maintain anything afloat in Bristol fashion. In Manchester, they included Ralph Burnham aboard the eight-meter yacht COCKADE and later the New York 32 GENTIAN; Gerry Smith aboard the Crocker-designed sloop MERCURY; Carl Maxner aboard Manchester 18 LIMPET; Pete Jensen aboard the motor-sailor NORTHSTAR; and Joe Ecklund aboard the schooner WHEN & IF.

Since its beginnings more than a century ago, the Manchester Yacht Club has remained a center of activity for sailing and racing small boats. As early as 1911, MYC member Guy Lowell, aboard CIMA, won the German-American Sonder Boat races at Kiel. The prize, an elaborately-woven silver basket, was presented by the Kaiser himself. Both the basket and a half-model of CIMA are now owned by the club. Other club victories include winning the Quincy Cup in 1900; the Sewanhaka International Challenge Cup in 1905; the North Shore

World War II censor has blocked out the hull numbers of this 110-foot wood subchaser (SC) built for the U.S. Navy at Walter B. Calderwood Yacht Yard in the early 1940's. She is being launched from the building shed into the waters of the cove between Norton's Point (background) and Cheever's Point where the yard was located. On the bow is rigger Charles McLauren, a long-time yard employee. As many as 125 persons were engaged in building these ships at what is today Manchester Marine. Security was tight. There were guards at the gate. Each worker was equipped with an identification card. In all, Calderwood's contributed eight ships to the war effort. Lack of room in the building shed meant that the superstructure and much other equipment were added while vessels were at the dock. SC's were manned by a crew of three officers and 25 enlisted men. Photo courtesy of J. Borden Foster.

Marina and shipyard of Manchester Marine Company in 1969. Then owned by Gordon Abbott, Manchester Marine, an early pioneer with fiberglass, built a number of running boats for the U.S. Navy, but was primarily devoted to storage and repair of yachts as well as a few commercial fishing vessels. At one time, the yard owned and maintained two 120-foot draggers, OCEAN WAVE and OCEAN CLIPPER. Crocker's Boat Yard, upper right, also engaged in storage and repair and built a number of yachts of wood construction whose lines were drawn by naval architect Samuel Crocker. This photo, which appeared in <u>The Boston Globe</u>, was taken by Globe staff photographer Harry Holbrook.

Junior Championships in 1927; the North Shore Women's Sailing Championships in 1934, 1935 and 1956; the Curtis Cup (North Shore Junior Championship) in 1955; the Frances McElwain Wakeman Trophy (Women's Massachusetts Bay Championship) in 1957; the National Midget Turnabout Championship in 1959; the North American Flying Tern Association National Championship in 1968, 1969, 1975 and 1976; the Rhodes 19 East Coast Championship in 1984, and the Rhodes Class Trophy for Marblehead Race Week in 1987, 1989, and 1990.

Since the 1920's, racing classes at MYC have included fleets of 13-foot Swampscott skiffs; Manchester 15-footers, the celebrated Manchester 17-footers which, with both gaff and Marconi rigs, were adopted by yacht clubs from Maine to Cape Cod; Manchester 18-footers (both the 17's and 18's were keel boats); Marblehead Class B (MB) dinghies; Penguins, Lightnings, 110's, 210's, Flying Terns, Turnabouts, Lasers, and Rhodes 19's. Following World War II and the spectacular growth in the number of cruising auxiliaries, Manchester Yacht Club skippers have ranged far and wide from Newfoundland to the Caribbean. Many have qualified for the Club's Trans-Atlantic Pennant. Today, wherever the Club's familiar white and blue burgee is seen it is viewed with admiration and respect. No mention of the Club would be complete without a salute to its professional captains, only five in a century of operation: Harry Mayo, Henry Hall, Fred Nataloni, Carl Magee and Jack Fadden. Their skilled and steady hands have maintained the club's floats, launches and other facilities through the years and in countless other ways have insured the success of its activities.

By 1942, America was at war and "wolf packs" of Nazi submarines were operating off the east coast sinking tankers and other merchant vessels at one point faster than they could be replaced. As a part of the effort to meet this threat to the nation's merchant marine, the Navy Department contracted with small shipyards throughout the country to construct a fleet of 110-foot wooden subchasers. In all, some 438 ships were built, eight of them at the Walter B. Calderwood shipyard in Manchester. At the height of the yard's activity, as many as 125 people were employed. They included Ernest Dalton (Doc) Richmond, Yard Manager in 1942, Charles Young, General foreman, Sturgis

Crocker, Edmund Mulcahey, Borden Foster and Jerry Noonan who later joined the Navy.

(Much of the information about the yard and its wartime contributions that appears here was taken from an excellent four-part series of articles written by Manchester's own Daniel A. Curran which was published in The Manchester Cricket in 1992. Curran, a graduate of the U.S. Naval Academy, was then Manager of International Marketing at the Raytheon Company. The articles are copyrighted by Raytheon which has kindly provided permission for their use.)

SUBCHASERS

110-Foot Craft Are Built for the Navy at Calderwood's; 2 Serve at Normandy

The keel was laid for the first ship, subchaser SC 692, in March, 1942. Like her sisters, she measured 110 feet overall with a beam of 18 feet, a draft of six and one-half feet and a displacement of 106 tons. Power on some of the vessels came from a pair of 1540 horsepower diesel engines, a new flat, radial "pancake" design produced by General Motors which could drive the hull at a top speed of 21 knots. Other ships, somewhat slower, were equipped with six cylinder diesels which delivered from 500 to 800 horsepower. Personnel requirements called for three officers and 25 enlisted men. Armament consisted of one three-inch deck gun, a single 40 millimeter and two 20 millimeter guns for anti-aircraft purposes. Most important, each vessel was equipped with 14 depth charges, the primary weapon used against submarines under water, and a sonar unit or echo sounder which could be used to calculate the range and bearing of a submerged enemy sub.

The hulls, deck and accommodations were constructed inside the building shed at Calderwood's yard. Because of a lack of room overhead, the ships were then launched and the superstructure and equipment added while they were alongside the dock. They then steamed to Boston where sonar was installed and were finally sent to Florida for training in anti-submarine warfare. As is often the case with new crews and new vessels, accidents happened along the way. One ship ran aground on Hardy's Ledge, two miles out of Manchester, and had to be towed to Gloucester for repairs. Another is reported to have had problems with her reverse gear in Boston and was damaged as she collided

Six, fin-keel sailing yachts built by Fenton & White are placed on Boston & Maine Railroad flat cars (three to a car) ready to ship to some unknown destination. Yard workmen secured the vessels for their ride on a siding next to the railroad station the roof of which may be seen just over the hulls of the boats. After Timothy White left to start his own yard on Ashland Avenue, David Fenton was joined by Maine native, Walter B. Calderwood who later bought out Fenton. Calderwood operated the yard until 1946 when it was purchased by Gordon Abbott, Sr. and christened Manchester Marine Railway and Construction Company. But although in the late 1950's, Manchester Marine, an early pioneer in fiberglass, was awarded a contract to construct some 50 glass running boats for the U.S. Navy, the yard primarily devoted itself to repair, rebuilding and maintaining yachts and selected members of the Gloucester fishing fleet such as the dragger FALCON. The days of building wood boats from scratch was over.

Steam yacht AZTEC owned for some 40 years by Albert C. Burrage, a long-time summer resident of Boardman Avenue, Manchester. Designed by William Gardner of New York who was also naval architect for the celebrated schooner ATLANTIC and the America's Cup sloop VANITIE, AZTEC measured 206 feet overall and was built by Lewis Nixon in 1902. From then until 1940, she would often lie in Manchester's outer harbor where she could be seen by the Burrages from their house. AZTEC served in both World Wars, first with the U.S. Navy and then with the Royal Canadian Navy. Photo courtesy of the Society for the Preservation of New England Antiquities.

with a dock. And one launched during the particularly cold winter of 1943 couldn't have made it to the outer harbor had it not been for the ingenuity of some yard employees who used dynamite to blast a channel through the ice.

One of Manchester's subchasers, SC 1358, took part in the invasion of Normandy in June, 1944. Two were transferred to the Soviet Navy. Another was later converted to an amphibious support ship. SC 692, commissioned in November, 1942, served in the Mediterranean and took part in the invasion of Sicily. The story of her wartime experiences appears in a book entitled Subchaser, written by her skipper, then 24-year-old Lieutenant (j.g.) Edward P. Stafford. It was published by the U.S. Naval Institute Press.

In May, 1946, with the war ended, Calderwood's yacht yard was purchased by Gordon Abbott, Sr. and rechristened Manchester Marine Construction Company. A former Boston banker and summer resident all his life, Abbott moved to Manchester year-round in 1939. Just out of the Navy where he had command of a five-ship division of 220-foot fleet minesweepers, he had won the Navy Cross for heroism on the "picket line" at Okinawa. He had owned boats all his life and understood their design and construction. His first efforts were to modernize the yard for the boom years in yachting that were to follow. He stuck primarily to service and repair although in an early adventure in fiberglass, he did build a number of 16-foot running boats for the Navy. During his 23 years of ownership, Abbott rebuilt the marine railway, erected a large 100-foot square storage shed, purchased the marina in the inner harbor, operated two, 120-foot fishing draggers—the OCEAN WAVE and the OCEAN CLIPPER—which were maintained by the yard and shared offices with Kirby Construction Company of which, with engineer Frank Kirby, he was a principle owner. Ready to retire, he sold the yard and marina with its then Boston Whaler, Evinrude and Mako dealership to Tom Sturtevant in 1969.

Sturtevant continued the modernization process adding a Travelift, constructing a new spar shed, dredging to create much-needed marina slips at the yard, rebuilding the railway, extending boat storage areas and expanding the retail store. For 20 years, the company operated successfully devoting itself still to service and repair. Then, on September 13, 1989, fire—a nightmare which haunts every shipyard owner—struck Manchester Marine. Thank-fully, only one boat was destroyed in the blaze but the offices of the corporation were a total loss. Much more of the yard would have been destroyed had it not been for the prompt and effective action of the Manchester Fire Department. Thankfully also, there was little wind that day to fan the flames. The yard recovered and continued. In 1991, after 22 years at the helm, Tom Sturtevant decided to sell. Manchester Marine was purchased by Northern Light Marine Group of Salem which, with Rob Hoyle as President, operates it today.

PERFECT TEAM
With Sam Crocker as Naval Architect, Son Sturgis Builds 38 of His Designs

Meanwhile, the yard next door had been engaged in building and repair since 1899. It was owned by the White Brothers—Timothy, Louis and their younger brother Charlie—all originally from Nova Scotia. In the 1930's, Charlie White, or Charlie LeBlanc as he often liked to be called, was not only a boatbuilder but a lobster fisherman as well. White's was well known for its construction of small sailboats—light, racing craft which were shipped by rail as far away as the Great Lakes. During World War II, with yachting all but at a standstill, the yard ceased operations and in 1946, White's was purchased by S. Sturgis Crocker who had worked at Calderwood's building subchasers.

The timing was perfect. Sturgis's father, Sam Crocker, was a distinguished naval architect who in his lifetime designed 344 boats, both commercial and pleasure. Sturgis was a skilled and dedicated boat builder and the partnership between father and son flourished. Sturg built 38 of Sam Crocker's boats from the 62-foot METACOMET and the 42-foot COUSIN ELIZABETH to the famous Crocker 20's and his own light-displacement, high performances 40-foot FIVE PLY, a design some 20 years ahead of her time. He is also the author of a handsome illustrated history of his father's designs entitled Sam Crocker's Boats published by International Marine Publishing Company. Today, with son Sam and daughter Kitty running the yard, Sturg can devote all his time to what he loves best—building wooden boats. CRICKET, a 33-foot Crocker designed sloop, was launched in 1992 and he is presently finishing a 30-foot tugboat yet to be named.

Wharf where the Manchester Yacht Club was built in 1895. This photo was probably taken between 1892 and 1895 as it shows the Paramus house at Gales Point which was constructed in 1892. Part of the property at Tuck's Point owned by Dr. Cyrus A. Bartol and purchased by the Town of Manchester in 1895, the wharf was sold by the town that same year to incorporators of the MYC. Note the steam launch at left and Long Beach pier, also visible. Original photo owned by Charlotte L. Read (Read's Island, Manchester). Frances L. Burnett Collection.

Annual Water Sports festival at the Manchester Yacht Club in 1897 shows a simple arrangement of floats. Canoe tilting is in progress and the pole which challenge swimmers to reach the small MYC burgee at its tip without getting wet may be seen in the foreground. Note that there are no boats moored in Proctor's Cove. It dried out at low water. A channel was dredged in 1896 but the coves which today are valuable mooring areas had to wait until later. Water Sports which continued until after World War II were always a popular social event which merited a story and photos in the NORTH SHORE BREEZE. Photo courtesy of Frances L. Burnett collection.

Since the turn of the century, there have been other small yards around the harbor which have specialized in both building and repair. They include Fenton's Boat Shop in the inner harbor; a storage yard located for a few years in the old Forster mill building at Bennett's Brook operated by Charley Hall, former Assistant Steward of the Manchester Yacht Club, and by then-retired yacht captain Ralph Burnham; Marine Enterprises, Inc. which, in 1950 turned a fish wharf in the inner harbor into a marina; Ashland Avenue Boat Yard which purchased property in the inner harbor between the railroad tracks and the marina in 1968; and Trysail Boat Company which at a number of locations in town including the marina, stored and commissioned small boats. Today, however, with new environmental, health and safety regulations enforced by the Federal government, boating is big business and only the larger yards seem able to survive.

In 1948, several distinguished citizens of the town decided that what Manchester needed was a boat club, which, according to one of its charter members, "was fashioned along the lines of a 'dory class' rather than the 'steamer class.'" The result was the Harbor Boat Club which today continues "to foster good fellowship, to promote and stimulate an interest in boating, and to encourage fuller enjoyment of the advantages of Manchester Harbor." Among its founders were George Lockhart Allen, Thomas Baker, Harrison Cann, Harry Collins, Sam Crocker, Stephen Hoare, Carl Needham and William Rudden. A special act of the State Legislature authorized the location of a pier and floats at Masconomo Park. In 1967, the club initiated the S.S. Crocker Memorial Race to pay tribute to one of America's premier naval architects. Today, the Manchester Harbor Boat Club includes some 220 members who are on the water throughout the season.

During the winter of 1960-61, thanks to the interest and efforts of Dick Villa, then President of Trysail Boat Company, Manchester joined Marblehead as a center for Frostbite sailing. Villa purchased a small fleet of O'Day Sprites to initiate a tradition which, despite occasional dunkings in ice-cold water, brought pleasure to scores of small boat sailors.

Another blessing to those interested in small boats was the establishment in the mid-1960's of the Manchester Sailing Association. It was agreed that an instructional program in sailing should be created which would be open to children throughout the community from 10 to 15 years of age. Early leaders of the MSA included Bob and Nancy Hopkins, David Gaunt, Sherry Proctor, and Moses Ware. The group was able to encourage sponsors to purchase some 20 Dyer Dhows which were also used for Frostbite racing. Bob McDonald, a North Shore school teacher, was the MSA's first professional instructor. The organization continues to turn out top-flight young sailors.

RUGGED INDIVIDUALISTS
Manchester's Fishermen Started with Dories; Diesel Power Replaces Oars

Despite overwhelming use of the harbor today for recreational boating, Manchester has always been proud of its fishing fleet which continues a tradition dating back to the 17th century. Few know more about its history than Pat Noonan who began fishing for lobsters here in 1934 as a freshman at Story High School. Those were the days of wood traps "and the first lathes we used to build them," Pat recalls, "came out of the walls and ceiling of the bowling alleys at the Masconomo House."

In the 1930's, fishermen, rugged individualists as they are today, were able to survive the lean years of the Great Depression. "I remember one man," Pat says, "named Charlie Bigwood. He had a camp on Little Ram Island. He was among the many then who hauled from a rowing dory. He probably had 50 traps and he caught more lobsters than we do today with 500. Then there was Carty Burnham who lived back of Knight's Coal Wharf. He hand-lined for cod and would take them around town in a wheel barrow to sell them. All winter, he'd spear eels. Milt Knight was another. When he retired he gave me the needle he used to knit heads [the twine entry to a trap]. I still have it today."

Decades ago, every fisherman built his own traps of wood laths and knitted his own heads. With pot warp, which was then made of sisal, heads would last one season and were replaced annually. Traps were weighted with four bricks and took a week or so in the spring to soak up water so they would sink. Pot buoys were made of wood and were painted as they are today with each man's distinctive colors. Usually, each pot was set separately. There were few trawls. There were fewer fishermen then as well, Pat recalls, perhaps five or six in the early 1950's. Prior to World War II, bait—filleted red fish or ocean perch—could be had for nothing in Gloucester. "We started buying bait—pogie, herring and mackerel—after the war," Pat says. "Some fishermen set fish traps off House Island, Misery Island or Kettle Island to catch their own bait. Wire traps for lobsters appeared in the early 1980's. They were lighter and easier to fish. Of course, we had plenty of bait to choose from. One summer I remember in the late 1920s, the entire harbor from Tenney's Creek [Bennett Brook] to the yacht club was filled with dead herring two feet deep. Although we put lime on them, they just lay there on the flats and rotted in the sun. It took more than week for the smell to go away!"

Inshore fishing boats in the early days varied from open skiffs propelled by oars or outboard and decked-over dories powered with one cylinder, make-or-break engines to boats up to 40 feet equipped with sophisticated auto engine conversions. Pat's first boat was built in 1940 by Adams Boat Shop, successor to Fenton, at the head of the harbor. A 28-footer with power by Chevy, she cost just $500. In 50 years of successful fishing with time out for service in the Navy during World War II, Pat owned three boats. In his first year full-time, he fished 150 traps. When he retired in 1992, he was fishing 450.

Lobster gauges, too, were different years ago. To determine counters from shorts prior to World War II, fishermen measured from the tip of a lobster's nose to the tip of his tail. Nine inches was a keeper. Today, anything shorter than three and three-sixteenths inches from the eye to the back of the carapace must be returned to the sea.

Other lobstermen of the late 1930's that Pat remembers include Stanley Thomas, Gus Ferriera, Harry Mercer, and, of course, the legendary Bruce LeSeine known affectionately as "Captain Dusty." In the late 1920's, Bruce worked for summer resident Albert C. Burrage, who each year used to arrive in Manchester from California aboard his private Pullman car which would be left on a siding downtown. Bruce was the chief steward. There was also a waiter and a cook. Accommodations aboard the car included seven staterooms, private baths, an "observation" or living room, a dining room and galley, and "quarters for the help" where Bruce lived throughout the summer. In 1929, however, the depression ended life as even many of the rich knew it, and Bruce found himself in Manchester out of a job.

As he told Richard Allphin, a summer resident of Baker's Island, in a recorded interview in 1988, "I went to Singing Beach, looked out at the ocean and said, 'There's money to be made out there.'" Thus began a career of some 53 years of fishing out of Manchester. From a rowboat he built himself, Bruce progressed to a series of small power boats including ultimately a 36-footer used not only for fishing but also to provide services for families at Baker's Island which he did for a number of decades. After he retired he owned a small seafood store on Summer Street.

Today, there are 35 full and part-time commercial fishermen in Manchester. Full-timers include Jay Bishop, Richard Burgess, Mark Chafey, Bob Hannah, Doug Heath (whose father, Harry, and uncle, Everett, fished here before him), John Herrick, Dan Marshall, Todd Pollock, Stanley Koch, David Ring, Frank Saco and Edward Smith.

MOORINGS SCARCE
Demand Exceeds Supply as Interest in Boating Grows Through the Years

Prior to World War II, with fewer boats and plenty of room for moorings, the administration of Manchester Harbor was in the hands of the Planning Board. But in 1947 as the number of boats began to increase, control was transferred to the Board of Selectmen. It created a Harbor Committee whose members, all volunteers, have worked closely with the town's Harbormasters through the years: Henry Hall, Roland "Pokey" Brooks, Bob MacDiarmid, and today, Peter Mains and Chief of Police Ron Ramos.

Since the war, the increase in recreational boating has been dramatic. According to Julie Harrison, town records show that 155 boats were moored in Manchester harbor in 1955. By 1966, just 10 years later, the number had increased to 475. In 1978, 600 mooring permits were issued and an additional 100 boats were moored at marinas. By 1994, the number of mooring permits had risen to 790. An additional 310 user permits were provided for craft at marinas and floats, making a total of 1,100 boats of different sizes and descriptions in Manchester harbor.

At this rate of demand what about the future? To help provide some answers, the Planning Board in 1993 appointed a special Harbor Planning Committee to study the harbor and to make recommendations related to its use and protection in the years to come. Among those who have contributed to its deliberations have been John Allen, Penny Gaunt, John Harrison, Rob Hoyle, Bob Jermain, Jim Justice, Joe Lombardi, Mary Waters Shepley and Lee Spence. As one committee member declared: "One of the most important things we can do for the future is to continue to maintain our dredging. Without the channel and mooring areas, which do silt in over the years, we'll be right back with the mudflats our forefathers had at Jeffrey's Creek."

PRIVATEERS: OUR SECRET WEAPON

During the Revolution and War of 1812, fast-sailing American privateers equipped with Letters of Marque which legalized their actions as independently-owned vessels, attacked and captured British merchantmen which were carrying valuable supplies for the Crown. Often schooner-rigged, they ranged far and wide taking the war even to England's shores where they were much feared as raiders. Supplies they captured during the Revolution were particularly useful to General Washington and his army. Here a privateer hoists her American colors as she escapes from an English man-of-war. The flag at her foremast proclaims boldly "Catch Me Who Can."

EARLY SEA POWER
Privateers Take the War to England, Raiding Towns, Seizing Shipping

The significance of privateers and their contribution to the success of American arms and the eventual defeat of the enemy, should not be underestimated. It's generally agreed by historians that these small ships "were a most important if not predominating feature of our early sea power" both during the Revolution and the War of 1812. The value of prizes taken by regular government vessels during the Revolution was less than $6 million; by privateers, $18 million. During the War of 1812, the ratio in favor of privateers is even greater: $6.6 million as compared to $39 million.

According to Edgar S. McClay's <u>A History of American Privateers</u>, articles in the British press during the War for Independence show that England was significantly more concerned about the impact of U.S. maritime forces, some of whom actually raided English towns and preyed upon shipping in English coastal waters, than they were with the Continental Army. Figures show that 800 British vessels, valued at $23.8 million, were taken together with 16,000 prisoners.

During the second war with England, prizes were valued at a total of $45.6 million with 30,000 prisoners captured. On the other hand, land forces of the U.S. during the Revolution captured some 22,000 prisoners with some 6,000 taken during the War of 1812. It's easy to see why England, despite the size and power of her own Navy, grew increasingly apprehensive about the growing strength and effectiveness of the U.S. at sea.

The contributions of North Shore communities in men and ships should also be recognized. Some 158 privateers sailed from Salem took 445 prizes, more than half of those captured, during the War of Independence. Colonel John Glover of Marblehead owned the schooner HANNAH which he kept at Beverly where, under the command of Captain Nicholas Broughton, she was commissioned upon orders of General Washington as the first ship of the new United States Navy. Some 60 privately armed merchant and other vessels, many owned by the celebrated shipping firm of J. & A. Cabot, sailed from Beverly. Marblehead, too, contributed an impressive number of privateers. Few vessels, of course, sailed from Manchester. The harbor here was little more than a creek which dried out at low water until it was first dredged in 1896. But the need and opportunities were such that in 1776 the schooner LUNCH, owned by Colonel John Lee (later Town Moderator), was commissioned in Beverly. To get her there from Manchester in February, the ice was chopped from around her by eight men. It took two days and reportedly more than a few gallons of rum to free her. Eighteen days later, with a "new topmast, square yard, cross trees and booms," she was towed to Salem where she was rigged and ballast put aboard. Her armament included two four pounders and four swivel guns. In May, she sailed for Portsmouth, NH, which became her home port throughout the Revolution.

Colonel Lee won fame also as captain of the privateer schooner HAWK. In 1776, according to an edition of <u>The Reperatory</u> published in Boston, in August, 1808, "after capturing a great number of British vessels, the schooner HAWK (Captain Lee) arrived in Bilboa with a part of the prisoners. She was seized...as acting without legitimate authority. But a memorial [memorandum] from the American master...being presented to the Spanish court, an order was given...to liberate the vessel and further to assure the captain...that his vessel and all those of his countrymen should be protected under their own flag in all the ports of Spain..." It was an early recognition of the new nation by a major European power.

EXTRAORDINARY TALE
Manchester Man's Ship Is Disabled Off George's Bank; Adrift for 261 Days

The sea has always played a major role in the history of Manchester. And there is little doubt that the true story of Nathaniel Allen and his survival is one of the most extraordinary and dramatic maritime adventures ever told.

A member of one of the town's earliest and most distinguished families and a hero of the Revolutionary War, Allen served in the Continental Army with Chief of Artillery, Colonel Henry Knox. He wintered at Valley Forge, crossed the Delaware River with General Washington and took part in the victorious battle of Trenton. He was also with the Army at Princeton.

When he returned home to Manchester, he decided on a life at sea and in October, 1780, he shipped out of Gloucester as a foredeck hand aboard the schooner AMERICA with five in crew and Captain Isaac Elwell in command. It was an easy passage to Point Petre, Guadeloupe, where they sold their cargo of fish and took aboard sugar, cotton, cocoa, coffee, rum and molasses for the voyage home, setting sail on December 19 that same year.

All went well until they reached the shallow waters of Georges Bank just southeast of Cape Cod. There, on December 31, they sailed into a winter gale of extraordinary ferocity. Buffeted by huge and breaking seas, AMERICA lost first her spars and then her rudder. Without steerage way, she drifted helplessly at the mercy of wind and wave. Although Allen and the others aboard were able to clear away the rigging and stay afloat, for the next two months they were swept by a series of winter storms from the west and northwest pushing them farther and farther out to sea.

Their one week's provisions soon gone, they turned to the cocoa and molasses and the occasional shark, dolphin and smaller fish that they were able to catch. They even devoured the remaining rats aboard. But their real need was water. One barrel was all that remained and for three weeks it failed to rain a drop. The cook died of thirst and each of them looked at one another not knowing who would be next.

They drifted in the Atlantic for an incredible 261 days or until September 17, 1781. With the Revolutionary War continuing, shipping was at a standstill, and in all that time, they had seen only three vessels. None had approached close enough to discover their plight. Although they signaled wildly to the nearest, she took no notice, changing course and sailing away. The next day, however, a brig appeared bearing down on them. Soon she had a boat over and a mate and two hands were pulling towards them. Once aboard AMERICA, according to a report published in 1839 in the <u>Salem Gazette</u>, the mate looked about and declared, " 'we saw you yesterday and wanted to come to your relief, but the captain was opposed to it; he said you were Americans and if we took you on board you would rise and take the brig.' (The Peace of Paris, which ended the war with Great Britain, wasn't signed until 1783.) Today we saw you again and as he had taken a 'stiff horn' and had gone to his cabin, we concluded not to let him know until we were near you.'

"The mate and the two men," the <u>Gazette</u> continued, "then returned to the brig and made their reports to the captain who immediately ordered the survivors to be brought on board. He told them

that if they behaved properly, he would treat them well; he would not make them prisoners, because he thought they had been prisoners long enough and had a hard time of it…The brig took from the wreck six thousand pounds of cotton, three hogsheads of sugar and two bags of coffee." Whatever happened to the casks of rum was never explained.

When Allen and the others on board AMERICA were rescued she was reported as being "twenty leagues west of the Western Islands." (As it's likely that she would have drifted with the Gulf Stream across the Atlantic towards England, these could have been the Scillys off Cornwall.) They had aboard for food and drink, 150 pounds of dried dolphin, a half barrel of water and one sea turtle. Miraculously, they had managed to survive for nine months catching what fish they could and collecting rain water.

Near the entrance to New York harbor, the captain gave them his only boat with a sail, oars and some provisions and "bade them God speed." Traveling by day, and by night sleeping beneath the boat ashore, they reached Black Cove Beach in [West] Manchester a week later. From there they walked to their homes, "so changed and emaciated that their friends hardly recognized them." Whether Nathaniel Allen ever went to sea again is not recorded, but the adventure had little effect on his health. He died in Manchester at age 84.

GUNNER DUNN

Our Indirect Link to USS CONSTITUTION; One Man's Tribute to His Friend

At first glance, it is a handsome model of the U.S.S. CONSTITUTION, the oldest commissioned warship in the United States Navy. But the story behind it is as filled with daring, bravery and adventure as the history of the ship herself.

It begins in early August of the year 1812. The United States was at war with England. Under the command of Captain Isaac Hull, the CONSTITUTION had returned from four years as flagship of the Mediterranean Squadron and had been overhauled at the Washington Navy Yard. On her way to Boston, she had nearly been captured by five British ships in a harrowing chase during two days of flat calm. By kedging (placing an anchor out ahead of a vessel and hauling her up to it) and by using the manpower of her pulling boats to tow her

The Trask House on Union Street became headquarters of Manchester Historical Society in 1925. It is named for Abigail Hooper Trask who purchased and remodeled the property in 1822 prior to her marriage to Captain Richard Trask, one of Manchester's best known merchant ship masters. For years, Abigail successfully operated a dry goods store located in the west wing of the house which for thirsty customers also dispensed copious amounts of rum. Records show that in one year this totaled 14 barrels! Photo by Richard Towle.

Painting of the full-rigged ship <u>ST. PETERSBURG</u>, flying her House Flag on her foremast (a white diamond on a red field) and signals at her mizzen, enters port with her lowers triced up and only one jib flying. In command of Captain Richard Trask of Manchester, and owned by Enoch Train & Company of Boston, <u>ST. PETERSBURG</u> was built in Medford in 1839. At 840 tons, 163 feet overall with 33-foot beam, she was at the time the largest vessel ever built in Massachusetts. With Captain Trask, she made three voyages to Liverpool and an equal number to Russia. Trask was also an investor in Train & Company. **Photo courtesy of the Manchester Historical Society.**

through the water, she managed to stay ahead of the enemy and broke free when the wind rose to enter Boston. With some 450 men and officers aboard, now at least somewhat seasoned, CONSTITUTION departed Boston on August 18, 1812. She ran to the eastward recapturing an American brig from the British sloop AVENGER. Captain Hull then sailed south intercepting a Salem privateer. She reported that she had been chased all day by a British warship named GUERRIERE. Anxious to engage the enemy, CONSTITUTION sailed throughout the night with a freshening breeze. Finally, at 10 a.m., there came a shout from the masthead. "Sail ho!" to leeward. Setting every bit of canvas he had and aided by a fresh nor'wester, Hull soon overtook what did, indeed, turn out to be H.M.S. GUERRIERE, a former Frenchman now commanded by Royal Navy Captain James Richard Dacres.

Backing her main topsail and taking in her topgallants, the Englishman readied for a fight. In ships, it was to be evenly matched—GUERRIERE, 49 guns, displaced 1,338 tons; CONSTITUTION, 50 guns, 1,576 tons.

The CONSTITUTION did have more men aboard, 456 to 272, but the British seamen were better seasoned. Hull had received his crew in Washington and it had no experience in battle. The weight in manpower would have made a difference if boarding had been the order of the day. As it turned out, it was not. For Hull wisely decided during the action that he could take GUERRIERE with his big guns alone without inflicting the high number of casualties that resulted from hand-to-hand combat.

Thanks to superb ship handling and seamanship, the celebrated skill of Yankee gunners who continually outshot the enemy, and spirited morale and leadership aboard CONSTITUTION, the day was soon hers. In less than an hour, the British ship, dismasted and burning, lay dead in the water. And Captain Dacres who had been wounded by musket fire as the two vessels came together for a moment during the battle, struck his colors and surrendered. Casualties aboard CONSTITUTION totaled 14 men; aboard GUERRIERE, 79.

In the heat of battle, one young seaman aboard CONSTITUTION, watching in wonder as a cannon ball bounced off her oak planks, cried, "Huzzah! Her sides are made of iron!" Thus it was that she came to be known forever as "Old Ironsides." This,

the first major engagement of the naval war of 1812, established the United States as a seapower to be reckoned with, not only by Great Britain, but by countries around the world. The English found the defeat of GUERRIERE hard to bear. It was, according to The London Times, the first time that an enemy frigate had defeated one of His Majesty's frigates in a battle between two ships.

Throughout the war of 1812, the accuracy and ability of American gunnery continued to confound the English. Gunners made up the largest single group of petty officers aboard a warship. On CONSTITUTION, a Gunner by the name of Richard F. Dunn was a hero of the battle with the GUERRIERE. Found after a barrage from the enemy with a severe compound fracture of the tibia, Dunn was carried below to the surgeon. There, according to his shipmate Moses Smith, who wrote about the engagement in his journal Naval Scenes in the Last War, his leg was taken off below the knee. "Dick Dunn," wrote Smith, "bore his amputation with a fortitude I shall always (remember). 'You are a hard set of butchers,' was all he said to the Surgeon as his torn and bleeding limb was severed from his body…" And, in those days, of course, without anesthesia.

Dunn must have been well liked aboard CONSTITUTION for one of his mates presented him with a model of the ship's hull carved from a piece of her taffrail shot away by the enemy. That model today is the property of the Manchester Historical Society. It was given at her death in 1925 by Mrs. Julian Low Curriea, daughter of Albert E. Low (1810-1906), a Deacon of Manchester's Congregational Church. Gunner Dunn was an uncle of her husband, Charles Morris Curriea, who purchased it from his estate. Presumably, Mr. Curriea had it rigged, or rigged it himself, and installed in its present case which has an attractive mural of the Boston skyline at the time as a background. An inscribed silver plate on the case sums up the dramatic story.

In 1925, a memorandum written by Herbert R. Tucker, then Historian of the M.H.S., tells how he interviewed Mrs. Eliza Leach, Mrs. Curriea's sister, then 89 years old. She recalled that "Uncle Dunn" as he was known, was often spoken of by the family. That year also, Herbert Tucker reported the Charlestown Navy Yard offered $500 for the model. In 1980, the Society contacted the U.S.S. Constitution Museum which confirmed, according to a diary of Dr. Amos Adams (quoted in the Journal of Connecticut Medicine) that Richard Dunn was aboard CONSTITUTION; was wounded in her battle with GUERRIERE; and did, indeed, have his leg amputated below the knee. The model is on display today in the Hattie Lee Harris bedroom of the Manchester Historical Society.

DAVID AND GOLIATH
Tiny U.S. Privateer Takes on Three Ships of a British Squadron in the Azores

Every American war has its share of extraordinary stories of patriotism and bravery, of capture and escape, and of victory against overwhelming odds.

One of these appeared in an article in The Manchester Cricket on August 6, 1898. Written by R.W. Allen, then the great-grandson of its hero, Captain John Allen, it describes how a lone American privateer, outmanned and outgunned, raised havoc with a British Squadron in the Azores.

Deacon John Allen, patriarch of the celebrated Manchester family, operated a tavern which was built near the corner of North Street and Washington Street in 1750. On September 25, 1814, the Deacon's grandson and namesake was serving as First Officer aboard the United States privateer brig GENERAL ARMSTRONG, Captain Chester Read in command. With nine guns and some 90 men aboard, she met up with three English warships in the harbor at Fayal which were bound for New Orleans to support forces of the King there about to engage General Andrew Jackson in a battle for the city.

The Squadron consisted of HMS PLANTAGENET, HMS ROTA and HMS CARNATION, 136 guns in all and with a total complement of some 2,000 men. Wary of what might happen, the American brig had anchored in shallow water close to shore.

Ignoring the rules of war which decreed that vessels of every nationality were safe in a neutral port, the British began their attack after dark with 14 pulling boats filled with armed men. The Americans opened fire and soon had the enemy on the run, seeking shelter behind nearby ledges. Seriously wounded by a rifle shot, Captain Read turned command over to his First Officer, Manchester's John Allen, who fought the ship bravely to the end.

Meanwhile, the story continues, HMS CARNATION, "being of light draft like the GENERAL ARMSTRONG," approached within range of the privateer to block her escape to the sea. At midnight, British cutters appeared again in the moonlight, and as before, the Americans opened fire with telling accuracy. Finally, after sizable losses, but still with overwhelming numbers, the enemy was alongside attempting to board. Enraged by the carnage afflicted upon his men by Yankee marksmanship, the officer in charge shouted "No quarters!"

Armed with pistols and long pikes, the Americans had also placed netting about the brig and British troops found themselves hopelessly tangled in it and easy targets.

At daylight, Portuguese authorities at Fayal ordered a stop to hostilities, but the Squadron Commander would have none of it. Indeed, he cried that he would have the privateer and the "damned Yankees," and if anyone tried to stop him he would sack the town. John Allen ordered wounded Americans sent ashore and the battle continued. This time, CARNATION opened with a broadside, but the privateer responded with devastatingly accurate fire from her Long Tom cannon, cutting down CARNATION's foremast and holing her below the waterline so that she had to retire. The other British vessels came to her aid, and the Americans, realizing they had done their best, scuttled their ship and rowed ashore to safety.

The score? The English suffered 120 killed and 180 wounded in the skirmish while the Americans lost just two men. Seven others were wounded.

John Allen went on to captain his own vessels but tragically, in 1823, he was murdered by pirates in the Caribbean. His exploits in the War of 1812, however, were well remembered among seafaring folk in Essex County for generations and were a fitting testimonial to the heroic stand put up by a small nation whose sailors fought so admirably and effectively against the world's mightiest naval power.

FAMOUS SKIPPERS
Captain Richard Trask, One of 50 Masters of Merchant Vessels Living in Town

By 1816, there were 50 Masters of merchant ships who were residents of Manchester. The harbor, of course, in those days could hardly offer their vessels shelter (prior to dredging in 1896, mud flats extended out beyond the second pair of channel buoys at low water). But whether they shipped out of Salem, Boston or New York, because of the character and charm of the community, they chose to make Manchester their home.

Commerce expanded rapidly after the War of 1812. By 1830, Boston, less than a dozen miles from Manchester by water, had become a city of 61,000 people and was running a close second to New York in trade with foreign nations. Yearly, an average of 1,500 sailing vessels entered its harbor from abroad. By 1844, as many as 15 came and went each day. Along the waterfront at India wharf and Rowe's wharf, at Central, Commercial and Lewis wharves, busy merchants brushed shoulders with sailors and stevedores. The sweet smell of tar and hemp mingled with the enticing odor of spices, tobacco and other imports in warehouses nearby. And sail and rigging were everywhere. On the waters of the harbor, schooners and brigs blended with barques and full-rigged ships. And in this magical world, no one was more important than the Captain. For as the owners of shipping firms knew well, it was he who would bring home cargoes safe, sound and on time. And this was where the money lay. A good captain was as important an investment as a good ship. And a combination of the two was unbeatable.

One of Manchester's best was Captain Richard Trask. Born in Salem in 1788, tragedy too soon filled his small world. His father, just 21 years old and chief mate on a vessel in the West Indies trade, died of illness in Havana before he could see his newborn son. His mother, shocked by the loss of her husband, became mentally deranged and was judged to be in no condition to raise a child. Thankfully, however, the baby came to live with a generous and caring family in Manchester named Lee who provided the affection and stability the boy needed. "Good Mrs. Lee," as William H. Tappan writes in his brief history of Manchester (1888), "supplied a mother's place to him and was rewarded with his affectionate helpfulness through the whole of her life." (There were many Lees in Manchester at this time. Just which Mrs. Lee this was is not known.)

THE DAYS OF SAIL
Foremast Hand as a Child, He Grew In Wisdom to Become a Captain

His adopted father, a fisherman, first took him to sea at age 12 aboard a schooner bound for the Grand Banks. As Tappan explains, Richard Trask "was remarkable for his great physical strength as well as for intelligence and sobriety, and when he was 18, he was unexpectedly offered a second mate's berth by a ship owner who was a total stranger to him but had heard favorable reports..." It was an opportunity he never forgot.

Like many lads of the day, he had little formal schooling, but while at sea he set about to teach himself the fundamentals of penmanship, navigation, and engineering. Soon he qualified as chief mate himself, and finally, there came an appointment to command the ship ADRIATIC owned by the Boston merchant firm of Loring & Cunningham. By 1828, he had accumulated means enough to purchase his own vessel and at the invitation of Enoch Train of Samuel Train & Company of Boston, Richard Trask helped to acquire the brig EDWARD which was to be employed in trade with Russia. Alas, she was soon lost off the Bahamas, but the relationship with Enoch Train was to last for the rest of his life. Shortly, the pair purchased the brig OREGON. The FORUM followed, this time with Richard Trask as Master combining the responsibilities of captain and merchant. Outward cargoes were generally Havana sugar or American cotton. The proceeds were invested in St. Petersburg in return for Russian hemp, sail cloth, cordage and feathers. Voyages were skillfully conducted and almost always profitable.

In 1839, then Enoch Train & Company turned almost exclusively to carrying cotton, and Trask joined the company in funding the construction at Waterman & Ewell shipyard in Medford of the full-rigged ship ST. PETERSBURG. At 840 tons, 160 feet overall with 33 foot beam, she was at the time the largest vessel ever built in Massachusetts. With her handsome square stern, painted ports, rich mahogany fittings below, and her officers' service of cut glass and solid silver, she won attention and admiration wherever she went. With Richard Trask in command, she made three voyages to Liverpool, and an equal number to St. Petersburg. By this time, however, Trask was ready to retire from the sea, but not from business. Until he died in 1846 at his home in Manchester, he remained an active investor in "Train's Line" of Boston to Liverpool packets.

The story of one of ST. PETERSBURG's voyages from Mobile, Alabama to Liverpool and return to Boston is told in a journal written by young Louisa Lord who for many years lived with Captain Trask, his wife Abigail and their son

Charles. All were aboard for the 40-day trip east and the 34-day passage home. Louisa wrote in her journal every day but Sunday. Her story, edited by Winifred Trask Lee, has been published by the Manchester Historical Society. Entitled <u>Miss Louisa Lord's Dairy of a Voyage on the Ship ST. PETERSBURG, 1840</u>, it tells a fascinating tale of what life was like for passengers at sea aboard a sailing ship in the mid-nineteenth century.

Handsome as she was, the ST. PETERSBURG was not a lucky ship nor as profitable as Train & Company hoped she would be. Struck by a sudden and intense storm off the coast of England in January, 1843, she found herself on a lee shore and despite the efforts of her captain and crew who cut away her masts and rigging, her anchors dragged and she was driven aground. Thankfully, everyone on board was saved. The following day, she was taken off by a steamer and towed to Liverpool where she was repaired and made ready for sea again. She completed one other voyage with Trask in command in 1845 carrying refugees from Ireland to the United States to escape famine caused by the potato blight.

A collection of letters from Richard to Abigail now at the Historical Society shows how upset he was that she wouldn't accompany him on a second voyage, but Abigail found the sea and its motion not to her liking. The letters also describe how when the ST. PETERSBURG was in New Orleans, her black cook and steward were taken off the ship in chains (this was a common occurrence in the South before the Civil War), held in jail and finally released days later. "So much for a free country!" wrote Trask.

TO SEA AT 9

Extraordinary Era in American Trade; 'Wooden Ships and Iron Men'

Another giant in the shipping trade from Manchester was Captain Thomas Leach. Born here in 1807, somewhat younger than Richard Trask, he was the son of a noted mariner who had "sailed the seas over" as Master of vessels owned by Salem merchant William Gray. At only nine years old, Leach went to sea with his father as cabin boy. Showing no favoritism, the Old Man saw that his son was trained in every aspect of a life at sea, below, on deck and in the rigging. By 1832, his abilities qualified him for command and he took

over the helm of the brig OREGON owned also by Samuel Train & Company of Boston. In his more than 51 years at sea, Thomas Leach completed 20 voyages to Russia, three to China and many more to other ports around the world.

A great spinner of yarns and tales, he loved to recount how on a voyage to East India, he escaped a blood-thirsty bunch of Malay pirates whose proa approached his ship in a calm with intentions that were obviously evil. Lining his men up on the rail, each armed with a cutlass, he rolled his cannon out and waited. The sight proved too much for the pirates who soon gave way and, with their sweeps, rowed off in another direction.

In 1874, by then age 67, he moved ashore to become Warden of the Port of Boston finally retiring in 1886. He died in the house in which he was born in December of that same year. He was 79.

That these were "iron men" is demonstrated by a story about Captain Leach when he was a boy serving with his father one winter in the North Sea. It was bitterly cold and he came on deck wearing a pair of mittens. "Tom," his father is reported to have asked, "what are those things on your hands? Let me see them." Holding them up, he exclaimed contemptuously, "Well, ain't these nice things for a sailor!" And with that, he tossed them overboard adding, "Don't let me ever see you with anything on your hands again!" For his half-century afloat, no matter how bitter the weather, Thomas Leach went barehanded.

FURNITURE MAKING MEANS JOBS, $$

Skilled craftsmen, Manchester's cabinet makers were widely known for their products. Here one works with a reeding and fluting machine to fashion what was perhaps a table leg. Machinery was rudimentary and much hand work was involved. Hey-day of the industry here was from the early 1800's to about 1850. At its peak, there were about 43 different furniture shops in town providing employment for hundreds of workers and steady wages for them and for their families. When the Civil War arrived, businesses closed and many joined the Union Army. Cheever photo from the collection of Eliot Crocker.

ANOTHER ERA

Manufacturing of Furniture Brings New Prosperity, Changes in Daily Life

While the fisheries and some farming characterized life in Manchester up to the Revolutionary War, it was furniture making that took the town into a new era from self-sufficiency and a dependence on resource-based activities to an industry involving hundreds of employees working together in mills and shops.

In the beginning, one or two craftsmen turned out simple, rustic stools, tables and chairs to satisfy a local market. Many of these works were individualized to bear the hallmark of some craftsmen who had special skills. More elaborate furniture was imported, primarily from England. But soon these pieces, too, were copied, enlarged upon and even improved, using native woods, to turn what had been a craft into art.

Individuals and small mills in Ipswich and Salem became famous first for their spindled chairs and later for beautifully carved furniture in Queen Anne and Chippendale styles with delicately upholstered seats. There were cupboards, desks and highboys, too, of birch, and cherry, pine and imported mahogany, all imaginatively carved and decorated to elevate them above the practical. Clock cases and gun stocks were inlaid with silver and different woods, all this to enhance and to add pleasure to everyday life.

In Manchester, the hey-day of the furniture industry was from the early 1800's to about 1850. A total of some 43 shops and mills of all sizes existed throughout the period providing work for hundreds of local people. The financial impact on the town was significant, creating new wealth and providing new opportunities for a growing middle class. There was a new emphasis, too, throughout the western world, on self-interest and on freedom for individuals to live better material lives than was enjoyed by those who came before them.

Between 1820 and 1860, this led to unprecedented economic and territorial expansion across the country. The Gold Rush of 1849 caused many to think, including a few in Manchester, that they could become rich overnight. But for most people, added income meant a chance to better themselves listening to lectures at Manchester's new Lyceum (established in 1830) or enjoying more leisure time with family and friends at picnics and celebrations such as Independence Day. Hard work was still a badge of honor, however, and usually paid off with success.

In the furniture industry, four cabinet makers here stand out. They were John Perry Allen, Moses Dodge (the Dodge dynasty lasted until the 1965), Eban Tappan and Charles Lee.

Allen worked first as an apprentice for Caleb Knowlton who moved to New Hampshire during the War of 1812 to escape the danger of British raids along the coast. In 1813, Allen, then unemployed, opened his own shop on what is now Union Street with one journeyman and one apprentice. Having exhausted the local market, he took two mahogany bureaus to Boston where they sold immediately and resulted in a number of orders. Ever the entrepreneur, he did the same for New York where the pieces were sold at auction with the same results. The problem now was to increase production to meet demand.

Shipped from Cuba or Honduras, mahogany was expensive and furniture makers of the era used it primarily as a veneer. This was originally sawed from a log by hand, a tedious and time consuming process. But Allen, now in a new mill located where Saw Mill Brook runs into the harbor, experimented with ways it could be done by machine. After the first two or three cuts, saw blades would heat up, steel would expand and cuts would become uneven. While replacing broken teeth on a veneer saw, the blades were placed farther apart, allowing them to cool more easily. The result? Perfect veneers and the beginning of a business which, thanks also to the existence of a new steam engine in 1825, was able to supply most of the furniture and piano factories in the United States.

Allen's four saws were so precise that they could divide a mahogany plank four inches thick into 60 strips of veneer. Although he was not the first in America to invent the process, for years his techniques were carefully guarded from the many furniture manufacturers who visited his plant to learn how they might do the same. Indeed, at the height of his prosperity, Allen's mills employed more than 100 men, a major industry in a small town like Manchester.

According to the Reverend D.F. Lamson, author of the first comprehensive history of the town written in 1895, John Perry Allen "was a man of great force of character and executive ability...While not a man of liberal education, he was a forceful speaker [with] impressive bearing...Few men have done more for the business interests of the [town]...or manifested...more indomitable pluck

Shop employees pose in front of a three-story cabinet mill on Elm Street possibly owned by Charles Lee. Note the Channel at right. Children are perched on wood stacked for manufacturing at left. Handsomely carved bedsteads on the second floor are varnished and ready to be crated for shipping. From the mens' dress, the photo appears to have been taken just after the Civil War. Lee served for three years with the Union Army. Following hostilities, he returned to operate the mill until 1868. Much of Lee's furniture was sent south as far as New Orleans.

In 1847, Cyrus Dodge built this steam-powered furniture mill between Desmond Avenue and North Street. Later converted to electricity, the structure cost $1,000. Thirty-five men were employed here in its busiest years. Cyrus specialized in the manufacture of mahogany parlor chairs in a style that would today be called Victorian. Dodge Furniture was founded by Moses Dodge in 1760. It continued to thrive throughout successive generations until Charles Dodge died in 1965. The mill building was razed that same year. Photo by Richard Towle.

in overcoming adverse circumstances." For in August, 1836, Allen's mills, his collection of woods from pine to mahogany, his own dwelling and several other houses, plus shops and out buildings, were all destroyed by fire. The loss was estimated at more than $60,000, a huge sum in those early days. Allen soon was back in business with a new mill, but the zenith of Manchester's role as a furniture manufacturing community had passed.

FIRST SHOP

In 1760, Moses Dodge Moves Here; Starts Making Furniture; Dies in Revolution

About 1760, Moses Dodge, a native of Beverly who moved to Manchester, began to construct furniture in his shop at 21 School Street for every day use by local residents. He thus lays claim to being the town's first cabinet-maker. A member of Manchester's militia, however, he failed to survive the Revolutionary War, dying in May, 1776 when his youngest son John was only three and one-half years old. A piece of his work, a handsome walnut tilt-top tea table still exists. On its underside, marked in chalk is an inscription. Written long after the table was built it reads: "Moses Dodge table made 1770. He was a Minuteman at Concord."

A sea-captain who's abilities were widely respected, John had five children, one of whom, Cyrus, became an apprentice at John Allen's mill in 1830. Soon he decided to go into business for himself and in 1841, for $1,200, purchased his own shop. According to a thesis entitled The Way We've Always Made It, The C. Dodge Furniture Company and the Cabinet-making Industry of Manchester, Massachusetts," written by Elizabeth H. Roessel in June, 1987, in partial fulfillment of the University of Delaware's requirements for the degree of Master of Arts in Early American Culture, Cyrus "specialized in the manufacture of mahogany parlor chairs in what today's collectors would refer to as early Victorian style. Dodge called them 'French chairs'" and they were evidently crafted in "the best quality and style."

His account book, Elizabeth Roessel writes "lists 11 chair makers and two upholsterers who assisted at various stages of the furniture-making process." Records show that in his first year he "mortised and tenoned approximately 1,400 chairs" which others assembled. Success followed success and in 1847, Cyrus Dodge built a steam-powered mill on North Street. Its cost: $1,000. At the height of its operation, it employed 35 men. But although the furniture industry prospered, its products were all but anonymous. Unlike others of the day such as watches, firearms and silverware, manufactures for the most part failed to label their work, frustrating many in later years seeking to determine their origin.

By the late 1870's, Cyrus' three sons, Cyrus, John and Charles, began to take over from their father and assume responsibility for the business. The firm's account books, now preserved by the Henry Francis Dupont Winterthur Museum, show that the mill completed orders for a sizable number of well-respected retail furniture stores in the region including Boston's own Paine Furniture Company which was celebrated for the distinction of its clients. Products of the mill included not only different kinds of chairs but "sofas, ottomans, bed rests and even a hat tree." As summer homes were built in Manchester, they were often furnished with locally built furniture, another market for the Dodges. One of the secrets of the mill's success was its ability to judge the fashions and demands of the day including reproductions of early American antiques.

In 1922, Charles asked his nephew and namesake, Charles Ernest Dodge, to join the firm and follow in his family's footsteps. A graduate of Massachusetts Institute of Technology, Charles was bound for a career in engineering, but trimmed his sails and in 1926 when his uncle died took over the Dodge mill. Quality reproductions of traditional styles continued to be the firm's specialty and, as Elizabeth Roessel writes, it "successfully supplied its customers with two valuable commodities... finely made furniture [and] a good dose of 'the way things used to be.'"

In 1956, a story about the mill and its history appear in The Gloucester Daily Times. It reported that there were three employees each of whom was more than 50 years old. One was 80. Charles Dodge himself was 67. The steam engine was still in place until 1935. The building's boiler happily celebrated its 75th birthday. Over the years little changed and furniture was still manufactured by hand in the good old-fashioned way which still pleased its purchasers. The business itself lasted until Charles Dodge died in 1965. The mill building of the C. Dodge Furniture Company, built in 1847, was finally razed that same year.

Furniture manufacturing shop owned by A.S. Jewett and G.W. Jewett was located at 10 Desmond Avenue. The Jewetts took over the shop in 1881. It was renovated in 1898. Note the bedsteads leaning against the building. A small table is also visible next to the wheel barrow carrying lumber. Employees of the company obviously posed for the photographer. Information from Frances L. Burnett. Photo from Manchester Historical Society Collection.

Originally built in 1871 as a furniture factory for Rust & Marshall, this structure on Elm Street was later occupied by Union Web Hammock Company of Gloucester and then by home builders Roberts & Hoare. It replaced a Rust & Marshall mill located on the inner harbor at Knight's Wharf (where Peale House Square is today) which was destroyed in a spectacular waterfront blaze that same year. The fire, which also burned neighboring mills and furniture warehouses, could be seen from as far away as Beverly and Gloucester. Old sails, wet down and draped over buildings nearby including Town Hall, enabled them to survive. By 1895, Roberts & Hoare had built 32 houses and 21 barns, many of them in Manchester, for the growing summer colony on the North Shore.

TAPPAN'S TORRENT

Craftsman Known for His Ships' Wheels Turns Out Our Earliest Fire Engine

Eban Tappan began his career in business with his father, Ebeneezer, who owned a store on Central Street. A man of many talents, he built sailing vessels engaged in coastal trade as well as a number of dwelling houses. But he made his mark as a skilled craftsman and cabinet-maker. Working at the same bench for more than 56 years, Tappan invented the first continuous turning lathe in Manchester. Furniture, however, was not his only interest. In his later years, he manufactured ships wheels for many a merchant ship sailing out of Boston. He then became fascinated with hand pump fire engines, known as "fire tubs," and in 1826 he began building them in his own shop entirely from his own plans. One of these, built in 1832, was christened TORRENT and became the town's first fire apparatus.

The iron work was done by a village blacksmith while the brass work was completed in Boston, all under Tappan's personal supervision. In 1836, after the Great Fire which destroyed a series of houses and mill buildings, the town was so pleased with the performance of TORRENT that it purchased it for the sum of $654.80. It came with 190 feet of hose and was used extensively until the first steamer was purchased in 1885. It was then placed in "ordinary" after 53 years of service. Fire department officials wisely kept the old pumper as a faithful relic of earlier days. In the 1960's, TORRENT was restored without charge by Manchester Marine Construction Company. The engine, with its fine lettering and striping, is now on display with Seaside 2, a 1902 horse-drawn steam pumper, at SEASIDE NO. I, a fire house erected on the Common in 1885 which is now a museum. For 76 years (1894-1970), the building also served as Headquarters for the Manchester Police Department.

Not one to spare a moment for relaxation, in 1818 Eben Tappan was active as Colonel of a Regiment of Militia composed of men from Beverly and Manchester. And from 1843 to 1844, he represented the Commonwealth and his community as a member of the Great and General Court. Much respected and admired, he died at age 82 in 1875.

Although the boom period in furniture-making generally had ended by the beginning of the Civil War, there was one notable exception, Charles Lee.

An apprentice to John Perry Allen, Lee had married his daughter Eliza in 1846. The couple had two children, Ella and Charles. In 1856, Lee began his own business, C. Lee Furniture, in a shop across the canal from the Baptist Church. Its location is clearly apparent on a 19th century town atlas.

Census records show that Lee's factory which employed some 18 men and was equipped with steam power, was in operation for about 12 years, from 1856 to 1868. Like many others, he served for three years with the Union Army returning at the war's end in 1865. Working with mahogany, rosewood and pine, he specialized in bedsteads, and in the year 1860 produced 400 of them worth about $20,000. Most of them, before and after the war, were shipped south to the port of New Orleans where the largest proportion was sold to residents of Louisiana and Mississippi. Matching parts of the bedsteads were apparently nested together, crated, and later assembled for the retail trade. As peace returned to the South, business was brisk. In 1867, Lee shipped more than 150 cases of furniture to 12 dealers in the city of New Orleans. Handsomely carved, they fetched a good price. And unlike many Manchester furniture manufacturers, each of his pieces was labeled "C. Lee" followed by a manufacturing number. Today, those still in existence, can sell for as much as $10,000 at auction. There is also a possibility that carving took place upon arrival, for early photos outside the mill in Manchester show bed rails and posts unadorned whereas examples in the south are often elaborately shaped and decorated in the style of the time, Rococo Revival.

SOLVING A MYSTERY

Search for 'C. Lee' Leads Scholar to Manchester Historical Society

In the early 1990's, Stephen Harrison, then a second year fellow at the University of Delaware's Winterthur Program in Early American Culture, found his way to Manchester after significant research for his master's thesis, The New Orleans Furniture Trade, 1840-1880: 'The Largest Assortment Constantly On Hand' which was completed in the spring of 1994.

As he started on the search for "C. Lee" whose name appeared on a number of beds he had examined, Harrison, a native of Louisiana, indicated in an article he wrote for Maine Antique Digest in

April, 1994, that speculation was widespread about who the mysterious manufacturer might be. "The most frequent and generally accepted [opinion], was that C. Lee was a free man of color," he writes, "who trained under and worked for Prudent Mallard...the greatest of all New Orleans craftsmen."

As Harrison explains, it was believed that Lee was granted his freedom and allowed to mark the beds he made with his own name, although always in inconspicuous places. And Mallard did, indeed, own a slave named Charles. Others speculated that "C. Lee" was a false name, a disguise for another cabinet maker. What was not in doubt, Harrison adds, was that records show that pieces marked "C. Lee, Chas. Lee or Charles Lee" appear on lists of goods imported by two large New Orleans furniture warehouses in the late 1860's.

The breakthrough came, he continues, when in the library at Winterthur, an article about a Charles Lee who lived in Manchester, Massachusetts was discovered in an obscure trade newspaper published in Boston in the early 1870's entitled The Cabinet Maker. "With renewed hopes," Harrison declared, "I braved the snow and headed north." Here at the Manchester Historical Society with the assistance of Librarian Mrs. Sherry Proctor, he found in both literature and photographs, information which enable him to finally identify the mysterious Charles Lee, "a maker of bedsteads for the southern market." A photo which appeared with the article in Maine Antique Digest shows a handsome half-tester bed now at Stanton Hall, Natchez, Mississippi, which was manufactured by Lee in Manchester.

Thus "the man behind the infamous stamp," Harrison concludes: "found on so many beds in the South, need no longer languish in anonymity or romantic speculation. He was an important participant in the 19th century furniture trade between the North and the South."

CIVIL WAR — MANY SERVE ITS CAUSE

Summer resident for many years at Sunset Hill in West Manchester, Henry Lee Higginson served as a Major in the First Massachusetts Cavalry during the Civil War. Wounded and left for dead after a skirmish with Confederate horsemen at Aldie Gap, he recovered and went on to become a huge success in the business world at Lee Higginson; to found the Boston Symphony Orchestra and to provide his alma mater, Harvard University, with the Freshman Union and Soldiers' Field, a memorial to fallen comrades. Photo courtesy of the Massachusetts Commandery Military Order of the Loyal Legion and the U.S. Army Military History Institute.

BLOODIEST DAY

Manchester's Julius F. Rabardy Recalls the Horrors of Antietam Creek, 1862

Emboldened by a striking victory at the Second Battle of Bull Run in August, 1862, newly-appointed commander of the Army of Virginia General Robert E. Lee with 40,000 troops shortly crossed the Potomac River into Maryland where he hoped to gather supplies and convince residents of the state to join the Confederate cause. But Union General George Brinton McClellan had other ideas. On September 17, with 70,000 men, he attacked Lee's forces at Antietam Creek, northwest of Harper's Ferry.

What resulted was the bloodiest day of the Civil War. Union forces suffered 2,108 killed, 9,549 wounded; Confederates: 2,700 killed, 9,029 wounded, a total of 24,378 casualties. The battle was a draw, but Lee took his army back to Virginia. The event, however, had long-reaching consequences. For with this demonstration of Union strength, European powers decided not to intervene in the war, and shortly thereafter Lincoln issued his famous Emancipation Proclamation.

One of those who took part in the Battle of Antietam was Julius F. Rabardy of Manchester, a Private in Company K, 12th Regiment, Massachusetts Volunteers. Born in France in 1833, Rabardy, a furniture maker, joined the Union Army at the age of 28. After the war, he became Postmaster and owner of the town's first monthly newspaper, Beetle & Wedge. In a letter, published in The Manchester Cricket in 1895, he tells first hand of the pain and horror of his experiences during that fateful and deadly day.

Action began at sunrise. Assigned with his Company to an area known as the "cornfield," Rabardy and his compatriots "fired at the Confederates well hidden in the big corn...I ran quickly over a oak fence," he writes, "enclosing young cherry trees, and fired from the SE corner until we were ordered forward...at this time, the guns [to] our rear fired too low and one of our men was shot [by friendly fire] while going over the fence. On through the cornfield we went till we came to a thin grove with decayed stumps...there I received the first wound which broke my leg near the knee...we had then been out about 40 minutes but had not seen a Confederate so well did they conceal themselves. Others were struck at this time. Two of my

Company carried me to the foot of a dead tree where wounded men were lying. Our skirmishers fell back and soon the Confederates advanced, trail arms, some passing close to the tree, cheering one another with their peculiar cry. They soon fell back [as well] and our men appeared and then retreated...the enemy advanced again with cautious yet strong steps of veterans...[suddenly] an officer with a breech loading gun which he used freely, [shouted], 'we are flanked boys, fall back!' Then our troops advanced. Their firing was terrific. The corn stalks fell as if mowed. The air is full of explosions and the smell of brimstone, missiles of all kinds strike the tree and dead branches fall among the wounded. I was shot through the right thigh [his second wound] by our own men...a poor fellow with uplifted arm begs for water. The arm is shot off and the man speaks no more...

"Another Confederate lies in front of me with a horrible wound. It is Hell. I close my eyes. It is probably that weak from the loss of blood, sick at the sight of such carnage, I became unconscious...When I recovered, all was quiet. The corn was trodden down. Many dead and wounded had been removed and 100 feet on the north of us stands in line, at order arms, a Union regiment. I ask its name. An officer answers, 'Second Massachusetts.' It gives me hope. I give the name of my regiment and beg to be removed to safer place which had been done in the case of other men, Union and Confederate. The officer answers that they were not allowed to leave the ranks. In the meantime, I saw a young man reel. He would have fallen if not for the help of his comrades. It was [a Gloucester boy], son of one of the men in our company who now lay dead on the opposite side of the tree. This young man had often visited his father. He knew my voice and my accent and from where he stood [he] recognized his father's body. He passed by it as his regiment went forward...

"I know nothing of the Confederate troops which passed by me [in the cornfield]...but in justice to those men I gladly say that when obliged to walk among the wounded, they did so in a careful way and though it was not a place for amenities, some even quieted our anxious looks by kind words..."

Private Rabardy was later treated and his wounded leg removed. But the loss of a limb did little to hold him back when he returned to Manchester. For not only was he a newspaper publisher but also Postmaster. He built the Rabardy block and founded what is today Floyd's store, operated until 2003 by his great-granddaughter, Alice Rice. In 1870, at his own expense, he established the town's first telegraph office. He died at age 97 in 1926.

'A LITTLE SHINDY'

Major Higginson Is Wounded, Left for Dead in Skirmish with Confederates

Another Manchester resident, albeit a seasonal one, was also wounded after a brief but fierce skirmish with Confederate cavalry at Aldie Gap, a narrow opening in the hills of the Blue Ridge near the Shenandoah. A graduate of Harvard College, Class of 1855, who after the war built a summer house at Sunset Hill, West Manchester, Major Henry Lee Higginson, was commissioned an officer in the infantry but was later assigned to the First Massachusetts Cavalry. Educator Bliss Perry, legendary Headmaster of Phillips Exeter Academy, tells the stirring story of his action in Life and Letters of Henry Lee Higginson published by the Atlantic Monthly Press, Boston, in 1921. Lieutenant-Colonel Greely S. Curtis, a friend of Higginson who also later became a summer resident of Manchester, is mentioned as well.

In his Reminiscences of the war Higginson writes: "It had been a hot, tiresome ride [in the June sun]. The men came along in pretty good order, although one of the regiments belonging to another brigade galloped about to get water and acted in a foolish way. Just as we came to the town of Aldie, we heard a little firing, and were ordered to the front…we turned to the right, went up by a little wood, and our regiment was put into a field close by a farmhouse and close by a road. There, Colonel [Greely] Curtis [a friend and soon to become fellow summer resident of Manchester], in command, left me with two squadrons, and went attending to something else. I rode up to the farmhouse and saw one or two soldiers jackets hanging at the door, and was looking about when I saw a regiment coming at full tilt down the road toward us.

"I immediately ordered one squadron into the road and we charged these men. They turned straight around and ran away. We came very near their rear, but could not reach them. They went down a hill and at the top I ordered a halt. Captain Sargent with two or three men, rode straight down into a valley after a few of the troopers we had been pursuing, and began fighting them. I yelled to him to come back, but he would not do so, and fearing that he would get into trouble, I rode down to give him the order, when right behind us came a whole regiment of Confederate cavalry at full speed.

"I shouted to Sargent and the two or three other men with him to ride for their lives and we galloped up a hill in front of us where we lost one man through the balking of his horse. We reached the top of the hill, and the Confederates had stopped, as we were not worth pursuing. Sargent turned around in his saddle and made faces at them with his fingers, whereat they pursued, and we rode down another very steep hill, and at the bottom they caught us, and we had a little shindy [slang for a row or brawl].

"Sargent was knocked from his horse and shot, as he thought, just above the heart. One of our men was killed and one lieutenant was shot through the side. In striking a man opposite to me who was using improper language, I was knocked from my horse and found myself in the road. Over me was standing a man who I had unhorsed, and who struck at my head. He then proposed to take me prisoner, but I told him I should die in a few minutes, for I put my hand under and found a hole in my backbone. He took what he could get of my goods, and rode off, leaving my horse which had been shot with four bullets.

"So in five minutes the shindy was over, and three of us were wounded and one dying. When they were out of sight, I ordered Captain Sargent to get up off the ground and come under a tree where I left him close by a little house. He declared he could go no further and should die in a few minutes. I crawled along to a brook, where I lay down and drank a pailful of water, then crossed the brook and got up into a wood. When I had nearly reached a fence, I heard some noise and lay down in the leaves and made a little memorandum in my notebook. Just then a solid shot [artillery] came down close by me. Presently, when all was quiet, I got up again, climbed over the fence, and walked in the direction where the fighting was still going on, and presently came in sight of our men, many of whom had been killed or wounded.

"I lay down on the ground, was presently put on a horse, which I could hardly bear, and taken to the hospital where Dr. Osborne looked at me and began to patch me up. He made a little slit at my back to see if he could find the ball, but could not;

Major Russell Sturgis of Manchester with saber on horseback at right with two other mounted officers. In the background, an infantry unit, perhaps from the 45th Massachusetts, is apparently engaged in close order drill. Tents indicate the officers and men are part of a military encampment. A loyal member of the Congregational Church where he taught Sunday School after the war, Sturgis generously made possible the construction of Emmanuel Church on Masconomo Street. A figure in the Allen Post, Number 67, G.A.R., he also collected a series of short personal histories written by local war veterans and published them as a tribute in a handsome, leather-bound volume which may been seen today at the Memorial Library.

Marching down the then-unpaved road between the old Police Station and Town Hall, veterans of the Civil War and members of Allen Post, Number 67, G.A.R, still have a spring in their step despite their obviously advancing years. This photograph may have been taken on Memorial Day about 1900, 35 years after hostilities ended. Originally known as Decoration Day, May 30 was designated a date to pay homage to those members of Union Forces who lost their lives during the War of Rebellion. The first celebration was in 1868. Today the tradition continues as a national holiday to honor the dead of all wars. Note that everyone in the unit seems to be in step (or out of step?) but the commanding officer!

as a matter of fact, I had a pistol ball in the sacrum [the posterior section of the pelvis], a good slash across the cheek, a punch in the shoulder, which was of little account, and a bad whack on the head, which also turned out to have no results except a sore. I was taken down to the village by Colonel Curtis—some men carrying the litter—and put into a house with one or two... prisoners, and left there for the night. I heard that my brother had been captured and [that] we had lost about half our regiment. But we had beaten the enemy back..." Actually, the day had been saved by three Union regiments which were brought up to assist the First Massachusetts Cavalry. They were the First Maine, the First New York and the Sixth Ohio.

'THANK GOD!'
Surgeon Probes for Bullet in the Major's Back; Finds It; He Finally Recovers

The next day, Major Higginson was taken by horse-drawn ambulance over painfully rough roads and later by train to a hospital in Alexandria. Higginson could stand or lie down but not sit. There he stayed for several days. Finally notified of his wounds, his father came to take him to Armory Square Hospital when Anna Lowell, a friend from Boston, was a nurse. A surgeon dressed his wounds, and the following day he was put aboard a train with other wounded, bound for New York. His wound was dressed again and finally he was taken home to Boston. There, as Higginson reports, "Dr. Cabot who had examined my wounds and had seen a piece of cloth and a piece of bone come out of my back, thought he had found the bullet. He had already probed for it and the second time, using a porcelain probe, he got the black mark of the lead, and then knew he had found [it]. So he gave me ether for the second time, and when I came to, the bullet was out, and he was sitting a chair saying, 'Thank God!' " If it had not been removed, Higginson feared he would have become paralyzed below the waist as was a friend and fellow officer who suffered much the same injury. As it was, he recovered quickly but was never well enough to return to active duty.

Many years later, while seated at dinner at the University Club in Boston following the dedication of the statue of General Joseph Hooker at the State House, Higginson was approached by General Rosser, one of a delegation of Confederate officers invited to the ceremony. He had always suspected that it was Rosser, then a Colonel, who had struck him across the face with his saber. Rosser approached the table and touched Higginson gently on the shoulder. "I want to see how good a job I did on your face that day at Aldie," he said with a smile. The Major, according to his son, "gave him both hands, and the two old men fraternized until the small hours of the morning."

After the war, Major Higginson rented a house in Beverly each summer from 1870 to 1875. In 1878, he built *Sunset Hill* in West Manchester.

Other reports about the experiences of Manchester residents during the War of Rebellion appear in an impressive leather bound volume entitled Personal War Sketches, presented to Allen Post Number 67, Manchester, Department of Massachusetts, by Major Russell Sturgis, 1894, Grand Army of the Republic. Collected by Major Sturgis as a tribute to the men involved, the accounts are fascinating. A few appear below.

Daron Woodbury, born 1835 in Essex, a Manchester resident, enlisted Salem, 1861. Private, Company H, 18th Regiment, Massachusetts Volunteer Infantry. Discharged 1862 for wounds received in battle.

Private Woodbury took part in the battle for Yorktown Peninsula. He was seven days on the line. While in Oak Swamp he was wounded "through the body. Was taken prisoner of the Rebels and put into Libby Prison. Transferred to Castle Thunder Prison, paroled and exchanged... went back to Newport News and finally to hospital in Baltimore. Then to the Stewart Mansion to the West Building. Discharged. While sick in Baltimore, my wife cared for me and to her nursing I owe my life. She tended me about three months and came home with me when I was discharged..."

George Edward Andrews. Manchester resident. Born 1836. Enlisted in Boston, 1863. Private, Company G, Third Regiment, Heavy Artillery of Massachusetts. Promote to Articifer Armorer [a technical rank involved in gun design and construction]. Discharged, 1865. Engaged at Harper's Ferry when Rebel General Jubal A. Early attempted his raid on Washington. "Later our company was detailed to guard a train [bound] for [General Ambrose E.] Burnside's armory. On reaching his wagons, we unloaded them onto his teams and rested near these till morning. About three o'clock a.m., five cavalrymen were seen riding slowly down to our camp. We remained quiet until they were within our circle, when we all rose up and they were captured before they could fire upon us. We made them prisoners and brought them to our camp at Alexandria, Virginia. We were told that the Rebel General Mosby was in camp about one-half mile from where we captured the five cavalrymen, just over the brow of the hill with 500 men, showing the we ourselves had a very narrow escape from being taken by him. We participated in the Grand Review in Washington, DC, after the close of the war when about 200,000 troops passed [in review] before President Johnson." Andrews died in 1918.

Thomas Atchinson Morse, Manchester resident, born 1841 in Essex. Enlisted in Salem, 1861. Private, Company H, 19th Regular Massachusetts Volunteer Infantry. Re-enlisted 1865. Discharged 1865 as Corporal. A fortunate survivor, Morse took part in an extraordinary number of battles: Yorktown, West Point, Fair Oaks, Savage Station, Mine Run, Robertson's Cross Road, Malvern Hill, Second Bull Run, Antietam, Fredericksburg, Chancellorsville, Gettysburg, Wilderness, Cold Harbor and Petersburg. He was wounded in the right arm in the fight at Deep Bottom prior to the Battle of Petersburg in June, 1864."With a few others, I was at the rear of my regiment making coffee for my breakfast when the Rebels, taking advantage of our faulty lines, made an assault on our left, capturing a large majority of my regiment and portions of four other regiments of our Brigade. The assaulting party came between me and my regiment and so I barely escape capture."

THEIR 'EARTHLY HOME'
Major Sturgis Moves to Manchester; Establishes Emmanuel Church

Major Russell Sturgis, a summer resident of Manchester, was born in Milton, Massachusetts in 1831. As a child, he lived in China with his parents, later attending Phillips Exeter Academy and in 1848 enrolling at Harvard College. Following graduation, he went to England with his father who then was employed by Baring Brothers but who subsequently joined Russell & Company in China as a Clerk and Acting U.S. Vice Consul. Back in Boston, Russell, with his friend Henry Saltonstall, established the business firm of Saltonstall &

Sturgis. Then, while still young—only 29—with the means to make it possible, he chose to retire. It was 1860.

Two years later, with the nation divided and embroiled in a bitter civil war, he raised a company of men for the Union Army here in Manchester and was chosen its Captain fulfilling the quota for the town. He served for nine months in North Carolina with the 45th Regiment of Massachusetts Infantry retiring with the rank of Major. Upon the death of his wife, he returned home and subsequently married again. He moved to Manchester year-round in 1858. He was a member of the Congregational Church and taught Sunday School. In 1882, he founded Emmanuel Church and it was his generosity that made possible the construction of the church building. "He never ceased to thank God for leading him to Manchester which is to him [and his wife and children, their] earthly home..."

FIRST MASSACHUSETTS
Greely Curtis Commands a Regiment of Union Cavalry at Gettysburg

Another who became a summer resident of Manchester, mentioned earlier, was Greely Stevenson Curtis. He was appointed a Captain of the Second Massachusetts Infantry early in the war, later becoming a Lieutenant-Colonel of the First Massachusetts Cavalry. His active life is described wonderfully and touchingly in a family biography entitled The Boldest Man I Know" The Life of Greely Stevenson Curtis written in October 2000 by two descendants, Joan Hopkinson Shurcliff and Arthur Asahel Shurcliff, II. Under Colonel Curtis' command besides his long-time friend Henry Lee Higginson, was Captain Benjamin Crowninshield of Marblehead who describes what the average Union soldier had to eat at winter quarters along the Potomac River in 1862. Hardly a balanced diet, it is a rare view of how the army of those days provided for its men.

"On a march, the regular food issued...consists of 'hard tack'...a square cracker, usually pretty good, but occasionally it had been stored for a long time. Age added to the hardness and distracted from the sweetness...Fat salt pork was the regular meat ration and sugar and coffee, the liquid stimulant. Rations were commonly given out for three days at a time...on the march the trooper had to be his own cook, while in the established camps

Brigadier General Greely Stevenson Curtis (1830-1897) by artist William Morris Hunt. In 1861, at age 31, Curtis joined the Union Army as a Captain and was assigned to command Company B of the 2nd Massachusetts Infantry. With his friend Henry Lee Higginson, he soon transferred to the First Massachusetts Cavalry and as a Lieutenant-Colonel fought following Antietam, at skirmishes along the Potomac, at the Battle of Brandy Station, at the Battle of Aldie and at Gettysburg. Disabled by malaria, he resigned from his regiment in March, 1864. Photo courtesy of Arthur Shurcliff.

Private Julius Felix Rabardy of Manchester served with the 12th regiment of Massachusetts Volunteers, a unit of infantry during the Civil War. Wounded and with a leg removed following the Battle of Antietam Creek in September, 1862, Rabardy, who had been born in France, returned to build the Rabardy Block, start what is today Floyd's Store, establish the town's first newspaper, the <u>Beetle & Wedge</u>, and accept appointment as Postmaster. Floyd's Store remained in the family, and until 2003, was operated by his great-granddaughter, Alice Rice. Rabardy died in 1926 at age 97.

Emmanuel Church, Episcopal, Masconomo Street, Manchester, in 1912. Built in 1882 in three months with funds provided by Civil War Major Russell Sturgis, Jr., it held its first service that year. The building which was a gift to his wife, was designed by his brother, architect Hubbard Sturgis of Boston.

cooking was done at a company cook house...The popular dish was prepared this way: hard tack would broken into small pieces and wet with water; then the soldier would take his half-canteen, put in his salt pork and fry it over the fire, [adding to it] the wet, broken cracker...judicious stirring [would] properly mix the fat...[and] before serving [he] would put some sugar on top. This dish received among the cavalry a designation unsuited to ears polite which old soldiers will readily recall. It was the standard food of both cavalry and infantry in the Army of the Potomac." Cavalry troopers, of course, could supplement their diet substantially by foraging food from farms nearby.

In between major confrontations, fighting went on. One particular and continuing responsibility was picket duty. Meeting with the Colonel, their commanding officer, Greely Curtis and Henry Lee Higginson were assigned the dangerous task of "clearing the country for three miles [in front of the brigade] of hostile inhabitants, spies, guerrillas, etc. A dirty job," wrote Higginson in his diary, "and one likely to injure us..."

He did, however, have faith in Greely's leadership. "The best in the division," he quoted another officer as saying, "and I believe so, too...no one in the service here has the marked ability for cavalry work that G. has..." At the time, Curtis, a Lieutenant-Colonel, was in charge of a regiment.

GETTYSBURG

Colonel Curtis and 1st Massachusetts Assigned to Picket Rebel Base

One of the most celebrated battles of the war began on July 1, 1863 at Gettysburg, Pennsylvania. It was to be a fight that the South hoped would defeat the Union army, cause Lincoln to lose the election, and bring England and France in on the side of the Confederacy. But, as history shows, that was not to be. A share of the Union victory was due in part to northern cavalry units which kept Rebel General J.E.B. Stuart from joining Robert E. Lee for more than 10 days. When Stuart finally did show up, he was soundly beaten by U.S. General David Gregg. Gregg sent the First Massachusetts Cavalry, including Lieutenant-Colonel Greely Curtis, east of Gettysburg to picket the supply base. Curtis reached the main battleground on the afternoon of July 3 just as General George Pickett's three brigades began their celebrated charge on Union lines. Following the battle, Curtis wrote to his friend Major Henry Higginson who was still recovering from his wounds in Boston.

"...It was a tremendous fight at Gettysburg and we whipped," he told Higginson. "The good old army of the Potomac fought splendidly. Thursday afternoon it went very hard with us and looked like a defeat. By the grace of God, a council of corps commanders decided to stand and fight it out the next day. Friday it was terrible, but we had a strong position and the slaughter of the graybacks—what shall I say—awful and splendid...I saw heaps of dead, 30 in a pile, touching. Now I suppose the Rebs are in full retreat. If the army from Washington will move up and cut off their retreat to Richmond, I see no reason why the war, up here, should not be over in three weeks. We have the hardest sort of work, but being in a manner detached we have managed to take pretty good care of the horses. Morse tells me that the 2nd Massachusetts Infantry never fought so well— 7 color bearers shot in about 20 minutes and the men jumping out of the ranks, vying with each other for the bloody honor of carrying it...

Just eight days later, on July 11, Colonel Curtis came down with malaria and on July 18 was forced because of illness to resign his command of the regiment. Replaced by Captain Crowninshield, he went home to Massachusetts on leave. Sick and worn out, he never returned to active duty. The victory at Gettysburg was matched by General Ulysses S. Grant's defeat of Confederate forces at Vicksburg, Mississippi. The tide of war had turned in favor of the North.

In 1866, Curtis and his wife Harriot, rented a summer cottage at Smith's Point, Manchester. The next year they purchased from a farmer named Kitfield, some 70 acres of land with one-half mile of ocean frontage east of property owned by Richard Henry Dana, Jr., a friend of some years. There in 1869, they built the Stone House that still stands today. In Manchester (during the winter they lived at 28 Mount Vernon Street, Boston), they raised a family of ten children, had three cows, two pigs, chickens, a stable of horses and a large vegetable garden as well as a 40-foot sloop, DREAM, which was moored at Kettle Cove. For most of his life after the war, Colonel Curtis, later promoted to Brigadier General, suffered from recurring bouts of malaria which weakened him and eventually led to his death in 1897. Till the end, his greatest pleasure was to meet monthly, usually at the Union Club on Park Street, with dear friends who had served as fellow officers during the War of the Rebellion. Members of the group always appeared in the full blue uniform of the Union Army.

During his life in Manchester, Greely Curtis and his wife Harriot would regularly take their children to visit with "Uncle Henry" as Major Higginson was known to the family, at the large house on the hill in West Manchester. Higginson would live until 1919.

TJC: HIS GREAT GIFT TO THE TOWN

Financier and benefactor Thomas Jefferson Coolidge, whose generosity made possible the construction of Manchester's public library in 1887, was 46 years old when this photo was taken 10 years earlier by Allen & Rowell, Portrait Photographers, Boston. A direct descendent of the nation's third President, Coolidge, impressed with the town's need for a new library building, engaged Charles Follen McKim, at the time one of the world's most celebrated architects, to draw plans for what became The Memorial Library and Grand Army Hall, named for those citizens of Manchester who had served with Union forces during the Civil War.

THE LIBRARY

Citizens Recognize Learning as the Way to Individual Fulfillment, Financial Success

By 1820, with the nation recovering rapidly from the effects of the War of 1812, there was new mood in America. Unlike Europe, where class structure restricted social mobility, every man was free to do as he wished within the laws of the land and this most often meant a devotion to bettering his lot in life economically.

As the nation grew, there were extraordinary opportunities for individuals to establish themselves and succeed in business and in manufacturing. And a new pursuit of self-interest was replacing an earlier emphasis on stability, tradition and unified protection of the public good.

There was a danger in this, of course, that selfishness could destroy social responsibility. But if ethics and morality could govern individual behavior, there was a growing faith that the development of a market-oriented society, could bring remarkable benefits to people everywhere. Indeed, between 1820 and 1860, this passion for individual financial achievement led to unparalleled economic and territorial expansion. It encouraged the migration of millions of Europeans to America. And it was a crucial factor in the move of population to the West.

It was soon acknowledged universally that one of the keys to self-betterment then, as it is today, was education, first in the public schools, then at home and in the community.

With new businesses now making furniture for markets locally and elsewhere, and creating steady jobs which provided predictable income, Manchester was taking part in the county's economic expansion. Unlike fishing and farming, manufacturing offered regular hours of work and there was more time not only for leisure but for learning.

One of the institutions which made this possible was Manchester's Lyceum founded in February, 1830. By definition, the Lyceum presented lectures and discussions ranging from topics dealing with the relationship between ownership of property and suffrage to systems of making and maintaining public roadways. There were talks on travel, on science, and on philosophy. One of the most popular lecturers was Manchester's own William Henry Allen. Widely traveled for the era (and the author of an early but brief history of the town), Allen spoke about life on the frontier, western Indian tribes and mining gold and silver. Typical of the era, the list of 120 members included "nearly all of the principal men of the town," apparently no ladies. Dues were 50 cents annually. Women could attend, however, by invitation. Members could purchase season tickets for 25 cents for "females only" and boys of a certain age.

Soon after the establishment of the Lyceum, enthusiasm grew for a library. It was eventually located at 12 School Street. Built in 1818, the structure (sited just west of the present fire station) housed not only books, but a school room, a fire engine (pumper), and until the new Town Hall was erected in 1868, an office for Selectmen. When the library was finally deeded to the town in 1871 (and the Lyceum disbanded after 41 years), it totaled more than 1,000 volumes. The gift was conditional. The town was required to provide funds "for the care and increase" of the library collection. In addition, three residents, Lewis N. Tappan, John H. Towne and Charles H. Trask, generously contributed $100 each for the purchase of books. By-laws were written and adopted and a governing board of three Trustees elected. Thus was the Manchester Free Public Library established. By purchase and by gift, it gradually grew until in 1878 it numbered more than 3,000 volumes which circulated some 14,500 times annually.

The need for a new library building had often been discussed, but it was only a dream until the arrival of summer resident Thomas Jefferson Coolidge. Born in Boston in 1831, Coolidge was the sixth and youngest child of Joseph Coolidge, Jr. and Eleanor Wales Randolph, a remarkable individual whose mother was Martha Jefferson, daughter of the President. "During my whole life," Coolidge wrote later, "I never met her equal in a woman, whether in cultivation of the mind or in the performance of her duties." On his father's side he was descended from John Coolidge who settled in Watertown in 1630. With a population of some 60,000 in those days, Boston was without plumbing, gas, electricity or even kerosene. Coolidge grew up with his parents in his grandfather's house on Bowdoin Street, then a fashionable part of town. It was lit by tallow candles and heated by wood and coal stoves.

HARVARD AT AGE 16

Coolidge Devotes Himself to Business and 'the Acquisition of Wealth'

According to a charming autobiography written for his family in 1902 (and reprinted and published in 1923 by Houghton Mifflin Company), Thomas Jefferson Coolidge was educated for five years in Switzerland while his father and mother were in China with traders Augustine Heard & Company. Upon their return, his schooling continued with his brother in Germany. Finally, at age 16 in 1847, he left Europe to join the sophomore class at Harvard College. Graduating at age 19 in 1850, he saw that "money was becoming the only real avenue to power and success" and he decided to devote himself, as he writes, "to the acquisition of wealth." In 1852, he married Hetty Sullivan Appleton, the attractive daughter of William Appleton of Boston, later a member of Congress. And at his father-in-law's invitation, he entered the milling industry becoming Treasurer of Boott Mills.

By the late 1850's, the dark shadow of civil war stretched across the nation. In 1859, John Brown attacked the U.S. Arsenal at Harper's Ferry. With war imminent and shortages sure to come, Coolidge wisely bought commodities, selling them later to make his first fortune, $100,000, a tidy sum in those days. Lincoln was elected President in 1860. The cotton states had all seceded, and by April, 1861, Fort Sumter had fallen to the Confederacy.

Abolitionism and the war were not universally popular in the North whose mills were kept running with southern cotton. As early as 1835, William Lloyd Garrison, native of Newburyport, Massachusetts, and later outspoken Editor of the famed abolitionist newspaper The Liberator, was nearly lynched in Boston for his radical views. Men of liberal intellect and wealth who showed sympathy for those who rallied against slavery, were viciously criticized and shunned socially for sabotaging what many felt was the common good which came from doing business with the south. Racial hatred and fear were also widespread. In the early 1850's, Manchester summer resident Richard Henry Dana, Jr., a Harvard educated attorney, heroically chose to defend two escaped slaves who were being prosecuted under the Federal Fugitive Slave Act. Dana was not only bitterly castigated by the public and the press, but he so shook his own circle that men he had known all his life refused to speak with him when they passed on the streets of Boston.

Coolidge, certainly part of the establishment, had not only been in the milling industry, but was closely connected to the South by family. His uncle, George Randolph, was a Colonel in the Confederate Army and later served Jefferson Davis as Secretary of War. In his autobiography, Coolidge writes disparagingly (as did many others) of the "vials of wrath [poured out]" in sympathy for John Brown by New England abolitionists Wendell Phillips and Ralph Waldo Emerson.

On the other hand, his brother, Sidney Coolidge, was a Major in command of the 16th Massachusetts Regular Infantry. Another brother, Algernon, Sidney's twin, was an acting assistant surgeon in the Hospital Service of the United States. Coolidge himself visited the front lines near Washington in 1861, but mentions no inclination to wear the uniform of Union Forces.

In 1863, then a battalion commander, Sidney was killed at the Battle of Chickamauga, part of the Western campaign. After a successful skirmish with the rebels, his unit was attacked near Bird's Mill and all but wiped out. Missing in action, his body could not be found, but a sword given him earlier by his brother Thomas Jefferson Coolidge, was finally returned to the family by a Confederate Brigadier. After Sidney's death, Coolidge writes that to avoid serving with the Union Army, "I paid seven hundred and eighty-five dollars for a substitute..." Actually, this was quite common in the North and well accepted at the time.

But why this reluctance to join the military? An admirer of Edward Everett, the great orator who served as Governor Massachusetts and as President of Harvard, Coolidge admits in 1865 that he agreed with Everett who "took the unpopular side" and endeavored to prevent the Civil War by counseling moderation, peace and justice.

"I had the same views," he adds,"and voted against the Republicans on the Whig side and after the end of the Whigs on the Democratic. But looking back I am convinced I was wrong. The country could not get on with slavery and the white men reared amidst slave institutions. Civil War could not be prevented and the country could not be saved except by suffering."

On April 3, 1865, Richmond fell to Union Forces and on April 9, Lee formally surrendered to Grant at Appomattox. After the war, Coolidge traveled in

Dedicated in 1887, this early photo from Union Street and Chapel Lane shows Manchester's Public Library around the turn of the century. The gift of summer resident Thomas Jefferson Coolidge in memory of those from Manchester who served with Union forces during the Civil War, half the building was devoted to Headquarters for the Allen Post, Number 67, G.A.R. Indeed, the structure was christened "The Memorial Library and Grand Army Hall." Coolidge, a Boston financier, also served his country as Minister to France and as a member of the Pan-American Commission. Note the two-story Franklin house on the Town Common to the right of the Congregational Church. Home for a retail store, it was razed with a neighboring structure in 1909.

Sons of Union Veterans, Allen Post 67, Grand Army of the Republic, pose for a formal photo in front of Manchester's Memorial Library around 1900. At that time many veterans of the Civil War were in their 60's. At far right is Manchester's first full-time Chief of Police, Thomas O.D. Urquhart. The police officer on the left may be Patrolman Leonard Andrews who, in 1902, was named the department's first Sergeant. His grandson, Police Sergeant Neil Andrews, follows in his footsteps today.

121

Europe for three years, returning to become Treasurer of Lawrence Manufacturing Company. Like many wealthy Bostonians, the Coolidges preferred to spend their summers elsewhere and in 1869, they occupied Nathan Appleton's house in Lynn.

'A WILD PROMONTORY'

Family Purchases the Goldsmith Farm at What Is Soon Called Coolidge Point

Four years later they purchased for $12,000 the old Goldsmith Farm on Millett's Neck just east of Kettle Cove and began to build "a country house at Manchester-by-the-Sea on a wild promontory surrounded by the ocean" which today is known as Coolidge Point. Of simple wood clapboard, the three story structure looked westward into the setting sun. It was in sharp contrast to the impressive elegance of the "Marble Palace" built in 1902 by his son T.J. Coolidge, Jr.

Coolidge was now also a Director of the Merchants Bank of Boston. Daughters Nora and Sallie were in the Boston Public School system and the family was well pleased with the quality of their instruction. On January 2, 1874, to celebrate Sallie's birthday, the Coolidges and "a large party" of 26 people took the train to Salem. There they boarded sleighs and "drove to my house at Manchester...The young men slept in the upper, and the girls in the first story. The weather became so warm that many of the men bathed in the ocean and both sleighing and skating came to an end, so we had to drive the girls in ox-carts to the station on our way home [to Boston]."

In July of the following year, Coolidge was appointed a member of the Boston Park Commission and, with his fellow commissioners, spent many days on horseback "laying out all of the parks around Boston" accompanied by planner and landscape architect Frederick Law Olmsted of Brookline. Included were parks along the Charles River and around Jamaica Pond.

By this time, Coolidge, who had also served for a short period as President of the Atchison, Topeka & Santa Fe Railroad, had done well enough in business to consider philanthropy. And in 1884 he announced a gift to Harvard College of $115,000 to build what was christened Jefferson Physical Laboratory, feeling "that no better use could be made of money than to facilitate in the college the teaching of physics..." Two years later,

in 1886, he writes, "I gave my adopted town, Manchester-by-the-Sea, a public library."

The idea had first come to him while listening to the town's librarian, Dulcea L. Bingham, Jr., coincidentally grandson and namesake of one of the founders of Manchester's Lyceum, cite the need for a new library building at the annual meeting of the Elder Brethren. "These gentlemen, as you know," Coolidge declared at the dedication of the new building, "console themselves once a year for being over fifty years of age, by eating chowder and making speeches. At this meeting, my friend Mr. Bingham made an impressive appeal for a new library building and a Memorial Hall. The words sank deep in me, and...I made up my mind to assist whenever the Town came to the conclusion that such a building ought to be erected."

What is interesting in view of Coolidge's political philosophies during the Civil War is that fully half of the new building was devoted as a memorial to those citizens of Manchester who served with Union forces. Indeed, it was christened at its dedication "The Memorial Library and Grand Army Hall at Manchester-by-the-Sea." It was also Headquarters of the Allen Post, Number 67, G.A.R., named in honor of brothers Isaac F. Allen and William H. Allen, as well as Edward F. Allen and Benjamin Allen. All four from Manchester had died during the War of Rebellion, Isaac at the Battle of Antietam, William and Edward as prisoners of war in Richmond, and Benjamin of wounds in a hospital at Washington.

In a most distinguished and successful career in public service as well as finance, Coolidge went on to serve as a member of the Pan-American Commission which recommended ways in which commerce between nations in the New World could be improved for the benefit of all; and as Minister to France from 1892 to 1893 during the last years of the administration of President Benjamin Harrison. He represented the United States with great distinction both as a diplomat and as an expert in international economics. While he was there, the French were involved in their unsuccessful attempt to build a canal across the Isthmus of Panama. He also defended American interests in the Bering Sea.

Upon his return home, Coolidge was appointed by the Governor of Massachusetts to a special committee to consider the issue of steadily rising state and municipal taxes. He was also considered a candidate for Secretary of the Treasury. In 1898, he was asked by President McKinley to serve on a Joint High Commission to settle disputes between Canada and the United States involving the fisheries; shared boundaries, especially in Alaska; and cross-border transportation of goods. Founder with his son of The Old Colony Trust Company which later merged with the First National Bank of Boston, he died in 1920.

LEGENDARY ARCHITECT
Memorial Library, Designed by Charles Follen McKim, Keeps Good Company

Another great figure who was responsible for the creation of Manchester's Public Library was its architect, Charles Follen McKim. Coolidge and McKim were friends, perhaps in part because the younger McKim in 1885 had married Mrs. Coolidge's niece, Julia Appleton. Born in Chester County, Pennsylvania in 1847, McKim was son of a Presbyterian minister who was a prominent abolitionist and one of the founders of the New York Nation. For one year, he studied at Harvard and then left for Paris and the Ecole des Beaux Arts from which he graduated with a degree in architecture in 1870. Returning to New York City, he was employed in the office of architect Henry Hobson Richardson (best known hereabouts for his design of Trinity Church in Boston) before forming a partnership with William Rutherford Mead. In 1879, with the arrival of Stanford White, the firm became McKim, Mead & White. It was the architect of many distinguished buildings.

These include in our vicinity only, Boston Public Library; Symphony Hall; with sculptor Augustus Saint-Gaudens, the Robert Gould Shaw Monument opposite the State House on Beacon Hill; Harvard University's School of Business Administration; Weeks Bridge across the Charles River; Harvard's Freshman Union; Robinson Hall, once occupied by Harvard's School of Design; the Algonquin Club on Commonwealth Avenue; many Class Gates around Harvard Yard; Radcliffe College gym and, again, with sculptor Augustus Saint-Gaudens, the statue of the Reverend Phillips Brooks on the grounds of Trinity Church at Copley Square. Obviously, Manchester's own Memorial Library and Grand Army Hall, a small but very distinguished design by McKim, keeps excellent company. It is also interesting to note that T. Jefferson Coolidge, Jr., fellow member

with McKim of the Pallachucola Club, employed McKim, Mead & White in 1902 to design his own summer dwelling, the "Marble Palace" at Coolidge Point. It was torn down in 1958.

One of the founders of the American Academy in Rome, McKim won international fame during his lifetime both in the U.S. and abroad. He received a Gold Medal in 1900 at the Paris Exposition and was awarded the King's Medal of the Royal Institute of British Architects in 1907. His personal life, however, was filled with sadness. Divorced from his first wife Annie Bigelow in 1878 after only four years of marriage, seven years later, as mentioned above, he wed Julia Amory Appleton of Boston. Tragically, 19 months later, Julia died in New York City and is buried at Mount Auburn Cemetery, Cambridge. McKim never married again but in later life became very close to his only child and daughter from his first marriage, Margaret. At meetings which he, of course, attended regularly, it is said he "was often observed fingering or contemplating the [wedding] ring he always wore—a circle of gold with two hearts [intertwined]."

The building he designed for Manchester is a gem. It's exterior of Ashlar granite with a natural seam face is said "to be French in character," according to a bulletin published on its 100th anniversary, "and the vaulted roof of the reading room to have been suggested by the twelfth century library at Merton College, Oxford." McKim was always one to embrace art in his designs and the Appleton and McKim coats of arms are carved directly above the archway leading to the stacks. Appropriate inscriptions appear in the woodwork as well and, as a surprise, the architect added a gift of his own. It is a window of exquisite quality which he himself designed, executed by world renowned artists Maitland Armstrong and Louis C. Tiffany. Its inscription reads: "In grateful acknowledgment of the munificence and public spirit of T. Jefferson Coolidge, his fellow townsmen have set this window."

'THE HONORED DEAD'
Building Is a Shrine to Those Who Gave Their Lives for Freedom

Speaking at the ceremony dedicating the library on October 13, 1887, Coolidge talked about the value of books, their role in expanding knowledge, and the importance of education. Then once again, honestly and openly, he also addressed his own relationship with the war which for four years had torn the country apart. "But this building is meant for other objects [as well]," he said. "We wish to commemorate the dead, the honored dead, who went forth when liberty was at stake, when the country was in danger, and endured the terrible hardships of war to the bitter end. I stayed home. I look back to it with regret; but my brothers joined the Union Army, and one of them laid down his life at the Battle of Chickamauga. His name stands engrossed in Memorial Hall at [Harvard University in] Cambridge.

"Like Cambridge, the Town of Manchester has not made the names of her sons illustrious by putting them in marble; they were illustrious before; but she has always shown that she appreciated her children and deserved to be the mother of heroes.

"The other room in the building," he continued, "is reserved for the soldiers who came through the war without losing their lives; and the best we can do, as long as they live, is to give them a comfortable room where they can meet to talk over old stories, to shoulder the crutch, and show how fields were won, and to assist one another by sympathy and good feeling."

Presenting Samuel Knight, Chairman of the Board of Selectmen, with the deed to the property and keys to the building, he concluded: "Please accept [them] as a sign of the affection I bear your sea-girt town, and of a desire to return the kindness I have met from all of you. I hope it may prove an incentive to study, that our children in acquiring knowledge may, at the same time, learn from its walls lessons of devotion and patriotism."

Although many words were spoken that day, none were more warmly received or better appreciated.

OLD GLORY

G.A.R. Post Members, Library Trustees Battle Over Whether to Fly the Flag

The story below comes from information wonderfully pieced together by Carl Triebs from letters of summer resident Thomas Jefferson Coolidge at the Massachusetts Historical Society; from minutes of meetings of Allen Post 67, Grand Army of the Republic at the Manchester Public Library; and from the pages of The Manchester Cricket. Former Treasurer of Manchester Historical Society, Triebs is known for his wide knowledge of Manchester's role in the War of the Rebellion.

It was nearly civil war all over again in March, 1892, as members of Manchester's Allen Post 67, Grand Army of the Republic faced the Board of Trustees of the town's Memorial Library.

At issue was whether the G.A.R. Post should be able to erect a pole and fly the American flag in front of the then five-year-old library building which also included Post Headquarters.

As one grizzled veteran expressed it: "There are 212 G.A.R. Posts in Massachusetts with 24,000 members and the Allen Post is the only one without a flag." Others recalled that they had followed the Nation's colors into battle and that many had died to preserve the Union which it symbolized.

To add another note of patriotism, it was proposed that a spar salvaged from the wrecked U.S. Revenue Cutter ALBERT GALLATIN which had gone ashore on Boo-Hoo Ledge that very year in a winter storm could be used as a flag staff. Best of all, it could be purchased from its new owner for $20.

But library trustees were unanimously opposed. Speaking for the board, summer resident Thomas Jefferson Coolidge, whose generosity had made the library, G.A.R. Memorial and Post Headquarters possible, wrote Post Commander Edward P. Stanley. "The question of putting up a flag staff in front of the library building is a question of judgment as to the effect on the building," he said in part. "...the...building in Manchester is copied from an ancient Norman library. It is true that a part of it is occupied by a Post of the Grand Army, but the outside effect was not meant to be military but literary and cloistral.

"With the greatest respect for the Post and for the flag of our country, you would not, I am sure," he continued,"propose to put up a military flag staff in a cloister of a convent. The flag staff would [do] great architectural injury to the building. It would jar the artistic feelings of all people. I have spoken to many who have the same opinion and I hope therefore that the Post will kindly consent not to put it in front of the library building, and by library I mean the whole structure..."

To support the trustees, Coolidge appealed to architect Charles Follen McKim for his opinion, but the Post stood firm and tensions grew.

By September, 1892, numbers of letters had been exchanged and Post members decided to appeal to the "citizens of Manchester," first with a petition and later with an Article in the Warrant at Town Meeting in March, 1894. Meanwhile, the

Post Quartermaster was authorized to purchase GALLATIN's foremast. (For more about the loss of GALLATIN, see REFLECTIONS.)

It was also suggested as a compromise that the flag be placed "near the end of the building" or behind it. But Post members would have none of it. "Our motto," they cried "is 'Flag to the Front!'" At Town Meeting in March, 1894, the issue was on the Warrant and remarks were exchanged like rifle fire on the battlefield.

Major Russell Sturgis, one of Manchester's most beloved senior officers, again stated his objection to flying the flag in front of the building. "I would like to ask the gallant Colonel of the 45th," Post Commander Edwin Stanley replied, "if the colors were ever at the rear? If they were, the Stars and Stripes and the building didn't amount to a snap. [Besides,]" he added, "there's as much beauty in the flagstaff as in the scrub tree there now."

Not all members of the Post, however, were in favor of the flag. Wounded Union veteran Julius Rabardy, who lost a leg at the Battle of Antietam, supported Coolidge's point of view and "thanked God he did not belong to the Post." Others expressed themselves in favor and opposed. Finally, the matter came to a vote. It was defeated, 61 to 56.

ULTIMATE VICTORY
Stars and Stripes Finally Raised; GAR Vets Win Their Battle for the Flag

As the smoke cleared and forces withdrew, additional meetings between parties led to a compromise in June, 1894. According to its minutes, the Post would be allowed to place the pole on the ground at the western end of the building. Evidently, no action was taken for three years. Then by March, 1897, the issue was again before Town Meeting. Thirty-four signatures were submitted on a petition in favor of the flag. Eighteen were members of Allen Post 67.

Once again, the battle began. This time the Post was victorious, 78 to 54. But at a meeting of its own later, it was agreed that without a unanimous vote of its members, the matter once again should be tabled. At the next meeting that same month, however, a committee of five was finally appointed "to superintend the making and erection of a flag staff in front of G.A.R. hall."

By July, 1897, "the staff was in position" and at sunrise on the morning of the fifth, the day following the holiday, Post minutes show that "the Stars and Stripes were raised thereon for the first time." Salutes were fired. There were other "patriotic exercises," and G.A.R. veterans celebrated with what must have been somewhat reluctant enthusiasm. The battle had been won but at what cost to the personal feelings not only of the donor of the building itself, but to the sensibilities of many others in town.

As Carl Triebs concludes, "At this time, I don't know when the flag staff was removed…Probably after 1927, when the the last G.A.R. member died…Minutes of the Post meeting in December, 1918, refer to an expenditure of $2.25 for repairs to the flag staff, so we can assume it was still in place at that time."

Today, peace reigns supreme on Union Street in front of the Library. And youngsters, who for years have enjoyed sitting on the wall, will now know about one of the final skirmishes of the War of the Rebellion which took place right here in Manchester.

WITH LAND, HE HAD A 'MIDAS TOUCH'

One of Manchester's earliest summer residents, Dr. Cyrus Augustus Bartol, minister of Boston's Old West Church, and his wife rented here for many years prior to the Civil War before building a home of their own at Glass Head. A great booster of the town with an uncanny eye for real estate values, Dr. Bartol purchased large portions of Smith's Point, all of Norton's Point and Tuck's Point which he later sold at a significant profit. On the land he also had built a number of sizable dwellings. These were first rented and then sold for seasonal use.

AN EARLY BOOSTER

Summer Resident Reverend C.A. Bartol Loved Manchester, Invested in It

Of all those interested in the establishment of Manchester as a summer resort, no one was more perceptive that the Reverend Cyrus Augustus Bartol.

Born in Freeport, Maine, in 1813, he was a graduate of Bowdoin College (1828) and in 1835 of Harvard Divinity School. A year before his marriage to Elizabeth Howard in 1835, he joined the Old West Church, Unitarian, on Cambridge Street in Boston (still standing today) as Associate Minister with the Reverend Charles Lowell. After Lowell's retirement, Bartol served as minister of the parish for more than 50 years.

Widely known and respected for his eloquence, scholarship and charm, he was an ardent abolitionist and leader in the Transcendental movement made popular in part by poet and essayist Ralph Waldo Emerson. Always a progressive, he was described as a "reverent radical, standing aloof with his church from all ecclesiastical entanglements by the flag of individual freedom of religion." His list of publications including sermons is prodigious. In 1859, he was awarded the degree of Doctor of Divinity by Harvard University.

A summer resident of Manchester for many years, staying first at Dame Cottage on Proctor Street, and later with the Crowell sisters at 21 Union Street, Cyrus Bartol finally purchased in 1870, a sizable portion of shorefront in West Manchester known as Glass Head Pasture which included what is now Tuck's Point west to the railroad bridge.

There on the bluff he built for himself and his family a three-story Victorian shingle-style house with a studio for his artist daughter Elizabeth, and an observation tower with a staircase to the top where, in a cozy room, he could survey not only his own holdings but the outer harbor, the islands and much of the surrounding countryside.

What caught his eye, however, was not only the beauty of the landscape, but its value as a most attractive site for seasonal housing. Perhaps with an eye to investing for retirement as well as a love for the land itself, in 1871 he purchased for $600 an acre, some 75 acres at Smith's Point which, after a few years slowed by the Panic of 1873, he readily sold to newcomers moving east from Nahant and Boston for nearly twice what he paid for it. He also acquired Little Ram Island, House Island and soon afterwards, in 1872, Norton's Point as well for $1,225, mindful of the fact, as he is reported to have told a parishioner, that the Lord created only so much shorefront property.

In 1895, he sold Tuck's Point to the town for $5,000 and an adjoining wharf for an additional $1,000. Later that year, the wharf and an accompanying strip of land, bought from the town, became the site of the Manchester Yacht Club.

In a number of cases, too, Bartol built houses for rental income such as the River House, the Moorings and the Fort House at Norton's Point. All three were designed by architect Arthur Little and built by Roberts & Hoare. The Moorings has been magnificently restored by its owner and was the star of a series of "This Old House," a television program regularly featured by public broadcasting station WGBH in Boston. A rebuilt portion of the River House is also still standing.

Besides his financial interests, Bartol was a genuine booster of the town and he convinced at least some of his friends and flock to settle here. Among them was celebrated author, editor and publisher, James T. Fields, who with his wife Annie built a home atop Thunderbolt Hill.

When Bartol first visited Manchester in 1842, the town, as he wrote in The Boston Advertiser, was "slow, sleepy, like a poppy gone to seed, only a little farming and fishing, with a few furniture factories being left. The old wharves [at] which once scores of schooners had landed mackerel, were rotting away. Earthworks thrown up against the British [during the War of 1812], had long borne not guns on their borders but spears of grass. Now by rail some 30 trains come and go each day for passengers and freight requiring a double track. Twenty houses crown the chief headland which half a generation ago was a wilderness of rock and bog, sand and bramble and barren waste."

During the last half of the 19th century, Cyrus Bartol helped as Manchester transformed itself from a simple coastal village to a thriving residential summer resort. As for his own involvement in land acquisition and development, seemingly inconsistent with the goals expected of the clergy, he did his best to explain it to his parishioners shortly after the 50th anniversary of his pastorate. His remarks appeared in a Boston newspaper with his obituary in 1900.

Brought up as a country lad in Maine, he said that he honestly loved the land and enjoyed the

The River House at Norton's Point was built in 1883 for Reverend Cyrus A. Bartol. Designed by architect Arthur Little and constructed by Roberts & Hoare, as were its two neighboring dwellings, The Moorings and The Fort House, it provided rental income until all three were sold. Famous for his success as a real estate investor, Dr. Bartol, minister of Boston's Old West Church, Unitarian, on Cambridge Street, also owned land at Tuck's Point and at Smith's Point. Double-ended launch at the dock flies the burgee of the Manchester Yacht Club founded in 1892. In 1895, the house was rented by J.H. Holmes, Editor of The Boston Herald. It was then sold to Walter Eaton of Boston who, in 1897, sold it to Conover Fitch, owner of the Waltham Watch Company. Mr. and Mrs. Fitch added a wing to the house doubling its size. Like so many of the great houses, the structure was modified following World War II.

128

healthy pleasure of working it "mowing, pitching hay, moving rocks, handling the ax, hedgebill and crowbar, trimming trees, cutting away thistles and bullbriers."

Although his neighbors locally and friends in Boston feared he had paid too much for properties and that his financial ruin would be the result, he said, in part, in the often intricate, indirect and formal language of the time, "None of my critics knew (and I did not tell them) what I was after; not my fortune but my life, in no act of which have I ever been more moved by a power above my own will…I am not entitled to credit for the sagacity…which I was charged with having shown…giving in charity [has] always consumed more than twice or thrice the sum of my salary…the prosperity which only by social influence and the prevailing need for purer than city air had been reached…furnishes no occasion for regret on your part. [And] on mine, no deep calculation or piece of good luck, but a gracious providence [and] relieved mental stoppage…Blessed be business, all of it I have had!"

REWARDING HOBBY

Dr. Bartol Loved His Dealings in Real Estate; Many Houses Still Stand

For 18 years, from 1872 until the year he died, Bartol was involved in real estate speculation with remarkable results both physical and financial. It was he who made possible the construction here of many of the great houses of the time. Although a devoted cleric, well respected for doing God's work, he must have also enjoyed bargaining with native landowners, dealing with building contractors, and profiting from his many ventures.

Others, too, were aware of the increasing value of real estate in Manchester, and in the nineteenth century, moved to acquire it as an investment. One of these was Boston financier and long-time summer resident, Henry Lee Higginson, hero of the Civil War and owner himself of Sunset Hill which he had built in 1878 in West Manchester. Higginson purchased wooded land in the vicinity of Jersey Lane listing it in his wife's name. A portion of the property later became Appletrees, an estate owned first by Girard Bement and later by Mr. and Mrs. Stephen Van Rensselaer Crosby.

With the filling and development of the Back Bay, the Old West Church lost many of its members. It could still be proud, however, that among the children who attended its Sunday School were Louisa May Alcott, later author of Little Women, and Charles William Eliot, who served for years as a great President of Harvard University.

Cyrus Augustus Bartol died in 1900 at age 87 leaving Glass Head in Manchester to his daughter Elizabeth. Sadly, the Old West Church closed its doors as a house of worship soon afterwards. An Asher Benjamin building (the architect, a disciple of Charles Bullfinch, designed the church in 1805), it was thankfully preserved and later revived as the West End branch of Boston Public Library. Then in 1964, with a newly-built city library only doors away, religion returned. The First Methodist Church of Boston which had merged with the Copley Religious Society acquired the structure and today "the congregation practices the heritage of civil and religious activism that is common to both United Methodists and the Old West Church's historical traditions," many of them established by the Reverend Bartol.

JEFFREY'S CREEK

A Story of People, Places and Events in the Town That Came to Be Known as Manchester-by-the-Sea

READING, WRITING & ARITHMETIC

STORY HIGH SCHOOL 1926

MAY 14

Story High School students posed for this picture on May 14, 1926. The high school building was located on Bennett Street at the top of the hill and was approached with a granite staircase which made a perfect grandstand for the photo. First used for educational purposes in 1874, the structure was added to in 1909 at a cost of $3,000. Another addition, this time significantly larger than the original school house, was completed in 1927, one year after this photo was taken. It cost $70,000. Abandoned and boarded up, Story High was torn down in 1953 and the land sold for residential use. Students moved to the former John Price School at Brook Street and Norwood Avenue where they remained until the new Junior-Senior High was built in 1962.

SCHOOL DAYS

In 1696, Two Schoolmasters Are Chosen to Teach Children in Manchester

Since its beginnings, leaders of the Massachusetts Bay Colony placed education high on their agenda. For Puritan New England, the ability to read was only a start, for it was believed that everyone should not only have personal access to the Bible but be able to understand and digest the lengthy and intricate treatises and sermons written and preached with weekly regularity in every parish in the region.

In 1647, the Great and General Court of the Commonwealth of Massachusetts ordered that in every town of more than 50 households, someone should be appointed to teach children to read and to write. When the community's population exceeded 100, the ordinance called for a grammar school to be established to "instruct youth so farr as they may be fited for [a] university."

In 1696, Town Records in Manchester show that John Siblee, Robert Leech and Thomas West were selected to choose a "Schoolmaster to teach our children to read & to wright..." (Obviously, early spelling differed from that used today!) It was a pay-as-you-go proposition, however, as each child was charged 5 [pence] per week to help meet the cost of the master's salary, "no more than 20 Pounds per yere."

All this changed in 1724. That year it was agreed that "ye town should be taxed ten pounds yearly...for the support of a free school..." Public school education for every child, boy or girl, had become one of the highest priorities of the Colony and inevitably, as time passed, both teacher salaries and tax assessments increased to meet the needs of a growing community.

In 1736, the town voted to support four schools. They were located at Newport, as West Manchester was then known; near the Meeting House downtown; at Plains, now the site of the Crowell Chapel; and at Kettle Cove, where the Dutch Bowl restaurant was once located. The Cove School was later moved to the corner of Forest and Summer Streets and was called Rowe School. Each was in its own district and each district was responsible for its school. It could raise the funds necessary to operate it. It could also own the building and the land upon which it stood.

Following the Revolution, in 1785, it was "Voted to Build a school hous...21 feet wide and 26 feet

Longe with an upright Chamber...where the old school hous Now Stands..." The first building to be devoted solely to education, it was sold in 1818, and moved to School Street near Saw Mill Brook, where it became a private dwelling.

That same year, it was decided to build another school house with one half to be paid for by the town which was to "become proprietors of the lower part," the other half to be paid for by the "district" which, as a corporation, was "empowered to hold property for the use of the schools." As Lamson writes, "the building was located on School Street on the site of the present engine house..." Awkward, cumbersome and divisive, the district system was abandoned in 1851 and all schools became the exclusive property of the town.

Following the War of 1812 and the growth of American shipping, there was a huge demand for education in seamanship and navigation. An independent vocational school devoted to this purpose was soon established in Manchester by Stilson Hilton, a resident "noted for his mathematical and nautical knowledge." It was a great success and many of the more than 40 Masters of merchant vessels who lived in town received classroom instruction at Hilton's academy.

By 1848, "a High School...for the benefit of the whole town" had been established. A High School System, much like ours today, also replaced the old "district system" which had provided unusual autonomy and authority for each school district. The first sizable and significant building devoted to education in Manchester was constructed in 1890. An impressive structure four stories high, located on Washington Street between North Street and Norwood Avenue, it was named for Dr. George A. Priest, a much-beloved member of the School Committee from 1868 until his death in 1888. Its facilities out of date, closed and deemed a fire hazard, the building was razed in 1954.

HIGH SCHOOL

Bennett Street Building Opened in 1874; Named for Much-Beloved Physician

The new high school, according to Reverend Lamson, was quartered in what was admittedly "not a new building" at the top of Bennett Street although its view of the inner harbor was impressive as were its surrounding stone walls. Opened in 1874, it was expanded extensively, first in 1895 and

Coach Tim Averill (center) with Sarah Gannett and Zach Leber, members of the debate team at then Manchester High School who in 1987 were undefeated winners of the National Forensic League Championship as well as winners of the National Tournament of Champions at Lexington, Kentucky. Today, Sarah is an attorney and public defender; Zach is a scientist and engineer involved in improving instrumentation for laser surgery.

Story High School (grades nine to 12), located on Bennett Street at the top of the hill, was opened in 1874 in an existing building. It was expanded extensively first in 1895 and then in 1909 to make room for a division of commercial studies. Finally, an addition much larger than the original building was constructed in 1927. Named for Dr. Asa Story, a long-time and much beloved member of the School Committee, it was razed in 1953. Photo courtesy of Betsy Sinnicks, a member of the Class of 1941.

then in 1909 to create a division of commercial studies. Finally, an addition much larger than the original building was constructed in 1927. Somewhat belatedly in 1895, it was named for Dr. Asa Story, also a longtime member of the School Committee, and was always known as Story High School. Obsolete and abandoned, it, too, was razed in 1953.

Voters at Town Meeting approved the construction of another school building in 1905. Located at the corner of Norwood Avenue and Brook Street, it was named for "Master" John Price (1808-1895), a much-respected educator whose methods of teaching and administration set new and improved standards in the Town of Manchester for many years. When the Bennett Street building was abandoned, Price School became Story High and served as such until the present high school was built in 1962. A handsome structure for which, after every consideration, no practical use could be found, it was torn down in 1965.

CHANGING SCENE
Growth Calls for New Schools After WW II; Then in 1999 We Regionalize with Essex

Memorial Elementary School was erected in 1950 following World War II as a new influx of residents arrived and Manchester began to grow as a community of commuters and a suburb of the City of Boston. Both Memorial and Manchester High have served the town well.

For more than 40 years, the town has discussed and debated the concept and the wisdom of establishing a regional high school at times with Ipswich, with Hamilton and Wenham and with Essex. Finally, in 1999, it was decided by voters at Town Meeting to join hands with Essex whose students now attend what has become Manchester-Essex Regional High School in Manchester and studies are underway which will lead to the construction of a new joint high school building.

DEBATE TEAMS
For Three Decades, Our Students Have Won Wide Honors Here & Abroad

Manchester has always prided itself on the quality of its education for both boys and girls and many students have gone on to attend the nation's top colleges.

Of particular excellence has been the High School Debate Team. Organized in 1971 by then newly-hired faculty member Tim Averill, it has won numerous national and international honors.

Interscholastic debate is directed by the National Forensic League which chooses debate topics annually for participating schools around the country. The topic this year, for example, deals with mental health. The secret to debating, as Averill explains, is research and the process must be thorough enough to enable team members to anticipate any argument their opponents may present. Participants are taught to produce rapid-fire arguments in favor of their contentions, a style of delivery that judges already approve of and understand.

Only in the so-called Lincoln-Douglas debates does oratory play a major role. There, too, speakers deal more philosophically with such topics as "when in conflict, the letter of the law should be more important than its spirit." A new debate series is named for Ted Turner, founder of CNN broadcast news, who provided its initial funding. Encouraging controversy, Turner debates tackle such topics as the use of affirmative action in college admissions, and limiting the amount of jury awards in medical malpractice cases.

All of this heady activity at Manchester-Essex High School is directed by Averill who also teaches Advanced Placement English and is head of the department. Bright, articulate, and deeply devoted to his subject and to his students, he is a midwesterner, a graduate of Topeka West High School where he was a member of the debate team, and of the University of Kansas. Migrating east, he received a master's degree in teaching at Harvard University's School of Education in 1971 and that fall joined the faculty at Manchester. In 1981, while on sabbatical, he also earned another master's degree in communication studies while at the University of Massachusetts at Amherst.

In his years here, he has helped the program grow from a club activity into what is now a credit course and a well-accepted part of the curriculum. Why has Manchester's debate team been such a success? As Averill explains it, "we have a lot of dedicated students, an excellent talent pool. We also receive unqualified support from the administration and from parents."

The record certainly proves it. In 1979, Charlie Brown and Martha Cutter reached the finals in competition in a tournament at the University of

Town House built in 1818 was located on School Street approximately where the Fire Station is today. One of Manchester's most ubiquitous structures, the Town House served as a school; as quarters for the Lyceum, the town's first library and lecture hall; as a storage garage for early pump fire engines (above); and, until a new Town Hall was built in 1868, as quarters for the Board of Selectmen. Sold to Samuel Knight in 1891, it was moved across the Channel to Elm Street. This photo was probably taken in the 1880's.

Massachusetts. In 1984, Hugh Bethell was the first debater to qualify for the Nationals. In 1985, Manchester finished second in the National Catholic Forensic League (NCFL) championships at Fort Lauderdale, Florida.

In 1987, team members Sarah Gannett and Zach Leber were undefeated winners of the National Forensic League Championship (NFL) as well as winners of the National Tournament of Champions at Lexington, Kentucky. In addition, Andrea Marston and Kirsten Bolten won trophies at TOC and at NCFL.

The following year, Gretchen Crosby won the National Lincoln-Douglas round-robin at Nashville, Tennessee. Four years later in 1992, Manchester represented the United States of America at the World Debate Championships at London, England, and Colleen Melia was Manchester's "first triple ruby" in the NFL.

With debaters all scoring well in national contests year after year, in 1998, Sarah Halpern-Meekin was chosen second place speaker at the National Tournament of Champions at Lexington, Kentucky. And in 2000, Pam and Celia Kiely celebrated the new century by winning the international debate tourney in Athens, Greece. (International debates are conducted in English.) Finally, last year, 2002, Matt Everett was victorious at the Harvard University Invitational Tournament and took part in the National Tournament of Champions.

Like many things in life, excellence in debate demands long hours of commitment and often weekends as well. "We start in September," says Tim Averill, and end in June. Support both from the school budget and from our annual appeal for charitable gifts, allows us to travel," And travel they do, around the U.S. to Atlanta, Chicago, Lexington, Kentucky, Washington, DC and, on special occasions, abroad. The schedule for the academic year 2002-2003 includes an amazing 41 separate competitive events. "Just getting to all these places is a challenge," adds Averill. "It often means 12 to 16 hour days."

All of this, of course, is an education in itself. One of the highlights, according to Tim Averill, while in Greece in 2000, "was sharing a bus for four days with Russian students while we drove around the Peloponnesus. It was a wonderful way to get to know each other and to learn about our two countries."

As for the outstanding youngsters who take part in the program and benefit from its remarkable learning experiences (as Averill says: "it prepares kids to be awesome college students"), they ultimately enter such distinguished fields as medicine law and education. Martha Cutter, for example, earned her Ph.D. and is now teaching at a college in the mid-west. Sara Gannett attended law school and is a public defender, providing legal representation for the needy. Zach Leber graduated from both Harvard and M.I.T. and is engaged in designing a comprehensive program for laser surgery.

Not all debaters, of course, have such unusual records. But with 20 percent of Manchester-Essex High School students taking the course, its benefits reach far out into the school community, offering everyone involved opportunities to learn to think critically and analytically, and to speak and write well.

Manchester can be enormously proud of the accomplishments of its debate teams. For a small school, it has won itself wide recognition and acclaim around the nation and, indeed, the world. Tim Averill has loved every moment of it, certainly one of the measures of his extraordinary success as organizer and coach. But in a few years, he retires. Hopefully, Manchester can find someone equally able to carry on its winning traditions.

For a small school, Manchester has also excelled in sports particularly under the legendary leadership and outstanding coaching of Joseph M. Hyland. Many times champion of the Cape Ann League, Manchester has won State-wide titles in football, basketball, baseball and tennis. A heady record for a small town. (See separate chapter.)

In basketball, field hockey, softball and tennis, Manchester's girls have also distinguished themselves with Cape Ann League Championships, an undefeated basketball team, and many invitations to State Tournaments where they have finished as semi-finalists and finalists. In tennis especially, individuals and teams have starred. Little League Baseball which started in 1952, and Youth Soccer, which began in 1979, have been major contributors to the quality of Manchester athletics.

Since Stilson Hilton's school for navigation, there have also been notable independent institutions of learning in Manchester. One "for the reception of pupils of both sexes" was established in 1836 by educator Master John Price who first taught in the public school system here for five years. Students paid $4 a quarter for tuition, 60

Rowe School at the corner of Summer and Forest Street, 1848 to 1927. Once called the Cove School, it was one of Manchester's four district schools authorized in 1736. The building was moved from the site of the former Dutch Bowl Restaurant on Summer Street. Residents of each school district raised funds necessary to support their school. Cheever photo courtesy of C.A. Fritz, Jr.

Cows graze in a field bordering the roadway in this photo of Summer Street at the junction of Magnolia Avenue taken around 1900. The building is the Cove School which was sold in 1932. Note that both streets have yet to be paved. Photo from the Frances L. Burnett Collection.

Built originally in 1905 to provide primary education for grades K through two, the Price School was named for legendary teacher "Master" John Price (1808-1895). When its Bennett Street building was vacated, Story High was moved to the Price School building at Norwood Avenue and Brook Street until the present high school was constructed in 1962. A handsome structure, the Price School was razed in 1965.

Named for a much-beloved member of the School Committee who served from 1868 until his death in 1888, the George A. Priest School was located between North Street and Norwood Avenue. An impressive, four-story structure built in 1890, it was the first building of its size in Manchester to be devoted to education. It facilities out of date, and deemed to be a fire hazard, it was razed in 1954.

cents a year for fuel and 15 cents a quarter for paper, pen and ink.

THE INDEPENDENTS
Brookwood School Established in 1956; Landmark Comes to Town in 1972

By 1885, according to Katharine S-B. Abbott, author of the chapter entitled Independent Schools which appeared in the 350th anniversary yearbook, Price's school, then in new quarters and a co-ed boarding academy, had an enrollment of 66 boys and 51 girls. Many were the sons and daughters of long-time Manchester residents. The Chapel School, as it was known, drew students from Salem, North Andover, Methuen, Roxbury, and Tamworth, New Hampshire, Price's home town. Two were from San Francisco, one from Santa Domingo and another from Latin America, sent to Manchester not only because of Price's reputation as a schoolmaster but also to escape the fevers common to tropical climates. Room and board, Abbott writes, "came to $176, so, in total, a student's tuition for the year was about $200."

One of the students at The Chapel School, a youngster from Cuba named Ernesto Miguel Machado, remained here after graduation, married a ward of John Price's brother, and, as a well-respected architect in Salem, designed the original structure built for the Manchester Yacht Club. In 1872 at age 64, Price decided to close his school and retire. He had taught some 1,700 children from all over the world. Active in town affairs, John Price served as a Deacon of the Congregational Church, as a member of the Board of Selectmen and of the School Committee, as Town Treasurer and, from 1830, as a member of the Essex County Teachers Association. He died at age 88 in 1895.

In the 50 years after World War II, with a new generation that increasingly saw young mothers and fathers both in the work place, there was growing demand for small, independent nursery schools. Mrs. Barrier's Play Group was started by Mrs. Louis J. (Agnes) Barrier in 1947. Marcia McDiarmid's Shore Nursery School opened its doors in 1953. In 1962, Rita Sullivan and Elinor Halloran established The Little School. Alice Newman also ran a preschool for some 30 years retiring in 1989. And in 1973, a group of young parents, anxious to become involved themselves in their children's pre-school education, founded Magic Years Cooperative Nursery School. A year later, Tara Montessori nursery school opened utilizing facilities of the Parish House at Sacred Heart Church.

In 1956, Abbott continues, "a [number] of North Shore parents agreed that an independent elementary school was needed in the immediate area..." It was to be more accessible than Shore Country Day School in Beverly founded in 1936. Villa Crest stables located in West Manchester and once part of the 36-acre estate of Walter D. Denegre which had been purchased by Mr. and Mrs. Charles B. Rimmer in 1949 was acquired in 1956 to house the new institution. It was christened Brookwood after the appealing name of its entrance roadway. Initial enrollment was 65 students. Philip Cutler, founding Headmaster, had taught at St. George's School in Newport, Rhode Island. In the early years, he, his wife Rose, who was a member of the faculty and coached athletics, and George and Renee Moniz, who took care of the buildings and provided lunch for attending students, were the mainstays of daily life at Brookwood.

Today, the school's enrollment totals more than 350 students ranging from pre-kindergarten through eighth grade. Forty-four full-time faculty members and 16 interns from Leslie School in Cambridge provide instruction in the classroom and coach sports which utilize the school's now extensive indoor and outdoor athletic facilities.

In 1972, following the death of Mrs. Charles B. Rimmer, the house at Villa Crest and some 20 acres of land was sold to Landmark School. Known as the North Campus today, it is used for elementary and middle school education. Landmark acquired another property in Manchester in 1976, thanks to the generous gift of Elsinaes, an imposing dwelling on Bridge Street and Highland Avenue once owned by Miss Elsie Hooper. Established in 1971, Landmark grew out of the Reading Research Institute of Berea, Kentucky and the Learning Disabilities Foundation of Massachusetts. Today it is attended by more than 300 students from ages 8 to 20. Its academic program "emphasizes achievement rather than grade placement." With a teacher-student ratio of one to three, and an average class size of six pupils, its curricula are designed to meet the needs of dyslexic children. A major portion of the campus of Landmark School is located in Beverly. The Hooper house solely provides living quarters for faculty.

FOREIGN EMBASSIES COME TO STAY

NORTH SHORE □ ☐ BREEZE □

Handsome dwelling at 47 School Street was the home of Charlotte Brown whose popular Brownland Cottages were located on Old Neck Road. In 1910, the house was rented to become summer headquarters for the French Embassy. In 1911, this photo of it appeared on the cover of the <u>North Shore Breeze</u>. The issue was dated Friday, April 7.

SUMMER HEADQUARTERS OF THE FRENCH EMBASSY FOR 1911
The Brown Cottage on School Street, Manchester

COOL BREEZES

Before Air Conditioning, Diplomats Flocked Here to Enjoy Manchester's Climate

By 1900, American foreign policy had gone from indifference and isolationism in the early 1890's, to engagement and expansionism. The war with Spain had ended in victory and with the acquisition of Cuba, Puerto Rico, Guam and the Philippines, the United States had become a world power.

In 1905, in the then most decisive naval battle in history, Russia would lose more than half her fleet to Japan and peace would be negotiated by President Theodore Roosevelt at nearby Portsmouth, NH. A year later, France and Germany were at odds over North Africa and once again, Roosevelt stepped in to force a settlement. Thanks to the President's initiatives, the U.S. also would complete the Panama Canal, a waterway linking the world's two great oceans. Roosevelt would be followed in the White House by William Howard Taft and Taft by Woodrow Wilson. And in a scant 14 years since the start of a new century, few could have predicted that Europe would be plunged into the darkness and horror of a World War.

Meanwhile, in the early 1900's, in this new era of internationalism for America, the North Shore of Boston, and particularly the Town of Manchester, became a welcome haven and retreat not only for such Presidents as Taft and later Wilson, but for scores of representatives of foreign embassies who made Manchester their summer home. Indeed, by 1910, 20 of the 39 European and other countries whose Ambassadors were accredited to Washington, had summer headquarters in Manchester or Magnolia.

Built in a reclaimed swamp beside the tidal Potomac River, Washington, DC, was all but uninhabitable during the hot months of the year and, like flocks of birds winging their way north, ambassadors, consuls and legation secretaries as well as embassy staffs and household retainers, came, seeking the quiet life, sea breezes (the only air conditioning of the day) and a dip in the cool and refreshing waters of Massachusetts Bay.

One of the primary attractions for foreign dignitaries here was the Masconomo House, a rambling, 230-foot, three-and-one-half story summer hotel with accommodations for 300 guests and a gorgeous water view. Built by producer and actor Junius Brutus Booth and his wife Agnes in 1877, the Masconomo House offered fabulous food and entertainment, tennis and billiards, and swimming at beautiful Singing Beach.

To this halcyon spot in June of 1899, fleeing the coming heat of nation's capitol, came the new Minister from Spain to the U.S., Jose Brunetti y Guyoso, Duke D'Arcos, and his wife the Duchess, Virginia Woodbury, an American woman and the only daughter of wealthy Archibald Lowery of Washington. Here for the summer, they rented one of the cottages at Masconomo House.

Familiar faces on the streets of the town, the Duke and Duchess had fallen in love while he was First Secretary of the Spanish legation 25 years earlier. The romance was not an easy one. Despite a distinguished lineage as both Marquis of Zahra and of Cadiz, and his obvious success as a career diplomat, the union was opposed by her family. It, too, could claim a celebrated ancestry including a member of President Andrew Jackson's cabinet and a justice of the Supreme Court. Finally, 18 years after the couple met and fell in love, her mother died and her father relented. The two were married at the Lowery family's summer house in New London, Connecticut. And the Duke, who had persisted in his love for nearly two decades, came from his post in Mexico, and was at last united with his American bride.

In between his correspondence and other duties to his government, the Duke, a handsome giant of a man with a magnificent beard, spent a portion of every day at the Essex County Club learning to play golf. Much in demand at social occasions, the Duke and Duchess formally opened the summer fair at Sacred Heart Church and were asked to every fashionable party in town. The couple and their entourage spent a delightful three months here (they returned for a number of summers, renting one of the Brownland cottages as well) and word soon got back to others in diplomatic circles that Manchester had a special charm all of its own.

That same summer of 1899, Jules Cambon, Ambassador to the U.S. from France, was in Cambridge to receive an Honorary Degree from Harvard. As guest of Henry Lee Higginson, he visited the Colonel's summer house at Sunset Hill, West Manchester, and was immediately captivated by its surroundings. The next year, France, too, would be added to the list of legations in Manchester. Perhaps learning about it from the Duke, Senor Azpiros, Ambassador to the U.S. from Mexico with

A montage from The Manchester Cricket in 1901 features the Minister to the U.S. from Spain, Duke D'Arcos, upper left, and, clockwise, one of the Brownland Cottages which served as summer home of the Spanish Legation; Duchess D'Arcos, wife of the Minister from Spain; and a photo of the imposing Spanish Embassy at Washington, DC.

One of the greatest attractions for foreign diplomats in Manchester was Singing Beach. This early photo shows a viewing pavilion which was located behind the bathhouse for guests of the Masconomo House. Dwelling at Eagle Head in distance was originally built in 1869 and was once owned by summer resident U.S. Senator from Michigan John McMillan.

his embassy staff, was also an early summer resident of the town as were the Russians. And thus began the parade of diplomatic representatives to a small, seaside community on Boston's North Shore. For The Manchester Cricket it meant delicious and never-ending opportunities to write about the activities, arrivals and departures of foreign notables. Most of the information here comes from The Cricket's pages.

By 1904, 11 foreign ambassadors had moved to Manchester for the summer. Besides the Masconomo House, its cottages and Miss Charlotte Brown's Brownland Cottages on Old Neck Road, which could accommodate up to 70 persons, there were houses to rent from wealthy families who had gone to Europe for the summer or who were travelling elsewhere. And then there were those who simply moved out of their homes to make money by leasing them, often for as long as from June to October. Legations and embassies through the years were a movable feast, occupying one house one summer and moving to another the next, whatever became available to rent. Many, however, were fortunate and were able to stay put in a favorite location for a number of years.

Nor were oceanfront mansions necessarily the most popular. Many diplomats such as Count Quadt, First Secretary of the German Embassy, who chose a house at 2 Windemere Park as his headquarters, were happy to be downtown and more a part of the local community. During the summer of 1901, when Ambassador Herr Von Holleben was abroad with his family, the Count took his wife to Italy and returned, as The Cricket put it, "to set up bachelor quarters" in Manchester.

Number 2 Windemere Park and number 6 were also occupied at one time by the Russians: Prince Nicholas Kondachef, Charge d'Affaires; J. DeThal, Gentleman-in-Waiting to His Majesty the Emperor of Russia and Second Secretary of the Embassy in Washington; Baron M. Kroupensky; and Naval Attache Mr. Vassilieff and his wife. The Italians, too, fancied Windemere Park and occupied number 4 with the Marquis Negrotto Cambriosa in residence, and number 10 with Charge d'Affaires R. Berghetti.

The German legation was located at one time at 112 School Street. And in 1910, The Cricket reported, Ambassador Count Von Berstoff was invited to speak on "German University Life" at the 114th commencement at Union College,

Schenectady, NY, where he also received an Honorary Degree.

The French, too, once summered at 89 School Street, later moving for some three years to the handsome dwelling at 47 School Street built in 1897 by Roberts & Hoare for Miss Charlotte Brown, proprietor of Brownland Cottages, and lived in today by Chris and Alice Nahatis who have owned the property for more than 50 years. By necessity, many members of embassy staffs lived elsewhere. For example, Oliver Taigny, Secretary of the French Embassy, Naval Attache Viconte de Faramonde, and Juan Roano and L. Pastor of the Spanish legation, were all at the Masconomo House.

In 1901, the Hemenway estate's Stone Cottage on Masconomo Street housed the British Embassy with Hugo Charteris, Honorary Attache, and George Young, MVO, Second Secretary, in charge. Later, however, the British Ambassador decided to summer at Newport, Rhode Island. In less than two decades, his successor would return to Manchester. Meanwhile, most other legations chose to move to or remain on the North Shore.

A cottage at Smith's Point was home one year to Ambassador and Madam Nabuco of Brazil. In another, it served as the German Embassy with Charge d'Affaire Haniel Haimhausen and his wife in residence. The elegant house at the corner of Beach Street and Ashland Avenue was home to the Argentine Embassy and Charge d'Affaire Jacinto L. Villagas.

LOTS OF ENTERTAINING
French Embassy Hosts a Dinner at Misery Islands Casino; Dinner Dance at Essex

Houses all over town provided shelter for representatives of foreign nations. The residence at 52 Bridge Street, also owned for nearly 50 years by Charles and Jane Gardiner, was home in 1913 for Baron Charles Freudenthal of the Austro-Hungarian Embassy, while His Excellency, Ambassador Dr. Constantine Dunba and Madam Dunba, occupied "River House" overlooking the harbor at Norton's Point, for years now property of Ann W. Brewer. More than a decade earlier, a second cottage on Bridge Street had been rented to the Austro-Hungarian legation, L. Von Callenberg, Charge d'Affaire, and his colleague Baron L. Ambrozy.

Another montage in *The Manchester Cricket* in 1901 shows from lower left, clockwise, Countess Quadt and baby, wife of the First Secretary and Hostess at the German Embassy; residence of the German Embassy in Manchester; Madame de Margerie, wife of the Secretary of the French Embassy; Senor Del Viso of the Argentine Republic; resident of the French Embassy in Manchester; Count Von Montgelas, Third Secretary of the German Embassy; and Count Quadt, First Secretary of the German Embassy.

In 1887, Manchester was a small town much beloved by embassy personnel of all ranks and stations. This view from Ocean Hill shows Jeffrey's Creek (foreground), railroad tracks and freight cars and, very prominently, the Congregational Church. House at lower right, 25 Tappan Street, known as the "Swiss Cottage," was built in 1872 for Mr. & Mrs. Henry A. Wetherbee of Boston.

Many of the choices involving where to rent and how lavish a life to lead here were related to economics. Although representatives of France were ensconced at a cottage on School Street, it was reported by The Cricket that "Ambassador Jules Jussier and his American wife are not expected to join the gaities this summer [as] they have no private fortune. France," The Cricket continued, "pays less than any other nation for the honor of maintaining an Embassy in America which makes extensive entertaining impossible."

Money, however, did not stand in the way when the French Embassy's Monsieur Potalis chose to host a dinner at Misery Island Casino for members of the Russian, Italian and German delegations. The first dinner dance of the season at the Essex County Club, according to The Cricket, was "a brilliant gathering with the club house taxed to capacity. Not only were there beautiful flowers and electric lights in red, white and blue, but all the important people [were there] including Captain D.S. Vasilief of the Russian Embassy [whose] table for 15 [was decorated] with Killarney roses and bunches of sweet peas at each plate.The German Embassy [also] had a table for 15 with three bouquets of mixed flowers. Among Count Wedel's guests were the French Ambassador, Count Portalis, Baroness Richofan, Italian Charge d'Affaire Paolo di Montagliari and Mrs. Horstman."

One windy day at Singing Beach, The Cricket reports, Italian Charge d'Affaire Montagliari and his Secretary, Roberto Centarro, used their wits and their strength to rescue two persons whose small boat had capsized in choppy waters and were in danger of drowning. The community hailed them as heroes.

By 1911, representatives of France, Italy, Germany and Russia had become a regular part of Manchester's summer colony. Legations from Persia and Siam occupied houses in Gloucester. Ever peripatetic, the British had moved once again, this time to Bar Harbor, Maine. They were accompanied by the Austrians, the Greeks and the Dutch. And by 1912, the Turkish Embassy had returned to the corner of Bridge and Harbor Streets to what is now the Old Corner Inn.

Throughout the "embassy era," the social scene must have been hectic. Parties were a babble of foreign tongues. English was spoken in stores and other establishments with a dozen different accents. And the town was filled with people of rank and title who were used to getting their own way. As Frank Floyd, legendary Town Clerk, Representative to the General Court and owner and operator of Floyd's Store, recalls in his history, Manchester-by-the-Sea, published in 1945, even the children of diplomats were demanding.

"It was a Sunday morning, and then, as now," he writes, "the New York papers were received in separate sections which had to be assembled before they could be sold. The Catholic Mass let out about the same time as the papers were received. Up to the front door appeared a fine span of horses drawing a victoria, in which was the Argentine Ambassador and his family. Out jumped his son; in he came on the run and said, 'I want the Ambassador's paper,' to which my [father] replied that it was not ready yet. 'But I must have the paper,' he repeated and again Dad said, 'I'm sorry but they are not ready yet.' Again, the boy said 'the Ambassador is waiting and must have his paper!' This was too much for my father and he wheeled around, looked right at the boy and said: 'I don't give a God damn if the Ambassador is waiting; put your ass on that stool and wait until I get ready to give you the paper.' The boy sat down!"

Somehow Manchester kept its sense of humor and perspective and survived. Of course, the legations provided merchants and the business community with lucrative seasonal returns. Demands for services, food and beverages were high and there was much employment to be had about town. But when fall came and the community was returned to its regular citizens, at least in some circles there must have been heard a sigh of relief.

SUMMER OF 1914
Shadow of World War I Darkens Embassy Life in Manchester; A Few Still Remain

In 1913, representatives of all the Great Powers, Germany, Austro-Hungary, Russia, France, Italy and England were in Manchester for the summer. British Ambassador and Mrs.Colville Barclay had rented a cottage at Smith's Point. But by the summer of 1914 the era was over. Serbian nationalists had assassinated the heir to the Austro-Hungarian Empire and World War I had begun.

To be sure a few legations remained. Plenipotentiary of the Argentine Embassy Roumbo S. Naon and Madam Naon were at "Windcliffe" on upper School Street, and as the U.S. was not yet at war

In 1905, Russian Ambassador Baron de Rosen spent a portion of the summer at Coolidge Point where he rented what was long known as the Marble Palace owned by T. Jefferson Coolidge, Jr. Baron de Rosen, who was appointed to succeed Count Cassini, previously served as Consul General at New York and as charge d'affaires at the Embassy in Washington during the first administration of President Grover Cleveland. He also served as Russian minister to Mexico and Japan. 1905 was not a good year for Russia. It was defeated by Japan's Admiral Togo in an epic naval battle at Tsushima Strait. Many Russian warships steamed halfway around the world to defend Port Arthur only to be sunk in a major fleet action. It was the end of the Russian Navy as a power in the Pacific.

The peace conference at Portsmouth, New Hampshire, in June 1906, following the Russo-Japanese War was attended by a "special correspondent" from The Manchester Cricket. Representing the Czar and the Russian government was Sergius J. Witte, pictured above, who The Cricket reported, "is a large man with bushy gray whiskers and very kind and attractive blue eyes." Arranged by President Theodore Roosevelt, who was later awarded the Nobel Peace Prize for his efforts, the conference took place at the Hotel Wentworth. Manchester's Masconomo House had earlier been discussed as a possible site but it was finally considered too small to house all those attending the event. Many Russian diplomats summered in Manchester during those years.

Staff members of the foreign embassies that moved to Manchester, and not a few Ambassadors and their wives, lived at the Brownland Cottages on Old Neck Road. Owned and operated by Miss Charlotte Brown, and a short walk to Singing Beach, they were immensely popular and could accommodate 70 people. Miss Brown also owned and had built by Roberts & Hoare in 1897 the handsome house at 47 School Street which for some three years she rented to the French embassy.

with Germany, General Consul Oswald Kunhardt resided at 92 School Street representing both his country and Austro-Hungary.

Kunhardt's story is unusual. He subsequently left employment as a diplomat and, with an office in Boston, became a representative of Berlin Analine Works, a New York corporation. When war with Germany finally was declared in 1918, he lived year-round in Manchester. However, now, still a German citizen, he was an enemy alien. And one hot July day when he returned on the train from Boston and unsuspectingly headed for a swim at Singing Beach, he was apprehended by Manchester Police Chief William H. Sullivan and told that he was wanted by the Justice Department. He was jailed and later sent to Washington where he was to be interned for the remainder of the war, sent home, or released. (See REFLECTIONS.)

THE CURTAIN DESCENDS
World War I Ends the Embassy Era; A Few Trickle Back in the 1920's

The war effectively ended migration of the diplomatic community to Manchester until the mid-1920's. Then, according to Who's Who on the North Shore, published annually for its readers, it was announced that the British were back in force. "The Embassy offices are located in the E.G. Black house in Manchester," the book declared showing a photo of the property. "Ambassador Esme Howard [is] making his home in Prides Crossing." Commander Harold A. Brown and family, Assistant Naval Attache, and Secretary of the British Embassy, Herbert W. Brooks and family, rented a house at University Lane. Military Attache Colonel C.E. Graham Charlton and Mrs. Charlton were at Windemere Park. Dr. and Mrs. Z.B. Adams were at Thunderbolt Hill and His Britannic Majesty's Minister to the U.S., Henry G. Chilton and Mrs. Chilton were at 38 Sea Street.

In June, 1926, The Cricket reported that Ambassador Howard and Lady Howard were back at White Lodge off Forest Street. Polish Minister to the United States, M. Jan Ciechanowski occupied a cottage in West Manchester. In 1928, the Howards returned again as did Ambassador Ciechanowski. Swiss Minister Marc Peter and Mrs. Peter had a house at Manchester Cove and later rented what was the Daniel Slade house on Allen Avenue.

And the new German Ambassador to the U.S., Friederich Wilhelm Prittwiz, returned, surely with some nostalgia for a happier past, to "The Hedges" on Old Neck Road. By 1929, only Herr Dr. O.C. Kiep and the German Embassy with no address, were listed in the North Shore's Who's Who. Those busy and wonderfully cosmopolitan pre-war years were gone forever.

Today, air conditioning makes living in the nation's capitol comfortable in every season and there is no need during the months of summer for legations to move to cooler climes.

Some of the information for this story of the "embassy era" was taken from a paper presented to the Manchester Historical Society in 1979 by Agnes Barrier. She credits an "anonymous" MHS member for the research and writing and she adds a personal note. In 1927, she says, no activities of any embassies were reported. "However,' she adds, "I have first-hand knowledge...that the British Ambassador and his wife resided at the Smith house at the corner of Beach and Masconomo Streets.

"A nice-looking, blonde young man was associated with the Embassy...I made every effort to meet him and four years later [we were] married." That "blonde young man" was Louis Barrier (actually of French ancestry) who for many years served the town as a member and then Chairman of the Board of Selectmen.

AMERICA: A LAND OF OPPORTUNITY

In 1937, attorney Edward Morley of Manchester was only five years out of Harvard Law School when he was appointed Justice of the District Court in Gloucester. A descendent of contractor Austin Morley, who with Dominick Flatley built Sacred Heart Church in 1907 as well as many other buildings throughout the town, Judge Morley was celebrated for his wit and wisdom as Moderator at Town Meetings. For many years, he was the youngest justice in the Commonwealth.

THE AMERICAN DREAM

From All Over the World, People Have Come Here to Begin a New Life

With the exception of native Americans, who had developed a number of complex cultures and civilizations of their own, our country has been, and still is, a nation of immigrants who brought with them the beliefs, the values and the cultural traditions of the European, Asian, African and Latin societies in which they were born.

First to arrive with Columbus were the Spanish whose huge western empire ultimately spread south throughout the Caribbean and included all of Central and South America but reached only as far north in the United States as St. Augustine, Florida and Santa Fe, New Mexico. The English, on the other hand, chose a different route, establishing their claims on the continent with the arrival in 1497 and 1498 of John Cabot, an Italian navigator and explorer employed by King Henry VII, in Newfoundland, Labrador and Nova Scotia.

Members of what was to be the first English colony here arrived in Virginia in 1585. Captain John Smith's exploration of the east coast of North America, including Boston's North Shore, took place in 1614. Six years later, the Pilgrims landed at Plymouth. And the Great Migration, of which our region was the beneficiary, did not begin until 1630.

Those who came to New England first, inhabiting scattered fishing settlements along the coast, were primarily English Puritans and it was they who established the social environment of the area. But there were also French, Walloons and Flemish Calvinists, many of them skilled artisans and thus much in demand. There were Scots and Irish, too, Ulster Presbyterians, and others from England's West Country, who inhabited the coasts of Massachusetts, New Hampshire and Maine.

Fiercely independent, ambitious for material gain, conservatively religious and yet radically committed to self-government, these were the people who in time ignored inherited cultural traditions to create a new breed of men and women that came to be known as New England Yankees. And as time passed, theirs was the kind of society that drew thousands and ultimately millions of others from the Old World to the New.

Manchester's first significant growth in population came from 1800 to 1850, when 522 newcomers, most likely attracted by jobs in the furniture indus-try whose heyday was during that half-century, increased the number of year-round residents from 1,082 to 1,604. To be sure, there were native-born newcomers which added to the whole, but by far the greater number here, as in the nation, came from immigration primarily from abroad.

Manchester's second great period of growth took place from 1890 to 1915 when its year-round population increased from 1,789 to 2,945 or by 1,156 people. Not incidentally, it coincided with one of the greatest waves of immigration the country has experienced. In the 25 years before the beginning of the Great War in 1914, 18 million people, 80 percent from southern and eastern Europe, landed on the shores of the U.S. Seventy percent of these came through the port of New York and were processed at a new facility called Ellis Island which had been constructed in 1892. Four out of five of the new arrivals settled in the industrial cities of the northeast including Boston and among their first thoughts was how to get a job.

By 1890, of course, Manchester was well on its way to becoming a watering spot for the wealthy. It was the Gilded Age, and with these new seasonal residents who had significant levels of disposable income, came a rising demand for goods and services. This meant work in the building trades as carpenters, masons and plumbers, for new houses seemingly rising everywhere in town. At the great mansions there also was a continuing need for caretakers, gardeners, chauffeurs and domestic help, not only to operate the new households, but to maintain their surrounding landscapes, lawns and greenhouses as well as barns, horses and carriages.

Most important, there were opportunities, too, for newcomers from abroad, as well as for others in town and throughout the region whose families may have been here in different trades for generations, to now start businesses of their own—grocery, fruit, hardware and drug stores, meat and fish markets, blacksmith shops and later garages to care for America's coming obsession, the automobile.

This new generation of settlers, however, came primarily, as Mary C. Kirby explains in her wonderfully personal account entitled Immigrants which appears in the 350th anniversary commemorative publication Manchester-by-the-Sea, 1645-1995, from Canada—New Brunswick, Nova Scotia and Newfoundland, and from Europe—England and Scotland, Greece, Ireland, Italy and Poland.

Purchased in the 1920's by Peter Brown as a dwelling for his family, this building was located at 20 Beach Street, Manchester. The photo was taken around 1918. Its first floor was always devoted to retail space, a restaurant in this era, and when the top two floors were occupied by the Browns, tenants were Cunningham Paints and Marguerite Beauty Shop. The lawn south of the house and the depot itself later became the site of Brown's Market.

Spiro Brown and an unidentified youngster in his cowboy suit pose for this snapshot in front of Manchester Fruit Store at 11 Beach Street, the second establishment owned and operated by Peter Brown. The sign over the store advertises Krueger Ale and Beer, Groceries and Tobacco as well as Wines and Daily Papers. Boxes in front, displayed daily, were filled with fresh fruit. Next to the original store, this building was purchased in the late 1940's. Photo courtesy of Connie Brown.

Their names were Crane, Bradbury, Dawes, Forward, French, Snow and Thompson; Demarkis, Filias, Kassanos, Psalidas (which later became Brown) and Nahatis; Boyle, Burke, Coughlin, Duffy, Flatley, Guinivan, Halloran, Henneberry, Hyland, Kenneally, Lomasney, Morley, Noonan. Wogan, and Wynne; Ambrifi, Capello, D'Agostino, and Nataloni; Bialecki, Kraczynski, Krakowski, Maijenski, Stasiak, Tomasewski, and Wrobel; Cruikshank, Doig, Emslie, Goodall, Jaffrey, McDiarmid, and Morrison.

HORATIO ALGER STORY

Hard Work, Honesty and Perseverance Pay Off as Many Achieve Success

They were hardworking, patriotic, and appreciative, as earlier settlers had been, of the chance to make it on their own and soon were considered among the community's most valued citizens. Like thousands before them, they brought with them the best of values: a belief in the unity of family; in the role of religion and the church; in the need for education; and in the importance of honesty, integrity and commitment. With them also came a faith in America and the opportunities offered them by a free society.

What they accomplished themselves and what they enabled their children to achieve is reflected best in the inspirational tales of Horatio Alger, Jr. (1832-1899), whose hugely popular books for boys described how hard work and a commitment to personal discipline leads inevitably to fulfillment and success.

Certainly among those families who most clearly illustrate what Alger was writing about are the Pasalidases or the Browns. Born in October, 1890 in Manary, Greece on the Peloponnesos, the family patriarch, Peter Anthony Psalidas came to the United States in his teens and started work for his uncle in Boston selling fruits and vegetables from a push cart.

Urged to settle in Manchester by his cousin, James Voutritsa, who owned a fruit store here, he and his brother Charles helped to operate the establishment until in May, 1918, when, like thousands of other young men in World War I, Peter joined the U.S. Army serving in Germany until August, 1919. By then his cousin had died, sad victim of the flu pandemic which swept the country in 1918. But Peter was able to purchase his share and soon became sole owner of Manchester Fruit Store.

Earlier, as his daughter Connie describes it, "my father was playing cards and one of the fellows said 'now that you are in America you should change your name to Smith, White, Jones or Brown.' He chose Brown and his brother, who continued to call himself Psalidas, never forgave him."

Meanwhile, Peter had fallen in love and in October, 1920, at age 31, with a Greek Orthodox priest officiating at Horticultural Hall in Manchester, he married Anastasia Synodinos, 25, also born in Greece and on the Peloponnesos. Devoted all their lives, the couple ultimately had 10 children: Anthony, Connie, Betty, Thomas (Spike), Paul, George, Jennie, Ted, Spero and Katherine.

The newlyweds first lived at Morse Court, then in an apartment at 1-3 Summer Street. But in the late 1920's, Peter had saved enough to enable them to purchase a home of their own at 20 Beach Street. It was located where Brown's Supermarket would be 40 years later and it marked the beginning of a series of real estate acquisitions which eventually included most of the properties on the west side of Beach Street to the railroad tracks, and along the south side of Summer Street to the brick building once owned by Manchester Electric Company.

The depression years were not easy either for the rich or for those struggling to earn their way in a new world. Of course, it was all relative. Following the collapse of the stock market in 1929, William B. Walker of Chicago, owner of Manchester's largest estate, was forced to lay off help and at least temporarily halt construction of a series of new greenhouses. While attorney Albert C. Burrage of Boardman Avenue, whose investments in Chilean copper made it possible for him to raise orchids and own one of the 10 largest yachts in the country, decided to give up the private railroad car which he used each year to bring his family to Manchester for the summer.

But for Peter Brown and scores like him in town, the Great Depression meant seeking to supplement the income he received from his store by signing up for a second job with the Works Progress Administration, or WPA. A public works program proposed by President Franklin D. Roosevelt, it offered such employment as building and maintaining roadways or repairing dams and bridges. Times were tight for those without money. If the bills weren't paid, phone and electric light would be shut off until they were. But welfare was out of the question for Peter Brown. Money came only if you worked for it. And slowly, as the economy improved, he began to recover and then to prosper.

He proposed the establishment of a businessmen's association to encourage people to shop in Manchester. It won unanimous support from those who worked "downtown." Then, in 1939, he opened a second grocery store at 3 Lincoln Street where children Anthony and Connie were in charge. And from 1943 to 1950, he leased a store building at the corner of Hale and Lothrop Streets in Beverly. Started by Connie, it was run by Betty, Spike and George and sold fruits, vegetables and meats.

"We didn't make a cent at Hale Street," Connie explains with a laugh. "My father wanted the stores primarily to keep us working, off the streets and out of trouble." The flagship establishment, of course, was at 9 Beach Street in downtown Manchester. It offered shoppers fruits, vegetables, bread, milk, cheese and tobacco products. Later a soda fountain was installed.

THE DOOR OPENS
Purchase of the B & M's Railroad Station Clears the Way for Brown's Market

Before Peter Brown died in 1953, he had acquired the Blaisdell Building at 11 Beach Street, whose second floor was occupied by the Manchester Club. It was used for storage while he continued renting number 9. Ultimately, however, as he grew older and his children assumed more responsibility for the business, number 11 was turned into a modern market with a new storehouse in the rear offering not only fruits and vegetables but meat and poultry and even "self-service" which was growing increasingly popular at the time.

Also in the 1940's, anticipating the needs of his growing family, Peter purchased houses on School Street and on Norwood Avenue. They were later sold. But the big boom in real estate acquisition came while the children were in charge.

In 1958, thanks to careful planning, some quick action and a key personal contact, they were able to purchase the depot and the land surrounding it which had been owned and operated by the Boston & Maine Railroad. They leased a portion to the then Esso Corporation for 20 years. The remainder of the property finally opened the door to a

long-held dream: the construction of a modern supermarket with adequate room for parking which would serve the community for many years to come. Thus Brown's Market was born. It opened in 1964.

With it came property at 7 Summer Street where Home Style Laundry is now located. A portion of that building once housed a Chevrolet dealership which was situated on the site of the Post Office and moved to its present location. Numbers 15 to 19 Summer Street, now home to Nor-east Cleaners and the office of dentist Dr. Thomas M. McDuffee, was once at the corner of Summer and Beach Streets and was again moved to its present site.

In 1978, the family also purchased the Pulsifer Block at the corner of Union and Beach Streets, the largest commercial building downtown. Before 1940, it had housed the U.S. Post Office (the present structure was opened in 1939), First National Stores (a food market), Bullock's Grocery and the Manchester Trust Company (this portion of the building is now owned by another party) as well as a toy and dry goods store run by the Misses Haraden. Today the building is home to Manchester-by-the-Book, North Coast and a retail landmark, the Stock Exchange. Abutting it are numbers 7 to 9, the site of which is a new Italian restaurant named Circolo.

Next down the hill, 11 Beach Street, is occupied today by Beacon Investment Management, Syndex Systems, Jewelry by Mahri and CB & Associates, real estate, owned and operated by George Brown's son, Christopher. The original warehouse addition, built in 1953, is rented today by Notus Arts, antiques.

In 1979, the family purchased the Dow Block built in 1894, and with builders Desmond & Larcom, completed the town's first miniature mall which includes off-street parking and tenants Cape Ann Savings Bank, Mila's Beauty Salon, Video Viewpoint, Manchester Barber Shop, and Photo Stop.

In 1985, the family acquired the Kimball Block, a four-story apartment building with nine units at 46 to 54 Union Street. It had been given to the Manchester Historical Society to be added to its endowment, and was in need of lengthy legal work to clear its title. Once this was done, it was sold. On the east side of Beach Street, Paul Brown also owns the apartment building where his real estate offices are located.

Contractor Dominick Flatley arrived in the U.S. from County Mayo, Ireland in 1899 and formed a partnership with his uncle, Austin Morley. The pair built Manchester's Sacred Heart Church in 1907. Later Dominick operated his own business here which was responsible for the construction of many private dwellings and much stone work and road improvements related to public safety. Here he is with his wife Nora and their family in the mid 1920's. Children standing from left: Mary Elizabeth Flatley (Greely), John William "Nick" Flatley, Margaret Mary Flatley (Foley), James Joseph "Joe" Flatley. Children in front of their parents, again from left: Katherine Cecilia Flatley (Walsh), Francis X. Flatley (who tragically drowned in Manchester Harbor in 1928), and William Dominick "Bill" Flatley. In 1988, Dominick and Nora's granddaughter, Ellen Flatley, was appointed to succeed her cousin Edward Morley as Justice of Gloucester's District Court. Photo courtesy Flatley family collection.

Sacred Heart Church at the corner of School and Friend Streets was built in 1907 of Cape Ann granite, some from a ledge at Kettle Cove, by local contractors Roberts & Hoare and Morley & Flatley. The cornerstone was laid by the the Archbishop of Boston, William H. O'Connell and the Governor of the Commonwealth, Curtis Guild, attended its dedication.

With the children getting older themselves and now another generation in the offing, after nearly 40 years it was decided, in 1996, to sell the market. "After all that time," as Connie says, "it was very difficult, but it was the right thing to do."

Of all the properties, the one most valued sentimentally is the lot bordered by Beach Street and railroad tracks which is now a part of the parking area for what has become Crosby's Market. For it is what Peter Brown always called his "corner of America," long sought by a young man from Greece who came here in the early 1900's with little more than the shirt on his back, but with a dream. If he had only lived long enough, how proud he would be to see what his children have accomplished.

SACRED HEART

Catholic Church Is Testimonial to the Skills of Local Stone Masons

There were others, too, whose abilities and initiative enabled them to enjoy the opportunities America had to offer. Austin Morley and his nephew, Dominick Flatley, both of whom were stone masons in Ireland, established their own contracting business and were responsible in 1907 for the construction of Sacred Heart Church. Morley, later on his own, was also subcontractor for the stonework and foundation at Horticultural Hall which was completed in 1917.

In 1908 he built his own family a home using concrete block. It was said to be the first of its kind in the county. Other houses and office buildings followed. They included the old headquarters of The Cricket Press and North Shore Breeze magazine on Summer Street; houses on Vine Street and on Norwood Avenue and Brook Street; and the building at the corner of Tappan and Beach Streets. During World War I, Austin Morley was in charge of food production for Manchester's Public Safety Committee which meant responsibility for the success of Victory Gardens throughout the town.

Born in Lecarrow, Ballyhaunis, a village near the town of Knock, County Mayo, Ireland, either (the records vary) on August 8, 1876 or September 4, 1877, Dominick Flatley, then about 20 years old, sailed for the United States aboard the CAMPANIA arriving at Ellis Island on May 13, 1899.

After working in Manchester with his uncle Austin, he returned to Ireland, finally coming to the United States again aboard the same CAMPANIA in May, 1904. Two years later he became an American citizen. In a happy coincidence, his naturalization ceremony (during which, as a descendant emphasized with a smile, "he swore to uphold the Constitution and to abjure all allegiance to every foreign Prince and Potentate, particularly [to] Edward VII, King of the United Kingdom, Ireland and Emperor of India") took place in the very courtroom in Gloucester presided over later by his cousin the Honorable Edward Morley and now by his granddaughter, the Honorable Ellen Flatley, who, in 1988, was appointed Justice of the Gloucester District Court to succeed Judge Morley.

Meanwhile, here in the United States, Dominick met and married Nora O'Connell Flatley (no relation) who claimed kinship with Ireland's Daniel O'Connell, the great Liberator and author of the Reform Act of 1832 which allowed the Irish to worship in their own way and to enjoy the fruits of education, rights they had previously been denied. The couple had seven children. Sadly, the youngest, Francis, died at age seven in a drowning accident in Manchester Harbor in 1928. The six remaining, who grew to adulthood, all attended college.

After the partnership of Morley & Flatley was dissolved, Dominick continued as a contractor on his own. According to his granddaughter Ellen, "he built a number of houses in the village including the stone house at 34 Vine Street where his children were born, and the stucco house at 41 Vine Street where the family lived in later years. He also built, among others, the houses at 21, 37, 30 and 32 Vine Street, his office building at 44 Norwood Avenue, the stucco houses at 55 and 59 Norwood Avenue, and the three houses numbered 1, 3 and 5 Arbella Street.

"He did much stone work around town," she continues, "and road work that improved public safety including the relocation of Pine Street and the widening of Summer Street near Hickory Hill." As a municipal project, he also piped and filled land just north of Beach Street which was known as Jeffrey's Creek. "He stored his equipment and took gravel from 'Flatley's Pit' on Lincoln Street which is now the site of Manchester-Essex Regional High School. His barn was located behind his house on land [presently] occupied by Manchester's Memorial School."

"Dominick started out," Ellen Flatley adds, "in the era of horse and wagon [and progressed] through the age of steam to the age of internal combustion. In the early years, with a team of horses, he brought an enormous granite boulder from Black Beach to the village green which [today still] holds a bronze plaque honoring citizens of Manchester who served with the Union Army during the Civil War. With little formal education, [he] was marvelously well read, articulate and well informed. He was a good businessman and politically savvy, contributing regularly to both the Republicans and the Democrats."

Finally, in another delightful coincidence, Dominick Flatley's great granddaughter, Katherine Ellen Flatley, is scheduled to be married in October, 2003 at Sacred Heart, the church he so lovingly built 96 years ago.

In 1920, Charles Nahatis and his wife Johanna arrived in Manchester and purchased a house on Beach Street for $1,095. On pilings, it bordered Jeffrey's Creek where the family kept a dory. In the years before World War II, Charles owned and operated the Sugar Bowl Restaurant in the heart of town at 7 Central Street and later, Park Confectionary on Beach Street which did a land office business during the warmer months selling hot dogs, hamburgers and ice cream as people came and went to Singing Beach.

"There was a tunnel under the road in those days," recalls his son, Chris, and my brother Mike and I would row the dory through it to go fishing in the outer harbor. During the summer, schools of mackerel would often find their way up past the house and end up stranded on the flats when the tide fell. There, baked by the hot sun...well, you can imagine the smell, so the town set about filling Jeffrey's Creek.

"And we did our bit to help," Chris added. "In 1939, when the present Post Office was being built, Mike approached the contractor and asked him to put the excavated earth behind our house. He was delighted to be able to dispose of it nearby. We even used to collect the ashes from neighboring coal furnaces and dumped these there, too, until the area was finally filled in."

Today Chris Nahatis, a born salesman who began his marketing career at age nine peddling Zanol home products throughout town, is widely known and much admired as a star of television commercials promoting kitchenware made by Saladmaster. He joined the company in 1951 and recently celebrated his 50th anniversary as the nation's leading spokesman for its products.

62 BEACH STREET
Park Hotel Offers Visitors Proximity to the Pleasures of Singing Beach

One of the earliest settlers of Greek ancestry to come to Manchester was Nicholas Kassanos, who owned and operated the Park Hotel at 62 Beach Street facing Masconomo Park. There, during the summer months, families would come to stay to enjoy sunning and swimming at nearby Singing Beach. A sizable, three-story structure which housed the Kassanos family as well, the hotel was destroyed by fire in 1932.

Kassanos was also co-owner of the Olympia Restaurant located where Al's Cafe is today. He shortly sold his interest in the Olympia to his partner and opened another eatery, the Liberty, on School Street opposite Hooper's Grocery. "I remember as a kid I would go to the Olympia," Chris continued, "where they had a Nickelodeon [a coin-operated player piano]. It was a real antique!"

The Filias family, too, were in the food business. Bill and Charles owned and operated a grocery store on Brook Street and later, the Dutch Bowl Restaurant on Summer Street. Prior to World War II, it had been known as Dutchland Farms, a precursor to roadside chain restaurants such as Howard Johnson's which grew to be so popular after the war. Nick, the youngest, became a builder of custom homes.

Athas and Efthelia, or "Effie" Filias, first came to Manchester in the early 1920's. Charles was born here in a house at 50 Beach Street in 1926. Earlier, the couple, both from towns on the Peloponnesos in Greece, had met in Lowell where they worked for Boot Mills. (Mrs. Filias was paid $1.50 per hour for a 12-hour day.) They soon moved to Maynard where Athas went into business for himself, to Manchester for a few years, and then to New Rochelle, New York, to manage a hat-blocking establishment.

Finally, in 1932, according to Charles, in the midst of the Great Depression, they moved back to Manchester, opening a successful shoe shine and hat-blocking business in the Kimball Block. Those were the days when people wore hats—felt in winter and straw in summer—and there was money to be made in their care. The shoe shine parlor soon expanded to become Filias Variety. Then in 1952, Athas died. He was 57 years old.

Park Hotel owner Nicholas Kossanos, top right, poses with Chris Nahatis in sailor's cap and others for this photo in 1937 at Singing Beach. Front row from left: Zoe Nahatis, Nick Filias, Mike Savas, Spero Brown. Behind Spero are Florence Savas and Jennie Brown. Second row: Mrs. Mary Savas, Cynthia Savas and Bessie Kassanos. Photo courtesy of Chris Nahatis.

Seated at center, Peter and Anastasia Brown pose with their family about 1951. Standing from left, Betty, Anthony, Thomas (Spike), Paul, George, Jennie, Ted and Speros. Seated from left, Connie, Mrs. Brown, Mr. Brown and Katherine. Photo by Robert G. Crosby, courtesy of Connie Brown.

Of the family's six children, Mary, Gregory and Alex moved elsewhere. Bill, Charles and Nick all chose to stay in Manchester. Today, their eight children are here, too, three generations in all. Effie lived into her 90's, proud of her brood and grateful that, unlike so many others in America, her children and her grandchildren lived nearby where she could see them and they could enjoy her company.

As Mary Kirby explains, some newcomers with a green thumb operated the gardens and greenhouses of the great estates, while others branched out and established related businesses of their own. One of these was William Emslie who became a landscape contractor. Others were Austin Morley, Jr. and Tom Cagney who together owned Magnolia Nurseries.

Another, according to Mary, was Leonard A. Capello. Born in Cellara, Italy, he came to the United States as a young man, working first at the Dexter estate and later at the Essex County Club where he was greens keeper for 47 years. He and his wife, Eliza Francis of Gloucester, were the parents of 10 accomplished children. Growing up at Essex, two of the boys had outstanding careers as professional golfers. Mary married Allen Andrews, Chief of Police here for many years. Ida, who owned a dress shop, was the wife of Manchester's longtime Superintendent of Streets, P. Edward Sweeney. It was in her memory that funds were raised to light the steeple of the Congregational Church.

Lena Mary Costello owned and operated a restaurant "opposite the old cemetery" at 35 Summer Street, Manchester, from 1924 to 1940. An advertisement which appeared in the <u>North Shore Breeze</u> in 1939 described, "The Sign of the Crane" as a "quaint, old-fashioned house, famous for its home cooking." It offered, among other delectables, "a fine selection of table candies" and cakes from the Women's Educational and Industrial Exchange, Boston.

Charles, an Army veteran of World War II, was employed by the School and Highway Departments of the town. His son, Leonard, while a Captain in the U.S. Navy, was stationed in Italy, with a house overlooking the Bay of Naples. Remarkably, as Mary Kirby concludes, its view included the area where his grandfather was born.

The original arrivals who settled here from the 1890's to the 1930's worked all their lives to benefit their children, some of whom were able to attend college and graduate schools, entering the professions and establishing businesses. As parents and as new citizens, they also successfully stressed the importance of service to the community, to the Commonwealth and to the Nation.

Many of their children, like Captain (later Colonel) Vincent Crane, pilot with the Army Air Corps, awarded the Silver Star, Distinguished Flying Cross and Air Medal, served with great distinction as officers and enlisted men and women in the Armed Forces of the United States during World War II. A few gave their lives to defend the principles of freedom that had brought their families here in the first place. Among them was Watertender Third Class Tony Santamaria, Story High School 1941, who was killed by enemy action while his ship was engaged in battles leading to the U.S. invasion of Okinawa.

SERVING THE TOWN
Some Become Police and Firemen; Others Are Elected Selectmen

Others like Jim Mulvey and Bill Hurley, became policemen and firemen to protect their town and to insure the safety of their neighbors. Tom Cagney, Charles Filias and Ben Stasiak were elected and reelected Selectmen—Stasiak for 14 consecutive years, a record which still stands. (Second in longevity was Louis Barrier who served a total of 12 years.)

Some, like Assistant Town Clerk Margaret Morley, worked for the Town of Manchester in offices at Town Hall. Others were employed by the Federal or State government such as Postmasters Jake Greenberg and Jerry Noonan (also for many years Chairman of the Board of Assessors) and Fred Nataloni, former Club Captain at the Manchester Yacht Club who was later appointed the Commonwealth's Commissioner of Marine and Recreation Vehicles.

Edward Morley, a graduate of Harvard Law School, served with great wit and wisdom for many years as Town Moderator, as did Joseph Flatley. Frank Flatley, also an attorney, was elected to the Planning Board and became its Chairman. Attorney George Brown became Town Counsel.

Over time, the demographics of the town changed, especially after World War II when another wave of newcomers arrived to make

Manchester a year-round commuting suburb of Boston. But those who settled here from the 1890's to the 1930's became, in their own era, and later with their children, the heart and soul of the community. Summer people were transients; they were here year round. The government of the town was their government (seasonal residents were not eligible to vote at Town Meetings), as were the schools, fire and police, other municipal departments and most, if not all, of the businesses and trades which kept Manchester going. To be sure, they worked to build a better life for themselves, but in doing so they built a better community for all.

WORLD WAR I: THE YANKS ARE HERE!

Holding an American flag, U.S. Army Private Peter A. Brown of Manchester (left), stands with a pal for this formal studio portrait at the time of World War I. As "Carte Postale" appears on the back of the photo, it was probably taken in France. Peter joined the Army in 1918 and served in Germany until 1919. The ribbon worn by both men may be the World War I Victory Medal awarded to troops following the German surrender.

LUSITANIA SUNK

Draft Is Initiated; Citizens Buy Liberty Bonds; Home Guard Drills

War began in Europe during the hot summer of 1914. But by August, despite Germany's efforts to quickly conquer France, forces on both sides were dug in short of Paris. Trenches stretched along what was now the Western Front and the bloody stalemate had begun.

The Wilson administration was determined to keep America neutral but it soon found that impossible. First, thanks in part to British propaganda, it became clear to the public that under no conditions was it in keeping with the interests of the United States for Germany to win the war. Second, after the sinking of the liner LUSITANIA in May, 1915 with the loss of 128 American lives, Germany's pledge to wage unrestricted submarine warfare, the torpedoing of four unarmed American merchantmen, and finally, German efforts to enlist Mexico as a belligerent on its side, the President had had enough. On April 2, 1917, he successfully asked Congress to declare that a state of war existed between Imperial Germany and the United States.

In Manchester, Memorial Day in 1917 had a special meaning. Newspapers had carried continuing reports of the terrible slaughter of trench warfare. Union veterans of the Civil War were aging, but still very much alive and homage was paid to the town's war dead.

There were stories in <u>The Manchester Cricket</u> about how to register for the impending draft of men 21 to 35 years old. Initially, men with dependents were exempt. A sale of Liberty Bonds expected to raise $75,000 locally, doubled that to $150,000. An appeal for $3,000 for the Red Cross raised $18,000. With Americans idealistically in the war to secure peace and not territory, a surge of patriotism swept the country and marchers in July 4 parades all over Cape Ann had a new spring in their step. In August, at Tuck's Point, the Elder Brethren began their meeting singing *America the Beautiful.*

In July, President Wilson incorporated Massachusetts National Guard regiments into Federal Service and locally it was proclaimed the "Last Week of Grace for Slackers" who failed to enlist or register. To prepare for the war, Manchester's Company of Home Guard was issued new rifles and uniforms. In a local tragedy, all but two of a truckful of Home Guard members, returning from an encampment in Lynnfield, were injured as their vehicle left the road and turned over. By the end of August, there was happier news that Horticultural Hall on Summer Street opposite the the railroad depot had been completed. It was dedicated in a special ceremony attended by Lieutenant-Governor Calvin A. Coolidge, who later became Governor and then President of the U.S. Boardman Avenue resident Wallace Goodrich was Master of Ceremonies.

The beginnings of the Home Guard, according to Manchester's military historian Carl R. Triebs, go back to 1863 when Governor Andrews and members of the General Court realized the need for a replacement for the militia which had been called to active duty with Union forces. Disbanded in 1865 after the Civil War, units of the Home Guard, then known as the Massachusetts Provisional Militia, were reactivated during the Spanish-American War. Then in 1907, the Massachusetts Volunteer Militia formally became the Massachusetts National Guard. And in 1916, with the National Defense Act, the Guard was designated a reserve unit of the Unites States Army.

Again at the Governor's request, in April 1917, just before the U.S. entered World War I, the legislature re-established a Home Guard which could provide security locally when the National Guard was called to Federal service. Volunteers had to be more than 35 years of age with dependents, although men physically unfit for service with the regular Army could be younger. By July, 1917, 135 companies across the Commonwealth, a total of some 9,000 men, had been enlisted and equipped.

Manchester formed Company I of the 15th Regiment of Home Guard. Captain Alexander Robertson was in command, assisted by 1st Lieutenant John P. Corley and 2nd Lieutenant Allan P. Dennis. Home Guard units drilled weekly, Triebs explains, supervised by retired National Guard officers. One of their missions was also to provide pre-induction training for men ages 18 and 19. Units of the Home Guard, including the 15th Regiment, were mobilized during the Boston Police Strike of 1919. They helped enforce the law in Boston from September through the end of the year. When the Massachusetts National Guard was finally returned to state service in December, 1920, the Home Guard, once again, was deactivated.

Scores of local residents including children worked in Victory Gardens during World War I to grow food for local consumption. These fields were located northwest of School Street. Number 78 School Street is located at left behind the flag pole. Numbers 79 and 75 are across the street. Contractor Austin Morley, a member of the Public Safety Committee, was in charge of Manchester's Victory Gardens during the war.

At the time of World War I, Manchester members of the Home Guard in campaign hats and puttees pose for a photograph in front of the John Price School at Norwood Avenue and Brook Street. Manchester's Company I was a part of the 15th Regiment of Home Guard. In command was Captain Alexander Robertson. He was assisted by first Lieutenant John P. Corley and 2nd Lieutenant Allan P. Dennis. The Home Guard was probably equipped with old Enfield rifles. Springfields, then the standard rifle of the regular Army, were issued to troops of the American Expeditionary Force overseas.

PRESIDENT HERE

Wilson Visits Manchester; Many Young Men Have a Rough Voyage Across

On Cape Ann in September, 1917, excitement grew as the Presidential yacht MAYFLOWER docked at Gloucester. On board were Thomas Woodrow Wilson and Mrs. Wilson escaping the heat of Washington. From there the President was driven to Manchester to meet with his friend, aide and confidant Colonel Edward M. House who was vacationing at Coolidge Point. The next day, President and Mrs. Wilson played a round of golf at Essex County Club in a foursome with Manchester residents Mr. and Mrs. Randolph Tucker. They then joined the Tuckers for lunch at their home at Norton's Point where the Italian Gardens were a showcase of the North Shore.

Even before the U.S. entered the war, some Americans were in combat. One was Edward C. Goodrich, born in Manchester, who as a soldier in the British Army had been wounded in the back but was recovering in England. By May, 1917, too, 31 men from Manchester including a number of summer residents, had joined the services. One was Frank Amaral who was later to be the first resident killed in action. According to The Cricket, Gordon Baker was serving aboard the battleship USS VIRGINIA; T. Jefferson Coolidge, II and Russell Codman were training to become Army officers at Plattsburg, NY; Gordon Slade, William Francis and Roland Kitfield were with the First Corps Cadets; and John Allen was aboard the USS ALABAMA.

By November, 1917, others were in France. Throughout the war, Isaac Marshall, then Editor of The Manchester Cricket, published letters from servicemen to their families under the weekly heading "Manchester Boys at the Front." They provide an intimate picture of what life was like primarily in the Army. Chronologically, the correspondents report from basic training, from troopships crossing the Atlantic, from U.S. bases in England or France and, finally, from muddy and dangerous trenches on the Western Front. Knowing the value of news from home, Marshall also used to send The Cricket free to each Manchester boy in uniform both in this country and abroad. To those far from home, it meant a lot. During World War II, Harry Slade, Sr., then Editor and Publisher, continued the much-cherished tradition.

Letters usually began "Somewhere in France." Manchester's Dr. F.A. Willis wrote on October 17, 1917 that he and another officer were living comfortably with a French family, Madame and Monsieur Voilleaux, who treated them to dinner with wine and champagne. "We get a little military instruction, but our time is much our own. Tomorrow I go on as O.D. or Officer of the Day. I have full charge of the camp for 24 hours. Every morning has been taken up by censoring letters. At first it was interesting, but now it's tiresome. I am my own censor but, of course, I have to abide by the rules...we are not allowed to write any names of places, dates of arrival or anything pertaining to the war. I wish the war was over. Tell Fletcher McCullom I am with Lt. Mallonsen of Gloucester. He is connected with Ambulance Number 2. They are right near us."

On October 23, 1917, Manchester resident Harry D. Baker wrote to his mother. "All OK. Wasn't it fine that I should be on the same ship with Irving (his brother) and Walter Smith? I have made quite a few friends and find that Co. B is not so bad as I thought it was. We entrained from Westfield (Massachusetts) on October 4, carrying rations to cover the journey. We traveled all night with curtains pulled when going through towns and cities. [We] finally crossed a long bridge guarded by Canadian soldiers, detraining at the Canadian Pacific docks. We were marched into large sheds and very soon boarded the ship, being assigned 2nd class staterooms. Walter was not so fortunate as his [Company] H was put in steerage. About 7 o'clock Saturday morning we started down the St. Lawrence...and on Tuesday, about 9 a.m. dropped anchor in the inner harbor at Halifax.

"The next Sunday, October 14, we had our last look at America...when sailing by the English [Navy] cruisers in the outer harbor we were given cheers and [aboard] one, the band played the *Star Spangled Banner*. We soon lost sight of land... Later, several started to contract that strange malady seasickness and made frequent trips to the rail. As fate would have it, neither of us experienced it at all although Irving said he felt funny a couple of times...Toward the latter part of our journey we struck some very rough weather...At meal times on these rough days, things were doing. One table, at which 10 men were sitting, slid over to the wall wrecking the setting and covering the men with tea, etc. In walking along the passageways, first you were flattened against one side and then the other and in the berths you were rolled about. How I got through without being seasick was a wonder. We are now lying safe and sound in port, only across the pond..."

Gordon A. Slade, Ordinance Department, 101st U.S. Engineers, American Expeditionary Force, wrote to his brother in Manchester obviously again from "Somewhere in France." "We get very little real news of the war except from soldiers home on leave. One thing they do say is that the Yankee is a d--- good fighter. Conditions here are much worse than in England. Most all of the people are in mourning...they are one brave race...you never hear them complain and they are fighting for their very souls..."

The Baker family, with two sons in the Army, Sergeant Harry D. Baker, Company B, 104th U.S. Infantry, and Sergeant Irving Baker of Company A of the same regiment, were generous with their news. On October 25, 1917, Harry wrote: "we are now at a Rest Camp in Southampton [England] but it doesn't live up to its name for me anyway. I worked all night with the cooks to prepare rations for the [train trip] the next day...We travelled through the rolling country...the inhabitants are either very old or very young. Everyone [in England] has a sad, determined look. America does not realize what they are going through over here. We passed factories where women in overalls do men's work. Women also run the cars...We are now at a YMCA and all the others writing at this table are Tommies [English doughboys]...we expect to [move again soon]..."

PARLEZ VOUS?

Oh, for a Little High School French! Letters Tell About Life in the Army

Harry's next letter is from "a small French village...We expect to be paid [shortly]. It seemed strange at first to handle English money, but now we have the French system which is much easier being more like our own. I wish now that I had taken an extra year of French in high school as I only catch a word now and then. We are fortunate, however, in having a cook who can 'parlez vous.' I don't suppose this will reach home until after Thanksgiving. Say, but won't that be a lonely day! Oh, I discovered that the mother of Lieut. Safford, who is charge of the headquarters section of our

company, spends her summers in Manchester at Tuck's Point..."

By November 1917, Russia was out of the war. Lenin and the Bolsheviks had taken power from the revolutionary provisional government, establishing a dictatorship, and Germany was now able to concentrate the full power of its forces in the west. In March, 1918, both the British and the French were battered by the German army's spring offensive along the Somme River. It was clear that America's help was needed more than ever. Back home, ladies silk stockings were on sale at Almy, Bigelow & Washburn's store in Gloucester. (How unlike World War II when every bit of silk that could be had was used for aerial parachutes or powder bags for the Navy's big guns!)

By February 25, 1918, Irving Baker had been commissioned a 2nd Lieutenant and Harry, still a sergeant, wrote home from "A Wine Cellar. Somewhere in France." "All safe and ok after doing our first bit in the trenches and believe me Sherman [General William Tecumseh] was mild in his description of war. I am writing this in a wine cellar of a town completely ruined by shell fire. My gas mask is the writing desk and the big guns furnish plenty of music...we traveled to the front in box cars...[sleeping] sitting up around the sides of the car with our feet together like a fan...at last came our initiation in the trenches...I was off duty [when] the barrage struck us...Zzz wang! Bzzz bang! and I said 'hit the hole!' The other two fellows beat me to it being nearer. It is all right to joke about it afterwards, but oh, my!"

In April, 1918, when he arrived in England on the way to France, Army Private Mark Lodge Edgecomb, a member of Company E, 77th Infantry Division, with everyone in his unit, was greeted with a copy of a special hand-written note from King George V. On Windsor Castle stationary, it read: "Soldiers of the United States, the people of the British Isles welcome you on your way to take your stand beside the Armies of many nations now fighting in the Old World, the great battle for human freedom. The Allies will gain new heart and spirit in your company. I wish that I could shake the hand of each of you & bid you God speed on your mission."

In combat, Private Edgecomb served as a runner carrying messages from one unit to another along the front lines. When the war ended, he returned safe and sound to Manchester where he served as Tree Warden for many years. On the way, he and his Division took part in Victory celebrations in New York City which included a giant ticker-tape parade down Broadway. His daughter, May Edgecomb Calnek and her family continue to cherish the letter from George V which was written now 85 years ago.

DREADED NEWS

War Department Telegrams Announce Casualties as Men Come Under Fire

Meanwhile, other news received here was not as cheerful. In May, 1918, James Coughlin of 15 Norwood Avenue, was notified by the War Department that his son, 29-year-old Private Michael Coughlin, Company A, First U.S. Engineers, had been killed on April 28. As his unit commander wrote: "Private Coughlin was seriously wounded by shell fire while near the company kitchen. He was given the best of medical treatment by an army surgeon at a nearby infirmary, but died of his wounds at 12:15 that day.

"He was buried by his company officers and comrades with full military honors the same night at Breyes (Oise), France, and his grave suitably marked. Private Coughlin was an excellent soldier and well liked by all who knew him. His loss in the field of honor for his country is one of the sad incidents in the history of our organization and his memory will long be fresh with his friends..." It was signed W.S. Corkran, Captain, Engineers, U.S. Army.

Coughlin was a graduate of Story High School who had worked as a carpenter for Roberts & Hoare. He later went to California where he enlisted in the Army. He was "the fourth Manchester boy to sacrifice his life in the present conflict."

By June, 1918, the U.S. Second Division was sent to... support the French at the Marne River and in its first major engagement, troops of the American Expeditionary Force stopped a German advance in Chateau-Thierry and drove the enemy back from Belleau Wood. At home in Manchester, aspirin tablets (12 in a box) were advertised for 18 cents. A bar of Cuticura soap could be had for 23 cents.

Sergeant Harry Baker again wrote to his mother: "Did I tell you of our Sunday afternoon ceremony when our regimental colors were decorated? One hundred and seventeen officers and enlisted men also received the Croix de Guerre.

Frank Amaral was one to receive the war cross but his place was a blank file. He did his duty nobly... Just remember that I was thinking of you on Your Day [Mothers' Day] and wish to send a whole lot of love. The other boys will have to buy the carnations this year..."

In August, 1918, Manchester once again welcomed President and Mrs. Wilson. The party, which included the President's personal physician, Rear Admiral Cary T. Grayson and representatives of the Secret Service, arrived on a special three-car train which stopped at Magnolia station. There Wilson was met by his aide Colonel House and driven to Coolidge Point where he stayed at the Marble Palace as guest of Thomas Jefferson Coolidge, Jr. who had offered the house to the Wilsons for a week. Soldiers in full battle dress with rifles and steel helmets camped out on the lawns providing the necessary security. The President and Mrs. Wilson, according to The Cricket, spent much of their time motoring around the North Shore, socializing with friends and playing golf at Essex County Club.

By the end of summer, 1918, General John J. Pershing, Commander of the American Expeditionary Force, had more than 500,000 men in Europe, a number that would double before the end of the war in November, and the Allies were ready to launch their final offensive against German lines. Meanwhile, Sergeant Walter N. Smith, who had been wounded, wrote to reassure his mother in Manchester. "My Dear Mother: Perhaps you are already wondering by this handwriting what is wrong with me...We went over the top and licked the stuffing out of the Huns. We took countless prisoners...[but] I hadn't gone twenty yards before a piece of shrapnel caught me in the right breast just below the shoulder. It is a very slight wound. [I] will undoubtedly be OK in a month or so...They took me to a dandy hospital; real American nurses here; believe me I was glad to get there. It was rather a bumpy ride...first time I had been in a real bed for nearly a year...

"It is impossible to write much as it hurts me so and I think I will make it short. Now mother don't you worry one bit because I am perfectly all right... the Lord has been pretty good to me and more so this time. Will close now with love and kisses to all."

Private Clarence Mackin of Company E, 302nd Infantry, American Expeditionary Force, also wrote from France to his parents in Manchester on August 4, 1918. "Last Tuesday the company rode down to Bordeaux [by truck] to escort General Pershing. As we stood at "Present Arms," [the] General and his staff rode past in autos. He looked just like the pictures you see of him."

OVER THE TOP
'Only Thing to Do Is to Keep Going,' a Young Man Writes His Sister

As fall approached, action along the Western Front grew in intensity as the Americans increased pressure on a now more vulnerable enemy. John J. Kinsella of Manchester had enlisted in the Army in February, 1917. A student at Boston College, he was 20 years old and had been assigned with his brother James, 22, to Company H, 18th Regiment. In late August, 1918, he wrote to tell his sister what it was like to go "Over the Top," which meant leaving the trenches and advancing towards German lines across "No Man's Land," a shell-scarred open area between the two warring sides, often strewn with barbed wire, criss-crossed by machine gun fire and always the target for artillery shells. Going "Over the Top" was the supreme test for any infantryman.

"We started from the edge of some wood where we had been holding the line for several days," the letter began. "We had to cross a wheat field on the other side of which was a town and beyond a hill held by the Boche. The attack started shortly after 8 a.m. and without any artillery preparation on our side. At the signal, we started from the woods in waves. I guess Fritz was so surprised to see us coming that the biggest part of our men were across the field before he had his barrage [artillery] working. But then he laid down a hot one.

"It is a queer feeling one gets on his first time over. Before we started I thought I was going to be about the most scared mortal on earth. But somehow or other, I didn't feel scared. The shells don't seem to bother me nearly as much as they sometimes do when I am crouching in a hole or trench, listening to them come over...Once you start over the top, the only thing to do is to keep going. It is strange what the shells sometimes do. I saw one land right in front of a soldier. I thought he was gone for sure. But all he did was to brush the dirt off his face and keep on going. A shell landed so close to one fellow that he turned a somersault. He got up with a laugh and [he, too,] kept going.

"Bill Francis of Manchester is over here with the Engineers. His company was in the attack with us. While waiting to start I heard a fellow mention his name and I asked for him but he had gone to the rear with some wounded men so I did not see him..."

In September, 1918, Sergeant Harry Baker, who had been in action with the first American units in Europe, was back home telling members of the Manchester Club what life was like on the Western Front. "Our first experience in the trenches was in February. Under cover of a heavy [artillery] barrage, we made the attack at 10 o'clock at night and it lasted for an hour...we were in this sector about a month and a half; we then went to Toul where we remained three months and saw much action...It was here that Corporal Amaral was killed...

"Cooties are the bane of a soldier's life... together with the rats which are as big as cats, [they] make life in the trenches miserable...soldiers are given two days ration at a time and the rats usually get most of it. The food as a rule is good...the drinking water is very poor and that is one reason why the French drink so much wine..."

Artillery, ranging from smaller field pieces and howitzers to gigantic railroad guns, played a major role in warfare at the time and Sergeant Baker explained that "shell shock" was one of the worst injuries that a soldier could suffer. Sometimes, he said, it was nothing more than shattered nerves, "but real shell shock is a terrible thing; something in the back of the head seems to give way and the victim goes insane."

Finally, on a personal note, he added: "I met Doc Willis one day. He looked fine and sent his regards to all the Manchester boys. He is in charge of dental supplies at one of the field hospitals...I also saw Gordon Cool and Pomp Francis."

Among the unsung heroes of World War I was an obscure unit of American volunteers called the "Reserve Mallet" of which James MacGregor Means of Manchester was a member.

Named for its French commander, Major Mallet (pronounced Mal-lay), the Reserve drove convoys of trucks for the French army (and later for the American Expeditionary Force or AEF) carrying guns and ammunition to the front lines to supply troops in combat as well as delivering food stuffs, barbed wire, shovels, picks and lumber to build and repair dugouts and other elements of trench warfare. At times, they were also called upon to

For the Second Battle of the Marne, Reserve Mallet Pierce-Arrow trucks shown here were used to carry seven-and-one-half-ton tanks to the front lines. Deep mud and shell holes made roads all but impassable, and in one area the five-ton trucks were not powerful enough to carry the tanks uphill. They finally made the grade with a tow from a French Renault tractor. Eighty percent of the tanks were destroyed by German mines. Photo from <u>The Hard White Road</u>.

Manchester resident James M. Means who served with the Reserve Mallet during World War I stands with his faithful Pierce-Arrow truck "somewhere in France." Means' Reserve uniform included leg-wrap puttees, a leather belt and French steel helmet with goggles to protect drivers from dust and flying stones. There were no windshields. Photo courtesy of Sally Means Loring.

move infantry units and even small tanks from one area to another. Their vehicles consisted almost entirely of U.S.-made five-ton, Pierce-Arrow trucks.

Why "Reserve?" According to a wonderfully readable history of the unit entitled The Hard White Road written and privately printed in 1923 by Alden Rogers who served with it in France, it was "because it was not attached to any particular Army, Army Corps or Division, but shifted from one part of the front to another according to where the pressure was greatest."

Means, whose family had moved from Swampscott to build a house off Proctor Street here in 1901 known as "Meadowledge" (it is still standing), was a graduate of Wentworth Institute and had volunteered to help the French before the United States entered the war in 1917. Later, when the Reserve was made a part of the AEF, he was commissioned a Second Lieutenant in the U.S. Army.

RESERVE MALLET
Manchester Man Joins a Special Unit Which Helps Supply Allied Troops

Like other volunteers, he had originally signed up with the American Field Service as an ambulance driver, but the need for supplies was paramount and, there to help the Allies in any way he could, he and hundreds of others agreed instead to drive trucks. A little larger than a battalion, the Reserve Mallet totaled about 1,100 men. Its convoys, organized according to the French system, were known as Motor Supply Trains. A Groupe, for example, consisted of four companies of about 40 men each (complement was always short) with 18 trucks to a company. There was considerably less emphasis on military discipline and drill than in regular fighting units, but care was lavished on the Reserve's collection of Pierce-Arrow trucks, said by French senior officers, according to Alden Rogers, to be "the best heavy truck of any they used and they have given them all a gruelling test."

Started by George N. Pierce in 1878 to manufacture bicycles, the company began making cars in earnest in 1906 at Buffalo, New York and from then until 1936, the Pierce-Arrow became one of the finest and most sought after automobiles produced in the U.S. In 1909, President Taft ordered two for the White House, a Brougham and a Landaulette, to be used for official occasions. The

vehicle of choice for celebrities, it was also driven by film stars, financiers and members of the Royal Family in Japan, Persia, Greece, Belgium and Saudi-Arabia.

But in 1915, the commercial division of the Pierce company began shipping hundreds of its trucks to Europe to be used by Britain and France on the battlefronts of World War I. Despite primitive roadways, mud, snow and shell holes, the Reserve Mallet and its Pierce-Arrows delivered the goods safely, on many occasions at night to escape attack by enemy aircraft. But on May 26, 1918, the Reserve and Manchester's Jim Means were not so lucky. It could, however, have been much worse.

The Germans had begun a huge offensive and were moving forward against the French. As Alden Rogers writes, "The following evening at nine came an order for 60 cars from the Groupe which were on the road five minutes later. They were to evacuate the headquarters and baggage of the Sixth Army from Soissons, for the town was doomed and everyone but the troops actually engaged in the fighting was leaving...

"During the loading, shells were slamming into the town at short intervals. Most of them were directed at the station three or four blocks away; others fell within the vicinity of the bridges on the other side of town; and still others whined overhead on their way to the railroad junction [on the outskirts.] Shortly before dawn we were loaded and left Soissons for Oulchy where the headquarters division was to be taken. The roads were crowded with troops going up into action and with refugees fleeing before the advancing Germans.

"During the afternoon, a convoy from [the Reserve's] Groupe Robinson and Groupe Bernhart were returning to camp. [As they passed] a French artillery train [formation] on its way to the front, suddenly, 10 or 15 Boche planes dropped down out of the sky and swept up and down the [column], raking it with their machine guns. The artillery suffered badly losing a number of horses and men, whereas the convoy came through practically unscathed. Several of the trucks had bullet holes in them but only one man, Jimmy Means, had been hit and he only slightly grazed by one of the bullets."

Means, of course, recovered from his wounds and went on to live to a ripe old age here in Manchester. His daughter Sally Means Loring, also a long-time resident, served as Curator of the

A memorial to those who lost their lives in World War I, this life-size statue of a "Doughboy" is located at Masconomo Park. Commissioned by the town and rendered by sculptor Philip S. Sears, it was dedicated in 1931. Its inscription "Lafayette We Are Here," pays tribute to the Marquis of Lafayette who left his country to help a young nation with its struggle for independence, as in 1917 the U.S. sent its own citizen soldiers to support France in its fight for freedom.

167

Manchester Historical Society and is married to G. Gardner Loring of Gid's Giddy Gang, a much-beloved jazz orchestra which has entertained at many town events. As for the Reserve Mallet, it was disbanded in June, 1919. As Alden Rogers writes, "in appreciation of [our] faithful work, the French recommended that the Reserve be decorated with the Fourragere de la Croix de Guerre, but American GHQ [General Headquarters] refused to let us have [it]."

James MacGregor Means, however, ultimately did receive a medal of recognition from the American Field Service. In his effects, his daughter also discovered a Victory Medal awarded to American Forces serving in World War I. On its multicolored ribbon above the medallion inscribed "The Great War for Civilization" are nine bronze clasps representing the remarkable number of battles in which her father took part: Cambrai, Somme Defensive, Aisne, Montdidier-Noyon, Champagne-Marne, Aisne-Marne, Somme Offensive, Oise-Aisne, and Defensive Sector. All just words to us today, they tell an incredible story of self-sacrifice, suffering and too often death endured by brave and patriotic young men who fought to restore peace and freedom to the world.

In October, 1918, the Allies, now bolstered by the Americans, launched what proved to be a final major offensive against German lines. U.S. forces attacked in the Argonne Forest along the river Meuse. Back home, Manchester's sale of Liberty Bonds topped $180,000 on its way to $500,000. By November, Austria-Hungary had collapsed and sailors of the German Navy had mutinied at Keil where in 1911, skipper Guy Lowell, representing the Manchester Yacht Club and sailing CIMA, had defeated the Germans in a Sonder Boat race. His prize, a silver basket still held by the Club, is inscribed: "Won by CIMA and presented by the Kaiser to Guy Lowell on board he HOHEN-ZOLLERN, June 29, 1911." How quickly the world changes.

Also in October, 1918, the U.S was struck by an epidemic of influenza which was to kill more than one million persons. Manchester, not to be spared, suffered more than 400 cases. Thankfully, most were mild and brave physicians and nurses cared for patients who were isolated at Horticultural Hall on Summer Street. With Mrs. William W. Hoare in charge, assisted by District Nurses Miss Long, Mrs. George R. Dean and Miss Claudia R.

Wilson, the building was filled with hospital beds and other medical equipment. Schools and churches were closed and lodge meetings and other social gatherings were prohibited. Food was prepared for those at home and representatives of the Board of Health visited every dwelling in town to make sure people knew how to recognize symptoms of the disease and how to treat it.

In November, the Kaiser was forced to abdicate following a general strike in Germany led by the Independent Socialist Party. The American army, continuing its advance, had reached the bank of the river opposite Sedan, and on the 6th, news of an armistice proved to be premature. But on November 11, 1918, in response to a telegram from Marshall Foche, the fighting ended.

CHURCH BELLS RING
November, 1918: Armistice Is Declared; Manchester Celebrates War's End

The news reached Manchester at 4 a.m. Charles C. Dodge awoke to hear the fire alarm in Salem which sounded "three times seven," which by pre-arrangement meant that an armistice had been declared. Dodge dressed, according to The Manchester Cricket, and went to the home of Fire Chief Clarence W. Morgan who agree to sound the same signal in Manchester. Dodge then proceeded to the Congregational Church where by 5 a.m. he had the steeple bell ringing out the good news as it did to announce the end of the War of the Rebellion 53 years earlier.

There were noises, cheers and flags on every hand in Manchester and in the evening an informal parade, headed by a drum corps, which included members of the Home Guard, veterans of the Civil War, Boy Scouts, members of the Women's Relief Corps, Sons of Veterans, members of the Arbella Club and scores of local men, women and children who marched throughout the town. Prayer services were also held at both the Congregational and Baptist churches.

Of the young men from Manchester who had responded to the colors, five failed to return. They were Frank B. Amaral (see earlier chronological section); Michael Coughlin, Edward Golthwaite, Ammi Lancashire and Joseph McNeary. The American Legion Post here is named for Amaral and Richard Bailey, the town's first battle casualty of World War II. In July, 1931, the bronze, life-size statue of a "doughboy," commissioned by the town and rendered by sculptor Philip S. Sears, was dedicated at Masconomo Park to those from Manchester who lost their lives serving in the Armed Forces during World War I. Its inscription, "Lafayette, We are Here," pays tribute to the Marquis de Lafayette who left his country to help a young people struggling for independence become a new nation, as in 1917, the U.S. sent its own citizen soldiers to support France in its fight for freedom.

No war in history had more battle casualties than did World War I. United States combat dead totaled 48,000 (an additional 62,000 died of influenza); Britain lost 743,000; France, 1,384,000, Russia, 1,700,000; and Germany, 1,800,000. An average of more than 5,600 servicemen died as a result of combat on each day of the four year conflict. The Great War was meant to be the "war to end all wars" but, alas, as we know, that was not to be.

SISTERS SHINE AT GOLF AND TENNIS

Manchester summer resident Harriot Curtis in 1905. In 1896, at age 13, Harriot, like her sister Margaret, a child prodigy when it came to the game of golf, won the Essex County Club Championship for Women. In 1906, then just 23, she swept all opponents aside to become Women's National Amateur Golf Champion. Margaret, two years younger, won the same title in 1911 and in 1912, the latter at the Essex County Club. Both extraordinary athletes, the sisters combined in 1927 to give what became the Curtis Cup, a trophy for international competition among women.

CURTIS LADIES

Summer Residents Harriot & Margaret Win State, National Championships

Although throughout its history Manchester's Essex County Club has attracted statesman and celebrities including Presidents William Howard Taft and Woodrow Wilson, banker J.P. Morgan, and singers Bing Crosby and Al Jolson, no one is closer to its heart than the Curtis sisters, Harriot and Margaret.

Summer residents of the town for all of their lives and daughters of Civil War hero Colonel Greeley S. Curtis who with his wife Harriot built Sharksmouth, a huge stone mansion just east of Dana's Beach in 1868, the Curtis sisters were remarkable athletes and pioneers in the games of golf and tennis at the end of the nineteenth century and the early years of the twentieth.

Both had been brought up in a family of 10 children, all devoted to outdoor sports and games. At 28 Mount Vernon Street in Boston, the back yard was flooded in winter for skating and in the spring and fall was the scene of games of every description. There was even a Curtis family baseball team. Margaret, as the youngest, was especially competitive perhaps fired by a need for recognition in a remarkably accomplished family. Harriot (named for her mother), quieter and more modest, according to her niece Isabella Halsted who wrote about The Aunts in a delightfully warm-hearted and loving reminiscence published in 1992 by The Sharksmouth Press, was "not a talker but a doer" and significantly less loquacious about her accomplishments than her sister.

With the Essex County Club just down the road, it was logical that the two would find their way to its golf course and tennis courts. Essex had formally opened in 1893 and a year later at the age of 10 and 12, Margaret and Harriot began to play golf. Both were naturals. Largely self-taught, they were stocky and strong and could drive a ball as far as most men. Margaret's short game was less impressive but in time it too improved markedly.

In 1896, Margaret, then just 13 years old, entered the USGA Women's Amateur Golf Championship held that year at Essex County Club. Paired with the defending champion, she lost but the experience was invaluable. In 1898, it was Harriot's turn and she won the Club Championship for Ladies. What was it like for experienced women golfers to be beaten by a child? As Isabella Halsted writes, one "vanquished opponent" is said to have replied, "She's not a child—she's a Baby Grand!"

As the years past, Margaret was often in the finals of National Amateur matches and did win the Massachusetts Women's Amateur in 1901. Finally, in 1906, a quirk of fate helped Harriot achieve her goal. Margaret, unable to play golf because of an appendix operation, decided to coach her sister as best she could. It worked, for that year Harriot, age 25, won the Women's National Amateur Golf Championship at Brae Burn Country Club in Waban.

The next year, with Margaret back on her feet, the two Curtis sisters dramatically faced each other in the finals of the Women's Amateur in Chicago. This time it was Margaret's turn. She won as she also did the Massachusetts State Amateur title. Reported The Boston Transcript: "The sisters played golf for all it was worth and the match was the most exciting of the tournament."

TWIN VICTORIES

Margaret Wins Two National Titles in One Year, Tennis and Golf

1908 was a banner year for Margaret. As National Women's Amateur Golf Champion, she and her neighbor on Beacon Hill, Evelyn Sears, who was Women's National Singles Champion in tennis, won the National Doubles Championship. Unfortunately, in defending her golf title later that year, she was defeated in the quarter finals. But her triumph in tennis, it is believed, according to the History of the Essex County Club 1893-1993 by George C. Caner, Jr., makes her the only person to have won both national titles in one year. Harriot, according to Caner, took the medal for the 1908 Women's Amateur which was held at Chevy Chase, Maryland, with an 85. It "was the lowest score to that date in the qualifying for any Women's Amateur," he writes.

Margaret was to win the national amateur golf championship on two other occasions. At the first in 1911, now age 28, she defeated the "unbeatable" Dorothy Campbell of Scotland at Balustrol. It was the first time Miss Campbell (then Mrs. Hurd) had been beaten in the United States. And to top the list of pleasures, it was Margaret's short game that made the difference. In 1912, this time again at Essex County Club, she successfully defended her

Margaret Curtis at age 11 looks tiny next to other players at 1896 Women's Club Championship at Essex County Club, but don't let size fool you. A formidable competitor, Margaret compiled an enviable record of championships in both golf and tennis. Her sister, Harriot, two years older, won the Club Championship for Women in golf in 1896. Harriot became the Women's National Amateur Champion in 1906. She was 23 years old. Margaret won the same title in 1911 and then in 1912 at the Essex County Club. The sisters combined in 1927 to give what became the Curtis Cup, a trophy for international competition among women. In 1958, at age 73, Margaret's extraordinary lifetime achievements were recognized as she received the Bob Jones Award for Distinguished Sportsmanship in Golf.

championship on home turf "taking her medal with an 88 and winning all her matches."

"With this victory," Caner states, "Margaret had won the National Amateur Championship three times in 15 tries, had been runner-up twice, and had been six times the medalist." She continued to "compete in the National Amateur through 1947, appearing in that championship 23 times over a 50-year span." The sisters continued their record performance in golf by taking additional Massachusetts State titles, Margaret in 1914 and Harriot in 1920. Margaret was on top again in 1947 taking the WGAM Senior Title at Brae Burn. It was an incredible record of achievement.

The sisters continued to support golf with the establishment in 1927 of the Curtis Cup to foster international competition and "to stimulate friendly rivalry among women golfers of many lands."

These extraordinary women had other talents as well. Both social workers in Boston for many years, Harriot was named a Director of the Associated Charities during World War I and afterwards served for four years as Dean of Women at Hampton Institute, a first-rate college for African Americans. Overseas in World War I, Margaret's organizational and administrative abilities won her the title of Chief of Refugee Affairs in Paris working with the Red Cross. For her accomplishments she was awarded the Legion d'Honneur by the government of France. It was the highest decoration that could be received by a civilian. After the war, she continued her work with refugees in Europe returning to Boston and Manchester at the start of World War II.

With their siblings, Harriot and Margaret had deep feelings about Sharksmouth and the wonderful times they had there together during their summers in Manchester. The town could feel a special pride as well for two remarkable women who chose to make it their home.

GRASS COURTS
Invitational Tennis Tourney at Essex Attracts Top Women Players

From 1924 to 1968, the Ladies Invitation Tennis Tournament at Essex County Club brought to Manchester the glamour—without the glitz—of international tennis, as well as the best women competitors the game had to offer. From Helen Wills to Billie Jean King, they came each summer to play on the emerald green grass courts that grace the entrance to the club.

It all started in July, 1924 when three of the top ten women tennis players in the country responded to an invitation to participate in a tournament at Essex sponsored by the United States Lawn Tennis Association. That year in the finals of the Singles, Leslie Bancroft of California defeated Essex County Club member Alice Thorndike, 6-2, 6-3. Climax of the affair was an elegant tea dance to honor visiting participants.

The "LITT," as George C. Caner, Jr. calls it in his History of the Essex County Club, 1893-1993, "was held annually thereafter through 1968 (except for World War II years) as a regular event on the Ladies Eastern Grass Courts Circuit, attracting almost all the major women players in the United States and abroad." From the mid-1930's on, the Ladies Invitational was timed to precede the National Doubles Tournament at Longwood Cricket Club in Brookline, both events attracting a wide audience from around the region.

It was an elegant era, especially before World War II. Photos of spectators in the 1930's and '40's, show ladies in light summer dresses and broad-brimmed hats and gentlemen in blue blazers and white flannels. After the war, skirts were briefer and clothing less formal. Shorts were popular and tennis star Gussie Moran shocked and fascinated the world with her lace "undies." But always there was the wonderful sight of athletes in white moving gracefully on a carpet of soft green grass.

Organizing and administrating the week-long annual event at Essex County Club called for a major effort which involved a sizable committee as well as other individual members. As Caner explains, it meant choosing "players to be invited; finding places for them to stay, mostly at members' houses; arranging transportation and entertainment—some form of dinner almost every night; putting out a program with features and advertising; seeding the players; determining mixed doubles pairings; making the draws; choosing prizes; recruiting ushers, linesmen, referees, ticket handlers and program sellers; arranging for ball boys; printing and selling tickets; and, finally, solving the myriad problems that always arose as the tournament moved along."

After World War II, new stands were erected to accommodate a growing number of tennis fans who came to watch the matches. One of the the thrills of

In 1897, the Women's Amateur Driving Competition was won by Manchester's Madeline Boardman here at the Essex County Club. Madeline, daughter of Essex County Club founder, T. Dennie Boardman of Boardman Avenue, winds up to drive her ball 137 yards.

Champion Nellie C. Sargent drives off the first tee at Essex County Club in 1897 during the finals of the Women's National Amateur Golf Championship. She finished second that year also winning the Club Championship while her brother George Sargent won the men's. Note that except for the caddie, straw hats and boaters for spectators seemed be the order of the day. Miss Sargent also was runner-up in the third women's Nationals.

Croquet was a popular pastime in the 1890's when this photo was taken showing the original club house. Shingle-style, the handsome structure was designed by the architectural firm of Andrews, Jacques & Rantoul of Boston and built by Roberts & Hoare of Manchester. Added to through the years, it fell victim to a night-time fire of undetermined origin in March, 1913. Staff members, lucky to escape with their lives, were trapped by the flames on the third floor. One heroically found his way over the roof to the ground outside and broke back into the locked building, rescuing his fellow employees. The following morning, nothing but the four chimneys remained. The present brick club house was completed and in use by December, 1914.

175

the tournament was the opportunity for male members of the club to play Mixed Doubles with some of the ranking women tennis players in the country. As many as 30 pairs were chosen and the excitement was intense.

Off the courts, there were teas, dances, beach picnics, songfests, clambakes and cookouts, as well as quiet breakfasts at home, which allowed members to mix with their famous guests in a wonderfully informal and personal way. But for every participant, the next day was all business.

In the Singles for the first few years until 1931, Helen Wills with four victories led the way. She was followed by Helen Jacobs and among others, Alice Marble (a three-time champion), Margaret Osborne and, finally, in 1942 by Louise Brough.

A NEW GENERATION

Younger Tennis Stars Take Over After WW II; Hospitality Still 'Fantastic'

After the war, the LITT attracted a new generation of players and Singles champions included such well known names as Margaret Osborne (now DuPont) again, Maureen Connolly, Margaret Smith (later Court), Shirley Fry, Althea Gibson (the first African-American woman to achieve a national ranking in tennis), Darlene Hard, Billie Jean King and, finally, in 1968, Maria Bueno.

In the Ladies Doubles, many of the above paired to win together. Top local players, too, were invited to participate. These included, according to Caner's history, Essex County Club members and Manchester residents Alice Roberts Connolly, Isabel Seyburn Harte, Catherine Coolidge Lastivica, Laura Curtis Cutler, and Lila Caner Mehlman.

Others from Manchester starred with the ladies in Mixed Doubles, winning their matches through the years. Among them were G. Colcott Caner, Frederick M. Bundy, Richard A. Buck, Hans H. Estin, George E. Putnam, Jr., Appleton King and Robert D. Mehlman.

But it was not only tennis that made the LITT so memorable and so enjoyed by visiting national tennis stars. It was also the hospitality, the parties and the fun that everyone seemed to have with each other. Many of the widely-traveled ladies who participated in the tournament wrote to express their feelings. Caner quotes portions of their letters. For Virginia Wade (Doubles Champion in 1966 and

1967), "it was 'like stepping into another world, [with] an abundance of friendly people—something that has disappeared from the large commercial tournaments. The club itself had a marvelous ambiance.' "

Helen Jacobs (1936 Singles Champion) wrote that "of all the tournaments in which I played during twenty years of competition, I remember none more enjoyable for its cordial atmosphere and the competence of its officials than the Essex County Club Tournament." Shirley Fry Irvin (Singles Champion in 1955 and 1956) summed it up: "one of my favorite tournaments," she declared, "the town was quaint and picturesque, the grass courts were well kept and the hospitality was fantastic."

Unfortunately, the "commercialization of tennis," as Caner explains, "brought an end to the LITT." In the late 1960's, open competition arrived with prize money for winners. Professionals were able to compete with amateurs. It was all too much for Essex, no longer able or willing to try to participate in what was becoming a very different world of sport.

The glory days of amateur matches were over and in 1968 the Club's Board of Directors reluctantly but realistically concluded that after 44 years it was time for the Essex County Club to end the Ladies Invitation Tennis Tournament which had been such a success and had brought so much luster to the Town of Manchester for so many years.

ATHLETICS: A REMARKABLE RECORD

1982 was a banner year for Manchester High School football. Led by Tri-Captains Michael Rooney, Darren Twombly and Charles Doucette, shown here from left to right, the team celebrated 10 straight victories during its regular season to lead the Mayflower League. It then went on to the Superbowl, played at Boston University's Nickerson Field, where the Hornets defeated Nantucket High School 28-6 to win the State Class D Championship. Coaching honors went to Fran York who had come to Manchester from Swampscott High just that year. In York's career here coaching football, he recorded an extraordinary 75 wins and 35 losses.

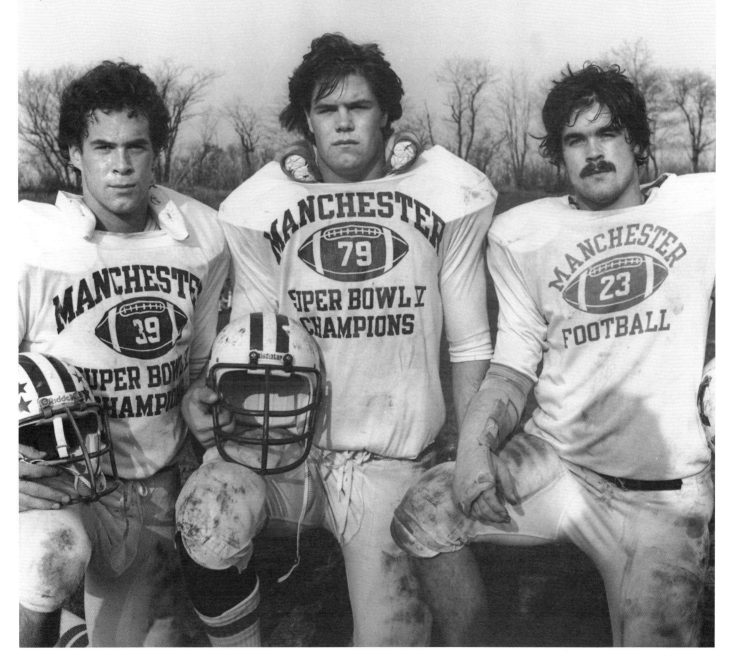

CHAMPIONS!

Since the 1920's, Manchester Has Compiled an Enviable Record of Athletic Victories

Information for this article comes from Joe Hyland's chapter entitled Athletics which appeared in the 350th anniversary book as well as from personal interviews with Joe himself and with Hardy Nalley, outstanding athlete and coach at Manchester-Essex Regional High School and presently its Director of Athletics.

Since 1922 when Tom Kelley, just graduated from Bates College in Maine, was hired to coach boys and girls sports at Story High School, Manchester has had an extraordinary record of achievement in athletics.

In football, basketball, and baseball, and later in tennis, field hockey and girls' basketball, it has often played the role of David, whose abilities, courage, and persistence have defeated many Goliaths on the playing fields of New England.

Few small town schools had organized athletic programs in the 1920's and Kelley, a native of Manchester, Connecticut, who was later elected to the High School Coaches Hall of Fame, found himself scheduling games with significantly larger communities such as Malden and Everett, and high schools in the cities of Beverly, Salem and Gloucester. In football especially, but in basketball as well, Kelley's teams compiled records that were admired far and wide, and set the high standards that were to be an inspiration for the years to come.

The man most responsible for Manchester's success on the athletic field in the past more than half-century, is Joseph M. Hyland. One of 10 children of Edward and Catherine Hyland, Joe was born here in 1916. At age eight, he contracted polio, which affected his legs below the knees. First came an operation at Children's Hospital in Boston, then metal braces on both limbs. But if his body was ailing, Joe's young spirit remained undaunted.

"We lived on Norwood Avenue opposite the playground in those days," he recalls, "and it included a lot of wonderful equipment from parallel bars to ladders and trapeze. I worked out every day I could to develop a strong upper body and to strengthen my thighs. I ran like a duck with a broken leg and wore those braces until my first year in high school!"

A natural athlete, Joe loved sports, especially baseball, and, as a youngster, he began to catch for the Town Team during batting practice. Finally, in 1931, his sophomore year, his parents agreed to let him play for Story High. "Those were different days," he adds, "and I was able to have [a team-mate] run for me after I reached first base. We played Rockport, Beverly, Salem, Danvers, Marblehead and Newburyport and we did well."

Because of his athletic prowess and his indomitable will to conquer his disability, Joe received considerable notice and in his senior year was offered a scholarship in physical education at Springfield College. But times were lean financially and it was not to be. He took courses at Boston University in math, science and the liberal arts and, most important, ran the program at Brook Street Playground where he taught youngsters not only to love sports as he did, but to learn basic skills and to become proficient especially in football and baseball.

In 1934, the school department hired Whitfield Kimball, a recent graduate of Dartmouth College where he was a football star, as a classroom teacher and coach. Kimball's record in football at Manchester was extraordinary: 21 wins in 26 games including a most satisfying victory over Newburyport, his own home town. Many of the youngsters, of course, who played for Whit Kimball had been taught the basics by Joe Hyland.

WELL DONE

Joe Hyland Started Coaching at Story High in 1937; That Year He Defeated Beverly

In 1937, Kimball was appointed principal of Story High School. One of his first acts was to ask Hyland, still at the playground, to coach high school sports. His salary was to be $1,200 a year. That spring, Joe's baseball team beat Beverly 5-0. In basketball, with only 37 boys in the entire school, Story High also defeated Marblehead, Swampscott, St. John's Prep and Danvers. "Four of the first five graduated," Hyland chuckles, "and the next year [1938] we were again undefeated!" Good coaching may have played a major role in his teams' successes, but Hyland is always quick to praise his athletes as well. "These were wonderful kids," he says. "I had known them since I coached them in the seventh and eighth grades. It was a thrill to watch them perform."

At the start of World War II, Kimball joined the Navy and ultimately attained the rank of

In 1966, Manchester's basketball team coached by Herb Schlegel, right, and assistant Bruce Magoon, was Class D champion at the Tech Tourney defeating Martha's Vineyard, 81-60; Dominic Savo, 79-53; Bellingham, 83-44; Hull, 78-69 and in the finals, Lincoln-Sudbury in a squeaker, 71-70. Brian Peters was captain. Number 20 in the back row is Ralph Kershaw who tragically lost his life in the attack on the World Trade Center on September 11, 2001. Photo courtesy of Hardy Nalley.

In the Golden Year of 1962, Story High School's baseball team, coached by the legendary Joe Hyland, won Class C and was crowned Massachusetts State Champion. Front row, from left, Coach Hyland, Eric Ericson, Hardy Nalley, Elliott Crocker (Co-Captain), Buddy Bachry, Peter Foster (Co-Captain), Joe Lazisky, Wayne Lynch, Manager Tom Burtt. Back row, Peter Hyland, Tim Logue, Skip Day, Dean Lynch, Stan Koch, George Mixel, Skip Cool, Wally Cammett, Paul Lasowski, Dan Slade. Photo courtesy of Hardy Nalley.

179

Commander. Other faculty members left for the war as well. Joe, of course, because of polio, was not eligible, so he served his country by helping its youth to build character and to learn the satisfaction of success both on the playing field and, by now, in the classroom. Determined to help with the war effort, too, during the summer months he worked as a welder at Fore River Shipyard in Quincy.

In basketball, in 1943 and 1944, tiny Story High was invited to compete in Division B in the state-wide Tech (Massachusetts Institute of Technology) Tourney in Boston. Led by Bob Bailey and Helmer Teodorson, the 1942 team played Winthrop at Tufts College. In 1943, Alex Kassanos and John Gilmore starred as Manchester faced Braintree High School at Boston Garden. Both the 1942 and 1943 teams, then members of the Cape Ann League, established in 1937, were undefeated.

A drop in student enrollment during the war years also led to a decision to shift to six-man football. At first, to find other six-man schools, Manchester had to travel far and wide in Massachusetts to Lancaster and Acton, and at times even further by car pool (fuel, of course, was rationed) to the towns of York, Dixfield and Eliot in Maine. Soon, however, interest developed locally and Essex Agricultural School, Hamilton, Georgetown and Topsfield were added to the schedule. During the 1940's and 1950's with Joe Hyland as coach, Manchester's six-man football teams won 80 percent of their games and remained undefeated at home for eight years. The undefeated 1946 team played before thousands at Manning Bowl in Lynn.

Hyland by this time was Athletic Director at Story High, although as he says, the title meant only more work. He was still coaching baseball and marking yard lines on the fields before games. But a new member of the faculty had arrived to take over football. He was Ed Field, a graduate of the University of South Carolina and varsity football player with a degree in English. "No man had more enthusiasm for the game," Joe adds, "or more love for the kids." Field quickly made his mark both in the classroom and on the playing field. In 1960, with new families in town increasing school enrollment, Manchester returned to the traditional, 11-man game and the next year, with co-captains Peter Foster and Hardy Nalley, the team won the State Class D Football Championship.

Hyland calls the 1960's the "Golden Years" for sports in Manchester. Joe's baseball team led the Cape Ann League in 1962. Remarkably, for the next eight seasons, in football with Coach Ed Field, in basketball with Coach Herb Schlegel, and in baseball with Coach Joe Hyland, Manchester finished first in the Cape Ann League. Joe retired from coaching in 1965. The School Committee, to express the town's gratitude for his many years of service, voted to name the field at Manchester's new Junior-Senior High School after Joseph M. Hyland.

Like the old playground program, organized sports at Memorial School, begun with the completion of the school building and its gymnasium in 1952, added immeasurably to the quality of athletics at the high school. Students from the fourth grade up learned the fundamentals, girls from coach Dorothy Sjorlund, a Navy veteran who served as an officer in the WAVES during World War II, and the boys from Joe Hyland. A Saturday basketball program was also initiated for youngsters in grades four to eight. Seventh and eighth grade boys played a full schedule with outside schools.

Fresh out of Salem State College where he played varsity basketball and baseball, Herb Schlegel joined the faculty at Manchester High School in 1957 to teach mathematics and to coach boys' basketball. It was a good choice. For three years, Manchester led its own Cape Ann League. Then in 1965, the team won the Class D Tech Tourney. Two years later, in 1967, Manchester was crowned State Small School Champions in basketball after defeating Rockport at Boston Garden. Ralph Kershaw, who tragically lost his life in the attack on the World Trade Center on September 11, 2001, was a member of the winning team. Richard Katherman set a tournament record scoring 176 points in five games. By this time, too, varsity basketball could play its home games in the new high school gym.

The next year with Schlegel on leave to take special academic courses, Harry Tozier stepped in to lead Manchester basketball to another Cape Ann League title and to the finals of the Class D Tech Tourney at Boston Garden. Unfortunately, the team lost to Rockport. Later, however, revenge was sweet as Manchester came back to defeat Rockport and again to win the State Small Schools Championship.

In 1961, Manchester began its second season of 11-man football. It was a banner year. The team finished with an unde-feated season of eight wins to lead the Cape Ann League and went on to become State Class D Champions. Coaches were Ed Field, Jr. and Arthur Edwards. Co-Captains were Peter Foster and Hardy Nalley (number 11). Nalley today is Athletic Director at Manchester-Essex Regional High School. Dan Slade was team manager. Seniors who celebrated their final year with the victorious team were Foster and Nalley, Elliott Crocker, John Heath, Don Macrae, Frank Glass, Eric Eric-son, Al Clapp, Pete Milner and Bud Backry. **Photo courtesy of Hardy Nalley.**

In 1999-2000, Manchester's Hornets were champions of the Commonwealth League in football and at the Superbowl won Division VI to become State Champions with an outstanding season game score of 10-2. Tri-Captains were Nick Ferraco, Dan McLaughlin, and Chris Murray. Dick Ananian was Head Coach. **Photo courtesy of Hardy Nalley.**

MAYFLOWER LEAGUE

In 1981, Manchester Football Finishes First; Defeats Dorchester to Win Class D

Victories continued to pile up in football as well and Manchester was now a member of the Mayflower League playing schools closer to its own size. In 1973, when Ed Field retired as coach, he was succeeded by Ira Yavner, a University of Massachusetts graduate, who had been coaching Manchester's Junior High. His varsity led the Mayflower League for two years. Charles "Chuck" Cook took over when Yavner moved to Wakefield High, and in 1981 Manchester again led the Mayflower League. That year also it defeated Dorchester High School in the Superbowl with a score of 49 to 6 to win the Class D State Title. The Boston Globe named Tri-Captains Eddie Field, Eric Bachry and Darren Twombley to its All-Star division team and Field was voted Most Valuable Player.

With a chance to coach football at a larger school, Cook moved to Hamilton-Wenham Regional. But with its apparently uncanny ability to select top-notch coaches, Manchester chose another winner named Fran York who had come from Swampscott High. Recommended by Principal Richard Howland and Hardy Nalley, York posted 10 straight victories in 1982, his first year, to lead the Mayflower League. The team's performance took it to the Superbowl at Boston University's Nickerson Field where it defeated Nantucket High School 28 to 6 to again win the State Class D Championship. Team leaders were Darren Twombley and Whitney Bower. York held a celebrated record here in football with 73 wins and 35 losses. Equally versatile in basketball, his 1993 team celebrated a Division II Cape Ann League Tri-Championship. After his stint here, York returned to coach at Swampscott. In 1999, Manchester High School, led by Coach Dick Ananian, won the Cape Ann league title in football and was crowned champion in Division VI at the Superbowl.

Organized sports for girls at Story High School began with field hockey and basketball in 1926. Coaches Tom Kelly and Marjorie Wilbur organized practices and games at Masconomo Park and on Friend Street at the "Old Catholic Church." In the 1930's, coaches Agnes Leonard and Dot Sjorlund took over and basketball was played at Horticultural Hall. Although it competed against larger schools, Manchester could be proud of its record.

Things really began to pick up steam, however, in 1965 when Nancy Bachman was chosen to teach physical education and to coach girls' sports. Once again, Manchester excelled, undefeated in field hockey for three years and for one in softball. Nancy, last to coach three sports, later moved to the Guidance Department. One of Coach Kay Volchko's softball teams qualified for the state championship. With coaches Frances Strazulla and Diane Coons, Manchester led the Cape Ann League in field hockey. For five years, coach M'Lena Gandolphi also took her field hockey teams to State Tournaments for Division II. For three years, they finished in the finals, losing to much larger Watertown High School. Another top coach, her overall record was 85-36-19. In 1984, her 8th grade girl's basketball team also finished its season undefeated. In 1995, 1997 and 1998, Manchester field hockey finished on top of the Cape Ann League and in 1995 also won the Division 2 North State Championship.

Three members of the 1993 field hockey team at Manchester High School went on to play in college: Kate MacLean at Wake Forest, Jenni Campbell at University of Maryland and Sarah Nalley at the University of Tennessee. It was easier for Kate and Jenni as varsity teams already existed at Wake Forest and Maryland. But Sarah, on her own, started Club Field Hockey at Tennessee. Soon they were playing outside schools such as Vanderbilt and Kentucky, and thanks to Sarah's early efforts, Tennessee will shortly recognize field hockey as a bona fide varsity sport.

Today, Herb Schlegel may be retired but he's been coaching girl's softball. The team has had an enviable record. From 1996 to 1999, Manchester's co-ed Swim Team, using pools at Gordon College and at Gloucester's YMCA, finished first in the Cape Ann League. The record recently for girls' basketball, too, has been outstanding including Cape Ann League titles in 1998, 1999, 2000 and 2001 as well as two Massachusetts Division II State Championships in 2001 and 2002.

TENNIS

In 21 Years, Manchester Wins 17 League Titles and Two State Championships

Always a tennis enthusiast (he was singles champion in his senior year at Story High and later regularly played doubles with Essex County Club pro Russell Dennis, Harry Slade and John Wynne), Joe

In Women's Tennis in the year 2000, the Hornets won the Massachusetts State Championship as well as the Cape Ann League with an extraordinary match score for the season of 20-1. Co-Captains were Caitlin Lombardi and Megan Routzong. Above from left, first row: Kara Powers, Alexandra deSherbinin, Paige Journey, Katie Steinhoff, Sara Rich. Second row: Katie McCabe, Gillian McCafferty, Mallory Miller, Caitlin Lombardi, Megan Routzong, Kelley Journey, Anne Angstadt and Marnie Powers. **Photo courtesy of Hardy Nalley.**

Men's Tennis in 1997-1998 was undefeated in a remarkable 21 matches. The team was crowned Cape Ann League Champions and Massachusetts State Tennis Champions. From left above are Karl Antons, Mikey Moylan, Darren Becker, Coach Zee Shanon, Alex Burgess, Chris Kelly, Sean Bresnahan, Eric Conrad, and Rudi Antons. **Photo courtesy of Hardy Nalley.**

Hyland started a program for girls and then boys in 1965 and 1966. In its first 21 years, Manchester won 17 Cape Ann League titles in tennis as well as two State Championships. In 1986, Manchester defeated Belmont, Haverhill, Needham and Framingham, all larger schools, but in the finals lost to Newton South. In 1990, Manchester girls led the Cape Ann League in tennis, won the Title for Division II North and were State Champions in Division II. In 1994, 1997, 2000, and 2001 four additional Cape Ann League titles followed. And in 2000 and 2001, the teams were Massachusetts State Champions in Division II with a win-loss record on the courts of 40 to one in those two years.

Girls' tennis has seen many outstanding players. Two deserve special mention. Joy Cummings, became statewide Junior Champion. Another, Johanna Sones, lost only two matches in league play in five years, later playing for William & Mary College where in her first year she was elected Most Valuable Player and still holds the record for wins in singles and doubles.

Boys' tennis, too, has had an extraordinary record. Starting in 1975 with Hardy Nalley as coach, it won three Cape Ann League titles in five years. It has celebrated a series of undefeated seasons, recently led its own Cape Ann League in 1998, 2000 and 2001, and in 1998 won the State Tournament for Division II as well.

Why has Manchester, a small town with a small school system, been able to excel in so many sports for so many years, often playing towns and cities several times its size? Good athletes, good coaching, to be sure, but Joe Hyland is a firm and practicing believer that playground programs, Little League Baseball, Youth Soccer, physical education for early grades at Memorial School, tennis clinics and the availability of sports facilities for pick-up, unscheduled games, have made the difference.

These important programs and opportunities for play teach not only a love of sports, but basic skills in the games of football, baseball, basketball, field hockey and tennis, which have helped provide the town with its extraordinary record in athletics. On the way, they have taught youngsters how to be great competitors as well as the meaning and importance of sportsmanship. They've helped to build character, confidence and poise in both boys and girls. And they have focussed attention on the value and the joys of physical and mental health.

None of the above would have been possible without the enthusiastic support of school administrators. Particularly, in Joe's day, these include Superintendent of Schools Foster Ball and Arthur Danielson and Principals Charles Ashley and Richard Howland. Hyland's roster of great coaches includes Tom Kelley, Whit Kimball, Richard Wilson, Ed Field, Herb Schlegel, Harry Tozier, Ira Yavner, Charles Cook and Fran York.

On his list of star athletes through the years, many of them playing three sports, Hyland mentions Sid Foster, Archie Gillis, Tom Carroll, Fred Cameron, Fred Cool, Dick Floyd, Phil Magnuson, Peter Foster, Joe Lazisky, Elliott Crocker, Dan Slade, Sr., Ed Field, Jr., Hardy Nalley (now Director of Athletics at Manchester-Essex High School) and Skip Cool.

Also, Ted Radack, Alex Kassanos, Bob Bailey, John Gilmore, Stu Bacus, John Koslowski, Craig McCoy, Fritz Coons, Peter Hyland, Rick Katherman and Power Fraser. Many of these then youngsters went on to play college sports as well: Dan Slade, Sr. at Syracuse University; Ed Fields, Jr. at Northeastern; Rick Katherman at Duke; Mark Needham at the University of Tennessee; Chuck Atwater at the University of South Florida; and Power Fraser and Darren Twombley at Boston College. John Koslowski, a star at Dartmouth College, tried out as a pitcher with the Boston Red Sox. Twombley played pro-football for the Patriots and later with the Green Bay Packers.

Manchester's success with sports excites not only parents of the kids involved but citizens of all ages throughout the town. It has helped to nourish town spirit and has made us proud of what our youngsters have accomplished. When the United Shoe Machinery Corporation was operating in Beverly, its employees came from communities all over the North Shore. "And I know for a fact," laughs Hyland, "that Manchester's football games with Georgetown, Topsfield, and Hamilton-Wenham, led to more betting than [did] the big game between Beverly and Salem!"

A LIVING LEGEND
Joe Hyland's Remarkable Record: 41 Years of Coaching; 80 Percent of Games Won

Today at 86, Joe Hyland is a living legend and a remarkable example himself of all he has tried to teach others. Despite a disability which could have defeated many, at an early age Joe decided to

Legendary athletic coach, teacher and mentor for hundreds of students during his 41 years with the Manchester School System, Joe Hyland's teams have won 80 percent of games played under his leadership. He is a member of the High School Coaches Hall of Fame and was elected a member of the prestigious National Honor Society for which he was proposed unanimously by the faculties at Memorial School and Manchester High School. A great athlete himself, as a youngster he overcame polio to play topflight baseball in high school and baseball and basketball with Manchester's Town Teams.

Since 1978, when Hardy Nalley was appointed Athletic Director, Manchester-Essex High School has won a total of 35 Cape Ann League Championships and 16 Massachusetts State Championships. A great athlete himself at then Story High School (Class of 1962), Nalley played on seven League-leading teams as well as winning two State titles. In his 35 years in education here, the Keene State College graduate has taught every grade from six to 12. An inspired successor to Joe Hyland, Nalley has been instrumental in selecting excellent coaches to help continue Manchester's extraordinary record of athletic victories.

Cheerleaders play an important role in athletic contests. Here during the school year 1961-1962 are Junior Varsity cheerleaders at Story High School. From left, Carol Cool, Susan Clopper, Pammy Bedell, Nora Hyland and Janice Nickerson. The new Manchester High School building also opened that year. The cheer dates back to Shakespeare's time and is known in countries throughout the world as a way to encourage and acclaim. Cheerleaders, both men and women at high school and at college, often perform acrobatics as they urge support for their teams and thus must be in as good physical condition as the athletes themselves.

commit himself to a life of sports. He learned to walk again and then to run. Refusing to give up, he played top flight baseball in high school, and went on not only to coach an impressive collection of winning teams in all sports, but to continue to play baseball and basketball as a member of Manchester's Town Teams.

UNANIMOUS ACCLAIM

School Faculties Propose Joe Hyland for the National Honor Society

For his achievements he was voted Most Valuable Player and elected to the Inter-Town League's Hall of Fame. He is also a member of the High School Coaches Hall of Fame. But the award that he treasures most is his election to the National Honor Society for which he was proposed unanimously by the teaching staff at Memorial School and at Manchester Junior High. The citation he received, presented by an official of the Society at a special assembly with students of both schools present, mentions his outstanding contributions to education throughout his career. Today, Joe Hyland sets an example for us all in character, in commitment and as an expression of the values which tell such a powerful story in America—overcoming initial adversity to reach a cherished goal.

Even in well-earned retirement, it was hard for him to give up helping others as he had throughout his life. Until recently, as a day-a-week volunteer, Joe and his wife Virginia were teaching boys and girls in Manchester's first grade to read. Helping to coordinate the Hyland's volunteer program was Sally McDonough, voted Manchester's "Most Outstanding Teacher of the Year 2001." Mrs. McDonough, Joe and Virginia's daughter, obviously continues the family's tradition of excellence.

Joe Hyland's record of service to this town and to its children is unrivaled: 41 years of coaching sports with an estimated 80 percent of games won. For 71 years in Manchester as a student, coach, teacher and Director of Athletics, he has been an inspiration to generations of youngsters and to his community as well.

PEARL HARBOR...'A DAY OF INFAMY'

Displaying a captured Japanese flag, Colonel, then Major, Vincent M. Crane, U.S. Army Air Force, of Manchester, stands in the cockpit of his B-25 bomber at a War Bond rally somewhere in the U.S. during World War II. B-25's, known as Mitchell bombers (named after Major General and aviation pioneer Billy Mitchell), took off from the deck of the aircraft carrier HORNET in April, 1942 to bomb Tokyo. It was the first air raid on the home islands of Japan. Colonel Crane, an Air Force pilot prior to Pearl Harbor, was a highly decorated veteran of 72 bombing missions in the South Pacific Theater. He was at Pearl when the Japanese attacked in December, 1941.

WORLD WAR II

An Uneasy Peace Ends as the World Is Plunged into Another Conflagration

By the fall of 1940, Americans had grown used to the war in Europe. At the Ware Theater in Beverly, at the North Shore in Gloucester and at the Strand in Ipswich, without television, films called "news reels" presented by "Pathe News" and the "March of Time" preceded the feature picture and offered the only up-to-date visual reports about what was happening around the world. Radio was hugely popular and there were still photos in newspapers and in LIFE and LOOK magazines, published weekly, but news reels told the story best.

France had fallen. German bombers were in the skies nightly over London as the blitz continued. Japan had conquered northern China and had its eye on the oil fields and rubber plantations of Southeast Asia. And in the U.S., President Franklin D. Roosevelt had decided to run for a third term. There was little doubt also that in the not too distant future, America would be in the thick of it herself. U.S. Navy destroyers were protecting Lend-Lease convoys to England and had orders to "shoot on sight" if attacked by Nazi submarines. Then on Sunday, December 7, 1941, in a surprise attack, planes from a Japanese carrier task force bombed the U.S. Naval Base and ships at Pearl Harbor, Hawaii. We were officially at war.

At Pearl in their honeymoon cottage, was First Lieutenant Vincent Crane and Mary Harvey Crane (sister of Dorothy Harvey Standley), his bride of four months, both from Manchester. A palm tree, felled by Japanese bombs, blocked the driveway, but minutes later Vince was at Hickham Field with orders to fly his B-17 bomber to safety at Wake or Midway Islands. Little did Mary realize when she kissed her husband good-bye that day that two-and-one-half years would pass before she saw him again.

At home, Vince's parents learned of the attack by radio as did most others here. But they had a special interest in the welfare of two young Americans. An agonizing week went by before they learned the couple was safe. After six months of volunteer work at a Honolulu hospital, Mary, like other dependents, was sent home. With her came her car. Its Hawaiian license plates caused quite a stir in Manchester.

Meanwhile, air raid wardens had already met with Director of Civil Defense, Police Chief George R. Dean and Deputy Chief Warden John F. Coughlin. To staff the aircraft observation tower on Town Hill behind the Manchester Historical Society an advertisement in The Manchester Cricket appealed for "men and boys" to volunteer as 24-hour-a-day plane spotters. A Rationing Board had been appointed to deal with the tightening supply of civilian materials which were needed for the war effort: gasoline (an "A" card, issued to everyone without special wartime needs, entitled the holder to three gallons a week!), auto tires, and even food such as meat and butter. And once again, recruiting offices were busy signing up volunteers, both men and women, for the Navy, the Marines, the Army and the Army Air Corps. Draft Boards in Manchester and other cities and towns were notifying young men that their numbers were up and that they had been chosen to serve Uncle Sam.

By mid-1942, to protect shipping along the eastern seaboard, Governor Leverett Saltonstall, had issued Blackout Regulations so that "no light whatsoever shall be visible from the outside." The top half of auto headlights were painted with black paint and every window in town had its blackout shades.

By November, 1942, L. Allan Andrews had been named Manchester's new Chief of Police as George R. Dean retired after many years of honorable service. Manchester boys, such as Bill Pembroke, were writing to Harry Slade, Sr. from England to thank him for sending The Cricket overseas and adding personal comments like this: "while there I saw Benny Stasiak and Bill Condon. You can take it from me that there is no place like Manchester!" That fall also the town said good-bye to another relic of its long history as the railroad station in West Manchester was torn down.

Although many servicemen and women wrote home, letters which appeared in The Cricket during World War II, apparently because of security concerns, revealed far fewer details about life overseas than did those in World War I. The best information came from government news releases which announced wartime accomplishments, awards of decorations, and, sadly, casualties, both wounds and deaths in combat.

B-17 IN ACTION
Two Planes Destroyed as a Manchester Pilot Scores a Hit on an Enemy Base

For those back home, it was comforting, too, to read in December, 1942, that we were finally taking the war to the enemy in the Pacific. One U.S. Army Air Corps B-17 Flying Fortress, piloted by Captain Vincent M. Crane of 114 Pleasant Street, Manchester, was reported to have strafed Japanese installations at Rekata Bay destroying two Jap seaplanes. While on the raid, Crane's aircraft was hit by a 37mm shell, severing one of its control cables, but with his crew he was able to land at Guadalcanal where he made temporary repairs before flying to the U.S. base in New Hebrides.

By July, 1943, Calderwood Yacht Yard had launched its sixth 110-foot wood subchaser for the Navy. Mrs. George A. Burchstead of Pleasant Street, an office employee at the yard, had been chosen unanimously by her fellow workers as sponsor. Felix "Pop" Radack, star athlete at Story High, was an air cadet in training to become a pilot for the U.S. Navy. After the war, Pop would become Chief of Police. There were also warnings about how to deal with poison gas should an attack take place. In World War II, unlike World War I, gas, thankfully, did not become a weapon used by Axis Forces.

The war was brought home to Manchester in May 1943 when it was learned that 24-year-old Augustus F. Forward, 3rd, an officer in the U.S. Merchant Marine, had escaped injury when his ship was torpedoed by a German U-boat. Although she sank in 20 minutes, her alert radio officer was able to send a message with her location. The ship's lifeboats were discovered by rescue aircraft and the crew later safely taken to Puerto Rico. Meanwhile, on Sunday, May 23, regular Army units and members of the State Guard held maneuvers and war games on the North Shore, seizing bridges and blocking roadways as if enemy forces had invaded the area.

Back momentarily from the Pacific after 72 combat missions, Manchester's Captain Vin Crane was awarded the Air Medal "for meritorious achievement" over Guadalcanal on Christmas Eve and Christmas day, 1942. Previously awarded the Silver Star and Distinguished Flying Cross, Captain Crane described the mission. "We had been flying constantly for three days," he said, "getting very little sleep before we took [off] on the Christmas Eve assignment.

"We wanted to give the Japs a Christmas present, and we did. We made three direct hits on a cargo ship and were returning to base when we hit a severe tropical storm. As we raced through the air, we noticed a large plane in front of us. The pilot [of] the other plane wiggled his flaps, a [sign] of friendship. We wiggled back but when we got close to the plane we noticed it was a Jap four-engine flying boat. We cut loose with everything we had, killing the tail gunner, silencing the number four engine, and forcing [it] to take cover in a cloud bank." Captain Crane, the citation read, "carried out his duties with remarkable skill and efficiency." At the time, he was 25 years old.

FIGHTING BACK
Early Days of the War: an Uphill Battle for the U.S.; Many Ships Are Sunk

The early days of the war in the Pacific were not easy. The Navy lost a number of major vessels to Japanese fire in battles both day and night. One of these was the cruiser USS HELENA. Aboard her was Manchester resident George Crafts, Musician 1st Class, who when home on leave told how the HELENA had been hit by torpedoes and sunk at Kula Gulf, near the Solomon Islands. Crafts, a four-year veteran of Navy service, was also at Pearl Harbor on December 7, 1941 and had taken part in 14 engagements including the landings at Guadalcanal.

Another pilot of whom Manchester could be proud was Lieutenant Ralph H. Lane of 16 Old Essex Road who was awarded the Distinguished Flying Cross for "extraordinary achievement" after completing 50 missions in the South Pacific. They involved "dropping supplies and transporting troops to advanced positions which meant flying at low attitudes over mountainous terrain under adverse weather conditions in a transport plane, often landing within a few miles of enemy bases." Seabee Gerard Leo Halloran of Manchester, Carpenters Mate First Class, also came in for praise and a Presidential Unit Citation for his Company's heroic action landing with U.S. Marines on a Pacific island under continuous shell fire as well as aerial bombardment and strafing. A beachhead established, the Seabees quickly constructed landing strips for U.S. fighter planes and with Marines, moved inland to help maintain Henderson Field which Japanese aircraft attacked regularly.

As American troops moved northward in the Pacific, island by island, in July, 1943 Staff Sergeant James A. Murray of 37 Central Street was recognized for gallantry in the campaign to seize New Georgia, with Guadalcanal, a part of the Solomon Islands chain, northeast of Australia. "Sergeant Murray," the citation read, "distracted the attention of the enemy by courageously exposing himself to machine gun fire while his squad withdrew from a precarious position. [He] then evacuated two wounded men by dragging them to safety between bursts of close range fire." He was later awarded a Silver Star for heroism and promoted to Technical Sergeant.

Murray, born in Manchester in 1911, attended Story High School and Vesper George School of Art in Boston. He enlisted in the Army before the war and was at Schofield Barracks, Hawaii when the Japanese attacked Pearl Harbor. He was later taken prisoner by the enemy in the Solomons but escaped to rejoin his unit, the 65th Engineer Combat Battalion, 25th Infantry Division. Many of these men, like Murray, in the first months of the war had signed up early for the service. It was they who held the line against huge odds in the Pacific Theater as America built up its forces and increased wartime production of guns, ships and planes to combat the Japanese.

At home, meanwhile, movies, sponsored by the Parent Teachers Association, were shown weekly at Town Hall. In July, 1944, the feature film was "Immortal Sergeants." That same month, the annual meeting of the Elder Brethren was canceled for the first time in the organization's long history "because of the exigencies of war." Clams for the traditional chowder were "prohibitive in price and practically unavailable." It was decided to "wait until another year." With an eye to post-war housing needs, members of the Planning Board, Finance Committee and Manchester's Businessmen's Association, were discussing the need for zoning to protect the qualities and character of the community.

The war in Europe, too, was growing in intensity. In 1942, the Allies invaded North Africa and American troops saw action for the first time with the British. The conquest of Sicily followed and from there Allied Forces invaded Italy. In February, 1944, Army Private Alfred W. Singer of 10 Pine Street, Manchester, was wounded in the battle for Rome and awarded the Purple Heart. He recovered and was soon back with his battalion, a part of the Fifth Army, which itself was one of the units honored with a commendation from Army commander General Mark Clark. In the same week, it was also announced that Lieutenant Ralph Lane of Manchester had won a second Bronze Oak Leaf cluster for his Distinguished Flying Cross.

'LIMITED DUTY?'
With One Eye, a Young Army MP Finds Himself Landing at Omaha Beach

A member of the Class of 1940 at Story High School, Ralph Hall was attending Northeastern University in 1942 when he tried to enlist in the U.S. Army. At age 11, however, he had lost sight in one eye in an accident playing baseball with the "Pine Street Gang" and thus was declared 4F, or medically ineligible to serve. Six months later he was drafted and assigned to "limited duty," meant to be primarily office work. But the war was increasing in intensity and the Army needed good men. The result was that, one eye and all, Ralph found himself a member of the 709th Military Police Battalion attached to General George Patton's Third Army. Six days after D-Day in June, 1944, he and his unit landed at Omaha Beach and with other GI's, fought their way to Paris. After the city's liberation, as luck would have it, he stayed there as a Corporal with the Military Police until peace came in May, 1945. Years later, after retiring from business, Ralph served as Treasurer of the Town of Manchester.

As the war progressed, The Cricket was filled with photos and stories of young men and women who were in the Armed Forces. The August 18, 1944 issue featured Lieutenant Marjorie Kelleher, Army Nursing Corps, who, the paper reported, had been overseas for 27 months in Australia and New Guinea. Her outfit had been through three campaigns and had received a Presidential citation for meritorious service. Lieutenant Kelleher graduated from Story High School and Carney Hospital School of Nursing. Also featured on The Cricket's front page was Anna Crocker Hooper, Yeoman 2nd Class, U.S. Naval Reserve who enlisted in the WAVES in July, 1943 and was then stationed at Kingsville Field, a part of the Naval Air Base at Corpus Christi, Texas.

Navigator Lieutenant Robert N. Hooper, U.S. Army Air Corps, third from left, stands with fellow crew members in front of their B-26 Martin Marauder. The twin-engine bomber was assigned to the 9th Air Forces' 323 Bomber Group and was involved in the Central Campaign over Germany's Rhineland during World War II. Hooper, a 1942 graduate of Story High School and Lead Bombardier for his squadron, was awarded European Campaign ribbons with two battle stars, the Air Medal with four oak leaf clusters and the Distinguished Flying Cross. Photo courtesy of Mrs. Robert N. Hooper.

The Purple Heart was awarded to Army Corporal H. Clifton Gott who was wounded in the shoulder serving with the Fifth Army in Europe. Gott, another of those who enlisted early in the war, was a member of the National Guard. He landed with his unit in Africa and then at Anzio and took part in the liberation of Rome. The news of casualties also sadly included those killed in action. One of these was Sergeant Charles Saco of 2 Elm Street, Manchester, who died while fighting in the India-Burma Theater of the war. A letter from his Commanding Officer to his parents states, in part: "It was my privilege to have known him; [he earned] not only my respect and appreciation, but the goodwill of the officers and his fellow men. His unit entered combat while displaying courage and devotion to duty and he met his death as a result of enemy action…My officers and men join me in offering condolences, and you have our solemn promise that we shall continue to remember him in our prayers…" Another early enlistee, Sergeant Saco, born in 1919, attended Manchester schools and joined the regular Army in 1939, serving first in Panama.

BOYS, GIRLS SIGN UP
Manchester Youngsters Join the Colors; Serve in Every Theater of War

Meanwhile, stories in The Cricket announced proudly that two Manchester families each had four sons serving with American forces overseas. They were Mr. and Mrs. Clifford F. Doane and Mr. and Mrs. John P. Corley. In November, 1944, readers were introduced to the Doane brothers: Lieutenant Clifford W. Doane, then stationed with the Quartermaster Corps in New Caledonia; Shipfitter 2nd Class Alfred S. Doane, a member of the celebrated "SeaBees" or Navy Construction Battalions; Private First Class Raymond "Tiger" Doane, U.S. Army Air Corps, then stationed at Gulfport Field, Mississippi; and Motor Machinists Mate 2nd Class Donald R. Doane, U.S. Naval Reserve, who had been serving at sea aboard a sub-chaser out of Key West, Florida.

William "Bill" Flatley, son of Dominick and Nora Flatley of Vine Street, served throughout the war with "Merill's Marauders," a special Army unit which often operated behind enemy lines in the China, Burma, India (CBI) Theater.

On March 9, 1945, The Cricket carried a story about the Corley brothers: Private First Class Joseph W. Corley, received the Purple Heart for wounds received in action in the Philippines and later was awarded the Bronze Star medal for "meritorious achievement in ground operations against the enemy, Pacific Theater of Operations on or about the ninth of January, 1945;" Corporal Edward F. Corley was stationed in England, France and Holland; Private First Class George W. Corley was with the Army Medical Corps in France; and Seaman First Class Richard Corley, U.S. Naval Reserve, then a member of the Naval Armed Guard, was aboard the SS JOHN SHARP WILLIAMS carrying vital war materials to England, Scotland and Russia. George Corley received two unit commendations "for outstanding work in the establishment of the 61st Field Hospital, Anderach, Germany," and for "guarding, screening, interrogating, discharging and transporting" back to their homes some 330,000 German prisoners of war in a period of three months.

By the end of 1944, the Allies were advancing both in Europe and in the Pacific. Southern France had been invaded, Paris had been liberated by French, British and American troops, many of whom had landed at Normandy in June. Landings at Kwajalein and Eniwetok had secured beachheads in the Marshall Islands and Guam and Saipan were in U.S. hands.

Private First Class Marshall E. Knowlton's B-17 Group attached to the 15th Air Force had been awarded a Unit Commendation for its role in a successful raid on an enemy aircraft installation at Memingen during which it was attacked by 200 German fighters. Without escort, U.S. gunners during the air battle shot down or damaged 65 enemy planes. Bombs destroyed an additional 35 on the ground. But the mission was costly. Fourteen B-17's were lost taking with them 143 officers and enlisted men.

Navy Lieutenant-Commander Edward S. Gilfillan, on a technical mission involving Naval ordinance, was with the Royal Indian Navy in Burma and later with U.S. Army fliers laying mines from the air. And for his bravery and daring in rescuing a downed Navy pilot in the Southwest Pacific, Quartermaster 2nd Class Robert W. Stanley was awarded the Silver Star. Stanley, aboard a PT boat in a narrow bay, was subject to enemy fire for two and one-half hours before the pilot was finally located and taken to safety.

In 1999, 54 years after the end of World War II, then Quartermaster 1st Class Robert Stanley (retired) was selected by the Surface Navy Association to represent all enlisted men who served in every Theater of the war. At a ceremony in Washington, DC, he was presented with the organization's Historical Remembrance Award by Rear Admiral Thomas Mastiak, USN. Stanley's craft, PT 489, completed 55 patrols and 10 specific missions. PT boats operated in the Atlantic and Pacific Oceans as well as in the Mediterranean Sea.

As 1945 arrived, Dorothy "Dot" Sjorlund, longtime teacher and coach at Story High School, was commissioned an Ensign in the WAVES and was stationed at the U.S. Naval Radio Station, Chatham, MA, as Welfare and Recreation Officer. And from Dutch New Guinea came news that T/4 Mabel Mantjouranis of Ashland Avenue, Manchester, had wed T/5 Clayton Sweatland of Burbank, California. Both were members of the U.S. Signal Corps.

For his "heroic achievements" in combat on Anguar Island, Palau Group, South Pacific Theater of Operations, Lieutenant Russell M. Dennis of 17 Vine Street, Manchester, was awarded the Bronze Star. Dennis, an artillery officer with the 81st Wildcat Infantry Division, "moved forward of [U.S.] infantry lines with two enlisted men just prior to darkness and mounted a tank." From there they were able to identify targets despite the fact that they were continually subject to fire from enemy small arms. Their action "materially assisted the early delivery of supporting artillery."

BRAVERY IN ACTION
Many from Here Are Awarded Medals for Heroism; Some Give Their Lives

As 1945 progressed, fighting intensified and news was received that Corporal William Marshall was wounded in Belgium and had received the Purple Heart. With General George S. Patton's Third Army, Marshall was a member of an Infantry battalion with the 6th Armored Division. By May 7, five months after the last German counter-attack at the so-called Battle of the Bulge, Hitler's armies had surrendered. Sad news, however, of Manchester men killed in action earlier continued to trickle in. One of these was Private First Class Otis H. Stanley who lost his life fighting with the Third Army in Germany on March 7. A graduate of Story High School in 1942, he had been an engineer with radio station WESX, Salem. Another was Army Corporal Harry Mercer who died in combat on

Leyte, Philippine Islands, January 11, 1945. Mercer was born in Newfoundland and came to Manchester in 1930 to live with his aunt. He had been a motorcycle officer with the Manchester Police Department as well as a member of the Fire Department. His commanding officer wrote that he had been in action in the vicinity of Villaba, Leyte, and was killed instantly by a burst of enemy machine gun fire. He was recommended for a Bronze Star and was about to be promoted to Sergeant.

Private John H. Gavin, Jr. of 60 Union Street, died on January 24, 1945 of wounds received in action with the combat engineers of the Seventh Army in France. A friend wrote to his family that Gavin had volunteered to repair a vital Command Post telephone line that had been cut by mortar fire. "They found one break and John told the other two fellows to take off...that he would fix the wire," his buddy wrote. "He did but a mortar shell hit close to him and jarred him at the time three burp guns hit him. He received a slug right through [his body]. He crawled back to our position and the medics took over...at the Battalion [aid] station he received 2,000 cc of plasma to bring him out of shock. He was then sent back to a hospital where he died...He was the best buddy a guy could have."

In April 1945, it was announced that Silver Star recipient Staff Sergeant James A. Murray (see above), born in Manchester in 1911, had died of wounds received in action on Luzon, Philippine Islands on March 15. Bad news, however, was at times tempered with good. Such was the case when Mr. and Mrs. R. Power Fraser of Brook Street opened a letter from their son, Lieutenant Redmond P. Fraser, Jr., U.S. Army Air Corps. Long a German prisoner of war, he had been liberated, he wrote, by Allied Forces. "I'm in France awaiting shipment back to the U.S.A.," he told his parents. "I'm in perfect health and couldn't feel better...You will get a full account of the details when I get back in two or three weeks."

Meanwhile, Quartermaster 3rd Class Jeremiah J. Noonan, aboard the Sims class destroyer USS ROE (DD-418), with four other destroyers and three U.S. cruisers, was engaged in action off Iwo Jima. The ships were bombarding the island prior to the invasion, when the ROE spotted a Japanese trawler inshore. She closed and with gunfire sank the enemy vessel. A Navy plane then observed a Japanese destroyer escort fleeing to the north and the ROE gave chase, the U.S. plane breaking off

Another 110-foot wood subchaser is launched in February, 1943 at Calderwood Yacht Yard, Manchester. The ice in the harbor that month was so thick that dynamite was used to break it up to provide the ship with open water. Among those who worked at the yard during the war years were Sturgis Crocker, who later built wood boats, many designed by his father, naval architect Sam Crocker, at his own yard next door. Others included Jerry Noonan and J. Borden Foster who took this and other photos of the SC's as they were called. Although wartime censors have blocked out the ship's number, it is believed she is SC 1358 which later took part in the Allied invasion of Normandy. Photo courtesy of J. Borden Foster.

because of a lack of fuel. At flank speed, she soon caught the enemy ship, sinking her with gunfire as well. It was all in a day's work for the USS ROE. She returned to station and began once again to bombard the beaches at Iwo.

In June, 1945, news was received that former Principal of Story High School Whitfield F. Kimball had escaped injury when his ship was hit and sunk by a Japanese Kamikaze pilot north of Okinawa. Kimball, a Lieutenant-Commander, was skipper of a Navy minesweeper which was struck at the waterline amidships by the suicide plane. All but two out of a crew of 68 survived despite the fact that the injured vessel rolled over and sank in minutes.

In May, 1945, Germany had surrendered unconditionally to the Allies and the end of the war in the Pacific seemed near as well. But on the Home Front, news of casualties continued to come in. One of these was summer resident Private First Class Charles Russell Lowell Sturgis, U.S. Marine Corps Reserve, who was killed in action in the South Pacific. A member of the Class of 1936 at the University of Virginia, he was married to the former Barbara Brewer. The couple were wed in 1937 at St. John's Church, Beverly Farms. Sturgis' brother, Howard, was also a Manchester resident.

Another summer resident, Navy Lieutenant Charles L. Burnett, son of Dr. and Mrs. Francis L. Burnett of Proctor Street, was awarded the Bronze Star for his role as a gunnery officer in the Pacific. "Performance of his battery," the citation read, "was credited with having contributed materially to the saving of his ship and others in the formation." Lieutenant Burnett's sister, Quitsey, was a Founder of the Manchester-Essex Conservation Trust and for many years a member of the town's Conservation Commission.

IN THE PHILIPPINES
For Gallantry Above and Beyond the Call of Duty, a Posthumous Silver Star

For extraordinary bravery, both Silver Star and Bronze Star medals were awarded posthumously to Corporal Harry Mercer who had resided with his aunt, Mrs. Bertha Snow of Forest Street. A member of the 305th Field Artillery, 77th Division, Mercer died of wounds received in action in the Pacific Theater on January 11, 1945. His Bronze Star Citation reads as follows: "For meritorious service in connection with military operations against the enemy near Leyte, Ormoc, Philippine Islands on 13 December 1944. Corporal Mercer, a Wireman with a Liaison Party of the Field Artillery, went forward with attacking infantry companies to lay wire for the Artillery Observer. In accomplishing his mission, it was necessary for him to cross an open rice paddy about 200 yards in width, carrying heavy, bulky wire and telephone equipment. In doing this, Corporal Mercer, without regard for his own safety, faced heavy enemy artillery and sniper fire which covered the paddy. His outstanding devotion to duty aided the effective deployment of artillery."

Mercer won his Silver Star some weeks later in exchange for his life. "For gallantry in action on 11 January, 1945 at Villaba, Leyte, Philippine Islands. Corporal Mercer, Liaison Corporal, Headquarters Battery, 305th Field Artillery Battalion, while accompanying a reconnaissance patrol which had come under intense fire from a well concealed and strongly entrenched enemy, volunteered to crawl forward to adjust much needed artillery fire. To do [so], he was continually exposed to fire from an enemy pillbox which was protected by intense and accurate machine gun fire. Though mortally wounded in this action, Corporal Mercer continued to adjust artillery fire with such effect that the enemy fire was eliminated or neutralized, and the patrolling company was able to withdraw successfully with important information [about] the enemy's disposition."

The awards were presented to Mrs. Snow by General William C. Crane in a special ceremony at Fort Devens. Mrs. Snow planned to send the decorations to Mercer's parents in Bay Roberts, Newfoundland.

A month before V-J Day, news was received by Mr. and Mrs. Paul Santamaria, 66 Pleasant Street, of the death of their son Tony. A Watertender 3rd Class, he enlisted in the Navy in January, 1942, attended "Boot camp" at Newport, RI, and served aboard the USS ELLYSON (DD-454), a Bristol Class destroyer where he was injured in an accident and hospitalized for 42 days. He was then assigned to a destroyer mine sweeper. He had seen action at Casablanca and in the Mediterranean. He was aboard one of the ships escorting President Roosevelt to Suez before being transferred to the Pacific fleet. There he continued to see action as his ship was involved in island invasions. He was killed at Okinawa where the Navy suffered heavy casualties from Kamikaze or Japanese suicide plane attacks. An excellent athlete, he graduated from Story High School in 1941.

Happier news arrived in August, 1945 when it was learned that Navy flier Herbert Hoyt of Manchester had been involved in a raid on Japan's naval base at Yokosuka which had heavily damaged the battleship NAGATO. Flying with Hoyt was Navy pilot George Foote of Boston, who later married Barbara Smith, daughter of Mr. and Mrs. Abbott Smith, longtime summer residents of Manchester. The NAGATO had been damaged by U.S. bombs at the Battle for Leyte Gulf.

On August 10, 1945, The Cricket featured another Manchester family with four members in the Armed Forces. They were Sergeant Arthur Gordon Cool, U.S. Army, who participated in the invasion of North Africa and later saw additional combat in Italy; Technical Sergeant Frederick R. Cool, U.S. Army Air Corps, a turret gunner in a B-26 Marauder with 60 combat missions to his credit who received the Distinguished Flying Cross, Air Medal with 12 Oak Leaf Clusters, and the Presidential Unit Citation; Technical Sergeant Samuel J. Cool, member of a U.S. Army Air Corps ground crew (mechanic) who was stationed in Alaska; and Lieutenant Mary Ellen Cool, an Army Nurse, who served in Hawaii and later in combat at Saipan. Their parents are Mr. and Mrs. John Cool of Pleasant Street.

In November, 1945 it was reported that 1st Lieutenant William J. Dean, Jr., U.S. Army Air Force, a Summer Street resident, had been awarded the Bronze Star "for meritorious service in support of military operations." An ordinance officer, Lieutenant Dean was recognized for his "eminently successful" supervising of the arming of B-26 aircraft. Stanley A. LaBroda, Boatswains Mate 2nd Class, USNR, of 86 Summer Street, serving aboard the battleship USS MASSACHUSETTS, was also honored with a commendation for "outstanding performance of the duties of his rating" which "materially contributed" to the fighting efficiency of his ship.

TOP SECRET
Manchester Woman Helps to Develop Vital Weapon: the 'Proximity Fuse'

Meanwhile, as peace returned to the world, activities which had been top secret during the war, were slowly being revealed. One of these was what was happening at Sylvania Electric Products in Ipswich which produced for the Navy and, later, for all of the Armed Services radio proximity fuses for anti-aircraft shells. The proximity fuse which automatically detonated the shell near the aircraft was called "America's second best kept secret of the war." Prior to its invention, gunners would set the range and bearing of each shot at a moving aircraft by hand, estimating the speed and altitude like firing a shotgun at a bird flying overhead. Proximity fuses increased the efficiency of anti-aircraft shells by a factor of eight to one. As Sylvania explained, "a plane might escape harm with a near miss of an ordinary shell, but a radio shell would explode and destroy the plane any time it got within 70 feet of it."

Key to the success of the proximity fuse were tiny radio tubes embedded in the nose of the shell which were designed to withstand the shock of firing the gun. A Navy contract called for the production of 400,000 tubes per day at Sylvania's Ipswich, Dover, New Hampshire and Buffalo, New York plants. So secret was the project that its real identity was kept even from the majority of those producing it. One of those who did know was Manchester resident Frances L. "Quitsey" Burnett who was in charge of a lab at the Ipswich plant during World War II.

According to Sylvania, turning the peacetime plant into a secret arsenal required a major upheaval. Production of florescent light fixtures was moved elsewhere and windows were painted so that no one could see what was going on inside. Guards were posted around the building and the classified production area was given a cover name: "the Appliance Department." Everyone who worked there was subject to an intensive background investigation. A resident staff of Naval officers, all engineers, served as liaison with the War Department and as inspectors. Even members of the town's Fire and Police Departments were prohibited from entering the buildings. The plant had its own fire fighting equipment and was guarded by a sizable unit of armed military police. It is generally agreed that only security for the development of the atomic bomb exceeded that for the proximity fuse. It is also agreed that possession of the device enabled the Allies to shorten the length of the war and to save a significant number of lives.

At the war's end, we also learned more about the bravery and extraordinary exploits of our fighting

A summer and later (1939) year-round resident of Manchester all his life, Gordon Abbott, Sr. was commissioned in the U.S. Naval Reserve and called to active duty in early 1940 before the nation was at war. Captain of three minesweepers in his five and one-half year naval career, he won the Navy Cross, the country's second highest award for valor, for action on the Picket Line as commanding officer of USS DEFENSE, AM 317, during the battle for Okinawa in April 1945. After the war he became President and owner of Manchester Marine Company and Kirby Construction Company.

Just graduated from "Boot Camp" at Parris Island (above), Private, later Platoon Sergeant and an Infantry Scout, Larry Kirby, Senior, of Summer Street served with the U.S. Marines' 3rd Division, 2nd Battalion, 9th Regiment during World War II from 1942 to 1945. A veteran of the battles to take Bougainville, Guam, and Iwo Jima, Sergeant Kirby was wounded by an enemy grenade at Guam. His decorations include the Bronze Star with V for Valor, the Purple Heart and the Navy Commendation Medal. Kirby's son, Larry Jr., served in the Army in Vietnam with the 101st Airborne Division, was also wounded and, as a squad leader, received the Bronze Star with V for Valor as well.

Electrician's Mate 2nd Class Pat Noonan at a U.S. Naval Base on the southern tip of the west coast of Greenland in 1944. Pat was there as a member of a team of 60 men operating high-frequency radio direction finders used in conjunction with sister stations in the U.S. to locate U-boats. Additional equipment also enabled Navy personnel to listen to German radio transmissions and to provide navigational information for ships and planes with newly invented and top secret, electronically operated LORAN. Don't miss the "No Women Allowed" sign. Where Pat was stationed there were none for thousands of miles!

Quartermaster 2nd Class, Jerry Noonan, here home on leave, served at sea board the USS ROE (DD-418) during World War II. A SIMS class destroyer, the ROE was commissioned in 1940 and was engaged in escort duty with convoys both in the Atlantic and the Caribbean, U.S. troop landings at North Africa, and the invasion of Sicily. In 1944, she joined the Pacific fleet and took part in escort duty and fire support during landings in the area of New Guinea and in the Marshalls and the Mariannas. She was also involved in the pre-invasion bombardment of Iwo Jima.

men and women such as Navy Lieutenant (j.g.) Harry J. O'Meara who graduated from Story High School with the Class of 1942. A pilot aboard the aircraft carrier USS YORKTOWN, O'Meara was in the air with his squadron hunting for a downed U.S. Army pilot when he spotted a Japanese seaplane. He broke off to destroy the aircraft and then, over land, also bombed and blew up four Japanese railroad trains. He was then shot down himself but managed to parachute into the ocean, a part of the Sea of Japan, where he was quickly rescued by a U.S. PBY amphibian. While on the water, it was chased by a nearby Japanese destroyer, but was able to take off in time to escape with Lieutenant O'Meara safely aboard and thankfully uninjured. All in all, it was an exciting day for the young pilot.

After V-J Day, O'Meara joined other Navy flyers who dropped food, medicine and clothing to Allied servicemen waiting to be liberated in Prisoner-of-War camps on the Japanese mainland. O'Meara's sister, Nancy, who also attended Story High School, was a Corporal in the U.S. Marine Corps Reserve serving in the Quartermaster Corps at installations in and around Washington, DC.

For their contribution to the war effort, few families in Manchester could rival the Conlons with five brothers in the Armed Forces serving in combat overseas. According to a story which appeared in The Manchester Cricket on November 16, 1945, Private First Class Dennis Conlon was with the 772nd Tank Destroyer Battalion during the Battle of the Bulge, Battle of Kolmar Pocket and the crossing of the Rhine River. Master Sergeant Francis Conlon, U.S. Army Air Corps, was Crew Chief for a squadron of B-29 bombers at Tinian Island. He was awarded the Bronze Star. Aviation Ordinanceman 1st Class John Conlon, U.S. Navy, was aboard the aircraft carrier USS ESSEX. He participated in raids on Wake Island, Truk, the Mariannas, Kwajalain, Rabaul, and Tarawa. He was awarded the Distinguished Flying Cross, Air Medal and Commendation Ribbon. Staff Sergeant James Conlon, U.S. Army Air Corps, served in radio communications in New Guinea and at Luzon in the Philippine Islands. And Technical Sergeant Thomas Conlon, U.S. Army Air Corps, was a radio gunner aboard a B-17 bomber serving in North Africa. He was wounded in action and received the Purple Heart. All are the sons of Dennis F. Conlon of Summer Street.

KAMIKAZE!

His Ship Is Hit Off Okinawa but the Bomb Fails to Explode; It's Safely Disarmed

Four days before U.S. troops went ashore at Okinawa Island, Japan, fortune smiled on the the cruiser USS BILOXI with Watertender 2nd Class Walter A. Sweeney of Manchester, aboard. At dawn, Japanese suicide planes appeared and although many were shot down by anti-aircraft fire, one kept coming. With the pilot apparently dead at the controls, despite a last minute maneuver by the ship, the plane struck, penetrating the deck aft. "Strangely, there was no explosion," The Cricket reported. Descending into flooded compartments, repair parties found the reason: the 1,100 pound bomb in the nose of the Kamikaze was, for some miraculous reason, still intact. Carefully, it was disarmed, hoisted topside and dismantled. It's reported that a portion was kept on the quarterdeck as a momento of the occasion.

As this chapter shows, the sons and daughters of an extraordinary number of Manchester families served in the Armed Forces. Mothers and fathers said good-bye to most and often all of their children as they left in uniform for foreign lands. There was no way of knowing when or whether they would return. And yet the cause was just and it was what persevered. Most of them saw combat. Many were decorated. Some were wounded and some gave their lives so that all of us and others around the world could live in freedom.

Another group of brothers who served with distinction overseas was the Scullys. According to a story in The Cricket on April 26, 1946, Electricians Mate 1st Class Francis T. Scully, U.S. Naval Reserve, was aboard USS NUTMEG in the North Atlantic before being transferred to the Pacific Theater where served until the end of the war. Sergeant James M. Scully, U.S. Army Air Corps, was a mechanic at Hondo Army Air Field in Texas where he maintained advanced training aircraft. Sergeant William P. Scully, U.S. Army Air Corps, was a member of a ground crew servicing aircraft in England, the Rhineland, France and Normandy. He was entitled to six battle stars on his European Theater ribbon. Private First Class Edward Scully served as a member of an infantry unit in Panama until he was transferred to Okinawa. All are the sons Charles H. Scully of Lincoln Street.

Two sons and a daughter of Mr. and Mrs. Michael Hurley of Manchester were also in the service of their country. Patricia J. Hurley was a Specialist 3rd Class in the WAVES assigned to flight duty. First Sergeant Thomas J. Hurley, U.S. Army, served with the Ozark Division in combat north of Aachen, Germany where he was wounded, hospitalized and awarded the Purple Heart. Chosen for Officers' Candidate School, he was commissioned Lieutenant and during the occupation, served as a member of a constabulary unit in Germany. Watertender 3rd Class William F. Hurley served aboard the battleship USS SOUTH DAKOTA at Ulithi atoll and during other engagements in the Pacific. SOUTH DAKOTA was the first battleship to bombard the Japanese home islands. Honorably discharged, Hurley served for many years as patrolman and then Sergeant of the Manchester Police Department. The story about the Hurleys appeared in The Manchester Cricket on May 10, 1946.

Also that year, Gordon Abbott, Sr., Commander, U.S. Naval Reserve, a resident of West Manchester, was awarded the Navy Cross, next to the Medal of Honor, the nation's highest decoration for bravery. Abbott, skipper of a 220-foot fleet minesweeper USS DEFENSE (AM-317) and Commander of five-ship MineDiv 10, had been stationed with other small ships (destroyers and destroyer escorts) on the so-called "picket line" north of the island of Okinawa to intercept Kamikaze aircraft as they flew south from bases at Kyushu to destroy larger U.S. ships such as carriers and transports with troops aboard readying for the invasion of the southernmost home island of Japan.

Abbott, then 42 years old, received the Navy Cross from Rear Admiral Morton L. Deyo who was acting for Admiral J.H. Yowers, USN, Commander-in-Chief, U.S. Pacific Fleet. The citation read: "For extraordinary heroism while serving as commanding officer of the USS DEFENSE on April 6, 1945, off Okinawa, when three enemy suicide planes made a simultaneous attack on his ship. One was shot down but damaging hits were made by the other two. Despite continuing air attack, he skillfully maneuvered his ship and picked up and gave medical aid to 50 survivors of a more seriously damaged ship. Then, by expert seamanship, he took in tow the badly damaged and disabled USS LEUTZE (DD-481) and towed her to safety.

His gallantry and determination in action were outstanding and his conduct was at all times in keeping with the highest traditions of United States Naval Service."

For more than two decades after the war, Abbott was owner and President of Manchester Marine Railway and Construction Company and an owner of Kirby Construction Company, both of Manchester. He also served the town for many years as Chairman of the Finance Committee. An early summer resident, his father purchased property here in 1901. Abbott had lived year-round in Manchester since 1939. He entered Naval service in 1940.

ATOMIC BOMB
Hiroshima & Nagasaki Hit; Japanese Surrender; WWII is Finally Over

In the summer of 1945, with the War in Europe over, President Roosevelt dead and Harry S. Truman in the White House, two nuclear bombs were dropped on Japan. One on August 6, destroyed the city of Hiroshima. The other, three days later, pulverized a greater portion of the city of Nagasaki. On August 14, Japan met Allied terms and surrendered unconditionally. Despite their initial devastation, it is generally agreed that the two nuclear bombs played a major role in forcing the capitulation of the Japanese Empire thus eliminating the need to invade the Home Islands, saving millions of lives on both sides.

Manufacturing companies throughout the nation played a crucial role in making components for the bombs. One of these was Metal Hydrides of Beverly where more than one local resident was employed.

In Manchester, news of the end of the war in the Pacific was received at seven p.m. on a summer evening. The first public announcement was a pre-arranged 2-2 blast on the fire alarm. Within a few minutes, as had been the case at the end of earlier wars, church bells all over town started ringing. The Civil Defense siren was also sounded celebrating the victory. People filled the streets and many special religious services were held to give thanks to God that peace had finally come.

Slowly but surely, veterans returned home, many to take up where they had left off years before, some to seek new directions, and others to take advantage of remarkable educational opportunities offered by the GI Bill which paid veterans' tuitions. Existing families were united, new ones begun, and people throughout the country prepared themselves to face a new and very different world.

(Much of the specific information in this chapter came from wartime issues of <u>The Manchester Cricket</u>. If there are inaccuracies, the author apologizes. The intent was to tell the story, now 60 years later, of the patriotism, the commitment, and the bravery of young men and women from Manchester who left the comfort of their homes and the love of their families to serve their nation and the cause of freedom in the Armed Forces. It is a record of which the town can be very proud. Equally important, it is a record which should be remembered and appreciated as the years go by.)

HOMELAND DEFENSE: WORLD WAR II

Early in World War II, this aircraft spotting tower was built on Town Hill, a property then owned by the Manchester Historical Society. Long before radar came into common use, volunteer observers manned the facility 24 hours a day. Equipped with binoculars and a telephone, they reported aircraft heard or seen to Aircraft Warning Service Headquarters in Boston where they could be identified as friend or foe. A second tower replaced the one pictured here in 1943. Significantly more comfortable for observers, particularly in winter, it offered a covered stairway and a heated shelter on top with windows facing in four directions. These towers, located in towns throughout the Commonwealth, were a part of the nation's first line of defense against enemy aircraft.

EARLY WARNING

In 1940, Before Radar, Volunteer Spotters Reported Airplanes Over Manchester

In December, 1941, shortly after the Japanese attack on Pearl Harbor, uncertainty and fear swept America much as they did following the terrorist destruction of the World Trade Center towers in New York on September 11, 2001.

Where would the enemy strike next? Would the Japanese bomb, shell or even invade the West Coast? Here in the East, would German submarines land espionage agents and saboteurs on our shores? Would foreign aircraft destroy our cities?

With help from Civil Defense officials and the U.S. Army Air Corps (the U.S. Air Force, a new service, was established after the war ended), a network of aircraft observation towers was created which could monitor air traffic and report airplane activity particularly in communities surrounding major urban areas. Radar, of course, had yet to be put into wide use and in 1940, even before the U.S. entered the war, an observation tower was erected in Manchester.

With the conflict raging in Europe and in the Far East, many Americans were aware that some day we would be in it, too. Preparations for war had begun and aircraft observation and tracking played a key role in protecting the country. It also gave local citizens the satisfaction of contributing to a larger, national effort.

The first tower was located on Town Hill, a property behind the Trask House then owned by the Manchester Historical Society. It was a simple wood structure with a railed platform on top open to the weather. Reached by ladder, it was operated from 1940 to early 1942 by volunteer members of Manchester's Frank B. Amaral American Legion Post.

Chief Observer, according to The Cricket, was H. Walter Heintz. He was assisted by Charles E. Dodge, Clarence H. Mackin, Leo S. Chane, Charles E. Smith, and Linwood Mitchell. Joining them were Robert Evans and John Murphy of Beverly Farms. John Karlen also served as Chief Observer. Many of these men, of course, saw active military service in World War I.

The second tower was more elaborate. It included a covered stairway, a viewing platform with sides for protection from the wind, and a small, heated shelter with windows facing in each of four directions. Its cost: $2,100, raised wholly from public subscription. By 1943, with the new tower in operation, more than 200 volunteers in Manchester kept watch for passing aircraft.

Equipped with a telephone, field glasses, and a wood stove to provide warmth during the winter months, observers manned the installation 24 hours a day during the war years. Planes sighted, or in bad weather and at night, heard overhead, were reported by phone to Aircraft Warning Service Headquarters in Boston. Early reports were sent to Mitchell Field, New York, operated by the U.S. Army Air Corps.

These towers were a part of the nation's first line of defense against enemy aircraft. No local radar facilities existed until later in the war. The concrete observation towers at Coolidge Point and at Gales Point, two of many along the nearby coast still standing, were designed to provide coordinates for aiming the big guns (as large as 16-inch) which were set in reinforced concrete emplacements to protect Boston Harbor. Their story follows.

Aircraft spotters were a part of the Ground Observer Corps and were issued blue armbands with winged insignia for identification. The information received from towers was plotted at Headquarters on a giant map of the region. It provided a continuous record of craft in the air and helped the Army decide between friend and foe. At air fields nearby, there were fighters ready to scramble at a moment's notice should an unidentified plane appear. Thankfully, there were no air raids on the East Coast during the war, but they were expected and, as mentioned earlier, there was considerable apprehension among coastal residents. But Manchester and other towns which operated spotting towers were watching and listening, ready to sound the alarm. According to Army officials, observation towers were "the nerve tip of the defense system."

The aircraft observation tower on Town Hill which rendered such gallant service during World War II burned down in the 1950's. Today the property upon which it stood is owned by Bill and Dee Burroughs. The Burroughs built their house on the hill in 1974. For many years, Dee Burroughs served as Secretary of the Manchester Historical Society.

TWIN TOWERS

Manchester's Other Towers Used to Help Sight Boston Harbor Field Artillery

Another kind of tower was also built in Manchester during World War II as a part of the Boston Harbor Defense Command. Square in shape and constructed of reinforced concrete, they still stand today. One is located at Coolidge Point; the other at Gales Point. Their purpose, which has excited imagination through the years, was obscured by the secrecy which surrounded them during World War II and subsequently was feared lost in the mists of time.

However, Craig Lentz, a corporate business consultant and now, with his wife Mary Jane, owner of the tower at Coolidge Point (the couple and their children occupy it as a part of their living accommodations) has completed significant research and written an excellent history of the structures which should put speculation to rest. It is reproduced in part below.

"Following the Revolutionary War, the nation began to erect seacoast fortifications to defend itself in case of attack. Forts were built of masonry beginning about 1800, using brick, granite and ultimately reinforced concrete. Many of these forts still exist. They include Fort Warren and Fort Independence in Boston Harbor."

By the end of the 19th century, improvements in artillery design included breech-loading guns, rifling (spiral grooves cut within the gun barrel which increased accuracy and velocity) and the adoption of bore sizes which allowed the use of shells up to 16 inches in diameter. "The largest of these guns," Craig writes, "had a range exceeding 25,000 yards or about 15 miles, which was equal to those in the batteries of battleships of the same era."

To enable the huge guns to accurately hit a moving target, he continues, "an elaborate system of fire control called 'base end stations' were located up and down the coast to support the gun emplacements. Once the target was located, common principles of geometry were used to determine range and bearing and to aim the gun. The Coast Artillery also used powerful telescopes known as 'depression finders,' central plotting rooms, and devices that were primitive forerunners of present day computers.

"At the beginning of the war, Boston with its Navy Yard and excellent port facilities, was high on the list of sites to be defended and several major gun batteries were constructed and armed in and around the harbor. A Coast Artillery battery typically consisted of two guns of the same type. Boston had 27 heavy caliber batteries placed within 13 forts and military reservations stretching from Nahant to Scituate, including several on islands in the harbor itself. In varying degrees, similar defenses existed at Portland, Maine, Portsmouth, New Hampshire, New Bedford, Massachusetts and at the entrances to Narragansett Bay, Rhode Island.

"The two structures in Manchester were a part of the Boston Harbor Defense Command. Each gun battery had several base end stations supporting it. The largest 16-inch guns may have had a half-dozen base end spotting towers stretching along the coast for as much as 40 miles. In addition to the two in Manchester, there were another eight base end stations on the North Shore from Nahant to Ipswich. Three, which were designed to look like private houses and are difficult to see without a trained eye, are located on the ocean side of Marblehead Neck.

"The towers in Manchester were built without any attempt to conceal them. Individual spotting stations were stacked on top of each other on separate floors reaching an elevation of more than 118 feet above sea level at Coolidge Point, and 165 feet at Gales Point. Walls were of military grade, reinforced concrete, 12 to 15 inches thick to protect against naval bombardment. Narrow, slit windows remained open when in use giving spotters a 180-degree view of the ocean. Manchester's base end structures supported several 16-inch batteries, the largest guns in the Army's arsenal.

"Both sites in Manchester were identified by the War Department as early as 1940 prior to the attack on Pearl Harbor. Sites were located on high points of land, not surprisingly on very desirable oceanfront properties which were taken by eminent domain as a "military necessity." An assessment was completed and the owner offered a fair value for the land. For example, the 10,000 square foot lot at Coolidge Point was transferred to the Federal government in June, 1941 at a price of $3,000, appropriate for the time.

"The five-story tower at Coolidge Point was officially known as Location 133, and was the base end station for Battery Gardner, two 12-inch guns at Fort Ruckman, Nahant; and for Battery Long, two

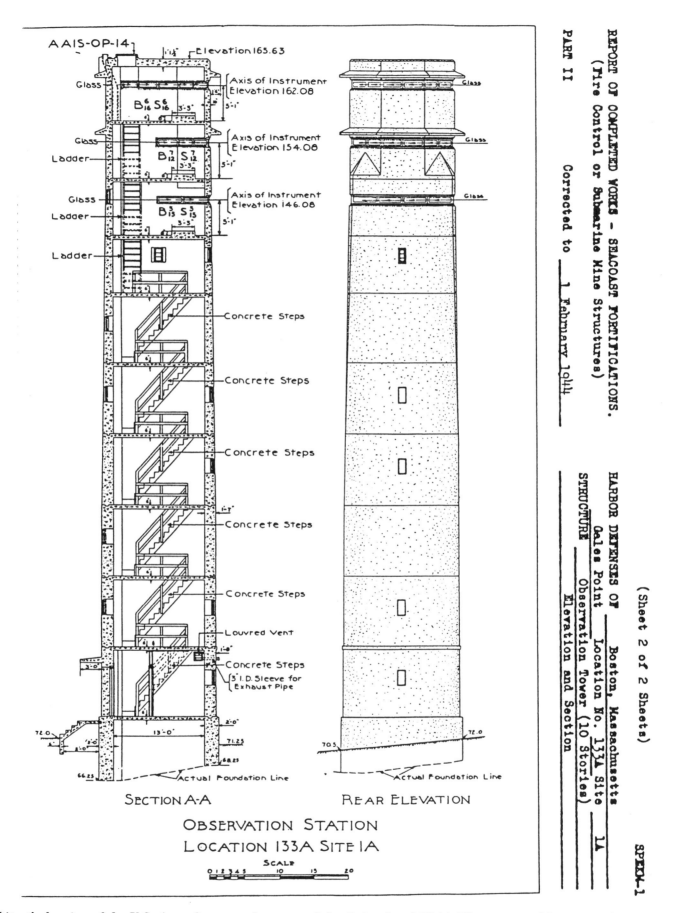

16-inch guns at Fort Duval on Hog Island, near Hull. (Hog Island now appears on the charts as Spinnaker Island.) The third station was never assigned, although it was planned for a gun battery at Portsmouth, New Hampshire.

WOOD BARRACKS

12 to 15 U.S. Army Technicians Housed Nearby; Coal Stove Provides Heat

"The 10-story tower at Gales Point, officially titled Location 133A, housed three base end stations and, near the end of the war, an early version radar system on its roof. It provided fire control for Battery Murphy, two 16-inch guns at East Point, Nahant; Battery 206, two six-inch guns also at Nahant; and Battery 105, two 16-inch guns at Fort Dawes, Boston Harbor."

Staff was needed, of course, to provide the coordinates and other information for gun crews in Boston and at Nahant, and wooden barracks with accommodations for 12 to 15 Army technicians were built alongside the two Manchester towers. Heated by coal stoves with unfinished interiors, their furnishings were sparse but they did the job.

"Several of the gun batteries in Boston," Craig adds, "may be seen today although the guns were removed after the war. Battery Murphy at Fort Dawes was located on what is now Deer Island. It was demolished at great expense to make way for a sewer treatment plant built by the MDC.

"Ironically, this system of land-based harbor defense became obsolete early in World War II due to the development of air power against which even these big guns were vulnerable. The Coast Artillery Corps itself was abolished in 1950 and the concept of heavy artillery defending the continental U.S. passed into history.

"Forts and military facilities like those in Manchester were either converted to other uses by the Army (some became sites for Nike missile defense systems during the early years of the Cold War), or they were declared surplus. Policy dictated that the land be offered to the original owner at its original cost plus the value of any "improvements" the government may have made. The transfer cost of the properties, including the concrete towers, wooden barracks and perhaps some outbuildings, totaled $12,800 at Coolidge Point and $29,400 at Gales Point.

The previous owner repurchased the property at Gales Point. The Coolidge Point site was subsequently sold at auction in 1953 by the government to another private party for under $14,000. Now 50 years later that same property has an appraised value of some $1,000,000."

Following its purchase in 1974, a 15-year "do it yourself project" enabled Craig and Mary Jane Lentz to turn the barracks building at Coolidge Point into a comfortable home for themselves and for their children. Much of the original construction was saved including the GI windows and the large ice box which now serves as a liquor cabinet. As for the tower, "the top or fifth floor," Craig explains, "is used as a family room; the fourth is a library; the kids' TV room is on the third; and we use the first and second for storage." Made safe for children, the family room is a popular place to watch sunsets as well as to view the Boston skyline.

HORSES, WAGONS AND UNPAVED ROADS

In 1895, as this photo shows, Central Street was not yet paved. A horse and wagon, carrying wood barrels, waits patiently outside the Police Station, now restored as SEASIDE NO. 1. Two ladies cross the dirt roadway which in dry weather was regularly wet down with water to control dust. Just above the wagon is a gazebo-like structure of decorative wrought iron which housed the town water pump. To the left of the Congregation Church is "Mother Hamilton's" store, site of Manchester's first apothecary, and the two-story Franklin building. Both were razed in 1909. In front of the church, surrounded by a black iron fence, is a young American elm planted in 1876 to celebrate the nation's centennial.

OLD DOBBIN

For Work and Pleasure, the Horse Played an Essential Role in American Life

Prior to the invention and widespread use of the motor car, the horse provided personal transportation for America and, indeed, the world.

Although wild horses existed earlier in history, domesticated animals date back to the Bronze Age. The horse appeared in Babylonia in 2000 BC and was perhaps first used by nomadic herdsmen in Central Asia, and was always considered important in war.

The use of horses for transport and tillage seems to have come about later. In Britain, for example, oxen, according to the Encyclopedia Brittanica, were used for plowing until the end of the 18th century.

Generally classified into three categories—draft, harness and saddle animals—horses were, in their own era, as vitally important and interesting a part of people's lives as automobiles are to us today. Except for railroad trains and steamers which offered mass transportation, they were the way to get about and Manchester was no exception.

In the 19th century, The Cricket regularly carried advertisements and reports relating to horses. They varied from simple announcements such as "P.H. Boyle, Livery and Boarding Stable, Summer Street" and "Horace Standley, Horseshoer and Jobber, Beach Street," to "R. Culbert, Harness Maker," who more elaborately proclaimed himself "Agent for McBride's Arabian Hoof Ointment and Liniment" and offered "whips and whip sockets, curry combs, brushes, assorted bridle fronts, fancy russet reins, bits, rosettes, and saddle cloths," every accoutrement for the knowledgeable horse owner.

Then, of course, there were carriages and wagons. Although many individuals owned saddle horses which they rode both for pleasure and for general transportation, it was the horse or horses which could be put in traces which were the most useful to a family.

Carriages came in a number of styles and types. For those who could afford them, there were the Chariot and the Brougham, both covered, and the Landau which was open. Most had four wheels, although there were those with two, such as the classic Handsome cab. And there were few sights that would turn more heads than a well-driven pair with an elegantly maintained carriage. For those who chose something less expensive, there were "buggies." Small, light, but still with four wheels, they offered far less fancy accommodations and decorations and were priced accordingly.

Stage coaches, which used to make their way along the North Shore to Boston, were largely replaced in the 19th century by trains and steamers. But carriages, "buggies" and especially commercial wagons, which delivered everything from freight to fresh milk, remained popular until well into the 20th century. Indeed, I recall Hood's milk, butter and cream being delivered in Boston by horse and wagon (granted with rubber-tired wheels) until 1940.

Most of the headaches we face today with automobiles—traffic jams, accidents and problems with parking—were common as well in the heyday of the horse. Take the summer of 1897 when Manchester's Chief of Police Thomas O.D. Urquhart announced "a crusade against teams standing in the streets and feeding horses, [especially] at noon time…" Wagons parked on Washington Street were a particular concern often blocking the flow of traffic, and horses, waiting for their owners, became a special nuisance when they nibbled at the bark of the town's shade trees.

Hardly a week went by that one team or another didn't end up in some sort of an accident. For example, one August day in 1897, a horse belonging to Samuel Knight & Sons, attached to a heavy commercial wagon and apparently annoyed by flies in the hot weather, suddenly took off at a gallop. Up Central Street the animal came at a good clip, the wagon bouncing behind him. In front of the Manchester House (opposite the Town Common), he overtook an open Landau carrying four ladies from Beverly. "There was a terrific collision," The Cricket reported, "and the [ladies'] carriage was overturned completely. [Thankfully] no damage was done beyond some bruises and a bad fright." The errant animal continued up School Street and was finally halted at North Street. Both shafts and its harness were in pieces.

A week or so later, two men driving an open wagon "with more exuberance of spirits than the time and place seem[ed] to warrant," The Cricket declared, "passed a team owned by Alma Haskell, and in doing so collided with the wheel of his carriage, frightening the horse and throwing both men

Carrying ice from Ayers Pond off Loading Place Road in the early 1900's, this wagon stopped at the Regent Garage located where Pine Street joins Bennett Street and Bridge Street. Blocks of ice were distributed by "ice men" wearing rubber cloaks to protect their clothing and carried into kitchens and pantries throughout Manchester where they were deposited in "ice chests," replaced by today's electric refrigerators. Blinders on the horse served to protect against distractions and to keep the animal on a straight and steady course. Horses, however, often had minds of their own and rarely a week went by that <u>The Cricket</u> didn't carry at least one story of a runaway.

Prior to the arrival of the automobile, transport around town of both goods and people depended upon the horse. Here, probably in the early 1900's, a wagon marked "Magnuson Flowers" is about to set off with its colorful content on display. In the background is the George A. Priest School. Wagons and carriages were everywhere then and just as some today take pride and pleasure in their cars, there were those who knew and loved horses and kept their harnesses and other equipment in mint condition. Photo courtesy Elliott Crocker Collection.

out [into the street]." The animal wheeled about and headed for town on his own. On the way, "he took to the sidewalk, left one wheel [there] and the other at Benjamin Tappan's, finally [running into] a tree. All that survived the wreck were the wheels. The remainder of the carriage was kindling wood."

Finally, "last Thursday," the paper continued, "School Street [where it enters Central Square] was pretty well filled up with carriages on both sides. A Tally-ho [a pleasure coach drawn by four horses] came along at a pretty good speed and the street, being narrow, [considerable] skill was required to pass…"

"Unfortunately, there was a collision and Mr. Pfaff's team with Mrs. Pfaff [aboard] waiting [at the curb] was struck." Their horse broke out of his harness but was stopped by Arthur Hooper who was nearby. Meanwhile, the Tally-ho, still traveling at a good clip, locked wheels with a coal wagon opposite Carter's store and dragged wagon, coal and horse up the street, on the way sideswiping a team from Bullock Brothers and another from Essex. No one was injured. An exciting day in downtown Manchester!

Of critical importance to anyone driving horses, as it is to those of us who use motor cars or bicycles, is the design and surface of a community's streets and roadways. Here in Manchester, those in charge of their repair and maintenance are the unsung heroes of our daily lives.

STREETS & WAYS
How Our System of Roads Has Changed from Unpaved Surfaces to Asphalt

When Benjamin J. Crombie retired after 38 years with Manchester's Highway Department in March, 1951, he had a store of memories. Not only did he begin work in 1913 when automobiles were just beginning to replace the horse as the primary mode of private transportation and dirt roadways were the rule rather than the exception, but he served with as many as four Superintendents of Streets.

In chronological order they were, first, his father; then George R. Dean, who later became Chief of Police; Ernest W. Dechene; and P. Edward Sweeney, for whom Sweeney Park off Summer Street is named.

Born at home on Pleasant Street, according to his retirement story in The Manchester Cricket, he

attended the Plain School and "recalled with pride his grand entry into the George A. Priest School." After a year of study at Story High, he left—which was not uncommon in those days—to join his father, then an independent contractor with wagons and two teams of horses. He was often hired by George Kimball, first Superintendent of the Highway Department. With a single team and tip-cart, he was paid $5 a day.

When his father was named Superintendent and he joined the Department as a youngster, Crombie was assigned as driver of its first gasoline-powered trucks, a Model A Ford, a two-ton Sterling and four Chevrolets. Prior to its acquisition of motor cars, the Department often hired local teamsters or used Fire Department horses for road work.

The streets in those days were generally surfaced with gravel and the town owned a stone crusher to maintain them. They then progressed, as Crombie explained, to a surface called "water-bound macadam." This was followed by "tarvia" and finally by asphalt or "hot-top." When it was dry, gravel roads were regularly salted and wet down by horse-drawn water wagons to control the dust. And, of course, in the spring, there was mud.

With municipal funds usually in short supply, unpaved roads were often left rutted and filled with potholes. This made travel by carriage or early motor car, then equipped with a minimum of springs, bumpy and uncomfortable for both passengers and driver.

In 1897, one frustrated resident of Ashland Avenue, hoping to get the condition of his roadway improved, finally wrote a letter to The Cricket expressing his feelings. It concluded with this poem:
"This road is not passable,
Hardly jackass-able,
He who would travel it,
Must turn out and gravel it…"
Winters were different then as well. Huge storms with up to three feet of snow were not uncommon and the town's first snow plow with a V blade was pushed by a 1916 Fordson tractor. In earlier days, snow was often rolled to flatten it for sleighs and pungs. And when it was deep or drifted, horses towed logs behind them to clear roadways. One resident today recalls that a horse-drawn plow was used to clear sidewalks as late as the 1940's. "I think the Highway Department had a pair named King and Chubby," he adds. "They were also used to rake Singing Beach." The Department, too, was the star

of many Manchester Parades and, as Crombie declared proudly, it had four trophies to prove it.

The importance of roads, streets and highways in America is often taken for granted. The earliest roadways were built by the Romans. Many of these, including the famed Appian Way (312 BC), still exist. During the 18th century in England, roads were in deplorable condition until John Loudan McAdam (1756-1836), a wealthy district road trustee in Scotland, experimented with road construction at his own expense. The result was a design which featured a well-drained way with a surface of crushed stone which, in honor of its inventor, was called "macadam."

Water-bound macadam, mentioned by Crombie as an early surface for roads in Manchester, was made from broken granite, trap or hard limestone. It still remains in use on lightly-traveled back roads throughout New England. But as it is not impervious to water (essential in colder climates where the freeze-thaw cycle exists), it is usually treated with a dressing of hot tar which is then often "gritted" with shingle. Asphalt is a brown or black tar-like substance which is mixed with sand or gravel to provide a smooth, waterproof surface.

29 MILES OF STREETS
Public Works Department Maintains Our Transportation Network

Bituminous concrete, a mixture of liquid asphalt and sand, is used to surface roads in Manchester today, according to Robert W. Moroney, PE, Director of Public Works and Town Engineer. Other more sophisticated mixes which include rubber are used on some surfaces such as airport runways to inhibit damage from spilt fuel. Popular road surfaces also include granite cobblestones which were used extensively for city streets in the early days; cement-concrete which was popular in the 1950's as a surface for major highways; and wood blocks set on end which appear in Europe on urban side streets. Roadways of the frontier or in wilderness areas were often made with logs laid side by side, a surface called "corduroy."

Bob Moroney reports that the Highway Division of the Department of Public Works maintains some 29 miles of downtown streets and other roadways in Manchester. To fulfill these responsibilities, Foreman Philip Gauthier and six other municipal employees are equipped with one back hoe, eight

trucks and a sidewalk snow plow. During the winter, vehicles from other departments help out with snow plowing as do private contractors who are engaged as needed. To provide for street drainage, catch basins, too, must be serviced. Through a system of pipes and drains, most of the run-off from rain and snow melt ends up in Saw Mill Brook, Cat Brook and Causeway Brook which eventually all find their way to Central Pond. It drains into the harbor over the spillway at the dam next to Seaside 1.

Records show that the first roadway which enabled settlers to reach Manchester from Beverly was begun in 1646. It included what is today Hale Street, Bridge Street and Bennett Street and was designed to join "the ferry at Salem, and the head of Jeffrey's Creek." According to Frank L. Floyd's history, Manchester-by-the-Sea, at Pine Street it headed northeast past Powder House Hill to Friend Street, then it came back down School Street toward the center of town and turned up North Street, continuing along Washington Street to Sea Street where it joined a road to Eagle Head (later abandoned) and provided access to what is now Masconomo Street, the way to Smith's Point.

In 1685, Floyd writes, a committee was appointed to lay out a road to Gloucester which ended up at Kettle Cove. And in 1728, it was decided to build a highway to Essex and Ipswich. Planning for other roads followed including in 1801, the construction of Summer Street, another main thoroughfare, over Crafts Hill to Forest Street. To spare horses the need to climb the steep hill at Bennett Street, a continuation of Bridge Street from Bennett to Pine Street was built in 1827. And it was not until as late as 1873 that Beach Street as we know it was built with a wooden trestle which crossed Jeffrey's Creek. The stone causeway was installed in 1888. In 1884, Floyd reports, Ocean Street was laid out as "a pleasure drive."

Roadways began as Indian paths in the days when traveling by water was an easier way to reach one's destination. They were improved by settlers who needed access to inland wood lots, public landings and nearby communities on horseback. As the use of carriages and wagons grew, their surfaces were stabilized and smoothed with gravel and crushed stone. Finally, with the appearance of the automobile, demands for speed and comfort led to the construction of a new kind of roadway whose curves had a wider radius and whose surface was much like the roads we use today.

JEFFREY'S CREEK

A Story of People, Places and Events in the Town That Came to Be Known as Manchester-by-the-Sea

CELEBRATIONS: WE LOVE PARADES!

A phalanx of Boston policemen leads the parade up Beach Street toward the Masconomo House in July, 1895 as the town of Manchester celebrates the 250th anniversary of its founding. Chief Marshall Russell Sturgis, a former Major in the Union Army, rides a white horse just behind them. Other officials on horseback follow. Note the formal dress of those watching on what was a warm summer day.

350TH ANNIVERSARY

A Splendid Series of Parties and Events Lasts Throughout the Year of 1995

It was to be the "Mother" of all celebrations. And, as Dan Senecal, Chairman of the 350th Anniversary Committee declared, "its goal was to to bring everyone of all ages in town together, allowing each individual and each organization to express the joy of the occasion in their own way."

It was to recall the long and distinguished history of Manchester and the contributions of more than 14 generations of men and women who lived here. It was to express love and affection for family and friends both past and present. And it was to commemorate the special character of the community itself which fortunately still provides residents with the pleasures and satisfactions of a small town. And unlike earlier anniversary observations, it was to be a series of events continuing throughout the year.

Members of the committee who made it all possible were Nina Adams, Connie Brown, Martha Brox, Gail Dudley, Harry Dudley, Reg Foster, Ed Halsted, Ruth Kelley, Tim Logue, Sally Loring, Nancy Nataloni, Lang Porter, Fred Rice, Dan Senecal, Betsy Sinnicks, Vin Terrill and Regina Villa. They were assisted, as the Board of Selectmen said in its letter to residents, by more than "1,000 volunteers from Smith's Point to Pine Street, from Black Beach to Tuck's Point, [who] offered their time, energy, expertise and importantly their finances to make the celebration a success." And a success it was, beyond the wildest dreams of anyone who took part in the initial planning. Like no other event in recent history, it seemed to pull people of every age and ilk together and give them a common pride and affection for their town and for each other.

And it was all recorded in words and photographs in a most extraordinarily handsome volume, two and one-quarter inches thick, whose hard covers measure twelve and one-quarter inches by nine and one-quarter inches. Titled Manchester-by-the-Sea, 1645 to 1995, it includes a section on the history of the town since its incorporation and a collection of photos, drawings and reproductions which record and recall the celebratory events of the anniversary year. It would not be surprising if everyone in town appeared in one or another of the photos.

The content of the book was exceptional and although credit must be given to all who contributed, three persons were responsible for the quality and attractiveness of the final product. They are Dan Senecal who coordinated and administered the process of production; Fred Nickless, who edited the copy; and Ed Halsted, who was responsible for graphic design, type, and placement of words and pictures.

An elegant publication, Manchester-by-the-Sea, 1645-1995 will forever be a cherished memento for each resident who took part in the celebrations. Halsted's artistic genius was also responsible for the attractive 350th Anniversary logo produced on a special 1995 calendar (which he also designed), stickers, posters, signs and even a mural painted on the concrete counterbalance at the top of the railroad draw bridge.

Events began with a Holiday House Tour on December 4, 1994. In January, a bonfire of Christmas trees at Brook Street Playground officially christened the start of the anniversary year. It was followed by a Valentine's Day dance sponsored by Manchester's Council on Aging; a Coloring Book Party hosted by the Friends of the Library; a concert in March featuring the Manchester Women's Chorus; a program entitled "Women of Manchester" presented by the Manchester Woman's Club; and a series of special dinners to acknowledge contributions of volunteers.

Also, a circular Neighbor-to-Neighbor Walk in May which passed through nearby towns and cities; a sidewalk decorating day with professional artist "Sidewalk Sam;" an Ecumenical Church Service at the First Parish Church Congregational which welcomed pastors of every other church in town, representatives of the Board of Selectmen and the American Legion; dinner and dancing at an elaborate Grande Ball at the Manchester Athletic Club in June which was attended by more than 600 joyful residents in formal attire and in appropriate costume; and a Celebration of Manchester History written and performed by members of the 6th grade at Memorial School.

Also in June, a Garden Tour followed by a gala Garden Party; a gathering at the Manchester Historical Society to open its exhibit of memorabilia from past anniversary celebrations; the always-festive Lions Club Red, White and Blue Breakfast at Tuck's Point on July 1; a series of events on

Spectators on Beach Street watch the parade in July, 1895 celebrating the 250th Anniversary of the Town of Manchester. Indians on horseback with full-feathered headdresses are followed by others on foot. Note the formal, heavy attire of both men and women viewers. Long sleeves and skirt, ties and jackets must have been sweltering in the heat of summer. But those were different days and informality was frowned upon. Note also the long hair in a braid worn by the lady seated on the carriage in the foreground who is mopping her brow. The girl, too, in white, has a handsome braid. And most everyone visible wears a hat.

Puritan ladies with their spinning wheels and loom are depicted in this float draped with white and drawn by two horses in the July, 1895 parade celebrating Manchester's 250th Anniversary. Behind them is another float transporting what appears to be a family scene. Horses are everywhere as the motor car had yet to make its appearance. Carriages and wagons were the way to get about. The fastest method of locomotion was the railroad train. Umbrellas are in use to shelter viewers from the hot summer sun.

Independence Day which included the traditional bonfire at Masconomo Park, the Fourth of July Parade, a Civil War Encampment including a candlelight tour and ham and bean supper; and a concert starring singer Arlo Guthrie and his son Abe which was attended by some 1,500 persons.

The Grand Finale was scheduled for the weekend beginning Friday, September 1, 1995. Earlier, as fate would have it, a full-size replica of HALF MOON, aboard which in 1609, Dutch explorer Henry Hudson discovered the river which bears his name, was hauled for repairs at Rocky Neck in Gloucester. Representing the same era as ARBELLA, she would do perfectly if she could be chartered for the occasion. A quick telephone call to Albany where she usually lay, told Dan Senecal that she was, indeed, available and all that was needed now was a sponsor. Thankfully, one stepped forward. He was Arthur Zafiropoulo, a former resident of Manchester who now lived on the West Coast. It was his generosity that for three days turned HALF MOON into ARBELLA which in 1630 with Governor John Winthrop, arrived in Salem Bay to establish the Massachusetts Bay Colony.

ARBELLA ARRIVES

Dignitaries Stop at the Manchester Yacht Club on the Way to Meet Masconomo

At Manchester's 250th in 1895, ARBELLA was also the highlight of the anniversary celebration. One hundred years earlier, however, using the hull of an old sloop, she was especially designed and built for the occasion. On Friday evening, a reception was held in Gloucester aboard HALF MOON which was now officially ARBELLA and the following day she got underway for Manchester.

Taking her cue from the 250th, she stopped first at the Manchester Yacht Club and next at Manchester Marine where on Sunday visitors were welcomed on board. Just ahead of her was the Navy's USS WHIRLWIND (PC 11), a high speed coastal patrol craft on a courtesy call to Manchester; the schooner WHEN & IF, once owned and sailed out of Manchester by General George S. Patton, dashing commander of the Third Army in Europe during World War II (Patton had her built "when and if" he was able to take time enough for a long-dreamed of voyage around the world); and U.S. Coast Guard Tug PENDANT.

Aboard ARBELLA in costume were Vice Chairman of the 350th Anniversary Committee Fred Rice as Governor John Winthrop, Lotte Calnek as Lady Arbella Johnson, Reg Foster as Isaac Johnson, Sam Adams as Thomas Dudley, Bill Saltonstall as his ancestor Sir Richard Saltonstall, and James Powers as the ship's Cabin Boy as well as other dignitaries. All were bound for Masconomo Park to meet the Great Sachem Masconomo himself played by Neil Andrews in the same manner as the delegation in 1895 was greeted by the then Chief of the Agawams Leonard Andrews, Neil's grandfather also, like Neil, an honored member of the Manchester Police Department. One hundred years ago, the part of John Winthrop was played by Richard Henry Dana, III, grandson of Manchester's first summer resident, who, like Dan Senecal, was Chairman of the celebration as well.

Featured as speaker at the ceremonies was U.S. Senator John Forbes Kerry whose parents, Richard and Rosemary Kerry, were long-time residents of Manchester. For the next two days at Masconomo Park, at Manchester Marine and throughout the town, thousands of visitors enjoyed Breakfast at the Beach, witnessed demonstrations and reenactments, toured visiting vessels, including ARBELLA, purchased special commemorative postage stamps, attended an art sale, inspected a display of antique autos and old-time bicycles, and listened to band concerts and a drum and bugle corps. One of the most popular attractions was a private railroad car called the "Texas Cannonball." Then on Monday morning at 10, the ceremonies over, ARBELLA got underway and became HALF MOON again as she departed Manchester harbor bound ultimately for the Hudson River and her berth at Albany, New York

It was, indeed, the "Mother" of all anniversary celebrations and one that we shall not see again in our lifetimes. Miraculously, every event was blessed with good weather. To make it possible, organizer Dan Senecal, the anniversary committee and other volunteers raised a total of more than $378,000, most of it from generous donors right here in Manchester. And in the future, for those who want to remember "the year that was," there is always the 350th Anniversary book, Manchester-by-the-Sea, 1645-1995. It will make happy reading for decades to come.

IN 1895

Masconomo House Is a Star of Town's 250th Anniversary Celebration

Although only a one-day affair, the town's 250th anniversary celebration which took place on July 14, 1895, was a party few who lived in that era would forget. At sunrise, residents awoke to the sound of church bells. At seven, a gun was fired to signal the gathering of Indian tribes: the Conomos from Manchester; the Wingaersheek from Gloucester; the Chickataubut from Beverly; the Naumkeag from Salem; the Ontario from Hamilton; and the Monotaug from Marblehead.

Soon, The Manchester Cricket reported, "the streets were alive with Indian Chiefs, squaws and papoose" awaiting the arrival of the Governor, John Winthrop, a role to be assumed, as mentioned earlier, by attorney Richard Henry Dana, III of Summer Street.

As in our own 350th, throughout the town, countless houses, stores and other buildings were colorfully draped in red, white and blue with flags, bunting, and pennants to celebrate the occasion. At the Police Station (now Seaside 1), bunting hung from the roof line and was drawn aside to reveal a shield with the commemorative dates—"1645-1895."

At the Masconomo House on Beach Street, the town's largest and most distinguished hostelry, streamers and flags of every description fluttered in the summer breeze. At Town Hall, an impressive ceremonial device with two Doric columns flanked a new front door made to look like white marble. And, as the early train wheezed to stop at the depot, it discharged the first of what was to become a crowd of 25,000 spectators (more than 11 times the size of the town's own population of 2,300!) who had come to watch the festivities. Many clutched a souvenir edition of The Manchester Cricket.

To help maintain law and order and "to protect people from being trampled by horses," Chief of Police Haskell had signed up 40 special officers. They included 20 from Boston, 12 from Salem and eight from Gloucester. To provide relief from the heat, temporary drinking fountains had been set up throughout the town.

By eight o'clock, "hawkers, hurdy-gurdies [hand organs] and snake charmers," according to The Cricket, were on every corner...and with the Hon. Henry C. Leach as presiding officer and Lieutenant-Governor Walcott seated with 2,000 guests in the arena behind Town Hall (Governor Greenhalge was reported occupied with "official business" in Boston), the band and vocal concert began. On the stage a group of children, dressed in red, white and blue, were arranged to replicate the Stars and Stripes.

By nine, just as it happened at our own festivities a century later, ARBELLA (or the reproduction thereof) arrived in the inner harbor having visited the Manchester Yacht Club. Her decks were crowded with joyful, costumed residents playing the parts of Governor Winthrop and his party. The town's formal greeting for the Governor included smoking a peace pipe with the Great Sachem Masconomo played by Sergeant Leonard Andrews, Manchester Police Department, and the presentation by a bevy of Indian maidens of birch bark baskets filled with strawberries. This latter detail of the ceremony celebrated the delights experienced by those Englishmen and women who, on their first day in the New World, went ashore on "the land of Cape Ann" to "gather a store" of the same wild berries.

At 10:30 a.m. after the chorus and the crowd sang the National Anthem and Manchester's own Hymn or Town Song, "The Same Tides Flow," written for the occasion by Nathan B. Sargent, a teacher and later a school principal, the speeches began. In those days before the arrival of radio and television, good oratory was a much appreciated art and audiences were willing to listen for hours to those who presented their messages with charm and erudition. During the 250th, however, speeches were generally short with the exception of that delivered by the Lieutenant-Governor who was billed as Orator of the Day. It may not have lived up to expectations, for the Reverend Darius F. Lamson, chronicler of the town's history, omits it entirely in his book "for want of room" while publishing every other address.

The much-anticipated Collation at Town Hall followed additional addresses by Alfred F. Jewett, Chairman of the Board of Selectmen, The Reverend Lamson and Richard Henry Dana. With an eye on his watch and on the afternoon's schedule of events, Dana observed: "the chairman said he had on his list the names of 12 other gentlemen who are to speak, [but] I will ask if they will please put off [their remarks] until the next celebration." One may suppose that his comment, as it might today,

Her carriage and harness trimmed with white poppies (foreground), Mrs. Gordon Prince was awarded a first prize for her decorations during the parade in 1895 (here on Bridge Street) celebrating the 250th anniversary of the founding of the town. Second prize went to Miss Madeline Boardman and her brother Reginald (Boardman Avenue). Manchester's Water Celebration, which took place on August 18, also included exercises and speeches, a River Carnival of boats after dark lit by torchlight, and a band concert.

Children and adults alike watch a summer parade around 1900 on School Street perhaps on July 4. Photo was taken at the corner of Brook Street. Number 38 School Street is on the left behind the gas lamp post. Street lights have yet to be electrified. First horse-drawn float celebrates the existence of Dodge Furniture Company. The mill's tall chimneys brush leaves of the American elm overhead. Another sign coming along reads "We Have Got a Pull." One wagon, center right, which may have nothing to do with the parade, is turning left. Again, everyone wears hats and is in formal attire for the occasion. Photo courtesy Fredrik D. Bodin and Manchester Historical Society.

was greeted with applause. In any event, after lunch it was time for the grand Floral and Historical Parade.

The procession formed at the Masconomo House on Beach Street. From there it was to proceed along Union, Washington and Summer Streets through the old "back entrance" of the Essex County Club, then along School and Bridge Streets to West Manchester. There it would double back along Bridge Street again to Central Street where it would disband. At 3:30 p.m., Chief Marshall Major Russell Sturgis, a veteran of the Union Army, still handsome in his blue uniform, raised his baton and the parade started. Astride a white horse, he was proceeded by a phalanx of 18 Boston policemen led by Lieutenant J.W. Butters.

Marchers, according to The Cricket, included the Salem Cadet Band, costumed Indians, veterans of the Grand Army of the Republic, a platoon representing the artillery men of the Old Continental Army, and the Lynn and Haverhill Cadet Bands, each, with Salem's Cadet Band, heading one of the three divisions of the parade. Next were scores of carriages carrying such notables as Lieutenant-Governor Walcott and Manchester's own benefactor and diplomat, the Honorable Thomas Jefferson Coolidge, State Representatives, Selectmen from Manchester and surrounding towns, Great Chiefs of the Improved Order of Redmen, and the celebrity of the day, Richard Henry Dana in costume as Governor John Winthrop.

FLOATS & FLOWERS

Horses and Carriages Crowd Roadways as Spectators Watch the Festivities

Behind the carriages came the floats—12 young ladies representing the Maumee Council; six young ladies perched prettily upon the Spinners' float; young men and women portraying the historic Boston Tea Party; a Fisherman's float; two yokes of oxen pulling a cart filled with 52 children supervised by teacher Miss Nellie Leonard; and, finally, pony carts, dog carts, covered phaetons, carriages and wagons, each decorated with flowers and flags. Freddy Prince held ribbons over the horses attached the historic coach used by Governor Eustis in which the Marquis de Lafayette rode in 1824. For her carriage, which featured a Russian hoop trimmed spectacularly with white poppies, Mrs. Gordon Prince won First Prize, a silver loving cup. What spectators remembered years later, were the hundred of carriages, not only in the parade, but those on the roadside along the way, filled with people who had come to watch the festivities.

After the parade, spectators visited the Art and Loan Exhibit at the George A. Priest School which featured a reproduction of a Colonial kitchen with its huge fire place, kettles, and trammel (used for raising or lowering the kettle) as well as a loom and spinning wheels. Also on display, to be returned to their owners, were priceless family heirlooms including silver, glass, manuscripts, coins, pictures and autographs, all of which told a fascinating story of the town's 250 years.

As darkness fell, streets were lit with Chinese and Japanese lanterns. A dazzling electric fountain simulated streams of falling water illuminated in many colors. Finally, at 8 p.m., a gigantic, hour-long fireworks display at the harbor's edge ended the day's festivities. Its closing set piece, lighting the night sky, spelled out the theme of the celebration: "1645 to 1895." There was a huge cheer from the crowd, and the activities were over. The depot was thronged until long after midnight with people leaving town for their homes after an extraordinary day.

In general, things went off without a hitch. One of the horses in the parade collapsed and tragically died of exhaustion. Another, frightened by spectators, was a near runaway. A waiter and musician fell ill and had to be cared for, but that was about it. As it was with our own in 1995, the success of the celebration was a glowing tribute to the cool heads in command, to the scores of skilled volunteers involved in administering and directing the events, and to the process of careful planning which had begun in January of the anniversary year.

There were other celebrations here in 1970 (for the 325th anniversary) and in 1975 during the Nation's Bicentennial. Just before the end of World War II, when most of her young men and women were still away in uniform, Manchester also chose to recognize her Tercentenary. On July 13, 1945 (Germany had surrendered but we were still at war with Japan), the town was once again decked with red, white and blue bunting. A committee of hardworking residents had organized an abbreviated program and festivities were meant to be held at Masconomo Park, but rain intervened and they were moved to Horticultural Hall opposite the depot on Summer Street. Committee members were Henry S. Tappan, Chairman, Frank G. Cheever, Frank L. Floyd, Grace M. Prest, Harry E. Slade and Eugene F. Wogan.

With Acting Chief of Police Jack Connors (Chief Allen Andrews was still in the Army) and his officers leading the way, the procession proceeded indoors to be welcomed by a chorus of local voices; to give thanks with appropriate prayers; to hear a letter from U.S. Senator Leverett Saltonstall, then in Washington; to listen to congratulatory messages from the Mayors of Salem, Gloucester and Beverly; and, finally, to enjoy the remarks of Governor Maurice G. Tobin, Honored Guest, who was the featured speaker of the day.

During the summer of 1945 as well, it having been canceled because of the war in 1942, 1943 and 1944, 225 members of the town's Elder Brethren revived their annual chowder outing at Tuck's Point. It was a sure sign that hostilities would soon be at an end and that life was getting back to normal.

WATER CELEBRATION
Full Day of Events Hails the Installation of Our Municipal Water System

Certainly, one of the most festive single events in the history of the town was the so-called Manchester Water Celebration which took place on August 18, 1892. Designed to commemorate the installation of a municipal water distribution system, it featured a gala parade which followed practically every main thoroughfare, finally ending up at the railroad station.

The procession included, according to the Reverend Lamson, the Germania Band and Baldwin's Cadet Band; both Gloucester and Beverly Light Infantry units commanded by Major Pew of the Allen Post Number 67, Grand Army of the Republic, Sons of Veterans; the Fire Department; barges (floats) with school children; the Magnolia Lodge of Odd Fellows; the Ladies' Relief Corp; and "coaches and private carriages decorated with flowers and bunting" followed by horses and wagons owned by local businessmen.

At 3:30 p.m. at the Town Common, there were speeches, songs "By the Children," and a recitation entitled "Our Treasure from the Flowing Springs" read by Shakespearean actor Joseph Proctor. At 4:30 p.m., the Fire Department presented a exhibition of its equipment and skills.

That evening, with the harbor illuminated by torch light, there was a parade of yachts and commercial vessels and a band concert. After dark, colored lights illuminated a temporary but symbolic water fountain installed at Town Hall.

Other celebrations here include the Fourth of July parade which with its colorful floats, marching bands, fire engines from surrounding towns, antique cars and local officials leading the way, is enjoyed by thousands of residents, and, in another season, the lighting of the Christmas Tree on the Town Common, a tradition which began in 1914. The sparkling new electric lights were provided by electrician Gus Knoerr. And thanks to the generosity of long-time summer residents Mr. and Mrs. William Hooper (whose home, Elsinaes, on Bridge Street is now a part of Landmark School), next to the tree was a collection of oversized toys which included Santa himself, a hobby horse, a bear and other stuffed animals.

"I remember the toys on the Common," Marion Preston Imbault wrote in an article which appeared in a newsletter of the Manchester Historical Society in 1987. "Mrs. Hooper [known to many as Aunt Elsie] was always doing nice things for the town. She organized the Arbella Club for little girls. As one [of them], I recall singing carols from the steps of the church. We wore little red capes...Mrs. Hooper supplied the fabric and we made [them] ourselves." A woman of considerable civic spirit, Mrs. Hooper was also responsible for a program during World War I which sent Christmas gifts to American servicemen overseas. Her niece, Elsie P. Youngman, a summer resident of Boardman Avenue was the author, with photographer George M. Cushing, of Summer Echoes from the 19th Century, Manchester-by-the-Sea. Published in 1981, the book includes a collection of photos of houses great and small from the early twentieth century when the town was one of the region's most popular "watering spots."

MANCHESTER'S BELOVED PHYSICIANS

General Practitioner Dr. Charles A. Herrick was a friend, counselor and physician to hundreds of Manchester residents of all ages for 46 years. One of the last family doctors to make house calls, he served in the U.S. Navy aboard ship and in combat during World War II. He was discharged with the rank of Commander. A graduate of Tufts College and Tufts University Medical School, he began practice in Manchester in 1932. Photo by Ed Wolkin.

SPECTER OF DISEASE

Small Pox & Typhus Haunt the Lives of Manchester's Early Residents

Fear of disease cast a dark shadow across the lives of Manchester's early settlers. Among the most dreaded of maladies was small pox and despite the fact that Dr. Zabdiel Boylston of Boston was vaccinating patients for it as early as 1721, records show that it appeared in Manchester in 1775.

As isolation was a known preventative, on March 20 of that year the town voted "to Choose a Committee of three men to Look out and purchase a place to sett a small Pox & smoak House upon and to agree with a Person or Persons to Build said Houses in the Cheepest manner [sic]." A house was also built at Grave's (Dana's) Beach in 1791 to isolate small pox patients. It was also available as a shelter for the poor when not in use for medical purposes.

In 1748, scores of children reportedly died of what in 1895 Darius R. Lamson's History of Manchester called throat distemper. "The throat swelled with white or ash-colored specks," he wrote "an efflorescence appeared on the skin; with great debility of the whole system, and a strong tendency to putridity." More modern medical theory indicates that the disease was probably diphtheria, an infection marked by high fever and difficult breathing. When news of the calamity reached Salem, William Gray, Jr., a generous merchant, sent money to Manchester and ordered that 100 bushels of corn be distributed to the needy.

Again in 1794, a memoir written by Edward Lee, reveals that another "great sickness," perhaps typhus fever, overwhelmed the town involving "every family but two." Records show some 90 persons died, just short of 10 percent of the then population of 1,000. It was difficult to get anyone to care for the sick and Dr. David Norwood is reported to have "labored excessively" to relieve suffering.

Certainly, the heroes of these early epidemics were the doctors of the community and those who worked with them to care for the ailing. Manchester was fortunate that dedicated physicians with demonstrable medical skills chose to live and to practice here. The earliest to arrive, according to Lamson, was Dr. Joseph Whipple. During the first year of the Revolutionary War, as befitting his status as a leader of the community, Dr. Whipple was appointed Captain of the Coast Guards. Besides practicing medicine, he was ordered with his soldiers to drill each day at the Town Landing; to carry muskets to meetings; to "walk the rounds at night" and to maintain three watches, one at Glass Head, another at Image Hill (just west of Eagle Head) and a third at Crow Island. Any soldier's failure to follow orders was met with a fine. Unfortunately, Dr. Whipple was a casualty of the war. As surgeon aboard the privateer GLOUCESTER, with 18 other men from Manchester, he was lost at sea in 1776 leaving behind him a wife and seven children.

Born in Essex in July, 1796, Dr. Asa Story was another of Manchester's early physicians. He began his education while working at his father's saw mill, walking three miles each evening to recite his lessons to an older friend and counselor. He later studied at Dartmouth College where he received his degree. (Dartmouth offered its first courses in medicine in 1798.) Dr. Story spent one year in Washington, DC and then settled down to practice in Manchester. Much beloved, he never refused, however inconvenient, to respond to calls for help. One bitter cold winter night, his son recalls, with the barn doors stuck fast with snow, he watched his father crawl in a window to reach a shovel so that he could clear a path for his horse and buggy and ride to the other side of town to see a patient who already owed him money and was unlikely ever to pay him a cent.

A long-time member of the School Committee, he was remembered in March, 1895 when Story High School, then located at the top of the hill on Bennett Street, was named in his memory by vote at Town Meeting.

Dr. Story was preceded by Dr. David A. Grosvenor who served the town from 1810 to 1820. Earlier, records show the names of Doctor Lakeman, here from 1801, and Doctor Norwood.

Born in Manchester in 1809, Dr. Ezekiel W. Leach attended local schools and graduated from Amherst College. He studied medicine with Dr. George S. Shattuck of Boston where he began his practice receiving his degree in 1835. Involved in activities with his church and with education, he also served for three years as a member of the State Legislature, but because of ill health was forced to resign. Seeking a milder climate than that offered by New England, he boarded a steamer for

After many years of devoted private practice in Manchester, Roger F. Greenslet, MD, was named Physician in Charge of Emergency Services at the Beverly Hospital. This photo, which appeared in a 1970 Beverly Hospital Aid Association newsletter, shows Dr. Greenslet at his desk. The primary purpose of the then-new Emergency Service was to provide "faster, more accurate medical care [for] the acutely ill" and to separate these often critical cases from persons using the Out-Patient Clinic for follow-up examinations and regular medical appointments.

Born in 1856, physician George W. Blaisdell, practiced in Manchester for 45 years, from 1881 to 1926. A graduate of Dartmouth College, he lived at 21 Union Street, a house occupied by many other MD's who followed him. His house calls were made by horse and buggy and later by automobile. Indeed, Dr. Blaisdell is said to have been the first physician in town to own one. Appointments were usually made with a note left at Lee's Apothecary on the Common. This formal photo of Dr. Blaisdell was taken at Cross Brothers Studio in Salem.

Handsome new ambulance for the Town of Manchester poses for a photo in front of the railroad station at right. The brick structure visible just above the vehicle's engine compartment is owned by the Manchester Electric Company. It's likely that this is the town's first motorized ambulance purchased in 1919. Previously, the town had been served well by an Abbot-Downing, horse-drawn ambulance acquired in 1902 upon the recommendation of Chief of Police Thomas Oliver Drinkwater Urquhart. Subject to the Chief's orders, it was kept at a stable nearby. Note the chains on the rear wheels of the ambulance which enabled it to navigate through winter snow storms and on dirt roads during the mud season.

Europe and sadly died of tuberculosis at sea during the passage. He was 33 years old. Much interested in the history of his home town, he was one of the first officers of the Manchester Lyceum and in his will he left a collection of manuscripts to the Massachusetts Historical Society.

PUBLIC SERVICE

Physicians Also Serve Their Town as Members of the School Board

In 1868, Dr. George A. Priest began the practice of medicine in Manchester. His office was located above D.T. Beaton's Hardware Store, just west of the Manchester House hotel and Floyd's. A fine physician, he was a much respected member of the School Committee. Elected in 1868, his first year here, he served on the committee until his death in 1888. As a tribute to his wisdom and his contributions to the welfare of the town, the George A. Priest School built in 1890 on Washington Street between North Street and Norwood Avenue was named in his honor. An imposing and elegant four story structure, it was torn down in 1954. An impressive monument marks Dr. Priest's grave at Rosedale Cemetery.

By the time of the Civil War, the practice of medicine had improved dramatically. There were a number of medical schools throughout the northeast and many young physicians were studying aboard. (Massachusetts Medical School was established as early as 1783.) The study of anatomy had opened up a new world of surgery. Hospitals and dispensaries had been established in most major cities. Vaccination was commonplace and pharmacology was developing.

Anesthesia had also been discovered and was in wide use. Massachusetts dentist William Morton was the first to use ether in the painless extraction of teeth in the 1840's. Dr. John C. Warren of Boston performed the first operation with ether at Massachusetts General Hospital in 1846. There were major advances, too, in public health and in pediatrics. (The first State Board of Health was established in Massachusetts in 1869.) And schools of nursing were soon to offer professional education for women.

But the family physician was still the lynch pin of American medicine especially in small towns such as Manchester. Babies continued to be born at home. And physicians treated accident injuries involving broken bones and sutures right in their own offices. During hard economic times, payment for medical services was often made in kind—the mechanic would repair a doctor's car, while the fisherman provided food for his table. In some cases, it was impossible for a family to pay at all, but care was never denied the needy.

Ambulances were horse drawn and in 1902 Manchester acquired its first. Thrifty citizens at Town Meeting talked about contracting for ambulance services, but Police Chief Thomas O.D. Urquhart thought the town should have one of its own. "You can't tell how soon any of us might be called to ride in one," he said. That turned the tide and the sum of $650 was appropriated to acquire a new Abbot-Downing ambulance to be kept in a stable subject to the order of the Chief of Police. It served the town until 1919 when it was replaced with a motorized vehicle.

In 1902, to provide immediate medical services, an emergency room and dental clinic were opened on Beach Street. In 1919, the charge for a visit to the clinic was 25 cents. The emergency room was closed in 1930 as facilities expanded at Beverly Hospital, and the dental clinic was moved to the George A. Priest School with Dr. Frank A. Willis as Director. A plaque now at Memorial School commemorates his service. The clinic was later administered by Dr. Robert Howard and Dr. Samuel Ina. Today, with youngsters taught the importance of dental hygiene early in their lives, and fluoride added to our drinking water, the clinic is no longer considered necessary. The need for continuing dental care for the remainder of us, however, is always present and Manchester may consider itself fortunate that among those practicing here are James J. Bacsik, DMD, Robert E. Howard, DMD, Dana K. Powers, DDS, Thomas M. McDuffee, DDS and Sophia K. Martz, DMD.

In 1910, thanks to the generosity of the Manchester Women's Club, the services of a visiting nurse were made available. By 1922, according to Dr. and Mrs. Roger Greenslet who wrote the chapter entitled "Medicine" for the town's 350th Anniversary book, comprehensive health examinations were instituted in Manchester schools. The position of school nurse is still important and continues to be funded as a part of the School Department budget.

In 1986, Charles A. Herrick, MD, a long-time and much beloved physician here, presented a paper to members of the Manchester Historical

Society which introduces many of the doctors who served here from the late 19th century to the present day. Much of the information which follows comes from Dr. Herrick's paper. In its introduction, he especially thanks Nathaniel C. "Nat" Andrews and Mrs. Dorothy Harvey Stanley for their assistance with its preparation.

DRUG STORE

Andrew Lee and Dr. Priest Establish Manchester's First Pharmacy

In 1881, Dr. George Blaisdell arrived in Manchester to begin what was to be a 45-year practice. Educated at Dartmouth College, Blaisdell, like a number of other physicians after him, purchased the house at 21 Union Street which he made both his home and his office. His first calls were by horse and buggy. Later he acquired an automobile and is said to have been the first physician in town to own one. With few telephones then in use, Dr. Blaisdell's schedule called for visiting patients in Magnolia two days each week. Those in Manchester who wished appointments would leave notes at the apothecary. Upon his return he would pick them up. Medications could be purchased from Andrew Lee.

Lee began life as a cabinetmaker. But with the decline of furniture manufacturing, he started studying medicine with Dr. George A. Priest. In 1856, the two opened the first apothecary or drug store in Manchester. In keeping with the era, a soda fountain was installed in 1862. Of white marble, it had one faucet and four syrup dispensers and cost all of $60. Andrew Lee retired in 1888 changing the name of the firm to Andrew Lee & Sons which finally became Allen's Pharmacy. For years, Allen's, then with a new and more elaborate white marble soda fountain, was located in the block at the east corner of School and Union Streets. The proprietor was Perry Allen, sodas were served by May Gray, and George Devon was pharmacist.

Like many Manchester physicians, Dr. Robert T. Glendenning served the town in other ways as well. He was active with the Historical Society and a member of the School Committee for seven years. A graduate of McGill University, Montreal, he arrived from Canada in 1894 and purchased a house on Church Street. Old-timers recall that he used to make his rounds by bicycle. Visiting one patient on Read Island off Proctor Street on a winter day in the 1920's, he had a close call when his bike slipped off the road and fell over the seawall at Proctor's Cove. Thankfully, his only injury was a pair of broken glasses. Like other physicians of his time, Dr. Glendenning brought many babies into the world at home and was on hand for the delivery no matter what the weather. He was also a hero of the flu epidemic here in 1918, caring for patients at Horticultural Hall. Three children died Manchester in what became a tragic national pandemic, killing more than one-half million people. In 1927, at the too early age of 57, Dr. Glendenning died from what was diagnosed as septic throat infection.

A graduate of Harvard Medical School in 1887, Dr. Waldo Tyler completed his residency at New York City's Bellevue Hospital before establishing his practice which he continued here for 40 years. Rugged and athletic, he took a special interest in baseball and was the umpire of many games at the Brook Street Playground. In fact, he is reported to have told one concerned mother-to-be that he would be happy to deliver her baby, but she must wait until the ball game was over. It is said that the infant (a boy) cooperated and that both mother and father were delighted with the medical services they received. Dr. Tyler was also a champion pool and billiard player with a regional reputation. He died in 1931.

In the 1920's and 1930's, Manchester welcomed Dr. William A. MacIntyre, Dr. Lawrence Mutty and Dr. Theodore Ely. Dr. MacIntyre arrived early in the 1920's. His home and office were first on School Street and later at Burnham Court. He practiced here for some 40 years and had a large following of devoted patients.

Dr. Mutty came to Manchester in 1931, establishing his home and office on Union Street. In the mid-1930's he moved to Cape Cod and died a few years later. Dr. Ely also arrived in the 1930's. A graduate of Yale Medical School, he practiced here with offices on Central Street until his death in 1939. He was succeeded by Dr. Edward Winsten who, shortly after World War II, left to accept a position at Danvers State Hospital.

Newly graduated from the Medical School at Tufts University, Charles Appleton Herrick, MD, arrived in Manchester in 1932 to begin a practice which lasted for 46 years. Born in Beverly in March, 1908, Dr. Herrick was a graduate of

The first drug store in Manchester serving physicians and their patients was established by Andrew Lee in 1856. It was located on the Town Common in the building in the shadows at right. The other two-story structure behind the drinking fountain was known as the Franklin House and was also the site of a retail business. Both buildings were razed in 1909. Lee started his professional life as a cabinetmaker, but later studied medicine with Dr. George A. Priest. When he retired in 1888, the name of the firm was changed to Andrew Lee & Sons, finally becoming Allen's Pharmacy and moving to the building at the far left at the corner of School and Union Streets in Central Square. Today, Allen's is located at Harbor Point.

Beverly High School and Tufts College. He interned at Cambridge City Hospital. Still single, he first leased space at 21 Union Street for an office, sleeping on his studio couch. (The house was owned by Dr. Blaisdell's widow.) In 1934, he married Esther Frost of Gloucester, then a nurse at Beverly Hospital, to begin a life-long relationship which included two children, John and Peter. Known as "Doc," John retired as Captain after many years with the Manchester Fire Department. Shortly after their marriage, Dr. and Mrs. Herrick were able to purchase the house at 21 Union which he continued to use as his home and office until after his retirement when he and Mrs. Herrick moved to Essex.

HOUSE CALLS

A Wonderful Tradition Is Abandoned in the World of Modern Medicine

With Dr. Roger Greenslet, Dr. Herrick was a member of the last generation to make regular house calls. He was even known to have visited Baker's Island to care for an ailing resident. A family doctor, he was also a neighbor, counselor and friend. Caring but with a professional bedside manner, he gave his patients confidence that they were receiving the best that medicine had to offer. During World War II, Dr. Herrick served for five years as a medical officer with the U.S. Navy on Atlantic convoy duty aboard the four-stack destroyer USS GREER (DD-145), and in the Pacific aboard the attack transport USS BURLISON which participated in the invasion of Okinawa. He retired in 1945 with the rank of Commander. He was also a member of the Building Committee for Memorial School. Mrs. Herrick was a founder of the Boosters Club. In October, 1978, then age 70, hundreds of former patients and friends attended a party to celebrate his retirement after a lifetime of caring for others. At the occasion, special thanks were expressed as well to those who ran his office for so many years, who arranged his appointments and who knew his patients almost as well as he did. They were Mrs. Wilbur "Dot" Stanley; Mrs. John "Mae" Saco, Mrs. Lester "Alice" Strangman and Mrs. Harry "Agnes" Slade. A scholarship is established in his honor at Tufts Medical School.

For a few months before he joined the Armed Forces in 1941, Dr. Leo Zentgraf opened a practice here on Beach Street. After World War II, Dr. Zentgraf studied anesthesiology at Lahey Clinic and was later appointed Chief of Anesthesiology at St. Elizabeth's Hospital in Brighton.

By the early 1940's, sulfa drugs had proved their effectiveness with infection and disease. Penicillin, too, had been discovered by Dr. Alexander Fleming. Polio vaccine followed and tuberculosis could be effectively treated with medication. The miraculous age of antibiotics had arrived.

During the war many younger doctors and nurses were with the Armed Forces and twice each week Red Cross volunteers in Manchester met to sew, fold and package gauze dressings and bandages for use in treating men wounded in combat overseas.

For three years during World War II, Sergeant Roger F. Greenslet served as a medic with the 45th Army Field Hospital in the European Theater and in Czechoslovakia. Ashore in France on D-Day plus two, his unit, which provided mobile surgical service to wounded front line troops, was also involved in the Battle of the Bulge. Following the war, he attended medical school at the University of Vermont, receiving his MD in 1953.

After residency at Beverly Hospital, he purchased a house at the corner of Lincoln and Vine Streets and in 1955 began practice in Manchester. Like Dr. Herrick, a devoted family physician, Dr. Greenslet often called on patients at home and, during his 14 years here, he and Mrs. Greenslet made many friends throughout the community. He, too, responded to calls for help from Baker's Island, and recalls crossing stormy seas to care for an ill child.

As physician for the Manchester School System, Dr. Greenslet regularly attended football games and other sporting events to be on hand to care for injured players. But no case involving his service to the schools matches one he describes in which a high school student's finger became stuck in a hole in his metal desk. After efforts by the teacher and custodians failed to budge the finger, the young man and his desk, still attached, were hoisted on strong shoulders and carried across Lincoln Street to Dr. Greenslet's office. There with much ingenuity, the finger was finally freed and treated, after which the victim was able to return to class on his own steam.

For reasons of health, as he reports, Dr. Greenslet reluctantly closed his office in 1969, later accepting appointment as Chief of the Emergency Department at Beverly Hospital, a position which he held until 1975 when, until 1986, he served as Medical Director for Sylvania/GTE Corporation. He and Mrs. Greenslet still live at 41 Lincoln Street.

In 1965, Dr. Allen R. MacLeod opened an office for the practice of medicine at Harold Street in Manchester. A graduate of Boston University Medical School with residency at the Beverly Hospital, Dr. MacLeod provided medical services here until 1975 when he accepted an appointment at the United Shoe Machinery Corporation in Beverly.

Today, of course, the delivery of medical services has changed markedly. Physicians rarely practice alone as they once did but band together to offer a variety of specialties. Technology with its extraordinary benefits has raised costs so that without health insurance, Health Maintenance Organizations (HMO's), Medicare and Medicaid, few would be able to afford treatment. It is difficult to remember when the process was once paid for out of patients' pockets.

BOARD OF HEALTH
Selectmen Turn Early Responsibilities Over to Professional Appointees

For years, Manchester's Board of Selectmen also served as its Board of Health. But in 1971, an independent board was established to assume responsibility for public health matters. Its members were Dr. Catherine Coolidge Lastavica, Gerald T. Donellan, and Dr. Samuel A. Ina, Chairman. Dr. Lastavica, a graduate of Johns Hopkins School of Medicine and a resident of Coolidge Point, is known nationally for her research with Lyme disease. Soon, Dr. William J. Otto, Jr. of University Lane, a graduate of Harvard Medical School, and Dr. Estill L. Caudill, a graduate of Vanderbilt University School of Medicine, joined the board. Dr. Otto, a radiologist, was Chief of the service at Beverly Hospital as well as Chief of Medicine.

Thankfully, Manchester continues to be served by physicians whose dedication to their profession and to their patients is still extraordinary. Starting in the 1970's, a new generation of younger doctors established practices in town.

They were Dr. Steven A. Barrett, Dr. Gregory Bazylewicz and Dr. David J. Bush. A graduate in 1969 of the University of Iowa Medical School, Dr.

Bush completed his residency at Hennepin County General Hospital in Minneapolis and came to Manchester in 1970, opening his office at the Old Corner Inn.

Dr. Barrett graduated from Harvard Medical School in 1972 and served his residency on the staff of the University of Colorado Medical Center from 1972 until 1975. The following year he began practice in Manchester opening an office first on School Street and later at the corner of Summer and Brook Streets.

A 1976 graduate of Northeastern University and Harvard Medical School, Dr. Bazylewicz received his resident training at North Carolina Memorial Hospital from 1976 to 1978, and at University Hospital, Cleveland from 1978 to 1980 where he was a Robert Wood Johnson Fellow in Family Medicine. Following tradition, he began his practice here in 1980 with an office at 21 Union Street occupied earlier by Dr. Blaisdell and Dr. Herrick, moving later to offices on Bridge Street. Today, 21 Union Street continues its historic role as a home and offices for James J. Bacsik, DMD.

Upon its completion in 1997, Dr. Bazylewicz, Dr. Barrett and Dr. Harlow LaBarge, all in Family Practice, moved their offices to the new Manchester Medical Building off School Street. They were joined there by eye physician and surgeon, Dr. John Gurley. The Medical Building is also headquarters for Sports Medicine North and Psychological Health Care Associates which includes on its staff Dr. Philip D. Cutter, also a long-time Manchester resident.

A number of Boston physicians who summered in Manchester some years ago also helped to care for its expanded seasonal population. They included Dr. George P. Denney who owned a house on Masconomo Street for many years, Dr. George Washburn and pediatrician Dr. John Davies.

The community is also proud of Dr. George W. Thorn, a summer resident of Coolidge Point, who is known throughout the world for his accomplishments in teaching, in-patient care, and in research, especially in the field of endocrinology. In 1986, the George W. Thorn, MD, Building for Medical Research was named in his honor by Harvard Medical School, Brigham & Women's Hospital and the Howard Hughes Medical Institute. More than 27 of Dr. Thorn's students have become heads of departments at medical schools around the country. Other distinguished physicians living here include Dr. Scott McDougall, surgeon at Massachusetts General Hospital; anesthesiologist Dr. Jon Jaques of Beverly Hospital, and orthopedic surgeon Dr. Charles G. Brennan of Salem Hospital.

Today, most Manchester doctors in family practice have staff privileges at Beverly Hospital. Established in 1888 by Dr. Samuel W. Torrey, and originally located at the corner of Union and Cabot Street, its six beds were for female patients only. By 1908, however, it had moved to Herrick Street where it is today. With 50 patient beds, it offered medical, surgical, obstetric and emergency services.

Responding to demand through the years, the hospital soon added new service centers: a pediatric wing in 1930; a school of nursing and nurses' residence; new operating rooms, a central supply and nursing office in 1941; additional surgical facilities, a new lobby and entrance, a pharmacy and administrative offices in 1957; new emergency and out-patient units, intensive care unit, and critical care unit in 1970; and in the 1980's, a new surgical pavilion, cafeteria and food facilities, more modern and expanded maternity services, and the replacement of four-bed rooms with two-bed and private suites.

BEVERLY HOSPITAL

Outstanding Medical Center Serves Residents of the North Shore

Widely respected for its innovations in medicine, Beverly Hospital was the first medical center north of Boston to have a full-time anesthesiologist and pathologist; the first to utilize the concept of a three-physician surgical team; the first to install oxygen and special piping for anesthesia in patient rooms; the first hospital in New England to provide operating room air conditioning; the first in Massachusetts to initiate training for Practical Nurses as well as Registered Nurses and to establish a Cancer Registry to track the continued health of earlier patients; and the first hospital in the country to create on its own campus, a free-standing Birth Center, staffed by Certified Nurse-Midwives.

But with its high level of professionalism, Beverly Hospital also historically recognized the importance of family. Peer P. Johnson, MD, Surgeon-in-Chief, for whom the Johnson Building is named, was the son-in-law of the hospital's founder, Dr. Samuel B. Torrey. In the next generation, Dr. Johnson's son-in-law, Richard E. Alt,

MD, also served the hospital as Surgeon-in-Chief. A building is named in his honor as well.

As time passed, each generation of physicians in Manchester found themselves able to offer their patients improved medical services because of the proximity of Beverly Hospital. Although the family doctor, now a primary care physician, is still the front line of modern medicine, specialists and continually developing technologies, offer new opportunities to treat disease at regional medical centers such as Beverly.

As staff members, many Manchester physicians have been leaders in helping to improve both the quality and quantity of medical services offered by Beverly Hospital. Few were more involved in this regard than Charles A. Herrick, MD who was appointed to the staff in 1933. Manchester's own Dr. Herrick served as a member of numerous hospital committees and was active as well with State medical groups. He took a special interest in the design and implementation of programs for the elderly. And like many other skilled and caring physicians who have served the Town of Manchester since its beginnings, he was an inspiration for younger doctors seeking to establish a practice of their own in family medicine.

THE ARTS: OUR OWN SPECIAL STARS

Herbert A. Kenny of Summer Street, veteran journalist and author of 13 books, was a reporter and editor of The Boston Post for 23 years. He ended his career after another 18 years with The Boston Globe serving as its Humanities Editor, a department devoted to books, music and the theater. Poet and writer of fact and fiction, Herb was a columnist for Boston Irish News and for 25 years was a member of Manchester's Board of Appeals. Photo courtesy of The Boston Globe.

THE CURTAIN RISES

Publisher James T. Fields; Junius B. Booth; Richard Henry Dana

Unlike its Cape Ann neighbors, the City of Gloucester and the Town of Rockport, Manchester is not widely known for its artists, writers or musicians. And yet through the years, several of its citizens have made significant contributions to the world of literature, to American painting and sculpture, as well as to musical composition and drama.

The first summer resident to represent appreciable accomplishments in the arts was James T. Fields, author and lecturer, but certainly best known as a publisher of books and magazines. Beginning in 1865, perhaps at the urging of his pastor, Reverend Cyrus A. Bartol, a Boston neighbor who had discovered Manchester earlier, he and his wife Annie rented here for many summers and finally, in 1874, built a home of their own on top of Thunderbolt Hill.

Fields, partner and later owner of Ticknor & Fields with headquarters first at Boston's Old Corner Book Store, could claim all but exclusive publishing rights to the works of an extraordinary list of the leading men and women of American letters. All were personal friends and many visited him here in Manchester. They included James Russell Lowell, Henry Wadsworth Longfellow, Harriet Beecher Stowe, Ralph Waldo Emerson, Henry David Thoreau, John Greenleaf Whittier, Sarah Orne Jewett, Celia Thaxter, Bret Harte, Mark Twain and Fields' Beverly Farms neighbor, Oliver Wendell Holmes.

A poet of note, author of articles in The Atlantic Monthly of which he was owner and publisher, and a popular lecturer, Fields, although not a college graduate, was awarded honorary degrees by Harvard and by Dartmouth for his accomplishments in the literary world. After his death in 1881, his wife Annie (herself an author) and her dear friend, Maine writer Sarah Orne Jewett (The Country of the Pointed Firs), spent many happy days at Thunderbolt Hill. (For more about James T. Fields see the section titled REFLECTIONS.)

At the time, Manchester could also point to other summer residents who were distinguished in the arts. One was Richard Henry Dana, Jr., son and namesake of the first summer resident, Richard Henry Dana, Sr., himself a poet and a founder of the North American Review. Dana, an attorney well known for his abolitionist activities, was the author of Two Years Before the Mast, a story of his voyage around Cape Horn to California as a seaman aboard the brig PILGRIM which became and still remains an epic of American literature. His father purchased land overlooking Graves Beach and built a house there in 1845. (See REFLECTIONS for additional information about the Dana family.)

Another summer resident at the time was actor and producer Junius Brutus Booth, Jr. who like James and Annie Fields, learned about the charms of Manchester in 1865 with the assistance of their friend and also summer resident, Benjamin W. Thayer, part owner of The Boston Theater. Booth, brother of the infamous John Wilkes Booth, assassin of President Abraham Lincoln, was one of three sons of a legendary theatrical family. His father Junius and brother Edwin were world famous particularly for their roles in the classical theater. John Wilkes was an actor, too, as was Junius. But his real abilities were as a producer and manager.

In 1869, he and his wife Agnes, a celebrated actress in her own right, built a house at the corner of Beach and Masconomo Streets joining what was to become a community of actors including such Shakespearean stars as Joseph Proctor and John Gibbs Gilbert as well as English actor Frederick B. Conway. Then in 1877, the Booths added on to their cottage a sizable structure which became famous as the Masconomo House, Manchester's great summer hotel with rooms for some 300 guests. It was there that visitors enjoyed not only the pleasures of elegant dining and bathing at Singing Beach, but dramatic productions as well such as Shakespeare's Midsummer Nights Dream and As You Like It. (Again, for more about the Booths see the section entitled REFLECTIONS.)

In more recent years, literary figures have included authors Charles D. Taylor, former U.S. Navy officer and prolific master of the naval adventure novel (Silent Hunter, Shadows of Vengeance, Boomer, Choke Point, First Salvo, Counterstrike and many others); Jack Leggett (The Gloucester Branch, Wilder Stone, Who Took the Gold Away). Leggett later became Director of the University of Iowa's Writers' Workshop; Gerald J. Gormley (The Doll, Dolphin in Summer,

Orcas of the Gulf), Larry Kirby (Stories from the Pacific, combat memories of a U.S. Marine); Ambassador John M. Cabot (First Line of Defense, Forty Years' Experience of a Career Diplomat); Richard J. Kerry (Star Spangled Mirror); Katharine Abbott (Nantucket Summers); Madeline Dewey Crane (poetry); Isabella Halsted (The Aunts); Gordon Abbott, Jr. (Saving Special Places, a 100-year history of The Trustees of Reservations; Abbott was also Editor of The Gloucester Daily Times and The Beverly Times); Darius F. Lamson (History of Manchester, 1645-1895); Ben Morrill, Jr. (History of Manchester, 1900-1990); former Town Clerk and State Representative Frank L. Floyd (Manchester-by-the-Sea, 1945); Elsie Youngman with George M. Cushing (Summer Echoes from the 19th Century); Robert L. Hooper and A.J. Rossi, Jr. (Pictorial Manchester) and Isaac Marshall, Harry Slade, Sr., Dan Slade and Dan Slade, Jr., all Editors of The Manchester Cricket.

Herbert A. Kenny, a long-time resident of Manchester, deserves special mention. A literary figure here and on the North Shore for many years, Kenny was a renaissance man in the world of writing. A graduate of Boston College, he was a lifelong newsman, working first for The Boston Post and later for The Boston Globe where he was a reporter, editorial writer and, finally, Book Editor and founder of The Boston Globe Book Festival. In 1956, when he was night city editor of the Post, he won the Robert Frost Fellowship in Poetry and followed this with a total of 13 books, both fact and fiction, including Newspaper Row: Journalism in the Pre-TV Era, Cape Ann, Cape America and Israel and the Arts. His love of Ireland and Irish writers led him to write Literary Dublin, a History and in his later years two novels, Paddy Madigan and Father, Forgive Me. He also produced popular books for children including Dear Dolphin and Alistair Owl as well as three books of poetry.

On top of all this, he served the Town of Manchester as a member of the Board of Appeals for 25 years and of the Board of Selectmen for one. He was Manchester's much beloved literary lion, and had a special interest in the town's public library.

YOUNG THESPIANS

Manchester Players and Summershow, Inc. Dazzle Audiences With Their Talents

In 1952, Manchester was a fast growing suburban community with a new population of younger residents. In their mid-twenties to early thirties, many of them were veterans of World War II who were beginning professional lives as well as starting new families. Some couples were creative enough to seek a way to express their talents with the Manchester Players which each year for almost a decade, presented a dramatic production at Memorial School, Horticultural Hall and even "on the road" at Gloucester High as a part of the Cape Ann Festival of the Arts.

The Players' performances included such well known Broadway productions as: Lo and Behold, All My Sons, Night of January 16, Bell, Book and Candle, See How They Run, Male Animal, Jane, The Torch Bearers, Rumpelstiltskin, The Wizard of Oz, Curse You Jack Dalton, The Bear, The Crucible, French without Tears and scenes from The Women.

According to Joan Devin, Marge Jackson and Nina Adams, who wrote about the Manchester Players for the 350th Anniversary book, The Crucible by Arthur Miller, produced in 1957, was the group's "most ambitious production." Its cast of 20 presented the traditional two performances in Manchester and then moved to Gloucester where it played successfully for two nights to an audience of nearly one thousand. The Players' some 50 members reportedly recall not only the pleasure and satisfaction of their dramatic performances, but with equal delight and nostalgia, the "never-to-be-forgotten cast parties" which celebrated each production.

Some years later, in 1972, Summershow, Inc. was created by Jim Kittendaugh, an imaginative and energetic teacher at Manchester High School. With his enthusiastic direction, a Broadway musical was presented each summer with Manchester teenagers taking part in every aspect of its creation. As many as 75 were involved in five performances.

In 1976, Summershow was revived by Manchester resident Lee Allen who for the next 16 years (until the curtain descended in 1992) followed the original model with teenagers presenting musical productions annually. In its final six years, Summershow, Inc. involved youngsters from other communities on the North Shore as well. Its financial support came entirely from tax-deductible contributions.

As Allen and Mary Jane Brown write in the 350th Anniversary book, in Summershow's total of 21 years, "nine directors, seven musical directors, seven set designers, and six choreographers...

[used] their professional skills, [to give] free training to Summershow participants…This unique youth theater program gained a reputation for quality and for wonderful entertainment as well as for providing young actors and technicians a place to hone their talents during the summer months."

SCULPTRESS OF NOTE

Kay Lane Weems Battles Tradition to Become a Distinguished Artist

Sculptress Kay Ward Lane Weems writes that she spent "long summers at The Chimney's, our country house [in Manchester] built by my Mother's brother, the architect Raleigh Gildersleeve, in one of the loveliest coves on the North Shore…"

Her memoir, Odds Were Against Me (Vantage Press), as told to friend and former editor of The Atlantic Monthly Edward Weeks (Weeks himself with his wife and family spent summers in Manchester during the 1930's), continues: "My parents were fond of open fires and there are seven fireplaces—hence the name—in our white Georgian house, which stands on a promontory above a…curving beach [Graves or Dana's Beach], looking seaward to Spain, but more closely to a small romantic island that curbs the force of the nor'easters. Wind, white sand, and the high tide surging over the rocks—it is a spot to invite the imagination, and here I would eventually have my studio…"

Born in Boston in 1899, Kay Lane was the only child of wealthy parents who encouraged her interest in art. She attended the School of the Museum of Fine Arts (her father was for seven years President of the Museum's Board of Trustees), and unlike many of her generation, she proposed to devote her life not to marrying and raising a family, but to becoming an accomplished and respected sculptress.

Her mother, sympathetic as she was, voiced concern about her daughter's choice of a career in an era very unlike our own today. "I wouldn't talk too much about your modeling," she said, "People will think it odd that you take it so seriously." From 1918 to 1919, Lane studied with Charles Grafly at the MFA, informally with Anna Vaughn Hyatt and then with Brenda Putnam in New York. After working with live creatures at the Bronx Zoo and earning recognition for a small bronze of a pygmy elephant, she decided to concentrate on the sculpture of animals.

By 1921, she had completed a piece she called Black African Rhinoceros and by 1924, she had begun to place her work on exhibit. Meanwhile, according to the chapter Thumping Wet Clay, part of a catalog published by the Museum of Fine Arts for an exhibit of the work of women artists in Boston entitled A Studio of Their Own, she wrote "I approached thirty with increasing confidence that after twelve years of apprenticeship, I had found what I was best qualified to do…it kept me absorbed and detached from matrimony…my Boston contemporaries who wanted to marry me would not accept my detachment and turned elsewhere…I needed time to prove that in sculpture I was not a flash in the pan…"

In 1926, her Pygmy African Elephant won a bronze medal at the Philadelphia Sesqui-Centennial Exhibition. The following year, her rendition of a jet-black champion racing whippet entitled Narcisse Noir received the Widener Gold Medal at the Pennsylvania Academy of Fine Arts. In 1930, a big commission came from Harvard University for a pair of sculptured bronze doors and a frieze of animals worked into the brick around them at the school's biology laboratories. She also produced a pair of monumental rhinos to guard either side of the doorway. The National Academy of Design awarded Circus Horse the Ellin P. Speyer Memorial Prize in 1931. In subsequent years, much recognition came her way including, in 1960, the National Academy of Design's Saltus Gold Medal. She was elected a chevalier of the French Legion of Honor and also designed the faces of the medal for the Legion of Merit presented by the Armed Forces of the United States.

In 1947, at age 48, Katharine Lane finally gave way to establishment expectations and married a long-time admirer, banker Carrington Weems. Like many of his generation, he was upset when in 1950, she marked pieces for exhibit with her maiden name. In 1980, long after her husband's death and at age 81, she finally had cast an image completed in 1926 she titled Striding Amazon, Rebellion and Revolt. One of the few human figures she created, it is of a "muscular woman intently poised with a rock in one hand and a look of anguish on her face…" dramatizing the frustration which many women of her day felt with the restrictions placed upon them by a more conservative and traditional society. It was a fitting expression of Katharine Lane's determination to

Dana or Graves Island in winter, portion of a watercolor painting (here in black and white) by artist Charles S. Hopkinson. Although Hopkinson was renowned as a painter of portraits (two U.S. Presidents), he was also widely acclaimed for his watercolors. A member of "The Boston Five," a group of young painters who sought to "explore the new possibilities of European modernism," Hopkinson's works were considered "shockingly modern" for his day. He lovingly painted this favorite view from his studio window in Manchester in each of the four seasons. It is owned by his daughter Joan Hopkinson Shurcliff of Ipswich. Photo courtesy of Charles Hopkinson Shurcliff.

Charming oil painting of Katharine Lane painted by her Manchester neighbor artist Charles Hopkinson in 1920 when she was 21 years old. (The image above has been tailored to fit the space available.) A noted sculptress, Miss Lane, who later married Carrington Weems, spent many happy summers at The Chimneys, her house overlooking Grave's Beach. There she had her studio. Hopkinson, a great portraitist, married Elinor Curtis whose parents lived next door at Sharksmouth. In reviewing a show in which the portrait appeared, one critic compared Hopkinson's work to John Singer Sargent. Today the picture is owned by the School at Boston's Museum of Fine Arts. Photo courtesy of Jane Lothrop Gardiner.

successfully overcome what she called in her auto-biography the "odds against me."

Also in 1980, still vigorous, she finished a marvelously dramatic sculpture, filled with motion, showing six, full-size dolphins playing in breaking waves. It is admired by thousands daily who visit the Aquarium on Boston's waterfront. She died at age 90 in 1989.

WORLD RENOWNED

With a Studio in Manchester, Painter Charles Hopkinson Wins Acclaim

Artist Charles Sidney Hopkinson was introduced to the charms of Manchester by his wife Elinor, daughter of Greely and Harriot Curtis who just after the Civil War had built a summer house at Sharksmouth (the shape of nearby rock ledges suggested its name) on the shore at Town Head east of Graves Beach. The couple were wed in 1903 and, except for a few winter months when they rented in Boston or Cambridge (the children even commuted to school by train), they spent most of their lives here. Still owned by the family today, the property looks southwest to Graves Island, south to Egg Rock and beyond to Massachusetts Bay. It is a view that fascinated Charles Hopkinson and one that he would reproduce in watercolors through each of the four seasons for more than half a century.

The scene also captured the attention of the artist's friend and fellow painter John Singer Sargent. Standing on the lawn and looking out to sea, he declared, according to Hopkinson's grandson, Charles Hopkinson Shurcliff, "Charles, what right have you to live in Paradise?"

Hopkinson made his mark, however, not just in watercolors but in oils as painter of portraits. Another grandson, Thomas Halsted, a former member of Manchester's Board of Selectmen and one-time fourth generation resident at Sharksmouth, tells how his grandfather was invited to Paris in 1919 following World War I with seven other artists to paint the portraits of Allied leaders attending the peace conference at Versailles. His work, now at the National Portrait Gallery, met with wide acclaim and led to other commissions which included portraits of Presidents Calvin Coolidge and Herbert Hoover and Supreme Court Justice Oliver Wendell Holmes.

Hopkinson painted members of the Harvard faculty as well as other great educators, businessmen of prominence and community leaders of his time. Today, as Halsted writes in his chapter titled Art and Artists which appeared in the town's 350th Anniversary book, his works are included in the "permanent collections of more than 50 museums and academic institutions including Boston's Museum of Fine Arts, New York's Metropolitan Museum of Art and the National Gallery of Art in Washington."

One of his most delightful paintings was of his neighbor's daughter, Katharine Lane, at age 21. When it appeared in the annual exhibition of the National Association of Portrait Painters in New York, a critic wrote that "Mr. Hopkinson has in the last year placed himself in a position where he rivals John Singer Sargent as America's greatest portrait painter. There are some," he added, "who believe he is greater than Sargent."

But there was another side to Charles Hopkinson, one which encouraged him to depart from the formality of classic portraiture and paint charming likenesses of his own family, his wife Elinor and her four sisters who continued to live next door, as well as his five beautiful and vivacious daughters. He also experimented in his studio at Manchester, overlooking the rocky shoreline and always restless ocean, with watercolors of the landscape around him which were dramatically different from his portraits in style and composition.

In the 1920's, he broke away from the conservative traditions of the "entrenched Boston School" and with four other artists of note (Marion Monks Chase, Carl Gordon Cutler, Charles Hovey Pepper and Harley Perkins) established what became known as "The Boston Five." As Leah Lipton of the Danforth Museum of Art writes in a catalog for an exhibit of Hopkinson's works in 2001 at Vose Galleries of Boston, all "were equally eager to explore the new possibilities of European modernism."

"Critics," she continues, "frequently singled out Charles Hopkinson for special praise when the work of The Boston Five was exhibited and evaluated in newspapers and magazines. His watercolors were perhaps the most abstract of the group, but they commanded serious consideration because of his reputation as a portrait painter." As Charles Shurcliff points out, Hopkinson's paintings were considered "shockingly modern in his day. He had four paintings in the Armory show of 1913, the show that woke America up to modern art." A champion of young and struggling contemporary artists, he established the Concord Art Association with sculptor Daniel Chester French, and with The Boston Five in 1927, the Boston Society of Independent Artists, and in 1928, the New England Society of Contemporary Art which he served as President. In 1948, TIME Magazine called Hopkinson "the dean of U.S. portraitists."

"Completely unworldly and innocent, he was in awe of the beauty of nature," writes his grandson Charles Shurcliff in a touching, personal sketch. "His goal was to try to capture it and convey his joy in it. He never learned to drive. Couldn't do math, but got through Harvard by filling his blue books with wonderful sketches of schooners. His idea of heaven [was] sailing around Egg Rock with a child in tow. Returning by train from his professional work at Fenway Studios in Boston at the end of the day, he would immediately [head for] the lawn to paint the setting sun, balancing his watercolors on his lap and showing his grandchildren how to see the true colors [of nature] by looking at the scene upside down through [their own] legs! He spent the evening making informal pencil sketches of his wife, children and grandchildren as they read or played in the living room. In sum, a very successful and loving life, not at all along the lines of what we think the artist leads."

Recipient of an Honorary Degree from Harvard in 1948, Charles Hopkinson was vigorous and active until the end of his many years. His one-man show in 1958 when he was 89 years old, attracted a "large and enthusiastic" audience. He died in 1962 at age 93.

SHIPS AND THE SEA
Sailor Himself, Thomas Baker Captures the Essence of Maritime Life

Born in Manchester in 1907, artist Thomas Baker fell in love with ships and the sea at an early age. He started sailing here as a youngster with the legendary class of Manchester 17-footers, later graduating to race R-boats in Marblehead. His grandfather, Edwin P. Stanley, was one of the original 11 members of the Manchester Yacht Club founded in 1892.

During World War II, then Lieutenant Baker, U.S. Coast Guard, was commanding officer of MADALAN, a magnificent 147-foot brigantine designed by Henry J. Gielow, Inc. and built originally in Italy as ILLYRIA in 1928 for Cornelius Crane whose father, Richard T. Crane, Jr. of Chicago established the Great House at Castle Hill and at Crane Beach in Ipswich. (Thanks to the family's generosity, both today are properties of The Trustees of Reservations.)

Like many other privately-owned yachts, MADALAN was commandeered, commissioned by the Coast Guard, and assigned to watch for German submarines in the North Atlantic from New York to Nova Scotia along the 100-fathom curve. Once a U-boat was sighted there was not much these ships could do but report its location by radio. Armed with little more than hand guns, they had no depth charges aboard as most were too slow to outrun the resulting explosion.

But despite the hardships of winter weather, the discomforts of often rough water, and the dangers of exposure to the enemy, Baker's experience offshore with the Coast Guard aboard MADALAN and later as navigator for the troop transport GENERAL GREELY, only added to his understanding of the reality and romance of life at sea, his knowledge of maritime traditions, and his interest in ships and shipping. It gives his paintings a quality few others can match.

Working with famed muralist Allyn Cox (whose house and studio today are headquarters for Essex County Greenbelt Association), Baker started painting in 1927 and ran his own commercial studio in Boston for more than 20 years during which he provided graphic design for catalogs and brochures as well as art for well-known board games such as CLUE and SORRY sold all over the world by Parker Brothers of Salem. In a story which appeared in The Beverly Times, Baker reported that he has "a fond memory of the person who encouraged him to make painting his life's work " when he was a young man. "I was down at [Singing] beach," he recalled, "and Frances [Quitsey] Burnett's mother [Mrs. Francis Lowell Burnett who was herself a Read of Read's Island, Manchester] saw me painting. She was the one who told me I should keep at it."

After work in San Francisco, Atlanta and other cities, Baker and his wife Mary returned to Manchester and to the house on Friend Street where he was born. Today, his paintings, which total more than 1,000, hang in the U.S. Senate Office Building and the Corcoran Gallery of Art in Washington, DC as well as in private collections throughout the country. For the Commonwealth's Bicentennial, he

Artist Charles S. Hopkinson at his easel about 1940. Married to Eleanor Curtis, daughter of Greely and Harriot Curtis, Hopkinson had a studio both in Boston and in Manchester at Sharksmouth, the house built by the senior Curtises after the Civil War. Proficient both in oils and in watercolor, Hopkinson's paintings are included in the collections of more than 50 museums and academic institutions. Photo by Margaret Noyes courtesy of Charles H. Shurcliff.

Artist Tom Baker in his studio at Manchester. An officer with the U.S. Coast Guard during World War II, Baker started sailing here as a youngster and later specialized in painting maritime subjects. His works are a part of permanent collections of art at the State House in Boston and at the U.S. Senate Office Building and the Corcoran Gallery of Art in Washington, DC. Photo courtesy of Mary Baker.

completed 14 watercolors representing each of the counties of Massachusetts which now hang permanently in the lobby of the State Senate. He also completed a series of watercolors of the Tall Ships for Sylvania. Other national corporations for which he worked on commission include Motorola, Salada Food, GTE and Ford Motor Company's magazine Ford Times.

Tom Baker died in 1986, but his watercolors live on for all of us to enjoy. Mary Kelly Baker, an accomplished musician, taught many Manchester youngsters to play and to love the piano. Today she continues as the organist at Sacred Heart Church.

Other artists, including Winslow Homer, visited Manchester as well. In 1870 Homer painted a watercolor entitled "Eaglehead, Manchester, Massachusetts," which shows three young women bathing at Singing Beach (the view looks east to Eagle Head). The painting was given in 1923 by Mrs. William F. Milton to New York's Metropolitan Museum of Art. Another local seascape Homer completed in 1868 is called "Manchester Coast" or "Rocky Coast and Gulls."

THE SOUND OF MUSIC
Early Harmony and Hymns Took Place in Churches; Band Concerts Follow

In the early days, the sound of music came primarily from Manchester's churches during their services on Sunday. Indeed, as Dr. Darius Lamson writes describing a typical Sabbath day in the 1750's, "The congregation settles itself...[and] from the 'singing seats' sounds the 'pitch pipe' and tenors and basses, trebles and contraltos, join in Mears or St. Martin's Dundee or Old Hundred, making such harmony as they can one of the paraphrases of Tate and Brady or of Watts' Psalms and Hymns."

Note is made that "Jacob Allen, probably grandson of William Allen and grandfather of John Perry Allen, "pitched the tune in the old meeting house on the Landing, for forty years without pay." Lamson also explains that "Watts' Hymns were published in England in 1707, and his Songs of David in 1719. They were introduced into the church in Manchester in 1753," he continues, "[and] were a great advance upon the often uncouth rhymes of Tate and Brady, and gradually supplanted that collection in the psalmody of New England churches..."

But there were ballads, too, often voiced informally, as indicated by Lamson's description of the close of a 18th century Sabbath: "As the stars begin to come out in the pure skies," he writes, "the young people join in the free-masonry of hearts as old as the race, tales are told [and] songs are sung..."

For many decades. the name of organist Bernice Baker Lipsett was synonymous with music at the First Parish Church Congregational. Today, the organ there is played by Donald R. Dunn. At Sacred Heart, as mentioned above, Mary Kelly Baker is organist and the choir is directed by Jane O'Brien. At the Baptist Church, the organ is played by Calvin Kline and at Emmanuel Church on Masconomo Street by Carolyn Skelton.

As time passed, there was music in the schools as well. The way was led by Nathan B. Sargent, teacher and later school principal (1866) who was also the author of what is called "The Manchester Hymn," actually titled, nostalgically, "The Same Tides Flow." Written for the community's 250th anniversary celebration in 1895, its words stirringly describe the beauties of the town and changes that have taken place since its beginnings: "Where the wigwam was once found, Stands the mansion rich and rare. Wealth and skill have brought their power, Everywhere their work we see; Love and beauty grace the bower, This is Eden by the sea."

As Priscilla Triebs writes in her wonderfully comprehensive review of music in Manchester which appeared in the book commemorating the towns 350th Anniversary, it has been a part of the school curriculum for a century and a half and students have presented scores of concerts through the years. On top of this, an operetta written by Nathan Sargent was produced in 1884. The Ladies Social Circle and Manchester's Women's Club performed musicals and pageants. A violin concert was held at Horticultural Hall in 1929. And, of course, the Masconomo House offered dancing nightly to the music of a professional orchestra.

Band concerts, too, were a happy part of summer evenings at Masconomo Park and at Tuck's Point. At one time, there was a Grand Army of the Republic Band, a Citizen's Band, a Veterans of Foreign Wars Band, and a Boy Scout Drum Corps. Dance bands organized by John Donelan and by Gardner "Gid" Loring were, and are, in great demand. Minstrel shows were popular after World

Teacher, school principal (1866) and song writer, Nathan B. Sargent is best known for encouraging music at Manchester schools and as the author in 1895 of what is known as "The Manchester Hymn." Written for the community's 250th anniversary celebration, it proclaims the changes that have taken place in town while its chorus celebrates the eternal beauty that surrounds us: "But the same tides flow, And the same stars glow; And the waves sing the same wild glee. Just the same the seabird's screech, And the shining Singing Beach, Takes the kisses of the same old sea."

A summer resident of Coolidge Point for many years, artist Ernest Wadsworth Longfellow, son of the poet, was a well-known landscape painter. He studied in Paris. His works were exhibited in museums in New York, Brooklyn and in Boston at the Museum of Fine Arts. Among them were those influenced by a visit to Japan in 1903. Born in 1845, Longfellow died in 1921. This portrait of him, dated 1892, is by English born artist Julian Russel Story, 1857-1919. The Museum of Fine Arts received it as a bequest from Ernest Longfellow. Photo courtesy Museum of Fine Arts, Boston.

Composer Gardner Read has lived in Manchester for nearly half a century. Composer-in-Residence and Professor Emeritus of Composition at Boston University's School of Music, he has also served as conductor of many of the nation's major symphony orchestras. With more than 150 musical compositions, he has won a series of prestigious awards, and is the author of nine books which are considered classics in the field.

War II and in the late 1950's, a group of energetic and creative young residents organized a pair of singing groups they called the Masconotes (women) and the Helmsmen (men) which presented major concerts each year. They were joined by the Harmonettes which much earlier had originated with the Harmony Guild of the Congregational Church and later became The Manchester Women's Chorus. Today the chorus includes men and women and is called The Manchester Singers.

A highlight in the lives of the Masconotes and the Helmsmen came in the late fall of 1962 when they presented an original musical entitled "Yes, My Darling Damsel." Music and book were written by Tom Cooke, with lyrics by Cooke and Jane O'Brien. Sponsored by the Manchester Women's Club, the two evening performances provided support for the Nathan B. Sargent Scholarship and the Alice Forbes Perkins Hooper Nursing Scholarship. The production was directed by David Poch and Katy Schlaikjer.

Music, too, played a major role in expressing the mood and sentiments of the 1960's. Civil rights, the war in Vietnam, reaction against an increasingly technical and insensitive bureaucracy, and the women's movement, all gave rise to the songs of protest, hugely popular, written by such stars as Pete Seegar, Woody Guthrie and Bob Dylan and sung by Joan Baez, the Kingston Trio and Peter, Paul and Mary.

With folk song festivals at churches in Manchester and around Cape Ann, adults tried to reach out to disaffected youngsters. Much of the music, sad, plaintive and beautiful, struck a chord with older Americans as well who were searching themselves for directions during a turbulent time in the country's history. The use of drugs was on the rise. Old values had little appeal to teenagers, but as the decade passed, disorder ended and with Presidents Nixon, Ford and Reagan, society reestablished itself as less individualistic and more conservative. Folk music, however, now on the national stage, was here to stay.

MAESTRO!

Gardner Read and Richard Emery: Two Celebrated Composers in Our Midst

Today, Manchester can be proud of its own composers. They include Gardner Read and Richard S. Emery who wrote the <u>Manchester Anthem</u> (words by Herb Kenny) for the town's 350th anniversary. A composer of choral music for Phillips Exeter Academy, Emery's works have been performed at Boston University, at the Boston Conservatory of Music, in Canada and in Europe. In 1996, his opera "death in Wallowa Valley" was performed in Gloucester at St. John's Episcopal Church.

Gardner Read, a resident of Manchester since 1954, has had an enormously distinguished career in music as a composer, teacher, conductor and author. His interest began as a high school student in Illinois. In 1932, he was awarded a four-year scholarship at the prestigious Eastman School at Rochester, NY. Following graduation, a fellowship made possible further study in Rome with Ildebrando Pizzetti and briefly with Jan Sibelius in Finland until war broke out in 1939. During the summer of 1941, he was at Tanglewood with American composer Aaron Copland who was teaching at the Berkshire Music Center.

From 1941 to 1948, Read was head of the composition departments at the St. Louis Institute of Music, the Kansas City Conservatory of Music, and the Cleveland Institute of Music. He was appointed Composer-in-Residence and Professor of Composition at the School of Music at Boston University in 1948, retiring 30 years later in 1978 as Professor Emeritus. In 1966, he was invited to become Visiting Professor at the University of California at Los Angeles.

From 1943 to 1944, he was Principal Conductor with the St. Louis Philharmonic Orchestra. He has been guest conductor with our own Boston Symphony Orchestra, as well as with the Philadelphia Orchestra, the Kansas City Philharmonic and a number of university orchestras. In 1957 and in 1964, with a grant from the U.S. State Department, he conducted and lectured in Mexico.

He has been a Fellow at the McDowell Colony in Peterborough, New Hampshire and at the Huntington Hartford Foundation in California. In 1964, he received an Honorary Doctorate in Music from Doane College. Other awards include first prize in the 1937 American Composers Contest sponsored by the New York Philharmonic Symphony Society for his Symphony No. 1, performed by the orchestra conducted by Sir John Barbirolli; first prize in the 1943 Paderewski Fund Competition for his Symphony No. 2, Opus 45, first performed by the Boston Symphony Orchestra conducted by the composer; and first prize in the 1986 Art Song Competition sponsored by the National Association of Teachers of Singing for his Nocturnal Visions, Opus 145. He was also honored in 1986 by his alma mater with the Eastman School of Music Alumni Achievement Award.

Many of Read's more than 150 musical compositions have been recorded as LP's and CD's. They include Gardner Read: Works for the Organ; The Sacred Trombone; American Hymn Preludes; CRI American Masters: Gardner Read; New York Legends: Thomas Stacey, English Horn and Gardner Read: The Art of Song.

He is also the author nine books some of which are considered classics in their fields. Among them are Thesaurus of Orchestral Devices; Music Notation: A Manual of Modern Practice; Compendium of Modern Instrumental Techniques; Style and Orchestration; and Pictographic Score Notation.

As musicologist Nicholas Sloninsky wrote in part in 1978: "In American music, the name of Gardner Read is synonymous with the best traditions of modern classicism and inspired romanticism..."

A man of many musical talents, his teaching has influenced hundreds of young composers and his work as a scholar in the field has won him wide admiration and acclaim. In this small town, he is a giant in our midst whose quiet presence we acknowledge with gratitude and respect.

PARKS, OPEN SPACES KEEP US RURAL

A giant glacial erratic, Agassiz Rock was officially christened by the Essex Institute of Salem in 1874. It and its companion, Big Agassiz, an even larger boulder left by the glacier more than 10,000 years ago, were named for Louis Agassiz, a celebrated naturalist, appointed Professor of Natural History at Harvard University in 1848. Both boulders are a part of Agassiz Rock Reservation, a property of The Trustees of Reservations, located off School Street north of Route 128 in Manchester. This photo, probably taken around 1900, shows a relaxed visitor enjoying his pipe.

WONDERLAND

1878: 24-Year-Old Alice Towne Initiates Land Conservation in Manchester

Twenty-four year old Alice North Towne was a young woman of considerable energy, intelligence and perspicacity. Like many summer residents in 1878, one of her favorite pastimes was driving her horse and carriage through the back roads of Manchester, especially on School Street and Southern Avenue which lead through the woods to Essex.

In the old days, all of that area was cut to provide timber for shipbuilding and firewood. Records show that as early as 1710, a series of wood lots was parceled out to residents of Chebacco Parish, Ipswich, which later became the Town of Essex. In much the same way, land was subdivided into wood lots for Manchester residents as well.

Fearful that her beautiful forest land might be destroyed by logging, Alice spoke with family friend Thomas Jefferson Coolidge, who, with Henry Lee of Boston and Beverly Farms, agreed to purchase for preservation purposes property along either side of the scenic roadway. It was among the earliest efforts in the region to protect open land for public enjoyment. (Nearby Ravenswood Park in Gloucester, now owned by The Trustees of Reservations, was established in 1890. The Trustees of Reservations itself was founded in 1891.) Included in the acquisitions was property in Manchester known as Cathedral Pines.

Ultimately, benefactors saw that the land was given to the towns of Manchester and Essex. Funds set aside for its benefit are today held in Manchester in the Woodland Park Trust and in Essex in the Coolidge Trust. Many years ago, to celebrate Alice Towne's foresight and initiative, a bronze plaque was affixed to a glacial boulder nearby. It bears these words: "To the Glory of God and for the Benefit of Man These Woods Are Preserved Forever, 1879."

Alice was the daughter of businessman and philanthropist John Henry Towne of Philadelphia and his wife Maria. In 1867, the Townes purchased some 25 acres of land at Eagle Head where in 1869 they built a house overlooking the ocean. It was later owned successively by U.S. Senator James McMillan of Detroit, Michigan, and in 1921, by Ira Nelson Morris, former U.S. Minister to Sweden. McMillan was chair of the McMillan Commission which, in 1901, was instrumental in restoring the L'Enfant Mall in Washington, DC. Members of the Commission were leading architects and artists of the day. The project had the unqualified support of President Theodore Roosevelt.

To commemorate the town's 250th anniversary in 1895, Alice, her brother Henry and sister Helen, gave the town, in memory of their parents, the stone drinking fountain (made of Lanesville granite) located in front of Town Hall. Alice married Boston attorney Roland C. Lincoln in 1888. Lincoln Street was named in his honor as a tribute for all he did to help provide Manchester with its first municipal water supply in 1892. As a seasonal residence, the couple purchased an 18th century house on Summer Street (number 388) where they lived for many years.

Today, throughout the area north of Route 128, where during the warm days of summer Alice Towne and others drove their carriages more than a century ago, some 1,000 acres of land have been protected as open space thanks primarily to the Manchester-Essex Conservation Trust founded in 1963 by Frances L. Burnett, Albert M. Creighton and George G. Loring. (Originally known at the Manchester Conservation Trust, it recently added Essex to its name.) The site has been identified as a "Wilderness Conservation Area" and biological surveys show it is a prime habitat for rare plants. Much of the information in this chapter comes from Helen Bethel, Executive Director of the Trust for many years, a former member of Manchester's Conservation Commission and one of the region's leading figures in environmental conservation.

Also in the woodlands and wetlands north of Route 128 is land owned by Essex County Greenbelt Association, Manchester's Conservation Commission and Agassiz Rock Reservation, a property of The Trustees of Reservations, the nation's oldest regional land trust. Named for Harvard University's famed Professor Louis Rodolph Agassiz (1807-1873) who first recognized the scientific value of the huge glacial boulder (Little Agassiz is located at the top of the hill; Big Agassiz, another glacial erratic, in the wetland at the bottom), the Reservation, which totals some 110 acres, was acquired in 1957. Agassiz Rock was officially christened in 1874 by The Essex Institute of Salem which owned another great glacial boulder, Ship Rock in Danvers.

Swiss-born Louis Agassiz, appointed Professor of Natural History at Harvard's Lawrence Scien-

Postcard photo shows Singing Beach in the 1920's with its row of wood bathhouses from one end to the other. Note boardwalk in front of bathhouses at far right. Strong winds, a high tide and spectacular surf during the great winter storm of January 28, 1933, destroyed nearly every bathhouse along the beach. Some were swept out to sea while others were simply torn apart and turned into kindling. The few that did survive were moved off site, and were converted to tool sheds and utility buildings. One ended up in New Hampshire as a privy. A couple of the original Singing Beach bathhouses still exist in Manchester.

Visitors admire the harbor from the Rotunda at Tuck's Point in 1896. On Smith's Point the houses from left are Webber, 1886; J. Warren Merrill, 1881; J. Warren Merrill, 1880; Winch, 1890; Stevenson. The Rotunda or Pavilion, the harbor's most distinctive man-made landmark, was designed by architect E.A.P. Liscomb of Boston. Built in 1896 by contractors Roberts & Hoare of Manchester, it cost $1,820. Note that its cap originally included a decorative pole which disappeared sometime in the 1950's perhaps in a storm or hurricane and was never replaced. Photo from the collection of Frances L. Burnett courtesy of Helen C. Sears.

tific School in 1848, was the leader of the natural history movement in America. A vigorous, stimulating personality, he lectured to thousands throughout the East. Agassiz also began the collections which later became Harvard's Museum of Comparative Zoology. He was the author of <u>Contributions to the Natural History of the United States</u>. Its four volumes were published between 1857 and 1863 and include his <u>Essay on Classification</u> which opposed Charles Darwin's process of natural selection. Agassiz's wife, Elizabeth Cary Agassiz, was a founder of Radcliffe College and served as its President from 1894 to 1902.

TUCK'S POINT
Named for a Revolutionary Hero, Park Is Enjoyed by Thousands Yearly

Thanks to ordinances promulgated in Colonial times, Massachusetts residents have had access to the tidal shoreline between mean high and mean low water for "fishing, fowling and navigation." Seacoast communities, too, provided settlers with ways to reach salt water with the establishment of "Public Landings." In early times as well, there were favorite overlooks and picnic sites which by common and prescribed usage (adverse possession) often later were acquired by purchase or eminent domain to become public parks, specifically set aside for recreation.

One of these in Manchester was Tuck's Point. Owned by Cyrus A. Bartol, minister of the West Church in Boston and a summer resident since the 1850's, its 5.4 acres were bought by the town in 1895 for $5,000. An additional $1,000 was paid for an existing wharf now site of the Manchester Yacht Club. Mention of the property first appears in town records in 1732. That year it was agreed that a road and a public landing should be constructed to provide for public access to Pitts Cove or Whittier's Cove.

The story of the structures at Tuck's Point—the Chowder House, the Rotunda, the original bath house and rest rooms and their replacement—appears in detail in the chapter about the harbor and waterfront. Needless to say, for more than a century, Tuck's Point has provided pleasure for the people of Manchester. It is the site of the annual gathering of the Elder Brethren, the Red, White and Blue Lion's Club Breakfast, high school prom parties, weddings, band concerts, outings for both Democrat and Republican Town Committees

and picnics for individual families as well as fraternal and other organizations.

In recent years, thanks to the efforts of the Board of Selectmen and a special Tuck's Point Advisory Committee, the old bath house has been replaced with an attractive new structure designed by Manchester architect John Olson; the Chowder House has been restored and the landscape improved with the addition of new plants, shrubs and trees according to a plan devised by landscape architect Victor Walker. Restoration work is scheduled to begin on the Rotunda as well.

Tuck's Point was named for Captain William Tuck, a local hero of the Revolutionary War whose house still stands nearby. Owner and Master of the 18-gun privateer REMINGTON, he was a man of many talents. Customs Collector of the Gloucester District, he was also a Justice of the Peace, and even successfully practiced medicine. Married four times, he was the father of 23 children. He died in 1826 at the age of 86. (See chronological history of Manchester to read about his escape after capture by the British.)

When problems with Great Britain began to fester again in 1810 (the issues involved freedom for American merchantmen to sail the seas without fear of impressment by the King's Navy), coastal towns armed themselves to prepare against raids and foraging parties from British ships.

Militiamen could keep their muskets with them at home. What was needed was a safe place to store gun powder and it was decided in 1810 to ask Colonel David Colby and his son to build a brick powder house on top of what today is known as Powder House Hill. Manchester had only one opportunity to defend itself against a British landing (see chronological history) and the episode used very little of the powder which was left safely in its brick magazine until it was removed in the 1850's.

One hundred and twenty-one feet above sea level, the property today is parkland, partially owned by the town (45.6 acres) and partially by the Manchester-Essex Conservation Trust (9.2 acres). Powder House Hill was also the site of the town's first water tower.

MUSICAL SAND
Singing Beach Is Known Far and Wide: Masconomo Is an Olmsted Park

Singing Beach, with its musical crystals of white sand (see chapter on harbor and waterfront), is

The traffic circle at Singing Beach around 1910. Rock Dundy is just offshore. In those days, wood bathhouses lined the edge of the dune which formed the back of the beach itself. Also included was a gazebo with a roof and fenced porch where visitors could climb stairs and admire views of the beach, ledges and and boating activities on Massachusetts Bay beyond. All were destroyed and many swept away by high tides, surf, and gale force winds in a fearful winter storm in January, 1933. Note the vintage car has extra spare tires for flats were a common inconvenience.

One of Manchester's most historic families, the Allens, are shown above in a reunion celebrated in 1906 at the Chowder House at Tuck's Point. William Allen came to Cape Ann in 1624 and settled in Manchester in 1640. An early selectman, he was a carpenter who built the first frame house in town. Samuel Allen, born in 1701 was a merchant, father of 13 children, town clerk and also a selectman. Captain John Allen built the brick house on Washington Street that bears his name. Other seafarers included Ben Allen as well as John, James and Samuel. Malachi Allen, 2nd, writes the Reverend Lamson, was "a man of much dignity of character with an inquiring mind who at age 89 could [still] cut up a codfish like a [boy]." Nathaniel Allen, also a sailor, crossed the Delaware with Washington, fought at the battles of Trenton and Princeton, and after the Revolution went back to sea for more adventure. Finally, there was John Perry Allen, cabinetmaker and mill owner in Manchester, who pioneered work in cutting veneers for use in furniture manufacturing.

one of Manchester's most popular attractions. In private hands until 1892, it was appropriated by the town as public park land using authority granted by the so-called Park Act, Massachusetts General Laws Chapter 154, Acts of 1892. Singing Beach totals 12.2 acres. A court settlement in 1899 awarded the owners $111,434.02, effectively the price paid for the beach. There was little disagreement at the time that it was a wise and prudent use of public funds and an investment that would pay huge dividends in the future.

In 1903, however, the proposal to acquire what ultimately became Masconomo Park met with some opposition at Town Meeting. Purchasing such an "isolated spot" seemed "crazy" to a number of voters, but the will of the majority prevailed and the town paid $19,300 for property known as Tappan marsh and mud flats.

By 1908 it had a name. In a letter to Selectmen that year, Mrs. William (Alice Forbes Perkins) Hooper wrote "I see by the Breeze [the North Shore Breeze, a magazine which called itself a Weekly Journal Devoted to the Best Interests of the North Shore], that the question of a name for the park-by-the-sea is to be brought up at the next Town Meeting and I should like, through you, to offer a suggestion to our townspeople [that it be called] 'Masconomo' "after the Great Sachem of the area. The proposal won unanimous and enthusiastic approval.

Park Commissioners engaged the firm of Olmsted Brothers in 1910 to prepare plans to transform the area into a country park. Principals of the firm at the time were the two sons of famed landscape architect and planner Frederick Law Olmsted, F.L. Olmsted, Jr. and John Charles Olmsted, who had worked with their father on designs for New York's Central Park.

In the next five years, some 23 drawings were produced. They envisioned an area of the park for active recreation such as baseball; another area for picnicking and listening to band concerts; and finally, a series of winding paths and roadways which would provide views of the harbor for pedestrians and for those in horse-drawn carriages. The Olmsted plans, which included extensive modifications of the topography of the site, major additions of fill and 500 feet of stone retaining wall, were only partially followed.

Park Commissioners did approve the addition of a "large amount of fill" primarily in what is now the "playing field area," according to a publication

entitled Masconomo Park Workbook prepared in 1995 by landscape architect Margaret Coffin. As testimony to the growing popularity of the park, a bandstand was built there in 1923 to replace one which for years had been located on the Town Common. Another feature was added in 1931: a bronze life-size statue of a World War I "doughboy" rendered by sculptor Philip S. Sears and standing on a handsome granite pedestal. Commissioned by the town to honor those residents who had given their lives for their country in the Great War as well as those who served, it was placed at the entrance to the park on Beach Street.

By the 1940's, officials still seemed interested in the Olmsted plans and a letter from the firm in the files contains suggestions about plant materials. By 1977, however, a new plan had been drawn by landscape architect Robert L. Mackintosh of Manchester to meet the needs of a very different era in which the automobile now played a major role. This plan, too, called for a pedestrian path around the outer edge of the park to enable visitors to better enjoy views of the harbor. Today, thanks to the interest of Selectmen, the efforts of a volunteer committee appointed in 1995 and the results of a design competition won by landscape architect Charles Shurcliff, the walkway is finally in place, attractively landscaped with numerous benches along its perimeter. Like Tuck's Point, detailed maintenance of the park is made possible with charitable contributions.

WINTHROP FIELD
Magnificent Open Space Gives Pleasure to Thousands Who Pass It Regularly

One of the great pleasures that hundreds of residents and visitors enjoy each day is the view from Bridge Street across pasture land to wooded hillsides at what was once Winthrop Farm. A wet meadow and wildlife habitat, it is today known as Winthrop Field in honor of Clara B. Winthrop whose generosity led to its preservation in 1970. The land, some 13.9 acres, is owned by the Town of Manchester. Miss Winthrop and Gardner and Vail Read, also made possible the establishment of Winthrop Nature Preserve off Jersey Lane, some 6.9 acres, owned by the Manchester-Essex Conservation Trust.

The property was purchased in 1894 by Miss Winthrop's father, Robert C. Winthrop, Jr. On it was a huge 80-room, 150-foot long, stone house which the family lived in until Miss Winthrop had it razed in 1952. Much earlier, in 1908, she had built for her own use a modest, six-room cottage. An inveterate traveler, she was there in the "off season." The stable, farm cottage, barn and green-house were built by Roberts & Hoare and still stand today. Clara Winthrop died in March, 1969. She was more than 90 years old.

Another substantial parcel of land is preserved stretching south of Summer Street to Eagle Head subdivision. Acquired by the Town of Manchester as a possible site for a new high school, it was deter-mined to be too wet and unstable to be suitable for building purposes. Today it includes Sweeney Park with its athletic fields, named for veteran Superin-tendent of Streets P. Edward Sweeney, as well as some 27 acres of small ponds, wetland, glacial ridges and mixed pine and hardwood forest. A wildlife habitat for small mammals and birds, it is a coastal stopover area during times of migration. The property includes a trail which leads past a small pond where waterfowl are often seen.

By 1953, Route 128, eastern Massachusetts' post-war circumferential highway, had been fin-ished as far east as Manchester. And a new bridge over the Annisquam River named for Congressman A. Piatt Andrew, a resident of Eastern Point, would soon provide high speed access to Gloucester and complete the road to Cape Ann. The highway bridge at Pine Street had been named for Seaman Richard E. Bailey, U.S. Navy, missing in action after the loss of the cruiser USS QUINCY in the Battle of Savo Island in August, 1942. The bridge crossing School Street was dedicated to the mem-ory of Corporal Frank B. Amaral, who died as a result of wounds received in action on the Western Front in April, 1918. Both men were the first bat-tle casualties from Manchester during the two world wars.

To many, the new roadway inspired dreams of "limited commercial development" located north of the town center between Route 128 and the Town of Essex in landscaped industrial parks which would offer job opportunities and new tax revenue. Others felt the land should be preserved as open space to be enjoyed for its scenic beauty and environmental values. Thankfully, much has been accomplished towards the latter. While the remainder of Route 128 is scattered with industry and shopping malls, the section of the roadway from Route 22 east to Route 133 is still wonderfully rural much as it was a century ago.

And although there were those who opposed the construction of Route 128 in the 1950's, imagine what life in Manchester would be like today if Route 127, which passes directly through the cen-ter of town, was the only access to Gloucester and Rockport to the east and to Beverly, Salem, Peabody and Danvers to the west. Our streets would be clogged with traffic and the town would be a very different place indeed.

ZONING
Selecting Land Use Patterns for Town Is the Role of Planning, Zoning

Mention of the town's open spaces, their impor-tance to the attractiveness of the community and the still rural character of its landscape, cannot be made without a reference to zoning which plays such a critical role in governing the uses of land everywhere. Discussions of zoning here began as early as 1944 with a proposal that two districts be established, a general district which allowed for unrestricted use, and a residential district which was restricted to single family homes.

It was presumed correctly that after the war, major estates would be subdivided and that Select-man Frank Floyd's prediction that Manchester would become a year-round residential community for suburban commuters would be realized. Among the first major subdivisions in the early 1950's were one for 39 house lots between Summer Street and Forest Street; 17 house lots at Eagle Head; and one for 38 house lots on a portion of the Charles Walker estate to be known as Highwood. As demand for housing grew other subdivisions followed at Woodholm Road, Walker Road, Deer Hill Road, Crooked Lane, Ledgwood Road, Hick-ory Hill and Forster Road.

One of the earliest took place in 1885. In 1872, according to research conducted by Shepard Brown, a longtime Manchester resident, John H. Towne (Alice's father, see story above), a summer resident from Philadelphia, purchased a sizable amount of land near Kettle Cove and at Eagle Head. The latter he used as the site for a home of his own overlooking the ocean. The former parcel, some 92 acres of upland and two of salt marsh, was, after his death in 1875, conveyed by his estate to the University of Pennsylvania of which he was

Sunset Hill, home of Major Henry Lee Higginson towers over Black Beach, West Manchester in this photo taken around 1900. Major Higginson became a summer resident of the town after the Civil War where he was wounded serving with the First Massachusetts Cavalry. The railroad station which then had a full-time ticket agent sits alongside the tracks. Note that the sea wall had yet to be built. There were far fewer trees in those days and by the look of the dories moored there, the cove was used by hand-line fishermen of which there were many. Photo from Peabody-Essex Museum collection.

Built prior to 1810, the brick Powder House atop Powder House Hill off Elm Street served the town during the War of 1812. Although firearms could be kept at home, muzzle-loading rifles and cannon of the era used gun powder which, for safety's sake, was stored in bulk away from population centers. The magazine most likely contained wooden kegs of black powder which could be parceled out to troops as needed. Today the Powder House still stands and the area, which totals more than 50 acres, is parkland open to the public. Smith's Point is visible in the background in this early photo taken by George W. Dodge's Photograph and Tintype Rooms, Washington Street, Boston.

a great benefactor. Ten years later, the university subdivided the property located in Manchester and in Gloucester. Records show that most of the lots were sold between 1884 and 1900, although five remained unsold until 1926. The area today is known as University Lane.

Zoning dictated the size of residential lots and for decades, until 2002, Residential A remained at one acre maximum. That year, however, it was decided by Town Meeting to rezone shorefront lots into two acre parcels to retain the open and scenic "estate character" of properties still remaining. It was a wise decision which some felt should have been made years earlier. Also thanks to the efforts of many and with the assistance of The Trust for Public Lands, a national organization devoted to the preservation of open space, negotiations have led to the design of large lot subdivisions at Dexter's Pond and off Highwood Road, for example, which have reduced building and other structural densities and protected woodlands and natural areas. Today, thanks to its size as one of the Commonwealth's smaller towns (7.84 square miles), few places are left in Manchester where major subdivisions can take place.

Besides its coastal conservation areas which also include salt marsh at Chubbs Creek in West Manchester (partially protected by Essex County Greenbelt Association and the Town of Manchester), at Bennett's Brook at Bridge Street, at Day's Creek and at Kettle Cove as well as Black Beach and White Beach off Ocean Street (originally town landings confirmed by the Land Court to be still public in 1921), Little Crow Island and Black Cove Beach at Boardman Avenue, West Manchester, the town has also taken steps to protect its freshwater ponds, streams and brooks.

These include Central Pond, 2.1 acres on Sawmill Brook between Elm and School Streets behind the Fire Station acquired for fire fighting purposes in 1873; Brickyard Pond, 2.6 acres which border Summer Street (Route 127) just east of Sweeney Park given to the town in 1943 by Mrs. G.M. Lane, Mrs. T.J. Coolidge and Mrs. F.M. Whitehouse; Cranberry Pond and Rattlesnake Den, 12.7 acres, off Forest Lane and Loading Place Road given to Essex County Greenbelt Association by Marion and Stephen C. Hall; and Dexter Pond Conservation Area, 19.4 acres, given to the Manchester-Essex Conservation Trust by Irving W. and Frances Colburn. The Colburns also

very generously gave to The Trustees of Reservations conservation restrictions protecting selected areas of their property which has ocean frontage and wetland along Summer Street.

Much of the watershed of Millet's Brook and Saw Mill Brook are protected by 13-acre Millet's Brook Reservation; by land along Saw Mill Brook and by selected ponds such as Central and Brickyard; with conservation restrictions (the land remains private property but development of any sort is prohibited); and by the Weems Conservation Area, 12.3 acres off Summer Street, gift of Katharine L. Weems. In 1965, the first parcel of what today is known as Wyman Hill Conservation Area was given to the Town of Manchester by United Shoe Machinery Corporation. Many generous people followed with other gifts until today the area totals some 90 acres. And in 1985, the Trust acquired Owl's Nest Woodland and Nature Preserve, some 23 acres, as a gift from R. Forbes Perkins.

Other properties acquired for preservation include Jack's Hill, 14.2 acres between School and Pine Streets along Route 128; Moses Hill, 7.3 acres, 18 acres, a gift from Pygmalion Partners; 118.3 acres, gift of a conservation restriction from Phillip deNormandie; and 23.5 acres given by William L. and Jane Saltonstall.

BENEFACTORS
Again, the Coolidge Family Rewards Manchester with a Special Gift

In 1871, Thomas Jefferson Coolidge of Boston, great-grandson of the third President of the United States, purchased for $12,000 the old Goldsmith Farm in Manchester on Millett's Neck, a point of land just east of Kettle Cove. There "on a wild promontory surrounded by the ocean," Coolidge, most appreciated here for his gift of our public library, and his wife, the former Hetty Sullivan Appleton, had built a "country house" in 1873.

For his own summer place on the point, Thomas Jefferson Coolidge, Jr. chose a house of dimensions very different from his father's. As architects, he engaged the celebrated firm of McKim, Mead & White which designed in 1902 what became known locally as the "Marble Palace" built of brick and white marble. This was torn down in 1958 and replaced by a far simpler single-story brick house shortly before the death of T.J. Coolidge, III. It was lived in by his widow, the former Katherine H.

Kuhn, for many years until her death when it, too, was razed.

Today, thanks to the generosity of Dr. Catherine Coolidge Lastavica, and her brothers, T. Jefferson Coolidge, IV and J. Linzee Coolidge, more than 57 acres including the Ocean Lawn, most of Clark Pond and its shoreline, woodland paths, carriage trails and a portion of Magnolia or Gray Beach, are preserved for environmental purposes in perpetuity. Coolidge Point Reservation is a property of The Trustees of Reservations. The remainder of Gray Beach located in Manchester is privately owned.

OUR NEWEST PARK
Two Acres of Public Open Space On Manchester-Gloucester Border

Manchester's newest public park is located off Raymond Street, Manchester, and Magnolia Avenue, Gloucester. Shared with the City of Gloucester (the boundary gives Manchester about two-thirds of the land), it is named after the Surf Restaurant which was located at the site for many years. A plan for the landscape of Surf Park has been prepared by Carol R. Johnson Associates of Cambridge. Its two acres were acquired in 2001. Generous gifts plus a contribution approved by voters at a Manchester Town Meeting, made purchase of the land possible. Funds raised include an endowment which will pay to maintain the property as well. The new open space will provide citizens of Manchester and Magnolia with a restful and attractive area for walking, views of Massachusetts Bay and Kettle Island, and a recharge area for rain water which used to drain down Raymond Street and through a culvert to Clark's Pond significantly affecting its water quality.

Organizations, individual citizens and public officials have worked hard through the years to balance the development of housing, commercial and municipal uses of land and open space conservation. That Manchester is still a "country town" is due in large measure to their efforts to protect the rural character of the community.

There is still need for additional land conservation as there is a need, particularly as property values rise, for "affordable housing." Thankfully, steps continue to be taken to fulfill both objectives.

ISLANDS: EMERALDS IN A SHINING SEA

Looking south from Great Misery, visitors see the single light at Baker's Island across Salem Channel. It was through this passage that the ARBELLA passed in 1630 leaving Little Misery to starboard as she ghosted in to Salem Bay. During the 20th century, Great Misery became the site of a summer colony of houses, a nine-hole golf course and a luxurious club house. Most buildings were destroyed by fire in 1926. At Baker's Island, the summer colony is still thriving. Today Great and Little Misery Islands are a day-use recreation area owned by The Trustees of Reservations.
Photo by David Ryan.

THE MISERYS

More Manchester Than Salem, These Islands Frame Our Outer Harbor

As ARBELLA coasted into Salem Bay on Saturday, June 12, 1630, her log notes that she "passed throughe the narrowe streight between Baker's Isle and [Little Isle] & came to an Anchor..." off what is presumed to be Plum Cove on the Beverly shore.

On her starboard hand was Misery Island and Little Misery (Little Isle) which she left close aboard as she would have today following the main ship channel. Since its first mention in those early days, Misery has been a part of the City of Salem. But like Baker's, also under the jurisdiction of Salem, its geographic location (it's much closer to us and helps to shape and protect our outer harbor) and its social history have made it feel a part of Manchester as well.

Just how Great and Little Misery Islands got their names is still a mystery. They were referred to in early records of the Bay Colony as "Morton's Misery" and "Moulton's Misery." Robert Moulton was a master ship's carpenter sent here by London adventurers in 1629 to encourage shipbuilding. All of the islands of the bay in those days were heavily wooded and speculation has it, although there is no evidence that Moulton owned the islands at any time, that he could have leased them for a supply of timber, easily rafted to the nearby shore. Heaven knows the problems he may have endured carrying out his work, but the name Misery has stuck ever since.

According to Saving Special Places, a history of The Trustees of Reservations, now owners of the some 90-acre property, at one time, the land on the islands was farmed, and during the nineteenth century, summer houses, as many as two dozen, some elegant, some modest, were built on Great Misery. The islands also served as the site of a fertilizer plant until about 1900 when they were purchased by the Misery Island Club as a summer resort.

A comfortable club house was constructed on the bluff above the cove which faces Manchester harbor. Two stories high, it had three gables and a wide veranda where members could relax in rocking chairs and overlook the busy waters around them. During its brief heyday the Club flourished. Dues were $25 per year. Many members were summer residents of Manchester. Access was provided by a pair of naptha launches, JOSEPHINE and LIZZIE, which ran to and fro from a pier at West Beach. Water was piped from the mainland to a tank on the island. A restaurant, a skeet-shooting range, a nine-hole golf course and a swimming pool at the beach which captured salt water at high tide allowing it to warm in the summer sun, added to the club's attractions. With more than a dozen bungalows and homes filled with happy families, Great Misery Island soon became a thriving summer colony. There was even a cottage dedicated as the Misery Island Station of the Manchester Yacht Club. Misery Island Club also had its own attractive burgee, green, red and white with a crest featuring a seahorse and fouled anchor and a Latin motto: "Te Salutamus Miseria Comitatum Amat."

A commemorative mug, discovered some years ago in an antique shop, shows that at least one Harvard College class celebrated its 25th Reunion at the club. But the venture was not a financial success. The summer colony, however, was and following foreclosure, the club house was christened Mystery Isles Casino. (I have a portion of a plate discovered on the island which bears the name.) For the next few years, happiness reigned until the arrival of the Great War in 1917. Now, in a very different world, with many of its members in the Armed Services, the Casino closed forever.

Godfrey Cabot, founder of the Cabot Corporation and a summer resident of Beverly Farms, built a hanger for his Burgess-Curtis float plane and, on active duty with the Navy during the war, kept an eye out for German U-boats in Massachusetts Bay. The plane was built by Greely Curtis' brother, Steen, son of Colonel Greely Curtis, an early summer resident of Manchester who lived at Sharksmouth on the water off Summer Street, and well-known naval architect Starling Burgess who had formed a partnership to construct aircraft in a factory at Marblehead. The two built planes for England's Royal Air Force throughout World War I, but in 1918 fire destroyed the plant.

In 1926, fire also changed a way of life at Misery Island. A caretaker, burning brush in the fall at the north end, accidentally lost control of the blaze in a strong, northwesterly wind. It swept the length of the island destroying the Casino and most private homes. Needless to say, the summer colony was never the same again.

But it was a proposal to locate an oil tank farm on Great Misery in 1935 that shocked residents of the

251

Headquarters of the Misery Islands Club overlooking Misery Cove in 1894. Also shown is the Caddie House and the third putting green of the island's nine-hole golf course. Visitors were transported to the island by naphtha-powered launch from West Beach. The Club House was comfortably furnished with a large area for dining and a sitting room. One of its cottages was dedicated to the Misery Islands Station of the Manchester Yacht Club. Activities at the Club included golf, trap shooting and boating. Sailboat races were a regular feature. The Misery Island Club had its own attractive burgee, green, red and white with a crest which displayed a sea horse and fouled anchor.

Dressed in the style of the era which included a long skirt and a hat, this lady is trying her hand at trap shooting on the range at Misery Islands Club in 1894 while her male companions watch. The range was located at the south end of Great Misery Island overlooking Baker's across Salem channel. No guns larger than 10 gauge were permitted on the range and specific rules carefully described what counted as a score. Club dues then totaled $25 a year. Water was piped to the island from the mainland and stored in a wooden tank. Its granite supports may still be seen today.

region and spurred them to action. Angry and concerned, many of them owners of shorefront property which looked directly at the islands, they banded together as North Shore Associates and proposed purchasing the property with contributions, the size of which, ingeniously, would be in direct proportion to their own real estate tax payments.

The appeal was an immediate success. The 68 acres acquired for a reported $15,000, were given to The Trustees of Reservations with the promise of an endowment to follow, to be preserved forever as public open space. Some years later, Little Misery was also purchased and preserved.

During World War II, the islands were "occupied" by the U.S. Coast Guard to prevent saboteurs from landing there and on the mainland and were off limits to visitors. Slowly, through the decades, fire claimed all of the remaining houses, now abandoned by their owners. But there are grown men and women today who remember as children, the romance and adventure of exploring the empty dwellings, the fascination of furnishings that had been left behind, reading old magazines in the attics, and even playing a piano which remained in one of the last houses to go.

Today, The Trustees of Reservations finally owns the two islands in their entirety. Long-time Superintendent of the property David A. Ryan, a Manchester resident, now retired after many years of teaching science in the schools here, set the standards for management which make the islands so popular as a passive recreation area. On summer weekends, scores of boats lie at anchor in the coves as visitors walk island trails.

TWO GRAND LADIES
Side-Wheel Steamers Meet Their Fate on the Rocky Shores of Misery Islands

On the shores of Little Misery in the channel between the two islands, lie the remains of the steamer CITY OF ROCKLAND which in 1924 was towed there and ignominiously burned. Her story appeared in a recent issue of Down East magazine. Built in 1901 by William McKie Shipyard in East Boston as a member of the celebrated Boston to Bangor fleet, CITY OF ROCKLAND was hailed as "the largest side-wheeler ever launched in New England." Planks used in her construction were 70 to 90 feet in length. With paddlewheels 25 feet in diameter, she was able to reach a speed of 20 knots.

But fog led to her undoing. Her first grounding came in July, 1904, when bound for Rockland in thick fog, she ran up on Gangway Ledge in Muscle Ridge Channel. Two years later, again in the fog, she collided with her sister ship, CITY OF BANGOR, off Portland Head. In 1912, while steaming in fog off the New Hampshire coast, she collided with the collier WILLIAM CHISHOLM. But her denouement came in 1923 when running from Bath to Boston. Once again in the fog, without visibility, she piled up on Dix Island in the Kennebec River to finally become a total loss. Despite her checkered career, she never lost a passenger in an accident, although many who were aboard at the time of her groundings may have later switched to rail to reach their destinations.

Sold as scrap for $3,100 to a shipyard in Salem, CITY OF ROCKLAND was stripped of her furnishings and anything else of value, towed to the channel between Great and Little Misery, and grounded once again. There on October 24, 1924, she was set on fire as a hulk. At low tide her ribs, now covered with ghostly layers of rockweed, still show above the water.

Earlier, in 1904, another grand lady met her fate in the fog at Misery Islands, this time under her own steam. Throughout her life, the side-wheel steamer MONOHANSETT was a handsome and important member of the fleet which serviced the islands of Martha's Vineyard and Nantucket. Built in 1862, she displaced 289 gross tons and measured 174 feet overall with a 28-foot beam. At one time, she was called "the best sidewheeler on the Atlantic coast." During the Civil War, she was used to carry government dispatches to ships of the Union Navy blockading the waters off Cape Hatteras and the entrance to Chesapeake Bay.

When the war ended in 1865, MONOHANSETT returned to the island service for which she had been designed. For years, she was known as "the regular Vineyard boat." She made occasional trips to Nantucket over the next two decades particularly in winter, forcing her way through the ice to bring supplies and mail to island residents all but marooned by the cold.

In 1900, she was sold to the then New Bedford, Martha's Vineyard & Nantucket Steamship Company to be used for passenger service in Massachusetts Bay. She became a regular on the North Shore providing service from Gloucester to Salem Willows. But on Wednesday, August 3, 1904 disaster

Paddlewheel steamer MONOHANSETT, 174 feet overall, was steaming from Gloucester to Salem Willows on August 3, 1904 when she lost her way in the fog and ran up on the shore in the channel between Great Misery Island and Little Misery. No one was injured. The steamer EMPRESS was called to help the 50 passengers aboard complete their voyage. Despite efforts to remove her, MONOHANSETT was holed badly enough to make her a total wreck. She never sailed again. During the Civil War, she delivered messages to Union ships blockading Southern ports. After the war's end, she served as ferry to Martha's Vineyard and Nantucket and was known as "the regular Vineyard boat."

View of the cove at Misery Island looking south about 1907. The roadway at the head of the cove ran to the Club House which was to the photographer's right. The fresh water pond beyond still exists. The island also included a nine-hole golf course, a skeet shooting range, and a pool where visitors could swim in salt water warmed by the sun. Notice that hardly a tree or shrub is in sight.

struck as she ended up on the rocky beach on the south side of Great Misery Island.

With 50 passengers aboard and Captain Frank Cates and Pilot Stillman Kenney on the bridge, MONOHANSETT left Gloucester at 3:45 p.m. It was a hot, gray day and fog soon shut in. Visibility of 10 feet was reported as she crawled past Whaleback Ledge "stopping every now and then" as a story in a contemporary issue of The Salem News explained, "to try to find some buoy or mark from which to lay her course." Too late, the lookouts spotted a black mass ahead, and despite the order to "Back Full," she slid gently up on the beach at high water. "There was no excitement among the passengers," The News reported. "Many regarded the grounding as something of a lark."

That, however, could not be said of Colonel William Stopford, the owners' representative who was also aboard. With some assistance, the Colonel was able to get to the beach and to walk to the Misery Island Club where he phoned to Beverly for help. The steamer EMPRESS returned all passengers to Salem Willows by 7:50 that night. Captain Cates, Pilot Kenney, the Colonel and Stewardess Daisy Thrower remained on board.

It was thought that MONOHANSETT could be floated easily on the next tide. But although no one knew it at the time, the ship had passed over a sizable boulder on the beach and when the tide fell, with all her weight, the boulder broke the back of her keel and dislocated her boiler. A total loss, she never floated again. The next day, the tug ELSIE and a lighter were sent from Beverly to remove everything aboard that could be salvaged. The remainder, her hull, boilers and engine, were then sold for scrap.

As The Salem News pointed out, it was high water and if MONOHANSETT had been 10 feet south of her course, she might have been able to slip safely through the small channel between Great and Little Misery Islands, but that was not to be.

MR. & MRS. BAKER

Twin Lights Once Marked Baker's Island; "Baby Baker" Used to Cry in the Fog

There had been a number of wrecks in the area—the tug HONEYBROOK on Dry Breakers and the tug MONTANA ashore at Baker's Island—and the feeling in nautical circles at the time was that these and the grounding of MONOHANSETT

might have been prevented if there had been a steam operated fog horn at Baker's Island. As early as 1876, a bell warned mariners of its presence in the fog. In 1907, the bell was replaced by a siren. The present air horn was installed in 1959. When there were twin lights on the island, they were known affectionately in Manchester as "Mr. and Mrs. Baker." The siren, it was said, was "Baby Baker" who cried in the fog.

Baker's Island has a rich history of its own. First mentioned by John Winthrop in the log of ARBELLA like Great and Little Misery, it was granted to the City of Salem in 1660. By 1670, there were two dwellings on the island and by 1731, it had been purchased for 130 Pounds and its 55 acres divided between two tenants. During the Revolution, British soldiers arrived from Boston, burning buildings and seizing cattle.

By 1791, the bay was busy with merchant shipping and the first beacon to be used for navigation purposes was erected. For $500, the U.S. government purchased 10 acres and in 1798, erected two lighthouse towers. The second keeper of the lights became a hero of the War of 1812, piloting USS CONSTITUTION safely into Marblehead Harbor as she sought refuge under the guns of Fort Sewall from two British frigates, HMS TENEDOS and HMS JUNON.

By 1877, Baker's had been caught up in the fever to escape the city during the summer months and that year its first cottage was constructed for seasonal occupancy. Others followed as Dr. Nathan R. Morse, who had recuperated from an illness himself on the island thanks to the generosity of one of his patients, purchased all of the island land except for the government's 10 acres. By 1888, Dr. Morse had given away and sold a number of house lots and had enlarged his own farmhouse to create Winne-Egan ("beautiful expanse of water" in Indian), a 75-room summer hotel.

A steam ferry linked Baker's with the mainland and in 1893 some 700 passengers visit the island in one day. In 1897, Dr. Morse's son added a nine-hole golf course to the pleasures offered to guests at the hotel. But as the century changed, so did life on the island. By 1906, the hotel had been destroyed by fire. In the years between 1909 and 1914, 20 more houses were built for the growing summer community as well as a meeting hall and a store. In 1910, 30 charter members voted to establish Baker's Island Association. Six years later, a telephone line

Twin lights at Baker's first erected in 1798, warned mariners of the hazards stretching south of the island, Northeast Breakers. The second keeper of the lights became a hero of the War of 1812, piloting USS CONSTITUTION safely into Marblehead Harbor as she sought refuge under the guns of Fort Sewall from two British frigates. One of the towers was later removed. This photo was taken by Metropolitan News Company in 1905.

The Winne-Egan ("beautiful expanse of water" in Indian) Hotel at Bakers Island was built in 1888 by Dr. Nathan R. Morse who, following his recovery from an illness on the island, purchased all the land except that owned by the Federal government for the twin light houses. Much enjoyed by visitors, the hotel had been sadly destroyed by fire by 1906.

led underwater to the lighthouses and by 1926, there were 58 houses on the island. Telephone service and electric light soon follow.

For a small community, Baker's Island has a remarkable record of patriotism. During World War I, 14 of its summer residents served in the Armed Forces. One died in France. In World War II, the number serving grew to 22. Three were killed in action, one in the Pacific Theater, two in Europe. The issue of real estate taxes has always been a sticky wicket for homeowners. Paid to the City of Salem, they yield few services in return. To protest, in 1946, a group of residents filed for tax abatements. The city responded with an offer of $1,000 for "various island projects" and the appeal was withdrawn.

PORT OF CALL
Manchester Is the Jumping Off Spot for Residents of Baker's Island

Today, many residents reach Baker's Island aboard their own boats from Manchester (more than two dozen for the purpose lie in the inner harbor), and the Post Office here continues a long-time tradition of providing a postal box for island mail. As is indicated elsewhere in the story about health and medicine, Manchester physicians also have been called upon to provide care for ailing islanders of every age and they have responded willing. Bruce LeSeine, a legendary Manchester lobsterman, also served some decades ago as caretaker and his boat as ferry for a number of island homeowners.

Other islands which help to shelter Manchester's outer harbor include House Island and the two Ram Islands as well as the ledges—Whaleback; White, which breaks at low water; Half Tide and Sauli's. Chubb Island, almost on the boundary line between Beverly and Manchester, adds another dimension to the mix of beach, rocky headlands and coves which make up the town's shoreline.

East of the harbor are Graves Island, Kettle Island and Crow Island, connected with a causeway to the shore, as well as a series of visible ledges: Pickett, which also shows itself at low water; Rocky Dundy, just off Singing Beach; Salt Rock and Little Salt Rock; Great Egg Rock and Little Egg Rock. Seas also break on Boo Hoo Ledge, upon which many a vessel has foundered, and during winter storms even on Gale's Ledge,

generally five feet under water at low tide. The Breakers, south of Baker's Island, which stretch for a mile almost out to Newcomb Ledge, are usually white with foam at every low water whenever a sea is running.

House Island, a sea bird nesting site for Herring Gulls, Blackback Gulls, and, at one time, for Black Crowned Night Heron, Snowy Egret and Glossy Ibis, was privately owned for more than a century. However, in 2003, thanks to the generosity of a few local residents, it was purchased and presented as a gift to Massachusetts Audubon Society which will manage it as a refuge for wildlife.

Inner Ram Island has traditionally been a part of the westernmost property at Smith's Point. Outer Ram, on the other hand, is considered to be owned by the Town of Manchester. Chubb Island is also in private hands as is Graves Island off Graves or Dana's Beach. Kettle Island, a nesting area as well, is also the property of Massachusetts Audubon Society.

Islands and ledges add immensely to the pleasure of those who sail along the shore. They also provide a fascinating diversity for the coastal landscape of the Town of Manchester.

A LIFE DEVOTED TO PUBLIC SERVICE

Governor and Mrs. Herter and their family posed for this photo in 1952 at the Herters' summer house on Proctor Street. The Governor was later named U.S. Secretary of State by President Eisenhower. Standing from left: E. Miles Herter who, with his wife Lee, has been a resident of Manchester for more than 50 years; Adele Herter Seronde of Arizona; Christian A. Herter, Jr., also a summer resident here for some 20 years and Frederick P. Herter, MD. of New York City. Purchased by the Herters in 1950 the Proctor Street property, which overlooks Manchester harbor, was sold in 1980. Prior to that the family rented here each summer beginning in the late 1930's. Photo by Welsh Photographic Studios.

LEGISLATOR, STATESMAN

Christian A. Herter, Long-time Summer Resident, Served in Many Roles

Although throughout its history Manchester can claim a number of distinguished regular summer residents, honors for the highest rank on every count must go to statesman and legislator Christian Archibald Herter.

As State Representative, Speaker of the Massachusetts House, U.S. Congressman, two-term Governor of the Commonwealth, and finally as U.S. Secretary of State, he and Mrs. Herter spent more than 30 happy seasons at their house on Proctor Street overlooking Manchester's inner harbor. There, especially in his later years, suffering from arthritis, Herter would sit happily by the pool enjoying the cheerful if noisy company of his children and grandchildren. He also regularly took part in community activities, one year speaking at the 50th anniversary of the Manchester Club and in another riding as guest of honor in the annual Fourth of July parade.

Although often considered a classic Brahmin with Boston roots, Chris Herter was far from it. Born in Paris in 1895, he came from artistic parents and spoke German and French before he knew English. His father was a widely respected muralist whose paintings appear in many public buildings (including the Massachusetts State House where his art depicting the beginnings of the Bay Colony decorate the House chamber); his grandfather, a popular and successful German architect whose clients included J.P. Morgan, William Vanderbilt and Mark Hopkins. When he was nine years old, Herter came to the U.S. with his family settling in New York City. He attended Browning School and later Harvard College graduating with the Class of 1915. After a year at Columbia University School of Architecture, he entered the Foreign Service of the United States.

Posted to Berlin, he was one of the last Americans to leave Germany as war was declared in 1917. In fact, he was arrested, held as a spy and threatened with execution but managed to convince his captors that he was a member of the diplomatic service. At the end of the war, Herter served in Europe as staff to the American commission negotiating the peace at Versailles and was assistant to Herbert Hoover when the future President was directing the American Relief Adminis-

tration and later back in Washington when Hoover was Secretary of Commerce.

Fed up with government during the Harding era, he returned to Boston in 1924 to enter the publishing business and to teach government and international relations at Harvard. But by 1930, politics beckoned and Herter was elected to the State House of Representatives from the "blue stocking" district of Back Bay and Beacon Hill. He served as a state legislator for 12 years, the last four as Speaker. In 1942, he ran for Congress from the 10th District and was successfully elected for five consecutive terms, heading a Select Committee of the House on European relief that laid the foundation for the Marshall Plan. Always interested in diplomacy, when he won the Collier prize in 1948 for distinguished service in Congress, he generously gave its $10,000 award to benefit the Foreign Service Education Foundation. And it was he who led the successful campaign to approve the Marshall Plan in the House while Senator Arthur H. Vandenberg of Michigan did the same in the Senate.

Returning to Massachusetts in 1952 after joining the team that convinced General Dwight D. Eisenhower to run for President, Herter, against the better judgment of his friends, decided to enter the race for governor. His opponent was Democratic incumbent Paul A. Dever. Herter won by a narrow 14,000 vote plurality and became famous in his first year for cutting the cost of government by $8.7 million and eliminating the need for a rise in taxes. He also was the first governor of the Bay State to establish a Department of Commerce and Industry to encourage successful corporations to settle in Massachusetts. Two years later he was reelected to a second term.

GOVERNOR HERTER

An Early Supporter of Eisenhower, He Became U.S. Secretary of State

In 1956, still as Governor, he was speaking in support of President Eisenhower when a renegade group of Republicans proposed to dump Richard M. Nixon and nominate him for Vice President during Ike's second term. Herter would have none of it. Indeed, at the convention, it was he who nominated Nixon for a second term thus ending the matter once and for all. Nixon responded by helping to get Herter appointed Under Secretary of State instead of the lesser post (Assistant Secretary) that had been proposed. When Dulles resigned because of ill health in 1959, Herter was chosen to replace him as Secretary. In an extraordinary show of bipartisan support, the Senate waived its seven-day rule and confirmed his appointment in just over four hours. Although it took Ike a while to get to know his new cabinet member, he soon grew to respect both Herter's abilities and his integrity. "When you look at him," Ike once said, "you know you are looking at an honest man."

Unfortunately, Herter's 21 months in office were filled with frustration. Instead of being able to initiate positive steps to improve U.S. relations with countries around the world, he found himself dealing with increased Soviet pressure on Berlin; facing a deteriorating relationship with Cuba's Fidel Castro; and on the eve of what was to be a summit conference with President Eisenhower and Premier Khrushchev, learning that Soviet anti-aircraft fire had shot down an American U-2 spy plane over Russia and with it hopes for the summit. As The New York Times reported, "The conference, so patiently prepared [for] and so anxiously awaited, expired in an atmosphere of gloomy foreboding about world tensions." In July, fighting broke out in the Congo and Khrushchev demanded that the United Nations Secretary General be replaced with a three-member directorate. Finally, shortly before January, 1961, the Eisenhower administration severed diplomatic relations with Cuba as the island nation allied itself with the Soviet Union.

AFTER IKE, JFK
Herter Asked to Head Delegation to Deal with the Common Market

But despite his disappointments, Herter was not through with public service. In November, 1962, President John F. Kennedy appointed him "the Government's chief planner and negotiator on foreign trade." His primary task was to head a delegation to deal with the European Common Market.

On December 29, 1966, he died unexpectedly at his home in Washington. He was 71 years old. An editorial in The Washington Post paid this well-deserved tribute: "Few men in public life," it declared, "did more to put an end to the sterile isolationism of the years between the wars. Few worked harder or more effectively to persuade the people of the United States to endorse and approve the active employment of American power to shape world events...he used his enormous influence, great talents and personal charm in the constant pursuit of peace through collective international efforts..."

Herter's oldest son, Chris, Jr. also a summer resident of Manchester for more than a decade, continued the family's commitment to public service. He was elected a member of the Governor's Council here in Massachusetts, served in the State Legislature and as a member of Richard Nixon's staff, accompanied the Vice President on one of his trips abroad. Herter's youngest son Miles, and his wife Lee, have lived year round in Manchester since 1952.

5 DISTINGUISHED U.S. AMBASSADORS

U.S. Ambassador Joseph C. Grew, a Manchester summer resident for many years, chats with tennis star Maureen Connolly at Essex County Club in 1953. Grew, a much-celebrated career diplomat, was Ambassador to Japan in the decade leading up to World War II and was at the U.S. Embassy in Tokyo when Pearl Harbor was attacked on December 7, 1941. Connolly, a great national champion, won the Ladies Invitational Tennis Tournament at Essex in 1952 and 1953.

JOHN M. CABOT

40 Years in the Foreign Service; First to Open a Dialog with Red China

Home to a glamorous collection of European ambassadors during the "Embassy Years" from 1899 to 1914, Manchester can also happily boast of having its own company of regular summer residents who served with distinction in the Foreign Service of the United States.

They include U.S. Ambassador John Moors Cabot, U.S. Ambassador William H.G. FitzGerald, U.S. Ambassador Joseph Clark Grew, U.S. Minister Leland L. Harrison and U.S. Ambassador Richard Bowditch Wigglesworth.

In his 40 years as a U. S. Foreign Service officer, John Moors Cabot held an extraordinary number of different diplomatic posts around the world. He was Chief of Mission or Ambassador at five of these and was also named an Assistant Secretary of State and Deputy Commandant of the National War College. It is a record few can equal.

During his career he was posted to Lima, Santo Domingo, Mexico City, Rio de Janeiro, The Hague, Stockholm, Guatemala City, Buenos Aires, Belgrade, Shanghai, Helsinki, Stockholm (again), Bogota, Brasilia, Warsaw and Washington, D.C. His achievements, too, match the variety of his assignments. As Counselor of the U.S. Legation in Belgrade in 1947, he was the first Foreign Service Officer to urge Marshall Tito of Yugoslavia to begin formal talks with the West which later led to his break with the Soviet Union. And as Ambassador to Poland from 1961 to 1966, he helped open the door to Red China beginning the first U.S. contact and conversations with Communist leaders in Beijing. Each of these initiatives contributed in their own way to maintaining peace and stability throughout the world during the uncertain and often dangerous era of the Cold War.

As Consul General in Shanghai, Cabot was present when the Communists took over in May, 1949, and, as Red Chinese troops advanced, it was he who persuaded retreating Nationalists not to destroy the city's electric power plants which would have meant hardship for millions of poorer residents.

Born in Cambridge in 1901, Jack Cabot attended Brown & Nichols School, graduated from Harvard College with the Class of 1923, and received an advanced degree from Oxford University in England. He spent his summers in Beverly Farms. His father Godfrey, a brilliant and legendary figure, was founder and President of Boston's Cabot Corporation. (At age 54 he took up flying, purchasing a seaplane which he kept in a hangar at Misery Island. As a Lieutenant in the Naval Reserve during World War I, he piloted the craft around the waters of Massachusetts Bay looking for German U-boats.)

His son Jack entered the Foreign Service in October, 1926. And then, as the Ambassador said in a New Yorker magazine Profile which appeared in 1961, "Since I was studying French and knew no Spanish, [I] was naturally sent as vice-consul to Lima, Peru." The assignment marked the beginning of a career during which Cabot became one of the State Department's best informed experts on Latin America. He was assigned to seven different countries within the region, serving as Ambassador to Columbia and later to Brazil, as Chief of the Division of Caribbean and Central American Affairs and as Assistant Secretary of State for Inter-American Affairs. He was also the first of his contemporaries to receive two double promotions in grade during his career as well as many personal commendations.

According to the New Yorker, Mrs. Cabot, the former Elizabeth Lewis (the couple met while both were on the staff of the U.S. Embassy at Mexico City), "had the reputation in the Foreign Service of being the perfect diplomat's wife." As she explained, "It's a lovely life but it's important to start young as we did. You see beautiful things and you're always meeting old friends and making new ones wherever you go."

Principled and courageous, Cabot was not afraid to speak up when it mattered. At some risk to his own career, he expressed outrage and indignation at the way many of his colleagues in the Foreign Service were treated during the "Red baiting" scares of the McCarthy era. And, too early for many, he urged initiating communication with Red China, which was only to come successfully years later during the Nixon Administration. On numerous occasions, too, he stood firm during discussions with senior military officers who he felt may not have understood crucial political considerations.

He was always one as well to try to understand the people—not just their representatives—in the countries to which he was assigned. He and Mrs.

Cabot would make it a point to travel outside the capital cities where they lived, to talk with farmers, small businessmen, local officials and students to learn first hand about the problems they faced from day to day.

As Deputy Commandant of the National War College at the end of his professional career, Ambassador Cabot well understood that the ultimate security of a country depends upon the strength and quality of its armed forces. But he was a firm believer that the nation's "first line of defense," as his autobiography is titled (First Line of Defense, Forty Years' Experiences of a Career Diplomat, published by Georgetown University's School of Foreign Service) is its "diplomatic representatives abroad—a trained and dedicated Foreign Service Corps, headed by a wise, experienced and observant group of chiefs of mission [who] must understand the country where they represent us...report without fear or favor...seek to secure and maintain friendly relations...warn us in case of aggression and be aware that although we want no military domination of any part of the world, a takeover by another power may be a threat to our security."

After the excitement and accomplishments of their lives both in the Nation's capitol and abroad, the Cabots found a happy tranquillity at Manchester. Following World War II, when they were looking for a place of their own, it seemed fitting to return to the North Shore. With their children, they chose to settle overlooking the sea in a house once owned in the nineteenth century by Jack Cabot's great uncle Walter.

There, on leave and in retirement, the Ambassador would relax in his poolside sauna (which recalled pleasant moments in Stockholm and Helsinki) discussing world affairs with friends of all ages. Warm, cheerful and outgoing in nature, he and Mrs. Cabot loved to entertain, especially their four children and grandchildren. Winters were still spent in Washington. John Cabot died in 1981; Mrs. Cabot in 1992. Their house today is occupied by their son John and his wife Carroll.

WILLIAM FITZGERALD

U.S. Ambassador to Ireland, He Brought a Refreshingly New Kind of Representation

Unlike other Ambassadors mentioned here, Bill FitzGerald, a summer resident of Manchester since 1962, is not a career Foreign Service Officer. "I'm no diplomat," he admits candidly. And yet his almost two years (1991-1992) as head of the U.S. legation in Ireland brought a refreshingly new and different kind of representation from the United States to Dublin. For FitzGerald is a hugely successful businessman and an imaginative administrator and entrepreneur who has served his country in many ways.

Appointed by President George H.W. Bush (Senior), he encouraged a growing number of U.S. firms to invest in Ireland bringing new capital and new jobs to the country while benefitting from being next to the European market and enjoying the lowest corporate tax in the region. "It is a wonderful place to build a plant," he says. "The Irish speak our language; they have the same kind of common law; and their average level of education is higher than our own!"

By the time he left, more than 160 U.S. corporations had offices, manufacturing facilities or research labs in the Republic of Ireland. Unlike other Ambassadors who confined their activities to diplomatic circles, FitzGerald also took it upon himself to visit scores of cities and towns throughout the country, meeting with Mayors and Councils and talking with ordinary citizens to learn first hand about their concerns.

A graduate of the U.S. Naval Academy, Bill FitzGerald has led a remarkable life, much of it in public service. He attended Harvard Law School and during World War II, he was in uniform working alongside such figures as the Navy's Hyman Rickover (later Admiral Rickover, father of our fleet of nuclear subs), helping to modernize U.S. submarines so that they could better compete with Germans U-boats and the Japanese. "In 1942," he says, "the Germans especially were light years ahead of us in submarine design." After the war, he entered private industry, beginning what was to be an extraordinary career in which he owned and operated companies engaged in engineering, agriculture, banking, the production of fine wines, investment counseling and prefabricated housing.

In 1956, at the request of then Under Secretary of State Christian A. Herter, a long-time summer resident of Manchester, he volunteered to serve his country once again as Deputy Director for Management at the International Cooperation Administration which evaluated U.S. aid programs throughout the world. In 1988, too, asked by then

Career diplomat John Cabot (left) accepts credentials from an old friend, Secretary of State Christian A. Herter in connection with his appointment as U.S. Ambassador to Brazil in 1959. Both men were long-time summer residents of Manchester. Cabot became one of the State Department's best informed experts on Latin America, serving in seven different countries within the region. Photo by U.S. Department of State.

U.S. Ambassador Richard B. Wigglesworth presents his credentials to His Excellency The Right Honorable Vincent Massey, P.C., C.H., Governor General of Canada in Ottawa in 1958. During his tenure, Ambassador Wigglesworth, a long-time summer resident of Manchester, visited every Canadian province. Friendly and sympathetic, he did much to increase understanding between the U.S. and its neighbor to the north. He was also involved in matters of mutual defense during the early years of the Cold War. Photo from <u>Richard Bowditch Wigglesworth, Way Stations of a Fruitful Life</u>, courtesy of Ann Wigglesworth.

Vice President Bush, he took time out of his business life to become Vice Chairman of the African Development Fund, which successfully bypassed local government red tape to get financial aid directly to village leaders in 42 sub-Saharan countries. "The fund made a big difference," he says. "Congress was so impressed that it added money to our budget every year."

An avid tennis player, still active in his 90's, he is Honorary Chairman of the International Tennis Hall of Fame. And although he had built a grass court at the American Ambassador's residence in Dublin, he was never able to find a moment to play on it. "It usually rained in the mornings," he explains, "and because of the time difference between Dublin and Washington, I was at my desk every afternoon and evening!"

Now retired, his major interest is in education and aiding the disadvantaged. "I've been fortunate in my life," he says, "and I think it's most important to help others." In the 1960's, he was an early supporter of tennis for urban youth in Washington, DC. Today, the William H.G. FitzGerald Tennis Center welcomes thousands to tennis matches which annually attract top-flight pros such as Andre Agassi and Andy Roddick. A portion of the proceeds benefits Washington Tennis and Education Foundation which seeks to improve the prospects of youths from lower-income communities who, through tennis and as FitzGerald Scholars, learn discipline and self esteem which can help them improve performance at school. Arthur Ashe was an early participant and an outstanding role model for many area youngsters.

There are also now four FitzGerald Scholars each year who graduate from the U.S. Naval Academy and are selected to attend Oxford University in England where they are able to meet and mix with future leaders of the world community like themselves. Finally, there are annually six to seven children of university faculty members who receive aid as FitzGerald Scholars to attend world-renowned Harvard College whose tuition might be beyond the reach of an individual faculty family. In all, there have to date been more than 1,000 FitzGerald Scholars, an extraordinary record of generosity and philanthropy.

JOSEPH C. GREW
In the Dark Days Before World War II, He Warned of a Japanese Attack

Also a summer resident of West Manchester as early as the 1920's, Joseph Clark Grew was U.S. Ambassador to Japan during the decade leading up to World War II. He is perhaps best known for his warnings to Washington which came as early as November, 1941, that Japan could attack the United States at any moment. In December, 1937, when Japanese forces in China bombed and sank a neutral U.S. Navy river gunboat, the PANAY, with a loss of two killed and 30 wounded, Grew delivered the U.S.'s demand for apologies, reparations and a guarantee that there would be no further aggression against American forces in the Far East.

A year later, acting for Secretary of State Cordell Hull, Grew also protested Japanese violations of the nine-nation Open Door Policy in China and refused to recognize the Empire's "New Order" in Asia. In September, 1940, the Ambassador once again warned his superiors in Washington that Japan might retaliate militarily in response to an embargo on oil. Finally, with a more moderate government swept aside by new Premier Hideki Tojo, the war that neither side really wanted arrived early on a Sunday morning in December, 1941.

An "old school" diplomat, Joseph Grew attended Groton and graduated from Harvard College in 1902. As Chief of the Division of Western European Affairs during World War I, he had seen the tragedies and the futility of global conflict. After the war he served as Ambassador to Turkey before being posted to Japan. An article which appeared in Yankee Magazine in January, 1942, written apparently before Pearl Harbor, describes his personality. "His suavity seldom fails him," it says, "his integrity is unassailable, and he is perfectly at home crossing wits at one of the Emperor's famous twelve o'clock luncheons…He is humorous and kindly but adamant when he feels Japan oversteps her rights. Cognizant of the problems, chaos and waste of the last war [he] believes in negotiated, not bloody victories…" Unfortunately, despite the

Ambassador's best efforts, diplomacy failed to keep peace between the two nations.

One can't help wondering, however, how much better we might have fared at Pearl Harbor, or even if the sneak attack could have been apprehended, had we paid more attention to Joe Grew's persistent warnings from Tokyo that Japan was on the warpath and determined to strike at the United States.

In August, 1946, when peace had been restored in the Pacific, Grew was asked to speak at an event sponsored by the Welfare Committee of Boston's Children's Hospital (two local ladies, Mrs. Alexander Wheeler and Mrs. Kirke A. Neal were cochairs) which was to take place here at the Congregational Church. His remarks, which appeared in <u>The Manchester Cricket</u>, provide a vivid and disquieting picture of his treatment at the hands of the Japanese.

"In my 43 years of living in countries all over the world," the Ambassador began, "it's nice to find myself [enjoying] a summer in Manchester where I spent my boyhood days."

With that he added, "I have been asked to speak tonight on Japan. When we arrived in Japan in 1932, we were tendered a dinner and I was asked to speak, which I did, and explained the friendly relations between my country and Japan. I was followed by a Japanese military man who proceeded to belittle me and the United States. At the end of his talk with a few brief remarks, I left the hall. Our reception to Japan was cold indeed.

"I soon found out that the Japanese military machine was built for war and that they looked for war and wanted war. The war lords were teaching the Japanese people that the A.B.C.D.—America, Britain, China and the Dutch—were out to strangle Japan. From observation I soon learned there were two factions in Japan, the war party and those who didn't want war. Among this latter group my wife and I had many friends for whom we still hold a great respect.

"At the time of the invasion of China in July, 1937, I sent a note to Secretary [of War] Stimson explaining the situation. From then on things grew steadily worse. The Japanese attacked one of our ships in the Yangtze River in China [USS PANAY].

"On the night of December 7, 1941, December 6 here, I listened [on] the radio to a message being sent by the President to the people of Japan. The next day a message was directed to me by Secretary [of State] Hull for delivery to the government. It was received in Tokyo at 12 noon, but was not delivered to me until 10:30 p.m., four hours after Pearl Harbor.

"The next day, Tojo thanked me for what I had done to preserve the peace, but said nothing about Pearl Harbor. The first I learned that we were at war was when I went out on the street and read it in the paper.

"We were immediately seized as prisoners of war and treated like a bunch of criminals. Some two to three hundred Japanese police, with a mob of people, came down the street and stopped in front of the Embassy, shaking their fists and shouting. Colonel Babcock who was attached to the Embassy, went out on a small verandah, smiled at them, took out his handkerchief and waved it at them and they went off down the street.

"There were 63 of us at the Embassy including servants. I told these servants that if they [remained] loyal to us they would be treated like criminals by their own people. But they stayed and were willing to take their chances. This kind of personal loyalty one can't find everywhere.

"In June of 1942, arrangements had been made for our transfer, on an exchange basis, back to the United States. And on June 25 we set sail from Yokohama, following several days of anxious waiting aboard ship in the harbor."

LELAND L. HARRISON
Minister to Switzerland During WWII; An Extraordinarily Sensitive Post

As U.S. Minister to Switzerland from 1937 to 1947, Leland Harrison manned a listening post of crucial importance to America and the Allies during World War II. Mrs. Harrison and their two daughters, Ann and Helen, were summer residents of Manchester during the war years (he getting away when he could) and afterwards until 1951. Winters were spent in Washington, DC. (Ann, with her husband and children, remained a summer resident, a practice which she continues still.)

Educated at Eton College in England, at Harvard and at Harvard Law School, Harrison entered the diplomatic service in 1908 and was appointed Third Secretary at the U.S. Embassy in Japan. Following posts in Beijing, London and Bogota, in 1918, at the end of World War I, he was named diplomatic secretary to the American Commission to negotiate peace at Versailles where it was likely he knew future Manchester summer resident Christian A. Herter. In 1921, Harrison returned to Washington as an assistant to the Conference on the Limitation of Armament. Named Assistant Secretary of State in March, 1922, he served until 1927 when he was appointed Minister to Sweden. His other posts included Minister to Uruguay and Minister to Rumania.

It was as U.S. Minister to Switzerland, however, that Leland Harrison was provided with unique opportunities to serve his country. As fellow diplomat William Phillips, a resident of North Beverly, writes, "He devoted himself to fostering friendly relations between neutral Switzerland and belligerent America and thus conserved for the Allied cause and our own benefit the secret though necessarily reserved loyalty of the Swiss government and its invaluable services in the protection of Americans and American interests in enemy and enemy-controlled countries…

"Realizing that the United States was entirely dependent upon Switzerland for the supply of synthetic jewel bearings for instruments, under the very eye of the Germans, he was secretly able to keep our Defense Supplies Corporation regularly [equipped] throughout the…war." In appreciation, the War Department awarded him the Medal of Freedom.

On August 14, 1945, he found himself responsible for transmitting Japan's acceptance of unconditional surrender. The note was handed to the Swiss Foreign Office by the Japanese representative in Bern, who turned it over to Leland Harrison. He read its text over the phone to then Secretary of State James F. Byrne.

As Secretary of State Dean Acheson declared following his death in 1951, "All who have intimately known Mr. Harrison, and especially those who have had the good fortune to serve with him, will remember him for his outstanding ability in the performance of his duties in whatever post he served throughout the world….During his long tour of duty in Switzerland [during] World War II, he frequently was obliged to make exceptionally important decisions on his own responsibility, and through his good judgment, was able to render valuable service to his country."

As Ambassador Phillips concludes: "Throughout the whole period Harrison was guided by serene faith and unswerving optimism. Not once was ruffled that calm and confident poise which was one of his outstanding characteristics."

RICHARD WIGGLESWORTH

In Congress for 30 Years, He Became U.S. Ambassador to Canada

A football star both at Milton Academy and later at Harvard (Class of 1912), Richard Bowditch Wigglesworth continued his winning ways in Congress for 30 years before becoming U.S. Ambassador to Canada. As an undergraduate, Wigglesworth was quarterback and, at only 156 pounds, celebrated victories over Yale and the U.S. Military Academy at West Point. A badly broken ankle finally sidelined him, but what he learned on the gridiron stood him in good stead for the rest of his life.

According to a delightful personal biography entitled Richard Bowditch Wigglesworth, Way Stations of a Fruitful Life written by Sinclair Weeks, he attended Harvard Law School, was an Assistant Coach of Harvard football and a practicing attorney in Boston when he was called to active duty as a First Lieutenant in the U.S. Army in October, 1916. During World War I, then-Captain Wigglesworth commanded Battery E of the Third Battalion of the 303rd Field Artillery in France. With its 155-millimeter howitzers, it was in action at Bois de Haudronville during the final days of the war.

When peace arrived, an offer to serve in Washington as legal advisor to the Assistant Secretary of the Treasury in charge of Foreign Loans and Railway Payments won out over remaining in Boston. This and four years in Berlin and Paris with the Dawes Commission, appointed to help restore fiscal stability to Germany, provided extraordinary experience in international finance, but perhaps most important, helped Wigglesworth discover that public service was what interested him most.

At this moment in his life, fate also intervened and he found himself presented with a rare and challenging opportunity. Supported by family, friends and finally by the Republican State Committee, he was named the party's candidate for Congress from the 14th District to take the place of former Congressman Louis B. Frothingham who had died unexpectedly in office only a few months earlier.

Despite his lack of experience with politics, Wigglesworth proved a natural on the campaign trail and was elected handily in 1928 to the seat he held for 15 terms or until 1956. In the House of Representatives for nearly three decades, he served under Presidents Roosevelt, Truman and Eisenhower as a member of the Committee on Appropriations as well as the Sub-Committee on Foreign Aid in the crucial years of the Great Depression, throughout World War II and the beginnings of its aftermath, the Cold War with the Soviet Union.

During this time, he, his wife Florence and their three daughters, Ann, Mary and Jane, spent many happy summers at their house in Manchester at the top of the hill on Old Neck Road which looks out over Singing Beach to the waters of Massachusetts Bay.

In 1958, just when he may have been wondering what he was going to do next with his life, Richard Wigglesworth was selected to serve as U.S. Ambassador to Canada thanks initially to a suggestion made by then Under Secretary of State Christian A. Herter, also a summer resident of Manchester. In the short two years before he succumbed to illness, it is said that his "quiet and friendly manner and eager interest in all things Canadian [won] new friends for the United States and for U.S.-Canadian understanding."

While at Ottawa, Ambassador Wigglesworth helped to create a joint plan for the development of the Columbia River Basin and, always interested in the military, laid the foundations for what became the comprehensive U.S.-Canadian program for the defense of the North American Continent. He died at age 69 in October, 1960, after two years in office.

A Story of People, Places and Events in the Town That Came to
Be Known as Manchester-by-the-Sea

STUFFY: A LEGEND LIVING NEXT DOOR

*From 1949 to 1954, Manchester's Stuffy
McInnis, right, coached varsity baseball at
Harvard. Here he is in 1953 talking with Jack
Barry, also a member of the famed $100,000
infield who played third base for the Philadelphia Athletics. At the time of the photo, Barry
was coaching at Holy Cross and the two
old teammates found great pleasure in their
college rivalry.* <u>The Boston Globe</u> *photo
by Charles Dixon.*

WORLD SERIES WINNER

Tappan Street Resident Played First Base for Connie Mack's '$100,000 Infield'

He was a quiet man, modest about his success, and few who saw John Phalen McInnis on the streets of Manchester would have guessed that he was a baseball hero and once a member of Connie Mack's legendary "$100,000 Infield."

A resident of Tappan Street until his death in 1960 at age 69, "Stuffy," as he was known, played first base for the Philadelphia Athletics and the Boston Red Sox. Born in 1890, he joined the A's after graduating from Gloucester High School in 1908. Only five feet, nine inches tall, he started out at shortstop, but quickly showed he could play first base with the best. "I got tired of watching those six footers who only had to reach for the ball," he reminisced in later years. "I figured I could get those balls by timing my jumps and getting plenty of spring in my legs. I went to Mr. Mack and told him so. And in 1911, I landed on first base." Replacing Harry Davis, he never looked back.

The quartet of McInnis at first, Eddie Collins at second, Jack Barry at shortstop and Frank "Home Run" Baker at third, led the Philadelphia Athletics to three pennants (1911, 1913 and 1914) and three world championships before Mack began breaking the club up in 1916.

McInnis was the eighth player to be sold to Boston in a three-year period. Showing his winning ways before a home town crowd, he helped lead the Red Sox to the American League pennant in his first year with the team (1918) and was the star of the World Series win over the Chicago Cubs. In 1925, he played first base with the Pittsburgh Pirates and was key to another World Series victory. Later he went on to play with the Boston Braves and the Cleveland Indians.

"He had a great pair of hands," one newspaper article quoted his Philadelphia teammate, Jack Barry, as saying. "He overcame his [size] with his ability…He was a tiny man among the greatest giants the game has ever seen," the paper continued. "Ruth and Jackson, Cobb and Hooper, Speaker and Lewis, Ed Walsh, Carl Mays, Dutch Leonard and Walter Johnson…the latter the best pitcher [Stuffy] ever saw."

"We never worked, we only played," recalled Eddie Collins many years ago. "Stuffy used to yell at us during practice, telling us not to make the throws so good…'make me reach for them,' he said."

One of the crowning moments of Stuffy's career came with the Athletics during the World Series in 1925. It was the fifth game with Washington leading three games to one. Pittsburgh morale was at a low ebb. McInnis was put in at first. With inspired play, he turned the club around and the A's went on to sweep the next three games to become World Champions.

Those "great hands" that Jack Barry describes helped Stuffy set two major league fielding records for first basemen that still stand today. In 1921, with the Boston Red Sox, wearing the small, round mitt of his era, he played for the entire season, 152 games (1,300 chances), and was charged with only one early season error, a .9993 fielding average. On another occasion, he played 163 consecutive games, handling the ball 1,625 times, without committing any errors. In 19 years as a major league ballplayer, his fielding average was a remarkable .990.

He could hit, too. His lifetime batting average was .306. He batted over .300 in 12 of his 19 seasons and in each year from 1910 to 1915. Internet information reveals that "he was a right-handed, line drive, pull hitter [who] could punch the ball in the opposite field as well." In 1922, McInnis struck out just five times in 142 games. He gained his nickname as a youngster in the Boston suburban leagues where his spectacular play brought shouts of 'that's the stuff, kid!' " Connie Mack reportedly once called him one of the steadiest players ever to wear a major league uniform. He could play golf, too, and many say he could have made his living at it as a pro if he had chosen to.

As Boston sports writer Jack Denny wrote: "Mack's famous $100,000 infield [would that be $100 million today?] did not acquire its name and fame until McInnis arrived on the scene as a young boy and took over the anchor spot at first base. Mack was once quoted as saying that before McInnis [showed up], Home Run Baker at third had one of the most erratic throwing arms in the business and Eddie Collins at second could heave a bad throw with the best of them. It was the quiet young boy from Gloucester who settled them down and helped make this famous infield a legend that will never die." During his career, Stuffy played in

2,128 games, hit 20 home runs and was credited with 1,060 RBI's.

After his retirement as a player, McInnis served as Manager of the Philadelphia Phillies in 1927 and resigned after finishing in last place in the league. The next year, nearer home, he led the Salem club in the old New England League. During World War II, Frank D. Ashburn, Headmaster of Brooks School in nearby North Andover and captain of the baseball team himself during his senior year at Yale in 1921, asked Stuffy if he would help coach secondary school students at Brooks. His two years there led to a coaching appointment at Amherst College in 1949 and finally to Harvard University where as coach of baseball he stayed for five years until 1954. At both colleges, one of his greatest pleasures was playing against Holy Cross, coached by his old teammate, Philadelphia shortstop Jack Barry. Earlier Stuffy also coached in Nova Scotia and at Norwich University in Vermont.

Journalist John C. "Finney" Burke, a lifelong resident of Manchester, former Editor of The Beverly Times and now retired Assistant Managing Editor of The Boston Globe, remembers Stuffy well in his retirement years. "Every day," he recalls, "he would leave his house on Tappan Street, cross the freight yards and head for Beach Street where he would pick up his newspaper at Peter Brown's Manchester Fruit Store."

HE LOVED KIDS
After the Major Leagues, Stuffy Turns to Coaching at Amherst, Harvard

Often he would linger in the back room and there, when they were young, Burke and his pals Ted and "Spike" Brown (Spike went on to become a popular radio sportscaster at Salem and in Boston), would "shoot the breeze" and listen to tales of the big leagues as they sat around with others often much older than themselves.

Finney, a ballplayer himself as a youngster and later manager of his team at Story High (Coach Joe Hyland tagged him with the nickname—Lou Finney played right field and first base for the Red Sox), said that once when Hyland was ill, Stuffy stepped in for a couple of weeks to coach not baseball but basketball. The team went on to win the League championship. "He was a great athlete himself and had a wonderful way with the play-

ers," Finney adds, "and he always took time to talk with kids who loved sports." A handsome man with salt and pepper hair, he often wore a Harris tweed jacket and button-down shirt with tie in keeping with his Ivy League associations.

While at Harvard he was interviewed by The Boston Herald's William F. Homer. "Baseball's different today," Stuffy mused. "We hit against the spitball, the shine ball and the emery. Pitchers would even use the ball to knock the mud off their spikes. We'd try to keep the old ball in play until it went out of the park. Now it's thrown out if it gets a hard look."

His daughter, Eileen Littlefield, remembers him as a kind and loving father who was understandably often away from home. Her mother, the former Elsie Dow of Manchester (the couple were wed in 1917), held the household together while Stuffy traveled from city to city by train and Pullman car as everyone did in those days. "He was wonderful with kids of every age," she recalled, too, "and made a lot of friends wherever he went. But he was basically a shy person. I don't think he ever really enjoyed the spotlight."

Somehow there was money owed the members of the great 1918 Red Sox team, perhaps because of World War I and its impact on the season, and in the 1990's, Eileen, Babe Ruth's daughter, and other descendants of team members, were invited to Fenway Park. There they watched a game and in a special ceremony, management presented them with a check which represented each players share of earnings which they had not received at the time. "Mine was for $250," said Eileen, quite a difference, indeed, from what ballplayers get today.

As sports columnist Jack Denty declared: "It was a grave injustice that Stuffy McInnis passed away without being welcomed into the Hall of Fame…Maybe he was punished for his lack of color. One thing for sure, he was not judged fairly on his record."

But in Manchester today in the hearts of many who remember him, Stuffy McInnis will always be a hall of famer not only for his accomplishments on the ball field, but also for his warmth and kindness as a neighbor and his interest in young people throughout the town.

2 GENERATIONS 'ON ACTIVE SERVICE'

Harvey H. Bundy of Manchester (second from right in civilian clothes), Special Assistant to Secretary of War Henry L. Stimson during World War II, salutes the colors at a 1944 Fourth of July ceremony in Rome, Italy. In the group of senior officers with Secretary Stimson, far left, and Bundy were Major General Harry H. Johnson, Lieutenant-General Jacob L. Devers and Lieutenant-General Mark W. Clark, Commander, Fifth Army. U.S. Army photo.

'TACT & DISCRETION'

Harvey H. Bundy Becomes an Indispensible Advisor, Aide During Two World Wars

Harvey Hollister Bundy's extraordinary career in public and private service began in Grand Rapids, Michigan where he was born in 1888. Migrating east, he graduated from Yale and then from Harvard Law School where he compiled a distinguished record as a member of the Law Review and advisor to the Ames competition.

Not only the brightest of the bright, but as his son McGeorge writes "a man of unusual tact and discretion" throughout his life, he was asked in 1914 to clerk for Supreme Court Justice Oliver Wendell Holmes. The decision took him to Washington and started him on a career in which he became an aide, indispensable advisor and personal friend to some of the nation's most important and influential people for a period just after World War I and throughout World War II.

Bundy's arrival as a summer resident of Manchester was occasioned by his marriage to Katharine Putnam whose family for years had owned a house at Smith's Point. The two were wed in 1915 and subsequently raised five children: Harvey, Jr., William, McGeorge, Harriet and Katharine Lawrence, known throughout her life as Laurie. Bill Bundy and McGeorge also had distinguished records of government service. In 1950, Mac, as he was called, married Mary Lothrop, a former Associate Dean of Admissions at Radcliffe College and later a Radcliffe Trustee for 18 years, uniting two long-time Manchester families.

Harvey, plagued with bad eyesight like his father, served as an Army officer in the Pentagon during World War II, entered business after the war and lived year round at Smith's Point with his wife Edie. A Certified Public Accountant, he was Vice President and Treasurer of Gorton's of Gloucester, Vice President of Cape Ann Bank & Trust Company and a founder of Gloucester Bank & Trust as well as President of the National Fisheries Institute. He also served as a member of the School Committee here for two terms.

Harriet, who became Dean of Admissions at Radcliffe and was later a Trustee, married Boston attorney Don Belin, a partner of Choate, Hall & Stewart. Laurie was a Trustee of Barnard College; her husband, Hugh Auchincloss, a surgeon in New York. All, with the exception of Bill, continued to spend their summers in Manchester.

After a year in Washington with Justice Holmes, during which he met and mixed with many young men who were to make their names in the world later, Harvey Bundy returned to Boston to practice law. War clouds were on the horizon, however, and by 1917, the US could stand by no longer. Bundy had spent the previous summer at Plattsburg, New York, training to become an officer. When war was declared he tried to sign up, but underweight and with poor eyesight, the Army wouldn't have him.

Instead, he went to work for the Justice Department as a special agent of the Federal Bureau of Investigation, following up on German aliens. But he had his eye on something more exciting where he could make a greater contribution with his knowledge of the law. The opportunity came when he was asked to serve as one of four assistants to Herbert Hoover, later to become 31st President of the United States.

As U.S. Food Administrator during World War I, Hoover, or the "Chief" as he was known affectionately, was building a legal department to deal with regulations and producer contracts. Another of his assistants was Bob Taft (son of President William Howard Taft who summered on the North Shore and visited Manchester often to play golf), who Bundy knew at Yale and who was to become a U.S. Senator from Ohio and later a candidate for President himself. The job was not only interesting, but exposed him to problems faced by business and industry, experience which was to come in handy for the rest of his life.

After the war, in 1919, Bundy returned to Boston and private practice where one of his closest friends from Yale was poet Archibald MacLeish. He became a specialist in wills and trusts, serving as Trustee for a number of wealthy Bostonians and putting together business investments and transactions. He changed law firms, too, becoming a partner of Choate, Hall & Stewart, where he knew the managing partner, John L. Hall, also a summer resident of Manchester and a graduate of Yale. During the stock market crash of 1929, he was busy helping investors and brokerage firms borrow money to survive.

Then in 1931, he visited a friend in Washington who was Special Assistant to then-President Hoover's Secretary of State, Henry L. Stimson,

Army Lieutenant McGeorge Bundy of Manchester may be seen just over the shoulders of Major General George S. Patton of Hamilton and Rear Admiral Alan G. Kirk, just after Kirk had engineered Patton's Third Army's successful crossing of the Rhine River. Bundy served as an intelligence aide to Kirk, Commander Naval Task Force and a key figure in Operation Overlord, the cross-channel invasion of France. Well versed in amphibious operations, Admiral Kirk had earlier commanded Amphibious Forces, Atlantic Fleet. After the war, Bundy became Dean at Harvard University and later served as Chairman of the National Security Council during the Kennedy Administration. Photo courtesy of Mary Bundy.

Mr. and Mrs. Harvey H. Bundy in Manchester with their grandchildren in 1952. The Bundys were long-time summer residents of the town. As special assistant to Secretary of War Henry L. Stimson during World War II, Harvey Bundy was much involved with super-secret operations including the development of radar, intercept intelligence and the Manhattan Project which gave birth to the atomic bomb. Photo courtesy of Mary Bundy.

also a Yale man, Class of 1888, and a graduate of Harvard Law School. The Secretary himself came to lunch and was most impressed with both Harvey and his wife Kay. Because of a death, there was an opening for an Assistant Secretary of State and, as an attorney who had experience in business and financial matters, Bundy was offered the post. His job would be to deal with problems of international debt including debt incurred by other countries such as England and France during World War I.

As a former aide to Hoover and a supporter of his bid for the Presidency, Bundy's political affiliations met every expectation and he was soon confirmed. He also worked with the Secretary on questions arising from the Japanese invasion of Manchuria in 1931. With the election of Franklin Roosevelt in 1933, however, the Bundys again left for Boston and Harvey rejoined Choate, Hall & Stewart.

In the fall of 1940, Roosevelt was elected to a third term as President. Barely 23 years after the armistice had ended World War I, Germany had conquered France and the Low Countries and had invaded Russia. The Royal Air Force was winning the Battle of Britain, but victory overall was far from certain and few people doubted that the U.S. would eventually join the Allies.

Now in his seventies, and a supporter of many of FDR's foreign policy programs, Henry Stimson had been named Secretary of War in 1940. His need for a top aide—someone he knew personally, liked immensely, could trust implicitly and with whom he could share his confidences—led him directly to Harvey Bundy. Prepared to stay for a few months to help where he could, Bundy ultimately served as Stimson's Special Assistant for four and one-half years until the end of World War II.

'FIRST TEAM'

Bundy Serves as Facilitator for Secretary of War Stimson During World War II

With immediate access to the Secretary in all matters, he became as Stimson said himself, "my closest personal assistant." As such, as Mac Bundy writes in Stimson's biography On Active Service in Peace and War (Harper Brothers, 1947), "[Harvey] Bundy served as his filter for all sorts of men and problems." He was also the point man for the Secretary "in dealings with scientists and educators, two groups whose importance was as great as it was unfamiliar in the new army of machines and civilian soldiers."

Other members of the War Department's "first team" besides Bundy were Robert P. Patterson, John J. McCloy, George Harrison and Robert A. Lovett. The five, all civilians, were men of extraordinary ability and "absolute integrity" which they had proved in private life. As Stimson's "eyes and ears," Bundy was involved with and helped facilitate such top secret projects as the development of the atomic bomb, the use and improvement of radar and the management of intercept intelligence.

His responsibilities kept him in constant contact with such major figures as Army Chief of Staff General George Marshall as well as other General officers; chief administrator of the Manhattan Project, General Leslie Groves; and science leaders Vannevar Bush and former Harvard President James B. Conant (the Secretary was very interested in science and its contributions to winning the war).

On inspection trips with Stimson, he met and talked with Winston Churchill and Generals Eisenhower and Patton, and attended the meeting of Heads of State at Potsdam. With the war over in 1945 in both Atlantic and Pacific Theaters, Stimson retired from the then Truman Cabinet in September. Bundy retired with him, returned to Boston, and once again took up his responsibilities as an attorney and trustee. He had a lighter side as well which should be noted, as his daughter-in-law Mary Lothrop Bundy recalls. A man of "infinite charm," she says, he was a "marvelous dancer," had a "good singing voice and played the mandolin in college as well as [having] great gifts in encouraging younger people."

Son William Bundy, whose wife Mary was the daughter of former Secretary of State Dean Acheson, an old family friend, graduated from Yale and spent the war years in cryptology as commanding officer of an American unit assigned to work with the top secret British Ultra team at Bletchely Park which was reading German code.

After the war he attended law school at Harvard, practiced law in Washington and then, in 1951, joined the Central Intelligence Agency. He soon became top assistant to the organization's Deputy Director for Intelligence. A rocky moment in his life occurred when he was asked to appear before the McCarthy committee of the Senate to be quizzed about his contribution to the campaign to defend Alger Hiss, accused of spying, but who many today still believe was innocent. At issue was the larger question, however, of how a covert agency could operate effectively if its employees were subject to Congressional subpoena. To escape Washington and the responsibility of testifying, with the approval of his superiors including President Eisenhower, Bill chose to visit his parents in Manchester where he had grown up. The weekend was a long one, but in the end, both the CIA and Bundy won out.

In 1960, Bill was asked to direct the staff of President Eisenhower's Commission on National Goals. Its well-received report became a blue print for President Lyndon Johnson's Great Society. Always a Democrat, Bundy now had his eye on a possible appointment with the new Kennedy administration, and when he was offered the post of Assistant Secretary of Defense for International Security Affairs, he accepted.

Meanwhile, his younger brother Mac, also a graduate of Yale, who had received an Army commission after he memorized the eye chart (like his father and older brother, he too had poor eyesight), served in Europe during World War II as an aide and Ultra officer providing classified information about the enemy to U.S. Rear Admiral Alan R. Kirk. At his own request, he was later transferred to a combat division which was to take part in the U.S. invasion of Japan. Thanks to the atomic bomb, however, Mac and millions of other young Americans were spared that necessity as peace finally came in August, 1945.

After the war, he joined the faculty at Harvard, helped Henry Stimson write a lengthy memoir about his experiences in public life, and authored a much respected and influential article in Harper's Magazine defending the administration's use of the atomic bomb as a weapon to end World War II. In 1953, he became Dean of Harvard, all the while living in Cambridge and, with Mary and their four boys, summering in Manchester which he enjoyed throughout his life. A familiar figure to many in his white shorts and shirt, he often played tennis at the Essex County Club and at the Bundy court.

PRESIDENT'S CHOICE

Mac Bundy Is Named Kennedy's Special Assistant for National Security Affairs

Then, in 1960, like his older brother Bill, he too joined the Kennedy Administration in Washington as the President's Special Assistant for National Security Affairs. Few advisors were as close to the Oval Office or had more influence with Kennedy. The two thought alike—both Mac and the President were men of action—and became close friends. Both Bundys were deeply involved with the extraordinary tensions of the era: the invasion at the Bay of Pigs; the Cuban missile crisis, the Soviet's isolation of West Berlin; the construction of the Berlin wall; efforts to end testing of nuclear weapons; the assassination of President Kennedy; the succession of Lyndon Johnson; and, of course, the increasing intensity of the war in Vietnam.

Bill and Mac, who spent their formative summers in Manchester, served the nation with loyalty and distinction. If there are those who criticize their advice and opinions about Vietnam, there are others who explain and defend them. It was a painful era which tore the country apart and which will create debate and controversy for years to come.

Mac went on to become President of the Ford Foundation and later a Professor of History at New York University. He was the author of three books: Secretary Stimson's memoirs, On Active Service in Peace and War; The Pattern of Responsibility, a defense of Secretary of State Dean Acheson's foreign policy; and Danger and Survival which dealt with the history of U.S. nuclear policy. Throughout his life, for him and for his family, Manchester played an important role as a place he was brought up, as a refuge from the intensity of Washington, and as a quiet antidote to urban life in New York City. After his death, Mary continues to summer here today.

Manchester can also be proud of another Bundy, Harvey, Senior's younger brother Frederick M., "Fritz," who lived here until his death in 1989. A graduate of Yale (1921) and Harvard Business School, he was at various times President of Gorton-Pew Fisheries in Gloucester, President of Cape Ann Bank & Trust Company and President of Essex County Club. His widow, Betsy, is still active in the community as is his son, F.M. Bundy, Jr.

In 1906, Eben D. Jordan, Jr., son of the founder of Jordan Marsh stores, built this tudor-style summer house overlooking the outer harbor in West Manchester. An opera lover, Jordan was president of the Boston Opera Company and provided funds to build the Boston Opera House. An earlier dwelling on the site was razed to make way for the new "cottage" which was some 185 feet in length. Constructed by Connolly Brothers of Beverly Farms, the house included accommodations for 12 female staff members but allocated them only one bath. On the floor below, the footman and butler, both male, of course, had the luxury of a bath of their own. Today, the house has been beautifully restored to its original glory by its present owners.

Once owned by Charles Stedman Hanks, a founder of the Essex County Club and one-time President of the Misery Island Club, Elsinaes, as it is called, was purchased in 1899 by Alice Perkins Hooper (Mrs. William) who paid $6,500 for the house and nearly three acres of land. Located at the corner of Bridge Street and Highland Avenue, the property which includes 38 separate rooms, has been a part of Landmark School since 1970. Elsie P. Youngman, author of <u>Summer Echoes from the 19th Century, Manchester-by-the-Sea</u>, published in 1981, was Mrs. Hooper's niece and spent summers there both as a child and later with her own children.

Elegantly designed, the Italian gardens at the Coolidge estate, Coolidge Point, Manchester, were a showplace of the North Shore. Walled and terraced, they reflected life in the villas of Italy where the formality of sculptured landscapes were a striking decoration. Nearby was the main dwelling, known as the Marble Palace, a magnificent summer house of brick and white marble built in 1902. It was torn down in 1958.

Magnificent six-story Oceanside Hotel was a magnet for Manchester summer residents prior to World War II. The village itself boasted an elegant Main Street–Lexington Avenue–lined with fashionable shops such as Lord & Taylor, DePinna, Tiffany's, J.J. Jonas and Frederick's, all with other branches in New York City, Paris, London and Palm Beach. Also nearby was the Magnolia Casino, a glamorous, seaside nightclub. The Oceanside, which also owned 18 "cottages" offered for rent, was part of a chain of hotels which included The Vendome in Boston, the Gasparilla Inn at Boca Grande, Florida and Forest Hills Hotel, Franconia, New Hampshire. The Oceanside was destroyed by fire around 1960.

278

Services were first held in Manchester's Baptist Church on School Street in February, 1844. Earlier, in 1842, parishioners met in the town library which was located where the fire house now stands. In 1843, 13 men and women, baptized by the Elder Elan Burnham of Essex, formed a congregation and were soon joined by 57 others. In 1848, during the pastorate of the Reverend P.R. Russell, the church officially joined the Baptist denomination.

The first Catholic Church was located on School Street and Burnham Lane in Manchester. In a practice common in its day, the building included two parts of the Craft house moved from the corner of Union Street and Church Street by Frederick Burnham. The first Mass was celebrated on Christmas Day in 1872. In 1904, the structure was moved again, reduced in size, and converted to a private home. Sacred Heart Church at the corner of School and Friend Streets was built in 1907.

Long admired as the most beautiful building in Manchester, the Orthodox Congregational Church was built in 1809. The product of devoted furniture makers and ships carpenters, it is a work of art and cost just $8,500. The pastor at the time was the Reverend James Thurston. As architect Stephen Robert Holt writes, the design of the structure was believed to have been inspired by drawings which appear in Asher Benjamin's book *The American Builder's Companion* published in 1806. With Samuel McIntire of Salem, Benjamin was one of the leading carpenter-builders of the era whose style set the tone for new American architecture. This striking photo was taken by Richard E. Towle in 1969.

Owner and Proprietor of J.F. Rabardy, Postmaster Julius Rabardy (white coat) poses in August 1892 in front of his store decorated with bunting for the parade scheduled to celebrate the completion of a new public water supply and distribution system for the town. Note chairs for sightseers on the second floor between the bay windows. Signs on either side of the central star read "With joy shall ye draw water" and "Honest water which ne'er left Man i' the mire." The building on Central Street which was home to Floyd's (Rabardy's stepdaughter married Lyman Floyd, grandfather of Alice Rice), was built in 1884. A Union veteran of the Civil War, Rabardy lost a leg at the Battle of Antietam Creek. Photo courtesy of Mrs. George Rice.

280

Spectators gather on the morning of January 18, 1906 to view damage caused by fire which struck the Pulsifer Block at the corner of Beach and Union Streets the night before. Windows are broken and a fire hose may still be seen at right crossing the street from a hydrant. On the first floor facing Union Street behind the ladder is the entrance to Bullock Brothers, groceries. After the blaze, it was decided to remove the second story and restore the first which still stands today. Prior to 1939 when the present brick structure on Beach Street was erected, the Post Office was located in the Pulsifer Building. The Pulsifer family were among the early settlers in Manchester.

Manchester was a quiet country town in 1879 as this photo taken from a stereopticon slide indicates. The view which shows residents on the sidewalks, boys in the street, and girls in long dresses sitting on the curb, perhaps all waiting for a parade, looks down Union Street towards Beach Street. At left is the fence in front of the Trask house, now home to the Manchester Historical Society. At right is the Franklin building which housed a retail store. It was razed in 1909. The Memorial Library, which was dedicated in 1887, had yet to be built. At the end of Union Street is the Kinsman house. Located at the corner of Union and Beach it was torn down in 1903. Note the American elm trees which provided welcome shade.

BIBLIOGRAPHY

Abbott, Gordon Jr., Saving Special Places, A Centennial History of The Trustees of Reservations: Pioneer of the Land Trust Movement, Ipswich, Massachusetts, The Ipswich Press, 1993

The Autobiography of T. Jefferson Coolidge 1831-1920, Boston and New York, Houghton Mifflin & Company, The Riverside Press, 1923

The Book Committee, A Baker's Island Chronicle 1964-1988; Salem, Massachusetts, Baker's Island Association, 1989;

Chapell, Howard, The History of American Sailing Ships; New York, W.W. Norton & Company, 1935

Day, Mrs. Arthur, A Scrapbook of magazine and newspaper clippings of Manchester residents who served in World War II

Dedication Services of the Memorial Library and Grand Army Hall at Manchester-by-the-Sea October 13, 1887; Boston, Rand Avery Company, Printers, The Franklin Press, 1888

Floyd, Frank L., Manchester-by-the-Sea, Manchester, Massachusetts, Floyd's News Store, 1945

Garland, Joseph E., Boston's North Shore, Being and an Account of Life Among the Noteworthy Fashionable, Wealthy, Eccentric and Ordinary, 1823-1890; Boston and Toronto, Little Brown & Company, 1978

Garland, Joseph E., Boston's Gold Coast. The North Shore, 1890-1925; Boston and Toronto, Little Brown & Company, 1981

Halstead, Isabella, The Aunts, Manchester-by-the-Sea, Massachusetts, The Sharksmouth Press, 1992

Lamson, Darius F., History of the Town of Manchester, 1645-1895, Manchester, Massachusetts, Town of Manchester, 1895

Maclay, Edgar S., A History of American Privateers; New York, D. Appleton and Company, 1899

Meinig, D.W., The Shaping of America, A Geographical Perspective on 500 Years of History, Volume I, Atlantic America 1492-1800; New Haven and London, Yale University Press, 1986

Merrill, Benjamin B., A History of Twentieth Century Manchester; Manchester, Massachusetts, The Cricket Press, 1990

The Misery Island Club, Beverly Farms, Massachusetts, Boston, The Farrington Press, 1900

Morison, Samuel Eliot, Builders of the Bay Colony, Boston and New York, Houghton Mifflin Company, The Riverside Press, 1930

Morison, Samuel Eliot, The Maritime History of Massachusetts, 1783-1860; Boston and New York, Houghton Mifflin Company, The Riverside Press, 1921

Rogers, Alden, The Hard White Road, A Chronicle of the Reserve Mallet; Buffalo, New York, Privately Printed, 1923

Senecal, Dan, Ed Halsted, Fred Nickless and Deb deSherbinin, Manchester-by-the-Sea 1645-1995; 350th Anniversary Committee, Manchester, Massachusetts, 1995

Shurcliff, Joan Hopkinson and Arthur A. Shurcliff, II, The Boldest Man That I Know The Life of Greely Stevenson Curtis, Privately Published, 2000

Slade, Harry, Dan Slade, Editors; The Manchester Cricket, a weekly newspaper published at Manchester, Massachusetts; various editions

Stimson, Henry L. and McGeorge Bundy, On Active Service in Peace and War; New York, Harper & Brothers, 1947, 1948

TIME Magazine, January 13, 1967

Weeks, Sinclair, Richard Bowditch Wigglesworth, Way Stations of a Fruitful Life, Privately Published, 1964

Weems, Katharine Lane, Odds Were Against Me, A Memoir, as told to Edward Weeks; New York, New York, Vantage Press, 1985

Youngman, Elsie P. and George M. Cushing, Summer Echoes from the 19th Century, Manchester-by-the-Sea; Rockport, Massachusetts, Don Russell, 1981

Note also Bibliographies which appear in copies of REFLECTIONS

REFLECTIONS

Written and edited by the author of this book and published by the Manchester Historical Society all but annually for the past decade, REFLECTIONS are a series of papers which present selected topics of Manchester history. Because they are mailed only to some 400 Historical Society members and contain much valuable information, it was agreed that they be included as a part of this publication. Six issues have been reproduced. They tell the story of <u>Masconomo and his Indians</u> and how Native American and early English colonists interacted along the North Shore; our first summer residents, <u>the Dana family</u> and <u>the great Sea Serpent mystery of 1817</u>; <u>our gallant firefighters</u> and their heroic actions since the days of hand-pumpers and the famous TORRENT, built in 1832 and preserved today at SEASIDE NO. 1; the story of <u>the Booth family</u>, the theatrical community in Manchester and the building of <u>the Masconomo House</u>; Manchester's "Finest," an account of <u>our brave police officers</u> and their activities since the department was formally established in 1897; and, finally, a history of <u>the Manchester Electric Company</u>, of <u>celebrated shipwrecks</u> off our shores, and the life of <u>publisher extraordinare James T. Fields</u>, summer resident here with his wife Annie from the 1850's through his death in 1881, who was a father figure for writers throughout the nation.

REFLECTIONS

MANCHESTER HISTORICAL SOCIETY

SUMMER 2001

MANCHESTER, MASSACHUSETTS

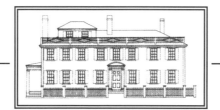

OUR HEY-DAY IN THE LITERARY SUN

INSIDE: MANCHESTER SHIPWRECKS;
OUR OWN ELECTRIC COMPANY

Manchester's own James T. Fields in his later years. The much respected and beloved publisher was photographed in an accustomed pose with books in hand and on the table. Beards and mustaches were very much in fashion. (The Boston Athanaeum photo)

CELEBRATED AUTHORS

Extraordinary Collection of Great Writers Visit Manchester as Friends of James T. Fields

In the last half of the nineteenth century, Manchester and this small section of the North Shore served as a summer home for such luminaries of their day as nationally-acclaimed stage actor and producer Junius Brutus Booth, Jr.; attorney Richard Henry Dana, Jr., celebrated author of Two Years Before the Mast, a breath-taking, trend-setting adventure of life at sea published in 1840; and Oliver Wendell Holmes, physician, teacher, and writer of a regular column entitled The Autocrat of the Breakfast Table which he produced for the then brand-new Atlantic Monthly magazine from his summer home in nearby Beverly Farms.

But for success in the literary world, few could rival the accomplishments of publisher, sometime author, poet and lecturer James T. Fields who, with his wife Annie, rented in Manchester for many summers and finally, in 1874, built a house of their own on top of Thunderbolt Hill. Fields, ultimately partner and later owner of Ticknor & Fields with early headquarters at the Old Corner Bookstore, School and Washington Streets, Boston, could eventually claim all but exclusive publishing rights to the works of an extraordinary list of the leading men and women of American letters.

They included James Russell Lowell, Henry Wadsworth Longfellow, Nathaniel Hawthorne, Harriet Beecher Stowe, Ralph Waldo Emerson, Henry David Thoreau, John Greenleaf Whittier, Sarah Orne Jewett, Celia Thaxter, Bret Harte, Mark Twain, and his near-town neighbor, Dr. Holmes. English authors, whose works he published in Boston for America readers, included Charles Dickens, Robert Browning, Matthew Arnold, Leigh Hunt, Alfred Lord Tennyson and William Makepeace Thackeray.

Fields and his wife Annie were not only publishers for these renowned authors, but their personal friends as well, and the Fields' houses at Manchester and at 148 Charles Street, Boston, were open to them all. They came with pleasing regularity for breakfast, lunch, tea or supper. They found enjoyment in the good companionship of each other buoyed by the warm hospitality, humor and genuine affection they held for James and Annie Fields. Many were friends before they met the Fields. Hawthorne and Longfellow, for example, were classmates at Bowdoin College. And Lowell and Longfellow both lived in Cambridge and taught at Harvard. Others, including Charles Dickens, became life-long friends through their literary associations.

Despite his remarkable achievements, James Thomas Fields had humble beginnings. He was born in Portsmouth, New Hampshire of Scotch-Irish ancestry in December, 1817. His father, Michael, of whom he saw little, was a sea captain engaged primarily in coastal trade. He died when James was only two. Thankfully, his mother, Margaret, left a widow at age 28, was a woman of great strength and character. Alone, she brought up two sons, James and his brother George. Devoted to his mother (Fields didn't marry until after her death when he was 32 years old), Jamie grew up like any normal American boy, exploring the streets and by-ways of the old city, attending church and Sunday School, and discovering the surrounding countryside on foot. After a sailing accident in which a classmate had drowned, however, he was not allowed to venture on the water. But unlike many of his contemporaries, Jamie Fields showed an early love for books and learning and, in his twelfth year, an ability to write poetry. He also read voraciously, browsed the bookshops of the city and, thanks to the generosity of selected elders, was able to utilize the resources of the public library, the Portsmouth Athanaeum, still as much of a fixture today as it was in the 1820's.

In 1831, at 15 years old, Jamie graduated from high school. It was hoped he could attend Harvard but college tuition was far too expensive for his widowed mother who still had his brother to care for. The other alternative was work and Portsmouth, whose shipping days were over, offered little to an ambitious young man. A family friend, however, came to his rescue and procured a position for him in Boston as an apprentice at Carter & Hendee's Bookstore. It couldn't have been a better choice and James was delighted.

At the time, Boston was growing in importance as a center of trade, industry and culture, and many a promising youngster, who 20 years earlier might have stayed on the farm or found a job in the small cities of the region, was drawn to major metropolitan centers nearby such as Boston or New York. As cities grew with migration from the countryside and with the addition of a steady stream of immigrants from Europe, it marked the beginning of urbanization and a new era for America. There were those, to be sure, who, perhaps with their parents, migrated west or south to the Frontier, but for those blessed with some connections as well as ability, Boston offered opportunity and even wealth.

And so it was in April, 1831, that James T. Fields hugged his mother good-bye, boarded a horse-drawn coach in downtown Portsmouth (the railroads, already in the planning stages, were to arrive a few years later) and traveled over rutted, dirt roads, arriving in Boston just before dark.

As the fourth largest city in the nation, Boston was quite a contrast to Portsmouth, New Hampshire. It was a center of shipping and finance. As many as 100 vessels in one day entered and left its harbor. Its streets were filled with carriages and wagons and young men like Jamie, out to seek their fortunes in a wider world, found lodging at one of the many rooming houses in the city, most probably with one of those for whom he worked. Within a year, his employers, Carter & Hendee, had been acquired by another book seller, Allen & Ticknor, and Jamie moved in with William D. Ticknor, who had just married, beginning a relationship, both personal and professional, which would last until the end of Ticknor's life in April, 1864.

SPECIAL THANKS

Of all of the sources used for information about chronology and events in the lives of James T. Fields and his wife Annie Adams Fields, two particularly stand out. One is author W. S. Tryon's epic biography entitled Parnassus Corner, A Life of James T. Fields, Publisher to the Victorians. It was published in 1963 by Houghton Mifflin Company, The Riverside Press, Cambridge. The other is a collection of notes compiled by historian Frances L. Burnett who transcribed from the voluminous Diaries of Annie Adams Fields now held by the Massachusetts Historical Society, those sections which pertain to Manchester-by the-Sea. I am enormously grateful to them both. G. A., Jr.

Of all of the attributes of James Fields' character, his personal charm seems to have been most admired. He spoke well. He was amusing. He cared genuinely for other people. And he was blessed with a fine intellect, literary abilities, good judgment and a commitment to hard work and to his chosen profession. As author W. S. Tryon states in his wonderfully comprehensive and delightfully readable biography Parnassus Corner, A Life of James T. Fields, Publisher to the Victorians (Boston, Houghton Mifflin Company, 1963), "Always friendly, always good-natured, people liked him, said his wife many years later, because 'his real interest is in what interests another.' ...Fields developed irritating characteristics as he grew older, but this charm of friendliness he never lost. It was founded in his desire to please others and explains in no little part his success in later years."

As Fields widened his acquaintances, he became a member of the Boston Mercantile Library Association, only a few doors from the Old Corner Book Store, which drew each evening to its unassuming quarters young men like himself of many occupations who could find books of their choosing as well as debate the issues of the day. For many of them, it served as the college experience they never would enjoy. It enabled them to educate themselves and to mature intellectually. James lectured to the group and recited his original poem, "Yankee Ships," which may later have been published as others of his were, in Boston newspapers.

At the organization's celebration of its eighteenth birthday, Fields was chosen poet for the occasion and shared the stage with the redoubtable Edward Everett, Governor of the Commonwealth. A former member of Congress; once President of Harvard College; Vice Presidential candidate in 1860 for the Constitutional Union Party; a former editor of the North American Review, and the principal orator at the dedication of the Federal Cemetery at Gettysburg (Everett spoke for two hours plus; President Lincoln, for five minutes), Edward Everett was a formidable figure. In such imposing company, James' presentation was well received and earned him high marks. He was 21 years old. Indeed, his employer, William Ticknor, thought enough of his Clerk's work to published the Governor's address and James' poem together in a special commemorative booklet.

A CANNY MOVE

At Fields' Urging, Old Corner Takes a New Tack as Publishing Becomes Its Primary Mission

As time passed, it was clear that Fields' life and the future course of the Old Corner Book Store were one. In fact, as W. S. Tryon writes in Parnassus Corner, "so inextricably woven was the career of the man and his business that the biography of one is virtually a history of the other." In describing the book trade in America in the 1830's, Tryon observed that its "functions were unspecialized, the scope of its business was local..., and the books with which it dealt were entirely 'miscellaneous' in character." With imagination, dedication, a flair for recognizing what the public would find interesting to read, and an uncanny ability for promotion and marketing, Fields would revolutionize the publishing world within the next 20 years.

First came 10 years of apprenticeship under Ticknor which involved publishing a few volumes and a series of periodicals aimed at both juvenile and adult readers. In most cases in the trade, books were published with no idea of who might buy them or how to create sales with advertising and promotion. There were no long-term relationships between writers and publishers. No attempt was made to contract with successful authors providing them with royalties for every volume sold. Indeed, in many cases, authors paid for publication themselves, happy finally to be in print. All this was to change as Fields gently helped turn the Old Corner Book Store from its traditional retail business into what was to be one of the greatest publishing houses in the northeast if not the nation.

It began with Fields convincing Ticknor, who was unusually cautious but respected the ideas and opinions of his senior clerk, to publish a new edition of Horace and James Smith's volume of poetry entitled Rejected Addresses. Fields knew that the store had received numbers of requests for the book, and that the last American edition had been issued in 1813. It was no blockbuster, but its first printing of 1,000 copies sold out within a year. Fields was thrilled, and with other additional small successes, he felt confident enough to recommend that Ticknor agree to publish the then quite controversial work of English poet Alfred Tennyson.

Competition for Tennyson's work was considerable. But Fields persuaded Ticknor, as W.D. Tryon explains, "not only of the advisability of publishing the work but also to take the unprecedented step of paying Tennyson 10 percent of the retail price for the entire printing—in this instance $150." The poet was delighted and from that moment on his loyalty never wavered. Thanks primarily to Fields' initiative and imagination, the rules of the game had changed and as the firm grew in reputation and new capital was invested, Fields was the beneficiary of a junior partnership.

His goal, which he set about to achieve in a quiet and respectful way, was to make his house known and admired for publishing the best literature available in England and America. He knew also that it was as important for his authors to make a profit as it was for the firm which published their works. By promoting sales and by providing royalties, he would encourage his authors' production. And with a new relationship based more upon the concept of partnership, he would be able to cement their loyalties so that they would choose Ticknor and Company as exclusive publishers for all of their works.

Among the early authors Fields discovered was a little-known poet from Newburyport named John Greenleaf Whittier. And in 1842, with an English partner, he published a book of poetry by Dr. Oliver Wendell Holmes. It was an immediate success and soon Ticknor & Company had sole rights to publish another volume with the author receiving royalties of 10 percent. Holmes and Whittier never forgot Fields' efforts and joined a growing list of distinguished authors, which was soon to include Henry Wadsworth Longfellow, who published only with Ticknor.

Longfellow and Fields had met earlier, enjoyed each others company and visited back and forth. And in 1847, when the time came to publish Longfellow's epic work Evangeline, Ticknor and Company offered the poet 20 cents for every copy sold. Press run for the first edition totaled 2,000. "Evangeline was a sensational success," according to W.S. Tryon. "No poem ever before published in America had enjoyed such popularity or such sales." Longfellow, too, was impressed and forever after, his friend James T. Fields was his editor and publisher.

In 1844, James' life took a new turn. He fell in love and was engaged to be married. The young lady was Mary Willard, daughter of Simon Willard, Boston's well known clockmaker, and his wife, Eliza. The Willards lived nearby and like James, were members of the Brattle Square Church. Sadly, the relationship ended too soon for Mary suffered from consumption and died at the age of 22 (she was six years younger than Fields) in the spring of 1845. In his sorrow, James turned to his work with more determination than ever. Then, in 1847, at the invitation of a relative in Portsmouth, who owned the ship NEW HAMPSHIRE, he sailed aboard her for a visit to England. It was to last five months, involve a significant amount of work meeting English authors (including William Wordsworth), making new friends, and developing a love affair for English life and the island's historic landscape.

Upon his return, once again he was asked to address the Mercantile Library Association, this time to celebrate its twenty-eighth anniversary. The primary speaker was Daniel Webster, but once again Fields rose to the occasion, and in his poem paid due tribute to the great orator. His presentation was loudly applauded and acclaimed. On top of this, Ticknor chose to make him a partner in his own right. Legally the firm still remained William D. Ticknor & Company, but the public now knew that James played a key role in its activities.

Flushed with his success, he chose to publish a volume of his own poems, and although it was pleasing, it was far from perfect as many of his friends agreed among themselves. As a writer, he was, to be sure, above average, but his real skills lay in publishing. By 1850, he had brought out the complete works of Thomas De Quincey in a unique, uniform edition and two volumes of the poems of Robert Browning. Other works of Tennyson, Whittier and Longfellow followed. James Russell Lowell, unhappy with his present arrangement, also chose to have his writings published by W.D. Ticknor.

That same year, Field's unerringly realized that The Scarlet Letter, by yet-to-be-acclaimed author Nathaniel Hawthorne, a friend who Fields believed had great promise, should be a full-length novel and not just another short story. Indeed, after reading a precis of the manuscript, he promised Hawthorne a printing of 500 copies above the usual 2,000 and a royalty of 15 percent, not the regular 10. The Scarlet Letter proved enormously popular and was testimony again to Fields' good judgment.

These years before the Civil War, marked a period of immense creativity in the country, sometimes called the American Renaissance. Native writers and artists were proclaiming their independence from Europe and yet were still in awe of its ancient cultures and traditions. With ease of transportation increasing, many traveled abroad (Washington Irving was living in England when he produced his quintessentially American tales Rip Van Winkle and The Legend of Sleepy Hollow), but they were discovering their own idiom, increasing linked to the character of their own country. Thomas Cole, Asher Durand and other painters of the "Hudson River School," sought to idealize the American landscape. James Fenimore Cooper, told the story of the frontier and of the lives of Native Americans in his Leatherstocking Tales (published 1826 to 1841). Nathaniel Hawthorne's The Scarlet Letter and The House of Seven Gables, prodded discussion of the conventions, sentiments and morality of the day.

Popular New England poets, men of intellect and learning, chose down-to-earth subjects. Longfellow wrote about the village blacksmith and the wreck of a sailing ship off Gloucester. Whittier famously described the beauties of a winter snow storm. And Lowell invented an imaginary homespun character called Hosea Biglow who spoke satirically in a Yankee dialect about the politics of the era.

James T. Fields had an uncanny appreciation of what did become the popular literature of the day and of the men and women who produced it. His publishing house benefited from this wisdom and now could count many of America's greatest authors as its own. But tragedy still stalked Fields' private life. Close to the Willards since the death of Mary, he fell in love again, this time with Mary's younger sister, Eliza and the two were married in March, 1850. The pair were blissfully happy, but soon, Eliza, too, came down with tuberculosis, the same malady that had so disastrously infected her sister. In a few short months, she was dead, married just more than a year.

Fields, who had been ill as well, was beside himself. "I am still so bewildered with my affliction that my mind refuses to act in the old channels," he wrote. On the advice of friends and with the wholehearted support of William Ticknor, he once again sailed for England. Visiting France and Italy as well, he was entertained in literary circles everywhere. Back in England, he looked for writers whose work might be worth publishing for American readers. He visited with Mary Mitford, dined with Robert Browning and his wife, the more celebrated Elizabeth Barrett, talked with Thomas Carlyle, and persuaded William Makepeace Thackeray to plan a lecture tour of America. But Ticknor, buried with work and carrying a double load since Fields had left, begged him to return. After all but a year abroad, he did, arriving in Boston aboard ship to a warm welcome from relatives and friends.

In the years that followed, Fields honed his talents as a promoter of the books he published, using newspapers and periodicals for advertising and working with editors for favorable reviews. In Boston, the favorite was the Transcript, which then and for years afterwards was the daily newspaper of the intellectual and social elite. In almost every case, reviews of Fields' books were favorable that is until The Boston Traveller was sent a copy of Longfellow's The Song of Hiawatha. The paper's comments were not complimentary. Fields was outraged, expecting naively that the dollars he spent for advertising would result in better treatment in the editorial columns. It was a mistake which generated an outpouring of comments about freedom of the press and criticism of the book publisher who expected a quid pro quo. Newspapers, and there were a half dozen in Boston at the time, battled with each other over the issue. Faced with many of the same practices, papers in New York City joined the fray. But finally, Fields, acting on good advice, let the matter go and became more prudent about how he dealt with reviews in the years ahead. Like most controversies over a work of art or literature, the publicity generated enormous public interest and sales of Hiawatha climbed dramatically to some 13,500 copies.

TICKNOR & FIELDS

James Becomes a Named Partner in the Firm; Falls in Love and Is Wed Once Again

The year 1854 marked another turning point in Fields' life. First, with his purchase of additional equity, the firm became Ticknor & Fields, and although still a junior partner, James' accomplishments had earned him signal recognition. Second, he had fallen in love once again, this time with Annie Adams, daughter of a well-known and much respected Boston physician, and first cousin to Mary and Eliza Willard. In November, the two were married at Kings Chapel. Just over a year later they moved into a new house of their own at 148 Charles Street at the foot of Beacon Hill, an address that was to become well known and much appreciated by friends and fellow authors in the years to come. Financing for the purchase was made possible by the generosity of William D. Ticknor. The firm picked up the mortgage. Fields paid back the loan with the rent.

Annie, although seventeen years his junior, was a rare find and a perfect compliment to Fields' personality and profession. Like James, she was charming, outgoing and gracious. She was young and beautiful and a perfect hostess. She had great presence and although she rarely claimed the limelight, her sensitivity and understanding enabled her to make the extraordinary number of celebrities who regularly became her guests, feel appreciated and at home.

All this entertaining—and there were a series of famous breakfasts for authors, editors and critics—of course, promoted the firm and its work, drawing stars of the literary world together. Hawthorne, Whittier, Holmes and Lowell, had now been joined by jurist Rufus Choate, Henry Ward Beecher, Professor Louis Agassiz, Charles Sumner and Julia Ward Howe. In 1854 and 1859, Ticknor & Fields began publishing works of Henry David Thoreau and Ralph Waldo Emerson. By 1860, Fields would add William Cullen Bryant, Harriet Beecher Stowe and England's much beloved Charles Dickens.

As testimony to his extraordinary abilities and accomplishments, in 1858, the once poor boy from Portsmouth, New Hampshire who couldn't afford to go there, was awarded an Honorary Degree of Master of Arts by Harvard. Thirteen years later, always sentimental about his past and ever aware of where he came from, he sent his Harvard degree to Portsmouth High School. There it served to tell other youngsters how one of their own, with the classic virtues of honesty, integrity and hard work, reached the pinnacle of his profession.

Annie, of course, had never visited James' beloved England and so part for pleasure and part for business reasons, in June,1859 they sailed for Liverpool aboard the Cunard Line ship CANADA. Amid the social whirl, Fields had his eye set upon meeting with Dickens to discuss the possibility of an American tour which later became a reality. The couple traveled through the English countryside, visiting writers, and then were off to Paris with more writers, ending up in Florence for the winter. That spring, a year after they had left, they returned to Boston.

By then it was 1860. The country was in turmoil. Lincoln had been elected President. South Carolina would be the first state to withdraw from the Union in December, and on April 12, it ordered the bombardment of Fort Sumter in Charleston

Portrait of Annie Adams Fields based on a daguerreotype taken by Southworth & Hawes in Boston about 1855. Mrs. Fields rests her arm on a balustrade inscribed with the verse: "And she in whom sweet charities unite, the old Greek beauties set in holier light." (The Boston Athanaeum photo)

Harbor. The Civil War had begun. It was to change America's way of life forever.

Fields had little or no interest in politics, but in the beginning of the war, like so many of his fellow merchants, he deplored abolitionism as a threat to trade. Indeed, the southern market was about to be lost and the west was dubious at best. Publishers everywhere curtailed their lists. But Ticknor & Fields did expand to add one new enterprise: the <u>Atlantic Monthly</u>. With James Russell Lowell as editor, the magazine had an excellent reputation as a literary journal, but was not much admired for its profitability. In 1861, James T. Fields became its editor. Because of his wide acquaintanceship with authors, he was an excellent choice. He also knew that to make the <u>Atlantic</u> financially successful, he would have to find some way to increase its appeal beyond the narrow confines of intellectuals. Throughout the war, the magazine became more political. It supported the Union cause and published such enduring pieces as John Greenleaf Whittier's <u>Barbara Frietchie</u>, Julia Ward Howe's stirring <u>Battle Hymn of the Republic</u>, and Edward Everett Hale's epic, <u>The Man Without a Country</u>.

Lean years, however, soon gave way to a new prosperity generated by the war and book publishing benefited with everything else. As W.S. Tryon writes, "The war made an ardent patriot of Fields and nowhere was the mood reflected more transparently than in his growing bitterness towards his beloved England." With others, he published a number of his own poems in the <u>Atlantic</u>, but he was beginning to realize that his real skill lay in telling the story, as only he could, of his beloved authors. Annie, too, was writing. First, an Ode to help dedicate the organ for Boston's new music hall. And second, a novel which Fields chose to publish.

It was also at this time that the Fields were drawn to the North Shore of Boston and its oceanside towns for rest and relaxation and to escape the heat of the city. During the war, they spent each summer at a boarding house in Pigeon Cove, Rockport. But in 1865, they moved to Manchester, renting cottages until 1874 when they purchased land on Thunderbolt Hill and built a house of their own.

Meanwhile, in 1864, Ticknor had died on a trip south with Nathaniel Hawthorne. Both men, ironically, had taken the voyage to improve their health. But neither got farther than Philadelphia. Fields, now senior partner, moved quickly to bring the firm into a new era. First, the retail book business and property at Washington and School Streets known as the Old Corner Book Store, was sold to E.P. Dutton, another Boston book seller. And Ticknor & Fields rented more spacious quarters, for additional room was urgently needed, at 125 Tremont Street opposite the Park Street Church. It housed not only elegant new offices for Fields himself, including a special room where authors and publisher could meet in comfort, but quarters for his junior partners: Howard Ticknor, representing his father; James R. Osgood, with a personality much like Fields himself who he had hired years earlier; and John S. Clark, who ran the financial end of the business.

MAGAZINES

With the ATLANTIC a Success; Fields Reaches Out for Juveniles and Charles Dickens

Encouraged perhaps by the performance of the <u>Atlantic Monthly</u>, now a lucrative producer for the firm, Fields decided to purchase the oldest and one of the most distinguished magazines in the country, the <u>North American Review</u> which was barely holding on to its historic reputation for excellence. It was jointly edited by Charles Eliot Norton and James Russell Lowell. At this time, also, Fields began a monthly aimed at juveniles entitle <u>Our Young Folks</u>, followed by a weekly publication, <u>Every Saturday</u>, and, finally, by a yearly journal of collected writings called <u>Atlantic Almanac</u>. Ticknor & Fields was in the magazine and periodical business in a big way. The war had brought inflation and the cost of doing business as well as the cost of books had risen significantly. Fields was forced to cut corners. He chose to go in two directions, producing cheaper, less attractive volumes for a new and larger market,

and for those who could afford them, and there were many, editions still elegantly bound and printed. As the firm expanded, so did the responsibilities of the senior partner and at times Fields felt overwhelmed. He was growing older, of course, and although that was a part of it, times were changing as well and life everywhere, as competition grew, was getting more hectic. It was time for Fields at least to retire as editor of the <u>Atlantic Monthly</u>. To take his place, he chose young William D. Howells who had worked for the <u>Saturday Press</u> and the <u>Nation</u>. By necessity, as the firm expanded, James was increasingly beginning to delegate.

Charles Dickens was one of the most popular, if not the most popular, author of his day both in England and in the United States. To engage him in a lecture tour of America was a crowning achievement. But Fields also sought another goal: publishing rights in this country for all of Dickens' work. The Great Man knew there was an immense market for his books on this side of the Atlantic with accompanying profits. So the desire to work something out was mutual. After months of discussions and negotiations with the author and his agent, it was agreed. And in November, 1867, Dickens arrived in Boston aboard the Cunard Line's CUBA.

The tour, which lasted some six months, was a huge success drawing capacity audiences everywhere. Lecture receipts and paperback book sales made it also a financial bonanza for both parties. After a final dinner in New York for more than 200 at Delmonico's, Dickens sailed for England, hugging Fields tearfully as he said good-bye. For James and Annie, perhaps the best part of the trip was the personal experience, the joy, the exhilaration, and the immense satisfaction of getting to know Charles Dickens and of being able now to truly call him a friend.

As inflation and unemployment increased and the country approached what was to become the devastating Panic of 1873, Ticknor & Fields, like other businesses, found itself in heavy financial seas. It cut back on the number of works published and, once again, produced a series of less expensive volumes. The firm's magazines, with the exception of the <u>Atlantic</u>, failed to make a profit. But somehow the company weathered the storm. One of another nature, however, even more revolutionary, led to its reorganization, the purchase of Howard Ticknor's interests, and a new name, Fields, Osgood & Company. James R. Osgood, as Fields declared "is the one on whom I have always leaned most."

But despite the aggravations and uncertainties of running a larger operation in an uncertain world as Fields grew older, perhaps the most unpleasant experience he suffered in a lifetime of publishing was an intensely disagreeable and harsh conflict with one of his authors over money. The matter was long and protracted and left Fields disillusioned and depressed. Part of the cure was another trip to England. This time, he and Annie would take with them Mabel Lowell, the poet's daughter and only child. Like the others, the trip offered a whirlwind of entertainment, breakfasts, luncheons and dinners with Dickens, who moved to London to be near them, with writer George Eliot and her husband George Lewes, with Anne Thackerary and with an up-and-coming young poet named Algernon Swineburne who was to make a considerable impact upon the world of letters. A quick visit to the Continent and the couple were back in Fields' beloved England. Then, six months after their departure, they sailed for Boston.

AN ERA IS OVER

Fields Sells Firm to His Partners; Becomes a Lecturer; Then Dies Too Soon in 1881

That winter was a cold one and James' health suffered. They looked forward to the spring in Manchester but somehow life and the world around them seemed different. Times had changed. The congeniality of the old days between publisher and author, which Fields so enjoyed, was gone. Now it was money that made the relationship. The responsibilities for administration with all its headaches had taken much of the fun out of day to day activities. Fields was 54 years old and perhaps, indeed, the time had come to retire. Both James and Annie knew it and negotiations began for the other partners to purchase Fields' interests in the firm. On the first day of the year in 1871, Fields met in his office with a few dear friends including Holmes, Longfellow, Whittier and Emerson, to make it official.

With his life far from over, Fields decided to strike out in a new direction. Recalling the pleasures and successes of earlier days, he wrote and organized a series of lectures primarily about the celebrated authors he had worked with and known as friends during his professional years. Two talks, which were among his most popular, adhered more to his philosophy of life and character than to his experiences in business. They were entitled A Plea for Cheerfulness and Master of the Situation. He presented both again and again to delighted audiences.

But as W.S. Tryon writes in Parnassus Corner, "The content of the lectures scarcely seems commensurate with the heroic efforts Fields made to deliver them. He was no longer a young man but in his fifties. Success, dinner parties, rich food and wine, had made his body heavy. He dressed in expensive but weighty tweed or broadcloth. The hair on the top of his head was still luxuriant but the black was streaked with gray. Over his face, indeed nearly hiding it, was a thick beard which flowed down over his chest."

For a man in his senior years, travel at the end of the nineteenth century, was hard work. It meant waiting outside on station platforms for trains in weather that was windy and cold or dusty and unbearably hot. Staying in strange and often unattractive hotels where accommodations and food were far below the standards he was used to. But Fields kept at it, visiting cities, large and small, from up-state New York to as far west as Wisconsin. He lectured at colleges and universities and in 1874 was pleased to receive from Dartmouth another Honorary Degree, this time Doctor of Laws. His audiences loved him. For the most part, they were not intellectuals, but citizens of the nation from all walks of life. And he in turn loved them. His lectures, too, provided more than adequate remuneration

Victorian furnishings fill the long library at 148 Chestnut Street. Sitting figures are Annie Fields and author and friend Sarah Orne Jewett. After James died in 1881, Miss Jewett lived with Annie both in Boston and at Thunderbolt Hill in Manchester. (The Boston Athanaeum photo)

both in pecuniary terms and in personal satisfaction. But his age, the stress of travel and his grueling schedule were taking their toll and soon began to affect his health. As a result, in 1876, he curtailed his his lecture program and turned once again to writing.

Just after retiring, he had produced a series for the Atlantic about his relationships with the literary figures of his day and readers loved them. James R. Osgood & Company, his old firm, published the collected pieces in a book entitled Yesterday With Authors which enjoyed equal success. He kept on writing until his death. His books included a collection of his poems and a comprehensive anthology of British poetry. Watching the output of James R. Osgood & Company, he was concerned that firm's standards were slipping, a view shared by others including Bret Harte and Harriet Beacher Stowe. The company was having a hard time of it as well and, as a last straw, lost its building with hundreds of others in the great fire which swept downtown Boston in 1872.

In 1878, Osgood, according to W.D. Tryon, was merged "with Henry O. Houghton's Riverside Press and its publishing subsidiary, Hurd & Houghton. The partnership was known as Houghton, Osgood & Company. It was an uneasy relationship of only two years. Osgood retired and the successor firm was Houghton, Mifflin & Company, which took over all the stock, plates and copyrights, and so far as it was feasible, the authors of Houghton, Osgood. Even the children of William Ticknor eventually joined the partnership. Thus is was that Houghton, Mifflin & Company became the direct heir of Ticknor & Fields."

In April, 1881, the end came. Fields died suddenly and unexpectedly in his beloved Charles Street house with Annie at his side. He was buried at Mount Auburn Cemetery, Cambridge, in the Adams family lot. From friends in England and throughout America came letters of sympathy. Newspaper columns here and overseas carried the news of Fields' death and editorials praised his contributions to the publishing world. His friend, preacher and fellow Manchester resident Reverend Cyrus Bartol eulogized his passing: "having known him well for forty years and lived with him summer after summer in the same house, I must swear I have not known a better tempered man..." From Rome, his Manchester neighbor Richard H. Dana declared, "Manchester-by-the-Sea became a new place after he made it his summer home..."

Fields' will dictated that everything he owned, all his assets, both physical and financial, should go to Annie, including the house at Thunderbolt Hill in Manchester where she had and was again to pass so many happy summers.

THUNDERBOLT HILL
James and Annie Fields Fall in Love with Manchester; They Rent and Then Build

To escape the heat of the city during the summer months, and to enjoy moments of peace and quiet in their busy lives, both James and Annie Fields were attracted to the tiny rural towns outside of Boston. High on their list of favorites was Campton, New Hampshire. During the first years of the Civil War, they rented a house in Rockport, Massachusetts at Pigeon Cove.

But in 1864, perhaps at the urging of their pastor, Reverend Cyrus Augustus Bartol, they discovered Manchester. Bartol was pastor of the West Church on Cambridge Street in Boston, an easy walk from the Fields's home at 148 Charles Street. Earlier, he had built a summer house at Glass Head in West Manchester. A great booster of the town, he went on to purchase and develop Norton's Point and a major portion of land at Smith's Point.

Annie Fields, although wife of Boston's most distinguished publisher of books and periodicals, was a considerable figure in her own right. A fabled hostess, she was widely known for her wit and charm and contributed much to her husband's professional success. Annie was also bright, observant and articulate, and had unusual literary gifts herself. Well read and well educated, she was the author of several books including Under the Olive (1881); How to Help the Poor (1883); Authors and Friends (1896); and The Life and Letters of Harriet Beecher Stowe (1897) and Letters of Sarah Orne Jewett (1911). James T. Fields, Biographical Notes and Personal Sketches (1881) was a tribute to her husband. Most deliciously for many, from 1863 to 1876, she kept a personal diary of her thoughts and daily doings. It's entries provide an intimate glimpse of life in those days and an early view of the beauties of nature and the special attractions of Manchester, Massachusetts.

Until 1874, when the Fields purchased land at the top of Thunderbolt Hill for a house of their own, they stayed first at Dame Cottage, as the west end of the old Smith farmhouse on Proctor Street was known, and then with the Crowell sisters at 21 Union Street, a handsome house which still stands today between the Coffee Cup Restaurant and Sovereign Bank.

It is obvious from her diary that Annie Fields fell in love with Manchester . What seemed particularly to appeal to her was the opportunity to be close to nature. The summer of 1864 had been a dry one and on August 17, 1864 she writes: "Easterly fog and rain. Until this—except an hour's rain one evening—no rain since we came. The drought and heat have been almost unprecedented. Last night wonderful moon and walks on the beach [Singing Beach, as yet unnamed] and rows on the bay [by which she must have meant the harbor] with Mr. Bartol..."

On August 30, 1864 she notes: "Passed at Hamilton in the woods and driving [with horse and carriage] about with Mary Dodge." Daughter of a prosperous farmer, Mary Dodge was educated at Ipswich Female Seminary, taught school for a while, a later became a writer, taking the pen name of Gail Hamilton. For two years she served as co-editor of a popular juvenile magazine entitled Our Young Folks which had been established by James T. Fields.

Oil painting of the cottage at Thunderbolt Hill, Manchester, owned by Mr. and Mrs. James T. Fields. After the death of James Fields in 1881, Annie Fields spent summers in the house with author and friend Sarah Orne Jewett until her own death in 1915. (The Boston Athanaeum photo)

Travel to Manchester was made easy by the railroad which ran as many as 12 trains each day. Rail service began in 1847. It took just 40 minutes for an express to reach Boston while other trains took a more comfortable hour. The fare was 65 cents. Annie and James Fields visited Manchester often. "Passed the morning alone in Dana's woods [probably reading]," she writes on September 1, 1864 and on September 15, "Returned from Manchester, the weather blue and gold."

Both Annie and James were here also for an event in 1865 which changed the course of history. "Forever memorable." she writes on April 3. "Our armies entered Richmond...In the afternoon we went to Manchester. The bells of the little town were ringing out the joyous news and the sea and sky were in exquisite unison. Returning home..." Six days later at Appomattox Court House, Lee surrendered to Grant and the long-fought, bloody and bitter War Between the States was over.

Life in Manchester for the Fields was filled with lovely walks and wonder at the natural beauty surrounding them at every moment of the day. For Annie and a friend to walk from Dame cottage on Proctor Street to town was quite a hike. With the estuary at the head of the harbor, salt marsh stretched up past the railroad station. It was not filled and bridged to create Beach Street until 1873. Travelers thus had to follow Masconomo to Sea Street, climb the hill, cross the railroad tracks, ascend another hill, and enter town by way of Washington Street and North Street to Union Street. With dirt roads, wearing long skirts and petticoats, it took time.

One of their objectives was the west end of Gales Point where rocks drop down to the sea below. As Annie notes on July 16,

1866, "we walked to 'The Cliff' in the morning and lay for an hour on the rock under the Cedar...[that] night was starry and moonlit, too warm for the house...we sat in the little apple orchard watching the reflections of the moon on the quiet cove..."

Other adventures took them farther afield. On Thursday, July 19, 1866: "Today cloudy but later cool and magnificently beautiful. Went over to Dana Island where a superb natural aquarium has been found holding hundreds of anemones..." That Sunday, " the sunset was full of golden promise. The tips of the apple trees were touched with gold and the surface of the sea shimmered in bright glory..."

The next day, Monday, they walked once again to town. "As we approached the small post office, we heard the Postmaster who lost a leg in our war. singing so loud that the whole village might hear first the 'Marsellaise' and afterwards Italian songs of patriotism..." The Postmaster, of course, was Julius Rabardy, hero of the Civil War who lost a leg at the bloody Battle of Antietam, publisher of Manchester's first newspaper Beetle & Wedge, builder of the Rabardy block, and founder and operator of Floyd's store later taken over by his step son-in-law, Lyman W. Floyd.

The easiest way to cross the harbor from the depot to Dame cottage on Proctor Street was by boat, except, of course, in winter when it was frozen. And, indeed, good use was made of small craft both for purposes of practical transportation and for pleasure. As Annie writes on Tuesday, August 6, 1866, "Jamie stayed in Manchester and Dr. Bartol rowed us across the bay and pioneered us to woodlands more beautiful than any I have before seen hereabouts."

Thankfully, in Manchester there are still some things left unchanged by time. One of these is Floyd's Store. A century and one half ago, just as today, it was a magnet for children. On August 8, 1866, Annie walked to the post office once again. "It was odd to see the nonchalance of the man [again, Julius Rabardy] who played the part of shopkeeper, bookkeeper, errand boy and Postmaster," she notes. "I was obliged to wait...until the youthful population had satisfied itself with candy and nuts..." (In the 1940's, I used to row to town with friends where we, too, visited Floyd's to "satisfy" ourselves with Skybars, Milky Ways and the latest editions of Famous Funnies and other comic and Big Little Books.)

FEW TREES IN SIGHT
Spectacular Views of Sea and Town from Every Hilltop in the Late 19th Century

During the summer of 1867, Annie reported that they came "to Marblehead for eight weeks" but by July 31 were back "in dear old Manchester. We were wretchedly homesick in Marblehead," she added, "and are now housed in Miss Crowell's comfortable cottage in the village behind a tulip tree." Maiden ladies, the Misses Crowells operated a guest house at 21 Union Street. Their brother, Colonel Benjamin F. Crowell, went west to make his fortune, returned to Manchester and bequeathed his estate to his sisters. In 1904, Susan Crowell offered the town a gift of B.F. Crowell Memorial Chapel which was constructed at Rosedale Cemetery and is available today without cost to "all people and all creeds for mortuary services."

On Saturday, August 10, 1867, they covered a lot of ground. "In the afternoon we went to the hill-top and sat by the out-worn little powder house [built to store gun powder during the War of 1812 and still in existence] with the sea in the distance. Walked over to Mr. Dana's [off Summer Street]...Mr. Dana, Sr. [in 1845, Manchester's first summer resident] to be 80 in September, and afterwards walked up to view some land back of Eagle Head with a wondrous view for which we have made an offer. There is not much hope that we shall get this land," Annie wrote, "and if we do not I shall think all is for the best."

It must be remembered, as views around town are described in Annie's dairy, that a century and a half ago, there were far fewer trees than there are today. They had been harvested to provide fuel for household heaters. Woodlands were cleared as well to provide fields for agriculture. This meant that the ocean was clearly visible from many more places than it is today.

Diagonally across the street from the Crowell sisters was the Trask house, now headquarters of the Manchester Historical Society. And that same August 10 in 1867, Annie and one of the Misses Crowells called upon Abigail Trask to pay their respects. Mrs. Trask was the widow of Captain Richard Trask, master of the ST. PETERSBURG, 860 tons, in her day the largest merchant ship that had been built in Massachusetts. "A noble and benevolent citizen she is," Annie

observes, "and a wonderful specimen of health and strength for her years. She thinks of going to town [Boston] to hear Mr. Dickens read when he comes."

Although the Fields obviously divided their time between a busy life with authors and publishing in Boston, by 1870, Annie was writing again of the joys of Manchester. "This village in which we live is very pretty. A bell rings stoutly from the white steeple at 12 o'clock and one fire engine has lately been introduced [a horse-drawn steam pumper]; the two noisy elements of the place if we accept the railroad. Between the hours of arrival and departure of the trains, we are for the most part as quiet as if we lived in the middle of the meadow yonder near the sea. There is a tulip tree outside my window now in blossom whose rich green leaves tell of a warmer one than the one it has found..."

The idea, too, of having a home of their own seemed increasingly desirable. In July, 1870, she writes, "Jamie and I have had a thought of buying a bit of land here, hoping if everything else should go, to have a 'pied a terre' here by the shore we love so much. It is all a fancy I suppose but we had a delightful excursion with that thought in our minds towards Norman's Woe..."

The town and countryside that James and Annie Fields now surveyed from their lofty perch atop Thunderbolt Hill was filled with fascinating and worldly people. They included the celebrated actor Joseph Proctor, widely known for his roles in the romantic theater, who had purchased the house on Sea Street once owned by Sally Allen Samples, founder of the town's first retail store. There was also theater empressario Junius Brutus Booth, brother of famed Shakespearean actor Edwin Booth and of the infamous John Wilkes Booth who in 1865 shot and killed President Abraham Lincoln. Junius and his wife Agnes, a popular actor in her own right, lived on the corner of Beach and Masconomo Streets where they later had built an elegant and luxurious hotel known as the Masconomo House. Other actors were nearby. John Gibbs Gilbert, owned a summer cottage on Old Neck Road. Frederick B. Conway and his wife, actress Sarah Crocker, built a house on Ocean Hill above Sea Street. And her sister, Elizabeth, wife of the late actor David B. Bowers, lived only a few doors away from the Conways on Old Neck Road.

As was said earlier, author, physician and "Autocrat of the Breakfast Table" Oliver Wendell Holmes lived nearby in Beverly Farms. It was a rare moment when the Fields were not entertaining such literary figures as James Russell Lowell, Sarah Orne Jewett or Henry Wadsworth Longfellow whose sister-in-law married Bostonian and Manchester summer resident, former Civil War General Greely Curtis.

The Curtis mansion off Summer Street overlooking the ocean was described by travel writer of the time Bayard Taylor as "a castle by the sea built of gray stone, and of very original design."

Story also has it that Longfellow was in Manchester staying with the Fields or with his brother-in-law Greely Curtis when, inspired by a true story of the loss of a sea captain and his tiny daughter, he wrote Wreck of the Hesperus which made famous the ledge known as Norman's Woe off the Magnolia shore.

AUTHORS STILL VISIT

Sarah Orne Jewett Living with Annie at Thunderbolt Hill; Willa Cather a Guest

After the death of James Fields, Sarah Orne Jewett, a close family friend, a client of Ticknor & Fields, and Maine-born author of <u>The Country of the Pointed Firs</u> and other works, lived for many years with Annie both at Thunderbolt Hill and in Boston. The relationship was close one, according to M.A. DeWolfe Howe in his <u>Memories of a Hostess, A Chronicle of Eminent Friendships Drawn Chiefly from the Diaries of Mrs. James T. Fields</u>. (Boston, The Atlantic Monthly Press, 1922). "For a longer period than she was the wife of James T. Fields, she was...his widow. Through nearly all this period the need of her nature for an absorbing affectionate intimacy was met through her friendship with Sarah Orne Jewett...In the friendship of these two women," Howe adds, "it would have been impossible to define either one...as the giver or the receiver. They were certainly both sustained by their relation." Fields himself, according to Howe, before his death in 1881, seemed to know that Sarah Jewett was "the ideal friend to fill the impending gap in the life of his wife." Indeed, in 1939, when the Thunderbolt Hill was purchased by Mr. and Mrs. Kirk Neal, keys were found in the house with a label still marked "S.O.J.'s Room."

A paper about the house written some years ago for the Manchester Historical Society by Charlotte Frasier also states that "windows with peaked tops in Mrs. Neal's dining and living rooms are said to have come from the Congregational Church, taken out when it was being done over...the four tops of the little Gothic windows are in the dining room while the bottom sections are in the living room. In one window," Mrs. Frasier writes, "there are 64 panes of glass."

According to the paper, when the structure was first built it included McIntyre mantels [for the fireplaces] in each room, collected by the Fields who were admirers of the great Boston architect. A inscription from the past, apparently left by one of the original carpenters, was also found when work was being done later behind the bookcases in the library. It read: "Andrew Stanley, December 24, 1874."

Writer Willa Cather (1873-1947) recalls the pleasures of life at Thunderbolt Hill. Famed as author of among many others <u>My Antonia</u> (1918) and <u>O Pioneers</u>! (1913), both novels about her state of Nebraska and life on the then closing frontier, Cather visited Annie Fields in her now later years. "At Manchester," she writes in <u>Not Under Forty</u> (1936) , a collection of essays, "when there were no guests Mrs. Fields had tea on the back veranda overlooking a wild stretch of woodland. Down in this wood, directly beneath us, were a tea table and seats built under the trees, where they used to have tea when the hostess was younger...now the climb was too steep for her..." "...in Boston," Cather continues, "tea was the most happy time for ...[but] in Manchester it was at the breakfast hour that they were most likely to throng. Breakfasts were long, as

Celebrated artist John Singer Sargent (1856-1925) painted this portrait of Annie Adams Fields in 1890. Mrs. Fields was 56 years old at the time. The top of the painting is signed by the artist and inscribed "To Mrs. Fields." Born in Florence, Italy, Sargent settled in London in 1885. A frequent visitor to the United States, he was in considerable demand as a portraitist. His murals may be seen today at the Boston Public Library and at the Museum of Fine Arts. (The Boston Athanaeum photo)

country breakfasts have a right to be. We had always been out-of-doors first and we were very hungry...small dinner parties and luncheons were a part of the regular routine when [Sarah Orne Jewett] was with Mrs. Fields at Charles Street or at Manchester-by-the-Sea..."

At Annie's death in 1915, her nephew, Zabdiel Boylston Adams, inherited the house at Thunderbolt Hill. He lived there with his family or rented it until 1939 when it was purchased by Mr. and Mrs. Neal.

LUNCH AT MRS. FIELDS'

Two Young Ladies Are Invited to Meet Charles Dickens' Granddaughters

I cannot refrain from reporting that as a girl, my own grandmother, Esther Lowell Cunningham born Esther Lowell Burnett, aunt to Miss Francis Lowell Burnett known affectionately to many in Manchester as "Quetsie," was invited to lunch with Mrs. Annie Fields at Thunderbolt Hill probably around 1910. My grandmother's mother was the daughter of poet James Russell Lowell, a great friend and intimate of James T. Fields who had published much of Lowell's work. JRL had also been editor of Atlantic Monthly magazine which was a property of the publishing house of Ticknor & Fields.

The invitation came to my grandmother's cousins George and Hattie Rantoul who had rented a house for the summer overlooking the harbor in Manchester. "The girls" (my grandmother and her sister) were living with their grandfather in Cambridge and, according to the story which appeared in the book Three Houses, A Narrative, written by my grandmother in the 1950's, took "The Fisherman" a fancy train which included a parlor car, to Manchester the next day. But let my grandmother tell the story. If she will forgive me, I have shortened it a bit to make it fit this issue of REFLECTIONS.

"Here's a letter for you girls," said Cousin Hattie. I opened it and said, "It's from Mrs. Fields. She wants us to come to lunch tomorrow to meet Mr. Henry Dickens (the author's son) and his daughter and niece, the granddaughters of Charles Dickens. They are visiting at Thunderbolt Hill." "Of course you'll go," said my Cousin Hattie. "But perhaps you'd better let Mr. Boyle take you there...Mr. Boyle and Mr. Swett ran the only livery stable in town...

"Mrs. Field's house was shingled with a broad covered piazza almost surrounding it. The roof of the piazza was supported with by cedar posts with the branches lopped off about a foot from the trunk...The posts served as a trellis for the profusion of climbing nasturtiums which almost completely covered them, and whose perfume, mixed with the smell of the sea, provided a pleasant welcome for visitors.

"I remember Mrs. Fields sitting in the back of this piazza where she was protected from the east wind. She was dressed in a timeless but lovely fashion of her own. Her dress with a long flowing skirt was of soft gray or white woolen material, made sometimes of the Chuddah shawls brought from India. The sleeves were wide and at her neck was a silk or muslin scarf. She always wore a piece of fine lace draped over her gray hair, which was worn parted in the middle and covered her ears in Victorian style.

"Of course, I knew her when she was an old lady, but I don't think that even in her younger days she would have been considered a beauty, as she had rather a large nose and a wide smiling mouth, but her lovely eyes and serene brow gave her face a look of charm and individuality...[but] it was Mrs. Field's gift as a hostess that always [enabled her guests] to "put their best foot foremost."

"Well, my sister and I endeavored to 'put our best foot foremost' when we alighted from Mr. Boyle's carriage. The front door was immediately opened by a smiling Irish maid who had evidently heard the sounds of the wheels as we came up the hill. She ushered us into the front room where Mrs. Fields was awaiting our arrival. The two young ladies were still upstairs, but Mr. Dickens, a rather stodgy Englishman, rose as we entered...'These are the granddaughters of Mr. Lowell,' said Mrs. Fields. 'Mr. Lowell was a friend of your father.'

"We shook hands and I couldn't help remembering that my mother had once told me that Grandpapa thought Charles Dickens a first-rate Charlatan and could not abide him; but I trust when I [met] Mr. Henry Dickens. that my face gave no indication of what I was thinking at the moment...we were about to sit down when there was a loud clatter on the stairway and into the room bounced two English girls about 17 or 18 years old. Mrs. Fields rose from her chair and introduced us to the young ladies, Miss Enid and Miss Monica Dickens. As she led the way into the dining room, she apologized to Mr. Dickens saying: 'I am sorry that I wasn't able to get another gentleman to keep you company with all these females.' 'Please don't mind that,' Mrs. Fields, said he, 'I really am quite used to having the ladies all to myself and I like it!'

"As we entered the dining room I was again conscious, as I always had been, of the artistic arrangement of everything that belonged to Mrs. Fields. The walls of the room were covered with gold paper, taken from the wrappings of the large sea chests which in those days were brought from China to Boston. The golden walls gave a glowing background to the mahogany table, whose shiny surface, instead of being covered with the usual damask tablecloth, was decorated with a strip of Persian embroidery, in silks of crimson and yellow, bringing out the colors of the centerpiece, a large bowl of nasturtiums.

"We seated ourselves and as I lifted my napkin I noticed the Italian pottery plate in front of me set on a mat made of brown leather cut and embossed to represent a large leaf. The mats may have come from Japan, as Mrs. Fields and Miss Jewett (author Sarah Orne Jewett who lived with Mrs. Fields) had traveled extensively in the East.

"Mrs. Fields's cook had been trained in the making of foreign dishes, the recipes of which had been gathered by Mrs. Fields when she was abroad, and on this day we sat down to a delicious repast. The two Misses Dickens—they were cousins—kept up a steady flow of conversation, telling us all about their travels.

" 'Of course,' said Enid 'we tried not to be burdened with too much luggage, and before we left home we thought it all out very carefully!'

" ' Yes,' said her cousin, 'when we were having some dresses made for the trip, the dressmaker had a marvelous idea. Two bodies for each skirt. She made a low body for evening and a high body for the daytime.' 'You see, one skirt would do,' Enid piped up. 'You know skirts take up so much room in packing.'

"And I agreed with her, for I wore to this luncheon party a costume composed of a voluminous white pique skirt, with a white shirt waist. 'Body' was the [English] name and 'shirt waist' the American for what we a call the blouse...and I might add, blessed is the female traveler today, for in those days with our ruffled petticoats —in fact, all our underwear was ruffled—we had to travel with large trunks to carry our wardrobe.

295

James T. Fields house at Thunderbolt Hill, built in 1874, is on the far ridge at center right in this photo taken from the steeple of the Congregational church about 1876. Large house on the left is owned by actor Frederick B. Conway. On the right is the cottage of Junius and Agnes Booth, prior to construction of the Masconomo House which opened in 1878. To reach Smith's Point from town, residents walked down Beach Street in center of photo, turned left on Tappan Street at the foot of the hill in the distance, and right on Sea Street, which you can just see, and followed Masconomo Street to Proctor Street. Note the tidal salt marsh beyond Summer Street which turns immediately left from Beach Street. This was later filled and bridged to form that portion of Beach Street which we know today which runs past the head of the harbor and Masconomo Park to Singing Beach. The railroad runs along a portion of Summer Street. A flat car and a box car are visible on a siding in the center of the photo, on Beach Street. The depot, which was built in 1852, is out of the photo to the right. (Manchester Historical Society collection; photo originally a glass negative by Proctor Brothers, Gloucester)

"The conversation of our [English] visitors describing their travels went on in a steady stream. 'Our steamer docked at Montreal. We stayed a while in Canada. On our way to the States we stopped to see the Falls at Niagara. What a magnificent sight,' gushed Miss Enid. 'All that water pouring over the edge!'

"A pause, and then one of the young travellers turning to my sister remarked, 'Have you ever visited Niagara Falls? No, I'm sorry I haven't.' replied my sister. 'But I might plan to go on my honeymoon. Oh,' said Miss Enid with typical British candor, 'if I were you I shouldn't wait as long as that!'"

My grandmother, Mrs. Stanley Cunningham, my mother's mother, for decades a resident of Milton, lived in Salem for a number of years at the end of her life where she could be close to two daughters, one in Manchester, one in Marblehead. It was there that she wrote <u>Three Houses</u>, her memories of Deerfoot Farms, Southboro, where she grew up; Elmwood, her Grampapa Lowell's house in Cambridge (for many years now the residence of the President of Harvard University); and Quinta Esperanca, a house in Funchal, Madeira, which the family rented for a year on doctor's orders to improve her Mother's health. My grandmother died in 1966 at age 87. (Gordon Abbott, Jr.)

Stone monuments mark the graves of Annie and James Fields at Mount Auburn Cemetery, Cambridge, MA. Inscriptions read: "In loving memory of Annie Fields, wife of James T. Fields, born 6th June 1834, died 5th January 1915, The charities that soothe and heal and bless are scattered at the feet of man like flowers; Here lies the body of James T. Fields, April – 1881. Rejoice evermore."
(A. Haskell photo)

MANCHESTER SHIPWRECKS
Without Electronic Aids, Navigation Many Years Ago, Relied on Different Skills

Electronic navigation today makes it possible for a ship to fix her position within feet of her actual location in any weather, foul or fair. Sixty years or more ago, however, it was a different story. Then, without radar, GPS, Loran, and recording fathometers, the only instruments available, other than the magnetic compass, were the sextant, a rotating log of some sort, a leadline or weighted sounding machine, and the stadimeter, which, when there was visibility, could tell you how far you were from an object of known height such as a lighthouse.

The primary methods of navigation were celestial or dead reckoning. Celestial, of course, worked only when the sun or stars could be observed. Dead reckoning could plot quite accurately how a ship traveled through the water, but often made a less than precise determination of how she had moved over the bottom. Ocean winds and currents could push a ship sideways so that in the fog or in winter snow storms accidents happened and vessels of every size and description ran ashore.

During the days of sail, another danger every skipper faced was finding himself and his ship on a lee shore. Early sailing vessels, especially those with square rigs, were not as able to move towards or up the wind as well as those with improved rigs which came later.

Thus they could be blown helplessly to leeward where too often they were swept onto rocks, sands or shoals.

The stories that follow tell of some notable shipwrecks which occurred in Manchester waters. Much of the local information comes from <u>The Cricket</u>.

A BITTER NIGHT AT SEA
Four-masted Schooner, Lost in a Snow Storm, Strikes Egg Rock; All Aboard Escape

Although square rigs had all but disappeared by the 1930's (an occasional barque arrived in Gloucester with a cargo of salt), a few "fore and afters"—three, four and five masted schooners—were still carrying freight in New England waters up to the 1940's and the start of World War II. Primarily engaged in coastal trade, these wonderful vessels delivered ice, lumber and coal, granite blocks and paving stones, fertilizer and salt fish to ports in Canada, the eastern U.S. and the Caribbean.

Typically, some 200 feet overall, displacing from 800 to 1,000 tons, they were heavy and slow, but threading their way through the islands and spar buoys of the coast of Maine or in open water under full sail with topsails set, they were a sight to stir the soul of seafarers everywhere.

The joy of a coasting schooner was that she could be operated with far fewer men than ships with square sails. Indeed, in later years many schooners put to sea with as few as three or four men, for knowledgeable hands were scarce as sail wound down and steam took its place.

In Portland, Maine on Wednesday, January 6, 1923, the schooner ALICE M. COLBURN, a four master, prepared to make sail. She undid her stops, hoisted her main, mizzen, spanker and foresail, and with a tug gently nudging her toward mid-stream, she slowly gathered way and moved down channel past Spring Point towards the bay. She was riding high—"in ballast"—without specific cargo aboard, and she was bound for Hampton Roads, Virginia between Portsmouth and Newport News at the mouth of the James River.

The day was a gray one. It looked like snow. The wind,

Four-masted schooners like the LADLOW, shown here in light air with her topsails set, carried lumber, ice, coal, granite, dry cargo or liquid in barrels to ports up and down the east coast of the US and Canada right up to the beginnings of World War II. At times, they would reach as far south as the Caribbean. Inexpensive to operate, they could be handled by a captain, mate, cook and four to six men. Many were built with huge centerboards, offset from the keel, which made them sail better to weather. Steam engines on deck handled cargo and helped raise sails and anchors. Some were equipped with auxiliary power, but usually a tug was on hand to meet them when they entered port. Measuring from 180 to 250 feet overall, "four posters," with their clipper bows and long bowsprits, were a striking sight underway. Masts, including topmasts, could reach as high as 149 feet. Shipyards in Nova Scotia, New Brunswick, Maine, New Hampshire, Massachusetts (including especially nearby Essex) and in Virginia, turned out hundreds of these handsome vessels in a century and a half. Sadly, scores also were wrecked on the rocks of New England and on the sands of North and South Carolina. (Peabody-Essex Museum photo)

from the northeast, was fair and while it held it promised a quick trip. Visibility was good, but off Boone Island, the weather began to change. The wind increased and seas began to build. Snow started to fall, first in large, fleecy flakes which turned to rain. Then, with temperatures falling, snow began again, this time as powder which filled the air like fog. A lookout was stationed at the bow, but he could see only a few yards. It was clear at this point that a blizzard was in the offing. Typical of the season, it was a January northeaster,

The wind was now gale force and reaching before it, even with shortened sail, the schooner could have been moving at 12 to 15 knots. Instead of staying off shore where she would have been in open water, the ALICE COLBURN must have lost her way. For in the darkness, shortly after passing Cape Ann, she ran up on Egg Rock, less than a mile off Manchester's Dana's Beach. There she stuck, hard and fast.

About nine pm, it was reported that "a large vessel" was ashore and from Dolliver's Neck, a US Coast Guard surf boat was launched and got underway to initiate a search. In the blinding blizzard, she got as far west as Misery Island, returning at 12:15 am without seeing a thing.

During the night the seas moderated. Crew members were able to launch a pulling boat and the skipper and 10 men made their way to the lights on Coolidge Point where they "were taken in and kindly cared for" by Mrs. T. Jefferson Coolidge's caretaker, N. G. Ericson who discovered the group as they sought refuge from the storm.

Between the crew of the Coast Guard surf boat and the keeper of Baker's Island light, there was no shortage of heroism that night. The lighthouse keeper reported that he had heard a prolonged "steamer's whistle" off Whaleback Ledge. Whereupon he called the Coast Guard in Gloucester and put off in a dory to see if he could help what he presumed to be a ship in distress. It later turned out that the "steamer's whistle" had come from a Boston & Maine railroad train whose warning signal had stuck open as it was leaving the station at Beverly Farms. Thankfully, the brave keeper made it safely back to Baker's.

In the morning, after the weather had cleared and the storm had blown through, the schooner was clearly visible. She was upright, her masts were all standing and following inspection of her hull, her captain felt she could be salvaged. But first, he telegraphed her owners in Providence for funds to enable his crew to take a train back home.

That afternoon, Thursday, a US Revenue Cutter from Boston appeared on the scene. She made several attempts to pull the schooner off the ledge, but the ALICE COLBURN wouldn't budge. The cutter stood by to wait until the next high tide. Once again, she was unsuccessful. The wind, meanwhile, had risen and salvage teams were afraid the schooner would break up in the surf.

A few days later, in a last ditch effort, a tug, also from Boston, tried once more to pull her off the ledge. But this attempt, too, ended in failure. There the schooner sat until another winter storm drove her further inshore west of Eagle Head. Now sunk, she was abandoned as a total loss. Few of these vessels, of course, were equipped with radio communications which would have enabled them to at least call for help.

The storm, according to The Cricket, "was one of the worst Manchester had experienced for some years." It took the town three days to dig out and a Ford tractor, borrowed from the Manchester Motor Company, was needed to clear side streets. Manchester Motor Company, located at the old Baker Farm where School Street now crosses Route 128, was owned by Cyrus Bagley, a resident of Forest Street.

Within a few years, steam had replaced sail for carrying cargo along the East coast. According to The Last Sail Downeast by Giles M.S. Todd (Barre Publishers, 1965), schooners which had once earned on one voyage more money than it took to build them, were lucky to receive $1 a ton for taking coal from Norfolk to to Boston. When the Florida land rush began in the mid-1920's, the fleet rallied to deliver lumber to Miami. But a few years after the building boom had ended, many of the shipping firms declared bankruptcy.

Steamers could go up the wind in almost any weather. They were faster and they could charge less. And, finally, there was the matter of finding qualified crew. Fewer and fewer younger men were turning to sail. The wages were too low and working conditions too demanding.

BOO-HOO LEDGE VICTIM

US Revenue Cutter Runs Aground; Blizzard Reduces Visibility to Zero: Crew Is Safe

On November 20, 1874, the US Revenue Cutter ALBERT GALLATIN was assigned for duty at Boston. An all but new vessel (she was built in 1871 at a yard owned by David Bell at Buffalo, New York), GALLATIN measured 137 feet overall. Her beam was 23 feet, six inches. She drew eight feet of water and displaced 250 tons. A sister ship cost $65,000.

Steam driven with a riveted iron hull, she was equipped with a Fowler patent steering propeller, "a six bladed screw with a separate engine for steering and reversing." It proved "uneconomical" and, according US Coast Guard records, both machinery and propeller were replaced in 1874.

Named for the Secretary of the Treasury who served both President's Thomas Jefferson and James Madison, GALLATIN was a handsome vessel with a clipper bow and bowsprit to match. Like many steamships of her day, she could carry sail as well. These included three squaresails on the foremast as well as a gaff-rigged foresail; and on the main, a staysail which was set forward of the mainmast and a gaff- rigged mainsail. Both fore and aft sails were also equipped with topsails. Indeed, her rig was classed as a "topsail schooner" for she operated with power and sail. Between the two masts were the bridge and deck house and a tall funnel. Her complement was seven officers and 33 enlisted men. She carried one deck gun and several boats in davits.

An official US Coast Guard photo, shows that underway she flew the vertical stripes which are now characteristic of the familiar Coast Guard ensign. The Revenue Cutter Service (it was originally called US Revenue Marine) was proposed by Secretary of the Treasury Alexander Hamilton and established by Congress in 1790. It's job was to apprehend smugglers trying to evade paying Federal taxes, receipt of which was vital to the financial well-being of the new Republic. It was not until January 28, 1915, that Congress adopted legislation which combined the US Revenue Service and the US Lifesaving Service to create the US Coast Guard.

At Boston, GALLATIN had replaced the cutter WOODBURY. Her duties consisted of patrolling waters from

At anchor, US Revenue Cutter ALBERT GALLATIN with her running boat alongside is a handsome vessel. Location of photo is unknown, but note the masts and yards of other ships on either side of the harbor or river. Built in 1871 in Buffalo, New York, the GALLATIN was 137 feet overall with a beam of 23.6 feet and a draft of eight feet. Steam driven, she was originally equipped with a 34-inch diameter Fowler patented six-blade steering propeller which required a separate engine each for steering and reversing. It shortly proved uneconomical, however, and was replaced with compound cylinders. Her hull was iron and she carried an auxiliary rig as a topsail schooner. Sails are bent and furled on all spars. Her complement was seven officers and 33 enlisted men. Her sister ship, the HAMILTON, cost $65,000 to construct. The GALLATIN was assigned to Boston and patrolled waters from Portsmouth, New Hampshire to Holmes Hole, Massachusetts. She was lost off Manchester on 6 January 1892. (US Coast Guard photo)

Portsmouth, New Hampshire to Holmes Hole, Massachusetts. In the spring of 1887, GALLATIN was ordered to New York to receive a new boiler. Work was completed that summer and in October she returned to Boston. The next year, her area of responsibility was extended from Portsmouth to Rockland, Maine.

Four years later, on Wednesday, January 6, 1892, she met her end on an underwater ledge just south of Manchester's Singing Beach. Most hands aboard made it to shore safely and, according to The Manchester Cricket, "found shelter and refreshment at the Manchester House." There, Captain Eric Gabrielson told The Cricket what had happened to his ship. A dramatic story, it appears in remarkable detail which brings to life, as if they had occurred yesterday, the tragic events of that moment more than a century ago.

"We left Kittery this morning," Captain Gabrielson said, "and [were] bound across the bay towards Provincetown. At 8:50 o'clock, we passed the Dry Salvages off Cape Ann and laid our course South. I went into the cabin to mark off our course on the chart. At 9:55, Lieutenant Dimock came below and called me on deck. The weather was thick and it had begun to snow. I made up my mind to run for Eastern Point and find shelter in Gloucester Harbor. [We] took in part of sail and stationed an extra lookout, stowed the engine and commenced soundings.

"At about 11 o'clock we made land, a rocky island ahead. We sounded and were in 12 fathoms [72 feet] of water, enough to float anything. Stopped and back, I went into the pilot house and asked the Pilot what he made out the island to be. He replied that it was Kettle Island. It was then hard-a-port. 'Are you sure?' I asked. 'Yes, I am,' he replied. All right then, start ahead and ring her up. I relied upon the Pilot supposing that he knew where he was, as I had been on this shore but a few times and he had been in here hundreds of times. I knew that if it was Kettle Island, an easterly course would fetch us to Eastern Point and we started on that course.

"At about 11:15 o'clock, after running at a fair rate of speed, she [hit] heavily on a sunken ledge. We stopped and backed but found the vessel fast and she was pounding heavily. I went to the cabin to get some more clothing, but the water was over the cabin table and I could not get down [below]. I called the crew to man all the boats. She was rolling heavily and filling rapidly. Blew off steam. She was rolling from side to side badly. The seas breaking over her carried away [her] skylights. The after part filled rapidly. The smoke pipe went by the board to starboard, striking, as it fell, J. Jacobson, the carpenter, who was in the bow of the cutter (pulling boat) at the davits. It struck him on the head and his body was carried overboard and lost.

"After taking to the boats, we sighted land on the port hand and pulled in affecting [a] landing on Eagle Head in a rocky cave. [The site is still recognizable today on the east side of the headland.] Three of the boats landed on the rocks and were destroyed before we could save them. The other was beached to the west on the sand and was saved. We found shelter at the house on the bluff, Mrs. J.F. Babcock kindly caring for us. Mr. Babcock being sick, [however], afterwards all hands came to the Manchester hotel, Mr. Benjamin Marble bringing us up with his horse and wagon. Mr. Knight of the Board of Selectmen has been very kind, dinner being given to us by the Selectmen of the town. The crew [was] sent to Boston by the Boston & Maine Railroad free of charge."

That afternoon as darkness arrived, Captain Gabrielson visited Singing Beach to look once more at his stricken ship. "At 4:30 pm, he reported, "the vessel was broken in two. The foremast and the main fore topmast remaining standing. The officers and the crew lost everything," he added, "including all personal effects, nothing being saved except what we stood in. She filled so rapidly it was impossible to remove anything from below."

The rock which GALLATIN struck is appropriately named Boo-Hoo Ledge, for it has caused tears to rise in many a mariner's eye. Modern charts show it just submerged and thus invisible at calm low water. Although the wind was blowing hard from the northeast, Captain Garbrielson stated that "there were no breakers" in sight, perhaps because the tide was flooding at the time. He also said the ledge "was not down on the ship's chart." As the story of the wreck was pieced together, it appeared that what the pilot had identified as Kettle Island was actually Salt Rock located some 1,000 yards south of Eagle Head. The 137-foot Revenue Cutter had lost her way, passed Gloucester Harbor and most likely had been set by the current in towards Singing Beach.

Crew members of GALLATIN identified by The Cricket included Captain Gabrielson, F.H. Dimock, Acting First Lieutenant and Executive Officer; A.R. Hanson, Third Lieutenant; A.L. Churchill, Chief Engineer; F.E. Owen, First Assistant Engineer; H.W. Speare, Second Assistant Engineer; H.E. Wooster, Pilot; J. Jacobson, Carpenter; Thomas Larson, Boatswain; and Anthony Sears, Master at Arms. Also aboard were two quartermasters, two coxswains, 10 seaman, and six coal passers and firemen. Jacobson, the Carpenter who was lost while attempting to abandon ship with the others, was, The Cricket, reported, "a Russian Finn about 38 years old." Unmarried, he had served aboard GALLATIN for four months.

Throughout the seacoast community of Manchester, Captain Gabrielson was much praised for "acting coolly, standing at his post, calmly giving orders while his ship was going down." In the best traditions of the sea, he was the last to leave her decks. He had been in command of GALLATIN for 15 months prior to her loss and earlier had been her Captain for some three years.

Boo-Hoo Ledge, The Cricket continued, takes its name from the peculiar sound it makes at times as a heavy sea "works over it." Unbuoyed, it was at the time considered a hazard to navigation. About 50 feet in length, the rock is two feet underwater at mean low tide. Some 18 years earlier, a yacht owned by summer resident Greeley Curtis had also struck the ledge. Shortly afterwards it was marked with a spindle but this disappeared some three years later in a winter storm. Early reports of the grounding of the GALLATIN reached Manchester about 9:45 am. By noon, the ship's officers and men, with one sad exception, were safely ashore.

The traditions of the US Revenue Service reach far back into the history of the region. One of the first 10 cutters authorized in 1790 was christened MASSACHUSETTS. She was built at Newburyport by William Searle. Some 40 feet in length, these smart little ships were schooner-rigged, fast and lightly armed, manned by a captain, lieutenant and six seamen.

Seven years later, another class of cutters was built. Again, they were rigged as schooners, but this time they measured some 58 feet overall. By 1807, the Service had its first GALLATIN, a schooner purchased in Norfolk for the Charleston, South Carolina Station. By the time of the Civil War, steam was beginning to replace sail in the Revenue Marine, but sailing cutters still existed until the 1870's.

Another activity, now also a mission of the US Coast Guard, involved saving lives of those who were shipwrecked along the nation's coasts. The first lifesaving station in America was established across Massachusetts Bay in Cohasset in 1807. One of the most decorated members of the US Life Saving Service was Joshua James, keeper of the station at Point Allerton in Hingham who died at age 75 as he stepped ashore after a rescue. Perhaps James' most celebrated life saving event took place off Hull in 1888 when he and his crew got 29 persons from five different vessels safely ashore during a bitter November gale.

The US Revenue Service and US Life Saving Service, both organizations with a rich history, became a part of the US Coast Guard in 1915. Since then the responsibilities of the Coast Guard have broadened dramatically. Today they include missions which vary from the enforcement of motor boat regulations to the International Ice Patrol and from drug interdiction to the protection of the fisheries and the marine environment.

GALLANT OLD LADY ABLAZE

Fire Strikes a Former U.S. Ship-of-the-Line Under Tow; She Drifts Ashore in 1923

Bathers at Singing Beach on that hot Wednesday afternoon in late July, 1922, watched with a gathering crowd as smoke and flames destroyed what appeared to be a sizable ship under tow, headed east, some three miles south of Kettle Island.

First to notify authorities, according to The Manchester Cricket, was caretaker W.W. Soulis who spotted the ship at 9 a.m. She was trailing what was then a thin wisp of smoke which grew rapidly into a sizable blaze. Soulis called the US Coast Guard Station at D'Olliver's Neck, Gloucester, which reported that a boat was already underway to the scene.

All that afternoon and throughout most of the night she burned, while scores of Manchester residents watched, the southeasterly wind pushing her towards Graves Island off Dana's Beach. There she finally grounded and sank, a total loss.

Earlier, she had been identified as the former USS NEW HAMPSHIRE, originally designed as a full-rigged, 74-gun ship-of-the-line, 196 feet, three inches overall with a draft of just over 17 feet. Built in 1817 at the Navy Yard at Portsmouth, New Hampshire, and now old and decrepit, she had been sold to salvors and was on her way to Eastport, Maine to be broken up for scrap.

According to the Naval Historical Center, the ship was authorized by Act of Congress on April 29, 1816 and her keel laid in June, 1819. She was to be christened ALABAMA (the state also first entered the Union in 1819), but for lack of finances she was never completed. Amazingly, she lay in the stocks unfinished and covered over for nearly half a century until 1863. With the Civil War then raging, she was obviously obsolete as a sailing warship of the early nineteenth century.

With the arrival of steam, those days were gone forever. But the Union Navy ordered her completed as a store and supply ship carrying 10 guns, four 100-pound Parrott rifles and six, nine-inch Dahlgren smooth bores. According to Official Naval Records of the time, her speed was listed at 10 knots. She displaced 2,633 tons and her complement included 820 officers and men.

She was re-named USS NEW HAMPSHIRE and placed in commission at the Portsmouth Navy Yard on May 11, 1864. With Commodore Henry K. Thatcher, USN in temporary command, she carried men and stores to Port Royal, South Carolina and joined the South Atlantic Squadron (relieving USS VERMONT) which was then blockading Confederate ports under command of Rear Admiral John A. Dahlgren. (Dahlgren was considered the father of modern Naval gunnery. It was weapons of his design that were used aboard the MONITOR in her epic battle with the iron-clad MERRIMACK.)

Foremost among blockade runners were the English who, desperate to keep their own mills in operation, traded guns and ammunition to the Confederates for cotton which was worth three times as much to them back home. The British government did little to discourage the trade and Rebel armies benefitted hugely, according to Admiral David Dixon Porter's The Naval History of the Civil War, as much as what was shipped included European field guns and small arms with rifled barrels, better than most of the smooth-bore equipment made in northern US factories which were sent to Union forces.

As Porter explains, however, "Blockade runners were captured in large numbers, and the vessels and cargoes condemned by our Admiralty Courts without protest from the British government." Indeed, many were taken intact, renamed, armed and commissioned as US naval warships.

After the Civil War, NEW HAMPSHIRE served briefly as flagship for Commodore Inman. She then returned to the Navy Yard at Norfolk, Virginia, where she was converted into a Receiving Ship, never again going to sea under a full commission. From 1876 to 1881, she served as a store ship at Port Royal, SC. Later, she was stationed at Norfolk and then ordered to Newport, RI, where she became flagship for Commodore Stephen B. Luce and his newly-formed and much-needed Apprentice Training Program for the professional Navy. For 10 years, she served as a Receiving Ship for Boys (trainees) both at Newport and at New London, CT.

On June 5, 1892, 73 years after her keel had been laid in Portsmouth, the gallant old lady was decommissioned as a ship of the US Navy and transferred on loan to the New York State Naval Militia. As the only institutions offering courses in basic training, Militias were vitally important in times of crisis. New York alone furnished nearly 1,000 officers and men for the Navy during the Spanish-American War.

Militia-trained volunteers were essential to the war effort as Secretary of the Navy John D. Long declared. "They rapidly acquired on shipboard the knowledge necessary for their efficiency. Considering their lack of experience, the services rendered by them were so valuable that the country has been amply repaid for the money expended in their instruction and training."

Nineteen years to the month after Naval volunteers had been called to serve in the war with Spain, the US was at war with Germany. Again, State Naval Militia provided the only men trained and equipped for immediate Naval service. During World War I, more than 14,000 officers and men were called to active duty as National Naval Volunteers.

Then Secretary of the Navy Josephuis Daniels was as effusive in his praise as was his predecessor. "When war was declared," Daniels said, "this body of men who had enjoyed practical training were at once available for duty. They were given important assignments ashore and afloat, in the fighting zones in ships of all types. In administrative positions, and as leaders and instructors of newly enlisted reserves, they rendered timely and useful service." Later, in his book <u>Our Navy at War</u>, Daniels expanded his remarks. "Never again," he wrote, "will men dare to ridicule the volunteer, the reservist, the man who in national crisis lays aside civilian duty to become a soldier or sailor…They fought well. They died well. They have left in deeds and words a record that will be an inspiration to unborn generations." The same could be said for volunteer members of the US Naval Reserve in World War II. So despite her age and the anachronistic qualities of her design, as a school ship for training volunteer sailors, NEW HAMPSHIRE rendered the nation invaluable service.

On November 30, 1904, her name was changed to GRANITE STATE so that a new ship might be christened

USS NEW HAMPSHIRE. Built by New York Shipbuilding Company at Camden, NJ, the new NEW HAMPSHIRE was a CONNECTICUT class battleship, BB-25, which was commissioned on March 19, 1908. She was as different from her earlier name-sake as could be imagined. Four hundred and fifty feet in length, her gigantic steel hull displaced 16,000 tons. Her armament included four, 12 inch and eight, eight-inch breech loading rifles. And her twin-screw, vertical triple-expansion engines drove her at a top speed of 18.7 knots.

Although commissioned too late to join the epic voyage of The Great White fleet which, with orders from President Theodore Roosevelt (and CONNECTICUT as flagship), sailed around the world starting in 1907, USS NEW HAMPSHIRE was afloat at Hampton Roads, VA to welcome the fleet home in a full-dress review as it returned to the US in 1909. She continued to serve her country until she was stricken from the records and sold in November, 1923.

Alas, the first of two tragedies overtook the old GRANITE STATE on May 23, 1921. While lying at New York as a training ship for the State Naval Militia, she caught fire at her pier and was burned all but to the water line. Sunk, she was sold where she lay for salvage to Mulholland Machinery Corporation on August 19, 1921. Finally floated, she was being towed to Eastport, Maine, for scrapping when she again caught fire

In happier days, USS NEW HAMPSHIRE lies at anchor off Newport, Rhode Island. There in the late 19th century and early 20th, she served as flagship for Commodore Stephen B. Luce and his new Apprentice Training Program for the professional Navy, the equivalent of today's "boot camp." Before that new recruits were simply sent aboard ships in the operating fleet and received their training there in the school of hard knocks. NEW HAMPSHIRE continued as a receiving ship for "boys," as apprentices were called, for 10 years both a Newport and at New London, Connecticut. (US Naval Historical Foundation photo)

off Manchester on or about July 27, 1923. Despite every effort, she had to be abandoned, finally drifting ashore where she grounded and sank on the south side of Grave's Island off Dana's Beach. The cause of either fire could not be determined.

Since 1958, the former USS NEW HAMPSHIRE has been a mecca for skindivers who anchor off Grave's Island to explore her remains. As one SCUBA club writes in a release, "clear water and a sand and rock bottom reveal the timbers and sections of the deck of the old frigate, now broken up and strewn about the ocean floor. Here and there a few ribs stab towards the surface. A few of the [copper] spikes, stamped "US" to indicate they had been approved for building purposes by the Navy, along with square bronze nails and other artifacts." Today, however, the wreck has been all but picked clean and fewer dive boats are seen anchored nearby.

Some decades ago, divers led a successful campaign to have the wreck listed on the National Register of Historic Places. It has also been said that NEW HAMPSHIRE's copper fastenings and sheathing were manufactured by Boston metalsmith Paul Revere.

ANCHORS DRAG
Lumber Schooner Fetches Up On Chubb Island Bar; Little Damage, Crew Safe

A three-day northeaster brought more than a foot of snow to Manchester in early February, 1899. Temperatures dropped below zero. Schools were closed. And with weeks of cold weather earlier, the harbor was frozen from Town Wharf to House Island. Ice fields even extended "in irregular lines," according to The Manchester Cricket, to Misery Island.

The only casualty of the storm, however, was the schooner AVALON, whose pride, thankfully, was damaged more than the rest of her. A two-master of 116 tons, hailing from St. John's New Brunswick, AVALON, had left Portland, Maine, on Tuesday morning bound for New York City with 175,000 board feet of lumber.

That night at about 10:30, it began to blow hard and the snow grew thicker. The schooner safely passed Thatcher Island and Eastern Point, but with only a few yards visibility, she saw neither the land or the lights. Soon, with the vessel laboring in the seas, she identified Baker Island and the skipper decided to seek shelter at Salem.

As The Cricket reported: "The lead was kept going, and as the water shoaled rapidly and [surf] could be heard, AVALON anchored," first with her port and then with her

Now a sad hulk, the former USS NEW HAMPSHIRE and GRANITE STATE, badly burned topside, is under tow through the ice. Fire struck the vessel in 1921 as she was lying at New York as a training ship for the State Naval Militia. She was then sold for salvage. In 1923, she was being towed to Eastport, Maine for scrapping when mysteriously she again caught fire as she and her tug were passing Manchester on their way east. Abandoned, she drifted ashore to ground and sink on the south side of Graves Island off Dana's Beach. The cause of neither fire has been determined. (US Naval Historical Foundation photo)

starboard bower. For a while, they held, but then, with winds now reaching storm force and seas breaking in the shallow water, she began to drag. Soon, she was "brought up on the bar between Chubb Island and the Manchester shore, about 100 feet from Boardman Point."

Her crew of six escaped safely in a dory. But, as The Cricket continued, "that the vessel escaped destruction before reaching this point seems miraculous as it is thought she must have passed through the narrow channel between big Ram and House Island, which is obstructed by a large ledge in the center and would be exceeding [difficult] to navigate under the most favorable conditions [because] of several additional ledges beyond."

Overnight, the storm blew itself out but temperatures stayed at zero or below. On Thursday morning at high water, a tug appeared and soon AVALON was afloat again, little damaged from her experience. Later that day in Salem, her crew joined her and she was underway again for New York.

TWO MEN LOST
Schooner Ashore at House Island in Wild Storm; Police Chief Is a Hero of Rescue

The year 1889 is best known for the famous gale of November 26 and 27 when the Steamer PORTLAND was lost off Cape Cod with all 140 persons aboard. But Manchester had it own tragedy that year as the two-mastered schooner BESSIE H. GROSS went ashore at House Island.

Once again, a wild, weekend storm in early December brought blinding snow and gale force winds to the North Shore. "Few there were who slept through the night [on Saturday]," reported The Manchester Cricket, "for the roaring of the wind which rocked houses…broke down trees and overturned everything moveable, made sleep impossible. There were no Sunday papers to read, something unprecedented, and no services were held at the churches. There were no trains after the up train which labored after the snow plow. It was due [to leave] at 8:11 am and went up at 10:15 am. There was nothing over the rails until a snow plow came down [on] Monday afternoon. The Sunday papers also arrived [then] over the road at about two o'clock. The no-school whistle sounded at eight o'clock. The first train arrived here from Boston at 9:15 [on Monday] evening and [nothing] like scheduled time was obtained until Tuesday afternoon."

Wet, heavy snow, with drifts in some places up to six feet in height, made clearing streets and ways a difficult and time-consuming task. Horse-drawn plows were all but useless and most roads had to be shoveled by hand. Sidewalks weren't cleared until Tuesday. At Fenton's boat yard at the foot of Ashland Avenue, scores of yachts covered and stored on winter cradles were blown over by the winds and a new shed was demolished. Other casualties of the storm included a giant American elm uprooted in front of Town Hall; the stone sea wall at Black Beach in West Manchester; and a number of white pines which fell blocking traffic on Bennett Street. More than 200 trees were reported downed at the estate of Greely Curtis. T. Dennie Boardman reported that he had lost as many as 40. At high tide, salt water invaded the cellar at Town Hall and extinguished the fire under the boiler. On

Magnolia Avenue, too, as many as 50 downed trees made passage impossible. In all, more than 100 men were put to work cleaning up after the storm. The wet snow packed and froze and the main road through town was finally broken out by a team of 12 horses pulling a huge log.

With winds from the north, Manchester's shoreline was spared serious damage, but at sea it was different. At about one a.m. Sunday, near the height of the blizzard, the two-masted schooner BESSIE H. GROSS, lost her way and struck the rocks on the east end of House Island. Out of Deer Island, Maine, she was bound for Boston carrying a load of stone. With a high sea running and a pounding surf, she began to break up almost immediately. Two of her crew of four made it safely ashore. Two others drowned.

Frank Dillon, a resident of Smith's Point and caretaker for Paramore Place, according to The Cricket, was the first to notify authorities. As the snow began to let up at about 1:30 p.m. on Sunday, Mrs. Dillon saw one of the survivors on House Island and the couple sent their son to town with the message. Quickly, Police Chief Thomas O.D. Urquhart notified boat yard owner David Fenton and the two, with Fenton's brother, jumped into a dory and started down the harbor. It was about 2 p.m.

"The wind was blowing furiously," The Cricket reported, "and the boat ran before it, being almost at times taken bodily out of the water and shot forward. After a perilous passage," the three men managed to reach the island but the sea was running so high that they found it impossible to land. With snow beginning again and little let up in the wind, they were forced to beach the boat at Smith's Point and walk back to town.

At daylight on Monday, the storm had past and Chief Urquhart heroically started out for the island again. With him in the dory this time, according to The Cricket, was David C. Jones.

The seas had subsided and although the rocks were covered with snow, the men succeeded in getting ashore. After a brief search of the woodlands, they found two survivors, huddled together for warmth, who now had spent two nights and day on the island in below freezing temperatures. They were, the Chief said, "in pitiable condition." Somehow, Urquhart and Jones managed to get the pair into the boat. They then rowed to the Police Station at the head of the inner harbor. There, wrapped in blankets and warmed by the coal stove, the two received food, water and medical attention.

They were identified as Hezekiah Robbins and Neil McDonald. Lost in the wreck of the BESSIE H. GROSS were her Captain, Wallace Thurston and his father, Thomas, who served as cook. Both were from Rockland, ME. Robbins told the harrowing tale of the disaster to police and to Isaac M. Marshall, Editor of The Manchester Cricket.

"We sailed from Wood Island [Biddeford], Maine, Saturday morning," Robbins explained, "and all went well until 8 o'clock that evening when were off Thatcher's Island. The storm struck us suddenly—almost without warning—and at 9 o'clock the snow shut in thick. The wind blew at hurricane [force] and although the BESSIE GROSS had a new set of sails, she was completely stripped of every yard of canvas and we were at the mercy of the wind and sea. We were driven before [it] until about one o'clock Sunday morning

With a bone in her teeth, the small two-masted coaster E.T. HAMOR built in 1889 in Eden, Maine, catches a fresh breeze. Schooners are a uniquely American rig and one of our most successful. Fast and easier to sail, especially up-wind, than square rigged vessels, schooners have been active as privateers, in the slave trade, in the fisheries, and in coastal cargo carrying. By 1790, the schooner was the predominant rig used in the US and Canada. Coasters like the HAMOR above were beamier and could carry bulkier cargo than the New England fishing schooner which was designed with a turn of speed to get her back from the Banks to market. (Peabody Essex Museum photo)

when she struck on the rocks. The Captain and McDonald were washed into the hold. McDonald managed to get out, but we never saw the Captain [again].

"I could swim and succeeded in getting on to the rocks. McDonald couldn't swim a stroke but he was brought ashore on the crest of a [30 foot wave]. His escape was miraculous. The dead body of the cook was washed ashore, [too], and I dragged it up on to the rocks, but the big seas took it off again."

Robbins, who was 19 years old, also told Marshall and police how he survived for more than 30 hours in sub-freezing temperatures. He had no hat, Marshall reported, "so he put a thick coating of snow on his head and let it freeze there. Having no mittens, he pulled off his stockings…drew them up over his hands and filled his boots with salt water. As fast as the water became chilled, he emptied his boots and filled them up with a fresh supply.

"The other man [McDonald], took the opposite course. As his boots became filled he would empty the water…wring out his stockings and put them on again. As a result, he was…badly frostbitten, while Robbins [was spared frostbite

altogether]." Both men were about to give up any hope of rescue when they saw the dory approaching. It was Robbins' third shipwreck and, as Marshall wrote, "he thinks he [may] be satisfied to stay ashore in the future."

Manchester was the first community in the area to have telephone service restored after the storm. And residents of both Salem and Beverly used Manchester's exchange to reach Boston. A generous citizen provided $15 which enabled McDonald and Robbins to purchase railroad tickets and return to their homes in Maine.

Heroes of the occasion, of course, were Police Chief Urquhart, David Fenton, Fenton's brother, and David C. Jones who risked their lives in two efforts to rescue the stranded survivors by dory. Suggestions were made that the town should have a boat ready at Black Cove Beach (which it did in earlier days) or it should construct a shelter stocked with food and blankets at House Island for shipwrecked sailors. This was finally done a few years later thanks to generosity of Miss Elizabeth Bartol, daughter of the Reverend Cyrus Augustus Bartol of Glass Head, West Manchester.

Manchester resident Tom Spang surveys wood timbers from an old shipwreck which washed up on Dana's Beach or were uncovered by a storm in 1998. Could they be from the USS NEW HAMPSHIRE?

MANCHESTER ELECTRIC

For 80 Years, 1903 to 1983, We Had Our Own Electric Power Distribution Company

This article could not have been completed without reference to one written about the Manchester Electric Company in 1953 by Daniel F. Slade, who later with his brother Harry, was owner of The Cricket Press, publisher of The Manchester Cricket. Dan's story never appeared in print. The one below, considerably enlarges upon the original and brings the history of the company up to date.

Today, as residents of Manchester, we send checks for our electric bills to Massachusetts Electric Company in Westborough. But only 18 years ago, we had our own electric company which exclusively purchased power for the town.

Indeed, from 1903 to 1983, Manchester Electric with its Summer Street sub-station and final offices at 35 Beach Street (where Beach Street Cafe is now located), provided the

electricity which enabled residents to light their homes and business establishments, operate their appliances, and the town to serve all of its municipal needs and facilities.

By early 1902, both Beverly and Gloucester were generating their own electricity, while in Manchester, streets were illuminated with Wellsbach gas lamps, each of which had to be lighted and extinguished daily. Homes still glowed with the soft, warm light of kerosene. Town Hall and a few seasonal residences had their own private gas plants. One, at least, of the latter had chance to regret his choice as a gas leak explosion destroyed much of the house and the resulting fire consumed the remainder. But the push was on to modernize.

As one frustrated resident declared at a special Town Meeting that year devoted to the subject: "…when I go out of town, I blush for Manchester who still clings to her old kerosene lights. I am sick and tired of them. I invite friends to my house for a whist party. Before the evening is half over, the oil is burned out of the lamps, the girl has gone to bed [domestic servants were an essential part of most even middle income families at the time], and there we are in darkness and the guests have to go home because there isn't any light…I think we can improve on this with electricity!"

The first formal step towards bringing electric service to Manchester was taken at the Annual Town Meeting on March 3, 1902. At the time, discussions focused on the construction of a town-owned generating plant and voters approved an article to appoint a committee of five persons to study the proposal or, as an alternative, "to allow such of its citizens as may desire, the opportunity to construct [such a plant themselves] and [to] operate under a franchise by the Town." Committee members appointed were Henry T. Bingham, Chairman; Raymond C. Allen, Secretary; and Franklin K. Hooper, James Hoare; Charles L. Norton and Oliver T. Roberts.

The idea of bringing electric power to Manchester was not universally favored. There were concerns about cost particularly as it related to demand and the Town's population which grew dramatically during the summer months and shrank with equal intensity during the winter. Some favored keeping kerosene lamps as a symbol of a simpler, less hectic life. Some proposed maintaining Manchester's independence with its own generating plant. Others called for purchasing electricity from Beverly or Gloucester.

But throughout the ups and downs of the arguments for electricity, there was universal agreement on one basic concept: that transmission lines, when they eventually arrived, should be run through conduits underground to maintain the scenic charm and rural character of the town.

Much mention also was made of the establishment of Manchester's municipal water supply which was inaugurated with great fanfare and delight a decade earlier. Skeptics then, were believers today and it was considered that the two events had this much in common.

By the turn of the century, Manchester was growing in popularity as a summer resort. Seasonal population in 1890 totaled 1,789 persons. By 1910, it had reached 2,673, a growth of some 50 percent. Boston was only 50 minutes away by train and although horse and carriage was still the primary mode of transportation locally, streets were being paved with asphalt and the motor car was making its appearance. As a sign of summer affluence, the Manchester Yacht Club was founded in 1892 and the Essex County Club in 1893.

Sizable, seasonal homes were being constructed, most notably by town builders Roberts & Hoare, at Smith's Point, at Norton's Point and in West Manchester. And, according to Oliver T. Roberts, most, if not all, were being wired for electricity.

At a Special Town Meeting in July,1902, the committee recommended that pursuant to the General Laws permitting such an arrangement, the town should "construct an electric generating plant within town limits for the distribution of electricity for furnishing light for municipal use, and light, heat and power for [the use of private residences and business establishments]." It was proposed that the generating station be located on Vine Street (specifically, what is now the southeasterly corner of Vine and Norwood Avenue, the latter not being extended at that time).

Sentiment ran heavily in favor of acquiring electricity. Differences centered upon whether the town should build its own generating plant or purchase power from one in another community.

Colonel Henry Lee Higginson, partner of Lee, Higginson, founder of Boston's celebrated Symphony Orchestra and a resident of Sunset Hill in West Manchester, said that the town's "excellent water and low taxes" have been drawing cards for summer residents. As for electricity, he said, "Put the wires underground and buy it from Beverly or Gloucester. They can make it more cheaply than we can."

"We don't want to go to Gloucester for electricity," one voter quickly added. "A good many go there for fire water and, if appearances mean anything, it's pretty poor stuff. Their electricity may be poor, too!"

Herman Thiemann, authorized to speak for US Senator John McMillan of Michigan, a seasonal resident of Eagle Head, said, " the Senator would have at least 50 lights on his grounds...you say they are only here in the summer; that is right, charge them enough to pay for it. Why if we had electric lights, they would play golf at the Essex Country Club all night! Give them what they want. Money has nothing to do with it."

Year-round resident, William Johnson, who said he was the oldest person present, told the meeting that "two weeks ago I had a pain in my back. I saw an electric pad advertised and I sent for it. I put it on the bottom of my foot," he continued, "and went to bed and didn't know anything until morning...when I woke up the pain was all gone and I haven't felt it since. Electricity is a wonderful thing!" Left unexplained, however, was where he got the power for an electric pad. Finally, an informal vote authorized the circulation of a questionnaire and showed that of the 122 residents present, all were in favor of acquiring a source of electric power.

With a second Special Town Meeting scheduled to discuss the issue on October 13, 1902, letters pro and con began to appear in The Manchester Cricket. A lengthy one signed by builder Oliver T. Roberts of Roberts & Hoare, is fun to read even today. It reviews in some detail the history of the town from its involvement in fishing, farming and furniture-making to the arrival of its summer residents. "I can remember," Roberts writes, "when Smith's Point was used only as a pas-

ture and not a particularly good [one] at that. Today, it represents an expenditure of nearly $2 million."

With an understandable interest in his clients' welfare, he continued: "There will be erected in our town within one year from this time, from $500,000 to $600,000 worth of new buildings, all of which will be thoroughly wired, the owners of which expect to be furnished with [electricity]. The taxes on these buildings alone will take care of our proposed plant. That is, pay any deficits after all expenses are paid, and retire the bonds as they mature...if we cannot or will not give [electricity] to them, they will go where they can have these things."

"It will be a comfort and convenience," he wrote with enthusiastic eloquence, "to those who take it and will put dollars in the pocket of the working man. Let us then, each and all, turn our faces to the rising sun of progress and vote to give the people, the whole people, light!"

Continually more conservative than the majority, furniture maker Charles C. Dodge, expressed concern about the cost of the project and warned of recessions yet to come. He also extolled the virtues of natural gas. "A grocery firm in a neighboring city paid $120 a year for electric lights and now pays $27 for gas...we should have something like gas that nearly all can afford...or wait until electricity can be made and distributed cheaply so as to be within reach of all. "

PEOPLE WANT IT
Scores of New Summer Houses Spur the Demand for Electric Lights, Appliances

But demands for power to light the increasing number of new houses being built for seasonal residents was a powerful force in favor of acquiring electricity. As The Cricket reported, Roberts & Hoare had been awarded contracts for an impressive number of structures. They included a house, The Chimneys, for financier Gardner M. Lane on the Dana Estate; a house, Glendyne, for banker W.J. Mitchell on Magnolia Avenue; a "cottage" each for F. M. Whitehouse, Crowhurst, and President of Jordan Marsh department stores E.D. Jordan,The Rocks, the latter with stable; a stable for Lester Leland, Treasurer of Boston Rubber Shoe Company; an addition to the Henry Lee Higginson house on Sunset Hill; and a contract to build Crowell Memorial Chapel of stone at Rosedale Cemetery.

On the list of new structures also was a house for H.P. Squires to be constructed on "the hill near the Tenney homestead off Pine Street;" an addition to the cottage owned by William A. Tucker of Tucker, Anthony, bankers and brokers; a stable for Mrs. Harriet Fellner on Blossom Lane and two major, two-story additions to the club house of the Essex County Club. Also mentioned was the possibility of the construction of another luxury hotel (plans had been drawn showing a building of brick) to serve the greater community in company with Manchester's celebrated Masconomo House which had been built in 1877 and was to last until 1920.

On October 13, 1902, 238 residents gathered in the auditorium at Town Hall. Henry T. Bingham, speaking for the electric light committee, reported to Town Meeting voters that, as directed, it had, first, asked both the cities of Beverly and Gloucester how much each would charge to provide electric power for Manchester with contracts for one, five and 10 years. Beverly, he added, had yet to respond. Gloucester indicated it would charge six cents per kilowatt hour "upon the condition that the amount used shall not be less than the amount estimated by the committee."

Second, Bingham said that the committee had sent a circular to every Manchester taxpayer asking recipients if they favored the introduction of electricity for lighting and other purposes, and if they would use electric power if it was offered. Responses to the circular totaled 236. These represented an assessed value of $4,600,968 or 50.5 percent of the town's total valuation for real estate tax purposes. "Of these answers, Bingham said, "191 are in the affirmative or favorable, and 126 would be consumers to a greater or lesser extent." Those in favor totaled 91 percent of the valuation represented in the replies. It was also explained that the average house in Gloucester pays $25 a year for electricity

E.P. Standley moved that the Committee's report be accepted. It was and conversation quickly return to cost. At the suggestion of committee member Oliver Roberts, summer residents were "offered the courtesy of the floor" to express their opinions. Once again, discussion centered upon whether it was wiser and more cost effective to purchase electricity elsewhere or, as had been recommended earlier by the committee, for the town to construct and operate its own generating plant. It was estimated that this would cost taxpayers $161,000.

Summer resident Thomas Jefferson Coolidge, Jr., Chairman of Boston's Old Colony Trust Company, again emphasized that "the people on the shore want electricity. "However," he said, "It is ridiculous to think that Manchester can build its own plant and manufacture [it] as cheaply as another plant that has only to add a little to its present [capacity]. I am almost ready to stake my reputation as a businessman that I could get the Gloucester company to accept an offer of five cents and waive the guarantee."

Year-round resident Charles Dodge still persisted in his support of natural gas. "Electricity is expensive stuff," he warned, "and out of reach of people with small means." Samuel Knight disagreed. "I want it in my stable, in my home and in my office," he said. "Ninety percent of the people have responded in the affirmative. They want it."

"We want electric light. We want it underground," declared Henry S. Grew of Harbor Street, President of Boston's National Union Bank. "And we are willing to pay the fiddler." His remarks were greeted with applause. Banker, President of Boston's Old Colony Trust Company, and resident of West Manchester Gordon Abbott added: "Like most of the gentlemen [here], I am a firm believer in electricity, but it seems there are two distinct propositions before the meeting. First, shall we manufacture electricity [ourselves]? Second, shall we buy and distribute it? I believe it is a bad thing for the town to go into the manufacture of electricity. When it comes to the other proposition, I believe it can be handled to good advantage. Gloucester has probably bid a sum in excess of what it is willing to take. It is a great mistake from an economic point of view for the town to own its own plant." F.K. Hooper disagreed. In favor of the town generating its own power, he said "I am opposed to anyone getting a franchise or hold in Manchester. I hope we shall

vote for the plant."

In the end, summer residents won the day. They included many with distinguished careers in finance and business. Their logic and weight of argument helped defeat the motion made early in the meeting that the town proceed to construct its own generating plant. A two thirds majority or 160 votes were necessary for approval; 127 were recorded in favor; 111 opposed. Thus, although the committee's report was accepted, its recommendations were not.

There was obviously work being done between meetings to implement the proposal that electric power be brought to Manchester. After failing to reach the two-thirds vote necessary to accept the first committee's recommendation, a new committee was appointed with the same mandate. Its members, named by Town Meeting Moderator, were Professor C. L. Norton, James Hoare, Raymond C. Allen, Henry T. Bingham, and Oliver T. Roberts. A motion made by James Hoare resulted in the Moderator himself being reluctantly added after protesting that he was busy enough with the general activities of the town to have time to do the appointment justice.

WIRES UNDERGROUND

Manchester's System Was Unique; Cables to Be Buried to Preserve Scenic Beauty

Summer residents, too, had organized to present a formal counter proposal which would enable the town to purchase electricity from neighboring sources. At the adjourned Town Meeting on April 18, 1903, Article 26, filed earlier for the warrant, was read as a motion before the meeting by F.J. Merrill. It proposed: "That the Selectmen be and are hereby are advised and authorized to grant a location for poles, wires, and underground conduits for electric lighting to a corporation now in process of formation, upon such terms as the Selectmen may approve, provided that such corporation shall give the town an option to purchase its property at any time within two years from the time of operating the plant, at cost, with interest at the rate of five percent per annum, less any dividends declared by such corporation." Merrill then spoke in favor of the motion.

"It is well known" he said, "that a party of gentlemen, summer residents, have associated themselves for the purpose of furnishing Manchester with electric lights and had the plan compensated as far as they could go, so the next move is to be made by us and it seems an easy solution of a matter that presents many hard features."

Spokesman for the group was summer resident and Boston attorney Philip Dexter. "Some of the summer people thought it rather a pity," he said, "that the town voted as it did last autumn. Colonel Henry L. Higginson took a lively interest in the matter...and proposed that some of our people get together and form a corporation...Sufficient money has been subscribed to do this and we have adopted essentially the same plan which the town proposed which is plan number two.

"We can contract with the Beverly Gas & Electric Company to buy the current and they are competent to give us good service. We propose to put in an underground system. If the town doesn't agree to the plan, it is alright and nobody will feel hurt...We hope to light the streets of the town and also to furnish light to private houses at a rate of one cent a lamp an hour to yearly subscribers and one and one-half cents to others.

"To purchase from Beverly…they will want a 10-year contract which we think is reasonable as they would be obliged to install considerable new machinery. If we buy their generators within two years, we would be getting the same thing that we would have had if we had put in our plant."

In response to questions, Dexter said he thought that the plant in Beverly which was to to serve Manchester might be in operation next autumn. Samuel Knight declared "this seems to me a very liberal proposition…we ought to be satisfied with the two years…" F.K. Swett proposed that it be extended to five. Dexter replied that he thought the matter could be adjusted and perhaps ought to be left to the Selectmen.

Knight said he was "heartily in favor of the proposal. If we should vote for a plant, it would take a year or more before it was in operation. Now these men out of the goodness of their hearts have stepped into the breech and agreed to assume all costs and all responsibility and are willing to turn it over to us at cost—and I don't doubt that they can do it 25 percent cheaper than we can—and what is there better that we could ask?…I wish I could vote with both hands instead of one!" The motion was carried unanimously.

It authorized Selectmen to grant a franchise to the newly-formed Manchester Electric Company, a private corporation then in the process of formation, permitting it to install poles, conduits and other equipment to distribute electricity within the boundaries of the Town of Manchester. On April 16, 1903, the Commonwealth of Massachusetts granted a charter to the new corporation listing its directors. A combination of year-round and summer residents, they were: Oliver T. Roberts, George C. Lee, Jr., Gardner M. Lane, Charles E. Cotting, Philip Dexter, Gordon Abbott and Raymond C. Allen. On September 18, 1903, the Board of Selectmen, William H. Allen, William E. Kitfield and Fred K. Swett, signed the permit which put the Manchester Electric Company in business. Now all that was needed was funding. The next day a hearing was scheduled at the State House on a petition filed by the company to allow it to issue capital stock with a par value of $116,500. Before the year end, a contract had been signed with Beverly Gas & Electric Company and construction of a distribution system had begun.

With Austin A.Cushing, Manchester Electric's first General Manager, located in an office at Town Hall, things began to happen. Anxious to make progress before the ground froze, in late October three carloads of piping to be used as conduit for electric wiring, the first of some 20 carloads expected, arrived at the railroad siding in Manchester. At first it was planned to use the same trench occupied by town water mains. But with water department objections, a trench on the opposite side of roadways was selected.

More than 100 "Italian laborers" also arrived to dig the four-foot deep ditches required. According to The Cricket, they were housed at the bowling alley on Beach Street and accommodations were sought for 100 more. The contract for the installation of wires was awarded to G.M. Guest & Company of Springfield. Specifications called for "on the bottom [of the trench], broken stone and cement laid to make a solid foundation. On this, clay tiling conduits are laid and covered with more cement." By mid-November, 150 feet of conduit had already been installed and workers had begun to construct a 42 by 22 foot building to house electric company offices and sub-station machinery.

Manchester's acquisition of electric power started others thinking as well. Both Beverly and Gloucester had electric street railways, although tracks were prohibited on Hale Street which bordered prime residential land. Manchester wisely recognized that a street railway would destroy not only its scenic beauty but its rural character and thus its appeal as a summer resort community. Indeed, it had voted to oppose the concept of a street railway at Town Meeting and its contract with Manchester Electric Company, specifically forbid the sale of electricity for that purpose. But the Gloucester, Essex and Beverly Street Railway Company had other ideas.

In February, 1904, it sought repeal of that part of its charter which restricted its expansion, especially to Manchester. Opposition, however, led by State Representative Franklin K. Cooper, a Manchester resident, prevailed. At Cooper's urging, and in executive session, the Committee on Rules voted not to concur with the action of the House which had waved the rules earlier and admitted the street railway company's petition. The committee's action ended the issue. Thankfully, it was never to rise again.

'JUICE' TURNED ON
West Manchester Is Lit First; Rest of the Town Follows; What a Convenience!

Winters were different in the old days, and with snow piled high on Manchester streets, temperatures near zero, and the ground frozen solid, work digging trenches for electric power lines in 1905 began again only in March. One laborer was injured in April as his pick hit an unexploded charge of dynamite. He was treated locally and then taken to Beverly Hospital where his injuries included the loss of one eye. By June, The Cricket reported "trenching is being done on Washington Street, on Union Street, and on the Smith Point road to the Masconomo House hotel." Work parties on Summer Street had started at either end and were nearing each other. By June 24, G.M. Guest & Company had installed power lines on Raymond Street and was ready to repave the area with what in those days was called "macadam." Named for Scotch engineer J.L. McAdam (1756-1836), the process called for successive layers of small, broken stones which were rolled into a smooth and durable road surface.

Finally, in late June, 1904, the "Locals" column of The Manchester Cricket reported that the "juice" was turned on for the first time for the West Manchester circuit. At the end of the line, "Gordon Abbott having the distinction of having the first light from this system. New circuits are being opened as fast as completed," continued The Cricket, "and by the last of next week the [town] Center will be connected." By July 4, 1904, electric lights were also lit for the first time at the Essex County Club, and after dark a new glow filled the club house and illuminated its grounds and driveways.

Work was still being completed at the Central Station on Summer Street, but although technical, The Cricket attempted to describe for its readers how electric current reached Manchester and was distributed to houses and businesses throughout the town. "The current is received over a main cable from Beverly," the paper explained, "coming into the station at 3,300 volts, passing into high tension oil-break switches, then passing into the transformers where it is reduced to 2,400 volts. From here it passes to the switch board which is of polished slate about seven feet high and 15 feet long, and is sent out over the various circuits. In the man holes", the article continued, "it is reduced again to 220 volts, and again divided, entering the houses at 110 volts."

What was unique about Manchester entering the age of electricity was its decision to install its distribution system underground. Poles and overhead wires would have cost a quarter of what was spent digging trenches and installing conduits, but unlike other communities, particularly Beverly and Gloucester where a thick skein of pole-supported wires wove through trees and marred the skyline overhead, Manchester wisely chose to preserve the age-old character of its streets and by-ways and the simple beauty of its countryside. It is a policy which has persisted until today although in recent years, larger corporations now delivering power to the town, have used cost as an argument to break with tradition

and place unsightly poles and wires overhead. Telephone, too, not subject to underground restrictions, is carried in many areas by pole.

It can well be imagined what the arrival of electricity meant to Manchester residents. Kerosene lamps were quickly stored in closets for emergencies and instead of matches needed to provide light at the end of the day, a simple switch on the wall but most likely on the light itself, did the trick. To be sure, in the early days, there were few lights in each room, perhaps one, at most two, and almost certainly no more than one outlet or plug per room. But what a convenience!

As the town grew in population, so did the Manchester Electric Company and its system reached farther out from the town's center. Then, too, came a national increase in the invention and use of electric utensils which dramatically changed life at home. Gone was the drudgery of doing everything by hand. First, came the electric iron which replace flat irons heated on a coal stove in the kitchen. The toaster and washing machine followed about 1915. By 1925, the ice man was beginning to disappear and many houses here were equipped with electric refrigerators and even oil burners. It

Celebrating the installation of a new transformer at the Manchester Electric Company's sub-station on Summer Street about 1965 are, from left, George Burchstead, General Manager, Bill Shomph, Pat Corliss, and the company's consulting engineer. The so-called "step-down transformer" reduced current coming to the sub-station from 23,000 to 2300 volts. It then could be distributed to smaller transformers underground around town where it was further reduced in voltage for use by homes and businesses.

was a revolution in living assisted by electricity which led ultimately, except in the wealthiest of households, to the end of domestic help.

In March, 1915, also, residents at Town Meeting voted to award the contract to light the streets of the community to Manchester Electric Company. Since the late 1890's, natural gas, provided by Wellsbach Lighting Company, had done the job. Earlier, in 1879, voters had provided a small sum for the purchase of a few kerosene lamps and fixtures from the Globe Light Company. Now, a ten year contract was proposed which would give the town an underground electric system serving 250 street lights. The lamps themselves, according to Arthur Lovering, then Manchester Electric Company Manager, "would use an ornamental iron post with a radial reflector. A 40 candlepower light," Lovering explained, "would give as much light as a 60 candlepower gas light. [Besides], "he added, "New York City has changed from gas to electricity for lighting Central Park and gas is being abandoned everywhere." As for expense, electricity would cost the town $36.30 per light per year; gas, $36.50.

With courtesy due a long-time supplier, the Moderator congratulated Wellsbach for improvements in service and asked its representative if he would like to speak. He acknowledged his company's mistakes, said it had served Manchester for 18 years and "would feel badly to kicked out." Sentiment, however, ran in favor of the home team.

One of Manchester Electric Company's directors, Oliver T. Roberts, urged voters that if they chose to act, now was the time to do so "before the streets are put back into shape again." The argument was summarized by A. C. Needham. "This is a simple [matter]," he told voters. "We are in the market to buy lights; we have two propositions: one gives us better light at less cost. Which is the best to buy? To my mind, electricity is what we want." His remarks carried the day. There were 142 votes for a decade-long contract with Manchester Electric, and 39 votes to stay with Wellsbach natural gas.

In 1928, the town's Water Department also contracted with Manchester Electric for power to drive pumps once operated by gasoline motors. An underground cable three and one-half miles long was installed from the Manchester Electric Company sub-station on Summer Street to Gravel Pond pumping station. Also that year, the overhead line from the generating station in Beverly, which was regularly subject to damage from downed tree limbs and branches, was replaced with a 24,000 volt cable buried along the railroad right of way to Gloucester thus making all service to Manchester underground and far less subject to the ravages of weather.

Since 1903, Manchester Electric Company has increased its sub-station capacity on at least three occasions. In the fall of 1953, following a post World War II boom in suburban growth, it installed a new transformer increasing capacity to 3,000 kilowatts. Cables were enlarged and extended to service additional new housing developments. From 1947 to 1953, more than 100 new houses in Manchester were provided with electric service. And scores more followed. By mid-1981, some 2,300 customers received power from Manchester Electric.

From 1904 to 1916, the offices of Manchester Electric Company were located at its sub-station at 21 Summer Street. By 1917, it had moved its offices to 4 School Street where it added for sale a line of electric utilities such as lamps, irons, toasters, cooking stoves and washing machines. In 1919, it moved again this time to the Bingham building in Central Square, adding to its retail offerings radios, then battery operated, and the earliest of refrigerators. Needing additional space in 1925, it moved to the Blaisdell building on Beach Street. And in 1928, Manchester Electric Company finally purchased the building at 35 Beach Street (now the Beach Street Cafe), which it remodeled to provide modern office space and a show and sales room for electric appliances.

CHANGING TIMES
Expenses and Sophistication Catch Up with a Small Company; Merger Inevitable

As the years went by, more and more customers and new inventions such as air conditioning and growth in the number and use of household appliances created an increasing demand for electric power. The business of delivering it also grew more sophisticated and expensive. In 1973, the Arab oil embargo shook utilities to their core and the rising cost of fossil fuels caused electric bills to soar. Manchester Electric was no exception. It was then purchasing power from New England Light & Power Company, and was forced to pass on its increases in cost to consumers throughout the town. One enterprising citizen applied for a permit to erect a tower for a wind-driven generator, but was told the proposal was in conflict with the town's zoning by-laws.

In late December 1981, bitter cold winter weather froze underground lines and overloaded circuits forcing delivery of electricity to portions of Manchester to cease altogether. Thanks to heroic measures, however, blackouts were short-lived—Memorial School lost heat and light for one hour—and even with temperatures at five below zero, power was soon restored. Engineers at the company's sub-station bypassed relays on circuit breakers and even asked police to broadcast, at least to those with battery-operated radio scanners, an appeal to cut back on the use of household appliances. The next day, relays were adjusted to minimize the affect of demand overloads. But signals were flying that the company was standing into danger. Underground cables were aging and many needed replacement. Other capital improvements to the system were necessary as well and it was clear that costs ahead would be significant for a small corporation now operating in a new and different era.

Thus it was that in May, 1983, that a hearing was held at Town Hall by the State Department of Public Utilities (DPU) to discuss the proposal that Manchester Electric Company merge with Massachusetts Electric Company "as quickly as possible." Paul Reynolds, President of Manchester Electric and also a Vice President of Massachusetts Electric, was asked to speak.

Reynolds announced that both companies had sought DPU approval to merge. The advantages? Two, he added, addressing Manchester residents. "First, you will pay lower rates. Second, you will receive better service.

"Once Manchester Electric becomes part of Massachusetts Electric, you will benefit from the service provided by a larger, more modern, more efficient organization. To be sure, you won't have line trucks [garaged] in Manchester, but they will be based [next door] in Beverly. And Massachusetts Electric has personnel on duty around the clock and an expanded communications system."

A rate increase was promised whether the merger went through or not. "A utility company," Reynolds continued, "must have enough revenue to pay all its operating expenses and all its fixed costs and still make a reasonable return for its stockholders. Manchester Electric hasn't been doing that.

"In 1980, the DPU found that 11.3 percent was a reasonable rate of return for Manchester Electric. In 1982, the company earned only 6.6 percent, and the stockholders only 5.3 percent. So far in 1983, the situation has become worse and in March, the Board of Directors voted against paying any quarterly dividend.

"If Manchester Electric can merge with Massachusetts Electric," he concluded, "the company and its customers can enjoy the benefits of a large scale, efficient, modern utility operation and the service and economies that go with it."

Earlier, in a move which harked back to discussions in 1902, R.W. Beck Associates, electric utility consultants, were engaged by Selectmen to examine the question of whether it was prudent for the Town of Manchester itself to purchase Manchester Electric Company. The study, entitled Engineering Report—Acquisition and Operation of Manchester Electric Company by the Town of Manchester, was sent to a special committee whose members included Selectman Louis Ranieri, William Dalton and Robert Dennis.

Speaking for the committee, Ranieri told the hearing that it did not recommend the town's purchase of Manchester Electric Company. But he urged that the town strive to obtain at least as favorable a rate structure as other customers of the New England Electric Company and that Massachusetts Electric continue to maintain the town's traditional underground delivery system.

Although operating successfully at the moment—there was no crisis in sight, either financial or physical—the time had come. Manchester Electric's cables, wires, transformers and switches would need modernizing. Its fixed and operating costs were rising and its profits shrinking. A significant investment of capital, more sophisticated management and a higher level of engineering and technical support were necessary if the service the company provided was to survive in the years ahead. Merger seemed the obvious way to go. Thus in 1983, after some 80 years of successful operation, Manchester Electric quietly became a part of Massachusetts Electric Company.

During its nearly eight decades, its Managers included Austin A. Cushing, Arthur Lovering; Thomas A. Lees, Albert W. James, George W. Burchstead, Reginald H. Smith, Jr. and Charles T. Campbell.

"What made Manchester Electric great," recalls Reginald Smith, now a resident of Hamilton, "was its crew, both operations and maintenance. There was a terrific spirit and great teamwork." At one time, he recalled, it was company policy that employees should live in town so that they could be at the scene immediately in case of emergencies. "But that had to change," he added, "as real estate prices increased."

Manchester resident William A. Temple, Sr., now retired, recalls his some 30 years with Manchester Electric. "We worked nights and weekends," he said, "but the most exciting time we had was during the 1978 blizzard. "I was driving the big truck to Black Beach where we'd been asked to shine our headlights out to sea to help the CAN DO, the Gloucester pilot boat that was lost in the storm. When I passed the Lodge on Summer Street there was a lady out in snow who was having a baby. She was looking for a ride to the Beverly Hospital! The ambulance soon arrived to help her. During that storm we worked around the clock."

Reggie Smith and Bill Temple remember other members of the Manchester Electric team who made such a difference in the old days. They included Foreman Bill Shomph, Tiger Doane, Pat Corliss, Skippy Marr, Pat Scully, Norm Crombie and Scott Haverty.

"It was a family affair," explains Pat Corliss, "We were committed to the company. I remember working to repair an outage at Sea and Tappan Streets. We'd been at it since 3 am. We had a new foreman. At seven, he said let's break for breakfast. We said, no, we don't leave a job until we've restored power. We worked that way all the time. In the big snow storm of 1978, many of us worked three days without sleep. We went home, took a two hour nap, and were back on the job. Big companies don't operate that way."

It is hard to believe, but there were no wiring diagrams for the town's electric distribution system. "George Burchstead, who grew up with the company, knew it upside down and backwards," said Corliss. "When we had a failure, he'd stay in the sub-station [to direct the operation]. Ninety-nine percent of the time we'd locate it immediately."

That the town was well served over the decades by Manchester Electric Company there is no doubt. And the wisdom of its founders who insisted that wires and cables be installed underground has been demonstrated again and again as cities and towns around us have lost electricity with downed overhead lines in hurricanes, storms and blizzards, while power in Manchester has continued uninterrupted.

Today, grateful, to be sure, for the modernization of the system brought to us by Massachusetts Electric, many of us here in town fondly recall the days when we had our own electric company, run by local people, most of whom were our neighbors, who had a rare commitment to public service and to a work ethic which meant doing a job right the first time around. Why in the old days we could even purchase a new Hot Point dishwasher or kitchen range at competitive prices right here in town from a handsome store and showroom at 35 Beach Street!

WHAT IS ELECTRICITY?
Early Experiments Begin in 1700's; Edison, AC Generators, Make Wide Use Possible

Despite the legends that surround him, Benjamin Franklin did not discover electricity. Our earliest ancestors experienced the powers of the electric eel and the torpedo fish, but it wasn't until the 17th century that man began to understand the technicalities of static electricity, the electrical effects of heat and of chemical action, current electricity, and electro-magnetism.

That amber, for example, after being rubbed, can attract materials such as a piece of straw or a feather was known by the Greeks in 600 BC. William Gilbert (1544-1603), physician to Queen Elizabeth I, found that other substances possessed the same power and it was he who coined the word "electric" after a Greek word meaning "amber." In Latin it became more recognizable as "vis electrica."

In the early 1700's, according to the Encyclopaedia Britannica, Fourteenth Edition, 1929, experiments found that some materials were conductors and others insulators. Machines were developed that could create electric sparks. In 1745, in Lyden and in Kummin, independent researchers trying to charge water in a glass bottle, found that if a wire, kept live by an electrical machine, was dipped into the water, a person who held the bottle in one hand and touched the charged conductor with the other, received a significant electric shock.

Franklin (1706-1790), continued research with the so-called Lyden jar which became a critical tool in the development of modern electricity. In 1752, he undertook his celebrated experiment with a kite, flying it in a thunderstorm with a key attached. It created sparks which charged a Lyden jar, thus establishing the difference between atmospheric electricity and ordinary electricity. All of these experiments captured public interest in the subject and as early as 1746, John Winthrop, IV, presented a series of lectures on electricity at Harvard College.

In Europe, meanwhile, research continued unabated by scientists whose names today are still connected with the terms used in the study and application of electricity. In 1790, Luigi Galvani led studies of current electricity. Experiments by Alessandro Volta in 1800 led to the development of the electric battery. In France, Ampere helped to identify electro-magnetism, and George Simon Ohm published a paper describing the flow of electricity through conducting wires which led to the establishment of Ohm's law.

Other discoveries were made by Faraday in 1831 whose research created the laws of electrolysis; by Lord Kelvin; and by Heinrich Hertz. Faraday's copper disk, rotating between the poles of a magnet, generated a steady current and was the forerunner of the modern electric generator. Alternating current generators were introduced about 1883. Soon, the concept of transmitting power using electricity was seen as a possibility and, in this country, Thomas A. Edison especially was instrumental in making it a reality.

By 1882, electric trams and street cars came into use, and across the U.S., electric motors began to drive machines of all sorts and sizes. That same year in New York City, Edison established the first central generating station in the world. And by 1928, single generators capable of producing as much as 50,000 kilowatts, or nearly 70,000 horsepower, were in common use.

In 1879, Edison's invention of the modern incandescent lamp with a carbon filament contained in a vacuum chamber of glass made it possible to manufacture a light which could be sold in cities throughout America wherever electricity was available. The lamp was first commercially used aboard the steamship COLUMBIA owned by the Oregon Railway and Navigation Company. The original installation of about 180 lamps lasted in good working order for 15 years.

During the two years from 1881 to 1882, more than 30,000 of these lamps were sold to light homes, factories, stores and offices. By 1906, tungsten filament lamps immensely improved the efficiency and power of earlier incandescents. The light bulb hugely increased public demand for electricity as did the invention of the electric stove in 1896, the electric iron in 1882, the electric sewing machine in 1889 and the electric washing machine in 1907.

The availability of electric power generation on a large scale was made practicable by the development and refinement of steam turbines. In 1897, a steam turbine had been successfully used to power a destroyer for the Royal Navy. In 1903, a Curtis turbine was installed by Chicago Edison Company to drive an electric generator with a capacity of 5,000 kilowatts. By 1930, 65 percent of U.S. electric power needs were met by steam-driven generators. The remainder came from hydro-electric generation or water power.

By 1902, when Manchester expressed its first interest in bringing electricity to town, Beverly was already using electric power and the art of power generation was well on its way. Prior to that, natural gas had provided for street lighting. In the evening, each gas street lamp was lit by hand and, as morning arrived, had to be extinguished.

The greatest monument to power generation on the North Shore today is the giant Salem Harbor Station of Pacific Gas & Electric Company (PG&E). A part of the Northeast Power Grid, it was constructed in 1952 for New England Power. The plant's two original units could each produce 85,000 kilowatts of electricity. To meet consumer demand, a third generating unit was added in 1958 and a fourth in 1972, boosting the Station's present generating capacity to a total of 775,000 kilowatts.

According to PG&E, the plant burns an average of 14,000 barrels of oil and 2,400 tons of coal each day. In 1984, to reduce dependency on costly foreign oil, generating units one, two and three were converted to coal. Tankers and colliers, a familiar sight entering and exiting Salem Bay, deliver the necessary fuel. Concerned with the environment and the need to maintain clean air, PG&E operates three ambient air quality monitoring systems. One is located in Salem, one in Marblehead and the other in Beverly.

Salem Harbor Station, which employs some 225 persons, can supply electricity to 14 cities approximately the size of Salem. In 1996, it paid about $8.5 million in taxes to the city. Electricity generated by the huge plant is distributed by the company's transmission grid which connects with other electric generating systems in New England as well as in New York State, and in New Brunswick and Ontario, Canada.

BIBLIOGRAPHY

W.S. Tyron, Parnassus Corner, A Life of James T. Field Publisher to the Victorians; Boston, Houghton Mifflin Company, The Riverside Press Cambridge, 1963; Dairies of Annie Adams Fields, original collection on microfilm at the Massachusetts Historical Society, Boston; Notes on the Diaries of Annie Adams Fields transcribed by Frances L. Burnett of Manchester, Massachusetts; Joseph E. Garland, Boston's North Shore, Being an Account of of Life Among the Noteworthy, Fashionable, Wealthy, Eccentric and Ordinary,

1823-1890: Boston, Toronto; Little Brown and Company, 1978; M.A. DeWolfe Howe, <u>Memories of a Hostess, A Chronicle of Eminent Friendships, Drawn Chiefly from the Diaries of Mrs. James T. Fields</u>: Boston; The Atlantic Monthly Press 1922; Annie Fields, <u>Authors and Friends</u>: Boston and New York, Houghton Mifflin and Company, The Riverside Press Cambridge, 1897; <u>Paper</u> prepared for the Manchester Historical Society by Charlotte Frasier; Janice Goldsmith Pulsifer, <u>Gail Hamilton, 1833-1896</u>; Salem, Massachusetts: Essex Institute Historical Collections, July, 1968; Fields, James Thomas, <u>Biographical Notes and Personal Sketches, With Unpublished Fragments and Tributes from Men and Women of Letters</u>, Boston, Houghton Mifflin and Company, The Riverside Press, Cambridge,1882; Bartol, Cyrus A., <u>A Discourse in West Church, Boston</u>; Boston, A. Williams & Company, Old Corner Bookstore, The Riverside Press, printed by H.A. Houghton and Company, 1881; Barbara Rotundo, <u>The Literary Lights Were Always Bright at 148 Charles Street</u>: American Heritage magazine, 1971; Esther Lowell Burnett, <u>Three Houses, A Narrative</u>: Boston, Thomas Todd Company, 1955;

Charles Todd Creekman, Captain U S N (ret.), Executive Director; J. C. Reilly, Jr. Head, Ship's History Branch, Naval Historical Foundation, Department of the Navy, Building 57, Washington Navy Yard, 901 M Street, SE, Washington, DC 20374-5060; Robert Browning, Historian, US Coast Guard Headquarters, 2100 2nd Street, SW, Washington, DC 20593-0001;

Howard I. Chapelle, <u>The History of American Sailing Ships</u>: New York, W.W. Norton & Company, 1935; historic editions of <u>The Manchester Cricket</u>; Raymond H. Bates, Jr., <u>Shipwrecks of Boston's North Shore</u>, a map, Marblehead, Massachusetts, 1988; unpublished paper about the Manchester Electric Company written in 1953 by Dan Slade, owner and publisher of The Cricket Press and <u>The Manchester Cricket</u>; Information from notes and clippings collected by Miss Frances Lowell Burnett of Manchester; and files of the Manchester Historical Society.

PHOTOGRAPHS

The Boston Athanaeum, 10½ Beacon Street, Boston, MA 02108; Mount Auburn Cemetery, Cambridge, Massachusetts; Peabody Essex Museum, East India Square, Salem, MA 01970; Department of the Navy, Photo Service, Naval Historical Foundation, Building 57, Washington Navy Yard, 901 M Street, SE, Washington, DC 20374-5060; Historian, US Coast Guard Headquarters, 2100 2nd Street, SW, Washington, DC 20593-0001; photo collection, Manchester Historical Society; A. Haskell; Gordon Abbott, Jr.

REFLECTIONS, a publication of the Manchester Historical Society, is written and edited by Gordon Abbott, Jr., a member of the Board of Directors

REFLECTIONS

MANCHESTER HISTORICAL SOCIETY

SUMMER 1999

MANCHESTER, MASSACHUSETTS

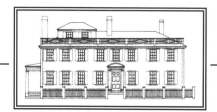

MANCHESTER'S 'FINEST' – 1897-1999

Manchester Police Department, July, 30, 1948. Front row, from left: Officer Jack Connors, Chief Allen Andrews, Officer Fred Lear, Officer Alex Backry; second row: Officer Felix "Pop" Radack, Officer Donald Doane; top row: Officer George James, Sergeant Dan MacEachern. In front, "Poozie" Radack.

A FORTUNATE TOWN

Our Police Have a Remarkable Record of Achievement and Commitment

Unlike a busy city where crime is frequent, police work in a small town such as Manchester is often tedious in its peaceful monotony. Understandably, this could breed complacency on the part of law enforcement officers. The history of the Manchester Police Department, however, fortunately for all of us, shows that this is not and never has been the case. Whenever on those infrequent occasions that vigorous response has been required, Manchester police officers through the years have answered the call immediately in an efficient, effective and thoughtful manner, often risking their lives to enforce the law and to make their community a safe place for others to live. Most important, between these climactic events, they have maintained an alertness and a professional presence which has resulted in the thwarting of many crimes and misdemeanors before they could begin. Finally, they have also used good judgment and sympathy dealing with young people in their formative years, guiding them away from bad influences, helping them to build character, and to become honest and upright citizens. I have also been impressed with the years of service contributed by many officers in the past century, and with the number who have attended Manchester schools and who have been life-long citizens of the town. We are blessed to have had so many who have given so much.

For this collection of stories about the Manchester Police Department since its establishment in 1897, I owe great thanks to Chief of Police Ronald W. Ramos, to Sergeants Leonard Niel Andrews and Alan Gilson, Clerk Frank Wood and to many of the members of families of former long-time police officers: Mrs. Mary Andrews, widow of Chief L. Allan Andrews; William Radack, son of Chief Felix "Pop" Radack; Mrs. Doris Connors, widow of Officer and Acting Chief Jack Connors; Mrs. Howard Towle, daughter of Sergeant Byron Bullock; Mrs. Arthur B. Collins, daughter of Officer Fred Lear; Mrs. Alex Backry and Major Michael S. Backry of the Essex County Sheriff's ' Department, widow and son of Officer Alex Backry; Francis Jess James, son of Officer George James; Sergeant David Towle, North Shore Community College Police, grandson of Byron Bullock and a former Manchester police officer; former Police Officers Craig McCoy and Al Powers; former Sergeants Bill Hurley and Jim Mulvey; Dog Officer John Saco; John C. Burke, retired Metropolitan Editor of The Boston Globe; John J. Coen, son of former Motorcycle Officer Joseph M. Coen; Gloucester Police Officer and department Historian Larry Ingersoll; Meredith Fine, Editor Gloucester Daily Times; and, finally, to Dan and David Slade without whose kind permission to access historic issues of The Manchester Cricket dating back to the 1860's, this paper could not have been written. — G.A. Jr.

FIRST FULL-TIME CHIEF

Thomas O.D. Urquhart Takes Reins as Department Is Established in 1897

By the end of the nineteenth century, Manchester was well on its way to becoming one of the most sought-after summer communities in the Commonwealth. Seasonal homes, many of sizable proportions, were being built everywhere. The Essex County Club and the Manchester Yacht Club were in full swing. In a few years, the town's popularity would give rise to the construction of the Masconomo House, a more than 100-room hotel. Indeed, residence in the community was so prized, that it became the seasonal site of many foreign embassies and consuls. Year-round population, too, was increasing, and by 1900 would reach a record 2,522 persons.

As the number of people grew, so did the need for law and order. In Colonial times, public morals and public safety were often considered more important than personal liberty.

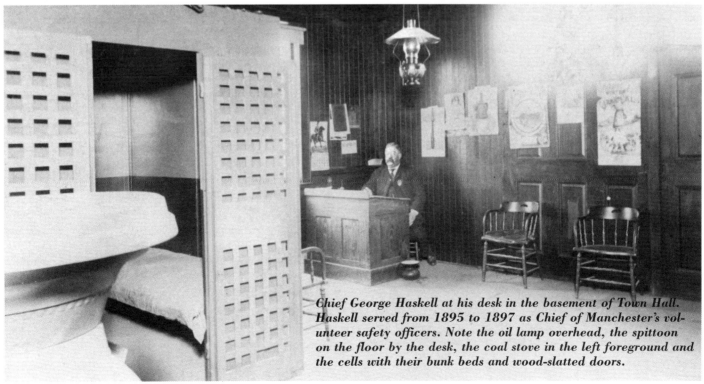

Chief George Haskell at his desk in the basement of Town Hall. Haskell served from 1895 to 1897 as Chief of Manchester's volunteer safety officers. Note the oil lamp overhead, the spittoon on the floor by the desk, the coal stove in the left foreground and the cells with their bunk beds and wood-slatted doors.

Indeed, as the Reverend D.F. Lamson points out in his History of Manchester, 1645-1895, "our fathers believed in good manners and self-restraint, and found them an excellent schooling and conducive to public comfort, respectability and safety." But even at the end of the nineteenth century times were changing and like today, personal liberty was playing a more important role in peoples' lives. Early rules and regulations in town prohibited smoking in public, especially near barns used for the storage of hay; playing ball within 70 yards of public buildings and dwellings; discharging guns or pistols within one mile of the "compact part of town;" driving carts and carriages faster than "a foot pace or common walk;" and behaving in a rude or disorderly manner, using indecent or profane language, or vandalizing fences or buildings.

Ever the preacher, Dr. Lamson declared "we may smile at such 'paternal' government, but we might be better off if we had a little more of it. It is possible that in some particulars, our fathers were sometimes over-governed. But the children are now making up for it by not being governed at all." Although this was written in 1895, there are many today who would agree with the sentiment wholeheartedly. After all, Dr. Lamson continued, "the most singular thing about these old By-Laws is that they were made to be enforced and not simply to adorn the records."

To provide for law enforcement, as early as 1864, the Board of Selectmen named 20 leading members of the community, each a volunteer, to serve as "Policemen" to enforce local By-Laws as well as the laws of the Commonwealth within the boundaries of the town. The list indicates what most bothered the good citizens of the day.

All persons were on notice "to take cognizance of all violations of the laws, respecting the observance of the Sabbath, and the disturbance of public meetings on that or other days,—respecting the use of profane and obscene language, of any loud or boisterous noises in any of the public streets or highways of the Town,—respecting the obstruction of public travel by persons standing in large numbers at the corners of streets and on the sidewalks,—respecting drunkenness, gaming, quarreling and fighting, and the assembling of disorderly persons in the nighttime, in any of the streets, highways or other public places, and respecting all other disorderly conduct which may tend to disturb the peace and order of the Town."

Residents "aggrieved or annoyed" were asked to "give immediate information" to the Board of Police. Dated March 24, 1864, the notice was signed "George A. Brown, Chief of Police."

By 1895, George Haskell was Chief (Brown had been followed by J.P. Carter) and the Police Station was located in the basement of Town Hall. There, at a slant-top desk with a spittoon on the floor beside it, sat Chief Haskell. Also in the room were wooden chairs, a kerosene lamp overhead, a pot-bellied stove and a block of cells with a bed bunk and slatted wood doors. In 1894, the fire department moved to new quarters on School Street and the small building on the Common which had once housed Seaside 1, the horse-drawn steam pumper, was assigned to the Police Department. It was to be its home for the next 76 years.

On March 31, 1897, the Board of Selectmen decided it was time to establish a full-time police department to provide professional protection for life and property.

Thomas O.D. (Oliver Drinkwater) Urquhart was appointed Chief with a salary of $2 a day. A native of Gloucester and a two-year veteran of the Gloucester Police Department, Urquhart was, according to The Cricket announcement, "highly recommended as an officer and a gentlemen." He moved his family to Manchester and began work on April 11, 1897.

Manchester's first full-time Chief of Police was Thomas Oliver Drinkwater Urquhart. A former Gloucester police officer, Urquhart was paid $2 per day. The Chief was widely known and respected for his prowess and persistence as an investigator.

His duties as described by Selectmen were to serve as "Keeper of the Lockup…to have the care of tramps [vagrants]…to provide police protection at all Public Entertainments in the Town Hall [and] to enforce the Town By-Laws." He was authorized "to carry a revolver and billy [club] while on duty." Equally important, Selectmen appointed Manchester resident Leonard Andrews as the town's first, full-time patrolman. He was assisted by Reserve Officers George E. Hildreth and Clarence W. Morgan.

(In 1904, three additional permanent officers were appointed: Jacob W. Lee, Thomas Sheehan and Robert Stoops. Charles Lucas served as a Reserve patrolman. Later appointments included Byron L. Bullock, 1909; L.N. Cook, 1912; John P. Connors and L. Allen Andrews, 1930. Sergeant Daniel N. MacEachern, Officer Fred Lear and Officer George James served with this second group.)

A man of enormous physical presence (he weighed some 265 pounds and stood over six foot, three inches tall), Chief Urquhart was honest, principled, hardworking and imaginative. One of his first tasks was to equip the new Police Station with a half dozen or so cells which he acquired from the Naval Prison at Portsmouth, New Hampshire. With wide bands of latticed steel on their doors, they were menacing looking, six by four foot cubicles with dark, uninviting interiors, just large to hold one individual. As you entered the building, there was a desk at the far end to the left. The cells were along the back or west wall facing the dam. Thus the officer on duty shared the space with whatever prisoners were incarcerated. Ultimately, to provide an office for the chief, a wall was built which enclosed the desk but this came much later. Heat during the winter months, was provided by a large pot-bellied stove, but the building was rarely comfortable even when steam radiators were installed.

KNIGHTS OF THE ROAD

Without unemployment insurance or a welfare system, vagrants, hobos or tramps were common at the turn of the last century. Mostly men, many middle-age, down on their luck, they wandered aimlessly from town to town, some picking up odd or seasonal jobs here and there, never staying in one place long, and often begging food at back doors from kind-hearted housewives or cooks at summer mansions. Known romantically as "Knights of the Road," they were rarely criminals and had a distinctive culture all their own. Always on the move, they walked, hitchhiked, or rode the rails in empty freight cars around the nation. Their songs, which today are an important and fascinating part of our folk heritage, describe their lives, their hopes, their dreams. They were often pictured in baggy and tattered clothing, carrying what few belongings they had in an colored handkerchief tied to a pole slung over their shoulder, and cooking their meals with an open fire using a old tin can as a pot. To some Americans of the time, frustrated by the worries of the work-a-day world, the life of a Knight of the Road was an expression of independence and of freedom from care and responsibility. But the reality was far less glamorous than the perception.

Manchester, perhaps because of its prosperity, seemed to be a particularly popular destination for tramps. Indeed, from 1894 through 1896, police logs show that an extraordinary yearly average of 464 homeless men were apparently happy to spend the night in the town lock-up. Released early, they would find their way to back doors nearby and there beg their breakfasts. With numbers like this, however, they soon became a nuisance and a concern grew for public safety.

Chief Urquhart, however, had an idea. Why not change the time of release to 11 a.m. when breakfast was over? Remarkably, it worked. The number of "tramps" noted in the department log dropped each year until 1903 when only 119 were recorded. As years passed, times changed and tramps and hobos became part of another era.

OLD FASHIONED SLEUTHING

Strangers stand out in a small town and when six arrived at the Manchester House early one day in November, 1901, as The Cricket reported, "they soon attracted the Chief's eagle eye."

Later that day, he received a circular from police in Dedham which announced that three men were wanted there for forgery. Urquhart checked the hotel register and, sure enough, two of the three names matched. "Scenting trouble ahead," The Cricket continued, "the Chief resorted to a little strategy and sent word to the two that they were wanted on the telephone at the police station. When they arrived, they were placed under arrest on a charge of forgery." They soon identified and described the third member of their party and Urquhart returned to the Manchester House. There he found the man who had registered under an assumed name. He, too, was brought to the station and arrested. The Chief then notified Dedham of their capture.

When Gloucester police called, according to The Cricket's report of the incident, "and said they had been looking all day for the men...the Chief had the satisfaction of [reporting] that [they] were already safely behind bars..." That night Dedham Police Inspector Donald arrived on the midnight train (there were no cruisers in 1901) and took two of them back with him, again on the train, the following morning. The third was freed for lack of evidence.

"The men came here ostensibly to canvas for a Chicago picture firm," The Cricket story concluded, "but they lit out the next morning. The Chief is certainly deserving of great credit for the quickness and neatness with which the round up was accomplished."

In 1902, Patrolman Leonard Andrews became the department's first Sergeant. Head of the "first family" of Manchester police officers, he was the father of Chief L. Allen Andrews and the grandfather of present-day Sergeant Neil Andrews.

A FIRST-CLASS INVESTIGATOR

A top-notch officer, Chief Urquhart possessed all the qualities of a first-class professional. As an investigator he was without peer. Take the example of the Means Case. Following the explosion of a tank of acetylene gas used for purposes of lighting, and the accompanying fire at the summer residence of James Means, it was ascertained that although a quantity of jewelry had been recovered, many valuable items were reported still missing. Suspected in the loss was a former coachman. A story which appeared in The Manchester Cricket on October 9, 1901, reported that "two weeks ago while the Chief was laboring on another case, he unearthed a quantity of old silver in a second hand store in Boston which he immediately recognized as coming from the Means fire."

With the assistance of Boston police, "a rigid search was made among the pawn shops which brought to light more property." From descriptions furnished to the Chief, suspicion at once focussed again on the coachman and enough evidence was compiled to justify issuing a warrant to search his Boston apartment. The results were inconclusive but during the process he was asked to help recover the valuables. He failed to do so and following a second visit with Inspectors Shields and Hart of the Boston Police Department, the coachman was arrested and taken to police headquarters where, The Cricket said, he admitted his guilt.

"At 3 p.m.," the story continued, "the Chief left headquarters with his man in a cab (horse-drawn) and arrived at Union [now North] Station. While he was paying the cabby, [his prisoner] broke away and [began to run]. Here started one of the liveliest sprints on record in which [the coachman] forgot to reckon with his host…Through the crowded depot and on to Causeway Street they sped. The Chief, although balancing the scales at 265 pounds, does know a thing or two about running…[in seconds] he overtook his man and before astonished onlookers, soon had him safely in irons and aboard the train, arriving here [Manchester] at 4:13 p.m." In court Monday, [the prisoner] pleaded not guilty, but was held in $1,500 bail. Unable to produce it, he was taken to jail in Salem.

FIRST CALL BOXES

An able investigator whose work with Officer and later Sergeant Andrews solved many a local crime, Urquhart also proposed a number of significant improvements which enabled his department to better serve the needs of the growing community. In 1901, Town Meeting voters, at his request, authorized the installation of a series of telephone call boxes thus establishing the town's first police communications system. Located strategically throughout the community, call boxes were used by officers on foot patrol to phone headquarters at regular intervals or in an emergency. The location and the time of the call were automatically recorded. Some 6,500 calls were made in the first year of the system's operation. A long distance telephone was also installed at headquarters. Prior to this, police officers crossed Union Street to use the phone at the store owned by Julius F. Rabardy.

With the support of both year-round and summer residents, at the Town Meeting in 1902, Chief Urquhart urged the purchase of a horse drawn ambulance. Many voters said they would be happy to contribute funds to get one. There was some talk about contracting for ambulance services, but the Chief thought the town should have one of its own. "You can't tell how soon any of us might be called to ride in one," he said. The sum of $650 was authorized to acquire a new Abbot-Downing ambulance to be kept in a stable subject to the order of the Chief of Police. It served the town until 1919 when it was replaced by a motorized vehicle.

THE DARK SHADOW OF POLITICS

In 1900, Chief Urquhart resigned "to accept a more lucrative position at Charlestown State Prison." The town, however, wouldn't hear of it. Two petitions were circulated urging him to stay. Influential residents pleaded that he change his mind. Finally, he did and, with an increase in salary, served the town for another three years.

But on March 4, 1903, Urquhart wrote to the Board of Selectmen that he meant to resign in earnest effective April 1. Unfortunately, politics were blamed for forcing an effective, unbiased, energetic Chief of Police to move on. As The Cricket explained: "The resignation of the Chief was not unexpected when the results of the election [were announced]…two new members of the board were elected to dethrone him…Like all active officials in this capacity, he has called down the venom of certain people…the trouble had its birth some five years ago when a wholesale arrest was made…" A letter also printed in The Cricket in March, 1903 elaborated: "…here is a man," it declared, "who because he did what he was sworn to do, gained the dislike of a certain [faction] which is found in every community…

"…his recent activity in suppressing the liquor element in Manchester [is partially responsible]. [Then, too,] some five years ago, he [caught] nine or 10 young fellows, belonging to prominent families in town, playing poker. He prosecuted them as he should have done, but from that time [on] efforts [began] for his removal. Last year the townspeople held a meeting and insisted that the liquor laws be enforced. [They were] to the discomfort of several of the…politicians in town. This performance of his duty was his curfew…the liquor elements linked forces with the followers of the gamblers and elected two selectmen who promised to oust the Chief. Rather than be ousted, [he] resigned."

Many distinguished summer residents, it was reported, were upset, but little could be done. Urquhart left Manchester to become Chief of Police first in South Framingham and then in Arlington where he served a total of 25 years. There he was responsible for the installation of the first system of remotely controlled traffic lights. Operating in sequence, they were designed to maintain an even and continuous flow of vehicles.

Chief Urquhart's replacement as Chief was Samuel Sumner Peabody, 47 years old, of Middleton. Formerly in the hay and grain business, he was well thought of but had no police experience. His son, Allan, was a resident of Manchester. Both men, however, were to make their mark in law enforcement.

THE MISSING CAKES
Police Work in the 1890's Seemed Less Violent Than It Is Today; A Smaller World

Police work at the end of the last century involved itself with issues quite different from today. In the 1890's and early 1900's, almost every issue of The Manchester Cricket reported one or more runaway horses, most attached to a wagon, and many causing injury not only to the animal involved but to pedestrians as well. There were petty thefts from houses such as one in January, 1894 at the railroad gatetender's cottage at Babcock Crossing. It was broken into and "two valuable razors and a Baldwin apple" stolen. But although it was reported to police, it took a wily landlady to solve the case of the missing cakes.

An excellent cook, she regularly baked cakes which were hugely popular with her boarders. One day, however, she noticed they seemed to be disappearing at a faster rate than normal. Sensing that one of her tenants might be guilty of appropriating more than his share, she seasoned the tops of the next batch with snuff, and, as The Cricket reported, "sat up to await developments." They were not long in coming. "All had retired to rest, but soon from one room came the sounds of fearful sneezing. The door was opened and the party then and there was obliged to plead guilty to the crime."

FOR SALE: 3 POLLOCK

In 1892, according to a story in <u>The Cricket</u>, police "had a queer lodger at the station on Monday night. He was rather a rough-looking customer, having on a pair of rubber boots and overshoes to protect them. He had a basket on his arm containing three pollock which he was trying to sell. He said he had just arrived from George's [George's Bank, an off-shore fishing ground] and was going to Boston where he could get a better price for the fish. In the morning, he started out again calling from house to house to sell the [pollock] but without success. He was last seen going through West Manchester towards the Hub. He was evidently ," <u>The Cricket</u> concluded, "a trifle out of plumb!"

CATCH ME IF YOU CAN!

Liquor also was a major factor leading to arrests, and dealing with its victims often had its lighthearted moments. During the 1880's when the town's police force was composed of volunteers, it was led by Captain J B. Carter. According to a story in <u>The Cricket</u>, "two of our businessmen are to run for police chief next year in opposition to Captain Carter, being encouraged in their decision by their brilliant experience in handling a prisoner a few evenings since. These two gentlemen," <u>The Cricket</u> continued, "were standing in front of Captain Carter's store when along came Officer [Edward] Lendall having in charge three drunken prisoners on the way to the police station [then located in the basement of Town Hall]. Having his hands full, Mr. Lendall asked the two [would-be] officers if they would be kind enough to escort the third prisoner to the station for him. The readily agreed…one gentleman took his left arm, the other his right. They had proceeded but a few steps when the prisoner…suddenly made up his mind to go the other way which he [did] in an exceedingly lively manner leaving his escorts clinging hopelessly…to a coat and vest which their [man] had neatly slipped out of and left for them to remember him by. The last seen of him, he was running up the street like a deer, calling back over his shoulder, 'Catch me if you can!'"

A CITIZEN MUST ASSIST

In those days as well, it was the duty of any citizen to provide assistance to a police officer if the officer sought it. Take the case in 1897 of Manchester Police Officer Clarence Morgan who arrested a local resident for drunkenness. A struggle ensued on the street and Mr. Morgan asked a passer-by to help him subdue his prisoner. The man refused and after Officer Morgan had finally landed his charge at the station single-handed, Chief Thomas O.D. Urquhart ordered the arrest of the citizen who failed to come to Morgan's aid. The next day in court, the prisoner was sentenced to two months. Thanks to the Chief's pleas for leniency, the citizen was fined a nominal $1 but the judge made it quite clear that next time a police officer seeks help, the law requires citizens to respond.

OF CURFEWS & HURDY-GURDYS

One of the social highlights of the early 1900's were regularly scheduled dances at Town Hall. Usually on Saturday nights, they drew crowds of people young and old. At times, however, attendees were somewhat too young, and at Town Meeting in 1901, it was proposed that a curfew be established to keep youngsters from six to 10 years old at home where they should be instead of gawking at their elders on the dance floor. Was a curfew a good idea the Chief was asked? Perhaps, he said. But a general lack of enthusiasm throughout the audience, indicated that the responsibility for controlling the nocturnal activities of the town's youngsters belonged to their parents and not to the Police Department. The motion to establish a curfew was defeated.

There was also a proposal to ask the Police Department to prohibit the early morning arrival of hurdy-gurdys (a instrument played by street musicians with a crank, often called a barrel organ). Summer residents especially had complained that the sound awoke them "before it was time to get up." But wiser heads prevailed, declaring that the coming of hurdy-gurdys to town was a harbinger of summer and thus should be looked upon with some benevolence. This motion, too, failed to receive the necessary majority.

'SCORCHERS' A MENACE

The Auto Car Arrives: a Unique Speed Trap Is Invented in Manchester in 1907

The motor car first made its appearance in France as early as 1770 when Nichols Cugnot invented a three-wheel, steam-powered vehicle which just managed to travel short distances at two and one-half miles per hour. Steam continued to be the primary propellant until the internal combustion engine was patented by Gottlieb Daimler in Germany in 1886. The first motorized vehicles manufactured for sale in the United States were built by the Duryea Motor Wagon Company in 1895 and from that moment on the industry never looked back. The age of the automobile had arrived.

In the first decade of the 20th century, automobile manufacturing increased a dramatic 3,500 percent with comparable increases in the demand for steel, alloys, glass, rubber and petroleum products. Fuel oil production rose from 300 million gallons to 1.7 billion gallons. Roads paved with asphalt and concrete grew in mileage from 161,000 in 1905 to 521,000 in 1925. Passenger car registrations in 1900 numbered 8,000. By 1913, they reached 1,258,062. That year, too, using an assembly line, Henry Ford invented "continuous flow production" which made it possible to provide cars at a price which most Americans could afford and still turn a handsome profit. By 1930, auto registrations throughout the U.S. had reached an extraordinary 26,545,281.

STUTZ AND PACKARDS

Car company products included Stutz motors cars, Reo motor cars, the Franklin, Pierce-Arrows, Packards, F.B. Stearns motor cars, Nash motor cars, Buicks, LaSalles, Cadillacs, and, of course, Fords and Chevrolets. The first automobiles were open-bodied vehicles and driver and passengers dressed accordingly to protect themselves from road debris (surfaces were still primarily unpaved) and the weather. A hat or cap, goggles and a long flowing cotton or linen garment known as a "duster" were commonly worn by every occupant. About 1910, closed vehicles began to appear which were hugely popular and provided significantly greater comfort.

Since their first introduction at the turn of the century, departments of police everywhere, with Manchester no exception, have been interested and involved with the automobile and how it affects public safety. At risk with a new vehicle which could propel itself up to 60 miles per hour, were pedestrians, horses and carriages, roadside structures, and the occupants of the autos themselves as well as other engine-driven vehicles which might come into contact with them.

In these early days, people were used to moving a slower pace (except for travel by rail). On foot, they walked at two to three miles per hour; by carriage, they travelled from five to 10 miles per hour; and with a bicycle they averaged somewhere in between. That created a level of alertness which was far below that needed to cope with a car even traveling at 20 miles per hour. Drivers of these new vehicles, too, were handicapped for they were used to more gentle speeds, and steering wheels and brakes, often not reliable mechanically, took some getting used to.

In 1901, voters at a Manchester Town Meeting approved a By-law which prohibited any vehicle from exceeding a rate of 10 miles per hour "within three-fourths of a mile of the Town Common." In court on May 5 of that year was an out-of-town resident who had been charged by Police Chief Thomas Urquhart for driving his automobile on Central Street faster than the law allowed. Both sides presented witnesses. Supporting the Chief's contention were the owner and operator of Swett's Livery Stable at the corner of Pine and Bennett Streets who saw the vehicle approaching town, and L.W. Floyd, whose place of business was opposite the Common itself. Floyd testified that he would "set the speed at 30 miles an hour." Other witnesses testified in favor of the defendant's contention that his vehicle, bound for Singing Beach, could not possibly reach a speed of 20 miles per hour and at the time was travelling only four to five miles an hour as it passed the Congregational Church. It was one man's word against another's. Judge Safford, deciding that the issue was in doubt, dismissed the case.

INFERNAL MACHINES

Meanwhile, here and in other cities and towns around the nation, the number of autos was increasing annually, as was the record of complaints about the "infernal machines" whose speed and recklessness was angering citizens and disturbing public peace. "Scorchers" they were called, and Chief Samuel S. Peabody of the Manchester Police Department, undoubtedly frustrated himself by many court experiences similar to the one described above, decided that something should be done to provide clear evidence that a vehicle was exceeding the town's speed limits.

On the job for just two years, the Chief in 1907 turned to his mechanically-minded son, Allan S. Peabody, then caretaker at the estate of Philip Dexter. Soon Allan had devised an ingenious system. It consisted of two sentry boxes designed to look like dead tree trunks, located exactly one mile apart. Within each box was a Manchester police officer equipped with a stop watch and a telephone. (The necessary wires were run underground between boxes.)

When a vehicle which the first officer suspected might be speeding passed his observation point, he started his stop watch and phoned his partner with a description of the car and its license number. The second officer immediately synchronized his watch which he then stopped on the second the unsuspecting driver passed his station. Quickly consulting a rate, time and distance table, he determined whether the law had been broken. If it had, the "scorcher" was stopped by a third constable, also in touch by telephone, posted somewhat

Chief Samuel S. Peabody served from 1903 to 1910. He and his son Allan invented a timed speed trap which became famous throughout the East and was so effective that it was adopted by the City of New York in 1905.

further on. Thus was the "speed trap," so familiar to us today, born in Manchester, Massachusetts.

"You can get some idea of the work were are obliged to do," said Chief Peabody, "when I tell you [that] during the months of July and August there was not a Sunday afternoon that we did not time more than 1,000 cars." (Week-end driving was, indeed, a popular pastime!) Speed traps were so successful that two were established in Manchester. One was on Bridge Street opposite Winthrop Farm in West Manchester. The other was in the so-called "cove" section on Summer Street on the Magnolia side of town. The problem of 'scorchers' was finally under control.

NEW YORK INTERESTED

One of the many public officials who were impressed with Chief Peabody's apparently fool-proof system of trapping speeding motorists was William McAdoo, Police Commissioner of the City of New York who, at the time, was vacationing at Magnolia. Indeed, Commissioner McAdoo was so interested in learning more about how he might transfer the technology to his own community that he invited Allan Peabody to meet with him in New York. On September 16, 1905, Allan left Boston on the midnight train, arriving at Pennsylvania Station the following morning. Reported a New York City newspaper: "Allan S. Peabody, the Massachusetts constable who traps scorching automobilists, is here to have fun with speed maniacs. It would be impossible to imagine anyone less like a constable than this quiet, self-reliant, wide awake, young gentleman.

"'I can't give you all the details we use in Manchester,' said Mr. Peabody, 'for that might interfere with Mr. McAdoo's plans. I am not sure it will be used here but I am going to look over the ground as soon as it stops raining. I have simply combined several things long in common use and made a way of determining with absolute certainty just how

Manchester police on parade around 1914. From left, Sergeant Leonard Andrews; Officer Thomas Sheehan, Officer (later Sergeant) Byron Bullock; Officer Jacob Lee (two stripes) and Officer Robert Stoops. Leading the contingent is Chief William H. Sullivan who served from 1909 to 1910 and from 1913 to 1923. Over Officer Sheehan's left shoulder is a Manchester Veteran of the Grand Army of the Republic who served in the Civil War.

fast a car is running. The results are so accurate that it is impossible to dispute them. We have found up in Manchester that the [inevitability] of being caught and fined if they break the law has cured all of our automobilists of the wild speeding habit. I guess it will cure New York scorchers, too.'"

Allan stayed in New York City for three weeks, a guest of Commissioner McAdoo at the Astor Hotel. Trial runs of the system on upper Broadway were a huge success. Instead of the "woodchuck" arrangement, however, using artificial tree trunks to hide police officers, McAdoo chose to erect two booths with their purpose clearly marked upon them. Similar "speed traps" were installed at Staten Island and at Coney Island Boulevard and The Manchester Cricket reported that Allan Peabody was expecting another invitation to visit the city to expand the system further. Chicago had also expressed interest.

140 WARNINGS ISSUED

According to an article in Yankee Magazine by Rufus Jarman, New York City police officials were elated. Said one: "Last month, 3,200 automobiles passed this station [upper Broadway]. We issued 140 warnings, but we did not make an arrest. The warnings are enough. Offenders do not care to monkey a second time with this buzz saw." Collier's Weekly had added praise for Allan's invention and what it had helped to accomplish. "The number of machines has increased by the thousands in the past three or four years," it wrote, "while the number of arrests or disasters has been steadily reduced." Today, the concept of speed traps, now using sophisticated radar devices, is used throughout the world. And to think it all began in Manchester!

A DAPPER THIEF
'North Shore Raffles' Invades Publisher's Home in 1905; Steals Jewels, Money

Boston publisher James T. Field, one-time editor of Atlantic Monthly magazine and founder of Ticknor & Field, owners of the Old Corner Book Store, was a leader in the community of distinguished artists and writers who owned summer homes in Manchester. In 1874, he and his wife Annie, celebrated in her own right as one of Boston's most gracious and witty hostesses, built their cottage on Thunderbolt Hill where they spent many happy seasons.

In 1905, however, according to a story in Hearst's Record American, a bold and dapper second-story man, referred to colloquially by the newspaper as a "North Shore Raffles" (from the old French, meaning the act of snatching) invaded the sanctity of the Fields' house and nearly was able to help himself to anything he wanted.

It was shortly after 5 p.m. on a warm summer afternoon, Mrs. Fields told the paper. "The first [we knew] of his presence was when he opened the door of a room on the second floor which was occupied by a member of the household. [She] asked, 'Who is there?' The man played his part well. With no hesitancy he said, 'I am looking for a relative by the name of____who lives in a house near here, situated as this is upon a high hill and I thought this was his residence. He is my cousin and I took the liberty of walking in and looking for his family, finding that bell did not ring and that the outer door was unfastened.'

"I should say," Mrs. Fields explained, "that the robber or whatever he may be, was passably well-dressed, easy in manner, and that he carried [out] his part of the performance better than even an expert thief. He was certainly intelligent though I should not say intellectual. We [escorted] him downstairs...showed him to the door and watched his retreat down the winding gravel walk to the street [Summer Street] below. When we tried the doorbell afterwards, we found it in good order."

HE LOOKED LIKE A GUEST

If he had failed in his mission at the Fields', however, he was successful a half hour later when he entered the home of William Hooper some miles away stealing both jewels and money. While the robbery was taking place, Hooper was playing tennis on a court nearby. Walter Denegre, a next door neighbor, told the Record American that he "saw a man saunter up the walk and enter the door [of the house]." He supposed he was a guest.

Chief of Police Samuel S. Peabody, the Boston paper continued, suspects that the "Raffles" in question was a man recently released from State Prison where he served time for a number of thefts. The Chief was reported to have a photograph of the young man acquired from a woman in Gloucester at whose house he was a boarder. Inspector Sullivan of the Gloucester Police Department also told Chief Peabody that a man answering the same description was in Gloucester the day before the robbery took place in Manchester. With the photo, Chief Peabody expressed optimism that he would able to "trace the thief through pawn shops [in the region] and eventually succeed in arresting him".

If Mrs. Fields had notified Manchester police immediately after discovering the man in her house, it is likely that the robbery at the Hooper's could have been prevented.

PRESIDENTS TAFT, WILSON

Manchester Police Provide Security for Chief Executives in 1912 and 1918

To escape the heat and humidity of the nation's capitol, Presidents William Howard Taft and later Woodrow Wilson chose Boston's North Shore as a place to settle for the summer. From 1909, just after he was elected, until 1912, President Taft, his wife Nellie and their three children, summered in Beverly.

For pleasure and relaxation, despite his size and girth, one of Taft's favorite pastimes was the game of golf and while on vacation he would play four to five mornings a week either at Myopia or at Manchester's Essex County Club often with his long-time friend John Hays Hammond of Gloucester. Taft actually became an Honorary Member of Essex and Locker number 11 was reserved in his name. For four years, while his son, future U.S. Senator Robert Taft, and his daughter, Helen, made use of the tennis courts, the President and his party enjoyed the greens and fairways.

In August, 1918, President and Mrs. Wilson came by train to Magnolia and thence by car to Manchester where, thanks to the generosity of Mr. and Mrs. Thomas Jefferson Coolidge, for two weeks they occupied the Coolidge mansion overlooking the sea at Coolidge Point which was known as the Marble Palace. Wilson, too, played golf at the Essex County Club with his friend, aide and counselor, Colonel E. M. House who regularly summered nearby in Gloucester.

There were, to be sure, Secret Service agents and even a handful of the U.S. Army camped in tents nearby, providing personal protection for both Presidents. But members of the Manchester Police Department were also asked help. Thus it was that Chief Thomas Urquhart, Sergeant Leonard Andrews and Officers Jacob Lee, Thomas Sheehan and Robert Stoops, were members of security detachments detailed to protect President Taft. A half dozen years later, President Wilson could also count on the services of Sergeant Byron L. Bullock and Officer L. N. Cook.

AN UNUSUAL ARREST

German Consul Is Apprehended on Singing Beach in 1918 as U.S. Enters WW I

One of the most extraordinary arrests in the history of the Manchester Police Department occurred in July, 1918. With the United States then at war with Germany, Chief William H. Sullivan was asked by the U.S. Department of Justice and the Secret Service to maintain under surveillance a former summer resident, then living in Manchester year-round.

He was Oswald Kunhardt, a German citizen and former Consul-General for Germany and Austria in Boston, who was considered an enemy alien, according to a news story in The Manchester Cricket which appeared on July 27, 1918.

Kunhardt, obviously without a hint of what was to take place on that summer afternoon, boarded the 3:20 p.m. train from Boston where he represented Berlin Analine Works, a New York corporation with offices at 124 Pearl Street. When he arrived in Manchester, it being sultry weather, like many others he went directly to Singing Beach. There the Chief found him in the company of two "ladies of the summer colony and a gentleman friend." Calling him aside, Sullivan informed him that he was wanted by the Department of Justice. He was taken by car first to the police station and then to his "boarding place [with] a private family on School Street." There, presumably he changed his clothing and was driven to Boston while, The Cricket reported, "two Secret Service men were left to search his rooms and effects."

Meanwhile, other members of the Secret Service were busy investigating "two prominent summer estates" and a house in the village [of Manchester] where two women boarders had also been under surveillance. Although little information was made available, The Cricket learned that "certain pieces of signaling apparatus" were discovered "as well as valuable papers."

Kunhardt, The Cricket continued, "is of [a] most prepossessing appearance and would readily pass as an American." Forty-two years old, he had resided in the U.S. for some 19 years but had shown little interest in becoming a U.S. citizen or in returning to Germany. Since the start of hostilities, The Cricket continued, "certain [activities] aroused suspicion and a close watch [was kept] on all of his actions." Indeed, Chief Sullivan spent "days and nights" on the case which meant he could take little part in other police activities.

When Kunhardt arrived in Boston, he was turned over to Federal authorities and taken to Cambridge where he spent the night in jail. No bail was allowed. He was to be detained there until orders were received from Washington possibly for his internment in a camp for enemy aliens or his release.

Manchester Police Station in 1919. Note the bulletin board and poster which advertises the motion picture "Out of Luck" starring Dorothy Gish who, with her sister Lillian, was one of the heart-throbs of the day. Sheldon's Market is in the building at right. At left are the coal sheds of Samuel Knight Coal & Lumber Company.

DREADED TELEGRAM
World War I Touches Home as Police Chief Sullivan Delivers the Sad News

The responsibilities of a police officer extend in many directions and one of the most heart-rending during the First World War, was notifying a family that a husband, son, brother or father had been killed or was missing in action.

Such was the news, always terse and unflinchingly to the point, that in April, 1918, Chief William H. Sullivan delivered in the form of a telegram from the War Department to Mrs. Virginia Perry of Manchester. "Corporal Frank B. Amaral," it read, "died April 15 of wounds received in action." It is not difficult to imagine the emotion and the grief experienced, of course, by the recipient of such sad news, but also by the bearer who may well have known Mrs. Perry personally and, as Sullivan was Chief of the department from 1913 to 1923, may also have been acquainted with Frank Amaral himself. Whatever the case, such assignments were not easy.

Born in Gloucester and orphaned at an early age, Amaral was brought up by Mrs. Perry, according to <u>The Manchester Cricket</u>. For six years, he was an employee of summer resident William Hooper whose estate was located in West Manchester. He then joined the United States Army seeing immediate service on the Mexican Border. Later, he was among the first "dough-boys" to be sent to France with Company H of the 104th Regiment.

Corporal Amaral, who was 24 years old at the time of his death, was later awarded the Croix de Guerre by the Government of France. The citation read: "For conspicuous coolness and courage in the direction of his squad under heavy fire. He inspired his men until he was killed in action on April 13, 1918." Amaral was Manchester's first casualty of the Great War. The local American Legion Post is named in his memory.

1918 FLU EPIDEMIC
Sergeant 'Bunk' Bullock and Other Brave Police Officers Sacrifice Life at Home

Byron "Bunk" Bullock, a member of the Manchester Police Department from 1910 until the 1940's, was the town's first motorcycle patrolman. Fellow officers at the time were William H. Sullivan, Chief, Jake Lee, Leon Andrews, the department's first Sergeant, and Tom Sheehan. In 1935, Sheehan retired after 33 years of service during which he provided personal security for two Presidents, William Howard Taft and Woodrow Wilson while on their vacations in Manchester. Sergeant Andrews retired in 1933. Bullock was then appointed Sergeant.

"I thought my father was the handsomest man alive," recalls his daughter, Mrs. Janet Bullock Towle. "On Sundays in the early days the traffic here was so heavy, he was on his motorcycle from 8 a.m. to 8 p.m. And I remember that during the influenza epidemic in 1918, he was gone for several weeks. We could only wave to him out the window. He was on the ambulance bringing people down to Horticultural Hall which was set up as a contagious disease center. I remember he told all of us that we had to behave to set an example for other children.

"Once, after I was older, a summer resident of Gale's Point complained that my father had stopped her for speeding on Craft's Hill. 'I think he would arrest his own Mother!,' she exclaimed. But she did admit that although he was strict, he was also fair. And he kept that motorcycle shining. I earned a nickel if I polished the spokes. It was an Indian like most of them in those days."

In 1919, Bullock was granted a six-month leave of absence to join United Shoe Machinery Company in Beverly. At the time, his duties as a motorcycle patrolman were taken over by 20-year-old Manchester police officer Joseph M. Coen. A veteran of World War I and a charter member of the Amaral-Bailey American Legion Post, Coen had served in the U.S. Army as a motorcycle messenger on the Western Front in France. A policeman for one year, he later became a Vice President of Borden Foods in Dallas, Texas.

Mrs. Towle had other wonderful memories of her youth. "We lived above my grandfather's bakery on Washington Street,' she said, "and one month after my father joined the police force, the bakery burned and we were forced to move out. The house was one of the first in Manchester to have electricity and I can remember before it arrived we used to study with kerosene lamps. Back then, too, there were dirt roads and carts were used to water the streets when it was dry to keep down the dust.

CONTINUING TRADITION

Byron Bullock's grandson, David Towle, continuing family tradition, served as a Manchester Police Officer himself for some 15 years. A 1965 graduate of Manchester High School, David became a Reserve Officer in 1972 and a permanent Patrolman in 1975. Although he passed the Civil Service exam with ease, David said he was one-quarter of a pound underweight when it came to meeting the physical standards required. The examining officer, David reported, "said that she was sure that by the time I was on the job I would have gained that one-quarter pound and she passed me!"

Those were lean times for the town financially and Towle had to pay not only for his uniform but for his own gun. "My first night on duty,' he recalled, "the other officer said 'I'll be out in Car 3' and there I was, alone at the desk with no conception of what to do. Twenty minutes later there was an accident on Route 128. You learn fast."

In 1981, David graduated from the State Police Academy in Topsfield and in those days had to prosecute each of his own arrest cases. This is done today by a District Attorney. "Again," he said, "it was on the job training. I had a pretty good conviction record." He also helped the department get new radios in the 1980's. "With the old ones," he said, "we often had to leave the scene of an accident to get back in range so we could call for an ambulance." Earlier in his career, he was finally issued an old 38 caliber Police Positive Special revolver. "I traced its original ownership," he said, "back to my grandfather, Byron Bullock." With that ancient lineage, however sentimental, it was not the weapon he wanted to carry and depend upon.

David left the department in January, 1986 to become a Security Officer at Hammond Castle Museum. In 1993, he joined Manchester police once again serving as a Reserve Officer until 1998. Today, he is a Sergeant and member of the police detachment at North Shore Community College with campuses in Beverly, Danvers and Lynn.

Sergeant Byron "Bunk" Bullock heads back to the Police Station on his motorcycle in the early 1930's. This photo of Central Street taken by Sergeant Bullock's daughter, Mrs. Howard B. Towle, shows the Pulsifer Building with the dry goods store owned by the Misses Haraden; Bullock's Market; the Manchester Trust Company; the homes of Dr. and Mrs. Charles Herrick and Miss Ethel Hooper (where Fleet Bank now stands) and the Library beyond.

'DIRTY DANCING'

Police Act in 1923 as Jazz Age Youngsters Pick Up on the Fast Fads of the Era

Public morality as well as public safety was the responsibility of the Police Department as indicated by this story which appeared in The Manchester Cricket in August, 1923.

"A near roughhouse was narrowly averted at Town Hall Wednesday during a dance by the timely arrival of Chief of Police [William H.] Sullivan. Special Officer Chester Cook was on duty in the hall with orders to stop any of the newer dances that he might deem immodest. Late in the evening he observed a couple dancing in a way that did not meet with his approval and, quietly stepping to the young man's side, he requested him to stop, which request he complied with but followed it up with questioning the officer what it all meant [and so forth]. Officer Cook declined to answer or enter into any argument beyond telling the young man that he knew what it was for, which did not seem to satisfy him and he followed it up [whereupon] the officer started to remove him from the hall on the charge of using profane language, which he resisted quite strenuously. Quite a number of the young men present seemed to side with the offender and things were getting quite exciting as it began to get a little warm for the officer. At this critical moment the Chief happened in and the crowd assumed a threatening attitude and hurled some very uncomplimentary language at him. The Chief made a movement to draw his club and announced that he would lay out the first man that touched him. This had a cooling effect on the belligerents who beat a hasty retreat, falling all over themselves in a scramble to reach a place of safety.

"The offender was taken to the Police Station and given a little fatherly advice and permitted to go but subsequently entered the hall again and on order of the Chief, Officer Cook ordered him from the hall again which ended the unfortunate affair.

"Chief Sullivan wishes it understood that Bunny Hugs, Turkey Trots and similar modern fancy dancing that is popular in some places at this time, will not be tolerated in Manchester and the sooner those who wish to indulge in them realize it the better for all concerned."

Although the new dances of the Roaring Twenties shocked older generations, they soon became an accepted part of the social scene. It was an era of prosperity and a new freedom. Its role models came from Hollywood and its symbol was the "flapper" who with bobbed hair, painted face, cigarette and short skirt, gaily waved good-bye to earlier conventions.

RUMRUNNERS

Cases of Illegal Liquor Are Landed at Dana's Beach During the 1930's

Until the 27-year reign of Chief L. Allan Andrews (1942-1968), no chief of police had served the Town of Manchester longer than George R. Dean. A man "popular with all classes," as The Manchester Cricket put it, Dean had been a long-time member of the Board of Selectmen serving in 1913, in 1914 and again from 1917 to 1921.

First appointed Chief in May, 1923, Dean served until 1931. He was then named Superintendent of Streets. A for-

mer construction supervisor, he had earlier directed the building of a six-mile section of the Newburyport Turnpike in Topsfield. In 1933, he was reappointed Chief of Police and retired in January, 1942. Not a native of Manchester, Dean was born in 1878, graduated from Boston English High School and attended Boston University, moving here in 1905. During World War II, Dean also served as Chairman of the local office of Civil Defense. After his retirement, he joined the U.S. Army and, with the rank of Lieutenant, provided security for defense plants in Hartford, Connecticut. He died in August, 1947.

His 19-year tenure as Chief of the Manchester Police Department, saw a significant rise in the use of the automobile and thus in auto-related accidents and auto thefts. It also coincided with the beginnings of the Second World War which meant police and Civil Defense enforcement of nighttime blackouts, fuel, tire and food rationing, and preparation for possible bombing raids. But it is safe to say that no activity had a greater impact on police work in his time—and during the tenure of Chief William H. Sullivan (1913-1923)—than did what became known infamously as "prohibition."

Thanks primarily to nation-wide lobbying efforts by the Anti-Saloon League, on 18 December 1917, Congress passed and sent to the states for ratification, an amendment to the Constitution which prohibited the manufacture, sale, or transportation of alcoholic beverages (any liquor with an alcohol level of more than one-half of one percent). The 18th amendment was declared ratified on 29 January, 1919 and went in to effect on 16 January, 1920. It was finally repealed with the adoption of the 21st amendment to the Constitution, in 1933.

In the 14 years that prohibition was in effect, however, avoiding it became a full-time occupation for many. On one side were the "drys," committed to purging the nation of alcohol. On the other were the "wets", most of them ordinary people who felt that their right to chose whether or not could they have a cocktail in the evening before dinner was being abused. Many citizens made liquor at home. All it took was a little machinery, some alcohol (easy to acquire), and a bathtub.

Others, hundreds of thousands of them, depended for their supply upon bootleggers who bought liquor abroad and smuggled it into the country from Mexico, Canada and the French islands of St. Pierre and Miquelon just south of Newfoundland. A favorite way to get it to customers in New England was by boat. Fast, powerful craft called "rumrunners" which could often outdistance Coast Guard patrols, would land cases of liquor at secluded coves where they would be transferred to waiting vehicles and taken to distribution centers in Boston. A bonanza for organized crime, prohibition was a headache for local police departments charged with enforcing the law.

DANA'S BEACH

In Manchester, Dana's Beach was a favorite landing spot for illegal liquor. With the big houses which surrounded it closed for the season, there were few people in sight. Sheltered by the island to the east and a rocky headland to the west, it was often without surf and thus offered easy access. Manchester police, of course, were continuously on the alert for suspicious vehicles and unlikely visitors. And it was such a sighting one evening in 1932, that prompted Chief George

Chief George R. Dean monitors traffic in Central Square in 1936. In those days, the streets of the town were lined with magnificent American elm trees.

R. Dean to station Sergeant Leonard Andrews, Officer (later sergeant) Byron Bullock and Officer Thomas Sheehan at the town's Poor Farm in the so-called "Cove" area to keep an eye on two unusual cars which they had seen near White Beach. (Like most Massachusetts towns, Manchester had purchased—for $2,300 in 1839—land and buildings which could be used to help feed and house the poor.)

As Dean returned from the Police Station with Officer Jacob Lee, the two were passed by a huge, heavy Packard car lumbering up Ocean Street. Quickly placing the Dodge cruiser across the road, the Chief tried to stop a second Packard which appeared, but it swerved skillfully avoiding the road block and sped off towards Summer Street.

With Officers Bullock and Lee now with him, Dean, at the wheel, started in pursuit. Through the town they went, the officers, one on running board, firing their pistols at the fleeing vehicles. At West Manchester, opposite Harbor Street, police caught the first Packard, forced it over and arrested two men. The other vehicle was located nearby parked innocently by the side of the road. With a spotlight on him and shots over his head, the driver was persuaded to surrender after trying to escape across Winthrop Field.

"About 60 cases of whiskey, gin and champagne" were seized with the two autos, according to The Cricket. Returning to Dana's Beach, the officers found another 60 cases including 10 gallons of pure alcohol. The three men were arrested and jailed at the station. Later that morning when life had returned to normal, a crowd gathered, curious to inspect the

bullet holes in the back of the get-a-way cars. As The Cricket declared with tongue in cheek: "Chief Dean had lots of friends [in the gathering] who said they were very thirsty."

CRATES OF ALCOHOL

Earlier, in May, 1926, acting on a tip, Dean sent Motorcycle Officer Byron Bullock to a Dana's Beach estate where he found two men who failed to justify their presence in the area. Holding them, Bullock phoned the Chief for assistance. No sooner had he arrived on the scene when a large furniture truck appeared with two other men. Suspicious now that they had stumbled on to something big, Chief Dean opened the door of a nearby garage. There, piled to the ceiling, were crates of alcohol. All four men were placed under arrest while the Chief called Federal marshals. At noon that day, according to The Cricket, marshals removed 241 six-gallon cases of contraband. Bail was produced and the men scheduled to appear later in U.S. District Court in Boston.

In May, 1928, Dana's Beach was the sight of another seizure of illegal liquor and arrests by Manchester police. Again acting on a tip, and this time assisted by the U.S. Coast Guard and two Federal Customs Officers, Chief Dean, Sergeant Leonard Andrews and Officer Jacob Lee, quietly hid themselves in the shrubbery to wait until dawn. As the sun's first rays appeared in the east, the officers moved in, capturing some 20 men at gunpoint who were busy, as The Cricket reported, loading two waiting trucks with "sacks of liquor that had been landed on the beach from a boat [then] lying about 150 feet offshore."

Caught by surprise, the culprits began running in every direction to escape. A few shots in the air did stop at least eight men who were arrested and handed over to Coast Guard petty officers who took them and the boat involved, a 60-foot sloop, to Gloucester. As for the liquor, police counted a mixed 300 cases valued at $15,000. Another man involved in the smuggling operation was found later walking in to

Patrolman Jacob Warren Lee at Singing Beach. An 1886 graduate of Story High School, Lee joined in 1902, retiring after 35 years of service in 1937. He died in 1951. Note the bath houses in the background which lined the back of the beach in those days.

town. His excuse that he was a commercial fisherman without funds on his way to Boston did not meet police requirements for an adequate alibi.

WE ALWAYS GET OUR MAN

A handsome man with a tall and impressive build, Chief Dean reportedly tipped the scale at 265 pounds. Evidently, none of it was fat for in 1926 he proved his reputation as a sprinter by pursuing and capturing a man in Manchester wanted by Beverly police for assault. Dean chased the would-be prisoner out of his house, through bushes and brambles, until he captured him at gunpoint. Chief Welch of the Beverly Police Department was high in his praise for his fellow officer who, according to Welch, "did the 100 yards in 11 seconds flat." Dean, always modest about his accomplishments, told The Cricket, "we in Manchester have adopted the motto of the Northwest Mounted Police: we always get our man." The prisoner was found guilty and sentenced to six months in the House of Correction. The Chief, whose clothing was torn in the chase, was provided with a new pair of trousers.

A FRUSTRATING FIRE

Engines Balk at Responding to Winter Blaze at the Police Station in 1925

The building which served Manchester Police as Head-quarters for 76 years was constructed in 1885 to house SEA-SIDE 1, the town's new horse-drawn, steam fire engine. It cost $2,500. Town Meeting voters appropriated $5,000 which also included the steam pumper. SEASIDE II, a second steam pumper purchased in 1902, is now on display with the historic hand-pump TORRENT in what has become in recent years a museum to commemorate the bravery and dedication of both fire and police departments. More police memorabilia will be added shortly.

Meanwhile, the police station itself was nearly destroyed in a stubborn blaze which erupted at 4:07 a.m. on December 27, 1925. Seeing smoke coming from the rear of the building, the duty officer called in the alarm. At the engine house on School Street the blaze was to prove frustrating. Firemen first tried to start the Knox motor truck but it wouldn't budge. The Seagrave did respond but stalled once in the bitter cold on the way to the fire. Hoses were hitched to a hydrant nearby but soon these blew off "sending a geyser [of water] straight across the street which," according to The Manchester Cricket, "landed squarely on a stack of police uniforms that had been removed from the burning building and piled up on the platform in front of Beaton's [Hardware] Store to get them safely out of the way. The hydrant did a remarkably good job in wetting the uniforms down," The Cricket continued, "so there was no danger of them catching fire from sparks, but it took the rest of the week to dry them out so as to be fit for our patrolmen to wear without risking an attack of pneumonia…"

Firemen tried a second hydrant but this, too, was unsuccessful and they turned to using "pony chemicals and a garden hose." A window was smashed in the front of building to get at the fire and although the Seagrave was ready to pump water from the dam (ice had to be broken to get at it), it wasn't needed. The blaze was soon under control. Damage,

estimated at $1,500, was confined to the rear of the building and to club rooms on the second floor. It also included what was once the hose tower which is soon to be replaced as a part of the restoration of the now venerable structure. The blaze, The Cricket reported, was blamed on "an overheated smoke pipe in the back of the [building's] Arcola heater."

One cell was occupied at the time of the fire. As smoke filled the building, the door was unlocked and the prisoner told to move out. "He lost no time in obeying the order,' The Cricket added, "and made for School Street with never a look behind. He was reported in Essex later in the day still going strong…"

ALL IN A NIGHT'S WORK

At 5 a.m. on an April morning in 1936, Police Officer Jacob W. Lee was completing a quiet night assignment at the station on Central Street when through the doorway walked two obviously confused and agitated young men wearing only their bathing trunks. Lee sat them down and listened to their story. After an all-night party with three girl friends, they had decided to drive to Manchester to go for a swim at Singing Beach. When they came out of the cold water, neither the girls or the car were anywhere in sight and thus marooned, they decided the only thing to do was to walk to the police station and to seek help. Immediately, Officer Lee, taking every precaution, phoned State Police barracks in Topsfield to report that the car had been "stolen." A few moments later, however, on Central Street, he spotted a vehicle of the right description headed for the beach. In it were three young ladies. When he and the now shivering swimmers caught up, they learned that the girls, bored waiting while their dates were enjoying the surf, had decided to take off for a "joy ride." It was somewhat prolonged when they lost their way in Magnolia. With the reunion complete and feelings restored to normal, Lee left to notify Topsfield that the case had been "solved" and to turn over his post to his relief. For the veteran officer, it was all in a night's work.

A 'TOUGH COP'

Manchester's Jack Connors Is Judged by TIME magazine in 1937 to Be the Toughest

Of all of the legendary figures who served as members of the Manchester Police Department in the past half-century, few can compare in stature and reputation with Patrolman John Patrick Connors.

Throughout the last century, the town has been enormously wise and immensely fortunate in its choice of police officers. Almost without exception, they have been men of the highest professional caliber, strict but fair, honest and brave, and in enforcing the law, when logic suggested it and the statutes allowed it, understanding, kind and helpful, particularly with youngsters.

Connors, who served the town for 28 years from 1930 until 1958, had all of these characteristics in spades, but it was his uncompromising approach to dealing with those who broke traffic laws related to the protection of the safety of the public (and to their own well-being as well) for which he was most famous. He was "tough cop." So tough and so unwilling to comprise high principles, in fact, that word of his dedication to duty and commitment to seeing that justice was done was known throughout the nation.

Indeed, in its issue of August 16, 1937, Jack, as he was known locally, appeared in TIME magazine. "One of the toughest of the 'tough cops' in the U.S., according to connoisseurs" wrote TIME, "is Motorcycle Patrolman John Patrick Connors, whose bailiwick is small, attractive Manchester, [Massachusetts]. Residents of Cape Ann, among whom the name of Connors is a byword, accuse him of being not only a superfine and arbitrary legalist, but a misanthrope who hates automobile drivers."

COLORFUL EXAGGERATION

"Incorruptible, Policeman Connors has been threatened on at least one occasion," TIME continued, "by an irate driver with a shotgun, and was once about to be assaulted by a burly victim in the lobby of a motion picture theater when bystanders intervened. Truck drivers passing through Manchester became so irked at what they considered unwarranted pouncing by Policeman Connors that they threatened to bring him to grief by making sudden stops with their air brakes while he was following behind on his motorcycle. Standing joke in the region," concluded TIME: "It's too bad Connors' own family doesn't drive, or he'd spend all his time arresting them and let the rest of us alone."

Colorful exaggeration has often been a part of TIME's style of writing. Jack neither hated auto drivers or had it in for truck drivers. He simply enforced the laws of the town and the Commonwealth to everyone's benefit without fear or favor. As for being menaced by a "burly victim" in a motion picture theater—nonsense. Jack Connors was a big, tough handsome Irishman with a formidable physical presence. He could take care of himself in most any situation and didn't need "bystanders" to "intervene." But despite what many considered minor inaccuracies, Jack liked the article in TIME.

A native of Manchester, he was born in 1897 and attended local schools. His father was a coachman for Thomas Jefferson Coolidge and his family both in Manchester and in Boston. After high school, Jack graduated from Wentworth Institute as a machinist. But in 1918, with America at war with Germany, he joined the Army. The armistice, however, was signed before he reached training camp. For a while, he worked at a defense plant in Washington building airplanes, but then returned to Manchester. He was employed by a livery stable and later drove one of the town's first taxis. Then in 1930, he decided to join the Police Department. He was named a reserve officer and in 1932, appointed permanent patrolman by Chief Stewart F. Cooper.

From 1943 to 1945, during World War II, with Chief L. Allen Andrews serving with the U.S. Army, Connors was the choice of the Board of Selectmen to become Acting Chief of Police. But administrative work had little appeal. He was happiest while on his Indian motorcycle, patrolling the streets of the town, controlling traffic and maintaining law and order. In 1951, he married Doris Hoare, a graduate of Boston University who served as Town Librarian here from 1945 to 1980.

A 'SOFTIE' INSIDE

A smart-looking officer, Connors wore his uniform well, and despite his reputation as a "tough cop," according to his wife of 34 happy years, Jack was a softie inside who helped

Motorcycle Officer John Patrick "Jack" Connors who TIME magazine declared was "one of the toughest 'tough cops' in the US. Connors served as acting Chief of Police during World War II.

many a youngster stay on the straight and narrow. In 1958, after 28 years as a policeman he retired. During his career he helped solve a number of local robberies, captured a pair of run-a-way convicts at gun-point with Officer Fred Lear (see story elsewhere), and with Officer (later Sergeant) William S. Hurley, rescued two children from a fire at the Manchester House, afterwards dousing the blaze itself. Like many others in the 1960's, he was disillusioned by the rise in rampant individualism and the lack of respect for traditional values, especially among the young. Active in his later years, he held a number of jobs, each of which he enjoyed. All of them involved driving a truck or car. He maintained a close relationship with the police department, attending many reunions and retirements until he died at age 88 in 1985.

TO THE NORTH POLE

Officer George James Was a Radio Expert on Byrd's Epic Flight in 1926

To Officer George H. James (MPD 1936-1970) the excitement of police work in Manchester must at times have seemed routine when he recalled memories of his experiences with the Byrd Polar Expedition of 1926.

James attended Story High School and left in 1923 to become an aircraft radio engineer with the U.S. Marine Corps. Honorably Discharged in 1926, he helped install the high frequency receiver aboard Lieutenant-Commander Richard E. Byrd's flagship, the steamer CHANTIER. Then, as a radio technician and operator, he sailed with her to the Arctic.

From Trondhjem, Norway, the CHANTIER proceeded north of the Arctic Circle to Spitzbergen. The story of the expedition is told in an impressive full-page article published on June 20, 1926 which James and his fellow radio technician, Lloyd K. Grenlie, wrote for The New York Times.

Highlight of the adventure was the flight of an aircraft, christened JOSEPHINE FORD, to the North Pole and back. Its radio was designed by Michael Hanson of the Naval Research Laboratory in Washington and, as James and Grenlie write "was built by us just before we built the ship's high frequency, short wave transmitter."

If the craft was forced to ditch, the radio set was equipped with a hand-powered generator. The unit, James said, was about the size of a "can of gasoline." The transmitter was able to operate on the flight, but the receiver could only be used if the aircraft went down as there was too much interference with the plane's engines. The JOSEPHINE FORD left on its flight to the Pole on May 9. James and Grenlie were aboard CHANTIER as the messages came in. "We are 230 miles from the Pole. Nothing but ice everywhere. No signs of life. Motors going fine." Then: "We have reached the Pole and are now returning. One motor [has] a bad oil leak, but [we] expect to be able to make Spitzbergen."

PLANE RETURNS

That night with the plane safely returned, James writes, "we were wild with joy. No work was done and a celebration staged. Things then went along as usual with the spark transmitter working night and day sending news of the flight. The short wave radio sent some of the press dispatches directly to the United States."

The Times announced that a reception to honor Byrd and his crew was to be held at City Hall with the Mayor and members of Congress attending. Speeches were to be carried on stations WOR and WNYC. Addresses at a luncheon later at the Advertising Club of New York were to broadcast by radio station WOR. The age of radio had arrived.

George James, meanwhile, according to his son Jess, returned to Manchester a hero, and from 1926 to 1936

worked for Charles Dodge at Dodge Furniture Manufacturing. He passed the Civil Service exam and became a Reserve Police Officer in September, 1936 and was appointed a permanent Patrolman in July, 1943. Born in 1903, James was also a volunteer fireman and, earlier, had been a yacht captain. He also worked with the WPA (Works Progress Administration) and during the 1930's helped with the contract to widen Summer Street at Craft's Hill. In 1940, just before World War II, he was asked by then Governor Leverett Saltonstall to direct a civilian committee encouraging enlistments in the Massachusetts National Guard. With the advent of Selective Service (the draft), however, in late 1940, the committee was disbanded. James retired as a Manchester Police Officer in 1970 and died in May, 1980 after a remarkable and varied life.

1940: BULLETS FLY

Stick-up at Magnolia Casino; Two Officers Are Heroes of Famed High Speed Chase

Perched on pink granite ledges high above the Magnolia shore, the Casino in 1940, was Cape Ann's answer to the glamorous seaside night clubs of Cap d'Antibes. Next to Rafe's Chasm, it catered to the rich and famous and featured fine dining, headline entertainers, and dancing until the early hours of the morning.

Owned and operated by Frank Fishburne of Gloucester and bandleaders Sammy Eisen and Ruby Newman of Boston, the Casino was widely known throughout the region. Newman was the star and the night club's major attraction. With his orchestras and vocalists, he played at the Hotel Buckminster and at the Ritz Carlton in Boston, at the Rainbow Room in New York and at debutante parties everywhere. With an eye for talent, he helped introduce many personali-

One of the most popular night clubs of the northeast, the Magnolia Casino was located off Hesperus Avenue near Rafe Chasm. This photo appeared on the cover of the North Shore Breeze in August, 1936.

ties of the day including such celebrated vocalists as Hildegarde and Gordon McRae, actress Sonja Heine and comedian Burt Parks. He was the darling of Cafe Society and they flocked to Magnolia to listen to his music.

SUMMER ELEGANCE

In those days before World War II, Magnolia was also a hugely popular summer resort with its magnificent multi-story Oceanside Hotel. Fashionable shops lined Lexington Avenue: Lord & Taylor, DePinna, Tiffany's, J.J. Jonas and Sara Frederick's, all with outlets in such other sophisticated locations as New York City, Paris, London and Palm Beach. And parked along the curbs, often with waiting chauffeurs, were Cadillac town cars, Packards, LaSalles and Pierce-Arrows.

But if all this elegance attracted those with money to spend honestly, it also caught the eye of those seeking it in other ways as well. And on the morning of July 15, 1940, at about 11 am, four heavily armed men, masked to hide their identities, climbed the trellises of the Magnolia Casino and burst into the rooms where 17 staff members were still sleeping. Ordering them out of bed (they had been working until 4 am), the thieves forced them at gun point to reveal where the night's receipts were hidden, then bound and gagged them with tape, yanked out telephone wires, collected some $1,800 in cash (a sizable sum in those days) and fled to a waiting car.

As soon as the Manager could free himself, according to a news story in the Gloucester Daily Times, he ran next door to notify Gloucester police who immediately called State Police and police departments in nearby communities. One of these was Manchester. As the phone rang at police headquarters here, now Seaside 1, it was answered by Chief George R. Dean. In seconds, with Officer Leonard A. Andrews (who succeeded Dean as Chief in 1943), the two were underway in the cruiser or what in those days was referred to as the "patrol car," a black Dodge sedan.

HOT PURSUIT

Dean, drove up Pine Street and turned right into Pleasant thinking that this was the most likely route the bandits would follow (Route 128, of course, had yet to be constructed). Suddenly, heading directly for them, they saw a Packard convertible coupe moving at about 40 miles per hour. It swerved from Pleasant Street on to what is now Old Essex Road (then Essex Street) "nearly overturning" in the process as The Manchester Cricket reported. "The Chief's car was in hot pursuit,' The Cricket continued, "and it was a ride the police will never forget."

Soon both vehicles were on their way to Essex engaged in a high speed chase on a winding, gravel road. With stones flying and wheels skidding, driving was both dangerous and difficult. As Dean and Andrews began to gain on the Packard, the suspects opened fire on the two officers out of the back window of their vehicle reportedly with a sub-machine gun. Andrews, his 38 caliber Colt Police Special revolver in his hand, returned the shots as best he could as the car beneath him lurched and bounced on the rough surface. "One bullet [from the gangsters] struck the front seat [of the patrol car] just beneath the Chief," according to The Cricket,"... another tore into the back seat..." A third pierced the engine compartment. Fortunately, neither Manchester police officer was hit.

The Packard, significantly heavier and larger, soon outdistanced the smaller patrol car and when the Chief reached the main road in Essex, opposite what today is Bothways Farm, it was nowhere to be seen. The officers at once stopped at a house to phone State Police (there were no two-way radios then), providing them with a description of the get-away car and the number of its Massachusetts license plate.

Later that day, the Packard, which had been stolen earlier, was found abandoned near Lowell. Inspection revealed several bullet holes and blood stains on the rear seats, testimony to the excellent marksmanship of Officer Andrews. As the search widened, it was believed that the men had continued their flight to the north in another stolen vehicle and were possibly those linked with a number of recent robberies in Massachusetts and New Hampshire. Sadly, it was suspected, too, that one of the gang was a resident of the Town of Manchester, a young man, 22 years old.

HIGH PRAISE

When the cruiser returned, "Nothing but the highest words of praise," The Cricket declared, "were heard on every hand for the splendid courage and work of Chief Dean and Officer Andrews...fear had evidently not been given a thought by the officers of the law who were bound to do their duty whatever might happen."

At their next meeting, Selectmen added their own words of approval and admiration. Said Chairman Harry E. Slade: "It took a lot of courage going at 40 miles an hour over that rough and curving road to swap shots with desperate men. As a selectman representing the people of Manchester, I am proud to echo their praise of what Chief Dean and Officer Andrews did. They are both a credit to this town and to the nation. Risking their lives...in an effort to clear the highways of such public menaces, they proved themselves the type of law enforcers who inspire [public] confidence. I shall certainly vote for an official commendation for both officers."

The Chief, meanwhile, discussed the possibility of adding a sub-machine gun to his arsenal, especially as this was the second armed robbery that had taken place in neighboring Magnolia within six years. In 1934, thieves made off with more than $100,000 worth of gold and precious stones taken from a jewelry store on Lexington Avenue. Then, they bypassed Manchester, making their escape directly through Essex on Essex Avenue.

Less than a month later, on August 7, 1940, a headline story in the Gloucester Daily Times reported that after robbing a bank, shooting and wounding a farmer, and stealing a car, two men, both suspects in the Casino robbery as well, were arrested at gunpoint by State Police in Biloxi, Mississippi. One, 28 years old, was from Chicopee, Massachusetts. The other, 22, was from Manchester. Both were bound over to the Grand Jury with bonds of $25,000 double surety and were later indicted. Charges included thefts in New Hampshire as well as Massachusetts. Both were parolees from the jail in Concord, NH, released in April, 1940.

THIRD SUSPECT

On August 12, 1940, according to the Gloucester Times, a third suspect, 26 years old and a resident of Cambridge, was apprehended by State Police in Monson, Massachusetts. After being identified by five employees of the Casino as one of those involved in the robbery there in July, he was also held with bonds of $25,000 double surety (equivalent to $50,000 bail) and later bound over to the Grand Jury.

The first suspect to be captured, the Times continued, was seized at gunpoint on July 29 in Billerica, Massachusetts. More than 15 State Police were involved. Identified by four Casino employees, he was 26 years old and a resident of Arlington. Chief Dean identified him also as the driver of the bandit's car although the suspect never admitted it. He, too, was held on bail and bound over to the Grand Jury. All four were parolees from Concord. The $1,800 stolen in the robbery was never recovered.

Sadly, one winter afternoon in 1954, fire destroyed the Casino building, ending an era of glamour and excitement. The blaze started when members of a work crew, burning leaves and brush, left the site to eat lunch. A small fire broke out while they were away. When they returned, the entire structure was in flames.

VETERANS RETURN

At the End of World War II, Police Officers Return from Europe and the Pacific

When World War II ended in August, 1945, veterans slowly began to return home. Among them were the two sons of retired Police Sergeant Leonard Andrews, L. Allen Andrews and his twin brother Nathaniel.

Allen was a member of what is now the distinguished "first family" of the Manchester Police Department . His father, who served the town for many years, was the department's first, full-time sergeant. His nephew, Neil, follows today in his grandfather's footsteps with the same rank. He is also the department's Firearms Officer.

A 1925 graduate of Story High School, Allen joined the Police Department as a Reserve Officer in May, 1930. He became a full-time patrolman in 1933 and succeeded George Dean as Chief in November, 1942. In September, 1943, with World War II at its height, he joined the U.S. Army. After basic training at Fort Belvoir, Virginia, he graduated as an expert in demolition with the rank of T/5 (Technician Fifth Grade). Following further training at Fort Lewis, Washington, in April, 1945 he was sent to France. When the fighting ended in Europe in May, 1945, Allen and his unit sailed from Marseilles for the Philippines. There he landed at Luzon and with the surrender of Japan, like thousands of other GI's, he awaited transportation to the States. His brother Nat, a Technical Sergeant in the U.S. Army Air Force, and father of present day Sergeant Andrews, was stationed in the Middle East for 32 months where he served as crew chief and aerial engineer.

CHIEF ONCE AGAIN

Allen received an Honorable Discharge in December, 1945 after after two years and four months of service. On January, 18, 1946, he assumed his responsibilities once again as Chief of the Manchester Police Department.

Jack Connors, who had been Acting Chief in Allen's absence, returned to the rank of Patrolman once again. Although he provided the town with exemplary service during the later years of the war, Connors never did take to

Acting Chief of Police Jack Connors on the steps of Horticultural Hall with Governor Maurice Tobin who visited Manchester to help celebrate the town's 300th anniversary. Other well-known figures of the day surround the Governor.

administrative duties, preferring to be out on the street enforcing the law. In general, the war years were reasonably quiet ones when it came to police work. In June, 1945, there was one major robbery which involved the theft of silverware from a home at Smith's Point. Thanks to the good efforts of Acting Chief Connors and his department, two Gloucester men were arrested and held on $5,000 bail. Much of the silverware was later recovered in Gloucester. A set of elegant candelabras was finally found in Louisiana. Connors also officiated as Chief as Governor Maurice J. Tobin helped Manchester celebrated the 300th anniversary of its founding in June, 1945. Mrs. Connors, then Doris M. Hoare, was the author of a poem written for the occasion and set to music by Manchester summer resident Wallace Goodrich. Tobin gave the Tercentenary Address.

Church bells rang, the air raid siren sounded, and gleeful Manchester residents blew auto horns, as the town celebrated the end of World War II in August,1945. "An orderly crowd," as The Cricket reported, "gave police no trouble and caused no damage."

FOUR BATTLE STARS

Other veterans returning to Manchester included Watertender Third Class William F. Hurley, Story High School 1940; Aviation Electronics Mate Third Class Alexander F. Backry; and Chief Carpenters Mate Dan MacEachern.

Hurley joined the Navy in April, 1944, attended "boot camp" at the Naval Training Station at Sampson, NY, and was then sent to Ford Motor Company, Detroit, Michigan, for schooling as a machinist. Bound for the Pacific Theater, he shipped out aboard the GENERAL STURGIS and at Ulithi was transferred to USS SOUTH DAKOTA, the first battleship to bombard the home islands of Japan. The SOUTH DAKOTA also served as flagship for Admiral Halsey and led the parade of ships at the surrender ceremonies in Tokyo Bay. Hurley accompanied his ship home to Philadelphia. Entitled to four battle stars on his Asiatic-Pacific ribbon, he was discharged at Boston and in 1947 was appointed a Reserve Officer of the Manchester Police Department. He later rose to the rank of Sergeant, retiring in 1984 after 37 years of service.

Chief Allen Andrews at his desk at the old Police Station on Central Street. Because of the size of the building, the Chief's desk was also used by the officer on duty and for the department's two-way radios.

Backry, who joined the Navy in March, 1944, also trained at Sampson, NY and was assigned to the Naval Air Station at Philadelphia. There he worked on PBY's and PBM's, the Navy's famed amphibian aircraft, which were used for anti-submarine patrol on the East Coast and on the West for tactical observation as well as anti-submarine warfare. Born in Lowell in October 1914, Backry grew up in Salem and settled in Manchester after World War II when he, too, became a police officer here serving from 1947 to 1972. He died in October, 1978.

A NAVY CHIEF

MacEachern was born in Manchester in 1907, graduated from Story High School, and, after working as a tree climber for the Commonwealth of Massachusetts, joined the Manchester Police Department in 1932. In 1939 and 1940, he was appointed its motorcycle officer. During World War II, from 1942 to 1945, he served in the U.S. Navy. After "boot camp" he was sent to Dry Docking School in San Francisco and then to ARD-14, a floating dry dock which was based at Tulagi and

later at Leyte Gulf where it hauled and repaired submarines and destroyers attached to the Asiatic-Pacific Fleet. MacEachern, then a Chief Petty Officer (Carpenters Mate), served as Docking Officer, directing ships on to the blocks and bracing them before water was pumped from the dry dock itself.

Honorably Discharged in 1945, he returned to Manchester and was named Sergeant in 1946. A crack pistol shot, he won many medals for marksmanship. Much admired and respected as a leader, he died in December, 1966. A granite bench behind the old police station overlooking the inner harbor memorializes his life and his many years of service to the town.

POSSE HUNTS FUGITIVE

Officer Fred Lear Is the Hero of the Day as He Seizes the Man at Gunpoint in 1949

Police Officer Frederick C. Lear, helped by a "posse" of some 200 local residents in March, 1949, captured a prison parolee from Gloucester at gunpoint after a dramatic chase through Manchester woodlands. The man later admitted to stealing more than $2,000 from a Cape Ann fish plant. The funds were to have been distributed to employees as Christmas bonus payments.

The incident, according to a story in The Manchester Cricket on March 11, 1949, began as Officer Lear apprehended the 21-year-old for questioning after he had tried to change what store owners considered might have been counterfeit ten and twenty dollar bills at Floyd's News Store and at Sheldon's Market.

As Lear was leading the man to the Police Station for questioning, he broke away and fled up Elm Street disappearing in the woods. One shot in the air failed to stop him, but the chase was on. As word of it spread, scores of volunteers from nearby houses and businesses joined the hunt.

On duty at the station, Officer John P. Connors, who couldn't fire at the fleeing man for fear of hitting innocent residents, jumped into Chief Allen Andrews' personal car (Andrews and Sergeant Daniel MacEachern were in court in Salem with the only cruiser) and drove up Pine Street to Pleasant to notify residents to be on the alert for a fugitive. Lear and two volunteers returned to the station just as Andrews and MacEachern arrived from Salem. The Chief then assumed command. Sergeant MacEachern was to take the cruiser with its radio to Pleasant and Pine Streets. The others, Officers Lear and Connors and the two volunteers, were to follow the trail of the escapee up Elm Street and through the woods.

STUDENTS JOIN HUNT

By this time, more volunteers, including scores of high school students, had joined the man hunt as it spread out through the woodlands north of the community. Finally, Lear, pursuing the youth first by car and then on foot, captured him at gunpoint off Mill Street. He was exhausted and quickly surrendered. Taken to the Police Station, he was booked on suspicion of felony. The following day he confessed, taking officers to his home in Gloucester where he handed over $1,100 which he had hidden in the head of a doll owned by his eight-year-old niece. Lear also recovered $280 which the man had dropped on Elm Street. And a Manchester

High School student turned in another $95 which he had found in the woods during the chase. In all, police estimated that some 200 persons and 20 vehicles, almost all of them privately owned, had assisted in the man hunt. Officer Felix Radack (who later became Chief) was also involved in efforts to apprehend the suspect who appeared in District Court in Gloucester the following day. He was convicted and sentenced to a term at the State Reformatory in Concord for this theft as well as for a series of robberies from several Gloucester stores.

Hero of the chase, Police Officer Fred Lear, was born in Salem in 1904, but shortly afterwards his family moved to Lynn. There, in his teens, he worked at Graham Farm helping with a herd of 120 milk cows. He was originally trained as a pattern and model maker at General Electric Company graduating in 1925. But jobs were scarce and Lear found work where he could first in Boston and later in the midwest. Returning to Salem, he was hired by Atwood & Morrill, then by a shop in Lowell which made wood propellers for small aircraft, and finally by another which built washing machines. By this time, it was 1929 and the Great Depression had arrived. Business failures were common and there were thousands of unemployed. Fred, always imaginative, started an egg route and sold more than 150 dozen a week, according to his youngest daughter, Manchester resident Sandra Collins. He also built two houses on the family farm off Route 114 in Danvers and established an ice cream stand with his brother Ed which made more than 100 gallons a day. He then moved to Manchester.

JOINS FORCE IN 1932

In 1932, still lean times economically, Lear took the police exam and was appointed a permanent patrolman serving the town as a much respected and beloved law enforcement officer until 1962, a total of 27 years. In 1959, then age 58, he returned to his first love, pattern making, owning and operating Lear Pattern Works in Lynn until he retired again in 1974. Among his clients were such industrial giants as General Electric Company, Atwood & Morrill, AC Spark Plugs and the astronomical conservatory at Harvard University.

Always active in community affairs, Lear was a member of the Board of Selectmen, the Planning Board and various school building committees. His skills with wood and metal working as well as model making were legendary. According to The Manchester Cricket, he built "clocks, candle-powered carousels, and a scale model of the Congregational church steeple." He made the patterns for the decorative urns which are a part of the steeple itself and inside the church he constructed the pulpit, the lectern, the communion table and the railing around the second floor balcony. His models included one of the town's historic hand tub, the Torrent, and of its steam fire engine, Seaside One. He even built himself and his family a 26-foot cabin cruiser whose hull was designed by naval architect and fellow Manchester resident Sturgis Crocker, Sr. Fred Lear died in 1991 at the age of 87. As one friend and admirer wrote, as a police officer he was a "counselor/psychologist in uniform."

SPEEDING TICKET FOR 'S1'
Manchester Officer Enforces the Law Without Fear Or Favor

If Officer Jack Connors was known as a "tough cop" so was Officer Alex Backry. Indeed, Manchester police had a reputation for enforcing traffic laws without fear or favor. One summer's day in the late 1950's, according to his son Mike, now a Major with the Essex County Sheriff's Department, when Backry was in the cruiser near University Lane, he stopped a huge black Cadillac bound for Gloucester. "You were exceeding the speed limit," he announced to the driver who was dressed in State Police uniform. "Do you know who's in the back?" the driver asked. "I don't care if it's the Pope," Backry declared, "you were breaking the law." A ticket was written, handed over and soon the Cadillac with its "S 1" number plate was on its way. Its distinguished passenger was Massachusetts Governor John A. Volpe who was running late for a speaking engagement and luncheon at the Tavern in Gloucester. The Governor later called the station to apologize for his driver's transgressions.

Even in a small town, police face danger each day. In June, 1949, Officer Backry, while on desk duty at the old station, noticed smoke rising from a boat at the town floats. After a call to the fire department, he hurried to the scene to keep eager spectators, mostly youngsters, out of danger. Just as he boarded the boat to remove an extra can of gasoline from its cockpit, the fuel tank on the engine itself exploded. Suffering from burns on the face, Backry was taken to Dr. Charles Herrick's office nearby but not until he had seen that the fire was extinguished. Within the hour he was back on duty.

OFFICERS SAVE GUESTS
Six Are Led to Safety as Fire Engulfs the Manchester House in 1952

Two police officers were heroes of a major fire in May, 1952 which destroyed the Manchester House hotel on Central Street and damaged Beaton's Hardware Store (where Hunneman's real estate offices are now located) and the Town Shop.

The blaze, according to a story in The Manchester Cricket, started in the hotel Tap Room and rapidly spread to the remainder of the building. Responding to a cry for help, Officer Fred Lear pulled the fire alarm at 1:13 a.m. Officer Alex Backry, in the police cruiser, immediately responded and the two fought their way through thick smoke to rouse six guests on the second and third floors of the hotel and lead them to safety. Backry suffered from the effects of smoke inhalation but after medical attention, he returned to duty. In all, nine hotel guests escaped without injury.

Firemen fought the flames, which at times reached high into the sky, with the new aerial ladder truck. At 2 a.m., help was sought from the Magnolia Station of the Gloucester Fire Department. Two Manchester firemen, Wilbur Stanley and Richard Wogan, were injured during the fire.

Thanks to the efforts of scores of volunteers, valuable merchandise was removed from the Town Shop before it could be damaged by water or smoke. Members of the Magnolia Lodge of Odd Fellows helped Red Cross Chairman John

A delivery truck plowed through the fence on Bridge Street, overturned and crashed into the marsh below on the north side of Tenney's Creek in 1949. Again, note the number of shade trees, many of them American elms, which lined the streets of Manchester and other New England towns before the arrival of Dutch Elm Disease.

Eaton serve coffee and doughnuts to firemen and volunteers. Members of every town department—Water and Sewer, Highway, and Police as well as employees of the Manchester Electric Company—joined in to help quell the blaze. Also of great assistance was night telephone operator Charles Allen who called members of the fire department who were unable to hear the alarm. Finally, at 8:40 a.m., Fire Chief Richard A. Hammond sounded the all out.

Mrs. Eunice Nichols, proprietor of the Manchester House, said that the original building was constructed in 1712. A third story was added following an earlier fire in 1900. The hotel was never rebuilt.

TOWN IN SHOCK

1953: Police Chief Allen Andrews Resigns in Dispute with Board of Selectmen

In a move which shocked residents of the town in late August, 1953, veteran officer L. Allen Andrews resigned as Chief of the Manchester Police Department. At issue was a written order given to the Chief by the Board of Selectmen which directed him to station a police officer on School Street, at Lincoln Street and at Pine Street for three days "at the regular rate of pay" in response to complaints about speeding vehicles.

In his letter to the board, the Chief wrote that "due to heavy commitments already scheduled for the assignment of officers to Route 128 [then under construction], for traffic control on those dates, in addition to carrying out the regular duties of the department, the...order made it impossible for me to reasonably fulfill all of the above duties. I sought and received a feasible and courteous explanation from the Chairman of the Board of Selectmen...made known my displeasure in regard to the order and at the same time informed him verbally and later by letter that I was resigning as of this date...the Chairman...refused to accept my resignation and tore it up. No longer wishing to be in contention with the board...on matters pertaining to the administration of the Police Department, I decided to [again] submit my resignation..."

In view of the demand for police work, however, during the busy summer season and especially over the coming Labor Day weekend, Andrews loyally stayed on the job until his resignation was formally accepted.

One unusual factor in the relationship between the town's top elected officials and its Chief of Police was that the Chairman of the Board of Selectmen at the time was the Chief's twin brother Nathaniel Andrews. A letter in the <u>The Manchester Cricket</u> at the time, however, denied a "family feud."

336

BOARD DEFENDS ACTIONS

According to The Cricket a week later (September 11, 1953), in a story topped with another four-column headline, the board defended its actions and reported that it had met with the Chief and Town Counsel Judge Edward Morley to discuss the matter. However, little about the dispute could be resolved and selectmen declared that they felt they had no option but to accept the Chief's resignation. This they did "with reluctance."

Apparently, the passage of time and many conversations helped to pour oil on troubled waters, for in its issue dated September 18, 1953, The Cricket announced that things were back to normal. "Believing it to be [in] the best interests of the town," the news story said, "Chief Leonard A. Andrews and the…Board of Selectmen have agreed to confer on the matters relative to the Police Department which have been at issue. It is now felt that the problems with which the parties have been concerned can be solved in an amicable manner…The Board of Selectmen has rescinded its vote of Tuesday, September 8, 1953," the story continued, "accepting the resignation of the Chief, and Chief Andrews has withdrawn the resignation which he presented on August 27."

The issue, it appeared, was one of jurisdiction. The Chief had been hired to administer the Police Department. He believed that the Board of Selectmen, with its direct order, was usurping his authority as the department's chief operating officer and this he could not accept.

All ended well, however, and most residents heaved a sigh of relief that the incident was over and that life could get back to normal. Selectmen continued to execute their duties in the best interests of the community and for the next 15 years, until he retired in 1968, Chief Andrews provided the town with exemplary security services. In all, he was member of the Manchester Police Department for 38 years, two years longer than his father, Police Sergeant Leonard Andrews. The town has every reason to be grateful to the Andrews family.

ESCAPEES SURPRISED

"One Mentioned 'Walpole' and I Knew We Had Something," Said Officer Connors

What started out as a routine patrol of Coolidge Point early one Saturday morning in November, 1956, by Police Officers John P. Connors and Fred C. Lear, ended with the arrest at gunpoint of two convicts who had escaped from Walpole State Prison a few days earlier.

From their cruiser, the officers spotted an unoccupied vehicle parked by the side of the road and, as Jack Connors told The Manchester Cricket, "we knew 12:25 [a.m.] was a strange hour for a car to be in this now unoccupied…area, so Fred and I decided we'd better check into the matter." As they drove into a nearby avenue, they saw two men. "…when I got out of the cruiser, I had my gun drawn and cocked," Connors continued. "As soon as [the two] saw it, they threw their hands in the air. Then [one of them] mentioned 'Walpole' and I knew we had something."

While Connors kept them covered with his Colt Police Special 38, Lear frisked the two escapees and discovered that both were carrying "zip" guns, homemade pistols manufactured in

prison. Lear then wisely called for assistance and in minutes Police Chief Allen Andrews and Officer William Fraser arrived on the scene. With the convicts handcuffed to Officers Lear and Fraser, Connors then drove the cruiser to headquarters with Chief Andrews following in his own vehicle.

After questioning, The Cricket continued, it was learned from the two men that they had arrived in Manchester at 2 a.m. a day earlier and had pulled off the road to sleep until noon. That morning they discovered the house which was closed for the winter, and "decided it would be a good place to stay until things 'cooled down.'"

STEAK DINNER

"After cleaning up [they found a razor and soap at the house], they drove into town, ordered a steak dinner at the Town Sandwich Shop (where Seven Central is now located), bought a paper at Floyd's, and other provisions at Manchester Fruit and Grocery. Returning to Coolidge Point, they lost their way and with a dead battery, were forced to abandon their car." They found another, however, managed to start it and were parking this vehicle when they were apprehended by police. Discovered in the car were several items taken from the house as well as false drivers licenses and birth certificates which had been obtained from the prison print shop.

When they escaped, the two men had been hand-cuffed together in the custody of three prison guards. With their hand-made "zip guns" they threatened the officers and ordered them to drive to Franklin Park in Boston where they got out and hijacked a car owned by a Natick resident. It took them an hour to remove the hand cuffs. For the rest of the day, they rode the subway in Boston, stealing another car that night and arriving in Manchester about 2 a.m. Picked up by Manchester Police the following night, they were held on $21,000 bail each, photographed, and finally turned over to two prison Wardens and a Correctional Officer to be transported back to Walpole.

Officers Connors and Lear received formal commendations for their actions from Police Chief Allan Andrews. Wrote the chief, in part: "It is seldom we are faced with such an experience as…theirs—their accomplishment in apprehending these convicts is highly commendable [especially] in view of the fact that it was done on a routine patrol without prior knowledge [or information]… their instant recognition of the situation and efficient action bespeaks their fitness and capability as police officers…"

A GREAT DISASTER

Two Officials Are Nearly Trapped as Flames Roar Around Them in 1957 Forest Fire

One of the greatest disasters in the history of the town of Manchester was the week-long forest fire which took place in in May, 1957. It not only threatened the lives of scores of firefighters but could have destroyed much of the town itself.

First at the scene of the blaze, then a small brush fire off Forest Street, according to Bill Radack, were his father, Police Officer (later Chief) Felix Pop Radack, and Fire Chief Richard A. Hammond. "They nearly had it out," said Bill. "It was the size of two, four by eight sheets of plywood, but it got away from them." The two public safety officers were

Members of the Manchester Police Department in January, 1968. From left: Officers Albert Powers, Bob LaFreniere, Craig McCoy, Arthur Beaulieu, Sergeant Bill Hurley, Officer Tom Andrews, Chief Allen Andrews, Officer Alan Gilson, Sergeant Felix "Pop" Radack, Officers Bill Laskowski, Alex Backry and Jim Mulvey. Photo by John C. Burke.

lucky to escape with their lives as the flames, fanned by high winds, roared into life and threatened to surround them.

For seven days, the fire raged. Story High School closed and students joined others in battling the blaze. A Canteen was set up in the Congregational Chapel and more than 1,000 meals were served by Red Cross workers. Thanks to the efforts of firemen, police, members of other town departments, neighboring fire departments, Federal, state and county fire officials and scores of citizen volunteers, flames were finally brought under control. Although there were a number of close calls, no lives were lost, houses remained standing, and only minor injuries were suffered by firefighters. Chief Hammond was effusive in his praise for the assistance he and his men had received during the disaster. He had special thanks for Chief of Police Allen Andrews and his men as well as for Superintendent of Streets Edward Sweeney and members of his department. Police officers singled out for special thanks were Sergeant Daniel MacEachern and Officer Radack.

All in all, it was an extraordinary effort of coordination. The hero of the occasion was Chief Hammond who went without sleep for three days. He wisely, however, decided to share the responsibility for directing fire fighting operations with two other Fire Chiefs, Deputy Chief W. Elliot O'Hearn of Gloucester and Chief Kellerly of Beverly, thus insuring that

the communications center was in command of a senior fire official who was rested and could make clear and proper decisions. No one man could have run things for 24 hours a day for nearly a week.

Fire apparatus came to the assistance of Manchester from more than 25 surrounding cities and towns including units from Civil Defense in Boston and from the U.S. Air Force.

THE DIAL ARRIVES
Early Users Warned of Hoax Calls as new System Is Installed in May, 1960

Dial phones, the first major change in telephone service in 50 years, arrived in Manchester at 1201 on Sunday morning, May 1, 1960. And with them, based upon experiences in other communities, came a warning from police about anonymous calls, hoaxes, insults, and youngsters dialing numbers at random, calls which heretofore could be screened by a live operator.

Manchester's exchange was JACKSON. (Hamilton's was HOWARD.) Users dialed JA 2 followed by their party's number. The town's calling area included Beverly, Essex, Hamilton and Magnolia. To reach Gloucester, it was necessary to dial 3 and then to give the number to the operator still on duty. Selectman (later State Representative) George L. Allen placed the first call to Edward McCarthy of Magnolia. Veteran operator Miss Margaret Cooney closed down the old system with its plug-in jacks for each line and familiar "Number Please?," with a call to her sister, also a telephone operator, that ended 48 years of live, 24-hour service.

The first phone call in town was made in 1912 by Peter Brown, owner of Manchester Fruit and Grocery Store. The phone company originally rented offices in the Rabardy Block, and was later located in the second floor apartment of the Misses Haraden, both of whom served as telephone operators. The switch board was then moved to the second floor of the Abdo Block. From there it went to the second floor of the Pulsifer Block until that was destroyed by fire. It then moved to the first floor until the telephone company constructed its own building on Summer Street.

HANDS WERE UP

Two Men Surprised by Lone Officer and Owner of SURF in December, 1964

It was 3:15 a.m. on a late December day in 1964, when the alarm rang at Police Headquarters in Manchester. Alone at the station, Patrolman Alex Backry identified the signal as coming from the Surf Restaurant on Raymond Street. Immediately, he phoned Chief Allen Andrews, restaurant owner Al Lazisky and Police Officer Jim Mulvey who would cover for him at the station. He then climbed into the cruiser and sped towards the Magnolia line. There he met Lazisky. Both conferred for a moment and then entered the building, Backry with his service revolver drawn and cocked.

Meanwhile, the two men inside were unaware that the alarm at the Surf had sounded when they broke into the structure through a storeroom window. Apparently, however, they heard Backry and Lazisky approaching and hid in a closet. They were apprehended at gunpoint trying to escape through another window. "We pushed open the door," Backry reported, "and there they were—standing with their hands up."

The interior of the Surf showed the effects of their visit. Tables and chairs had been overturned, some of the coolers had been left open, a small sum of money had been taken from one of the cash registers, and an attempt had been made to rifle a cigarette machine.

With Chief Andrews now on the scene, the men were searched and arrested. Taken back to Manchester, they were jailed and charged with breaking and entering and larceny in the night. The following day in Salem District Court, both pleaded innocent. The case was continued and bail imposed of $2,500 each.

Later, the Board of Selectmen unanimously voted to commend Officer Backry for his courage, for his professional abilities and for his commitment to the best traditions of police work in capturing the pair. If either man had been armed, however, and had chosen an alternative to surrender, the story might have had a very different ending. Backry, who retired in 1972, was cited on four occasions for merit and bravery.

A CHIEF'S PLEA

1965: Additional Officer Sought; 'Department Is No More Than an Answering Service'

Officer Alex Backry's lone capture of two men in late 1964 who were arrested for breaking and entering at the Surf Restaurant, highlighted the need for additional patrolmen.

As Chief Allen Andrews wrote to the Board of Selectmen in his 1965 Annual Report, "...the one officer on duty had to call [me] and two others before he could respond. If it were not for the immediate assistance given by the owner of the establishment, the life of this one officer could well have been in jeopardy before [aid] arrived." The point was well made.

As Andrews explained, the size of the police department which at the time included nine men, had remained the same for the past 36 years or since 1929. Since then the town's population had more than doubled. Police coverage had increased from 20 hours per day to 24. On the other hand, the work week for police had been reduced from 56 hours to 40 hours, vacation time had been extended and sick leave opportunities established.

"Despite the introduction of a police radio system," the Chief continued, "to offset the curtailment of foot patrols and the elimination of the summer motorcycle patrol...the department with the complement at hand is no more than an answering service."

On many occasions, the Chief explained, citizens had be called off the street to staff the station so that the officer on duty could respond to a call for assistance. With only one cruiser, too, officers are even forced at times to commandeer a passing car for the transportation they may need to protect lives and property. This, the Chief said, is no way to maintain law and order.

FIGHTING FOR HIS MEN

In those days, before the present budgeting system and the appointment of a Town Administrator, department heads often had to take their pleas directly to Town Meeting. Andrews was famous for this, fighting for the needs of his men and for funding which would increase the safety of the public and the well-being of his fellow citizens. He asked for and got the addition of another regular patrolman and a second cruiser. He also sought the widening of downtown streets to relieve traffic congestion, and the codification and clarification of Town By-Laws, rules and regulations which the Police Department was charged with enforcing.

Allen Andrews served the town with distinction for 40 years, first for two years as a call fireman and then as a police officer from 1930 to 1968. He was appointed a patrolman the day his father, Leonard, the department's first Sergeant, retired. Named Chief in 1942, he was granted a leave of absence during World War II to serve with the U.S. Army in both Atlantic and Pacific Theaters. Following the war, he oversaw the introduction of two-way radios which revolutionized police work not only here but around the nation. To meet new and growing demands for professionalism in law enforcement, he began the first program which enabled officers here in Manchester to attend training courses offered by the Massachusetts State Police.

As Chief of Police and as a founding member of the Manchester Athletic Association, he also helped scores of local youngsters find their way through the difficulties of adolescence to later lead positive and productive lives. For 26 years also he was Secretary-Treasurer of The Manchester Club and a faithful attendee at its meetings. He died much respected in May, 1979 at age 71.

JUVENILE JOY RIDE

Two Teens in a Stolen Car Lead Officer On a Wild Ride; Pair Are Finally Captured

Responding to a report from Rockport police of a stolen vehicle in December, 1965, Police Officer Alex Backry stopped a car matching its description on Route 128 in Manchester. As Backry left his cruiser to approach the vehicle, the two youngsters in it started up and sped away. At Pine Street they turned off and headed for Hamilton past what was then the Town Dump. Bachry gave chase at speeds which at times reached 80 miles an hour over gravel roads.

When they reached Vitale Pit, the two took off on foot through the trees. Backry followed, shouting at the youngsters to halt and firing three shots in the air. Forty-five minutes later, the boys, both juveniles, were apprehended as they left the woods by Chief Haraden of the Hamilton Police Department. The youngsters had originally stolen a car in Fall River which they drove to Rockport. They then took another one there. One was charged with using a motor vehicle without authority. The other with operating without a license. Both were held in $3,000 bail to await juvenile session of District Court in Boston. Other Manchester police officers involved in the chase were Craig McCoy and George James.

PAYROLL ROBBERY

Thieves Hi-Jack Paymaster's Car; Bind and Gag Him; No One in Town Is Aware

Two armed bandits escaped with $8,000 in October, 1965 after stealing a payroll destined for employees of a construction company then building a house on Elm Street.

As the paymaster pulled up to the site, he was accosted by the two men. With pointed guns, they forced the him over to the passenger's side of his car, climbed in and sped away. On Pine Street just beyond Moses Hill, they bound and gagged him, took the money and his car keys and fled on foot. It was assumed that they had a get-a-way vehicle hidden nearby.

It took the paymaster, meanwhile, just five minutes to free himself. Fortunately, he had a second set of keys. He started his car and drove to the Police Station. There he reported the robbery. Neither the duty officer, only a block from the scene of the crime, or any Elm Street resident, was aware that the theft had taken place.

ILLEGAL DRUGS

650 Pounds of Marijuana Are Discovered in a Potting Shed Here in 1975

Each era of police work has had its own challenges: dealing with the arrival of the automobile at the beginning of the 20th century; enforcing prohibition during the 1920's and coping with the illegal use of drugs which began to proliferate

As a motorcycle officer in the mid-1950's, Officer Felix "Pop" Radack cut a dashing figure. Handsome and able, Radack served as a patrolman and sergeant for 16 years. He was appointed Chief of Police in 1968 and retired in 1984, after more than 38 years of police work.

in earnest during the 1960's, sadly involving too many of the young.

Of all of the issues which faced Felix "Pop" Radack during his 16 years as Chief of the Manchester Police Department, drugs were certainly among the most pervasive. One of the most spectacular drug seizures here occurred in October, 1975, when Sergeant James Mulvey and then patrolman (now Sergeant) Alan Gilson led US Drug Enforcement Agents to a potting shed in Manchester where they discovered some 650 pounds of marijuana and arrested two suspects. The men were a part of a gang of 14 persons, including six from Massachusetts, who were seized with some 8,600 pounds of marijuana worth some $1.7 million in an investigation and a chase which began at a farmhouse in Arkansas and ended here on the North Shore, Connecticut and Colorado.

SCORES OF US AGENTS

The pursuit by scores of Federal agents, described in The Manchester Cricket, involved radio-equipped cars and airplanes which followed the suspects' vehicles during a week-long odyssey as they made their way north and west. According to the DEA's Regional Director, "the trucks which left [Arkansas] had police scanners and citizen band radios…to determine if they were being followed, so we had to rely heavily on air surveillance." One truck with some 700 pounds of marijuana aboard was stopped near Denver where three persons were arrested. A second was halted in Connecticut. The third, a camper, was observed by aircraft following the Massachusetts Turnpike to Route 128 where it turned off and entered Manchester. There DEA agents in unmarked cars took over and were assisted in their search by Manchester police.

The house in Manchester and its outbuildings had been rented earlier by one of the men who found it listed in an advertisement in a Boston newspaper. The innocent owner was totally unaware of the use to which his dwelling was to be put. The two men seized here were arraigned at Federal Court in Boston.

As time progressed, marijuana gave way to harder drugs with street values significantly higher. In November, 1980, Chief Radack and Inspector Kenneth Sucharski, joined some 75 other police officers from Gloucester, Essex, Danvers, Rockport and Ipswich in what was reported to be the largest drug raid in the history of Cape Ann.

A five-month investigation which had the assistance of a State Police undercover officer, resulted in the arrest of some 38 people including four from Manchester. It was discovered that Class A and Class B drugs such as heroin, hydromorphome, oxycodone, phencyclidine, and cocaine as well as other controlled substances were being sold in the downtown area of Manchester. Ten additional arrest warrants were available for persons still at large.

HOUSES RAIDED

The round up began at 6:30 a.m. Arrest teams, The Cricket reported, consisted of two State Police troopers and a local police officer. Houses were raided and drugs, cash, firearms and stolen property confiscated. Three vehicles were also seized and turned over to the District Attorney's office. When the day was over, Manchester's Board of Selectmen wrote to compliment Chief Radack and Inspector Sucharski as well as other members of the police department for their role in the arrests.

Manchester police also joined Federal and State narcotic agents in another raid in May, 1981 which yielded an estimated $500,000 worth of heroin. Some $50,000 worth of the drug was seized here in Manchester. The remainder was taken into custody in Springfield.

Manchester police stopped two suspects in their car on School Street around midnight. They were charged with a series of drug offenses. A third was also arrested. All three were arraigned in Salem District Court.

The Cricket reported that a spokesman for the District Attorney's office said that details of the operation were first learned in October, 1980 in the raid described earlier which concluded with the arrest of more than 30 suspects on the North Shore. It was said that one individual apprehended was the source of foreign heroin for the states of New York, Connecticut, Vermont and Massachusetts. The drug seized by police and narcotic agents was also said to be more than 50 percent pure. Most heroin sold on the street, the DA's office explained, is between three and seven percent pure.

CRIME INTERNATIONAL

No longer confined to local issues, police work was now embracing crimes which may have had their origins as far away as Asia, Europe or Latin America. And drugs had so permeated society that in 1981 scores of concerned parents crowded into the Music Room at Manchester Junior-Senior High School to hear State Police narcotic agents tell about the types of drugs to which their children might be exposed.

Just last year (1998) alone, with the Cape Ann Regional Drug Strike Force, police in four North Shore communities made 201 arrests in connection with narcotic enforcement and interdiction and removed hundreds of thousands of dollars worth of illegal drugs from circulation. In the schools, with the assistance of a State grant of $6,000, the Drug Abuse Resistance Education (DARE) program continues under the direction of Police Officer David MacDougal. In today's changing law enforcement environment, a growing number of police hours are spent in the area of education to prevent crime and to reduce the number of injuries from traffic and bicycle accidents.

POP RADACK

Police Chief and Navy Veteran Served Town for 38 Years; Saw Many Changes

Police Chief Felix Radack was a man of many dimensions. Handsome (he was said to look like Hollywood actor Lee Marvin) and impressive in his uniform (he was a former U.S.

This cartoon drawn by Phil Bissell was presented to Chief of Police "Pop" Radack at his retirement dinner in September, 1984 by the Manchester Division of the Cape Ann Chamber of Commerce. One friend recalled that when Radack was riding a motorbike as a patrolman in the mid-1950's, he and his school chums used to refer to the machine as a "Pops-cycle."

Navy Chief Petty Officer), he was an able leader and administrator, tough when needed, but inside, filled with a deep compassion and concern for the welfare, safety and future of those around him especially the young.

He was known as "Pop" because as a child, according to his son Bill, he used to regularly "pop" in to the Highway Department garage next to where he lived and the nickname stuck. His record of service to the Town of Manchester totaled a remarkable 38 years and seven months. Sixteen of those years were as Chief of Police. Another 16 were as patrolman and Sergeant.

Perhaps the most moving story Pop told at his own retirement dinner in September, 1984 was one of a youngster he had first taken into custody at age 13 and who seven years later he had to lock up again. This time the then frustrated 20-year-old angrily flooded the cell block of the new police station. Exasperated, Pop said he wished that he was his father so he could give him the thrashing he deserved. "If you'd been my father," the young man replied sadly, "I wouldn't be here today."

CAPTAIN OF FOOTBALL

A graduate of Story High School (Class of 1937) where he was Captain of football, Pop Radack worked first for a summer resident as caretaker and chauffeur, but in January, 1941, months before the Japanese attacked Pearl Harbor, he enlisted in the Navy, signed up for pre-flight school and was sent to Peru, Indiana as an Air Cadet. A serious case of pneumonia, however, side-tracked his ambitions to become a Naval aviator and he served throughout the war as an aviation machinist aboard ship and at airfields in the South Pacific. In November 1945, he was Honorably Discharged as a Chief Petty Officer.

Like many veterans, Radack tried to find work he liked and was about to re-enlist in the Navy when then Chief of Police L. Allen Andrews urged him to join the department as a reserve patrolman. The date was February, 1946. The next year he received appointment as permanent police officer and the rest is history. Twenty years later he was promoted to Sergeant and then in 1968 when Andrews retired, Radack became Chief.

As he recalled, those were not easy years. Drugs, alcohol, political protest and dissension because of the Vietnam War were everywhere and among the young especially there was a new focus on individual rights and freedom and a particular disdain for law and order.

As a veteran of World War II, Pop was a patriot and one of his proudest memories was when he attended his son Bill's graduation from Marine "Boot Camp" at Parris Island. At a time when other youngsters were fleeing the draft and wearing the American flag on the seats of their pants, he said that Bill took him over to where a huge version of the Stars and Stripes flew proudly above the drill field. "Dad," he said pointing to it,"isn't that beautiful?" Later, Bill, back from Vietnam and now a decorated Marine Sergeant in dress blues, joined his father in Manchester's Memorial Day parade. For Pop, it was another great moment.

COMPASSION A HALLMARK

Chief Radack's compassion for the down-and-out, even those he had arrested, was widely known. In court one day when he was conducting a case (now this is handled by a Dis-

trict Attorney), he reported that the Judge leaned over the bench and whispered "are you the prosecutor or the defense attorney?" Times have changed, Pop sighed, but, he added, there are scores of local kids who got into trouble when they were young who are living productive lives today because of the way they were dealt with by the police department and by their families.

As Radack's friend John 'Finney" Burke explained, "a police chief's job is particularly difficult in a small town where he knows everyone." Burke, former editor of <u>The Beverly Times</u> and later Metropolitan Editor of <u>The Boston Globe</u>, used to cover police activities on the North Shore. "Pop," he added, "knew that what he did could have a marked effect on someone's life. He made his decisions with great sensitivity. Perhaps instead of Police Chief his title should have been 'Peace Chief,' for he felt it was his primary job to maintain peace, harmony and civility within the community."

Asked about major changes in law enforcement which took place during his era, Chief Radack cited the education and professionalism now required of police officers; the equipment, especially radio, which makes communication with other departments instantaneously available; the addition of uniformed women to police forces everywhere (Manchester's Joanne Graves and Colleen Smith-Pearson were among the first to enforce the town's new parking regulations); and Emergency Medical Technician training which enables police officers today to save scores of human lives.

NEW HEADQUARTERS

During Radack's career also, and after 76 years, the police department moved to new quarters at Town Hall. The old station was heated with a pot-bellied stove and Pop remembered running next door to Sheldon's Market to get orange crates to burn when it ran out of coal. The coal bin also was used as a backdrop for target practice. In the early days, too, after the war and before the use of two-way radio became widespread, a blue light shining on a pole above the station indicated to those officers in the cruiser that they should return to check in immediately. Before the construction of the Masons' building and Legion Hall, the light could be seen from Proctor Street across the harbor.

Hundreds of well-wishers attended Pop Radack's retirement banquet at the Surf Restaurant. Those present included Master of Ceremonies Chris Nahatis, Federal and State Legislators, Selectmen, fellow police officers and newly-named Chief Ron Ramos as well as friends and family. The evening concluded with everyone singing "God Bless America." Somehow, perhaps more than anything else, that emphasized the values that Pop had stood for all his life.

A 'DIRTY WHITE CAR'

Alert Officer Spots Suspects' Vehicle While Off Duty; Follows Up with Arrests

Difficult as it is to believe, in 1970, a Manchester woman had her purse snatched and stolen in front of her own house downtown. The thief, she reported, ran down the street, jumped into a "dirty white foreign car" driven by a woman and was soon out of sight. Duty Sergeant James J. Mulvey, III sent then Officer (later Sergeant) William Laskowski to the scene to talk with the victim, and radioed Officer Alfred

Powers in the cruiser to look out for the car. It was to no avail. The pair had vanished.

However, at 4:30 that afternoon, The Manchester Cricket reported, while Mulvey, then off duty, was driving to Wenham with his wife and children, he spotted a man and woman in a white Peugot sedan at the intersection of Larch Row and Route 1A. With the incident of the morning clearly in mind, he followed the car to Beverly where he picked up Patrolman Warren Kendall at the corner of Rantoul and Elliot Streets. Officer Kendall radioed for the Beverly cruiser. Arriving shortly, it stopped the couple, arrested them and returned them to Manchester where they were charged with larceny from a person.

Mulvey, who grew up in Manchester, attended St. John Prep in Danvers and following graduation entered the U.S. Army in 1958. Trained at Fort Cordon, Georgia as a Combat Military Policeman, he served in Korea and was discharged in 1962 with the rank of E4. At the suggestion of then Officer and later Sergeant Bill Hurley, he took the police exam and was appointed the eighth and first full-time patrolman to be added to the department in many years. In those days, he was on duty from seven p.m. to three a.m. and recalls working 96 days in a row without a day off. Named Sergeant in 1968, he graduated from the Massachusetts State Police Academy the following year. There he was President of his class and led 43 other students with a grade average of 97. He was also ranked third in a firearms and combat course given by the Police Revolver League. A founder of the Manchester Police Association, he retired on a disability in 1979 after serving for 17 years. Today, he continues police work as a private investigator in Salem.

LONESOME PATROLS

In the Early 1900's, Officers Walked Their 'Beats;' Horse and Railroad Used for Transport

Manchester's Police Department purchased its first patrol car or cruiser in 1924. As early as 1916, it acquired a motorcycle to enable it to have a more continuous presence throughout the community and to provide for a more rapid response to problems of public safety. The town's first motorcycle patrolman was Byron L. "Bunk' Bullock who later was appointed Sergeant.

Before the arrival of motorized vehicles, records show that the department did possess one Columbia bicycle, but to maintain law and order in the community in the early days of the century, policemen were assigned "beats" or regular rounds which they patrolled on foot, day and night, spring, summer, fall and winter. One officer, Jacob Lee, was responsible for the east side of town from the police station to the Magnolia Depot including the Cove area. Another, Robert Stoops, walked his "beat" from the police station to the Beverly line including West Manchester to the West Manchester Depot. And during the summer season, a Reserve Officer was assigned to a third area which included Old Neck Road and Masconomo Street.

For the most part, particularly at night and in the "off season," these were lonely rounds. Shelter was available at the Cove School at the junction of School Street and Magnolia Avenue and at the West Manchester Depot where patrolmen could warm themselves on a cold winter night and perhaps eat a sandwich. A generous housewife, too, or cook at a summer mansion would often invite an officer in for coffee. Until Chief Thomas O.D. Urquhart, with the consent of Town Meeting, ordered the installation of telephone call boxes, the only way a policeman could contact headquarters was to use a household phone, if one existed in the area, or commandeer a ride back to town by horse and carriage if, indeed, a team passed by. In most cases, a man was completely on his own.

For transportation over any distance, people used the railroad. It ran frequently, traveled faster than a horse and was more reliable. Prisoners, for example, usually handcuffed to a police officer, were taken to court in Gloucester by train. If it was necessary to go to Boston to pursue a lead in the investigation of a crime, as was often the case, the Chief or one of his officers, again, would travel by rail. Patrolmen would usually meet each train as it arrived in Manchester and would often be asked by the conductor to remove a passenger who might be drunk or disorderly. Even after automobiles became more numerous, police were slow to buy one of their own. But it was understood by most citizens and supported by law that an officer could order a car to stop and its driver to assist in an arrest if a pursuit was called for.

PHONE IN THE SQUARE: 1963

As late as 1963, according to The Manchester Cricket, police still depended upon the phone box located outside Jimmy's Sandwich Shop (now Seven Central). An extension of the phone at the police station, it allowed the officer on duty at Central Square to direct traffic and at the same time answer calls to police headquarters.

Of all of the areas in town, none was more dangerous for early automobiles than Craft's Hill, Duwart's Corner and "Dead Man's" Corner, all on Summer Street. A review of news stories in The Manchester Cricket in the early part of the century clearly indicates that the number of accidents, injuries and fatalities that occurred at these three locations easily exceeded all others in town. Because of steering failure or other mechanical problems, bad weather, excess speed, driver inexperience or intoxication, cars, trucks and even busses would leave the road with alarming regularity and crash headlong into a tree. Before safety glass was in general use, injuries would almost always include vicious cuts from broken glass. At Craft's Hill, the road was widened and the grade made more gradual in a major project completed by the WPA in the 1930's. At "Dead Man's" Corner, a new "pop corn" surface was laid down in the early 1960's to prevent skidding.

A major effort to increase automobile safety here occurred after World War II when formal courses in Driver Education were made a part of every high school student's curriculum. Autos with dual controls for driver and student were often contributed by local car dealerships. Bike Safety Days were also established to teach school age children how to ride safely with the increasing traffic on local roadways.

In 1950, Chief L. Allen Andrews accepted a Highway Safety Award in the town's name from then Governor Paul A. Dever and Registrar of Motor Vehicles Rudolph F. King for the community's freedom from fatalities during the previous year.

343

TWO-WAY RADIOS: 1946

Perhaps the most dramatic change to affect police activities after World War II was the improvement in communications made possible by the widespread use of police radio. Telephones and call boxes were abandoned in favor of instant and continuous contact provided by hand-held "walkie-talkies" developed for the armed services, and mobile radios in each cruiser which enabled officers to talk directly with the Police Station and later with other town departments and State Police throughout the region. Retired Police Sergeant Bill Hurley remembers that just after the war the only way to communicate with officers when they were on patrol in a cruiser was to switch on the blue light outside the station house. "That way we'd know we were needed for an ambulance run," he recalls. Now each officer is equipped with his own hand-held radio unit with which he is able to maintain constant contact with police headquarters.

Sergeants Jim Mulvey, left, and Bill Hurley use the phone at the old station which served as police head-quarters for 76 years. The building, Seaside 1, originally a fire house, is now a museum which commemorates the work of both fire and police departments.

During a renovation of the old Police Station (now restored to SEASIDE 1) in September, 1952, then Officer (later Chief) Felix "Pop" Radack discovered a piece of wood in the boiler room of the old building which had inscribed upon it in pencil this message: "Whoever brings this board to me after 1900 shall receive 25 cts. [signed] A. [Albion] Gilman, July 21, 1885."

ONE DAY OFF IN SIX: 1947

At Town Meetings in August, 1946 and in February, 1947, the sum of $1,630.79 was authorized to provide an increase in compensation for police officers and one day off in six. Although some voters wondered where the old motorcycle was (it had been sold by the Board of Selectmen for $40), it was agreed to purchase a new one for $655 as one cruiser was considered inadequate to effectively patrol the town. The motorcycle officer then was Jack Connors.

According to the Committee on Town Wages in 1947, salaries for a Patrolman and/or Driver were $48 a week. A Reserve Patrolman received 95 cents an hour; a Sergeant of Police, $52 a week, and the Chief (both Police and Fire), $57 a week.

In May, 1947, a 15-year-old Salem girl, reportedly assaulted in the Manchester woods, copied the registration of her assailant's vehicle in lipstick on a paper match container. Her vigilance resulted in his arrest.

$50 UNIFORM ALLOWANCE: 1955

In 1955, Town Meeting voters approved granting a $50 uniform allowance for police and firemen. A raise in salary that year was turned down. In 1957, Chief Allen Andrews proposed an 11 percent raise in salary for officers of the Manchester Police Department. Town Meeting voters defeated this motion but upon recommendation of the Board of Selectmen and the Finance Committee, did grant a five percent raise to all town employees. The 11 percent raise sought by the Chief, who was noted for his efforts to fight for the welfare of his men, would have set salaries at $78 per week for patrolmen; $83 a week for Sergeants; and $92 a week for the Chief. Andrews was concerned that low salaries drove members of his department to seek additional jobs to supplement their income thereby affecting their performance as police officers.

Manchester's 'First Lady Police Officer," according to The Manchester Cricket, was Mrs. Robert Lations Elso of North Street who in 1955 was appointed a traffic officer to provide protection for students arriving and departing from school. She was in uniform.

PERSISTENCE PAYS

L. Allen Andrews, Chief of Police from 1942 to 1968, had a remarkable memory for details and a persistence when it came to criminal investigations that almost always enabled him to "get his man" whether the case was large or small. Take the theft of a TV set from a house on Norwood Avenue. Armed with a description of a strange vehicle in the neighborhood (a blue Ford) and a jumbled series of possible license plate numbers, Andrews, with the assistance of then officer Felix Radack, traced the sequence through the Registry until they matched the identity of the car which, it was learned, had been rented from an agency in Salem. From there it was easy to locate and arrest the driver who had used his real name. Meanwhile, he had sold the TV, but the buyer had read about the theft in a local newspaper and reported to Salem police that he had the set in hand. Result? The TV was safely returned to its original owner in Manchester and the suspect and his accomplice, who were wanted in connection with a series of breaks, were turned over to Salem Police.

Manchester's first women police officer with the power of arrest was Coleen Smith Pearson. Appointed a patrolman in 1984 by Chief Ronald Ramos, Pearson was 21 years old at the time. A 1981 graduate of Manchester High School, she had received an Associates Degree in Law Enforcement from North Shore Community College and at the time was attending Salem State College where she sought a Bachelor of Science degree in Criminal Justice. She was also taking the Massachusetts Criminal Justice Training Course and receiving training as an EMT. The town's first uniformed woman officer was Mrs. Robert Elso (the former Eleanor Lations) who in 1955 joined the department to provide for traffic control and safety at community schools.

FIVE DAY WEEK: 1952

In 1952, at the urging of Chief L. Allen Andrews, despite the opposition of the Board of Selectmen, Town Meeting voters approved a five-day week for police officers. The count was 283 to 115.

In July, 1953, State Department of Public Works Commissioner John A. Volpe (who later served as Governor) and Manchester resident Charles Fritz, Chief of the Beverly Office of the State DPW, were present as the northbound lane of Route 128, then under construction, was opened to two-way traffic.

At a Town Meeting in 1955, Chief Andrews again sought the appropriation of $2,814 to provide a pay raise for police officers who he said were forced to hold two jobs to maintain their families. With the Board of Selectmen and the Finance Committee opposed, the motion was defeated 272 to 236.

With Governor Christian Herter in residence on Proctor Street during the summer of 1956, Manchester and State Police were assigned to provide extra protection because of a telephone threat on his life which was identified as coming from a pay station in Lexington, Massachusetts. The Governor continued to conduct state business as usual at his home overlooking the harbor.

In 1957, all town employees received a five percent raise in pay. The 11 percent sought for police by Chief Andrews would have meant that patrolmen would have received $78 a week, Sergeants, $83 a week and the Chief, $92 a week.

FIRST STOP: LOCAL DOCTORS

In the early days, following an auto accident, the injured were most often taken by police not to the Emergency Room of the Beverly Hospital but to the offices of a local physician. Through the years, many a victim was well attended to locally by Dr. George W. Blaisdell, Dr. Robert Glendenning, Dr. William MacIntyre, Dr. Roger Greenslet, Dr. Charles Herrick and Dr. Oliver Viera. More serious cases, of course, were taken to hospitals in the area.

Chief Andrews' Annual Report to the Board of Selectmen for 1964 noted 77 arrests, 19 less than 1963. 1964 was also the first year that all municipal departments were connected by radio.

In July, 1967, Selectmen agreed to add one permanent patrolman to the then nine member Manchester Police Department. It was also agreed that Officer Felix Radack (Radack later became Chief) should attend the Massachusetts State Police Academy.

In 1967, a basketball game between the Police and Fire Departments to benefit the Manchester Athletic Association ended with a 46 to 41 victory for police. High scorers were for the firemen, Donald Burgess, Ben Burgess and Norman Hersey; for the police, Jim Mulvey, Bill Laskowski and Craige McCoy.

In the 1980's, a proposal to consolidate the position of Chief for both Police and Fire Departments was defeated at Town Meeting.

In April, 1984, Police Chief Felix Radack proposed that Manchester join the Boston Area Police Emergency Radio Network (BAPERN) as another step towards completing a mutual aid program.

A LOBSTER LUNCH

Each year, the Manchester Police Association hosts a clambake at Tuck's Point. Among the 100 or more persons who attend are judges, clerks of court, towing service operators and key police from neighboring communities, all those with whom the department works throughout the year. Some time ago, with a number of lobsters left over, duty officers brought them to the station the next day for lunch. Out of the kindness of their hearts, an extra was given to a prisoner who had been arrested the night before. Some concern was expressed, however, that it might get around that Manchester was the place to be jailed. Not every police lock-up served cold boiled lobsters for lunch!

CAUGHT RED-HANDED

A police officer on the night shift many years ago, regularly used to help himself and his partner to doughnuts from the fire station. As the days passed, he grew increasingly confident that no one would discover who was responsible for the missing delicacies, but firemen had been doing some sleuthing of their own and decided to get even. The next night, just as he was tiptoeing back to the cruiser, they turned on every light in the building. Not only was he scared out of his wits, he was caught red-handed. Besides having to replace every doughnut taken for the past fortnight, he was compelled to suffer the ignominy of discovery and the jibes of his fellow public safety officers for days to come.

Many years ago, while one police officer was alone in the cruiser late at night near the Manchester depot, he dozed off momentarily and somehow knocked the shift lever into DRIVE. Up over the curb the car went. It struck some object and stopped dead. Now wide awake, the officer tried in vain to back up and finally called the station for a tow truck. "And bring an umbrella," he added. "It's raining." "It's not raining here," the duty sergeant shot back. It was soon discovered when the wrecker arrived that what the cruiser had accidentally run over was a fire hydrant.

TEENS RIOT

Group Menaces Two Officers in 1972; Entire Force Comes to Their Aid; Eight Are Arrested

The late 1960's and early 1970's were turbulent times for the U.S. and Manchester was no exception. There was active and often violent opposition to the war in Vietnam. Drugs were beginning to infect society and were particularly prevalent among the young. Teenagers, too, had developed a contempt for law, order and especially for establishment organizations such as the police.

As early as 1965, Manchester police officers received instruction in riot and mob control because of fears that students from high schools and colleges in the area, visiting nearby beaches in the spring, might become a threat to peace, tranquility and public safety.

But on a Tuesday evening in late March, 1972, Manchester had its own confrontation between students and police. More than 40 teenagers had gathered at the shopping center south of the railroad tracks off Beach Street, a favorite hang-out in good weather after school as was People's Park overlooking the harbor across the way. Sensing that the gathering might lead to problems, Sergeant James Mulvey and Officer Craig McCoy asked the group to disperse.

All but one youngster started to walk away. He, however, remained where he was, defying the officers' request. As the two moved to apprehend him, the group returned and suddenly Mulvey and McCoy found themselves surrounded. They radioed for help. Twelve off-duty police—the entire force, in

fact—responded immediately. Then, as the two groups came together, there was a scuffle. A few tried to upset the police cruiser. There were cries of "Kill the Pigs!" Ultimately, an additional seven teens were arrested on charges which ranged from drunkenness to assault on a police officer. All eight were arraigned at Salem District Court.

POLICE STATION INVADED

The following day, a group of still angry youths stormed the Police Station itself. There was no counter or secure area around the offices at the time and in seconds the place was filled with shouting teenagers. Officers on duty managed to clear the building and the group marched down to People's Park where members of the Board of Selectmen did the best they could to calm things down.

Reporting to the Board a few days later, Chief Felix Radack said: "Nobody was hurt and as a matter of fact, I let a few of the so-called gang [who] were quiet when they came here, stay in the hall at the station mainly to allow them to observe what was going on so there would be no talk of police brutality or anything like that. We've been through that before." Others would have been arrested initially at the shopping center, the Chief added, if more than just two officers had been involved.

A police officer here for 19 years, Craig McCoy graduated from Manchester High School in 1955. For three years he served in the U.S. Navy as a member of its famed "Sea-Bees" or Construction Battalion at Naval bases in Bermuda, Barbados and Argentina, Newfoundland. Discharged in March, 1958 as an Electrician First Class (he specialized as a tele-

phone lineman), he thought about joining the phone company until, as Craig said, "Fred Lear asked if I wanted a job." Jack Connors had retired and Allen Andrews, then Chief of Police, was looking for a replacement. McCoy was appointed a Reserve Officer in 1958 and became a permanent patrolman in 1964. He served until 1975.

Today, his son Mark, a 1995 graduate of Salem State University with a Bachelor of Science degree in Criminal Justice, continues family tradition as a Reserve Officer with the Manchester Police Department.

A DEAF EAR

Manchester Police Association Seeks 'Fair Treatment' with Benefits and Pay

Early members of the police department took their questions and grievances to the Chief who then, especially in the matter of salaries and benefits, spoke to the Board of Selectmen and later often directly to voters at Town Meeting. But during the early 1970's, the Manchester Police Association was established to represent the welfare and interests of members of the department.

In October, 1975, the MPA was on the defensive. The Town Negotiating Committee, it charged in a special statement published in The Manchester Cricket, "has failed in [its] duty to negotiate fairly!" The charges included "turning a deaf ear" to MPA requests, spending more on attorney's fees (a reported $7,000) than the extra benefits sought would have cost, and accusing the MPA of not signing a contract that had

Chief of Police Allen Andrews (on tracks at left) confers with Gordon Abbott, owner of Manchester Marine Construction Company at the Ashland Avenue railroad crossing following the collision of a car and train in July, 1953. The crossing was the site of numerous accidents through the years. Crocker Boat Yard is seen at far left. Today, flashing lights and automatic gates halt cars when trains approach.

been agreed to but, according to MPA representatives, had been altered by the Negotiating Committee's attorney before handing it back for MPA signatures.

History shows that the police department has struggled continually to fairly reward its officers for the services they render and to expand and equip the department so that it may provide the then growing community with the level of public safety it was believed it deserved. Both Chiefs Andrews and Radack were tireless advocates for their men and for improvements. And in the fall of 1975, the MPA was not about to surrender its ideals.

NO OVERTIME PAY

"The only benefit change we have received in the last ten years", it declared, "is an increase in our clothing allowance... [All] other departments receive overtime pay...we do not if we work overtime on accidents or other investigations...most other departments have 65 and 80 percent of their [health insurance] paid...we {get] 50 percent...75 percent of all other departments receive three weeks of vacation after five years of service...we receive two weeks up to 10 years and three weeks after 10 years...Regular Officers work six days in a row and then have one day off...and a long weekend every fifth and sixth weeks...but in a six week stretch there is only one week when we work less than six days in a row...Most other departments are now working a four on, two off work schedule...many departments receive personal time off, call back time, night differential pay and longevity pay...we receive none of these...we want to be treated fairly...like other [town] departments...we have nothing to hide from anyone!"

Slowly, thanks to the efforts of the MPA , the availability of funding, the wisdom of the Board of Selectmen, and the actions of Town Meeting voters, things have changed. Today, the Manchester Police Association is not only certified by the state as a collective bargaining unit, but also contributes widely to community causes. It sponsors the annual Bike Rodeo, helps to fund the DARE program, helps finance and

provide manpower for the annual mock prom accident rehearsal, and contributes to the high school yearbook. It also provided support for the new Honor Roll for Manchester's war veterans.

LESS POLITICS

Budget processes are also different today. Department heads submit their budgets to the Town Administrator who then meets with Selectmen and with the Finance Committee to review budget requests. It is far less political and certainly less personal and confrontational than it was in earlier years. Designed to be fair, objective and professional, the present process is still meant to provide funding within the town's ability to pay. But it assures citizens that each department gets a fair hearing and that Finance Committee recommendations embrace the needs of the community as a whole.

HOSTAGES ESCAPE
Armed Man Holds Two at Masonic Temple on Christmas Morning, 1979

While most residents were eating breakfast or opening Christmas presents on December 25, 1979, at 9:30 a.m. Manchester police received a report that the Master of the town's AF & AM Lodge, was being held hostage at gunpoint inside the Masonic Temple behind Town Hall.

Earlier, a Lodge member had gone to the Temple to get some chairs. When he entered, he was surprised by a man with a 22 caliber rifle who had broken into the building earlier. According a story in The Manchester Cricket, the intruder asked him questions about the Lodge and then demanded that he call the Master. When he arrived, he, too, was taken hostage, but in a subsequent struggle in which the gun was knocked to the ground, the other Mason managed to escape. The intruder, however, recovered his weapon in time to threaten the Master and to continue to hold him at gunpoint. The Lodge member went directly to headquarters to inform police. One shot was fired, but, thankfully, no one was injured. Shortly afterwards, the Master, too, was able to elude his captor. He broke free and ran from the hall out a back door.

Police Chief Felix "Pop" Radack, home at the time, was notified immediately by the duty officer. He called State Police and mobilized his own department. At the scene, meanwhile, Manchester Officers Joseph Aiello, Alfred Powers, and Ronald Ramos (now Chief of Police) continued to talk with the gunman. "I spoke with him first," said Powers, "but when he said he had a hostage, we backed off."

By 10 a.m., members of the State Police Special Tactical Operation Platoon (STOP) arrived. The man, however, refused to surrender and threatened to start shooting unless a television camera crew was called in to film the incident. He continued to blame the Masons, The Cricket reported, "for everything from Chappaquidick to the Iranian [hostage] crisis."

TROOPER GRABS ARM

When TV crews did arrive, the gunman was in the kitchen of the Lodge from which he passed coffee out through a window and addressed television cameras. As he extended his arm, it was grabbed by a State Trooper. Another seized his clothing and with the assistance of Manchester Patrolman (now Sergeant) Kenneth Sucharski, the prisoner was soon subdued and handcuffed. Officer Joseph Aiello turned the man's rifle over to State Police and the immediate danger was over.

The gunman was taken to the police station here and charged with assault and battery with a dangerous weapon, with possession of a dangerous weapon, with breaking and entering in the night time and with assault with intent to murder. He was brought to District Court in Salem by then Officer Ronald Ramos and two State Troopers. The Court Psychiatrist ruled that he was not able to comprehend the charges or their severity and thus was not competent to stand trial at the time. The Judge committed him to 20 days observation at Bridgewater State Hospital. He was due to be in court again on January 14, 1980.

Meanwhile, most of us in Manchester, unaware of the remarkably fortunate and courageous escape of the hostages, and of the bravery and dedication of our police officers, were still opening Christmas presents.

Officer Al Powers graduated from Gloucester High School in 1953. At the end of the Korean War, he served with the U.S. Army in Texas as an engineer and as a member of an armored division. Honorably Discharged in July, 1956, he moved to Manchester and became a sheet metal worker. In February, 1956, he joined the Manchester Police Department as a Reserve Officer. Appointed a permanent patrolman in 1957, he attended Massachusetts State Police Academy and served here until his retirement in 1986. Skilled with metal and wood, he rebuilt a portion of the interior of police headquarters to provide officers with additional security. He also helped to construct the building at Powder House Hill which contains the department's radio antenna equipment.

CHANCE MEETING

In 1981, Two Inquisitive Police Officers Stop to Ask Questions; Two Men Arrested

Good police work often depends upon luck and the alertness of the officers involved. Take the case of Manchester Police Officer David Towle who with Gloucester patrolman John Beaudette was returning from a friend and fellow officer's funeral in Andover (the three men were classmates at the State Police Training Academy) in April, 1981.

Towle and Beaudette, according to a news story in The Manchester Cricket, were traveling in an unmarked police cruiser and had turned down Mill Street from Route 128 when they saw two young men acting "in a suspicious manner" with a large metallic box which protruded from the trunk of their car. Both officers stopped and approached the two who at this point were trying to cover the box with a blanket. In response to Towle's questions, the men said that the box had been given to them, that they didn't want it and that they were dumping in Manchester. Advising them of the town's laws against littering, while Beaudette continued questioning the pair, Officer Towle circled the car and there discovered a safe, the bottom of which had been "jimmied and torn out." Both officers then asked the two for identification and radioed Gloucester police who called Manchester. Soon Officers Joseph Aiello and Alfred Powers were at the scene to assist.

Further conversation revealed that the men were from Beverly. Calls to area police also indicated that a safe had been stolen from a Beverly church and papers inside were identified as belonging to one of its clergy. At this point, The Cricket reported, both men confessed to stealing the safe. There were arrested for receiving stolen property and for possession of burglary tools. They were advised as to their rights and taken to police headquarters in Manchester where they were booked and later arraigned in Salem District Court.

MOTHER AND CHILD SAVED

Police Officer Braves Choking Smoke; Risks His Own Life to Rescue Two Others

Putting his own life at risk, Patrolman (now Sergeant) L. Neil Andrews rescued a six-year-old boy and his mother from a smoke-filled house in Manchester early one January morning in 1981.

Thanks to an alert neighbor, Officer Alan Gilson (now also a Sergeant) received the 911 emergency message at police headquarters. The caller reported that a smoke alarm was sounding in a nearby apartment. Gilson immediately radioed Officer Andrews and Officer David McDougall. Andrews, who was alone, arrived at the scene first.

Stepping out of the cruiser, he heard the alarm and the cries of young child. He entered the apartment to find it full of thick, choking smoke. Although hardly able to see where he was going, he followed the sounds of the boy's crying, found him upstairs, and carried him outside to safety. He then went back into the smoke-filled apartment to locate the boy's mother whom he also led outside to the safety and warmth of the cruiser.

Unable to ascertain whether there were others still inside the dwelling, Andrews went back a third time to search the entire building. He found no one. This time, however, he did discover the source of the fire—a burning sofa—which somehow he managed to remove. Officer McDougall soon arrived with fire apparatus and the blaze was extinguished.

The Board of Selectmen commended Officer Andrews for his heroism and for his successful rescue efforts which saved two lives. The incident obviously emphasizes also the importance of installing properly located, functioning smoke alarms.

EDUCATION & TRAINING

Today's Officers Must Be Highly Professional, Continually Trained in a Changing Society

In the old days, police officers were issued a uniform, a billy club and a pistol, some elementary instructions and ordered to walk their beats. Many of them, however devoted, brave and loyal they were, had graduated only from grammar school. They learned their profession primarily from older members of the department who were delighted to take younger men under their wings. It was, in effect, a school of hard knocks which, in its own way, was surprisingly successful.

Today, however, in a much more complicated and litigious society, police officers must be well educated, highly professional and continually trained. Nowhere is this better exemplified than in the backgrounds of two men appointed Sergeant and Inspector of the Manchester Police Department in late 1982. One of these men today is Chief. The other continues as Detective Sergeant. Both grew up here, went to school here, and thus, like so many police officers before them, have an understanding of the town and its traditions, and a sympathy and affection for its citizens, a large majority of whom they know personally.

VIETNAM VETERAN

Kenneth Sucharski joined the department in 1972. After his graduation from Manchester High School in 1967, Sucharski served three tours of duty in Vietnam with the U.S. Army as an Infantry Squad Leader where he was wounded in action. Honorably discharged with the rank of Sergeant, he attended North Shore Community College and Northern Essex Community College. He is a graduate of the Massachusetts State Police Academy and the Attorney General's Drug and Alcohol Abuse School. He is a member of the New England Narcotic Enforcement Officers Association and annually completes its two-week refresher seminars. Since 1978, he has been a nationally registered Emergency Medical Technician (EMT) and his personnel file contains two letters of commendation from District Attorney Kevin Burke. He was appointed Inspector in 1980.

Ronald Ramos, now Manchester's Chief of Police, was named in 1982 to take Sucharski's place as Inspector. A classmate of Sucharski's at Manchester High School, Ramos also joined the department in 1972 becoming a permanent police officer in 1974. The following year, he received an Associates Degree from North Shore Community College and in 1979, he graduated with honors from Northeastern University with a Bachelor of Science Degree in Law Enforcement. He holds a Master's Degree in Police Administration from Anna Maria College as well, and is a graduate of the Command Training School at Babson Institute.

All in a day's work. Chief of Police Felix Radack (far right) directs traffic at the scene of an auto accident at the Surf Restaurant on a Sunday morning in September, 1980. "Drive in Service at the Surf Lounge" quipped The Manchester Cricket *in its photo caption. The operator of the vehicle was arrested for driving under the influence. His passenger suffered a head injury.*

Present day uniforms contrast sharply with the tall hats, high collars and heavy coats of early years. From left, Police Officers Bill Maijenski, Sergeant David Matrano, Chief Ronald Ramos, Sergeant Neil Andrews and David Lynn. Photo taken in 1988 at Singing Beach.

Ramos has completed the 10-week course at Massachusetts' State Police Academy and has attended the Attorney General's Drug and Alcohol Abuse School as well as numerous drug and alcohol seminars and police science courses. He, too, is a member of the New England Narcotic Enforcement Officers Association and is a Red Cross Cardiopulmonary Resuscitation (CPR) instructor. He has been a nationally registered EMT since 1975. In 1984, following the retirement of Felix "Pop" Radack, Ron Ramos was appointed Chief.

JOINS NAVY AT 17

Sergeant Alan Gilson, whose father was a senior pilot for Trans World Airlines, grew up in Marblehead, Manchester, Wenham and Woolwich, Maine where he attended Bath High School. After working at Brunswick Naval Air Station, he joined the U.S. Navy at age 17 in 1960. Upon completion of "Boot Camp" at Great Lakes Naval Training Station, he shipped out aboard the USS GLACIER, AGB-4, a diesel-electric powered Navy icebreaker which was a part of two Antarctic Research Projects, Deep Freeze 6 and Deep Freeze 7. In 1962, with the rate of Engineman 2nd Class, Gilson transferred to a floating drydock in Davisville, Rhode Island which helped maintain destroyers for the North Atlantic Fleet. Honorably Discharged in 1964, he moved back to Manchester and for three years worked for Sylvania in Danvers.

During the summer of 1967, with then Police Officer Bob LaFreniere, he jumped overboard to save the life of a man involved in a boating accident off Manchester. Hearing about the incident, Chief Allen Andrews asked if he'd ever thought about becoming a police officer. "I started in June, 1967 as a Reserve," Alan recalled, "at $2.68 an hour. We worked a 70 to 80-hour week with no time and a half. Because of their hourly rate, Reserves often made more than Regulars." In 1968, Gilson was appointed Patrolman and a permanent member of the department.

Because of the crushing work week, little time off, no overtime, and less pay than comparable jobs, low morale plagued police in the late 1960's and early 1970's, resulting in a significant turnover of personnel. Because of scheduling, too, officers often had to spend their few days off each month in court where they received $4.20 a day no matter how long they had to be there. Men were working two jobs to earn enough money to pay their mortgages or rent. As a result, they saw little of their wives and children. Family break-ups were not uncommon.

EDUCATIONAL INCENTIVES

The coming of a four-day-on, two-day-off work week and overtime pay, however, turned things around dramatically as did State-directed educational incentives which meant that an officer could earn 15 percent more with an Associates degree, 20 percent more with a Bachelors degree and 25 percent more with a Masters. Gilson, for example, with the assistance of the GI Bill and State aid, received his Associates Degree in Criminal Justice from North Shore Community

College in 1977. Earlier, in 1974, he also attended Massachusetts State Police Academy in Framingham. The program of educational incentives was a benefit not only for the officers involved but for communities, providing them with new levels of police professionalism in an increasingly complicated law enforcement environment.

In 1981, Alan Gilson was made Sergeant. He had earned his EMT in 1975. Of all of the cases he remembers in his now 32 years of police work, one in which he and Bob LaFreniere captured two men who broke into Ellis Chevrolet on Summer Street stands out. "They had also stolen a million dollar collection of scrimshaw and it was sitting right there in their VW wagon. It was a great arrest" he added, "for two rookies!"

In May, 1985, David Metrano, then a 14-year veteran of the department, was appointed one of four Police Sergeants upon the retirement of Sergeant William F. Hurley. A graduate of Boston University with a Bachelor of Science Degree in Police Science, Metrano, too, attended the Massachusetts State Police Academy. Certified as a Firearms Instructor by the Massachusetts Training Council, he became the department's Firearms Officer. A six-year veteran of the U.S. Navy, Metrano received several special commendations for excellence in the performance of his duties.

CONTINUOUS TRAINING

Today's police officers must also maintain their hard-earned skills with with a remarkable array of continuing training exercises. With the assistance of Federal and State funding, Manchester police now receive a total of some 2,000 hours of "in service" training each year. This includes a quarterly session on the range with firearms and participation in courses offered by the Massachusetts Criminal Justice Training Council including constitutional law, motor vehicle law, domestic violence, child abuse, elderly abuse and crisis intervention.

Officers must maintain their status as EMT's and are certified each year in speed control radar, emergency vehicle handling and suicide prevention. They are also required to monitor designated courses offered on closed circuit TV by The Law Enforcement Training Network located in Dallas, Texas.

QUICK WORK

Top Investigative Skills Solve a $12,000 Safe-cracking Robbery in a Week

When thieves broke into Manchester's Richdale market one night in April, 1983, cut their way into the store's safe with an acetylene torch and stole more than $12,000, it took little more than a week for Manchester police to apprehend them.

Working with information gathered from several sources including Salem police, then Police Inspector Ronald Ramos (now Chief of Manchester's Police Department), arrested a trio of men from Beverly, Peabody and Salem.

One was taken in Peabody after a search warrant had been obtained for his home. Some $1,300 in cash was recovered. Another was apprehended at home in Beverly. And a third, from Salem, was arrested in Peabody by Inspector Ramos and Police Officer (now Sergeant) Neil Andrews on a warrant from Peabody District Court. Both Andrews and Officer Alfred Powers assisted with the investigation.

PRISON ESCAPEE

Federal Fugitive Is Discovered Here In 1984; He Is Captured in Central Square

In May, 1984, Manchester seemed to offer an ideal hiding place for an escapee from a Federal prison in Florida who was awaiting trial for drug trafficking. That is until then Inspector Ronald Ramos (now Chief of Police) received information that he might be in the area. Ramos was also warned that the runaway was armed, might resist apprehension, and should be considered dangerous.

Investigation revealed that a man renting a room in town fit the description of the fugitive and the net began to tighten. Several U.S. Marshals arrived and with local police, all in plain clothes, under the direction of Inspector Ramos and Sergeant Allen Gilson, surveillance of the man's resident began. He left the house shortly afterwards and when he reached Central Square, Ramos and a Federal Warrant Supervisor made the arrest. The man, who showed no resistance, was processed here and turned over to U.S. Marshals for appearance at Federal District Court in Boston. Local officers involved in the surveillance included Inspector Ramos, Sergeant Gilson, Sergeant Kenneth Sucharski, and police officers Matt D'Angelo, David Towle and now Sergeant Neil Andrews.

A subsequent search of the fugitive's room resulted in police finding a loaded 38 caliber revolver, 50 rounds of ammunition, a hunting knife and personal accessories such as clothing and a wig.

POLICE FIREARMS

Weapons Have Improved in Fire Power and Sophistication Since The Early Days

Firearms issued to Manchester police have improved over the years. In the early days, each patrolman carried a 32 caliber Colt, Iver Johnson or Harrington & Richardson revolver, not in a holster, according to Firearms Officer Sergeant Neil Andrews, but in the pocket of their great coats. Later, officers were equipped with Colt 38 caliber Police Positive Specials, also revolvers. Most then wore their sidearms holstered on their right hip, but Chief Allen Andrews preferred to cross draw his weapon and his holster was always on his left side. In the 1970's and 1980's, with Chief Felix Radack's permission, many officers purchased their own weapons. A favorite was a 357 magnum revolver with a four-inch barrel often manufactured in stainless steel by Smith & Wesson. But in 1985, Chief Ronald Ramos instituted a study which lead to an overhaul of the department's weapons program. Today, all officers carry Austrian-made Glock automatic pistols. These are 40 caliber with two, 15 shot clips offering maximum fire and stopping power. The department's arsenal also includes police pump shotguns. Each police officer carries handcuffs, a heavy-duty flashlight, either a Maglight or a K-Light, surgical gloves and a mask to protect themselves from disease, and often a Buck knife. In the 1970's, Mace was popular. Today, officers carry a pepper spray, at times a small billy club and always a Motorola, two-way radio.

THREE GENERATIONS

Andrews Family Has a Record of Distinguished Service to the Town

There is little disagreement that the Andrews family is the "First Family" of the Manchester Police Department. Its roots stretch back into the town's history. John Andrews came to Essex in 1635 and in 1637 settled in Manchester. Leonard Andrews, born in 1867, was appointed Manchester's first Police Sergeant. His father was a Manchester veteran of the Civil War. Leonard's son, L. Allen Andrews, served as Chief of the Police Department from 1942 to 1968, the first on Civil Service. Chief Andrews' nephew, Neil Andrews, graduated from Manchester High School in 1967. Educated as a machinist at Bryant College, he worked as a plumber for his father and joined the police department as a Reserve Officer in April, 1972. A permanent patrolman by 1981, he was appointed Sergeant in 1984. He is also Firearms Officer. The three generations of the Andrews family span an extraordinary total of more than 100 years of police service.

HARBORMASTERS

Unique Position Brings Order and Public Safety to the Town's Waterways

Manchester Harbor has always been one of the town's most precious assets and the role of Harbormaster through the years has increased in importance as the use of the harbor, and especially the number of moorings, has grown exponentially. Under statutes of the Commonwealth of Massachusetts, Harbormasters have limited police power and thus are subject to the partial jurisdiction here of the Manchester Police Department.

Manchester's first Harbormaster of record was Lewis Lations who served from 1904 to 1922. Following him were David Fenton, owner and operator of Fenton's Boat Yard, 1923 to 1925; Henry Hall, Captain and Steward of the Manchester Yacht Club, 1926 to 1955; summer resident and former Manchester Yacht Club Commodore U. Haskell Crocker, 1956 to 1957; Roland Brooks, 1958 to 1974; and Robert E. McDiarmid, 1974 to 1985. Although McDiarmid and those before him reported directly to the Board of Selectmen, he was also a Special Police Officer as was Henry Hall, Haskell Crocker and Roland Brooks.

Since the end of World War II, the increase in recreational boating here has been dramatic. Records show that 155 boats were moored in Manchester harbor in 1955. By 1966, just 10 years later, that number had increased to 475. In 1978, 600 mooring permits were issued and an additional 100 boats were moored at floats and marinas. By 1994, the number of mooring permits had risen to 890. An additional 310 user permits were provided for craft at marinas and floats, making a total of 1,100 boats of different sizes and descriptions in Manchester harbor.

Harbormaster Roland Brooks points to map of Manchester during a meeting. Brooks served as Harbormaster for 16 years from 1958 to 1974. He and his wife Helen who used to accompany him aboard the harbor patrol boat, HELEN G, were familiar figures in Manchester waters.

Today, Manchester's Harbormaster is its Chief of Police, Ronald Ramos. His deputy is Associate Harbormaster and Reserve Police Officer Peter Mains who operates the Police Boat and patrols Manchester waters coordinating his activities, including search and rescue, with other town and city Harbormasters in the region and with the U.S. Coast Guard in Gloucester and in Boston. Assistant Harbormasters are Sergeants Alan Gilson and Neil Andrews and Patrolmen Todd Fitzgerald and William Davidson. Mains also conducts classes in boating safety for adults and students.

The Police Boat today is a commercial-grade hull built by Boston Whaler. It offers speed, maneuverability and durability and is captained by Associate Harbormaster and Reserve Police Officer Peter Mains. Equipped with the latest electronic navigational and communications devices, the craft is able in a seaway and capable of search, rescue and security missions along or just off shore.

Police Force 1995: from left, first row: Sergeants Alan Gilson, Neil Andrews and Kenneth Sucharski; Patrolmen John Swallow, Bill Davidson, David Towle, Todd Fitzgerald; Chief Ronald Ramos; Associate Harbormaster Peter Mains; Lois Nagle, Secretarial Staff; Dick Towle, MPD Photographer; Betty Mulcahy, Dispatcher; Barbara Lane, Secretarial Staff; Frank Wood, Dispatcher; Second row, from left: Patrolmen Doug Puska, Richard Rizzo, Stephen Driscoll, Joe Aiello, John Kenney; Third row, from left: Patrolmen Tom Eagan, Dick Lysiak, William Maijenski and David McDougall. Photo by Laura Imbeault

SOME STATISTICS

Eight Police Officers Today Have Served the Town for More Than 20 Years

Police officers today with more than 20 years of service to the town include: Chief Ronald Ramos; Sergeants Neil Andrews, Alan Gilson and Kenneth Sucharski; Patrolmen Joseph Aiello, David McDougall, John Kenney and Richard Lysiak, and Clerk Frank Wood.

Since 1895, 14 Chiefs of Police have served the Town of Manchester. They are: George A. Brown, J.P. Carter and George Haskell (part-time, 1860's-1897); Thomas O.D. Urquhart (1897-1902); Samuel Peabody (1902-1909); William H. Sullivan (1909-1910); Michael E. Gorman (1911-1912); Frank D. Converse (1912-1913); William H. Sullivan (1913-1923); George R. Dean (1923-1931); Stewart F. Cooper (1931-1933); George R. Dean (1933-1942); L. Allen Andrews (1942-1968); Felix Radack (1968-1984); and Ronald Ramos (1984-present).

LANDMARK DATES

1864: Selectmen appoint 20 part-time volunteer police officers, first of three part-time chiefs appointed; 1894, SEASIDE 1, former fire house is designated police headquarters; 1897: Town Meeting voters authorize establishment of a full-time police department, Thomas O.D. Urquhart becomes Chief, Leonard Andrews its first patrolman; 1898: first phone acquired; 1901: first call boxes installed, police issue first ticket to automobiles for exceeding the speed limit; 1902: Leonard Andrews named first Sergeant of Police, Manchester acquires its first horse-drawn ambulance; 1903: Samuel Peabody becomes Chief and with his son Alan, he invents new trap to catch "scorchers", speeding motor cars which menace the safety of pedestrians and horse-drawn vehicles; 1909: all but Chief's position now under Civil Service; 1904: first Harbormaster appointed; 1909-1913: four chief's appointed, each serve one year; 1913: William H. Sullivan becomes Chief; 1916: Byron Bullock first motorcycle officer; 1919: police granted one day off in eight and 10 days paid vacation, town acquires its first motorized ambulance;

A DEADLY HILL; DANGEROUS CORNERS

1920's: at Craft's Hill, Duwart's Corner and Dead Man's Corner, auto, truck and bus accidents take a lethal toll each year; 1923: George R. Dean becomes Chief; 1924, police purchase first patrol car or cruiser; 1920's: Prohibition provides new challenges for police departments everywhere; 1925: fire at police station destroys old hose tower; 1929: Town Meeting vote authorizes pensions to be paid to retiring police officers, new uniforms adopted with two vertical rows of brass buttons and "choker" collars; 1930: Stewart F. Cooper becomes Chief; 1937: Jacob Lee, last of the original patrolmen, retires; 1933: George Dean become Chief once again; 1942: Allen Andrews named chief, World War II, Andrews joins U.S. Army, Jack Connors appointed Acting Chief; 1946: Andrews returns from the Pacific Theater to take over again as Chief of Police; 1950's: Police Department grows to 12 full-time officers including two sergeants, first two-way radios are installed in patrol car and at headquarters; 1955: first uniformed woman is appointed traffic control officer at schools; 1968: Sergeant Felix "Pop" Radack becomes chief;

DRUG ERA BEGINS

1960's: Drug era begins in earnest, major raids take place on Cape Ann; 1968: first radar unit purchased to measure speed of passing vehicles; 1970's: focus on individual rights, Miranda Law is initiated, Federal and State laws and financial grants initiate comprehensive new programs for training police officers at Massachusetts State Police Academy and elsewhere; 1970: new Town Hall and Police Station are completed; 1973: Manchester Police Association established, Teletype terminal installed, linking Manchester to other law enforcement agencies throughout the U.S., EMT training required for officers who operate the ambulance; 1974: "911" emergency call system starts; 1979: Breathalyzer device acquired to use in drunk driving cases; 1980: third cruiser added (unmarked) for police investigator; 1983: new communications system installed known as BAPERN, Boston Area Police Emergency Radio Network;

RAMOS NAMED CHIEF

1983: Sergeant Ronald Ramos becomes Chief of Police; 1980's: focus is on "proactive and preventive" law enforcement, training is expanded, DARE program and school safety programs enlarged, officers work with Cape Ann Regional Drug Strike Force, first uniformed woman officer with the power of arrest joins the department; bicycle patrol unit established, modern police boat acquired, animal control officer appointed, department continues to be professionalized.

PRICELESS MEMORIES

Nat Andrews, Brother of Chief Andrews, Recalls Some Wonderful Stories of the Past

In 1984, former Chairman of the Board of Selectmen Nat Andrews, son of Manchester's first police Sergeant Leonard Andrews and brother of Chief Allen Andrews, wrote a delightful personal history of the department which appeared in The Manchester Cricket on August 3. It included some wonderful stories of the old days told to him by his father. They are priceless part of the town's history and some are reproduced again below.

"The Townies (so called) had built a Fourth of July bonfire stack at the park in 1899. It was torched several days ahead of time by a number of young men from the summer colony. Three of these young men were apprehended in the act, taken to the station and their parents informed of the incident.

"One parent asked to speak with his errant son and when the conversation was ended the young man informed Officer

Today's sophisticated police cruisers with their pursuit engine packages and distinctive striping are a far cry from the Dodge sedan patrol cars officers used for transport in the 1930's. Manchester now has three cruisers including one unmarked vehicle used for investigative purposes.

Andrews in rather an agitated voice, 'My father wants to talk with you.' The boy's father politely asked how long his son could legally be kept in custody. He was told, whereupon he requested that his son be kept there every minute of it if possible. Officer Andrews told him that wasn't necessary and that the young man could be more use helping his fellow culprits rebuild the fire stack in time for Fourth of July eve. The parents of these boys and others who owned up to the torching saw to it [that] the "Townies" had another stack ready for the Fourth.

YOUNG LABORERS

"About this time [early 1900's], many summer estates were being developed. Local contractors were very busy and many laborers were needed. Many of them were from the "Auld Sod." They were excellent graders, sod layers, planters of shrubbery and good teamsters. Some would have a few too many on a weekend night and would of necessity be locked up for their own protection.

"Sergeant Andrews took a great interest in these men and would have a good stiff drink of their confiscated whiskey awaiting them on the condition that they go to work when released. He often said it was very seldom [that] any of these men let him down and the contractors were pleased to have [them] back at work. Many of these men, they were young then, and being in this country only a short time, led a somewhat lonely life.

THE CASKET DISAPPEARED

"The opportunity to attend a wake arose one summer's evening at a house not far from where I lived as a boy. This particular wake was held on the rear porch of the couple's house.

"As the evening progressed, so did the tempo of things in general. The police received a call, I presume, from an irate neighbor. When Sergeant Andrews and Officer Sheehan arrived at the scene, they were informed that the casket and its remains had disappeared. He looked the gathering over, had a word with Officer Sheehan who nodded in agreement. Sergeant Andrews, trying to keep a straight face, told them to have the casket with the deceased back in 10 minutes or the

At Police headquarters in the early 1970's. Seated, from left: Officer Bill Laskowski, Sergeant Jim Mulvey, Officer Arthur Day; Standing: Officers David Matreno, Craige McCoy, Kenneth Sucharski; Alan Gilson, Al Powers and David Towle.

wake was over. This was done and the wake allowed to continue in a more subdued manner. The deceased laid out in all its splendor in its own casket lined with purple satin, was promptly and suitably buried the next morning. It was the couple's pet bulldog who had died several days [earlier].

OUT OF UNIFORM

"Back in the early thirties when we were young, we often congregated in front of Doc Chaney's drugstore in Central Square. I happened to see a veteran police officer who was proceeding by foot to the Library. I hustled across the street to speak to him and made him aware of his headgear. He ducked behind the Library while I went to the station and got his regulation uniform cap and brought it to him. He was in full uniform but had forgotten he was still wearing a straw hat. I will say this, no one hooted or made any remarks and he later showed his appreciation by letting us sit on the Library wall once in a while.

TALL HELMETS AND GREAT COATS

"I'm old enough to remember the old-time uniforms. The single row of brass buttons...the wide black belts with the large circular buckle. The tall helmets, blue in the fall and spring, light gray in the summer time. The teamster-type felt hats with ear flaps in the winter time. The heavy winter overcoats with the heavy belt and buckle and later heavy overcoat with the double row of brass buttons. And last but not least, the high wing collars. They are gone forever...

TIME TO GO HOME

"I close with one of [Chief Allen Andrew's] favorite stories when he was a young rookie. The Launch Club at that time rented the former firemen's hall above the station. Their 'meetings' at times lasted until the wee hours of the [morning]. Several calls came into the station. The officer on the desk told an irate wife he would see to it [that her husband got her message to come home. He did this [when] a third call came in which the desk officer promised her he would soon be on his way home. The desk officer was J.W. [Jacob] Lee, a veteran of nearly 30 years at the time.

"He kept his word to the irate wife. He walked over to the fuse box on the first floor and removed the second floor fuses, plunging the hall into darkness. Soon steps were heard

Police Basketball Team, 1970. First row, from left: Alex Backry, Jim Mulvey, Craige McCoy, Bill Hurley; Back row: Alan Gilson, Bruce Hudson, Lou Gates, Arthur Day, Tom Bourke.

coming down the stairs. No police officer had actually seen what was going on upstairs. I rather bet that [the] man was a winner that night as I'm sure he caught it when he got home."

BIBLIOGRAPHY

Editions of The Manchester Cricket, 1870-1980; Edition of the Gloucester Daily Times, 1940; Article by Chief Ronald W. Ramos entitled Police Department, which appeared in Manchester-by-the-Sea, 1645-1995, published by the 350th Anniversary Committee, Manchester-by-the-Sea, Massachusetts, 1999; Lamson, Rev. D.F., History of the Town of Manchester, 1645-1895, Town of Manchester; Boston, The Pinkham Press, 1895; Records and Logs of the Manchester Police Department; Files of the Manchester Historical Society and personal interviews and other newspaper clippings (see introduction).

ILLUSTRATIONS

Archival photographs from the collection of the Manchester Police Department; photographs from the collection of the Manchester Historical Society; photo of Police Station, Manchester, Massachusetts, 1919, Society for the Preservation of New England Antiquities; photo of Officer Felix Radack with motor cycle by John C. Burke; photo of Magnolia Casino courtesy of the Peabody-Essex Museum, Salem, Massachusetts; and photos from the collections of Mrs. Arthur B. Collins, Mrs. Doris Connors, Francis Jess James, William Radack and Mrs. Howard B. Towle.

A RENAISSANCE

Christening a New Building at the Manchester Yacht Club Gives Rise to Many Memories

A shorter version of the article which appears below was presented by the author at the dedication and christening ceremony on Saturday, July 10, 1999 of the new building of the Manchester Yacht Club. For REFLECTIONS, it has been enlarged and expanded with added personal memories of earlier times. During the winter of 1998-1999, the club house, built for the Manchester Yacht Club in 1895, was razed to make way for the new structure which is scheduled to be completed in August, 1999.

We are here today to dedicate a new and very welcome building which will stand as the old one did — we hope and trust — for more than 100 years. A clubhouse is not a club. It's members are. But these facilities, these buildings, porches, piers, gangways and floats, are the welcoming stage which permit us access to the waters we love and which allow us to gather as friends and sailing companions in fair weather and foul to enjoy each others company.

It has always intrigued me that the original club house of the Manchester Yacht Club was built in little more than a month. The corner stone was laid in mid-June, 1895 and on Tuesday, July 16 of that same year, the property was open for use and dedicated in ceremonies much like these today.

As <u>The Manchester Cricket</u> reported: "The day was a stormy one, but the best cheer prevailed inside. Tea was served at five o'clock, a table being spread with many delicacies." The Club, of course, was organized, if not incorporated, in 1892. Its original members were yachtsmen from Manchester and members of the Beverly Farms Yacht Club who had been using a bath house at West Beach as their clubhouse.

In 1895, the Town of Manchester purchased what is now the some six acres of public land at Tuck's Point from Dr. Cyrus A. Bartol, a Unitarian minister who had a sharp eye for real estate and who at one time owned Norton's Point and much of Smith's Point as well as his own substantial dwelling at Glass Head.

As many of you may know, the point itself is named for Captain William Tuck who moved to Manchester from Beverly in 1760 and occupied the house on Harbor Street now owned by Past Commodore Tom Walker and his wife Ann. A colorful character, Tuck was owner and skipper of the privateer REMINGTON which took many prizes during the Revolutionary War. A man of considerable talents, he served as Customs Collector for the City of Gloucester, as a Justice of the Peace and as a practicing physician. Married four times, he was the father of 23 children, 14 of whom lived to maturity.

The town paid Dr. Bartol $5,000 for the property at Tuck's Point and an additional $1,000 for an existing wharf. It then conveyed to two MYC members, Gordon Prince and William A. Tucker, the wharf and a parcel of land about 30 feet wide at its northern end, pending the incorporation of

REFLECTIONS, a publication of the Manchester Historical Society, is researched, written and edited by Gordon Abbott, Jr., a member of its Board of Directors.

the Manchester Yacht Club. This took place at a meeting on June 10, 1895. Members then immediately voted to buy the land and the wharf and to authorize a mortgage on the property in the amount of $3,000. Architect Ernest Machado of Salem was chosen to design the club's new headquarters and to supervise its construction. The dry stone wall under the new club house is a part of the original pier which was known as Marster's Wharf after another early owner. Built prior to 1890, this sturdy foundation, which holds us up today, has withstood without damage more than a century of winter storms and hurricanes.

ADDITIONS PROPOSED IN 1903

By 1903, additions were already being proposed to the original buildings. Back of the "Boat House" (the small structure on the left as you then faced the old club from the water), a room was built which housed a galley with a kerosene stove, a sink and two Murphy beds which folded up against the wall. They were still there when I was a kid in the 1930's and were used by Henry Hall who served as Club Captain for 49 years, from 1911 to 1960, his brother Charlie and Henry's predecessor, Bill Cunningham.

In the early part of the century, until use of the automobile grew just prior to World War I, members arrived at the yacht club by horse and carriage. Whether there was a problem with parking as there is today, history does not reveal, but the Club's records do show that in September, 1895, a railing some 40 feet in length was erected "for hitching purposes."

Attempting to encourage the use of the club house in 1897, the Executive Committee on August 12, voted to authorize sale on the premises of such refreshments as "brandy, whiskey, beer, ginger ale, cheese and biscuits." Eighteen days later, however, on August 30, the Committee apparently thought better of its commitment, nullifying the motion, and repealing and declaring null and void its earlier action "concerning the sale of intoxicating liquor at the clubhouse." There has been no deviation from the policy ever since. Except at special events and private parties, the Club has wisely refrained from ever continually operating a bar or a restaurant. Through the years, however, there have been plenty of pleasant opportunities to "bring your own bottle."

By 1901, the club had installed a telephone and in June of that year it was decided that tables in the Reading Room which was housed in the larger structure on the right as you viewed the old club from the channel, should be equipped with pitchers of "ice water." Indeed, the Reading Room from which the By Laws specifically stated "no publication shall be removed," offered members, according to an old bill from Floyd's News Store, the enjoyment of perusing copies of "Harper's Weekly, Leslie's Weekly, Puck, Judge, Life, Forest & Stream, Outing and Rudder" magazines.

As early as 1897, the Club initiated its popular, annual day devoted to "Water Sports." Up to 300 people, dressed in their finery — ladies in long, summer dresses with broad-brimmed hats and gentlemen in celluloid collars and straw boaters — gathered on the porches and at the floats to watch their children, grandchildren and other youngsters walk the pole, in costumes of their choice, to reach the miniature MYC flag at its tip. Other events for boys and girls included tub races, canoe tilting, and swimming and rowing races.

Often, a string orchestra played on the porch and tea was always served as the afternoon ended. News of the Water Sports regularly appeared in the Society pages of the Boston Evening Transcript, the Brahmin newspaper of the day, and always, usually with a montage of photographs, in the North Shore Breeze, a weekly magazine devoted to the social doings of the summer colony. Water Sports lasted through the 1950's when somehow life began to accelerate in other directions.

Up to the arrival of World War I, the Club thrived, winning boat races locally, elsewhere on the East Coast and even abroad, and gaining a respect for its sailing abilities which was remarkable for its size. But in January, 1918 with war still raging in Europe, use of the club had dropped to a worrisome low. Finances were a major problem and the Executive Committee, with perhaps a bit too gloomy an outlook for the future, asked the membership "for permission to wind up the affairs of the club, provided that they can effect a sale of the property at a price which, in their judgement, is adequate."

Thankfully, cooler heads prevailed and the meeting voted "that the Club property should not be sold." The premises were opened again that summer "on a reduced scale of expense." When the war ended, a special committee, appointed by the Commodore, successfully increased the number of members and encouraged a new interest in yacht racing. The buildings, then 23 years old, heaved an appreciative sigh of relief and once again in the Reading Room, tea was served in the afternoons "on Saturdays, Sundays and Race Days."

FIRST JUNIOR PROGRAM

In 1921, the Club started its first program to teach youngsters to sail using its class of 13-foot, flat-bottomed, centerboard skiffs. G.N. McNaughton, billed as an "experienced yachtsman," was hired as head instructor.

The old Club House also had a front row seat during Prohibition watching one rum-runner with an illegal cargo of spirits aboard meant for a prominent resident of Beverly Farms, fetch up on Half Tide Ledges during the night. Another fast craft, loaded with cases of whiskey, found her way into Tuck's Point Cove. There she, too, grounded out at low water and was discover by Henry Hall, then Club Captain, the following morning. "I called the Chief of Police," Henry reported, "and we towed her up the harbor. The Coast Guard came over from Gloucester for the boat, but I never did find out what happened to all that liquor."

The Great Depression also took its toll on club activities. Pressed financially, a significant number of members resigned and for a while it was difficult to know whether funds could be found to pay Henry's salary. Fortunately, for all and for the future of the Manchester Yacht Club, they were, but these were still desperate years. As the economy improved, again in an effort to attract new members, construction of a swimming pool was proposed. Connolly Brothers of Beverly Farms designed one for the club and estimated its cost at $24,000. It was never built and only heaven knows where it might have been put!

Between the wars, the Club offered its members the opportunity to fuel their boats and there were two SOCONY gas pumps located near the bathhouses on the east side of the buildings. Those were the days of professional skippers and paid hands. I well remember many of them around the Club

who each day rowed out to their yachts which varied in size from Manchester 17 and 18-footers to eight and 10 meter boats. There they would chamois off the dew, shine brass winches, blocks and cowl ventilators, care for hemp and cotton sheets and halyards, and touch up hatches and trim whose varnished mahogany sparkled like diamonds in the summer sun.

Dressed in khaki with black ties, brown sneakers with white soles, and yachting caps with the MYC burgee and the owner's private signal crossed above their visors, these were the last of the real watermen and role models for each of us fortunate enough to grow up in that long-ended era. They could splice, hand, reef and steer like old-time sailors and thanks to their patience, understanding and good humor, we learned the art of marlinspike seamanship and how to handle small boats smartly and with precision in every sort of weather.

During World War II, because of fuel rationing, the Club launch was put to bed at Dion's Yacht Yard. Armed Coast Guard reservists patrolled the shorelines 24 hours a day on the lookout for saboteurs who could be landed by submarine. There were few adult males around and we kids were brought up by Henry, a Navy veteran of World War I, racing and sailing our own dinghies without formal instruction. For those four of us who hung out around the Club daily, there was a mix of summer pastimes — riding an old bike with a line attached down the gangway across the floats and into the harbor; digging clams with the high pressure hose at low water, and in our bathing suits, leaping from railings and roof tops when the tide was high. We spent hours when we were young in rowing dinghies in muddy coves and on the islands.

Henry was like a father to us (mine was far away in the Pacific from 1940 until just before I got out of the Navy myself in late 1946), giving us just enough rein to do what boys do before teaching us how to be responsible as well as rambunctious. As we grew to be older teens, we mixed our pleasures with summer jobs (I worked at Standley's Garage in the back shop for two years), but there was still time to collect storm-damaged lobster traps along the shore in winter, repair them and set them again using wood buoys marked proudly with our own colors. One season we had as many as 75 traps set and rarely did we haul one without at least two "counters." The boat we had — an old one of Henry's, one of the 13-foot skiffs — we propelled by oars, two pairs of them, as were many that were used for fishing in those days.

For added excitement after supper on long summer evenings, we would row out to the flats off Long Beach and there, at low water, we would spear flounders which we would take home, and sculpins, known as "grubbies," which we would not. With the war, there lots of girls around but no men, and to provide entertainment Yacht Club dances were regularly scheduled. Attended by scores of Naval officers, many of them British or French from ships being repaired at Boston, these were wild affairs. We would watch from a safe distance as quarts of champagne were iced down in the green wood tubs used for Water Sports and the swing music of the era lasted long after we were supposed to be in bed.

After the war, things returned to normal and a new generation of youngsters, far larger than our small group, was formally instructed in the arts of sailing and seamanship as part of a hugely popular, well-organized, Manchester Yacht Club operated, Junior Program. Indeed, many non-sailors joined the Club just so their kids could take part and there was a sizable waiting list for membership. Rowboats, too, were replaced by the luxury of launch service. The YOU-ALL, donated to the MYC by a generous member, was operated by Fred Nataloni who served as Club Captain from 1960 to 1968. In 1966, the Club purchased WHALEBACK and two years later, HALFTIDE. The decision to build TRIDENT was made in 1965. She was launched at Bass Harbor, Maine and brought home to Manchester the following spring. Finished and in commission, she cost the Club just more than $9,000.

Through the years, changes to the original buildings designed by Ernest Machado were slowly made to meet the demands of each era. Bathhouses and lockers were built on the west side of the Club. After World War II, the bluestone driveway and parking area were paved with asphalt, the deck in front of the gangway was partially extended to provide additional space for Club functions and an office was constructed for the Club Captain.

ORIGINAL ARCHITECTURE ALTERED

In the late 1950's, the original architecture of the Club, which was so beautifully proportioned, was all but destroyed by the construction of much-needed quarters for the Junior Program. By the 1970's, a planning study urged other changes which included an extension of the deck to its present size and the addition of a workshop for then Club Captain Carl Magee.

Somewhat earlier, the swimming porch (later known as the English Martini Porch, named for former secretary Bill English), was washed out to sea in an early spring storm further disturbing the integrity of the original design. Boxes and lockers were added on the deck as they were needed, as were bottles of LP gas for the galley and a container for trash barrels, both out front. Convenient, even necessary — yes — but still clutter on the surface and at the entrance of what was once a simple but elegant concept.

Old age, wear and tear, as well as storms and hurricanes also took their toll upon the buildings. Following the great February Blizzard of 1978, Connolly Brothers was called in to pour more than 100 yards of concrete to form a pad under the Club to provide needed support. Mark Clemenzi, working to build this new club house, was one of those with Connolly Brothers at the time. The three-day No Name Northeaster, only a few years ago, with its huge sea surge, also lifted the porch deck more than a foot and this, too, necessitated extensive repairs to the Club's foundation. It's a wonder as well that we didn't lose the Club to fire, for each administration from Henry Hall to Carl Magee found itself forced to douse flames started by paint guns and even by vandals in the trash receptacles by the galley door.

In 1995, Club buildings quietly observed their 100th birthday. Painting, patching, puttying and some replacement — always underway by members of the staff — kept everything standing in good geriatric order. Plans had been discussed for some time — actually as early as 1991 — which called for extensive repairs and restoration of the existing plant with the addition of several interesting features. An architect was engaged and, with understandable timidity about disturbing the original structures beloved by so many

generations of members, the Executive Committee edged forward. But it took an engineering survey to address the issue head on and to fire the first broadside in favor of economics and practicality.

AN ENGINEERING SURVEY

Because of the small size and age of the facility, and the condition of its outdated plumbing and electrical systems, the survey declared in October, 1996, it is recommended that the existing structures be completely demolished and that they be replaced with a new building. There were many in the Club who felt that such a step would brutally violate the history and traditions of more than a century. But there were others who believed, as I did, that the original buildings had been so altered over the years to meet changing demands that they had long since lost their original architectural integrity and charm. It was time to begin again.

There was a caveat, of course. The character of any new design should match the original in beauty and simplicity, reflecting the devotion to yachting and the water which has been the purpose of the Club for so many years. As the architect himself has stated: 'we tried to recreate the essence of what was there before, and yet design a building which meets the needs of the years ahead." Essence is a good word. Webster defines it as "the nature or flavor or something," and this new building, it seems to me, accomplishes its goals, preserving the best of the old — its scale, its general lines and its Greek revival waterside, while providing the best of the new — more room, more comfort, more efficiency and a more contemporary richness and grace.

It is still a collection of simple structures, neatly spliced together with details that reflect the past but do, indeed, offer new opportunities to enjoy the future. Not to be overlooked is that the chimney is the same that masons built in 1895. It is a comfort to know that it still faithfully anchors the Club in place as it always has. For more than a century, in the brisk days of spring and fall, its fireplace has warmed the backsides of many a generation of Manchester Yacht Club members.

Today, also, there seems to be a new spirit about the club, of which, in many ways, this new building is a symbol. We have a wonderful company of new members now to enjoy it. We have a new Club Captain, too, Jack Fadden, who bridges the old and the new, and who, with his associate Gordon Gilbert, will provide the new building with the necessary tender loving care.

TRADITIONS TO BE REMEMBERED

The House Committee, in its wisdom, will also provide ways to have the new Reading Room reflect the extraordinary traditions and accomplishments that have made the Manchester Yacht Club what it is today. For our burgee, which has flown on mastheads around the world, is much respected and admired wherever it appears.

I have only one regret connected with this happy occasion which I know that many of you share. It is that Carl Magee did not live long enough to see this building completed. That would have been a reward in itself, but many times last winter as I walked to this site, I thought of how much he would have enjoyed being involved in the details of its construction, for that was what Carl loved best.

In 1967, the Manchester Yacht Club observed its 75th Anniversary with a gala celebration which featured dinner and a special musical written by then Commodore Dick Preston. The theme song of the evening presentation was entitled <u>The 4th Prong on Your Trident</u>. It proposed a new era when the ladies would to take over the Club. They would be represented by another prong added to our Trident's traditional three. The final verse, sung by the Commodorables — wives of Past Commodores, who included my Mother — went like this: "We'll put a new shake in martinis, New braid for your cuff, A new shape in bikinis, An agenda that's tough. The fourth prong in your Trident, Will take in all that slack, Your

problems are over, So lie back in your sack, Don't react, Just back the 4th Trident."

I won't say that our problems are over, or even that the ladies will take charge although, who knows, they are now rightfully equal to men both in membership privilege and status, but I will say that with this wonderful building, we have reached a new beginning and, as we turn the corner into a new century, the way ahead looks very bright indeed. Thank you all.

Gordon Abbott, Jr.
Commodore 1974, 1975

Couple in a rowboat watch as a crane demolishes old Town Hall in July 1969 to make way for new municipal building which today houses headquarters of the Manchester Police Department.

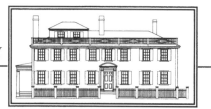

MANCHESTER HISTORICAL SOCIETY

NEWSLETTER

MANCHESTER, MASSACHUSETTS

SPRING 1998

OUR OWN CELEBRITY: J.B. BOOTH, JR.

Rare photo of the three brothers appearing in Julius Caesar performed on November 26, 1864 as a benefit for the Shakespeare Statue Fund at the Winter Garden Theater in New York City. John Wilkes Booth (left) as Mark Antony; Edwin Booth (center) as Brutus; and Manchester's Junius Brutus Booth, Jr. as Cassius. (Photo Harvard Theater Collection.)

STARS OF STARS

Junius Brutus Booth, Sr., Father of Manchester's Junius, Jr., owner of the Masconomo House

Much has been written over the years about Manchester's great summer hotel, the Masconomo House, but little has been told about its founder, Junius Brutus Booth, Jr. and his distinguished family's extraordinary contributions to the American theater. This then is the personal story of Manchester's own matinee idol, his early life, how he was affected by his brother's assassination of President Abraham Lincoln, how he came to love Manchester and settle here, and how he and his wife Agnes established the hotel and made it into one of the finest of its kind in New England.

The theater in America is as old as the country itself. In its early years it was somewhat inhibited by puritanical views of morality, but by the 1820's, stage presentations had become a popular part of American life. There were theaters in New York, Philadelphia, Baltimore, Charleston and Boston. Companies of actors traveled between cities presenting dramas which ranged from tragedy to comedy and farce with even occasional musical interludes.

People came to see the stars. The vehicle mattered less. And what stars they were! Edmund Kean whose performance as Richard III presented in November, 1820 is reported to have "brought forth almost hysterical praise." Charles Kemble and his daughter Fanny whose Juliet at the Park Theater in New York captivated her audience. And perhaps the greatest of them all, Junius Brutus Booth whose Hamlet, King Lear, Shylock and Richard III moved even such luminaries of the time as poet Walt Whitman to melodic heights of praise.

Born in England in 1796, as were so many of our early actors, Booth settled in Bel Air, Maryland, bought a farm and raised nine children. One of them, Edwin Booth, who starred as Hamlet for a then unequaled record of 100 consecutive nights, became a better known theatrical idol than his father, drawing adulation from around the world. (It was said, even by his family, that Edwin was Hamlet.) Another, John Wilkes Booth, handsomest of all his siblings, is best remembered not as an actor, but as the assassin who shot and killed President Abraham Lincoln at Ford's Theater on April, 14,1865.

A third brother, Junius Brutus Booth, Jr., the oldest, known as June, was an actor as well. He first appeared in 1834 at the age of 13 as Tyrrel in <u>Richard III</u>. His talents, however, he found later, lay primarily not on the stage, but with the management and promotion of the theater itself, and it was here that he made his name and reputation.

It was he who in 1869, fell in love with Manchester-by-the-Sea and built a cottage at the corner of Beach and Masconomo Streets. Eight years later, along side it, June and his third wife Agnes, an actress of considerable ability and charm herself, arranged for the construction of an impressive 240-bedroom summer hotel which they called the Masconomo House. Booth, who with his wife was well regarded by the community, died in Manchester in 1884 at

age 63. With his two young children, one of whom who predeceased him, he is buried in Rosedale Cemetery where his headstone may be seen today.

JUNIUS BRUTUS BOOTH, JR.

Manchester's member of the famous Booth family was born in December, 1821 at Charleston, South Carolina. His father, Junius, Sr., had left a wife, Adelaide, and a son,

Junius Brutus Booth, Jr., resident of Manchester and owner of the Masconomo House, in his later years. Photo Harvard Theater Collection.

Richard, in England to elope to America with an 18-year-old, dark-haired Covent Garden flower girl named Mary Ann Holmes who was to become June's mother. The couple made their way to Richmond, Virginia where Booth played Richard III, a role that was to propel him to stardom in the United States as it had in London. Then, following a tour of New York as well as a series of southern cities (including Charleston where Mary Ann gave birth to her first son), his father purchased a farm in near Baltimore which in time became home not only to young Junius but to nine brothers and sisters. Finally, in 1851, after Adelaide had agreed to a divorce, his mother and father were married. Junius Brutus Booth, Senior died the following year. Like their father, the boys of the Booth family shared a love of liquor, high living and beautiful women. There was a touch of madness, too, in the old man, which perhaps contributed to his genius on the stage but made him difficult to handle in ordinary life. And all of the children, it was reported, seemed to share a love of beauty, a general nervousness, and "capacity for melancholy never to be outgrown."

At first, June was assigned to rein in his father during his more exuberant moments. But he was soon replaced by his younger brother Edwin who, quite literally, became his father's keeper, traveling with him wherever he went. As author Gene Smith writes in <u>American Gothic, The Story of America's Legendary Theatrical Family</u> — <u>Junius, Edwin</u>

and John Wilkes Booth (New York and London, Simon & Schuster, 1992), "June…was practical and business-minded, a brilliant athlete [he taught his brothers swordsmanship]…[but] he was not suited to be a guardian…" Edwin, however difficult it was, profited by the association. Always fascinated with acting, he began with bit parts and ultimately became more famous than his father and is today the Booth that the world remembers. (Except, of course, for John Wilkes who made his name in quite a different way.)

All of the children but Edwin had attended school and were reasonably well educated.Their father continually proclaimed that he wanted none of his sons to become an actor. His remonstrances did little good, however. June was urged to study surgery but after a few months he, too, was on the stage. Heavy but handsome, Junius, Jr. soon married an actress. She was Clementine De Bar, 11 years his senior.

GO WEST, YOUNG MAN
1848: Gold is Discovered in California; the Booths Join Thousands Who Seek Their Fortunes

In 1848, gold was discovered in California and it changed the face of the nation. The prospect of immediate riches excited tens of thousands of Americans. Young and old, they left their parents, wives and children and journeyed west by wagon train and by ship around Cape Horn. Others traveled across the Isthmus of Panama, all braving the dangers of Indian raids, shipwreck, cholera and yellow fever until they reached the promised land. Among them, in 1851, was Junius Brutus Booth, Jr.

He sailed for California, not with Clementine and their then baby daughter Blanche, but with Harriet Mace, a pretty, young actress from Boston. Like his father before him, he had deserted his wife and child and moved in with Harriet. He had also realized that he was a fair actor but a far better administrator and he accepted an offer to become manager of the Jenny Lind Theater in San Francisco. He and Hattie were gone for 11 months and returned with fabled stories of the fabulous West.

The tune of the times was "Oh Susannah" with new words supplied by the Forty-niners which declared; "I'm off for Californy with my washbowl on my knee!" The pioneers came first with pick and shovel to pan for gold in the streams and rivers of the Sierra Mountains. They were followed by the profiteers who lived off those who had struck it rich and even those who hadn't but who, with a little money, would spend it on whiskey and beer, gambling at cards, wild women, fineries such as clothing, Cuban cigars, paperback novels by the most popular writer of the day, Charles Dickens, and the theater.

BURLESQUE AND SHAKESPEARE
In those days in the West, what took place upon the stage varied from displays of magic and wild animal shows to burlesque, pantomimes and actual dramas. There seemed to be no shortage of money and prices were wildly inflated.

Depending upon time and place, an apple could cost five dollars and a dozen eggs up to fifty. Rent for a store on Main Street could be up to $1,000 a week and when miners were pleased with a dramatic production they were apt to toss nuggets of gold upon the stage. When they were not, especially in frontier towns, there would be pistol shots aimed for the ceiling, loud and derisive remarks or boos and hisses.

Agnes Booth, a great actress herself, was hostess at the Masconomo House. Photo John and Olivia Parker Collection.

People often knew dramas, and especially Shakespeare, by heart. But there were those who didn't know what was coming next and when the heroine was being abused they often took it upon themselves to protect her, climbing down upon the stage and threatening actors until they were finally persuaded to return to their seats. The audience loved it. It was all a part of the show. Of course, in the bigger cities, life was more civilized. June established theaters in Sacramento as well as in San Francisco. Constructed of wood and lit with live candles, they often burned to the ground. But they were rebuilt overnight to the delight of their audiences.

JUNIUS, SR. JOINS HIS SONS
Shortly after he returned home to Maryland, June suggested that his father open an engagement at the Jenny Lind. The old man was intrigued. He was tired of fame and even of fortune; perhaps it was the adventure, one more world to conquer, that persuaded him. And in the spring of 1852, after an abortive earlier effort in which his father went off on a spree with a friend and forced them to miss the boat, June and Harriet, Junius Brutus Booth, Senior and Edwin, set sail from New York for Colon, Panama, aboard the sail and steam-powered vessel ILLINOIS.

From there they were polled up the Chagres River in barges, completing the trip by mule. On the west side of the Isthmus, the streets of Panama City were clogged with fortune hunters waiting for the next ship to depart for California. Hundreds had already died of fever and church bells tolled sadly throughout the days for those who would never to see their loved ones again.

Finally, passage was arranged, the Booths sailed, and soon arrived safely in San Francisco. News of their coming preceded them and every actor in town was at Long Wharf to meet them. Tom Maguire, owner of the Jenny Lind, had hired a brass band, and June and Harriet, said to be "the handsomest couple in 'Frisco," were greeted with cries of "Welcome home!" But attention centered on the tired but elegant figure of the great actor, Junius Booth, Senior, who met the gaze of the crowd with the confidence and composure of a man well used to adulation.

Up from the waterfront with its forest of spars and rigging, marched row upon row of wood frame houses. The Jenny Lind Theater was located at the corner of Portsmouth Square, the heart of San Francisco. Near it was the Bella Union, best known of the gambling halls. The company of the Jenny Lind included June Booth and Harriet who was accepted as his wife, as well as actors William and Caroline Chapman, brother and sister, who had been raised aboard their father's showboat on the Mississippi River. Junius Booth, Senior and his friend, actor George Spear, known as Old Spudge, who had caused the delay in leaving New York, were soon sampling whatever spirits they could get their hands on. They were out all night but were on time for opening rehearsal the following morning.

(The senior Booth was fond of alcohol. Indeed, the story goes that in Boston, Edwin locked his father in his room one afternoon to guarantee a sober performance that evening. But shortly before curtain time when he was finally let out, he was found to be hopelessly intoxicated. He had bribed a stage hand to feed him whiskey by way of the keyhole through which he had ingeniously thrust a straw.)

For two weeks the Booths, Harriet, Old Spudge and the Chapmans played to packed houses. Then, as Maguire had sold the theater building to the city for municipal purposes, June contracted with another hall in

Sacramento and the whole company moved 12 miles up river. Because of a sudden financial depression, however, they played to light audiences, and Junius Booth, Senior, who had spent what money he earned in San Francisco, decided it was time to go home. Unreasonably, he demanded that June pay him the full guarantee for the American Theater despite the fact that the company was in debt. June did as his father asked, however, and the old man sailed alone from San Francisco, just two months after he'd arrived. Edwin stayed on, now free to do what he wanted on his own. It was to be the last journey for the aging thespian for on November 30, 1852, aboard a river steamer bound from New Orleans to Cincinnati, he died. Edwin made his way from the mining camps where he was acting to his

Booth Cottage, built in 1869, with friends of June and Agnes Booth on the porch, front steps and lawn, posing for the photographer. When the Masconomo House was constructed in 1877 it was joined to the left side of the house. (Photo John and Olivia Parker Collection.)

brother's house in San Francisco. There June met him and the two embraced. They were the last members of the family to see their father alive. At June's house on Telegraph Hill, Edwin read two letters from his Mother urging both boys to stay in California for to her it was still the promised land.

EDWIN COMES INTO HIS OWN

Now out of his father's shadow, Edwin came into his own. Prosperity was returning and June, then manager of San Francisco Hall, a new playhouse built by Tom Maguire, offered his brother a contract. He played comedies of manners such as She Stoops to Conquer, as well as operettas, straight comedy and farce. People loved it. Finally, he tried more serious theater, Richard III and Hamlet. It was the latter that became Edwin's trademark. The reviews were ecstatic. He was only 19. June then cast his brother as Captain Absolute in The Rivals and then as Mr. Dombey in Dombey and Son. By the day, Edwin was gaining in experience and maturity. In May, he acted in Much Ado About Nothing. Soon, he was hired away by the owner of a new theater, the Metropolitan, much grander than little San Francisco Hall. And then Edwin thought he should visit Australia. But June, skeptical of the money his brother said he would earn, remained in San Francisco.

Back in Maryland, meanwhile, June's wife Clementine, somewhat understandably, was threatening to sue for divorce. In those days it would have created a scandal to be avoided at all costs, and taking Harriet and their daughter Marion with him, he made the long journey east to see his mother. There he managed to dissolve his marriage to Clementine quietly and discreetly, and return to San Francisco just as Edwin arrived from Australia. His brother had $10 in his pocket.

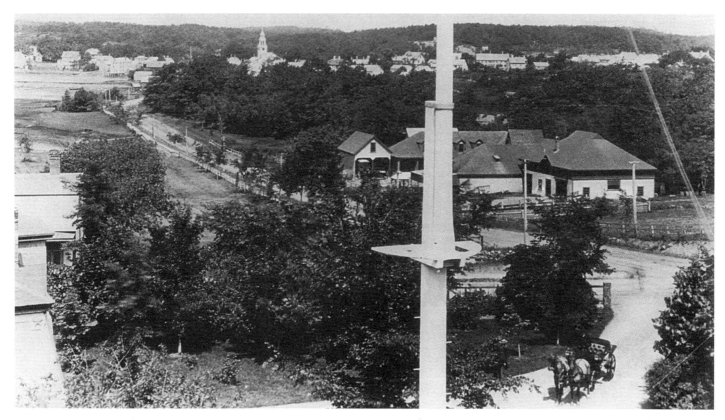

View from the roof of the Masconomo House looking down Beach Street, then unpaved, towards the town. Note the carriage approaching the hotel and the stables and barns where horses and wagons were kept. Photo George P. Smith Collection.

Edwin's poverty, however, was short-lived. A cross country tour took him to Boston (for the first time) and then to New York. In both cities his performances drew unprecedented applause from audiences and rave notices from the critics. But he was still billed as "Son of the Great Tragedian." In time this was to change.

JOHN IS HANDSOME

Among all of the brothers there was little disagreement, as among the young women who pursued him, that John was the most handsome. As an actor, he had a way to go, but as Eleanor Ruggles writes in her book, Prince of Players, Edwin Booth (New York, W.W. Norton & Company, 1953), "Restaurant waitresses swarmed to serve John. Hotel maids tore his bed apart for the ecstasy of making it up again." Even Edwin wrote to his brother Junius, "I don't think John will startle the world...but he is improving fast and looks beautiful!"

Junius, meanwhile, had lost his beloved Harriet who had died in California. He buried her under a monument embellished with a marble figure. It was marked with her name, age, date of death and the sad inscription "Don't Cry." Then with their daughter Marion, he headed home to Baltimore. There Edwin helped him find a business position in New York City at the Winter Garden which Edwin had leased for several seasons with his brother-in-law, John Clarke, husband to his sister Asia.

LINCOLN'S ASSASSINATION
John Wilkes Booth, Always a Southern Sympathizer, Shoots Lincoln; His Family is Surprised, Shocked

Unrest over the problem of states' rights and the issue of slavery had simmered throughout the country for more than a decade. By 1861, Southern states had seceded and on April 12 of that year, the pot boiled over. Unable to accept the presence of Union troops so close to the heart of the South, Confederate batteries at Charleston, South Carolina, opened fire on Fort Sumter, little more than a mile away. There, after 34 hours of bombardment, with his ammunition nearly exhausted and no relief in sight, Union Major Robert Anderson finally surrendered. The American Civil War had begun.

Edwin, Junius and Asia were on the side of the North, but as residents of Maryland, a border state, loyalties within the Booth family, were divided. Joseph, a doctor, served with the Confederacy and John Wilkes railed against the North and praised the South so vehemently that he was told "to shut up or get out of town." Only Joseph took part in the war itself, however. And although thousands of men, young and old, joined the forces on both sides, for thousands of others including Junius and Edwin, life went on much as it had before. John, too, stayed with the theater, his one ambition: to achieve a reputation for himself out from under the shadow of Edwin and his father. His sad moment in history, of course, was to come later.

Meanwhile, he continued to criticize the Union and was arrested and fined in St. Louis for remarking that he "wished the whole damn government would go to hell." With an actor's pass he traveled easily across the lines of battle reinforcing his allegiance to the South. But after four years of slaughter and destruction, the cause was lost and finally decided with Lee's surrender at Appomatox. The war itself was over but anger and bitterness lingered on. For John Wilkes and other conspirators, the moment of vengeance had arrived.

Junius Booth's grave at Rosedale Cemetery.

Memorials marking the graves of sons Algernon and Barton.

The play at Ford's Theater that April night in 1865 was <u>Our American Cousin</u> starring Laura Keene. John Wilkes was not on the playbill. As he entered the theater, he saw Lincoln's empty carriage waiting outside. Climbing the stairs, he reached the President's box. The soldier who had been assigned to guard it (the President generally scorned any measure of security) had slipped around the corner to a seat in the balcony to enjoy a smoke. A few seconds later, there was shot. Booth leapt upon the stage below breaking his left leg just above the ankle. In pain, he hobbled past startled actors down a back passageway to his horse in the alley. In seconds, he was away in the night.

Twelve days later, on April 26, John Wilkes Booth was discovered by a troop of US cavalry hiding in a tobacco barn in Port Royal, Virginia. The barn was immediately set on fire to drive him out. He was seen standing with a rifle in one hand and pistol in the other when a shot rang out and he fell. Troopers quickly pulled his body from the flames. A bullet had passed through his neck severing his spinal chord. Whether he shot himself or was shot by a cavalryman is still in question, but those who knew him best always maintained that he took his own life.

The story, told even in recent years, that Booth's body was secretly brought to Manchester and laid beside his brother Junius at Rosedale Cemetery, is contradicted by fact. It was buried first under the dirt floor of the US Arsenal in Washington. Later, in 1869, after Edwin, then restored to popularity, had written to President Andrew Johnson, the remains of John Wilkes Booth were returned to his family. They were finally interred with his father and grandfather in a new lot at Greenmount Cemetery, Baltimore where they lie today. By order of the President, no marker was ever to be placed above the grave of the assassin. Edwin, meanwhile, ever honorable, had repaid the farmer for the loss of his barn on the night that his brother had died.

IMPACT ON THE FAMILY

John's murder of Abraham Lincoln came as a dramatic surprise and an emotional shock to his family. Edwin Booth was playing in Boston where the manager decided to close The Boston Theater and drape its facade in black crepe. Junius was fulfilling an engagement in Cincinnati and was walking about the hotel lobby after breakfast when a clerk warned him not to step outside. There, according to Eleanor Ruggles' <u>Prince of Players, Edwin Booth</u>, an angry mob, "hungry for a lynching, had ripped down his playbills all over town. Junius," Ms. Ruggles continues, "looked simply bewildered." When he heard the news "'he was the most horrified man I ever saw,' the clerk told a ring of reporters.'…I suggested…that it would be better for him to go to his room and he did so. He had scarcely gone upstairs before the room he [had] left was filled with people. [There were] fully five hundred in number. They would have hanged Booth in a minute if they could have laid hands upon him. We finally smuggled him away.'

With the profession considered only on the edge of decency in those days, all actors were suspect. But, understandably, the Booths bore the brunt of it. The family received hundred of hate letters, many with threats of death. Asia Booth's husband, John Clarke, was arrested shortly after he turned over to police a sheaf of papers left with him by John Wilkes Booth simply because they had been in his possession. A detective was assigned to stay with Asia and read her mail.

Shortly before John's death, Junius had written to urge him to get out of the "oil business," by which he meant investing in oil stocks, but suspicious Federal agents locked him up as well in Washington's Old Capitol Jail. Because of political pressure applied by Edwin's friends, he remained free to move about as he wished although he was watched constantly. The entire family including John's mother, suffered most with the shame of it and the scar that would be forever left on its collective name.

EDWIN RETURNS TO THE STAGE

From jail Junius wrote "we must use philosophy...'Tis a mere matter of time...I feel sure Time will bring all things right ...that is as right as we have any right to expect." His predictions were accurate. Months passed, and after signing sworn statements of fact, both June and his brother-in-law, John Clarke, both unconnected with the crime in any way, were released from prison and began to live their lives again.

By 1866, Edwin dared to return to the stage at the Winter Garden Theater in New York as Hamlet, his great role. As the curtain rose, it revealed him, in black, seated in a huge chair. Slowly, the crowd began to clap. Then a cheer was heard. Finally, as one, the audience rose to its feet to applaud the slim, silent figure. After a few moments, Edwin rose and bowed deeply, his eyes filling with tears. He was back, his honor and his reputation restored.

BOOTH'S THEATER: DREAM OF A LIFETIME

By 1871, Edwin had realized a dream of a lifetime and was the proud owner of Booth's Theater in New York City. On 23rd Street between Fifth and Sixth Avenues, it had been built in two years earlier and was famous for its elegant interior and lavish stage sets. With a growing number of theaters, however, competition for audiences and for the approval of critics was fierce. There was also a new trend underway that led to the opening of music houses throughout the city featuring bevies of beautiful girls dancing and singing popular tunes of the day. Booth's Theater, however, stuck to what it knew best, productions of the classics. On Christmas night Edwin opened with Shakespeare's Julius Caesar casting himself in the role of Brutus. He was superb. Cassius was played by his brother Junius who had stepped in to replace actor Lawrence

Barrett. June lasted just two months. He was 51 years old and his figure no longer fit the "lean and hungry look" which the part demanded.

Edwin had been acting and serving as manager and was not only finding it hard to make ends meet but wearing himself out on the process. In financial trouble, he turned to his brother, June, who agreed to lease and operate the premises for five years. This would free Edwin to appear on the road where the money was better than in the competitive environment of New York City. But just as the arrangement started, the Panic of 1873 struck the country. Businesses everywhere failed. June struggled to stay afloat financially, but it was no use. At 40, Edwin found himself bankrupt and Booths Theater passed out of his hands. Ten years later, it closed its doors forever.

June, meanwhile, had other things going on in his life. Some years before, he had built a house in Manchester. He had a new wife, actress Agnes Perry, who at 26, was 25 years his junior. And, ever the entrepreneur, he had new ideas about how to make money.

Driveway to the Masconomo House wound past elegant lawns and flowers to the entrance. Note the awnings which could be lowered to protect guests from the heat of summer as they sipped iced tea on the porch overlooking Singing Beach.

MANCHESTER BECKONS
A Colony of Distinguished Actors Develops in Town; Junius and Agnes Booth Build a Cottage

The progenitor of the so-called literary and theatrical community in Manchester was James Thomas Fields, well-known and widely respected publisher, poet and editor (The Atlantic Monthly), who, as a resident of nearby Boston, discovered the charms of the seaside community in 1865. Nine years later, Fields and his wife Annie, a literary light in her own right who became famous for her Beacon Hill salons, stopped renting and built a summer house on Thunderbolt Hill off Summer Street.

It was Fields who is said to have coined the name "Manchester-by-the-Sea" and inscribed it on his letter paper. As Joseph E. Garland explains in his epic history Boston's North Shore, Being an Account of Life Among the Noteworthy, Fashionable, Wealthy, Eccentric and Ordinary, 1823-1890 (Boston and Toronto, Little Brown and Company, 1978), Fields' friends "reacted irreverently" to the appellation. Dr. Oliver Wendell Holmes, "Autocrat of the Breakfast Table," whose summer house was located near the railroad station in neighboring Beverly Farms, began signing his letters "Beverly-by-the-Depot."

But through the years the name Manchester-by-the-Sea stuck and a few years ago voters at Town Meeting with the approval of the State Legislature, adopted it as the community's official title. And it was the sea and the beauties of its shoreline which drew to Manchester not only the Fields but other writers and actors as well, especially those who had appeared at The Boston Theater on Washington Street, one of the region's most popular establishments.

As Garland explains, there were the noted Shakespearean players Joseph Proctor and John Gibbs Gilbert as well as English actor Frederick B. Conway. In 1864, Proctor purchased the historic Sally Samples house on Ocean Street. Four years later, Conway acquired land on Ocean Hill above Sea Street. But the man behind the scenes who helped Proctor and others connected with the stage discover Manchester, was Benjamin W. Thayer. A booster of the town and a summer resident himself, Thayer was an investor in Boston real estate which included The Boston Theater. Proctor, Edwin Booth and Junius Brutus Booth, Jr., all had played at Thayer's theater. By 1866, despite controversy surrounding the family after Lincoln's death at the hands of their brother, Edwin and Junius were back in popular favor. And that year, with Edwin and his brother-in-law John S. Clarke leasing three top-flight theaters in as many cities, June was asked to manage the property in Boston. The result was a great success.

Among the many fine actors and actresses June engaged was Agnes Land Perry of San Francisco, recently widowed. An early relationship between the two blossomed into romance and in February, 1867 they were married. Agnes was 25 years younger than June and three years younger than his oldest daughter Blanche. She had already had a distinguished stage career. For some years she had been the "leading lady" at The Boston Theater and was a principal as well in many of the magnificently successful productions at the Booth Theater in New York. Born in Sydney, Australia, her father was an officer in in the British Army who died shortly before her birth. Her mother married again, this time to a clergyman. Both parents expressed some dismay when, at the age of 14, Agnes (whose full name was Marion Agnes Laud Rookes) made her debut as a dancer. She came to the US shortly afterwards and joined John Wood's Company in Sacramento City, California. There, at age 16, she met and married actor Harry Perry who died the following year. From California, in 1865, she made her way to New York where, because of her talents, she soon became a favorite of theatergoers and critics alike.

Newly wed, June and Agnes spent part of time that summer with their friends Benjamin and Rachel Thayer in Manchester. They liked it so much that in the fall they purchased from him land of their own at the corner of Masconomo and Beach Streets overlooking Singing Beach. On it in 1869, they had built what became known as "Booth Cottage," a Victorian structure designed by architect William G. Preston of Boston, complete with towers and a delicate portico looking rather like a stage setting itself.

The construction of the house, according to an article in The American Architect and Builders Monthly, January, 1871, "is in wood, and is tinted in light cool colors, with the parapet rail picked out in gilt and chocolate." Its accommodations included a sitting room, a smoking room, a kitchen, dining room and butler's pantry, five bedrooms and a bath. On the third floor was a billiard room and tower rooms with magnificent views across "nearly a quarter of a mile" of lawn to Singing Beach and the bay with Kettle Island beyond. Also included was a stable and planting to decorate the landscape.

(Booth Cottage still stands today. The top of its towers have been removed and its entrance shifted from Beach Street to Masconomo Street. But otherwise the house - except for a bit of the hotel which still clings to its side - is much the same as it must have been more than century ago.)

In 1874, another actress at The Boston Theater, Mrs. D. P. Bowers, joined her fellow thespians in Manchester, purchasing a house near the Conways on Old Neck Road, thus completing, as Garland writes in Boston's North Shore, "the already famous actors' summer colony of Manchester known by then as 'Theater Lane.'"

THE FINANCIAL PANIC OF 1873

By 1872, Junius, on the lookout for a good investment, had joined with his friend Benjamin Thayer and others to create a land company to purchase Marblehead Neck for $250,000. But with the nation speculating in railroads, American industry and agriculture overexpanded, and European demands for U.S. products shrinking, the powerful banking firm of Jay Cook and Company collapsed taking with it security prices on Wall Street and creating the Panic of 1873.

Edwin called for Junius to help save Booth's Theater from bankruptcy. Giving up his job in Boston, June moved to New York that year but despite heroic efforts, the property ultimately was sold at foreclosure and Edwin went back to acting on the road. For June, it meant not only his last appearance as a theater manager, but the loss of a significant portion of the capital he had accumulated through the years. After a quick trip to Europe to see his daughter Marion, he was back in Manchester where he planned to take up permanent residence and retire from the stage. But there was to be one more effort to shore up his finances.

His plan was to return to San Francisco to sell some of his real estate there while Agnes was to appear in Romeo and Juliet at the California Theater. June was to be on stage for one night only in the title role of King John. Although Agnes was enthusiastically received, her engagement was not the financial success both had hoped for. The city had also changed and June deplored the wider streets and loss of intimacy in what was then no longer a frontier town, but a rapidly growing metropolis. On the way home, he stopped off in Nevada where he had contracted for a mock duel with a champion swordsman from France. The contest lasted for more than an hour and newspapers especially hailed June's ability with a foil.

STAGE PERSONALITIES WELL LIKED

Meanwhile, in Manchester, the denizens of "Theater Lane" had brought a new and very different glow to the community. Actors and actresses entertained others of their kind and although year-round residents may have been skeptical about those moving into their midst who lived a faster life on the stage, they appreciated how they supported and took part in town-wide charitable endeavors and how easy they were to live with.

Singing Beach with its collection of bath houses and the Masconomo House in the background is shown in this sketch from the booklet advertising the hotel. View is from Eagle Head. Note horses and carriages on the beach.

Indeed, one old -time Manchester resident recalled with pleasure playing with the Booth children as a boy. "We called Mr. Booth 'J.B.'," he is quoted as saying in Stanley Kimmel's The Mad Booths of Maryland (Indianapolis, New York, The Bobbs-Merrill Company, 1940). "He was a handsome man, very dignified but always pleasant. I was just a young fellow then and never talked with him very much, but I played a lot with his two boys, Sid and Wid (Junius, III). They had a raft anchored off shore from the…beach [Singing Beach] where we went swimming. The boys called that big island rock down there [Rock Dundy] Monte Christo. Wid told us about the play and we used to swim over to the rock and stage a little drama. We were all going to be great actors…the Booths were well liked by everyone in town. I never knew of Edwin Booth being at J.B.'s place, but I suppose he came sometime or other. Boston papers were always printing things about him. [Edwin had a house in Boston on Beacon Hill at 29A Chestnut Street.] I never heard J.B. speak of John Wilkes."

MASCONOMO HOUSE
Fabulous Food and Entertainment, Tennis and Billiards, Singing Beach and No Mosquitoes or Ticks

The end of the 19th century was the grand era of the great summer hotel, and with June and Agnes filling their cottage with friends every summer, they decided it was time to build one of their own in Manchester. In November, 1877, Julius F. Rabardy's Beetle and Wedge, the town's weekly newspaper, announced: "J.B. Booth, Esq., has contracted with Messrs. Phillips and Kilam for the building of a summer hotel in proximity to his house and that beautiful field by the sea…" Town records show that to pay for its construction the mortgage of $30,000 listed as collateral not only the land and buildings, but the furnishings of every room including bronze figurines and toilet seats.

The Masconomo House, as it was known, was a sizable structure. Joined to Booth Cottage at one end, it measured 230 feet long and 50 feet wide and included accommodations for 300 guests. In the shingle and clapboard style of the day, it was three and one-half stories high running parallel to Masconomo Street. Roofed with slate, its exterior was striking, painted "Indian red" with "bronze-green" trim. Its windows looked out across a broad field to Singing Beach. A few bathhouses were scattered along the beach bluff and then there was Kettle Island, Egg Rock, the Salt Rocks and the blue waters of the Atlantic Ocean stretching away towards Spain. It was a spectacular setting.

Visitors arrived at the Masconomo House first by rail (the Eastern Railroad offered a choice of four trains daily from Boston) and next by carriage, up Beach Street (then a dirt road), right on a gravel drive to the entrance.There they were met by a select few of the hotel's 50 staff members (some of them Harvard students working during their summer vacation) and escorted to their rooms. Transient rates were $3.50 per day. An illustrated booklet (which must have been given to every guest and also used for advertising) describes the hotel's surroundings and its celebrated neighbors. (It should be remembered that there were far fewer trees in the landscape then and fewer houses as well. Thus the larger ones, which were built along the shore and on its promontories, were visible for miles. Then, too, the population of Manchester totaled about 2,000 persons. Development was significantly less intense than it is today.)

"Thunderbolt Rock," the booklet declared proudly, "is nearby adjoining the hotel whence James T. Field's cottage looks down; farther away across the creek [Manchester Harbor!] the summer home of the Reverend Dr. Bartol with its lookout tower, shown in one of the sketches. Peeping from deep woods, or with broader and smoother bank surroundings, are cottages and sumptuous chateaus. Some of the better known residents of the locality are Messrs. Augustus Hemenway, Russell Sturgess, Jr., Mrs. G. H. Towne, Messrs. Caleb and Greeley Curtis, T. Jefferson Coolidge, Charles H. Trask, R.S. Boardman, Richard H. Dana, Jr., Alanson Bigelow, S.R. Rindge, Mrs. Anson Burlingame, Mrs. Bullard, President Eliot, Joseph Sawyer, Rev. Dr. Bartol, Professor O.S. Fowler, J.W. Merrill, L.N. Tappan, J.T. Fields [and] E.E. Rice…"

Besides taking comfort in the fact that they were able to at least view the houses of "some of the best known citizens of Boston, New York and Philadelphia," guests could also enjoy "a locality whose native hygienic features absolutely banish asthma and hay fever." Indeed, the booklet brags "There is no miasma [a poisonous atmosphere formerly thought to rise from swamps and cause disease]. There are no mosquitoes, no ticks in the woods, no venomous reptiles in the hedges, an enjoyment of the open sea in front, the safer pleasures of the cove (again, the harbor) in the rear, smooth lawns, drives, a wilderness at hand for the hardy pedestrian, choice shrines for the worshiper of Nature, 'the sea, the open sea' for the yachtsman, the locked bay for the timid and child sailor, with boats and sailing craft in skillful hands for all." To indicate the temperature of the water for those interested in ocean swimming, red, white and blue flags were flown from the staff on top of the hotel's bath house.

June is said to have paid particular attention to hygiene and public health, following "his plumber and sewer builder with a jealous eye." The booklet is careful to explain that "All refuse is carried to a distance, and put absolutely beyond reach as a harmful agent. All vaults and sewers are [located to prevent a] possibility of mischief. Everywhere is ventilation and the exercise of precautions too often neglected in localities that rashly invite summer guests. The water supply is from excellent wells and from vast cisterns that supply an abundance of filtered rain water."

Finally, came an appeal to discriminating palates. "The hotel table is…supplied each morning with fresh fish from the sea that have never had need of ice; with milk from cows on the farm. Mr. Booth's arrangements for his house supply, already in advance, cover a wide range in the most celebrated markets. His cook and his helpers throughout the establishment are carefully selected." Besides this, there were tennis courts, bowling alleys and billiard tables, a dance hall and a band stand. Down the hill towards the town, stood a collection of commodious stables for horses and barns to store carriages. The Masconomo House offered its visitors about everything they could want.

Together Junius and Agnes operated the hotel for five years. It was a huge success. There were gala parties in the dining room and theatrical productions on the lawn. The rooms were filled during the summer season both with regular visitors and celebrities. And, most important, the Masconomo House made money. The only sadness in their lives came with the deaths of their two young sons. Barton predeceased June in 1879. Algernon died in 1887. Both are buried at Rosedale Cemetery, Manchester. Two other boys survived to manhood.

THE CURTAIN DECENDS
1883: Junius Booth, Jr. Dies in Manchester; Edwin Lives Another 10 Years and Is Buried at Mount Auburn

In the fall of 1883, Agnes was in Philadelphia at the Chestnut Street Opera House playing the part of Mabel Ronfrew in Augustin Daly's drama Pique, when the news came that her husband was in critical condition. Junius had been suffering from Bright's disease for some time and had taken a turn for the the worse. She departed for home at once and arrived in Manchester on September 13 to find June in a coma. It was obvious the end was near. Joseph and Edwin were summoned to the Booth Cottage on Beach Street. Their Mother, too old and infirm to travel, stayed behind with Rosalie at Joseph's house in Long Branch, New Jersey. On September 16, June's conditioned worsened, and although news bulletins stated that he died at 11:10 that night, the "Book and Card Record" shows he died on 17 September "at the age of 61 years, eight months and 23 days."

According to "Comments", a special section which appears at the end of Stanley Kimmel's The Mad Booths of Maryland (Indianapolis, New York, The Bobbs-Merrill Company, 1940), "numerous discrepancies appear not only in the Book and Card Record but also in the inscriptions [on] the gravestones in the Booth lot at Rosedale Cemetery." Chief among them is the date of Junius' death which is recorded as September 15, 1884. "Mrs. Agnes Booth," Kimmel continues, "later married to John B. Schoeffel, and her mother, Mrs. Sarah Smeathman, who survived Junius, are buried [in Rosedale Cemetery as well] but not Junius, III, who killed his wife and committed suicide in England." Son Sidney Booth, who died at Stamford, Connecticut in February, 1937, was buried in Manchester the following spring.

"Junius," Stanley Kimmel writes, "inherited little of the elder Booth's genius for the stage. Of the three sons who followed theatrical careers, he showed the least [talent] as an actor…His ability lay behind the scenes." As a manager, he was widely respected both from within and without the profession. "He had been connected with several of the largest theaters," Kimmel continues. "and had known every stage celebrity of his time. His modesty, good nature, and keen sense of humor, had made him popular among his many friends." His funeral, which took place at Booth Cottage, was attended by scores of mourners many of whom came from Boston on a special train. His will left all of his estate, estimate at some $60,000, half of which was mortgaged, solely to Agnes.

Shortly after his death, Junius' daughters, Blanche De Bar and Marion Booth, brought suit and Agnes paid each $1,000 to settle their cases. Sidney, too, sued his mother as did Junius, III. Kimmel explains their actions, again in the "Comments" section of The Mad Booths of Baltimore. "S.H. Halstead and Alfred Clarke, who had been employed by Junius in operating the Masconomo House," he writes, "gave their testimony at this time. Halstead had been manager of the hotel and had attended to many of Junius' financial matters and had witnessed his will. He stated Junius told him, when making it, he wished 'Aggie' to have all of his property so that the boys would be dependent upon her, as she could tell what their dispositions were and whether they should have anything; that he had always consulted her and relied implicitly upon her judgment, both in the management of the property and care of his family, and that he had provided for his daughter Marion out of the proceeds of his California investments, and meant to leave nothing more to her..."

"The court found for the defendant and presented Sid with a bill of fourteen dollars and seven cents for the cost of the suit, which Wid (Junius, III) had to share. That ended the family litigation over the Masconomo property..."
Alfred Clarke, another employee of the Masconomo House, according to Kimmel, reported that sometime after Junius had signed his will he had mentioned that his boys "had set fire to the beach bank which he had carefully protected as the tides would otherwise have washed it out." It was an indication, Junius had said, that the boys were "careless and thoughtless" and could be controlled better by their mother [Agnes] if she had the property. They would have nothing to fear, Junius was said to have added, if "they behaved themselves and were good."

On June 7, 1893, Edwin Booth died at The Players in New York City, a organization for actors which he had founded. After a service at New York's Little Church Around the Corner, his body was taken by train to Boston and buried at Mount Auburn Cemetery in Cambridge and Watertown. Thus the curtain finally came down on the lives of America's most famous theatrical family.

HOTEL FLOURISHES

Masconomo House Continues with Agnes at the Helm; Married Once Again, She Finally Dies in 1910

After Junius' death in 1883, Agnes was married for the third time in February, 1885 to an old family friend who had helped her run the hotel while June was ill. He was John B. Schoeffel, manager of Boston's Tremont Theater. Under their direction, the Masconomo House continued to flourish. At no time was this more evident than during the summer of 1888 when a performance of Shakespeare's Midsummer Night's Dream was presented out of doors on the lawn in front of the hotel. Visitors began to arrive by rail in early afternoon and eager attendees continued to stream from the depot to the Masconomo House until the play began at eight that evening.

As The Manchester Cricket reported: "A better night could not be imagined." The approaches to the hotel and the stage were illuminated by more than 100 calcium lights. These were supplemented by 20 locomotive headlamps and scores of Chinese lanterns, all electrified for the occasion. The performance, which was designed to benefit the Boston Lodge of Elks, was compared to the previous year's presentation of As You Like It and was found somewhat wanting because of the noise of snapping branches caused by young men and boys climbing into nearby trees and bushes

to get a better view. Programs were printed on satin and sold for 25 cents each. The show was over by 10:30 pm and a special train was waiting to return guests to Beverly, Lynn, Swampscott, Nahant and Boston.

That summer, too, the hotel prepared for the arrival of President of the United States Grover Cleveland, and actress Miss Lillian Russell and comedian Nast Forrest both stayed for nearly a month. Celebrities arrived by sea as well. In 1890, The Cricket reported that the "world famous yacht AMERICA belonging to General Benjamin F. Butler [a controversial veteran of the Civil War, a US Congressman and a resident of Gloucester] sailed gracefully into Manchester harbor Wednesday, having on board the General's son who is stopping for a few days at the Masconomo House..." Retail magnate R.H. White, too, arrived with his yacht VIXEN to sample the establishment's hospitality. In 1891, records show visitors included the Duke and Duchess d'Arcos and the Minister to the US from Mexico.

Throughout the season, there were biweekly concerts for guests of the hotel presented by the Salem Cadet Band and special appearances by individual artists, both actors and musicians. Businessmens' groups and conventions met at the Masconomo House as well. Two rental houses had been constructed on hotel property and tennis courts, bowling alleys, and billiard tables were in constant demand. "A lady from Boston," reported The Cricket, "divided the honors [at the billiard table] among the gentler sex with a lady from Chicago, and the playing of both is not without envy on the part of the men." On July 21, 1889, The Cricket announced that a baseball team from Beverly Farms had defeated the Masconomo House Bellboys. And August 30, an excited Cricket reporter wrote: "Rumor has it that there are four young ladies boarding at the Masconomo House, each of whom is worth $15,000,000. Wake up young men!" There was evidently rarely a dull moment in the establishment at the top of Beach Street hill.

Because of Manchester's popularity with foreign representatives of the diplomatic service (11 different Ambassadors and their households, for example, lived here during the summer of 1904), the Masconomo House was considered as a location for the Peace Conference to be hosted by President Theodore Roosevelt which in 1905 was to end the Russo-Japanese War. It proved to be too small, however, for the massive number of delegates scheduled to attend and the conference was moved to the Wentworth Hotel at Newcastle, New Hampshire.

Agnes Booth Schoeffel died in 1910. Besides operating the hotel successfully and serving as its charming and much-admired hostess, she continued to act for most of her life. Paying homage to her talents, the National Encyclopedia of American Biography declared "In versatility and complete and admirable command of her art, she was one of the finest actresses of her time."

Agnes Booth Schoeffel poses in her Victoria which is drawn by two horses and decorated with pink and white astors with ribbons to match for the parade during the Water Celebration of 1892. The event marked the christening of the town's water supply system.

At a public auction in connection with her estate, her husband John purchased the Masconomo House for $72,000, according to the Registry of Deeds of Essex County. After Mr. Schoeffel's death, the hotel, now in the hands of Mr. and Mrs. Sullivan, remained open but times had changed. Around 1919, a portion of the building was destroyed by fire. Much of the remainder was torn down in 1920 and the furnishings sold at public auction. By 1931, concern for the future of the property and its possible development, prompted its purchase by the Singing Beach Trust. Ultimately, a portion of the land became what is now the Singing Beach Club. In 1944, the house and what remained of the hotel was sold to Charles Putnam Smith. Today, his son George and his wife Lelly own the property. The hotel is gone but the dwelling, despite alterations, is still charmingly and unmistakably, Booth Cottage.

BIBLIOGRAPHY
Gene Smith American Gothic, The Story of America's Legendary Theatrical Family — Junius, Edwin and John Wilkes Booth; New York and London, Simon & Schuster, 1992; Joseph E. Garland, Boston's North Shore, Being an Account of Life Among the Noteworthy, Fashionable, Wealthy, Eccentric and Ordinary, 1823-1890; Boston, Toronto; Little Brown and Company, 1978;Kimmel, Stanley; The Mad Booths of Maryland; Indianapolis, New York, The Bobbs-Merrill Company, Publishers, 1940; Eleanor Ruggles, Prince of Players, Edwin Booth; New York, W.W. Norton & Company, 1953; Gene Smith, Paper delivered to the Manchester Historical Society by Mrs. H.V. Carr and Mrs. Jay Schlaiker, March, 1960; historic editions of The Manchester Cricket and Cape Ann Advertiser; Information from Miss Frances L. Burnett, George P. Smith, the Harvard Theater Library and files of the Manchester Historical Society. Phone call with representative of Tudor Hall, Home of the Maryland Booths, Tudor Lane, Bel lAir, MD 21014.

ILLUSTRATIONS
Harvard Theater Collection, Pusey Library, Harvard University, Cambridge, MA 02138; John and Olivia Parker Collection, Manchester, MA 01944; George Putnam Smith Collection, Manchester, MA 01944; Sketches from booklet entitled The Masconomo House at Manchester-by-the-Sea, Essex County, Mass, J.B. Booth, Proprietor; Other photos from the Manchester Historical Society Collection.

The Newsletter of the Manchester Historical Society is written and edited by Gordon Abbott, Jr., a member of the MHS Board of Directors.

MANCHESTER HISTORICAL SOCIETY

NEWSLETTER

MANCHESTER, MASSACHUSETTS

WINTER 1997

OUR GALLANT FIREFIGHTERS

In 1895, members of the Manchester Hose Company pose in uniform with their wagon in front of the engine house on School Street (site of present fire station) to celebrate the 250th Anniversary of the town's founding. The building, then three years old, is draped for the occasion in red, white and blue bunting. That year the department's equipment consisted of horse and hand-drawn apparatus including a steamer, a chemical engine and a hook and ladder truck. There were 54 volunteer firemen. Additional hoses and ladders were stored elsewhere in town.

Of all of the accomplishments at the Manchester Historical Society during the year 1996, none surpasses the opening of SEASIDE 1. After more than 26 years of planning and discussion, the old fire house on the Common, now attractively restored as a museum, proudly exhibits the town's two historic fire engines. One is SEASIDE 2 (named after an earlier steamer, SEASIDE 1, for which the engine house was built in 1885), a Third Size, Amoskeag steamer (the "size" of a machine indicated the power of its pump measured in gallons per minute), manufactured by Manchester Locomotive Works, Manchester, NH and purchased in 1902. The other is the TORRENT, a hand pumper, constructed in 1832 by our own Eben Tappan and acquired by the town in 1836. For years, storage had been provided for both engines locally (thanks to a generous resident) and at the Essex Institute in Salem. Each piece of apparatus is a gem and it is with pride and pleasure that we welcome them home.

Much has been written about the engines themselves, but few tales have been told of the celebrated fires they helped to fight and finally to extinguish. What follows then are stories of some spectacular early conflagrations. They include, the heroic efforts of the Manchester Fire Department and SEASIDE 2 in Salem during the disastrous fire which struck that city in June, 1914, destroying in 13 hours more than 1,700 homes, businesses and factory buildings, and the Great Fire in Manchester in 1836 as well as other local blazes, subdued in part by the TORRENT and the efforts of scores of citizens and volunteers from surrounding towns.

It is important to note that it is not the intent of this newsletter to tell the full story of the Manchester Fire Department. This has been done wonderfully well already by Fire Chief Joseph O'Malley in <u>Manchester-by-the-Sea, 1645-1995,</u> a history of the town published in 1995 for its 350th anniversary celebration.

THE GREAT FIRE OF 1836

At about two o'clock on the morning of Sunday, August 28, 1836, fire burst from the steam furniture mill on Central Street owned by John Perry Allen and lit up the night sky.

The two-story, wood frame building, used to cut veneer, was located opposite Elm Street where Saw Mill Brook enters Manchester's inner harbor. It was soon a mass of flames which rapidly spread to cabinet shops and warehouses next door and threatened other structures nearby including a handsome dwelling house owned by Allen himself who was away at the time.

In those days, fire was a nightmare which haunted the dreams of every community. Houses, mills, warehouses and piers were all built of wood, and light and heat came from live flame. Extraordinary care was taken to see that damage from fire was kept at a minimum. Ladies were warned to watch their skirts and petticoats when they passed burning candles or fireplaces. Regulations restricted the use of bonfires, lamps and smoke houses. Chimneys were inspected regularly, but still catastrophes occurred.

Fires were fought by volunteers with buckets of water passed hand to hand from a nearby pond, stream or salt water cove to the blaze. Men were responsible for getting full buckets to the fire, while women returned empty buckets to the source of water to be refilled. But by 1836, like many other towns, Manchester not only had its own "bucket brigade" but two hand pumpers, the EAGLE which had been bought by the town in 1828, and the TORRENT, built in 1832 by local resident Eben Tappan (who in 1818 was a furniture maker and Colonel of a local Regiment of Militia). With a 125 gallon tank (which itself was kept filled by a bucket brigade), the TORRENT with its lead (metal) hose could throw a column of water more than 100 feet.

That August night, as the cry of "Fire!...Fire!" pierced the summer air and the bells of the Congregational Church rang to sound the alarm, citizens ran for their leather buckets (which were a mandatory part of each household) and reported to the scene. Meanwhile, the officers and men of Engine Company No. 2, established only the previous April, set out to get the pumpers which were then housed in a fire barn on School Street. With Saw Mill Brook and the harbor nearby, a good supply of water was at hand. But by the time firefighters got organized, more buildings were ablaze and flames soared high into the night sky. Indeed, the heat was so intense that the wood bridge across the brook was destroyed hampering efforts to reach houses and other buildings in the area.

For more than six hours citizens fought the fire and when morning dawned along the waterfront, the scene on both sides of Central Street was one of smouldering devastation. Losses totaled more than $50,000, a significant sum in those days. On August 30, 1836, The Salem Gazette reported that "upwards of 100 industrious men have been thrown out of employment, and several worthy individuals have lost their all" because of the fire. To blame, according to Reverend D.F. Lamson's History of Manchester, 1645-1895, was "a spark...falling into some mahogany dust [where it smouldered] for hours" finally bursting into flame.

Lost in the fire were not only Perry Allen's mill which cut veneers with a revolutionary new steam-powered saw he had invented, but his nearby shops; his house; Larkin Woodbury's cabinet shop on the Town Common; Dr. Asa Story's house and barn (Story High School was later named in the doctor's honor); Solomon Lee's house and barn (Lee was an elderly veteran of the Revolutionary War); the house and cabinet shop of Mrs. Lucy Marsters (widow of Captain Andrew Marsters) located on the wharf and known as the "Green Shop," and the stable and shed attached to the tavern owned by Nathaniel Colby. And if it hadn't been for the assistance of volunteers and other pumpers from Salem, Beverly, Gloucester, Essex and Hamilton, the results might have been worse.

After 53 years of dedicated service, the hand-pumper TORRENT, was finally retired by the Manchester Fire Department. Manufactured in 1832, it was used until 1885, a total of 53 years of service. Wisely kept in "ordinary" by the Fire Department for more than a century, the TORRENT has been restored and is now on display at the SEASIDE fire museum at Town Common.

Allen's losses alone amounted to some $60,000, but he was fortunate. A portion of his holdings was insured and he soon rebuilt the mill. At the time of the fire, both he and Woodbury, the Gazette reported, "were absent on a tour of the interior." (Manchester furniture was still much admired as far west as the Mississippi River, but the boom in production was to end with the arrival of the Civil War and the closing of southern markets.)

1838, 1871: MORE MILLS BURN

On the first of February, 1838, fire struck again. This time a spectacular blaze consumed John and Henry Knight's bark-mill and curry shop which contained more than $2,000 worth of harness leather. Miraculously, thanks in great part to the work of the TORRENT (which had been bought by the town in 1836 — it had been on loan before that), firemen did succeed in saving a barn filed with hay and bark located only six feet from the mill. (Cabinet shops with their heating stoves, glues, varnishes and steam-operated equipment, seemed particularly susceptible to fire and others were destroyed or damaged in 1843, in 1845 and in 1851.)

On April 25, 1871, Manchester's waterfront went up in flames again. A bark house, a sawing and turning mill and a cabinet shop, the latter each huge, three-story buildings owned by John Knight, as well as Rust & Marshall's workshop and warehouse, all on or in the vicinity of

Knight's wharf (where Peale House Square is located today) were destroyed in the fire. On neighboring Town Wharf, flames also leveled the coal shed of Thomas H. Kitfield. The report of the "Hook, Sail and Ladder Company," written in long-hand following the blaze, stated in part, "The buildings burned so fiercely together [and] made a flame so bright that its illumination [was seen in] Beverly. Steam fire engines from Beverly and Gloucester [came] to our assistance and did good service...coal on the wharf and the bark burned for several days..."

with a hose carriage and 1,000 feet of rubber hose. (SEASIDE 2, acquired in 1902 and now on view, was a Third Size steamer with a larger boiler and greater pump capacity.) From that day forward, the TORRENT was listed in the department's annual reports as a "spare" engine. It was an old soldier which had served the town well for 53 years. It had earned a rest and, as Fire Departments through the years thankfully agreed, it deserved to be preserved.

On Sunday, May 6, 1900, according to <u>The Manchester</u>

TORRENT Engine Company members pose proudly with their pumper and hose wagon in front of the Congregational Church on May 3, 1858. Early records show that the group voted "to have an AMBROTYPE of the Company and Engine taken at 7 cents apiece..." Uniforms had yet to be issued to firemen. Left of the church is "Mother Hamilton's" store building. Three years later, in 1861, annual expenditures for the fire department, primarily for wages, totaled $319.98.

Heat from the huge fire even scorched the west side of Town Hall as well as the front of a dwelling house and stores on the north side of Central Street. Sails, wet down and spread out over the building, played a major role in saving municipal offices. Fortunately, too, the wind was from the north and sparks were blown towards the harbor. Another spectacular blaze struck the Knight tannery in 1874 (the family seems to have suffered more than its share of fires through the years) and burned to the ground almost all of the buildings between Friend's Court and Saw Mill Brook.

It was the practice of firemen in the early days after a blaze had been extinguished to repair to one of the local taverns or hotels to celebrate and to thank volunteers from neighboring towns. But a bill for $30 received by the town for "refreshments" after a cabinet shop fire in December, 1845, caused considerable discussion at Town Meeting the following March. Voters finally agreed to honor it but warned that from that day forward "the town will pay no [other] bills for intoxicating drinks." By-Laws governing behavior were drafted for fire companies and posted inside the fire house although, as one wag reported, they were often turned "face to the wall!"

1885: FIRST STEAMER ARRIVES

By 1885, changes in technology led to the replacement of the faithful TORRENT. That year, Manchester purchased its first horse-drawn, steam-operated fire engine, SEASIDE 1. An Amoskeag, Fourth Size steamer, it cost $5,000 and came

<u>Cricket,</u> just after midnight, fire struck again in the center of town at the stable and storage building on Elm Street owned by Fred J. Merrill. Police Officer Leonard Andrews and two others were among the first at the scene and, <u>The Cricket</u> reported, "did the most excellent job in getting out horses, [wagons] and harnesses...with 12 horses in the building there was not a moment to lose...flames were fast settling down into the first story and the building was filled with smoke...all of the horses were gotten out safely although it was a question whether the last one could be gotten out in time..."

Although the wind was light, showers of sparks were carried across Central Pond to the east and soon wood shingles on the roofs of F.R. Rust's store, Mrs. Ira Baker's house and even on the fire station itself were ablaze. The chemical unit quickly extinguished these as well as a roof fire at David McKinnon's house as far away as North Street. Meanwhile, the steamer (SEASIDE 1) was pumping water from the pond through seven hose lines. At 2 a.m., coffee, crackers and cheese were sent over from the Manchester House to revive tired firefighters. Spectators grew in number as the blaze progressed until police had to establish fire lines. Finally, as dawn came, the stable fire was extinguished. Thanks to the department's efforts and skill, it was the only casualty. Losses, which totaled $7,000, included the building itself, hay and other feed stuff, and furniture stored on the third floor. For a moment, the blaze had threatened the entire business district. A number of coincidences, however, as

<u>The Cricket</u> pointed out, had worked in favor of the town that night. First, the wind was light. Second, it was a weekend, people were out later than usual — the theater train from Boston was about to arrive as the alarm sounded — and on Saturdays the barber shop was open till midnight. This alone accounted for the early discovery of the fire.

As the nineteenth century progressed, fire fighting grew significantly more sophisticated. As early as 1845, Manchester and other waterfront communities were collecting old sails which were wet down during a fire and used to cover nearby buildings. They were remarkably effective in preventing stray sparks from setting fire to neighboring roofs. (In 1852, Town Meeting voters agreed "to purchase a carriage for Sails and Ladders...") Indeed, sails were employed at fires with great effect until 1900. As time passed, chemicals (primarily baking soda and acid mixed with water) also became popular and Manchester was proud to own a two-cylinder chemical engine which was used extensively to extinguish chimney fires. It was known as "Lyman Floyd's Soda Wagon," affectionately named for its engineer. As a part of the process of fighting fires, explosive "hand grenades" were located in public buildings around town to be used to destroy a structure and create a fire break if necessary during a major conflagration.

A NEW HOME FOR SEASIDE 1
In 1885, the year that Manchester acquired its first horse-drawn steamer, new quarters were constructed for the engine on the west side of Town Common. The handsome two-story building (which was named after its inhabitant, SEASIDE 1) complimented the architecture around it and not only offered space to store firefighting equipment but on the second floor, a place for fire fighters to meet. Today the structure is owned by the town and leased to the Manchester Historical Society. Its second floor is used as a business office and is rented to a private tenant.)

SEASIDE 1 (again not to be confused with SEASIDE 2, a

second and larger steamer purchased by the town in 1902 and now on display at the restored fire house) was drawn by horses borrowed from the Smith Express Company. A team from the Samuel Knight Coal Company pulled the hook and ladder wagon. Later, a pair of horses named "Tom" and "Jerry" were acquired especially to pull the steamer. The hook and ladder was then drawn by a team from the Highway Department. Harnesses were hung from the ceiling of the fire house. When the alarm sounded, horses were backed in, harnesses were dropped and the team hitched up. It was then off at a brisk trot or a gallop, hauling the steamer behind. There were no sirens to warn other wagons that a fire engine was underway, just a bell under the driver's feet, rung with a hammer which he hit with his foot. Usually, a fire was started in the boiler before the steamer left the engine house. This meant that pressure would be available for the pumps when the apparatus reached the fire. It also provided us with those wonderful pictures of steamers racing to blaze, horses pounding at a full gallop with smoke belching from the stack.

By 1910, there were full-time firemen in Manchester (the first was reportedly hired in 1908 and worked a 144-hour week — six straight 24-hour days), firemen had been issued rubber coats, and the town had entered the automobile age acquiring a Knox motorized chemical and ladder truck from its manufacturer in Springfield, Massachusetts. Water supplies, too, had progressed from wells and ponds strategically located around town (Central Pond behind the present fire station was taken by the town in 1873 for firefighting purposes), to a town-wide system of hydrants. A whistle alarm had also been installed. And by 1892, an impressive, new, three-bay engine house had been built on School Street where the present station stands today. SEASIDE 1 was soon remodeled as headquarters for the Manchester Police Department, a role it served until the present Town Hall and Police Station were occupied in 1970.

1914: A MASSIVE CONFLAGRATION IN SALEM
Manchester Fire Department Plays an Heroic Role as Flames Destroy 60 Percent of the Central City; 13-Hour Blaze Leaves Six Dead, 60 Injured, 20,000 Homeless; Apparatus Sent from 18 Cities and Towns; Militia Is Called Out

The weather in the Witch City had been dry for weeks and on that fateful Thursday, June 25, 1914, it was another hot and windy, northwesterly day. Flags snapped in the early summer breeze and white caps covered Salem harbor.

Suddenly, at 1:30 p.m. on Boston Street, a series of explosions shook the factory building of the Korn Leather Company, a huge, three-story wood structure at Blubber Hollow. Worker Reuben Salkovitch was on the first floor when flames burst through the door of a shed where inflammable material was stored and almost simultaneously fire caught the entire side of the building. Reuben, his face and clothing scorched, barely escaped with his life. Men and women employees, some 300 of them, ran to the street. One, Charlie Lee, with burns on his hands, jumped from a third story window. He broke bones in both his feet but luckily he, too, survived.

Someone, meanwhile, had pulled Box 48 at 1:37 p.m. and four minutes later, pulled it again to signal a general alarm. As fate would have it, one-half of Salem's full-time fire

fighting force was at lunch. Unbelievably, too, all commissioned officers of the Salem Fire Department were at a drill some 12 miles away. But every engine in the city, sirens shrieking, was soon on its way to Boston Street. The first hydrant tried was out of order. But hoses were quickly hooked up to others and firefighters began to direct water at the flames.

By this time the entire block was ablaze. Wind-whipped sparks settled on wood shingled roofs, dry as tinder in the hot sun, and caught fire immediately. First the Quinn Block on the east. Then the Creedon factories on the west. Flames crossed Proctor Street, burning half the block occupied by the Sheridan Club. They soon swept down Boylston Street, until scores of houses, machine and leather shops were all ablaze. Alarms had been pulled everywhere and the Salem department now sought aid from outlying communities. This was a big one.
Dynamite was used to blow up five houses to create a fire break at North Pine Street but the flames raced on, swallowing up buildings more than a mile now from where

375

the blaze had started. Other factories and homes — the Orphan Asylum (100 children were moved to safety before the building burst into flames), the fire house at Ropes Street, the Saltonstall School, Salem Hospital (patients had been evacuated earlier), St. Joseph's Church — all were destroyed. At Union Bridge, Pickering's coal piles and wharves were on fire and at Lane's wharf, thousands of tons of coal were burning. At Naumkeag Cotton Mills, heat and flames drove firefighters back behind their engines. One Salem resident remembers, "the smoke was so thick that the streets were like night..."

An army of firemen from cities and towns throughout the North Shore — Lynn, Beverly, Peabody, Marblehead, Danvers, Wakefield, Swampscott, Chelsea, Reading, Stoneham and tiny Manchester-by-the-Sea, joined others from as far away as Boston, Lawrence and Newburyport — to battle what had become the most massive conflagration in the region's history. During the day, the blaze roared on, but by 7 p.m., Thursday evening, firefighters were able to take a stand at the substantial Salem Laundry building just west of Derby Wharf and to hold the flames from spreading there. Only a few hours later, however, at 9 p.m., equipment was rushed to North Salem where another major fire had erupted, damaging or destroying 23 homes and seriously threatening all of Ward 2 before it, too, was checked. Finally, just before 3 a.m., Friday, weary fire fighters at Lane's wharf, this time aided by a three story brick building with a blind wall to the east, held fast, and blazes everywhere were under control. The battle had been won.

Some 13 hours had passed since the alarm was first sounded. A half-dozen people were dead. More than 60, including several firemen, were injured. The conflagration had leveled some 250 acres and destroyed some 1,400 buildings in a swath which measured one and one-half miles long and one-half a mile wide stretching roughly from just east of what today is Salem State College to Derby Wharf and reaching from the waterfront to Canal Street. More than 20,000 people were left homeless. Some 10,000 had lost their place of employment and would be without work. Fifty-one streets had been wiped out completely and 48 partially damaged. In all, 60 percent of the central city had been destroyed including several major industrial districts.

One Manchester resident, Reg Foster, recalls that his father, 14-years-old at the time and living with his parents at Coolidge Point, told of seeing "a wall of flames lighting the night sky." It seemed, he said, as if the entire city of Salem was being consumed. Another resident, present day fireman Tom Andrews, reports that his mother, Annette Caron, who later married his father, William E. Andrews of Manchester, had vivid memories of the Salem fire. As residents of the city, her family lost their house to the flames. With her mother and father and 14 brothers and sisters, Mrs. Andrews walked all the way to Beverly, spending the night at the North Beverly Fire Station which is still there today adjacent to Henry's Market. She was six years old at the time of the blaze.

View from the High School shows the Salem fire raging at 2:30 p.m. on June 25, 1914. It was finally extinguished the following day at 3 a.m. During the night, Manchester firefighters "borrowed" coal from a railroad engine to fuel the boiler of steamer SEASIDE 2. The town's motorized chemical truck also distinguished itself. Photo from The Salem Fire by Arthur B. Jones, 1914.

Smoking remains of the Korn Leather Factory on Boston Street in Salem after the great fire of June, 1914. More than 300 employees fled for their lives. A sizable area of the city was destroyed in the blaze. 18 cities and towns including Manchester were asked to help the Salem department fight the flames. Photo from The Salem Fire by Arthur B. Jones, 1914.

Volunteer firemen pose with Manchester's horse-drawn Hook and Ladder wagon in the Cove area around the turn of the century. Seated fifth from right is fireman Nils Olsen, great grandfather of present day firefighter Bill Wilson. Mr. Olsen came to America from Norway in 1880 and built a house for his family at 7 Norwood Avenue. He worked as a carpenter for Roberts & Hoare, which constructed many of the town's most prestigious summer homes. Note that ladders had hooks at one end to secure them to buildings. Hooks with chains attached were also used to pull down burning walls of a structure to reduce a fire. Kerosene lamps were used on the wagon at night to alert other horse-drawn vehicles.

MANCHESTER RESPONDS
Steamer SEASIDE 2 and Motorized Chemical
Truck Speed to Aid Stricken Salem

Manchester received its call for help at 5:07 p.m. The town was eighteenth on Salem's list to summon for outside aid. Fire Chief James Hoare asked Assistant Chief Thomas Baker to take charge. Baker immediately started the Knox chemical and hose truck and, with driver Charles Chadwick at the wheel, Captain Ellery L. Rogers and firemen William Allen, Chester Cook, Frank Floyd, James Kehoe, Manuel Miguel (who later became Chief), John Riggs and one other man aboard, it left for Salem.

SEASIDE 2, the horse-drawn steamer which was housed with the Knox motor truck at the School Street engine house (and is now on display at Manchester Historical Society's SEASIDE museum), was hitched to a truck owned by Paine Furniture Company of Boston. It had been passing through town and was commandeered by Chief Baker to tow the 1902 steam-driven pumper to the fire.

Aboard the furniture truck were steamer engineer Charles Dodge and Manchester firemen Alfred Hersey, Edward Flynn, Louis Lations, Sumner Mason, and James Read. Other firefighters — Ralph Lane, Everett Smothers , Benjamin Stanley and Herman Swett — climbed into a taxicab owned by Manchester resident Alex Sjorland and found their own way to the fire to be met there by fellow firefighters Howard Stanley and Michael Kelleher as well as volunteers William McDiarmid, S.R. Stanley and Albert and Fred Smith.

The trip to Salem was not without its own excitement, according to a first-hand report written by Frank Floyd, owner of Floyd's News Store, and read many years ago at a meeting of the Manchester Historical Society. "For a short while it appeared to those of us who were riding on the Knox that we would never reach Salem, but I guess the good Lord was with us," he declared. "As we aproached the Beverly Farms railroad crossing the gates were down. The gate-tender, seeing us, started to raise [them, but] quickly brought them down [again]...as a train of flat cars loaded with Gloucester fire apparatus went by like a streak...

"From then on we made record time until we reached Town House Square [in Salem] where we had a flat tire at just 5:26. (The Knox's 60 horsepower engine would push the truck at 25 MPH on a grade and at 40 MPH on the flat.) While some changed the tire, the rest of us got into our rubber coats and boots. The department owned no helmets at the time. They came later with the uniforms and brass buttons.

"From the square we could see the flames reaching skyward...it was also here that one of our members [listed as 'one other man' above] went AWOL [absent without leave] and was subsequently discharged from the department...

"Our kit contained only a chemical tank, hand extinguishers, and 1,200 feet of hose so we were unable to do effective work until the steamer arrived. In the interim, we were directed to extinguish small roof fires. Buildings were being dynamited in the path of the fire...I never cared to

377

handle dynamite so you can imagine my feelings when an open touring car drove up, parked beside our truck...and there before us on the seats and floors of the car were dozens of sticks of dynamite together with detonating caps...[and] the driver [was no where to be seen]...

"Evidently, Charlie Chadwick didn't like [what he saw] any better than I did, for he immediately started to move the truck away from the scene...forgetting that some of our men [were up on a ladder] playing a hose against a dwelling...they had the presence to let go of the hose and Charlie and I went down the street dragging [it] behind us...with our tanks empty we were then dispatched to Canal Street to await...[the] steamer..."

Meanwhile, Floyd continued, "we had the soda and the acid and we felt [that] if we could find a pail or some container we could fill our tanks with water from the canal and be useful..." Luck was with them, for there, along the side of the street, was a row of "chamber pots" which had been rescued from the fire with other household items. A "pot brigade" was established and soon the tanks were full!

At 6:35 p.m., SEASIDE, its metal stack shining proudly in the evening sunlight, arrived and, Floyd said, "I wish you could have seen the smiles [on our mens' faces] when, as our pumps started working, all the water in the hydrant was sucked away from the Malden apparatus...they eventually were forced to shut down and move to another location..."

The heat from the wreckage of burned buildings was extraordinary. At one point, SEASIDE was working close to what had been a machine shop at the corner of Canal and Ropes Street. To cool off, Lations had removed his fireman's coat and hung it on the wheel of the steamer. Although the red hot metal in the ruins was some yards away, it soon began to melt the coat's rubber exterior which dripped on the ground below. As night came, the steamer ran out of coal to fire its boiler, but Dodge succeeded in acquiring an additional supply from a nearby locomotive. Many of the visiting steamers, which also ran out of fuel, burned whatever they could get their hands on including wood from picket fences which were still standing.

SEASIDE's proudest moment came when one of its two hose lines helped to contain the fire on Canal Street using as an

1. EDWARD P. FLYNN.
2. HOWARD M. STANLEY.
3. ARTHUR A. SMOTHERS.
4. JOHN E. RIGGS.
5. SUMNER A. MASON.
6. MICHAEL J. KELLEHER.
7. JAMES P. READ.
8. JAMES A. KEHOE.
9. HERMAN C. SWETT.
10. CHARLES C. DODGE.
11. LOUIS O. LATIONS.
12. ALFRED E. HERSEY.
13. ELLERY L. ROGERS. (CAPT.)
14. CHARLES E. CHADWICK.
15. THOMAS A. BAKER. (ASST CHIEF)
16. FRANK L. FLOYD.
17. WILLIAM H. ALLEN.
18. CHESTER D. COOK.
19. MANUEL S. MIGUEL.
20. RALPH H. LANE.
21. BENJAMIN L. STANLE

Heroes of the Salem fire are photographed shortly after the event in front of the fire house on School Street with their equipment: the steam pumper SEASIDE 2 and the Knox motor truck. Assistant Chief Thomas Baker, who led the brigade, stands in a white coat in front. Just behind him is driver Charles Chadwick. Engineer Charles Dodge stands next to the gleaming stack of the steamer. Just to his left, wearing a cap, is fireman Louis Lations whose rubber coat was melted by the heat of the flames. Frank Floyd, who wrote so vividly about the blaze, is seated on the Knox truck behind the bell. Standing behind Floyd with his hand on his hip is Manuel Miguel who served as Chief of the MFD in the 1930's.

assist, a brick fire wall which was a part of the factory building of the Lefavor Shoe Company. With its second line, which Floyd and other Manchester firemen bravely carried to the third floor piazza of an apartment house nearby, it also saved two cottages and the three-decker itself from the ravages of the blaze, although, as Floyd reports, "the house we were on was badly scorched." If it had burst into flames, the men could have been trapped three stories above the street.

A grateful resident of one apartment asked "Where are you fellows from?" "Manchester!" Floyd said they all replied in unison. "I didn't know there was apparatus here from New Hampshire," the lady responded. "We soon put her straight," Floyd continued, "but she couldn't understand how men from such a small town could do such a god job... [however] she was very grateful..."

At midnight, tired firefighters were revived when a Salvation Army truck appeared with coffee and doughnuts. And the next morning, the word was spread that baked beans were being served at City Hall on Central Street. "They sure did taste good," Floyd recalled.

At about 6 a.m., Manchester firemen were told to retrieve their hose lines, pack up their equipment and head for home. Their only loss in the blaze was one pony extinguisher. SEASIDE and the Knox truck (which perhaps towed the steamer) arrived back in town at 8:35 a.m. The men were dead tired and filthy dirty but proud and happy, as Floyd concluded, "that we had been of some assistance to our good neighbor."

Relief efforts began immediately and Manchester formed a special committee which over the next few months collected food, clothing, and money to aid the homeless and to help care for those who had lost everything they owned. The State Militia was called out to prevent looting as more than one million sightseers visited the city to view the ruins in the weeks following the blaze. Engineers reported that Wenham Lake was drawn down as much as two inches by pumpers using water to fight the flames. And damage estimates totaled $15 million, an enormous sum in those days.

For Manchester's Fire Department, it was the experience of a lifetime and the brave men who helped to save Salem never forgot the great fire of June, 1914.

RELIEF
Manchester Residents Rush to Provide Assistance for Children, Homeless

With her own men and apparatus at the fire and the night sky lit for miles around by the flames, Manchester was soon aware of the extraordinary extent of the damage in Salem, and particularly of the numbers of now homeless people who needed food and shelter.

"Early Friday morning [June 26]," according to the July 4, 1914 edition of The Manchester Cricket, "the call came for milk for...refugee babies. Boy Scouts were sent out to canvass the town and in a few hours, 150 quarts had been secured and iced and [was] on its way to Salem. Mrs. Gordon Abbott [grandmother of the author of this Newsletter]" The Cricket reported, "was early on hand and

was at Bullock's Bakery (then at the corner of Summer Street and North Street) with her auto when it opened...[she] bought all the bread supply on hand and other eatables which she took to Salem and also took personal charge of an infant that was found without care, which is but one illustration of the practical work being done."

Others donated and collected money to provide aid for families made homeless by the blaze. Some "$800 was collected on the first day," The Cricket continued, "along with $75 worth of provisions and $40 worth of clothing. People loaned cars [to help out] and the Boston & Maine Railroad transported food and clothing free of charge."

Suffering was everywhere. One couple, in their 60's, sat alone throughout the night at Salem Common waiting for daybreak. They had lost their house and with it everything they owned. "I'll have to begin all over again," the man said, "It's hard when you're 65." A younger woman whose home had also been destroyed was separated from her baby, just eight months old. The following day, according to a story in The Salem News, North Shore Babies Hospital reported that it did have one unidentified child which had been brought in during the fire. When the mother saw the little boy, she recognized him immediately and was overjoyed to have him returned.

The Red Cross, headed by Miss Mabel T. Boardman of Manchester, was the leading coordinating aid agency. In the five days after the fire, its milk station for babies was responsible for 736 feedings. On June 29, North Shore Babies Hospital counted 38 babies whose parents were homeless. Sadly, three babies were as yet unclaimed.

On June 26, the day after the fire, President Woodrow Wilson wired his sympathies "to the stricken people of Salem" and asked if the Federal Government could be of assistance. Neighboring cities and towns sent carloads of bread and provisions. Hood Milk Company offered 1,000 pints of milk a day free of charge. Many other provision firms were equally generous. Gardner M. Lane of Manchester was Treasurer of a special committee of 100 persons formed to aid survivors. A message was sent that Beverly would raise $100,000. Other communities pledged funds as well. By June 27, the State contributed more than one half million dollars and Congress had appropriated $200,000 to aid fire victims.

Tents were set up as temporary housing in open spaces around the city —100 here, 100 there. As many as 1,200 homeless family members lived in wood-floored tents at Forest River Park. The telephone company installed special phones and phone lines to meet the demands of relief workers. Public health officials worked wonders. Strict sanitary arrangements and excellent medical care virtually eliminated disease. And on Sunday, June 28, 1914, in front of a make-shift altar built of wood boxes, some 3,000 people gathered to celebrate Mass. As the heavens opened and the rain poured down cooling the last of the city's smoking ruins, they gave thanks to God for their deliverance.

On Saturday, the day before, barber John Frasier, who had saved one of his chairs from the flames, announced he was open for business — shave and a haircut as usual. Life was beginning to return to normal.

PRAISE FROM BOSTON CHIEF

Manchester firefighters received high praise for their accomplishments at Salem. With the town's steam pumper, SEASIDE 2 and the motorized Knox chemical truck, they were "largely responsible," according to The Manchester Cricket, dated July 4, 1914, "for saving the major portion of a huge shoe factory.

"It sounded good," The Cricket declared, "when the factory superintendent came along and said: 'Boys, you've saved [jobs] for 800 people!' Even the Boston Fire [Chief]," The Cricket continued, "said he had never seen better work...The auto chemical [operated in a way] that was not surpassed by any...After using up the chemical supply, [it] went to Canal Street where a hydrant connection was made and a determined stand taken...the fire was held at that point and an entire street of tenement properties saved thereby..." Charles Dodge, engineer for the town's steamer, extolled its performance as well although as a horse drawn engine it's days were numbered.

A DREAM COMES TRUE
Old Fire House Becomes a Museum After Efforts of 26 Years; Old Engines Now Back Home

When in 1970, Manchester's Police Department moved into its first professionally designed quarters next to Town Hall, a logical question was what to do with the small building on the west side of Town Common which the Police Department had called home for 76 years (1894-1970). In short order, the answer was to preserve it as an historic building and an architectural feature of the Common. The way was led by the Manchester Historical Society and its then President W. Merritt Miller who, with the early and continuing support of the Manchester Fire Department, proposed that the structure not only be made available for community use, but be restored as SEASIDE NO.1 to reflect its original purpose as a fire house built in 1885 for the town's first steam operated fire engine. The building was to serve as a museum and as a home for the town's two antique fire engines, the TORRENT, a hand pumper built in 1832, and SEASIDE 2, a horse-drawn, steam pumper that the Fire Department had acquired in 1902.

The Historical Society agreed to lease the structure from the town and to maintain it until sufficient funds were raised to complete the restoration. To help meet the cost of maintenance, the Society sub-let the building to a succession of tenants which included the Manchester Art Association and a number of private parties each of whom paid a small sum to use the space. Finally, in 1995, in conjunction with the 350th Anniversary of the town's founding and with the blessing of the Board of Selectmen, sufficient funds became available to undertake the long hoped for restoration.

Today, a dream of some 26 years has finally been realized thanks to the continuing interest and leadership of Merritt Miller, who also served as Chairman of the Seaside One Building Committee, Reginald Foster, President of the Manchester Historical Society, and committee members Carl Anderson, Esther Proctor, Dan Senecal, Dee Burroughs, Fred Rice, Sherry Proctor, David Forsythe, Joan Brown and Nina Adams. The elegant Palladian window is in place. The doors facing Central Street match those of the original

Steamer SEASIDE 2, purchased by the town in 1902, has appeared in numerous parades. It is on display here with a framed photograph of the brave members of the Manchester Fire Department who accompanied the engine to Salem on June 25, 1914 to fight the great blaze there which consumed nearly 60 percent of the city center. SEASIDE 2 was an Amoskeag engine manufactured by the Manchester Locomotive Company of Manchester, New Hampshire. It was a pulled by a team of two horses. When its older sister, SEASIDE 1, was purchased in 1885, there were some who thought horse-drawn engines, which galloped through town with bells ringing, horses snorting, and smoke belching from their shiny stacks, were a major hazard to pedestrians. There were instances in communities around the country where people were run over by apparatus hurrying to get to a fire.

fire station (with one exception: passers-by can see through a series of clear panels). The engines are safely inside and on display, and historic photographs of earlier fire department activities hang on the walls. Only one element is missing: the top of the hose tower with its cupola and steamer weather vane. It is the Historical Society's hope, now with a 10 year lease in hand, to replace these as well.

TWO LOYAL ENGINES
TORRENT Serves the Town for 53 Years; On Display with SEASIDE Steamer

SEASIDE 2 (now on display at the SEASIDE fire museum), was delivered to the Manchester Fire Department in October, 1902. The horse-drawn, steam fire engine was manufactured in Manchester, New Hampshire by the Manchester Locomotive Company which acquired the former Amoskeag Manufacturing Company, makers of fire engines, in 1877. A Third Size, double neck frame engine, SEASIDE 2 was listed in the company's 1902 catalog as an Amoskeag steamer which could pump 600 gallons of water per minute. First Size engines could pump 900 gallons a minute. In 1885, Manchester acquired, SEASIDE 1, a Fourth Size steamer which could pump 350 gallons a minute. It was later sold or traded to make way for SEASIDE 2. Amoskeag and Manchester Locomotive produced a total of 853 steam fire engines between 1859 and 1913. It was the third largest factory of its kind in the US.

Most of its engines went to big cities. Boston, for example, had 30; New York City, 56. Other steamer manufacturers included America-LaFrance of Elmira, NY; Clapp & Jones of Hudson, NY; and W.C Hunneman & Company of Boston.

The other engine on display at the newly restored fire museum is the TORRENT which was made by hand here in Manchester in 1832 by Eben Tappan who began in business as a ship builder and trader. Later he turned to manufacturing furniture and ships' steering wheels. He then became fascinated with hand pump fire engines, known as "fire tubs," and in 1826, he began building them in his shop entirely from his own plans. The ironwork was done by a village blacksmith while the brass work was completed in Boston, all under Tappan's personal supervision. The town purchased the TORRENT in 1836 for $654.80. It came with 192 feet of hose and was used to fight fires until the first steamer was purchased in 1885. It was then placed "in ordinary" after 53 years of service. Fire department officials wisely kept the old pumper as a relic of earlier days. In the 1960's, the TORRENT was overhauled without charge by the Manchester Marine Construction Company. The fine lettering and striping on its tub and wheels is the work of Edward French, Jr. of Andrews Avenue who was the shipyard's Chief Painter at the time.

MUTUAL AID
Volunteers Pitch In to Assist Neighboring Communities Yesterday and Today

Mutual aid has been a hallmark of successful fire fighting since the early nineteenth century. Volunteers from Salem, Beverly, Essex and Hamilton, with "hand tubs" that were pulled by manpower over dirt roadways, helped to extinguish Manchester's great fire of 1836. As early as 1830, according to a story which appeared in The Manchester Cricket on February 20, 1892, the pumper EAGLE (Manchester's first hand pumper which in 1828 came with 12 pairs of leather buckets) "was called to Gloucester and rendered valuable aid in the work of staying the conflagration that day which destroyed property valued at $150,000." With that kind of loss, it must have been a fire of huge proportions.

A history of the Manchester Fire Department written by Henry T. Bingham which appeared in The North Shore Breeze in 1898 reported that "the hand engine 'Perseverance' [from Beverly Farms] rendered great assistance" in 1854 during a stable blaze behind the Manchester House. In 1858, some perhaps overly enthusiastic young volunteers from Manchester, trying to return the favor, responded to a fire in Beverly Farms only to be turned back "at the line" with their pumper, the EAGLE, by a member of their own Board of Selectmen who wanted the equipment to stay in town. In June 21,1898, a horseman shouting "Great fire in Essex!" galloped through the streets of Manchester. "Everyone who could," said Henry Bingham, "went to Essex." Only two small buildings, however, were burned. And in 1914, Manchester was one of more than 20 towns called to help with the city-wide conflagration in Salem. Today, a system of mutual aid is in place throughout the region which provides for assistance from neighboring communities whenever a city or town finds itself faced with the dangers of a General Alarm fire.

ARRIVAL OF SEASIDE 2
A Day of Celebration; Steamer's Engine Tested; Lavish Luncheon Served at the Fire House

When a new piece of fire apparatus arrived in town at the turn of the century, it was an occasion for celebration, and Tuesday, October 31, 1902, was no exception to the rule.

Manchester had just acquired SEASIDE 2, its second horse-drawn steamer manufactured by the Manchester Locomotive Works of Manchester, New Hampshire. A test of the new machine had been scheduled and dignitaries and townspople had been invited to a luncheon banquet at the engine house on School Street. There were to be remarks, some serious some lighthearted. In all, it was to be a festive day.

With its eight-foot boiler, steam guages, levers and valves all nickel-plated, and its running gear — wheels and carriage — painted bright red and decorated with gold pin stripes, SEASIDE 2 was a work of art and glistened magnificently in the morning sun. A crowd of several hundred was on hand to welcome the new pumper. It included Fire Chiefs of surrounding towns, handsome in their blue uniforms and brass buttons (as, indeed, were the members of Manchester's own department) as well as town Selectmen, members of the Water Board, and W.C. Rust, veteran firefighter and former Chief of the Manchester Fire Department.

According to a report in The Manchester Cricket delightfully headlined "A Gay Day for Manchester Fire Laddies," SEASIDE 2 (now on display at the Seaside fire museum) first fired up and then, drawing water from Central Pond, played its hoses on the Town Landing. Pressure was tested with two lines and judged to be satisfactory. Two nozzles were used. The first measured one and one-eighth inches in diameter; the second, one and five-eighths inches. Both worked well with water from the pond and from a nearby hydrant. A high wind, unfortunately, prevented fire engineers from measuring the length of the streams but it was enthusiastically agreed, the Cricket reported, that "she is a good engine!"

(Unlike SEASIDE 1 which the town purchased in 1885, the new steamer was an Amoskeag Third Size pumper which was not only significantly more powerful but included an innovation which enabled firemen to control the intensity of the stream of water at the nozzle of the hose rather than notifying the engineer back at the engine.)

After the test, which drew wide admiration from those watching, the crowd of some 100 people met at the fire house for lunch. The fare was sumptuous: scalloped oysters, baked sea trout, roast turkey, and lobster salad were followed by banana fritters, ice cream and coffee. With cigars lit, guests then settled back in their chairs to hear the speakers. There was a succession, but Selectman William Allen probably said it best. "I joined the fire department when I was 16 years old" he declared, "and continued with [it] until I was 36 and so I can well call you brothers. I add my congratulations on this new acquisition. I feel that the department is fully equipped and second to none of any town in the state." With the proud record of Manchester's Fire Department through the years, the same could be said of it today.

Driver Charles E. Chadwick (now in fire department uniform) at the reins of Manchester's Hose and Ladder wagon in the early 1900's. The team may have been made up of horses from the Highway Department which were used to pull fire equipment. Later, a pair of horses, one called "Tom," the other "Jerry," was acquired by the department especially for the steamer. Note the soda fire extinguisher. The photo was taken in front of the ledge at the beginning of Pine Street. The steeple of the Congregational Church is just visible over the ledge at right.

LADDER COMPANY
Fire Strikes Building Where Equipment Is Stored; Five Horses Are Lost

On January 13, 1846, at the request of the Board of Selectmen, Manchester established its first Hook, Sail and Ladder Company. The equipment, which was to prove so useful at so many fires throughout the town, was kept for 19 years in a barn at the corner of Pine Street and Bennett Street (where the Gulf station is located today) occupied by Simeon J. Swett and owned by Miss Ella F. Lee. A fire in 1885 destroyed the barn. Five horses, harnesses, robes, blankets and grain as well as carriages and sleighs were also lost in the blaze. Apparently, the Hook, Sail and ladder wagon escaped harm. It's destruction is not mentioned in reports of the fire.

SEASIDE FIREMEN'S CLUB
The name SEASIDE is perpetuated today by the Seaside Firemen's Club which was founded on March 14, 1938 and is still going strong. Its membership is composed of all permanent and call firemen who meet once a month for training at the fire station. Retired firefighters may attend as well. The Club also sponsors a raffle and a food sale once a year, the proceeds of which provide scholarship aid for Manchester students. The Club's officers today Peter Briggs, President; Michael Powers, Vice President; Jack Briggs, Secretary; and Tom Andrews, Treasurer.

ILLUSTRATIONS
The illustrations in this Newsletter were primarily provided by the Manchester Historical Society and the Manchester Fire Department. Two photos of the fire in Salem were copied from those in a remarkable book entitled The Salem Fire. It was written in 1914, the year of the blaze, by Arthur B. Jones, who served as Assistant Chief of the Salem Fire Department and later as a member of Hose Company Number 2. Jones' book was published by The Gorham Press in 1914. A reprint is listed as available from Higginson Book Company, 148 Washington Street, Post Office Box 778, Salem, MA 01970.

BIBLIOGRAPHY
Lamson, Reverend D.F.; History of the Town of Manchester, 1645-1895; Boston, Massachusetts; The Pinkham Press, 1895; Floyd, Frank L.; Manchester-by-the-Sea; Manchester, Massachusetts; Floyd's News Store, 1945; Jones, Arthur B.; The Salem Fire; Boston, Massachusetts, The Gorham Press, 1914; Salem, Higginson Book Company, reprint; Clippings and papers of the Manchester Historical Society; historic editions of The Manchester Cricket; information from Miss Frances L. Burnett; Fire Chief Joseph O'Malley; Fireman Bill Wilson; Reginald Foster, III and Esther "Slim" Proctor, Librarian, Manchester Historical Society; also Conway, W. Fred; Those Magnificent Old Steam Fire Engines; New Albany, Indiana; Buff House Publishers, 1997; and Goodenough, Samuel; Fire! The Story of the Fire Engine; Secaucus, New Jersey; Chartwell Books,Inc., A Division of Book Sales, Inc., 1978.

The Newsletter of the Manchester Historical Society is written and edited by Gordon Abbott, Jr., a member of the MHS Board of Directors

A trio of ladies crosses Central Street about 1895 opposite the then "new" Police Station building (right) which had been constructed in 1885 as a fire station and a home for SEASIDE 1, the town's first horse-drawn steam pumper. When the three-door, three-story engine house was built on School Street in 1892, the Police Department took over SEASIDE 1 and used it from 1894 to 1970 when new headquarters were constructed next to Town Hall. SEASIDE 1 has just been repaired and restored by Manchester Historical Society and is now a fire department museum. Inside are SEASIDE 2, a second steamer purchased in 1902, and the venerable hand pump fire engine TORRENT, which served the town from 1832 to 1885. Note that the street is still unpaved and that to the left of the Congregational Church are "Mother Hamilton's" store and the two-story Franklin building which also housed a retail establishment. Both were torn down in 1909. In front of the church, surrounded by a black iron fence, is a young American elm planted in 1876 to commemorate the country's Centennial. Just visible to the left of the Police Station above the wagon is a decorative wrought iron structure which sheltered the town water pump. The building on the left just beyond the other wagon is the Manchester House, a hotel which burned in 1952 and was later razed.

MANCHESTER HISTORICAL SOCIETY

NEWSLETTER

MANCHESTER, MASSACHUSETTS

FALL 1997

THE DANAS: THEY LED THE WAY

Three generations of the Dana family spent their summers in Manchester. From left; Richard Henry Dana, Sr., the town's first summer resident; his grandson, R.H. Dana, III; and his son, author and attorney, R.H. Dana, Jr. The elder Dana died in 1879 at age 92. At that time RHD, III would have been about 28. This photo appears to have been taken in the mid to late 1870's. Photo from the National Park Service, Longfellow Historic site.

The Reverend Oliver A. Taylor, minister of Manchester's Congregational Church from 1839 to 1851, is said to have been responsible for the arrival of the town's first summer resident. Attracted by Taylor's reputation as a scholar and a writer, poet Richard Henry Dana, Sr., who then had a house at Pigeon Cove, attended a Sunday service here in 1844 to hear him preach. Afterwards, in conversation, the cleric is said to have suggested that Dana, who had expressed an admiration for the community, consider moving to Manchester.

Driving about the area in his carriage, the poet heard the sounds of surf and upon following an old wood road, found himself on a bluff east of town overlooking what is known today as Dana's Beach. A year later, in April, 1845, Dana's son, then an attorney in Boston, acted for his parent. "Father had spoken highly of a place on Cape Ann [then] called Graves Beach [after the Graves family farm of which it was a part], " he wrote in his Journal, "and seemed to think the owning of it would be almost too much delight for him to enjoy. I went to Manchester, examined the place and employed a man...the stage driver, to purchase it. This he did for $1,800..."

Richard Henry Dana, Sr. (1787-1879) was then 58 years old. A founder of the distinguished *North American Review,* he was not a great success in the literary world. In fact, he so alienated the *Review's* subscribers with his criticisms, that he left for New York to begin his own journal which he called *The Idle Man.* Two years later he gave this up as well. A perpetual procrastinator, he was said by fellow poet James Russell Lowell to be "so well aware of how things should be done, that his own works displease him before they are begun..."

In 1833, Dana did publish *Poems And Prose Writings* in two volumes. But for most his later life he was overshadowed by the accomplishments of his son. He did manage to have constructed on his property above the beach a simple, square, two-story clapboard house with magnificent views of Egg Rock, Kettle Island, and Massachusetts Bay. By the time he died in 1879, his holdings had increased to some 100 acres which Julius Rabardy's *Beetle And Wedge*, the town's weekly newspaper, later praised in an editorial (perhaps in reaction to the newly-manicured lawns and formal gardens which became the hallmark of so many of Manchester's great summer places)."Thanks are due to Mr. Dana," it stated, "for suffering his estate to remain in its original state of Nature...it is a genuine pleasure to get stuck in the brambles that grow unchecked in the wild woods..."

By the end of the 1840's, the character of Manchester was changing. To be sure, there were still rattlesnakes north of town and hunters had just been offered a $1 bounty for each successful kill. But in 1847, the Gloucester Branch of the Eastern Railroad had been constructed and it was far easier and more comfortable to reach Manchester by train than by stage coach, a long and dusty ride from Boston. Indeed, it was the arrival of the railroad that made seasonal settlement here possible. Many of the community's 1,300 residents, however, were not as ready as their neighbors in Beverly and Nahant to embrace the influx of summer folk that was about to take place. But, bit by bit, other families followed the Dana's example.

Richard Henry Dana, Jr. was as fond of Manchester as was his father. A resident of Cambridge and a successful attorney, he was often away from his family on business for days at a time, "his only...real recreation," his biographer and friend Charles Francis Adams wrote in 1890, "was in the summer when he and his family went to Manchester-by-the- Sea...the Danas, old and young, made one family at Manchester, and [it was there that] Dana passed some of the happiest and most enjoyable hours of his life...he threw away his books and cases and office cares," continued Adams, "and lived for the hour with wife and children, walking, bathing, driving, and sitting on the gallery of the house drinking in the air from that ocean always so dear to him and upon which he never wearied feasting his eyes...indeed, there was nothing in his life more genial or more pleasant to recall than those hours, far too few in number, most profitably idled away at Manchester-by-the-Sea."

Dana himself also wrote rapturously about the place. "It is inexpressively beautiful," he declared, "...the grand and ever-changing sea, the islands and lighthouses and indented coast, the beach at high tide, the beach at low tide, the rocks, the woods and their smells, the unbroken quiet and the moon upon the waters!"

In his two-volume story of Dana's life, *Richard Henry Dana, Jr., A Biography*, (Houghton Mifflin & Company, The Riverside Press, 1890), Adams describes the location of the land in a way which is delightfully familiar for anyone who knows that pleasant part of Manchester. "The acquisition of this property," he writes in classic, turn-of-the-century prose, "had been for the whole Dana family a veritable stroke of good luck. The attention of the elder Dana had been called to it as early as 1844, during summer sojournings on the north shore, long before that region had become a fashionable resort. It was then held as mere grazing land, stony cow-pastures, in a money point of view of little value.

"A few miles west of the entrance to Gloucester harbor and the reef of Norman's Woe, at the foot of the bold and wooded shore, lay a pebbled beach, upon which, as the wind varied from the fierce southeast to a gentle west, the waves of the Bay broke with violence or softly-lapped. The rocky upland commanded a wide ocean view to the southward, while to the west the eye followed a vanishing line of coast, until in the distance the blue Milton hills loomed up across the water over the islands which marked the entrance to the harbor of Boston. Beach and upland were part of a Cape Ann farm of fifty or more acres..."

Although he made a considerable reputation for himself in the law, Richard Henry Dana, Jr. was perhaps best known for his account of an ocean voyage taken in 1834 to improve his health (he had eye problems as a sophomore at Harvard following a bout with measles). He shipped out aboard the brig PILGRIM as an apprentice seaman, rounded Cape Horn and sailed to California where he worked loading hides, finally returning to Boston aboard the ship ALERT to re-enter college. His account of his adventures, published in 1840 and entitled *Two Years Before the Mast,* won him acclaim throughout the English-speaking world. The book was written in six months after graduation from Harvard Law School while Dana was waiting to pass the Bar exam. There is little doubt that its dramatic realism in an era of fictional melodrama created a host of imitators and greatly influenced the production of subsequent literature about the sea. Indeed, it's reported that the 45-cent edition of *Two Years Before the Mast* "revitalized" its publisher, "the house of Harper." The book's success was more than its young author (Dana was 25 years old at the time) could have imagined in his wildest dreams.

The popularity of *Two Years Before the Mast* and the subsequent ups and downs that Dana had during his career in law and politics have made some historians wonder why he chose that life instead of becoming an author where his talents were obviously immense. But Dana himself is said to have felt that writing was something a gentleman did outside of his profession. His literary works were thus limited to *The Seaman's Friend,* a guide designed to explain to sailors their legal rights and duties, his personal Journal, and *To Cuba and Back,* a story of his travels produced in 1859.

When he returned from the sea, Dana plunged into the law with characteristic vitality. Charming, talented and from an old Boston family (his grandfather was a Chief Justice of the Commonwealth), he soon collected a list of distinguished clients. He and his beautiful young wife, Sarah, with whom he had six children, were sought after "by a Boston society whose proverbial exclusiveness," it is said, "was never to be more completely realized than during this period." Dana had all the right credentials to belong to the inner circle of what was becoming Brahmin Boston. In ways, manners and breeding, he was a gentleman. Conservative politically, he was a graduate of Harvard and Harvard Law School. Later he was to become an Overseer or member of the university's governing board. He spoke well in public, he was well traveled, he was a member of the appropriate clubs, both social and intellectual, and he was active in the community with the Bar Association, as a Director of a number of banks and as a vestry man of his church. Dana's experience before the mast also gave him another dimension: he was happily at home with others who were not from his own class and who earned their living working with their hands. He was also a man of strong principle and this was to make life difficult for him at times in the years ahead.

HALF SLAVE: HALF FREE?
The Issue Divides the Nation; Emotions Run High in Manchester; Voters Act at Town Meeting

In the early 1850's, while the nation was rapidly expanding to the West, it was divided between those who opposed slavery and those who approved of it. Feelings ran high and in 1853 even Manchester's Town Meeting entered national politics, voting to demand that its representatives in Washington oppose a move in Congress to repeal the Missouri Compromise which excluded slavery from the territory of Louisiana.

Dana was an avowed abolitionist and a member of the Free Soil party which advocated ending all Federal sanctions of slavery, prohibiting it in the District of Columbia and excluding it from the new territories. He stood strongly against the Federal Fugitive Slave Law which required that slaves who had escaped to so-called free states be treated as personal property and returned to their owners. In Manchester, sentiment for the Free Soil party ran high. It was even discovered later that there was a secret organization of townspeople here who shielded and aided fugitive slaves and hastened them on their way to freedom which often meant to Canada.

In 1853, Manchester voters chose Richard Henry Dana, Jr. to represent their interests at a statewide Constitutional Convention. Dana was honored. "I had the compliment of being elected...by a clear majority...on the first ballot," he wrote in his Journal. At the Convention were many of the great public figures of the time including US Senator Charles Sumner of Massachusetts, attorney Rufus Choate and the outspoken Benjamin F. Butler who was to become a Union general and, after the Civil War, a US Congressman (and a summer resident of Gloucester) whose seat Dana would unsuccessfully contest. The constitutional technicalities in question involved the judiciary as well as town representation in the General Court. The battle was between Boston and rural interests throughout the state. From the start, Dana's eloquence, logic and independence of thought won the admiration of those he supported and even of those he opposed. But in most cases, out of principle, he broke with his conservative friends and sided with the liberals. It was a change in his life that was to have far-reaching consequences.

Meanwhile, the issue of slavery was growing more heated. The break-up of the Union and the war itself were still a half-dozen years away, but across the nation sides were being chosen. In New England, however, and particularly in Boston, the ruling gentry was inclined to look upon abolitionists as revolutionaries who threatened the establishment's comfortable status quo. Many Bostonians of Dana's station had financial interests in cotton mills doing business with Southern plantations. There was also an emotional tie to the "gentlemen and ladies of the South" who, outside of slavery, shared many of the cultural and intellectual interests of Brahmin Boston and certainly much of its admiration for its English ancestry.

Dana, on the other hand, was bitterly outspoken on the subject of slavery. In public, he ruthlessly castigated the great Daniel Webster for compromising with Henry Clay on the issue of free soil and the Fugitive Slave Act. Webster, fearful of secession and the war that would certainly follow, pleaded for a more charitable attitude towards the South. But Dana would have none of it. His conservative friends were aghast at his abusive criticism of the old Senator and at his vehemence, but Dana pressed ahead.

In 1851, he agreed to defend an escaped slave named Thomas Sims taken by authorities citing the Fugitive Slave Act. He lost the case as he had to under the law, but his actions so shook the establishment that men he had known all his life refused to speak to him when they passed on the streets of Boston. There were even pleas in the newspapers to boycott his law practice. As time passed, however, public attitudes — even those of the most conservative — changed dramatically.

By 1854, when Federal marshals in Boston arrested another fugitive slave, Anthony Burns, Dana once again took the case for the defense. This time, fed up with the South's intransigence and finally convinced that slavery was a major moral issue, his friends were with him as, indeed, was the entire community. Once again, however, "a tyrannical statute and a weak judge" won out and Burns was ordered to be returned to his owner in Kentucky. Despite a huge presence of Federal troops, citizens thronged the streets shouting "Shame! Shame!" as the slave appeared in chains and it was all US Marshals could do to get Burns out of town. It was obvious that Boston's sympathy with the South was at an end and that the question of slavery had divided the nation.

8,000 AT SMITH'S POINT
Huge Free-Soil Party Rally Stirs Residents; Dana Addresses Political Gathering

In September, 1856, the Free Soilers of Essex County convened in Manchester to promote the candidacy of Colonel John C. Fremont, "conqueror" of California during the war with Mexico, who ran for the Presidency as a Republican (the party was just two years old) on a ticket that opposed the expansion of slavery. (He nearly made it. A win in two additional states would have enabled him to defeat Democrat James Buchanan.)

An incredible 8,000 people gathered at Gale's Point for the occasion. There were bands, banners, slogans and buttons. Many of the town's residents decorated their houses in support of Free Soil. Huge tents were erected and scores of distinguished speakers addressed the crowd. Among them was Manchester's own Richard Henry Dana, Jr.

But by 1859, as the great Civil War was about to begin, Dana's health began to fail. At 44 years old, he left for Europe to recover. When he returned, he campaigned briefly for a young lawyer from Illinois who was running for the Presidency, and upon Lincoln's election he was rewarded with a relatively minor appointment as US District Attorney for Massachusetts. But one of the biggest disappointments in Dana's life came after the war. He was selected by President Ulysses S. Grant to become US

Ambassador to Great Britain, but old enemies prevailed. One of them was Representative Butler who never forgot an opponent (Dana ran against him for Congress). At the last minute, the Senate failed to ratify his appointment.

Finally, in 1882 at age 67, Dana died in Italy where he had gone with Sarah to retire. He was a man who was never quite able to come to grips with his real self. With equal fervor he embraced two vastly different worlds: Brahmin Boston with its conservative traditions of power and intellect, and the rough and tumble environment which he so enjoyed while serving before the mast as a young sailor. Then, too, there was, at such an early age, the immense success of his book, an accomplishment that in his later years he sadly admitted was never repeated. His son, Richard Henry Dana, III, continuing a family tradition, lived after him in Manchester and in 1895 was a featured speaker at the 250th anniversary of the town's founding.

SLAVERY DID EXIST HERE
Manchester Turns Against the Practice Early On; Helps Run-a-Ways Reach Freedom

Records of births, deaths and marriages show that slaves did exist in Manchester in the early and mid-1700's as they did in many other cities and towns throughout the Colonies.

For example, the town's early statistics list the death of "Taft, 'slave of Mrs. Lydia Lee,'" who died in Manchester on November 1, 1803 at age 76; the birth on October 19, 1788 of "Tyta, "a Molato boy Belonging to the Wid[o]w Sarah Cheever;" and the marriage on April 9, 1778 of "Seser and Philes, 'Belonging to Captain Sam'l Lee, Jr.'"

But in the North, the tide turned early against a human being of any color being the legal property of another. In 1775, a lecture was presented in Manchester entitled "The Beauties of Civil Liberty and the Horrors of Slavery" and after 1800 there are no public references to "servants" listed as taxable property. Indeed, those in town against slavery met frequently and engaged the best speakers of the day whose words and ideas convinced others to join the movement. Two abolitionist newspapers, the *National Era* and the *Liberator,* had many local subscribers. And Manchester was well known for its anti-slavery prayer meetings which, according to one member, "was one of the most singular...formed in Manchester or anywhere else." The services included prayer, sacred songs, readings from anti-slavery publications and discussions. In view of the early opposition to abolitionism, "it could not be urged," continued the attendee, "that this was an anti-church meeting. It was organized and conducted by church members and the services were always of a serious and religious character,"

As the decades passed, the Manchester Abolition Society was disbanded and its activities and commitments transferred to the Republican Town Committee which represented a party now involved with the issues of slavery on a national level. But in its time it accomplished much and because of it, Manchester was considered a leader among the towns in Essex County which were outspoken against the evils of slavery.

A small group of civil libertarians in town actually became involved with what was known as the "Underground Railway," a system of helping slaves who escaped from the South find their way to freedom.

Indeed, in the mid-1850's, as the Reverend Darius F. Lamson writes in his *History of Manchester, Mass., 1645 - 1895,* "two or three friends of freedom were willing to risk something to befriend a fellow human being in distress and danger, even though his skin was a few shades darker than their own..."

At the time, Congress had passed what was known as the Fugitive Slave Act which required free states to return run-a-way slaves to their masters as private property. As the story goes (and, of course, Reverend Lamson was writing in 1895, a time when memories of the late 1850's, 45 years earlier, were still fresh), one cold spring evening, a fugitive appeared in Manchester having apparently lost his way for Salem was the "main track" of the Underground Railway. "There was one home to receive him," Reverend Lamson continues, "and there was one friend to help him; wet and cold and trembling, he took him to his own house (and there) fed, warmed and clothed him. The next day, which was Sunday, the poor man's habiliments were repaired...a little money was collected, and early Monday morning, the grateful but still fearful stranger was guided on his way...he was afterwards heard from in Canada, safe beneath the protection of the British flag."

Among those who bravely and compassionately sheltered the run-a-way, according to the Reverend Lamson, were Daniel W. Friend, Deluncena L. Bingham and Thomas W. Gentlee. Not only did they place themselves in danger of being apprehended by Federal Marshals for aiding and abetting the escape of someone else's "personal property," but they risked incurring the wrath and indignation of fellow residents and even friends.

"It is difficult for us to conceive," the Reverend Lamson added, "the odium which attached to the early Anti-Slavery movement...fifty years ago [1855], to be suspected of sympathy for the slave was to be ostracized socially, politically and, in some cases, religiously. 'Mr. Eminent Respectability' regarded the whole thing as low and vulgar. The friends of Liberty were anathematized (as Richard Henry Dana, Jr. learned too well) as pestilent fanatics and disturbers of the peace. To oppose the slave power was to confront mobs, persecution and, sometimes, death. To attend Anti-Slavery meetings placed one outside the pale of polite society..."

But in five short years, times changed and attitudes changed with them. A growing number of Northerners were now united in their opposition to an all but feudal South, ruled by an aristocratic few and supported by slave labor, too often denigrated and abused. The North offered a different way — a society of independent, industrious and self-reliant individuals whose success or failure depended upon their own ingenuity, initiative, and ability. The West was to be the testing ground for these two ideologies. As new states and territories entered the Union were they to be slave or free? That was the fiery question which faced the nation just prior to the Civil War.

In the early 1950's, *The Manchester Cricket* printed a letter which had been sent to Manchester resident Paul Frazier. It was written by Archer M. Nickerson, then retired as a school principal in Dorchester. Seventy-four years old, he grew up in town and graduated from Story High School in 1894. Nickerson wrote that he recalled a conversation when he was young with a man named Friend who "lived on School Street, up about halfway from Lee's Drug Store to Pleasant Street..." The man said that he, too, had helped slaves on their way to freedom. "He showed me the farm wagon he used," Nickerson wrote, to take run-a-ways "to the next most convenient station."

Then, too, at the Lee House on School Street (built between 1720 and 1725), Sally Gibson, a much respected Historian of the Manchester Historical Society for many years, reports that "in the 1840's the house's owner, John Lee, was an ardent anti-slavery man and is said to have sheltered escaping slaves...with the help of a 'secret' staircase...which climbed behind the chimney to a hidden place on the second floor..." Born in 1813, John Lee was a member of Manchester's Board of Selectmen for 25 years. He also served as a State Representative. He died in 1879. Today, his diaries are a valuable part of the local history collection at Manchester's Public Library.

BOOK A MASTERPIECE

Two Years Before the Mast Is Enormously Popular; A New Style of Action Writing is born

In 1873, disappointed with what he had achieved in the world of politics as well as with many aspects of his life as a practicing attorney, Richard Henry Dana, Jr., then 57 years old, wrote a revealing letter to his son.

"My life," he said, "has been a failure compared to what I might or ought to have done. My great success — my book — was a boy's work, done before I came to the Bar." Dana started *Two Years Before the Mast* when he returned from the sea to Harvard Law School and completed a first draft in six months. The book was published in paperback in 1840 (a pocket edition, it measured about four inches by six inches) and was an instant hit. Today it is still considered one of the classic tales of life at sea in the great days of sail.

The experience that it recounts — shipping as a foremast hand in the brig PILGRIM (she was only 86 feet overall, 180 tons) to the California coast by way of Cape Horn to collect hides and returning 24 months later aboard the ship ALERT — had an enormous impact on the character and career of its author. He was in effect, a man of two personalities. One was completely at home with Brahmin Boston where he was a successful attorney, an Overseer of Harvard University and respected member of the Establishment. The other, tempered by hardship and adventure and the dangers and excitement of furling wet sails high aloft in a storm at sea, was able to relate and sympathize with the kind of brave and simple men he knew in the fo'castle who were often victimized and exploited by their masters. These two sides of Dana's nature were again and again to influence his choice of direction and commitment.

Herman Melville, it's reported, admired *Two Years Before the Mast* immensely and found it useful in the construction of his novels **Redburn** and **White Jacket**. But despite his obvious way with words and the appeal of his first book, Dana considered writing for a living unsuitable for a man of his background and education. Besides, he needed the money that a career in the law could provide to care for his aging father, his younger brother and sister, his wife Sarah and his own growing family (the couple ultimately had six children). His only other published works include **The Seaman's Friend** (1841), designed to tell sailors their legal rights and duties, and **To Cuba and Back** (1859), the story of another voyage (this time he was a passenger) which, unfortunately lacks the qualities of the first. After Dana's death in 1882, some of his more moving

addresses were collected in a book entitled *Speeches in Stirring Times* (1910). His Journals, too, have now been published. (A bit about them appears elsewhere in this Newsletter.)

While at sea aboard PILGRIM and ALERT, Dana made notes of his observations and experiences in a pocket notebook. Later, while off watch and when not working, he wrote a full story of the voyage. This, however, according to his son, Richard Henry Dana, III, who took over his father's law practice when his parents left for Europe, "was lost with his trunk containing sailor's clothes and all souvenirs and presents for his family and friends by the carelessness of a relative who took charge of his things at the wharf when he landed in Boston in 1836." Thankfully, the notebook survived and served as the basis for a second manuscript. There was a purpose for the book, too, which transcended the merits of the story itself. The flogging of two fellow sailors off the coast of California, stirred Dana's indignation and, as his son explains in the introduction to an elegant later edition of the book published by Houghton and Mifflin of Boston and New York in 1911, lying his berth the next night, he "vowed that, if God should ever give me

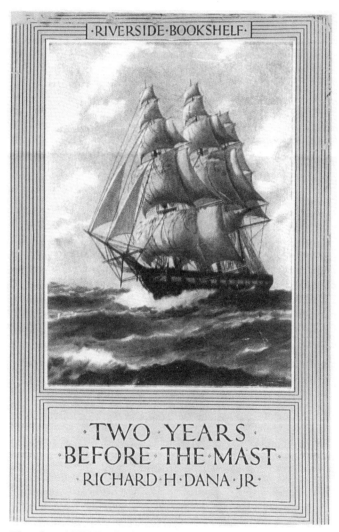

·RIVERSIDE·BOOKSHELF·

· TWO · YEARS · BEFORE ·THE·MAST· RICHARD·H·DANA·JR·

The ship ALERT which brought Richard Henry Dana, Jr, back to Boston in 1836 adorned the cover (dust jacket) of the elegant 1911 edition of Two Years Before the Mast published by Houghton Mifflin. The painting by artist Sidney M. Chase was then in the possession of RHD, III.

HARPERS'

FAMILY LIBRARY.

Nº. CVI.

TWO YEARS

BEFORE THE MAST;

A PERSONAL NARRATIVE

OF

LIFE AT SEA.

NEW-YORK:
PUBLISHED BY HARPER & BROTHERS,
NO. 82 CLIFF-STREET.

Cover of the 45-cent, first edition of <u>Two Years Before the Mast</u>. Measuring some three and one-half by six inches, the little volume was pocket-size.

the means, I would do something to redress the grievances and relieve the sufferings of that class of human beings with whom my lot has been so long cast..." The result, of course, was *Two Years Before the Mast*.

The manuscript was read by Dana's father and by Washington Allston, a poet and artist, who was his uncle by marriage. Both urged that every effort be made to have it published and the manuscript was sent to William Cullen Bryant (apparently a family friend), then a nationally acclaimed poet as well as Editor of the influential *New York Evening Post*. Bryant presented the book to a well known New York publisher who wanted to buy the manuscript but refused to offer royalties to its author. According to RHD, III in his introduction to the 1911 edition by Houghton Mifflin (which did not print the original), "The most...that the elder Dana and Bryant were able to get from the publisher was $250" and two dozen printed copies. Editions were also published in England and France. The honorarium sent to RHD, Jr. from England (no international copyright law then existed) exceeded the sum that he received from his original publisher in New York.

Finally, in 1868, RHD, III continues, "the original copyright expired and my father brought out the 'author's edition' thoroughly revised and with many important additions to the text including the "Twenty Four Years After..." the latter a description of a memorable and nostalgic visit to California, this time by steamer, as well as accounts of meeting with former shipmates, friends and acquaintances.

In the 1911 Houghton edition of *Two Years Before the Mast*, RHD, III provided a last chapter himself, this time entitled "Seventy-Six Years After by the Author's Son." He, too, visited California and retraced his father's steps. The year was 1880 and Richard Henry Dana, III was 29 years old and just married to Edith Longfellow, daughter of Henry Wadsworth Longfellow of Cambridge, one of the nation's most celebrated and beloved poets. Dana also added a brief biography of his father which included personal observations about his life and personality.

But it was left to Charles Francis Adams, a younger friend and admirer of RFD, Jr. to complete a definitive biography in two volumes which was also published by Houghton Mifflin Company in 1890.

As the years past, life at sea for those who manned ships, owned at least by Western nations, changed dramatically for the better and many who had a hand in these changes have said they were influenced by what they had read earlier in *Two Years Before the Mast*.

NOTES ON MANCHESTER
Dana's Journal Contains Many Mentions of the Beauties of the Shore and Sea

The Journal that Richard Henry Dana, Jr. kept from 1841 when he was 27 years old to 1860 when he was 45, provides us with an intimate, personal and candid picture of his life and times. Used partially by biographers and others over the years (it is preserved by the Massachusetts Historical Society today), it was first made available in its entirety in 1968. The excellent, illustrated, three volume set was edited by Robert F. Lucid and published by The Belknap Press of Harvard University Press.

In his introduction, Lucid writes that "Socially, professionally, politically, and literarily, Dana provides a wide assortment of primarily historical data..." He also emphasizes that the Journal "reveals more than enough to identify [its writer] as a wonderfully attractive personality."

The text is easy and fun to read and, as Dana rubbed shoulders with the social and intellectual elite of his era, it includes interesting comments about such notables of the day as Louisa May Alcott, William Cullen Bryant (who helped with the publication of *Two Years Before the Mast*, Ralph Waldo Emerson, Henry Wadsworth Longfellow and James Russell Lowell. Both Longfellow and Lowell were Cambridge neighbors. Abroad, Dana also met with writers Thomas Macaulay, William Makepeace Thackeray and Charles Dickens.

There are numerous references to Manchester, too, of which RHD, Jr. was deeply fond. He describes purchasing for his father a part of the old Graves Farm (see lead article elsewhere in this Newsletter). On July 28, 1845: "Ch., Father, Ned and I, all went together to the beach, Eagle Head, to select a site for the house. After nearly giving up in despair, we at last hit upon a spot in which we are all perfectly united, commanding a noble view both of sea & of shore. Spent the night at the Tavern, & came up to the city

First summer residence in Manchester was a substantial dwelling located off Summer Street overlooking Graves Beach. Richard Henry Dana, Sr. acquired the land in 1845 and built the house shortly thereafter selling his home in Cambridge. View from the porch where family members often sat listening to the waves on the beach below, looks east towards Town Head and Coolidge Point. Artwork by H. Billings. Engraving for Houses of American Authors, by L.V. Hunt.

[Boston] while the others went to Gloucester."

On August 28, 1852: "...reached the Shore at 7 o'ck [that evening]. Delightful bath in the surf, tea, walk, and enjoyment of the pure air, the piny smell of the woods, the rolling sound of the surf, & the still cheerful ray of the lighthouses {most likely Eastern Point and Baker's Island] lying over the water. Being unused to the sound, the surf kept me awake awhile, yet it was lulling."

August 16, 1852: "Spent the day here [Manchester]. Bath in surf before breakfast, 7 another at the end of a hard day's work in the woods, where I wielded the axe & bush scythe with energy.Just before sun-down, caught a few fish from the island. How beautiful this is! There is no place like it, that I ever saw — such a combination of green woods, brown and gray rocks, yellow beach, blue ocean and white sails and white lighthouses, with a beautiful indented coast studded with islands."

After his years at sea, RHD, Jr. thrived on hard work and exercise. One of the activities he enjoyed most at Manchester was cutting trails as evidenced by this report in the Journal late one September: "Returned from spending a week at Manchester — glorious weather. Worked hard, "he writes, "& made several paths in the woods with bush scythe. One from Hildreth's E. [east] wall, near the beach, to Craft's E. wall, leading to Shark's Mouth (a large boulder), another from the latter point, over the hill to meet the path that comes out near Craft's E. line on the road, near the top of the hill; another to connect this with the path over our own hill..."

Throughout its nearly 20 years, when America was emerging as a young nation, Dana's Journal includes intimate reflections on the details of his own personal life, observations on the world around him, and comments about the people of all stations with whom he associated. It reveals the activities and ideals of Boston Brahminism, then in full flower, as well as the intricacies of his law practice, his travels and his politics. And always, throughout the text, runs the thread of inner conflict between Dana's institutionalized existence in Cambridge and Boston and the

personal freedom, adventure, excitement and achievements of those two extraordinary years at sea aboard PILGRIM and ALERT.

He loved the ocean and its restless ways even giving Sarah Watson, his wife to be, in 1840, an emerald engagement ring. "It is the color of the sea, and among all the precious stones always represents the sea," he said to her, according to a family biography written by Henry Wadsworth Longfellow Dana years later in 1941. (***The Dana Saga, Three Centuries of the Dana Family in Cambridge***, Cambridge Historical Society, Harvard University Press.) "Whenever you look at it" he continued, "remember whatever associations you may have attached to the ocean, & among them, if you call to mind one who wandered over it, then unknown to you, why — it will be one reason for which I gave it to you."

This, too, certainly was among the many qualities which Dana loved about his life in Manchester. For it gave him a chance at least, especially in his later years, to be next to his beloved ocean if not on it as he had been as young man.

AN IDYLLIC LIFE
Summers with Grandfather Dana Were Particularly Important to the Children

"How we children looked forward to the summer with grandfather [Richard Henry Dana, Sr.] at Manchester-by-the-Sea, or at the 'Shore' as we called it!" wrote Richard Henry Dana, III. "He was the first man from the city to buy a place on the South Shore of Cape Ann," the younger Dana continues in a biography entitled **Richard Henry Dana, 1851-1931** by Bliss Perry (Houghton Mifflin, The Riverside Press, Cambridge,1933). "He [grandfather, RHD, Sr.] chose a beach with singing sands, a quarter of a mile long and rocks at either end. The beach was smooth and good for bathing at all tides. It had a double curve with a pretty, four acre, wooded island, accessible at low tide, over the bar where these curves met.

"On the mainland the trees, with forestlike density, came down to the edge of the rocks or the beach for the larger part of the frontage. In those woods the united family worked on pleasant mornings, clearing paths, after which we all went bathing. I so well remember the Sunday before going down to the shore, and how my mind wandered from the [church] service, with visions of forest, beach and sea, so excited was I with the prospect!"

As Richard (or Dick as he was known) grew older, he began to appreciate "the literary treat that was given us at the 'Shore.' "My grandfather," he writes, "was not only one of the founders of the *North American Review*...but was also a poet. There was reading aloud from the best new books, as well as from the old ones. I got my first taste for Charles Lamb from these readings and I listened to part of Don Quixote and the 'Lake' poets [Coleridge, Southey and Wordsworth]. The conversation turned frequently on literary subjects in a joyous, easy way. There were besides my grandfather, my father [RHD, Jr.] when he was able to be there (not half enough for me) and my Uncle Edmund [Dana], who got at Heidelberg a doctor's degree summa cum laude.

"My mother knew whole passages from Milton by heart and was better up in chemistry and geology than any of them, while my aunt, Miss Charlotte Dana, was little short of a genius with an unusual knowledge of philosophy,music and modern languages to say nothing for a good deal of Latin...[and] with all the serious side was mingled abundance of laughter and fun."

In those early days, the town was sparsely populated. Its coastal lands were still wild, its islands and beaches all but deserted which gave the Danas a little kingdom of their own. Small wonder they found such delight, enjoyment and satisfaction with their house at Manchester-by-the-Sea.

1817: A SEA SERPENT SIGHTED — NO KIDDING !

Scores of Perfectly Sane and Many Distinguished People Observed Ocean Monster Some 90 Feet Long Off Gloucester; Its Existence Is Supported by the Lengthy Report of a Learned Scientific Society; Beast Also Seen Off Nahant

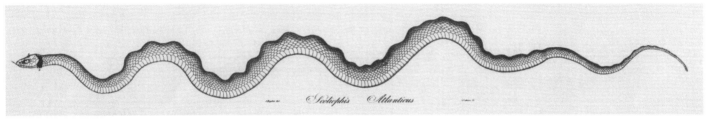

Drawing of Scoliophis Atlanticus *taken from the Report of the Linnaean Society, 1817. The engraving was "copied from the specimen in possession of Capt[ain] Beach." According to the report, "The dimensions of the animal, the number. size and proportion of the protuberances, are accurately preserved. The body is bent vertically to [show] its flexibility in that direction." The letters a, a, indicate "portions of the head and throat so far destroyed that their structure could not be ascertained."*

Many an eager whale watcher of today would be astounded to learn that in the early years of the last century there was another mammal which caught the fancy of those who lived on Massachusetts Bay.

In August,1817, a "sea serpent," some 90 feet long with a "head the size of horse" and a girth as big around a "half a barrel" was reported seen in Gloucester Harbor. In 1815, there were reports of sea serpents sighted in Plymouth. And in the summer 1819, off Nahant, the creature was seen again by hundreds who were gathered at Lynn Beach to swim. Like today's tales of "flying saucers," stories of sea serpents swept the North Shore.

Reports that a "sea serpent" had been sighted came not only from scores of ordinary citizens who wrote letters to their newspapers, but from mariners, fishermen, merchants and public officials, each of whom was considered sober, industrious, intelligent, of sound mind and of exemplary character. Such a one, for example, was Colonel Thomas Handasyd Perkins, a Boston merchant and clipper ship owner made famous by his successes in the China trade, who reported he had observed the serpent in 1817 in Gloucester. "As he approached us," he wrote, "it was easy to see that his motion was not that of a common snake...but evidently the vertical movement of the caterpillar. As nearly as I could judge, there was visible at a time about 40 feet of his body...I had a fine glass, and was within one-third to half a mile from him...The animal," he added, "was...of a chocolate color."

In a letter to Perkins, Samuel Cabot, whose direct descendents included two United States Senators, Henry Cabot Lodge, Sr, and Jr., wrote about his own experience with a sea serpent at Nahant in 1819: "My attention was suddenly arrested," he declared, "by an object emerging from the water which gave to my mind the idea of a horse's head...As my eye ranged along, I perceived, at a short distance, eight or ten regular bunches or protuberances...I returned to Nahant and in crossing the small beach, had another good look at him for a longer time...he moved more rapidly, causing a white foam under the chin, and a long wake...at this time he must have been seen by two or three hundred persons on the beach and on the heights on either side..."

But verbal descriptions — and there were many in the press — were not the only evidence presented that a sea serpent existed. Another Nahant resident, James Prince, a prominent Boston merchant and Marshal of the District of Massachusetts, actually drew a sketch of the animal as he saw it through his telescope. A number of attempts were also made to shoot and capture the creature all of which were unsuccessful. But the fever of interest and speculation was such that a shed was reportedly constructed near Faneuil Hall in Boston to display the serpent after it had been caught.

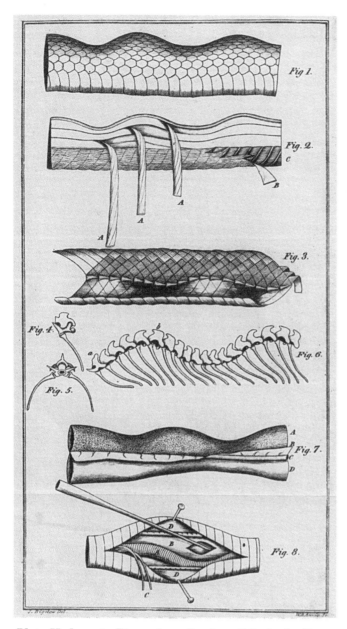

Plate II shows in Figure 1, a Section of the body; Figure 2, Dissection of the same on the opposite side; Figure 3, Inside view of the cavity of the ribs and spine with the internal muscles crossing the ribs; Figure 4, Side view of a vertebra; Figure 5, Front view of same; Figure 6, Portion of the spine; Figure 7, Portion of the viscera of the first section; and Figure 8 which represents an opening in the throat.

Those who reported having seen the sea serpent were, understandably, subject to some ridicule and disbelief by those who hadn't. In fact, some years later, Colonel Perkins confessed that he was one of the "unfortunate individuals" who had recorded his observations for public consumption. But there were so many seemingly authentic sightings in Massachusetts Bay that the Linnaean Society of New England (named for Carolus Linnaeas, 1707-1778, a Swedish botanist and originator of a system of taxomic classification), decided that the subject demanded further investigation and, if possible, verification of the existence a new species of marine mammal.

Its response was an illustrated, more than 50-page report published in Boston in 1817. A collection of distinguished scholars and scientists, the Society appointed a three- man committee "to collect evidence in regard to the existence and appearance of a Sea Serpent..." Committee members were the Honorable John Davis, Jacob Bigelow, MD, and Francis C. Gray, Esq. On August 19, 1817, the committee wrote to Lonson Nash of Gloucester, a Justice of the Peace, as well as to Samuel Davis of Plymouth asking each to interview some of those who had seen the animal and to take statements under oath from persons willing to provide them. For uniformity, each witness was asked to respond to a series of 25 specific questions. Included in the report as well, as supporting evidence, was an account of sea serpents said to have been seen frequently in the mid 1700's in the North Sea off the coast of Norway.

The final report, published in Boston by Cummings and Hilliard, concluded that the "testimony was sufficient to place the existence of the animal beyond a doubt." Scientists christened the beast **Scoliophis Atlanticus**. It was a somewhat more dignified appellation than that chosen by the newspapers of the day which referred to the sea serpent as "His Snakeship."

One of the most detailed depositions describing a sighting came from Matthew Gaffney of Gloucester , a ship's carpenter, who told the Linnaean Society: "That on the fourteenth day of August, AD, 1817, between the hours of four and five o'clock in the afternoon, I saw a strange marine animal resembling a serpent in the harbor [of] said Gloucester. I was in a boat and was within thirty feet of him. His head appeared full as large a four-gallon keg; his body as large as a barrel, and his length that I saw, I should judge [to be] forty feet at least. The top of his head was of a dark color, and the under part of his head appeared to be nearly white, as did also several feet of his belly...I fired at him when he was nearest to me. I had a good gun and took good aim. I aimed at his head and I think I must have hit him. He turned towards us immediately after I had fired, and I thought he was coming at us; but he sunk down and went directly under our boat, and made his appearance about [100] yards from where he sunk. He did not turn down like a fish, but appeared to settle directly...like a rock. My gun carries a ball of eighteen to the pound, and I suppose there is no person in town more accustomed to shooting, than I am. I have seen the same animal at several other times, but never had so good a view of his as on this day. His motion was vertical like a caterpillar." Mr. Gaffney also estimated that the serpent was travelling at approximately 15 knots. As other witnesses, he had with him in the boat that day his brother Daniel and Augustin M. Webber also of Gloucester.

Sightings were confirmed and sworn to as well by Sewell Toppan, Master of the schooner LAURA, who saw a sea serpent off Brace's Cove just east of Eastern Point; by William B. Pearson, who saw the animal off Webber's Cove in Gloucester Harbor; by Captain E. Finney, who saw a sea serpent in the outer harbor at Plymouth; and by the Reverend Abraham Cummings who reported a sighting in Maine's Penobscot Bay. Additional testimony included a statement from a Mr. Miller, who reportedly lived on an island in the Bay, that "about 1780, as a schooner was lying at the mouth of the river, or in the bay, one of these enormous creatures leaped over it between the masts — that the men ran into the hold for fright, and that the weight of the serpent sunk the vessel 'one streak' or plank. The schooner [which evidently survived the incident] was of about eighteen tons."

Excitement on the North Shore soared during the fall of 1817 when residents of Cape Ann discovered and killed two snakes near Sandy Bay in Rockport and at Loblolly Cove, Gloucester. Both were smaller serpents (one was three feet long), but unlike any other of their kind ever seen on land. It was thus "suggested ," as the Society's report states, "that [both] might be the progeny of the Sea Serpent...which was said to have been seen near the Cove where this snake was killed." The pair was offered to the Society whose scientists were able to dissect their "internatural structure" and describe in detail not only the animal's external appearance, but its muscles and its viscera. Particular attention was paid to the back-bone which showed an extraordinary "flexibility and an increase in strength in vertical motions" which enabled the creature to proceed, as observed, like a "caterpillar" rather than slithering like a snake.

It was also noted by the report that "the **Colubri** [non-venemouos snakes] without fangs was the species most nearly resembling the **Scoliophis**. (The sea sepent had a long, forked tongue.) [The former] are said by naturalists to be generally if not always oviparous (creatures producing eggs which hatch outside their bodies), depositing [them] in the sand in the spring or [at] the end of the summer, [and abandoning them to survive on their own]. These eggs are hatched by the heat of the sun often in less time than a month. The large serpents in our accounts and depositions," the report continued, "were seen near the shore and only in the month of August, excepting once at Plymouth in June."

Some concern was voiced about the disproportionate size of the smaller serpents, but it was explained by Linnaean Society members that the young of the giant Boa constrictor, for example, bore a close resemblance in size to the two snakes found along the shore. The report also observed that the smaller animals were likely to have remained in the tidal zone to protect themselves from deep sea predators. And that like other serpents, the young were" perfect in all their parts [resembling their parents] and capable of providing for their own subsistence immediately on being hatched."

Indeed, Society representatives agreed that the smaller serpents which had been captured as specimens were most probably "individuals of the same species [as the larger, thus entitling them] to the same name — **Scoliophis Atlanticus** — until, as the report concludes, "a more close examination of the great Serpent shall have disclosed some difference of structure important enought to constitute a specific distinction."

Shortly after the report had been completed, news of another sighting was received from Rye and Mamaroneck, New York. That, too, was published by the Society adding further evidence to the existence of sea serpents not only along the North Shore but in Long Island Sound as well.

It was obvious that the best minds of the day truly believed that one or perhaps more sea serpents had been seen and did, therefore, at least in the early 19th century, actually exist. Are we in any position today to assume otherwise? And, if not, why have no other sightings of such creatures been reported since?

Just perhaps as our children dig in the sands of Singing Beach, or we walk along the shore, we should be alert for signs of eggs or young serpents playing in the shallows. And when we look out to sea, we should be just a bit more aware of the possibility that **Scoliophis Atlanticus** could reappear after all these years.

BIBLIOGRAPHY

Lamson, Reverend D.F.; *History of Manchester, Mass., 1645-1895.*; Boston, Massachusetts; The Pinkham Press, 1895; *Report of a Committee of the Linnaean Society of New England, Relative to a Large Marine Animal Supposed to Be a Serpent, Seen Near Cape Ann, Massachusetts in August 1817*; Boston, Massachusetts, University Press Hilyard and Metcalf, 1817; Charles Francis Adams; *Richard Henry Dana, A Biography*; Cambridge, Houghton Mifflin & Company, The Riverside Press, 1890; *The Journal of Richard Henry Dana, Jr., Volume I*, Edited by Robert F. Lucid; Cambridge, Massachusetts; The Belknap Press of Harvard University Press, 1968; Clippings and papers from the Manchester Historical Society; historic editions of *The Manchester Cricket*; Longfellow National Historic Site, the National Park Service, Cambridge; Dana, H.W.L., *The Dana Saga, Three Centuries of the Dana Family in Cambridge*; Cambridge, Massachusetts; The Cambridge Historical Society, Harvard University Press, 1941; Perry, Bliss; *Richard Henry Dana, 1851-1931*; Houghton Mifflin Company, New York and Boston, The Riverside Press, 1933; *Houses of America Authors*; New York; G.W. Putnam & Company; 1853.

ILLUSTRATIONS

Three generations of Danas: Richard Henry Dana, Sr, RHD, Jr. and RHD, III. photo courtesy of National Park Service, Longfellow National Historic Site; Cover, first edition of *Two Years Before the Mast* from a private collection; Cover, 1911 edition published by Houghton Mifflin Company, Boston and New York: "SHIP ALERT, From a painting by Sidney M. Chase, [then] in the possession of the author's son, R.H. Dana [III];" engravings of the sea serpent came from the *Report of the Linnaean Society of New England* published by Cummings and Hilliard in 1817; steel engraving to the Dana house at Graves' Beach, Manchester, originally appeared in Homes of American Authors, G.W. Putnam & Company, New York, 1853. The drawing was by artist H. Billings; the engraving by L.V. Hunt.

The Newsletter of the Manchester Historical Society is written and edited by Gordon Abbott, Jr., a member of the MHS Board of Directors.

MANCHESTER HISTORICAL SOCIETY

NEWSLETTER

MANCHESTER, MASSACHUSETTS

SPRING 1996

MASCONOMO AND HIS INDIANS

In February, 1636, as they left the Fort, a band of Englishmen was surrounded in the forest by "two or three hundred Indians." The settlers fought back gallantly but the difference in numbers was too much. Some of the men escaped, two were taken prisoner and two were slain. Indian warriors were equipped with firearms as well as bows, arrows and tomahawks. Many settlers carried a sword as well as a musket.

On Saturday, June 10, 1630, after many weeks at sea, ARBELLA rounded up and dropped anchor in Manchester's outer harbor. Members of the ship's company ventured ashore to explore the land and friends from the settlement in Salem rowed out to greet them.

But by far the most interesting visitor to the ship must have been the Sagamore Masconomo, who, with another American Indian, John Winthrop writes, "came on board [on Sunday] and bade us welcome, tarrying with us all day."

The Indians in Manchester and in this part of Essex County were members of the Massachusetts Tribe which occupied the eastern portion of what is now the Commonwealth. They were a mobile people, settling along the shores of lakes, ponds, streams and bays during the warm months of summer, and moving inland during winter. Thus Manchester cannot claim Indians of her own as the town can claim residents today.

The Massachusetts (meaning "at or about the Great Hill," presumed to be Blue Hill in Milton) were a part of the Algonquin nation. On the North Shore, they divided themselves into three sub-tribes, or "sagamoreships." One of these was led by the Sachem Masconomo. Early English explorer Captain John Smith mentions sighting 11 of their

villages along the coast during his voyages here and indicates there were more than 20 Indian seaside settlements in what is today Essex County.

Until 1658 when their lands were sold to the English, there was a tribe in Ipswich known as the Agawams (fish-drying place). By 1658, however, the Agawams were almost extinct. To blame, according to early records, was a plague in 1617 and and epidemic of smallpox shortly thereafter brought to the area by Europeans. Other North Shore Indian tribes were also decimated by disease. Indeed, the Massachusetts tribe, it was reported at the time by English sources, was reduced from "from 30,000 to 300 fighting men." Besides disease, there were also the Tarrantine, a fierce tribe of warriors from southern Maine, which swept down upon coastal Indians, burning villages, killing men and seizing women and children as slaves.

With all but a handful of his followers remaining alive, it was little wonder that Masconomo was willing to sign a treaty with the English in 1644. The instrument called for his people to "bee true & faithfull to the government, ayding in the maintenance thereof...&...willing from time to time to bee instructed in the knowledge and worship of God." In return, the Indians expected and received protection from their foes.

Throughout the next century, residents of Salem, Beverly, Manchester and Gloucester lived in comparative harmony with native Americans. It was true that waterfront communities, including Boston, were easier to fortify and protect because of their geography. Here also was where the white population was most densely settled. But if friendly relations with the Indians existed along the coast, the same could not be said for the inland towns of Essex County especially to the west and northwest. These included Haverhill and Andover which then marked where the wilderness began.

HOSTILITY GROWS BETWEEN SETTLERS AND THE INDIANS
A Different Way of Looking at Land, Deceit on Both Sides, & the Sale of Indian Children

Religion played a major role in the life of the Puritans of the North Shore and conversion of native Americans to a Christian way of life was considered a part of their mission in the New World.

Understandably, this created friction although it must be said that the efforts of the ministry in many cases — Reverend John Eliot and his Praying Indians, for example — were remarkaby successful. Then, too, as settlements grew, the English soon began to usurp traditional rights of the Indians to the use of land. Hunting grounds were cleared to grow produce. Streams were taken over and houses and animal shelters appeared in fields once used by Indians to produce maize. Close to the heart of the matter was that European and Indian relationships to the land were very different. To the English, land was property to be held privately and used as its owner wished often not only for sustenance but for profit. To the Indians, land was a community resource, to be respected, as all of nature was, for the bounty it could produce for every member of the tribe. Then, too, many of the Puritans were traders with "a trader's conscience" which was used to rationalize underhanded financial and other dealings with their Indian neighbors. The latter, for example, whose culture it must be remembered was primarily Neolithic or Stone Age, had little understanding of deeds or money which too often led to their undoing. The township of Manchester-by-the-Sea, for example, was purchased for the sum of three pounds, 19 shillings. The town of Bradford cost the white man six pounds and 12 shillings. Ipswich was acquired for just 20 pounds.

Settlers hoodwinked Indians in other ways as well. One report tells of a trader in Groton "who claimed to have a foot weighing exactly a pound [which] he would put on one side of the scale while balancing it with furs on the other." But it was the sale of native boys and girls into slavery that most infuriated the Indians. Records show that in 1684 residents of Essex County purchased an "Indian maid" for 15 pounds and an "Indian boy" for 20. Friction soon grew into hatred, and, ultimately, hatred erupted into violence. One revengeful assault followed another and atrocities were common to both sides, white and Indian. Such was the unbelievable bitterness of the times.

Fear of Indian raids stalked every village in the County. Men took their muskets to work in the fields and even to

church. Women, just as brave, learned the use of the powder horn and the musket to defend their families. Indians, too, were equipped with modern weapons and ammunition which they had traded for furs and other goods and they quickly became proficient in their use.

As early as 1637, English settlers from Essex County were part of punitive expedition called the Pequot War arranged to avenge the murder of a white trader named John Oldham. In a surprise attack on an Indian village near Mystic, Connecticut, the force slaughtered some 600 men, women and children. Two white men were killed and about 20 wounded.

Although the town itself was free from Indian attack, men from Manchester-by-the-Sea rallied to help other communities. Serving under the gallant Captain Lothrop of

Beverly during the three-year war against the legendary King Philip (1675-1678), four Manchester men — Samuel Pickworth, John Allen, Joshua Carter, and John Bennett — were slain at the battle of Bloody Brook in central Masachusetts. On September 18, 1675, the troop had started from Deerfield to provide relief for the citizens of Hadley. On the way, they were ambushed by more than 700

A garrison house at York, Maine about 1645. Strongly constructed of heavy planks and timbers, houses such as this were used as refuges by English settlers when their towns were attacked by Indians. Gun ports in the overhang of the second floor made it possible to fire down upon the enemy if he tried to break down the doors or set the fire to the house.

Indian warriors. In all, 90 English settlers were killed. Throughout Essex County people reacted to news of the disaster with terror and dismay. Nearly every village had lost one or more of its residents. But the war against Philip continued and 70 additional men were drafted for the Essex County Regiment which at the time consisted of 13 companies of foot and one of cavalry.

Trained in the ways of the hunt, stealthy, often cleverer and as vengeful as his white neighbors, the Indian was a master of guerilla warfare. His mobility made him a dangerous and ever-threatening foe. As an observer wrote at the time: "From the woodland shadows he could [see] the movements of his [English] victims unconscious of immediate danger...by day or night no white man was safe. As [he] plowed or reaped, the fences along his fields were the crouching places of his...enemy...thickets by the roadside were likely at any moment to breathe forth a whisp of musket smoke when the fatal bullet would speed to his heart. The savage lurked in his barns and outhouses, and his terror kept pace with the days as they grew..."

Because of animosities among the tribes themselves, there were friendly Indians who fought bravely and gallantly with the settlers, often warning them of attacks to come and acting as scouts during battle itself. But it seemed impossible for either the red man or the white man to trust each other, their lives were on such different courses. One was fighting to defend his lands and a centuries old way of life against an invader who seemed to want to confiscate it all. The other, convinced of his own righteousness and empowered by his God, was determined to settle this new world in his own way, to protect his wife and family against all comers, and with others of his race and creed, to create a new and better life than that which he had left behind in England. It was a conflict of ideas that sadly could be settled only by the force of arms.

INDIAN RAIDS, MASSACRES AND ESCAPES
The Incredible Story of Hannah Dunston: How She Was Captured by the Indians, Transported to New Hampshire and Found Her Way Home Again to Her Loving Family and Her Husband Thomas in Haverhill

Throughout the late 1670's, Indians continually raided such towns as Amesbury, Bradford, Andover and Haverhill. To the west, the residents of Deerfield and Lancaster were slaughtered in their beds and their towns burned to the ground. Settlers everywhere were incensed and determined to avenge their losses. Indeed, according to the Reverend Increase Mather, when the war against King Philip was at its height in 1677, two Indians were captured and brought to Marblehead. There on Sunday, May 23, as "the women [of the town] came out of the meeting house, [they] fell upon [the] captives and, in a tumultuous way, very barbarously murdered them." It was considered by the authorities as just punishment.

Meanwhile, the raids continued. Newbury kept 51 people on watch each night. Settlers were picked off while working in the fields. Houses were burned after dark. Children were taken captive by the Indians and sold as servants in Canada. But it is the story of Hannah Dunston, her capture and her remarkable escape in 1697 which still excites readers today.

A resident of Haverhill with her husband Thomas, Hannah had given birth to the family's twelfth child only a few days before her house was attacked by some 20 Indians. Thomas managed to escape with the other children, but Hannah, in bed upstairs, was taken prisoner. According to The Story of Essex County published by The American History Society in 1935, "It is said that she had only time to secure one shoe before starting on her terrible journey. Such of the captives who could not keep up with the march were tomahawked [and] the Dunston's baby's brains were dashed out. [But] weakened by illness and grief as she was, Hannah...continued on through the cold winds, the mud and snow of March and arrived in good condition at the Indian camp on a small island [north] of Concord, New Hampshire."

As was the Indian custom with women, "she was treated with kindness" but not allowed to worship in her Protestant faith. It was also said that she would be sold to the French once the Indians reached Canada and that she would be forced to "run the gauntlet" naked at the next Indian town. This was too much for Hannah and she and an English youth named Samuel Leonardson who had been taken prisoner in Worcester earlier, decided to escape. Leonardson, who had been with the Indians so long they regarded him practically as a member of the tribe, had been taught how to use a tomahawk, a skill that he had discussed at some length with Hannah Dunston.

Seized by the Indians in a raid on Haverhill and carried to an island in Contoocook, New Hampshire, where they were kept as prisoners, Hannah Dunston, her friend Mary Neff and 14-year-old Samuel Leonardson, managed to escape by killing their captors while they slept. As proof of their story, they scalped the Indians and took the evidence to the Great and General Court in Boston where they were rewarded for their bravery.

One April night, an hour before dawn, Hannah, Mary Neff, who had been nurse to the Dunston baby, and Sam Leonardson, just 14 years old, attacked the sleeping Indians with tomahawks and hatchets killing all 10 of them, two men, two women and six children. Another squaw and a little boy escaped. The three prisoners then scuttled every canoe but one, collected a musket and what provisions they could, and set off down the river to freedom. Suddenly, it occured to Hannah that without scalps as proof, no one would believe their story and they returned to the island. There, according to an account of the day, "with a courage that speaks volumes for... pioneer women, she...scalped the 10 corpses and, wrapping her trophies in a piece of linen she had brought from home at the time of her capture," boarded the canoe again and continued her voyage home. Her husband and other children were both amazed and overjoyed to see her and news of her remarkable escape spread throughout the region. Both Tom and Hannah Dunston travelled to Boston with the tomahawk, the gun and the 10 scalps. There, with the evidence in hand, Hannah presented a petition to the General Court "for recompense on account of 'the just slaughter of so many of the Barbarians'" as well as for the loss of the couple's house and possessions in the Indian raid. They received 25 pounds, a goodly sum in those days. Mary Neff and Sam Leonardson were given 12 pounds, 10 shillings each. Although the merits of Hannah's accomplishments were, at the time, subject to some debate, most thought they were justified. By 1879, however, all doubt had vanished and 182 years after her escape, a statue of Hannah Dunston commemorating her bravery was erected on the Common in front of Haverhill City Hall.

As The Story of Essex County declares: "Today [1935] the red man no longer exists within the borders of our county; a whole race which with different treatment might have made a distinct contribution to American life has been wiped out." It is a sad story which led to extraordinary loss of lives on both sides.

MASCONOMO
**A Gentle Leader Welcomes the White Race and
Signs a Treaty of Peace and Protection**

There seems little doubt that Masconomo was the Sachem, Sagamore or leader of Indians in what is now eastern Essex County. Although records are scarce, history has it that he was chief of a small sub-tribe known as the Agawams which inhabited the area from Salem to the Merrimack River until their lands were sold to the English in 1658. He was known for his friendliness with the Europeans and it is said that the more than 150 ships which visited the North Shore each year before 1620 found his welcome so warm that the Pilgrims considered settling here instead of at Plymouth. French traders were more familiar with the area at the time than were the English which might explain the Indians cordiality for it is said that although "the French called the Indians wolves [they] treated them as friends, while the English called the Indians friends and treated them as wolves."

Although the dreaded plague of 1617 had reduced the numbers of his tribe to a mere handful of what they had been, Masconomo who was also known as Masconnoma, Masconomet and even by the Christian name of "John," was one of the most important Sachems of his Federation. It was he who guided Englishman David Thompson to an island in Boston Harbor with fresh water which today still bears the settler's name. And it was he who, shortly after meeting with John Winthrop aboard ARBELLA in 1630, agreed to a treaty with the English which included a pledge of allegiance

to "the only true God" and a prohibition of work on Sunday. In exchange, Winthrop and his men were to protect the Agawams from the predations of the Tarratine, a brutal, warring tribe of Indians which inhabited the coastal region of southern Maine. On one occasion, white settlers in Ipswich were warned by an Agawam and saved from attack.

But Masconomo, perhaps to test the extent and veracity of his relationship with the English, decided to right previous wrongs and raid a Tarrantine village himself. His men killed a number of warriors and captured women and children. Winthrop and his followers were shocked by this unprevoked assault and Masconomo was banished from English homes for a year by order of the General Court. The penalty for violating the order was payment of 10 beaver skins. In return, the Tarrantines, too, had their revenge killing seven Agawam braves and wounding many others in a return raid at Ipswich.

Town Seal shows Masconomo being paddled out to the Arbella to meet with Governor Winthrop and other English visitors to the New World.

When the attack began, according to an account at the time, some of the natives sought safety at Governor Winthrop's house and begged him to save them from the possibility of capture and death by torture. One of the favorite forms of brutality indulged in by the Tarrantines was to tie a prisoner to a tree. Members of the tribe would then each tear off bits of flesh with their teeth until the poor victim died. Little wonder the Agawams were concerned! By 1644, Masconomo and four other chiefs of neighboring tribes had signed a formal agreement with the Massachusetts Bay Colony, pledging their allegiance, vowing to alert the English to any conspiracy which they might discover and allowing themselves to be instructed "in the knowledge and worship of God."

As time passed, Masconomo became a Christian. His tribe dwindled to only a handful of men, women and children, and, like others of his race, he was given a small plot of land by the English to farm. In 1658 he died, "poor, disheartened and friendless, as a ward of the state." Despite his new religion, he was buried as an Indian Chief at Sagamore Hill in Hamilton with his gun, tomahawk and other artifacts used in life. Some years later, vandals dug up his grave, scattered his possessions, and marched around town with his skull at the end of a pike. The youths were taken to court and punished. Masconomo's remains were again interred and today a tablet marks his final resting place.

By 1730, a century after Winthrop arrived in the New World, the Agawams were all but extinct. In a salute to their past glories, on a cold and rainy Thanksgivingday in 1971, local officials led a delegation to the Chief's graveside. A wreath was placed on his headstone and the 23rd Psalm was read in Narragansett Indian. The site, given to the Hamilton Historical Society by former Superior Court Judge Standish Bradford, is maintained by the Hamilton Historical Commission and visitors may read the inscription on the memorial: "Musconominet, Sagamore of the Agawams. Died 1658. Erected on the tradtional site of the grave by the Heirs of W.H. Kinsman and J.F. Patch Le Baron, 1910."

STATUE OF MASCONOMO
A Likeness of Masconomo Is Revived After
Many Years and Is Now at Town Hall

Masconomo may have died unheralded and unappreciated in his own time, but there have been attempts at least in later years to recognize the roll he played in welcoming our forefathers. Hamilton has preserved and marked his last resting place. Here in Manchester there is Masconomo Park, Masconomo Street, and the Masconomo Council of the Knights of Columbus. Mention of the Chief appears in the town hymn. The name of Masconomo (or Masconomet) also appears in the title of the regional high school in Boxford.

Early in this century, members of Manchester's Elder Brethern, according to its centennial history written in 1978, proposed that a monument to the Sachem be erected at Masconomo Park. In 1938, the Brethern sought funds from the Federal Arts Project of the Works Progress Administration and by the end of that year sculptor George Aarons of Gloucester had submitted a plaster model of a life-sized statue which was to be cast in bronze. It's appearance, however, was very different from that which was envisioned by the Elder Brethern. Instead of a standard Hollywood Indian with feathered headdress and tomahawk, Aarons had sensitively sculpted Masconomo in an almost mystic state of repose, standing with eyes closed and arms folded, his long hair braided and touching his bare chest on either side. No feathers were visible (the Agawams rarely wore them). The Sachem's lower body is wrapped in a sleek and simple robe. It is a striking vision but one that is admittedly unconventional. In their letter rejecting the statue,the Elder Bretheren committee wrote: "The model reminds one more of a Jesuit priest in long flowing robes..." Others compared it to an Egyptian mummy or to an Indian squaw. So back it went to Aaron's studio in Gloucester.
In the summer of 1983, however, former Selectman Herbert A. Kenny, who had retired as Book and Arts Editor of The Boston Globe, wrote a letter to The Manchester Cricket which told the story of the statue and suggested that it be

purchased and displayed in town. The idea caught on immediately and with committee members Ted Brown (Chairman), Lucy Conley, President of the Manchester Historical Society, Nancy Southgate, former Town Librarian Doris Connors, O. Kelley Anderson, President of the Elder Bretheren, and Dan Slade, Editor of The Cricket, contributions to purchase the sculpture poured in. By this time, Aarons had died but the excellence of his work lived after him in private collections and in cities and institutions around the world. Five of his pieces, as Kenney explains in an article he wrote for the quarterly publication Essex Institute Historical Collections, were purchased by Boston's Museum of Fine Arts. In the end there was not only enough money to acquire the 30-inch model of Masconomo, but to have it cast in bronze directly from the plaster.

Today, the Sachem surveys us all from his pedestal at Town Hall and, thanks to Herb Kenny and to others who made it possible to reproduce his image, the town and its citizens pay homage to the man who first welcomed our forefathers to these shores 351 years ago and who helped to make their lives easier in new and strange surroundings.

STONE AGE CULTURE
What They Looked Like; How they Dressed,
and What They Produced for Food

Most Indian villages in Essex County were located along streams or near the ocean shore. There the tribe could hunt beaver, otter, mink, muskrats and other fur-bearing animals as well as build traps and weirs to catch both fresh and salt water fin fish. Their hunting methods were crude compared to those used by Europeans. But it must be remembered, that when the first settlers arrived in 1620, they were greeted by what were essentially a people living in the Neolithic era or what is commonly known as the Stone Age, a period of human culture which began about 10,000 years before the birth of Christ. Indian hunting implements consisted primarily of bows and arrows, the tomahawk and the noose. Later, of course, they acquired firearms and other weapons but in the early seventeenth game was so plentiful that it could all but be had for the asking. There were massive flocks of wild pigeon, duck and geese; huge herds of deer and somewhat farther north, thousands of moose and caribou.

Indian villages were often surrounded by stockades of logs with a small entrance which was easy to guard. Inside were a series of "long houses" shaped like Quonset huts of World War II and covered with bark shingles. Some 15 feet wide or more, these long houses varied in length according to the number of families they sheltered. As many as eight could be accommodated. Other dwellings somewhat smaller and of a different shape but constructed in the same manner were called "round houses." These usually sheltered one or two families. Long houses were used in winter as it was easier to keep them warm, while the round house became more popular in summer. The lodges and their contents were considered the property of the women of the tribe, while the men owned their weapons. Both sexes worked together to construct weirs for fishing and no village was without its mortar, a granite boulder with a slight natural depression which was worn deeper as tribal members ground corn and other grains with stone pestles. Many of these mortars still exist today and may be seen especially along the banks of the Merrimack River.

Based upon anthropological studies studies done by Dr. George Woodbury of Manchester-by-the-Sea among others, Herbert Milton Sylvester author of Indian Wars of New England, writes in 1910 that the New England Indian was generally "of tall, angular and stalwart physique...In peace and plenty [he] was calm and mild...In anger or unrest his features were as shifty as the sea in a whipping gale...As an expression of savagery, [he was] demoniac. [He was] at once brave, timid, detesting falsehood in others, and again courting it; haughty and insolent with those of inferior rank or power, [he was] most humbly docile in the presence of... superiors...The mood of the savage was kaleidoscopic..."

Indian dress and hair style depended upon age and station. Youngsters wore their hair long while King Philip's Mount Hope warriors trimmed theirs in the fashion of a cockscomb with either side of the head shaved smooth. Most shaved their beards with stone implements and many, both men and women, were tattooed. Robes and winter clothing were of fur using the skins of beaver, otter, wolf, raccoon, deer and moose. Men wore deerskin leggings, belts and and breech-cloths, and everyone wore leather moccasins. "Inside their shelters," early observers reported, "they wear very little covering. False modesty seems to have been instilled in the minds of the natives by Europeans...Indian women who wore rather short garments [in summer], lengthened them and always wore {these} in the presence of [the English]."

As for food, there was, of course, meat from hunting and fish fresh from streams or estuaries. Corn or maize was a favorite of every Indian tribe. There were also meals made from crushed acorns, hickories and chestnuts. Berries of every kind were available, and oysters and clams were often dried for future use. Each family had its own garden which produced corn, beans, pumpkins, squash, Jerusalem artichokes and tobacco. When it came to preparing a new patch of land for agriculture, trees were cut about three feet above the ground. Branches were piled around the stumps and burned. Corn was then planted between the stumps. Later, both stumps and roots were removed.

French explorer Samuel de Champlain reported that during his voyages in the early 1600's, he saw scores of Indian huts along the Massachusetts coast each with its own well-tended garden. Eating utensils, primarily bowls and spoons, were skillfully made of wood. Hemp and rush baskets and bags were also fashioned in great variety and number. Buckets, boxes and dishes were made from birch bark. One settler observed "their women are of comely feature, industrious, and do most of the labor in planting and carrying of burdens; their husbands hold them in great slavery, yet never knowing other, it is lesse grievous to them..."

Whatever their habits may have been at home, Indian men and women taught the English much about how to survive in this wild, new land. Without their assistance, there is little question that many European lives would have been lost to starvation.

INDIANS
Evidence of Indian Life in Manchester Is Discovered as Soil Is Excavated

The Agawams visited Manchester to hunt and to fish and, according to a paper written and presented to the Friendship Circle in 1944 by Manchester resident Grace M. Prest, Indian shell heaps have been found along the shore of Day's Creek. Early records also show that land where the Plains are today was fertilized with fish and seaweed and used by the Indians to raise corn, beans and pumpkins.

Chief Samoset became a fast friend of the Pilgrims at Plymouth in 1621. Unafraid to approach them, he granted them land and recalled the visit in 1614 of Captain John Smith. Remaining with the English, he spoke their language, if a bit haltingly, acted as their interpreter and taught them how to live off the land.

Three Indian "mounds" have been opened here in Manchester, wrote Miss Prest. "One was south of the Congregational meeting house [overlooking the inner harbor] on land belonging to Captain Thomas Leach." Another was discovered when land was prepared for Union Cemetery off School Street, and a third was located in what was then a field, across from the Lee house on School Street near Bell Court.

A former Selectman and town history buff, John Lee (1813-1879) was Miss Prest's grandfather. He told her particularly about these three sites. When workers were levelling the area for Union Cemetery, Mr. Lee explained, they found many places "where the earth had been burnt down by fires... deposits of ashes, charred wood and burned stones [lay] from 16 to 18 inches in depth...the [soil] for some feet around was of a reddish-yellow color, different from the natural earth." This, Miss Prest explained, was where an Indian settlement had been located.

The mound at the head of the harbor south of Town Hall "was about 150 feet in diameter," Mr. Lee told his granddaughter, "and about eight [feet] above the adjoining marsh. On it stood [a number] of large apple trees. It was of conical form and had a moat surrounding it which filled with water [during spring] tides. Large quantities of bones were found here, but very much decayed so that they cut with a spade or shovel as easily as the ground in which they were embedded. The bones appeared to have been interred promiscuously and in an erect position..."

In his own field, however, near what is now Bell Court, Mr. Lee reported, the discovery of a treasure trove of Indian remains. "When in the autumn of 1844 the gravel pit was opened into a sandy, gravelly knoll, four entire skeletons were [found] buried, three of adults and one of a youth. ("These were the skeletons [that] I was brought up with!" Miss Prest added.) One of the adults was of a very large size," Mr. Lee continued to tell his grandaughter. "They were found lying nearly side by side with their heads toward the west though they were raised so as to face the east. They...were about 14 inches below the surface [of the earth] which had been much cultivated. One of the skeletons had

Massasoit meets with Governor Carver to agree to a treaty of peace. The Chief was accompanied by his warriors, all unarmed for the occasion. At the pow-wow, it was reported that "some strong water [was] brought, the Governor drank to Massasoit, who in his turn 'drank a great draught, that made him sweat all the while thereafter.'" The treaty proposed that if either side attacked the other those responsible "should be given up to be punished."

its head resting upon a round piece of copper...about 16 inches in diameter and where the head touched the copper, the skin and hair adhered firmly to the skull. The hair was black and bright, about two and one-half feet long. With [the skeletons] was found an iron tomahawk and an iron knife blade much decayed by rust; some course cloth made of flags or rushes, a short-stemmed smoking pipe and a large number of bone [and stone] arrow heads, preserved by the copper in sound condition. There were also some lobster claws, a fishing line, in good form but very rotten; a portion of another line of larger size...made from some fibrous plant; a wood ladle or bowl and [a number of] wooden spoons." On other occasions, Mr. Lee said he had found "a round, smooth stone about 14 inches long probably used for crushing corn, and a round stone about the size of an eight pound shot. It had a groove around it in two ways, deep enough to receive a small rope or withe" (a tough, supple twig used for binding things together).
In 1844, "when my mother's oldest brother was about three," Miss Prest continued, "he was taken by his

grandfather to see a family of Indians" living in the hollow at the junction of Sea Street and Old Neck Road. While there, my great-grandfather bought [a] little canoe. I keep it [today] with my Indian things."

Finally, she added, "I have one more Indian legend [to tell you about Manchester]. "In Edward MacDowell's 'Sketches' for piano is [a piece of music entitled] 'From an Indian Lodge.' It starts in clump, clump, clumping along — very stately and solemn. It is said that it was written {about] an Indian warrior who had lost his sweetheart. He felt so [depressed] he finally left his lodge [which was located] on Image Hill and walked [along] Singing Beach to Eagle Head. The music brings out the booming of the surf on the headland. When he reached the top of Eagle Rock he kept straight on, over the cliff and into the sea, to [join his] Indian maiden in the Happy Hunting Grounds. So to the Indians, "Miss Prest concluded, "the tufts of trees on Eagle Head were not the feathers of an eagle, but the feathers on the [head dress] of a [devoted] Indian warrior."

A BARGAIN PRICE
Selectmen Purchase the Town for
What Is Now Pocket Change

To secure just title and to "avoid the least scruple of intrusion," Governor Endicott directed English settlers in Massachusetts wherever possible to purchase their lands from Indians tribes. On 18 December, 1700, a deed was acknowledged in Salem which showed that Indians Samuel English, Joseph English and John Umpee sold to Selectmen Robert Leach, John Knowlton and Samuel Lee, property which today is the town of Manchester-by-the-Sea. The price: three pounds and 19 shillings "current silver money." Needless to say, it was a bargain, worth today about $6.15.

According to the deed, reprinted in D.F. Lamson's <u>History of Manchester,</u> the Indians' agreement to sell was based upon the fact that "the township (Manchester) quietly and peaceably and without molestation [had] enjoyed the soil, & etc. for more than 60 years....by the consent and approbation of our grandfather Sagamore John of Agaawam — alias Masconomo, or Masquenomenit, and ever since by consent and approbation of his children, and by us his grandchildren, being now the surviving and proper heirs to our said grandfather Maquenomenit."

In 1718, the Great and General Court's "Act for the Regulating of Townships, choice of Town Officers and Setting Forth Their Power," enabled the Proprietors of Manchester to organize and to operate the town. The petition to "erect a village" at Jeffrey's Creek was made and granted in 1640. At that time, Manchester was a part of Salem.

Although the residents of Manchester may have waited until some 60 years after its settlement to obtain a deed from the Indians, Boston was equally tardy in the matter. According to an early history of the city, "it was not until half a century after the occupation of the Boston peninsula [by Europeans], that the citizens troubled themselves to obtain a deed of land from the grandson of Chickataubut. This was in 1780..."

Chocorua, the last of the Pequakets, with his young son, later poisoned by the English, mourns at the grave of his wife, Keoka. The Chief, for whom New Hampshire's Mount Chocorua is named, asked that a curse be brought down upon the settlers for killing his child. He was later slain himself.

ILLUSTRATIONS

The illustrations in this Newsletter are taken from a book published in 1851 by James H. Earle, Boston and Chicago entitled History of the Indian Wars of New England with Eliot the Apostle. Fifty Years in the Midst of Them, by Colonel Robert Boodey Caverly.

BIBLIOGRAPHY

Bonfanti, Leo; New England Indians, Volume I, New England History Series. Wakefield, Massachusetts, Pride Publications, 1971; Caverly, Colonel Robert Boody; History of the Indian Wars of New England with Eliot the Apostle, Fifty Years in the Midst of Them. Boston and Chicago; James H. Earle, 1851; Felt, Joseph B. A History of Ipswich, Essex and Hamilton; Cambridge, Massachusetts, 1834; Ipswich, Clamshell Press, 1966; Fuess, Claud M. and Paradise, Scott H. The Story of Essex County, Volume I. New York; The American History Society, 1935; Keenan, Alice. Oh, No, Masconomo; Ipswich Yesterday, Volume II. Ipswich, Sanachic Publishers, 1984; Kenny, Herbert. The Masconomo Statue, Salem, Essex Institute Historical Collections, January, 1986; Lamson, Rev. D.F. History of the Town of Manchester, 1645-1895. Prest, Grace M. Indians of Manchester. A paper delivered before a meeting of the Friendship Circle, Manchester, December, 1944; State Street Bank, Other Indian Events of New England, Volume II. Boston, 1941; Waters, Thomas Franklin, Ipswich in the Massachusetts Bay Colony. Ipswich, Massachusetts, The Ipswich Historical Society, 1905.

Manchester Historical Society Newsletter written and edited by Gordon Abbott, Jr.

ABOUT THE AUTHOR

A life-long resident of Manchester-by-the-Sea, Gordon Abbott, Jr. represents the third generation of his family (his grandfather purchased a house in West Manchester in 1901) to live here, first during the summers and later, in 1939, year round. A former school teacher and advertising copywriter, Abbott went on to become editor of two prize-winning daily newspapers on the North Shore of Massachusetts, the <u>Gloucester Daily Times</u> and the <u>Beverly Evening Times</u>. He also served for nearly 18 years as Director of The Trustees of Reservations, at the time, the largest private owner of conservation land in the Commonwealth. A 1950 graduate of Harvard, he received a Master's Degree in American Studies from the University of Massachusetts at Boston. In 1984-85, he was a Visiting Scholar at Harvard University's School of Design.

At the end of WWII, he served with the U.S. Naval Reserve as a Quartermaster Third Class aboard a minesweeper in Japanese and Korean waters and later as a Lieutenant (j.g.) with the Naval Reserve Unit at Salem.

Active as a board member of many charitable organizations, he has been an elected Director of the Harvard Alumni Association; a Trustee of Connecticut College, New London, Connecticut; of Brooks School, North Andover, Massachusetts and of Shore Country Day School, Beverly, Massachusetts; a member of the Board of Directors of Maine Coast Heritage Trust; and a Trustee and Secretary of the Board of Trustees of USS CONSTITUTION Museum, Boston. A founder and first Treasurer of the Land Trust Alliance, he also proposed and helped establish the Center for Rural Massachusetts at the University of Massachusetts at Amherst where he served as an Associate Director of the Center and as an Adjunct Professor of Regional Planning.

In Manchester, he is a former member of the Planning Board, of the Harbor Committee and of the Committee on the '90's (its recommendations led to the appointment of a Town Administrator) as well as a present member of the Advisory Committee for Tuck's Point. He is also a Past Commodore of the Manchester Yacht Club. An avid sailor and skier, he lives with his wife Katharine in the same house originally purchased by his grandfather in 1901 and which after World War II was occupied as well by his own father and mother. The couple has four children.